Literature for Today's Young Adults

Literature for Today's Young Adults

· ·

FIFTH EDITION

Kenneth L. Donelson
Arizona State University

Alleen Pace Nilsen
Arizona State University

LONGMAN

An imprint of Addison Wesley Longman, Inc.

New York • Reading, Massachusetts • Menlo Park, California • Harlow, England
Don Mills, Ontario • Sydney • Mexico City • Madrid • Amsterdam

Editor-in-Chief: Priscilla McGeehon
Acquisitions Editor: Virginia L. Blanford
Supplements Editor: Donna Campion
Project Coordination and Text Design: Ruttle, Shaw & Wetherill, Inc.
Cover Designer: Kay Petronio
Cover Photograph: PhotoDisk, Inc.
Electronic Production Manager: Christine Pearson
Manufacturing Manager: Helene G. Landers
Electronic Page Makeup: Ruttle, Shaw & Wetherill, Inc.
Printer and Binder: R. R. Donnelley & Sons Company
Cover Printer: Phoenix Color Corp.

For permission to use copyrighted material, grateful acknowledgment is made to the copyright holders on pp. 459–460, which are hereby made part of this copyright page.

Library of Congress Cataloging-in-Publication Data

Donelson, Kenneth L.
    Literature for today's young adults / Kenneth
L. Donelson, Alleen Pace Nilsen.—5th ed.
        p.   cm.
    Includes bibliographical references and indexes.
    ISBN 0-673-99737-5
    1. Teenagers—United States—Books and reading. 2. Young adult literature, English—History and criti-
cism. 3. Young adult fiction, English—History and criticism. 4. Young adult literature, English—
Bibliography. 5. Young adult fiction, English—Bibliography.
    I. Nilsen, Alleen Pace.   II. Title.
Z1037.A1N55   1997
028.5'5—dc20   95-26604
                                                                                                        CIP

ISBN 0-673-99737-5

2345678910—DOC—999897

DEDICATION

To the women in Ken's life—Marie, Sherri, Jenny, Joey, Valerie, Amanda, Jackie, and JoJo.

To Alleen's grandchildren in hopes that they will find many of the books we talk about here—Taryn, Britton, Kami, David, Lauren, Jim, and Luke.

And to Bob Carlsen from Ken and Alleen, our beloved teacher, critic, and friend, who never tired of telling his classes, "Good books people our lives," and who never stopped living that truth.

Contents

Focus Boxes

The People Behind the Books

Tables and Charts

Preface

· ·

As we said in the preface of the fourth edition of *Literature for Today's Young Adults*, doing another version is both an obligation and an opportunity because the field of young adult books is always changing. Since the first edition, multiculturalism has become a part of every teacher's and librarian's life. Defining the nature of the literary canon has confused our lives, but determining the "true" canon is no closer than it was 15 years ago or last month. And even 10 years back, who could have foreseen the emphasis on computers in schools and homes? But some things are eternal problems or opportunities for all of us—namely getting the best books out to kids and helping kids learn about the joy of reading.

Young adult literature continues to gain respectability, as shown by the establishment of the Margaret A. Edwards Award sponsored by *School Library Journal* and administered by the Young Adult Library Services Association. But then the best proof is the continued excellence of authors as good as Robert Cormier, M. E. Kerr, Robert Lipsyte, Katherine Paterson, Brock Cole, Lois Lowry, Peter Dickinson, Berlie Doherty, Gary Paulsen, and Francesca Lia Block.

Popular culture changes include an ever more explosive increase in the production of videotapes. People can now go to the corner rental shop and select a movie for viewing as easily as they can go to the library and select a book for reading. Worse yet for some teachers, students can replace reading a book by seeing it on videotape, although few students still understand that the videotape of a novel is not the novel itself.

In this revision, we've tried to take into account all these changes and balance them with the latest books that kids will want to read and to include the best in the field, no matter what the copyright date. We've continued to add many titles and brief descriptions of recommended books, movies, and magazines in "Focus Boxes" instead of the text. (Adults are encouraged to photocopy these focus boxes and give them to young readers.) We are often asked for lists of books dealing specifically with members of minority groups, so we've added more focus boxes in this area. We've tried to add focus boxes of all sorts to help as many teachers and kids as possible. If readers find areas that deserve focus boxes that we have missed, we would be happy to receive suggestions for the next edition.

As we've said before, we have many reasons for continuing to work on this book, but chief among them is our belief that it is needed and worth doing. When in the late 1970s we surveyed teachers of young adult literature in library science,

English, and education departments, an overwhelming majority expressed a need for a scholarly and readable book to provide history and background for the field. One teacher wrote that her major problem "in establishing and promoting the work of the course was the sometimes skeptical view of colleagues about the worth of this literature" and added that she would welcome a text to educate professionals in related fields about the growing body of good young adult literature. We hope our book answers some of these needs, not just for academic classes in young adult literature but also for librarians, teachers, counselors, and others working with young people between the ages of 12 and 20.

For our purposes, we define *young adult literature* as any book freely chosen for reading by someone in this age group, which means that we do not make a distinction between books distributed by juvenile divisions and adult divisions of publishing houses. Young people read and enjoy both, and we share in the obvious goal of moving teenagers toward reading more and more adult books.

Throughout the text, we present criteria for evaluating various kinds of books, but these criteria are tentative starting places. Developing evaluation skills comes only with wide reading and practice in comparing books and matching them to particular needs. Similarly, our lists of recommended titles are only a beginning and should be supplemented by your own judgments and by current reviewing sources and annual lists of best books compiled by the Young Adult Library Services Association, the editors of *School Library Journal, Booklist,* the *ALAN Review,* the *New York Times, VOYA,* the *English Journal,* and other groups.

Although we know that paperbacks are far more widely read by young people than the original hardbound books, in our book lists we show the hardback publishers (where applicable). We do this to give credit to the companies who found the authors and did the initial editorial and promotion work. Also, by relying on the hardback publishers, we are able to be more consistent and accurate. The paperback publishing industry is fluid, and a title may be published and then go out of print within a few months. To find paperback editions of any of the books we have listed, consult the most recent issue of *Paperbound Books in Print* published annually (with periodic supplements) by R. R. Bowker Company and purchased by most libraries.

A comprehensive Instructor's Manual, written by Elizabeth Wahlquist of Brigham Young University, has been provided by the publisher to accompany the text. It includes such features as chapter summaries, activities, discussion questions, glossary of literary terms, bibliography for glossary, and reproducible handouts.

For help in preparing this fifth edition, we acknowledge the support of the English Department at Arizona State University. We particularly thank Mary Jones for her word processing skills and her ability to keep Ken sane at the same time he seemed intent on driving her bonkers. We also thank friends and colleagues, those who toil the fields of adolescent literature and make it more fruitful and far more fun, those we love as friends and admire as colleagues, those whose ideas and words have probably found their way into our pages more than we realize. In no particular order of importance, we salute Mary K. Chelton, Don Gallo, Bob Small, Maia Pank Mertz, Dick Abrahamson, John Simmons, Anne Webb, Beth and Ben Nelms, Ted Hipple, Chris Crowe, Elizabeth Wahlquist, Gary Salvner, Patty

Campbell, Diane Tuccillo, Dick Alm, Terry Ley, Dorothy Broderick, Jerry Weiss, Bob Probst, Paul Janeczko, Ginger Monseau, Leila Christenbury, and Hazel Davis.

And anyone who has read much in the history of English Education will recognize how much we owe to the spirits of four great master teachers and writers, four people who were dedicated to reading and adolescent literature—Samuel Thurber, Dora V. Smith, Lou LaBrant, and Dwight Burton. Without them and their work, there never would have been a reason for a book like this.

We thank Nicolette Wickman for help with proofreading and indexing, and we thank critics of the fourth edition and the readers of our manuscript who saved us from more errors than we might have made otherwise: Mary Ann Capan, Western Illinois University; Leila Christenbury, Virginia Commonwealth University; Jim Haskins, University of Florida; Rodney D. Keller, Ricks College; Joyce C. Lackie, University of Northern Colorado; Sandra W. Lott, University of Montevallo; Robert C. Small, Jr., Radford University; and Elizabeth Wahlquist, Brigham Young University.

We also thank the young adult authors who contributed the "People Behind the Books" statements. Lastly, we thank Longman editor-in-chief Priscilla McGeehon for supporting us on this edition, and we thank Peg Markow of Ruttle, Shaw & Wetherill for bringing it all together.

More than a hundred years ago, Edward Salmon justified his work in children's literature by writing:

> It is no uncommon thing to hear children's literature condemned as wholly bad, and some people are good enough to commiserate with me on having waded through so much ephemeral matter. It may be my fault or my misfortune not to be able to see my loss. I have spent many pleasant and I may say not unprofitable hours in company with the printed thoughts of Mr. Kingston, Mr. Ballantyne, Mr. Henty, Jules Verne, Miss Alcott, Miss Mead, Miss Molesworth, Miss Doudney, Miss Younge, and a dozen others, and hope to spend as many more in the time to come as a busy life will permit.*

Today, it is heartening to consider how many talented people share Edward Salmon's feelings, and, like us, feel joy in spending their lives working in a field of literature that is always changing, exciting, and alive.

Kenneth L. Donelson
Alleen Pace Nilsen

* "Should Children Have a Special Literature?" *The Parent's Review* 1 (June 1890): 399.)

Literature for Today's Young Adults

Part One

Understanding Young Adults and Books

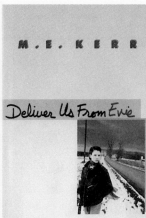

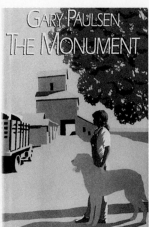

Chapter 1

Young Adults and Their Reading

. . . .

"Of all passages, coming of age, or reaching adolescence, is the purest, in that it is the loneliest. In birth one is not truly conscious; in marriage one has a partner; even death is faced with a life's experience by one's side," wrote David Van Biema for a special issue of *Life* magazine devoted to *The Journey of Our Lives.*

He went on to explain that going from boy or girl to man or woman is undertaking a "huge leap on the slimmest of information." The person who fails grows older without growing wiser and faces ostracism, insanity, or profound sorrow. Because such a debilitated or warped individual is a "drag on the community," the community bands together with the young person to see that the journey is accomplished.[1]

Initiation rites are one of the ways that communities help young people see the importance of leaving their childhood behind and taking on the mantle of adulthood. *Life* photographers traveled throughout the world to take pictures of young people undergoing such rites. Besides the expected communions, bar mitzvahs, junior proms, athletic competitions, cotillions, and graduation ceremonies, the photographers showed a virility initiation of a young boy being passed through a split sapling in an Italian forest, a boy on his first deer hunt with his father near the Pecos Bend Ranch in Texas, three Rastafarian girls partaking of "wisdom weed" (marijuana) in a Jamaican church, three Congolese Kota boys painted blue to symbolize the death of their childhoods, an Apache girl dressed in buckskin and beads and participating in a four-day celebration of her first menses, an Egyptian girl and a Turkish boy undergoing circumcisions, two Gabon girls painted white and secluded in a special hut because they had begun to menstruate, and several of Rio de Janeiro's teenage "surfers" riding the tops of speeding trains.

In affluent societies, books are one of the items that the community provides to young people in the hope of helping them succeed in their journey into adulthood. In the United States, we are just as anxious as any society to help our children in this passage, but we don't have the heart—or the faith that it would work—to isolate them purposefully from us, to put them in physically dangerous situations, to confuse or disorient them, or to indoctrinate them forcefully into following in their parents' footsteps.

Undoubtedly, there are teenagers in "advanced" societies who feel isolated and in danger as well as confused and coerced. This isn't because their societies have planned such conditions as rites of passage, however; rather, it is because the societies have been unable to prevent them. Most of us feel more comfortable in offering children an intellectual approach to growing up. We want them to read about more experiences than they could have on their own. And deep in our hearts, we're probably hoping that such reading will help young people mature intellectually and emotionally so that they won't feel the need to participate in the kinds of daredevil physical challenges that in one year cost the lives of 144 of the Rio de Janeiro train surfers. (A list of films on coming-of-age in various societies is found in Focus Box 1.1.)

The *Life* photographers did not show any teenagers reading books or any children getting their first adult library cards, a rite of passage that Robert Cormier remembers as "one of the great moments of my life, possessing my passport to a world that I still explore with wonder and delight." As a boy in the Leominster

FOCUS BOX 1.1

Films About That Dangerous Trip into Adulthood

Great Expectations (1946, 118 min., black and white; Dir: David Lean; with John Mills, Jean Simmons, and Martita Hunt)   The impoverished Pip finds happiness and disillusionment in this Charles Dickens story.

The Last Picture Show (1971, 118 min., black and white; Dir: Peter Bogdanovich; with Jeff Bridges, Timothy Bottoms, Ben Johnson, and Cloris Leachman)   A great script and a fabulous cast make Larry McMurtry's novel about a small, dying town in west Texas the perfect initiation film.

The Man Without a Face (1993, 114 min. color; Dir: Mel Gibson)   Gibson stars as the disfigured teacher who becomes Justin's friend as he secretly helps him study for admissions tests.

Member of the Wedding (1952, 91 min., black and white; Dir: Fred Zimmermann; with Ethel Waters, Brandon de Wilde, and Julie Harris)   The novel/play by Carson McCullers is about growing up and feeling unwanted.

My Life as a Dog (1989, 101 min., color; Dir: Lasse Hallstrom)   When his mother is ill, a 12-year-old boy is shipped off to relatives. Based on the Swedish novel of the same title (recently available in the United States) by Reidar Jonsson.

Pelle the Conqueror (1988, 150 min., color; Dir: Billie August; with Max von Sydow)   A father can't find work in Sweden, so he and his young son come to Denmark and find farm life and work far worse than they had expected. Mostly grim, but ultimately a touching portrait of the love of father and son.

Personal Best (1982, 124 min., color; Dir: Robert Towne; with Mariel Hemingway and Patrice Donnelly)   A young athlete trains for the Olympics and becomes involved in a lesbian affair.

Sons and Lovers (1960, 103 min., black and white; Dir: Jack Cardiff; with Dean Stockwell, Trevor Howard, and Wendy Hiller)   D. H. Lawrence's novel is the powerful story of a son trying to determine his rite of passage out of a coal-mining town.

Tex (1982, 103 min., color: Dir: Tim Hunter; with Matt Dillon)   S. E. Hinton's popular novel of two brothers finding their way in life. All of Hinton's young adult books have been filmed with varying degrees of success.

The Yearling (1946, 128 min., color; Dir: Clarence Brown; with Gregory Peck, Jane Wyman, and Claude Jarman, Jr.)   A fine cast and a great retelling of Marjorie Kinnan Rawlings' novel about a family, a pet, and survival.

Public Library, Cormier would sneak behind the circulation desk into the adult stacks and rub his hands across the "spines of books, reading the names of the authors." Because he couldn't check the books out, he would pull them from the shelves, and sitting on the greenish, opaque glass floor with his knees jackknifed and, his back against the wall, he would read. One afternoon, Miss Wheeler, the librarian, found him there and, after they "talked books and authors," issued him his library card.[2]

Undoubtedly, one of the reasons the *Life* photographers did not photograph young people reading books is that when people read, the action takes place inside their heads, which doesn't make for dramatic photos. In addition, except for textbooks, a relatively small percentage of the world's young people read books, and not all books for young people are written to help them grow into adults. Some writers simply want to share the pleasure they feel in words and story, others want to make money, and still others want to indoctrinate or educate their readers. Ever since the mid-nineteenth century, when—to the joy of the young and the anguish of the old—American publishers discovered that young people would buy dime novels by the millions, tensions have existed over which of these purposes books should serve.

The first American writers to gain national attention with books written for what today we call the "young adult audience," were Oliver Optic and Louisa May Alcott. Optic's didactic series books are almost forgotten, but Alcott's autobiographical *Little Women* is still read and loved. As famous as these two authors were in the 1860s, the terms *young adult literature, teenage books,* and *adolescent literature* would have been strange, even meaningless, because only within the last half of the twentieth century has literature for young adults developed as a distinct unit of book publishing and promotion. Even today, an optimist might describe the field as *dynamic;* a pessimist would be more apt to say it is *unstable.*

Because of the newness of the concept and practice, there are no longstanding traditions as in children's literature, and opinions vary on whether there is even a need for a specialized approach to teenage books. The creation of such books coincided with the developing concept of adolescence as a specific, unique period of life. Puberty is a universal experience, but adolescence is not. Even today, in nontechnological societies the transition from childhood to adulthood may be quite rapid, but in the United States, it begins at about age 12 or 13 and continues through the early twenties. This stretching out of the transition between childhood and adulthood followed the Civil War. Before then, people were simply considered either children or adults. The turning point took place about age 14 or 15, when children could go to work and become economic assets to the family and the community. But as the predominantly agricultural society in which children worked with their families gave way to a technological society in which people worked in factories, offices, schools, hospitals, research centers, and think-tanks, available jobs required specialized training. The more complex society became, the longer children had to go to school to prepare for their eventual adulthood. These children, waiting to be accepted as full-fledged members of society, developed their own unique society. They became *teenagers* and *young adults* or, as psychologists prefer to call them, *adolescents.*

Any change that affects this many people in such a major way demands adjustments and a reshuffling of society's priorities and roles. Such changes do not come automatically, and few believe that all the adjustments have been made.

What Is Young Adult Literature?

We recently heard young adults defined as "those who think they're too old to be children but who others think are too young to be adults." In this book, we use the term to include students in junior high as well as those who have graduated from high school and are still finding their way into adult reading. We should caution, however, that not all educators define young adults in this way. The Educational Resources Information Clearinghouse (ERIC), for example, defines young adults as those between the ages of 18 and 22, whereas the National Assessment of Educational Progress (NAEP), administered by the Educational Testing Service, refers to "young adults, ages 21 through 25."

We confess to feeling a bit pretentious when referring to a 12- or 13-year-old as a young adult. We shy away from using the term *adolescent literature,* however, because, as librarians have told us: "It has the ugly ring of pimples and puberty"; "It's like a conference about young adults with none present"; and "It suggests *immature,* in a derogatory sense." Still, most such college courses offered through English departments are entitled *Adolescent Literature,* and because of our English teaching backgrounds, we find ourselves using the term for variety, along with *teenage books.* We do not use such terms, however, as *juvenile literature, junior novel, teen novel,* and *juvie.* These terms used to be fairly common, but today they are weighed down with negative connotations. This is unfortunate because there is often a need for communicating that a particular book is more likely to appeal to a 13-year-old than to a 19-year-old. With adults, a six-year age difference may not affect choice of subject matter and intellectual and emotional response, but for teenagers even two or three years can make a tremendous difference.

By *young adult literature,* we mean anything that readers between the approximate ages of 12 and 20 choose to read (as opposed to what they may be coerced to read for class assignments). When we talk about *children's literature,* we refer to books released by the juvenile or junior division of a publisher and intended for children from prekindergarten to about sixth grade.

It wasn't until the 1920s and 1930s that most publishers divided their offerings into adult and juvenile categories. And today it is sometimes little more than chance whether an adult or juvenile editor happens to get a manuscript. Robert Cormier had never thought of himself as a writer for young people, but when his agent submitted *The Chocolate War* to Pantheon, the editor convinced Cormier that, as good as the book was, it would be simply one more in a catalog of adult books. If it were published for teenagers, however, it might sell well, and it certainly would not be one more in a long string of available adolescent novels. The editor's predictions came true, and Cormier later acknowledged that although his initial reaction to becoming a "young adult" author was one of shock followed by a month-long writer's block, he is grateful for the editorial help, which led to considerable attention from reviewers as well as his first financial success as an author.

The decade of the mid 1970s through the mid 1980s may come to be known as the golden age of young adult literature. We remember an editor in the 1980s telling us that whereas he used to count on one hand the number of young adult authors who earned their living exclusively by writing (most were teachers or were partially supported by spouses), he could now name 30 authors writing for teenagers who could accurately be described as affluent because of the way their books were selling.

Contributing to the change was the need by television and movie producers for stories that would appeal to a youth-oriented society. Also, in many schools, teachers who had previously scorned teenage books found themselves facing students who simply could not, or would not, read the so-called classics. Taking a pragmatic approach, these teachers concluded that it was better to teach adolescent literature than no literature at all. This made schools and libraries a primary market for young adult books, especially paperbacks, with the result that hardback publishers sold the rights for paperback editions of their successful books for what at the time seemed to be shockingly high prices. And as the book industry discovered that teenagers were willing to spend their own money for paperbacks, the financial base began to change. See George Nicholson's "People Behind the Books Piece" (pp. 8–9), which shows how the long-term results of such changes are not at all clear.

Although we talk more about some of these changes in Chapter Three, for now we cite just a few of the differences we have noticed in the mid-1990s compared with the mid-1980s. First, although educators' interest in young adult books has increased tremendously as shown by such things as the adoption of whole-language teaching methods, the creation and adoption of textbooks based on pieces from contemporary young adult literature, teacher attendance at workshops on contemporary young adult literature, and increased numbers of professional articles and books on the subject, the interest of publishers in young adult books has lagged. For example, several of the authors whom we invited to contribute to our "People Behind the Books" feature added some discouraging asides to their letters. One said he had just taken a $2000 cut in the advance for his next book because publishers told him that young adult books weren't selling anymore. Another said she was depressed by the fact that she could no longer just "tell a story." Before she could get a contract, she had to prove the book "filled a need." Several authors admitted that they were now writing for kids in middle schools because that's what their publishers wanted.

The most optimistic explanation we've heard for what we hope is a temporary slump is that young adult books are not selling as well as they used to simply because of demographics. There's a dip in the population for high school kids as compared to middle schoolers. In a few years when the large numbers of middle schoolers move up to high school, we'll be back to those brisk sales that encouraged us all in the 1980s.

More pessimistic explanations center around gloom-and-doom stories about kids no longer wanting—or being able—to read, and publishers no longer being interested in anything except the bottom line. Independent publishers have been

GEORGE M. NICHOLSON
On the History and Development of the Young Adult Novel

Richard Peck, in his new collection of essays *Love and Death at the Mall,* best defines the young adult novel as a "shot fired just over the heads of our readers. . . . Young adult novels test the boundaries . . . leading to the subtext of all our books: the responsibility for the consequences of actions." In a series of witty and often highly opinionated pronouncements, Peck splendidly conveys the passion of writers in the genre and the extraordinary faith they have in young people to carry on, to understand what is inside themselves, and to find hope in the future.

That hope is often hard to find for today's publishers who are battling the burdens of the bottom line and the eternal war over Art and Commerce.

That battle was not always so clear cut. The Young Adult novel was, of course, originally a librarian's classification for adult novels which young people might enjoy. Primary among these were Betty Smith's *A Tree Grows in Brooklyn* and, most dramatically, J. D. Salinger's *The Catcher in the Rye* which, along with Twain's *Huckleberry Finn,* are the classic voices of the American novel of coming of age.

In the late sixties and early seventies, a covey of brilliant new writers began to explore the outer edges of adolescent experience. Writers like S. E. Hinton, Robert Cormier, and Judy Blume, respecting their audience and understanding fully the moral crises young people faced, wrote of a world in which adolescents stood alone, desperately trying to find a place which substantiated their lives. A few titles—the film *Rebel Without a Cause* and the novel *The Outsiders*—clearly indicated the way they felt. Honest, if hyperbolic, emotion told the tale amidst a welter of "beach blanket" movies and innocuous fiction for teens.

During the sixties, however, an extraordinary commercial vehicle developed which served this new Young Adult novel, the chain bookstore. Over the next decade came the vast growth of the chains in nearly every mall in America, and the insatiable need for product, month in, month out. For the first time, the teenager had only to pick the book he or she wanted. No questions asked at the checkout counter, just cold cash, please. So, for years, the paperback "teen" novel flourished. From an industry which had responded mostly to the critical judgments of professionals who worked with young people in hardcover books sold in school and public libraries came, not only fine books, but, not surprisingly, the return of the pulp novel. Not since the heyday of the Stratemeyer Syndicate in the thirties, had such books been seen in such quantity. Series publishing found its natural partner in the chain stores yearning for new product.

By the eighties, publishing itself had changed. The gulf between paperback houses and hardcover houses had begun to shift. Each began to publish both hardcover and paperback. Sales and distribution divisions echoed the editorial changes. And, soon, fierce competition appeared among houses who had quietly tolerated one another for decades. Packagers entered the scene providing editorial and often marketing services when publishing and editorial staffs were too small to handle the volume. As the proliferation of material accelerated, so did the specter of failure and loss, heretofore almost negligible in responsible houses catering to the institutional markets.

Another curious result of this vast overproduction was the broadening of the sales base to include material for younger children. The very phrase "Young Adult" came to mean something different in trade bookselling. Children's booksellers who had not always been able to lure the teenager into their stores, as well as the chains, seemed to accept a diminished definition of the YA novel, whereas the label remained constant in the institutional field.

And thus came an increasing gulf between what would sell in larger numbers and what would not. Serious fiction was at a sales impasse, echoing the world of adult publishing. The writers in the field were troubled about whom they were writing for. Literary writers found themselves in the strange position of writing more complex titles and stretching the limits, to much praise and fewer sales. Writers who write primarily to entertain found themselves forced to lower their judgments in order to survive in the field. And some writers found themselves frozen out of the Young Adult novel altogether. Certainly the best of the older writers were taught in schools, but what of the new writer?

All of us who care about the future of the Young Adult novel now find ourselves in a most complex position. Publishers must clearly redefine what it is they wish to publish. Do they want the literary novel for the older readers which asks serious questions of its readers? If so, a new market and one largely unaware of YA material coming from children's publishers must emerge. A potential hardcover and paperback market is the adult librarians in the public library systems who have no YA coordinators and rarely see YA catalogs and promotions. Small houses like Algonquin Books of Chapel Hill regularly publish fine novels which reach the intelligent reader through adult distribution.

Better access to adult mass-market distribution is a desirable but tough goal. YA fiction should be a genre in the adult sections of paperback racks as are romances, westerns, et al., rather than afterthoughts in children's sections. The YA world has to confront honestly the tough aspects of teen life rather than adulterated and often hypocritical approaches to life. It is utterly foolish to think the average 12- to 16-year-old unable to handle serious subjects which they see in every other media. Two new YA writers, Francesca Lia Block and Chris Lynch (both HarperCollins), are publishing in new directions which explore the most intimate of their experiences, sex and family violence. Yet their sales do not approach their potential audience response.

So, are we left only with hope? The hope the writers convey to their readers? Yes, but hope tied to action. It is our job, each of us to redefine and relocate our goals. It can be done and the young people will be enriched. That recognition of ourselves as readers and caring human beings has served us over the decades. And it will do so again.

George M. Nicholson is currently a literary agent, but over the past three decades he worked as an editor for leading publishers of both hardback and paperback books for young adults.

purchased by conglomerates, and independent bookstores, which carried two or three copies of many moderately popular books published over the last several years, are being replaced by large chain bookstores. Rather than carrying a few copies of many books, the chains find that their profits are greater when they carry many copies of a few best-sellers. This encourages publishers to produce fewer books and to keep only the most popular in print. A downside for teachers is that they can no longer depend on having access to books they have found especially useful for in-class reading or thematic units, while a downside for authors—really for all of us—is that publishers are less likely to take chances on new authors and on subjects and styles that may not have the mass appeal wanted by the big bookstores.

A Brief Unsettled Heritage

Before those of us who love young adult books grow too discouraged over present conditions, we need to realize that the field as a whole is a relatively new area and that all literary scenes have their ups and downs. If we compare the total group of today's young adult authors with those of a generation ago, we can see tremendous progress. The field took a big step when on the basis of his Pulitzer Prize-winning play *The Effect of Gamma Rays on Man-in-the-Moon-Marigolds,* Paul Zindel was invited by Harper & Row to try teenage fiction. His first book was the well-received *The Pigman,* which both M. E. Kerr and Robert Cormier have acknowledged as a positive influence when they pondered the effect that writing books for teenagers might have on their own careers.

Don Gallo's *Speaking for Ourselves: Autobiographical Sketches by Notable Authors of Books for Young Adults* and its sequel *Speaking for Ourselves, Too* have statements from nearly 150 active, well-respected authors. As part of a Twentieth-Century Writers Series, the St. James Press featured nearly 400 authors in its 1994 *Twentieth-Century Young Adult Writers,* whereas Charles Scribner's Sons gave fuller write-ups to the 125 authors it decided to feature in its 1996 *Writers for Young Adults* edited by Ted Hipple.

We should be encouraged not only by the numbers, but also by the variety. Today's writers for young readers include men and women from all socioeconomic levels and from all over the world writing about life experiences of every possible kind. The first time we solicited author comments for our "People Behind the Books" features, we had a hard time getting comments from anyone other than white, middle-class Americans. That wasn't true for this edition, in which we are especially pleased at how many British authors are included. The world truly is shrinking with young adult literature becoming an international field. One of the "global village" tidbits that we picked up in the course of our correspondence was learning that "our" American fantasy writer Robin McKinley is married to "their" English fantasy writer Peter Dickinson. We're not sure what this means for young adult literature, but it seems to say something in favor of trans-Atlantic communication.

Other tidbits illustrating the variety of people committed to writing fiction for teenagers include the fact that Judie Angell and Fran Arrick are actually the same person, with Angell choosing lighter topics than does Arrick. At the 1994 National

Council of Teachers of English conference, it was fun to listen to Gary Paulsen, Will Hobbs, and Theodore Taylor swap stories about their childhoods spent in places as varied as the Panama Canal Zone, the Philippines, and Cradock, Virginia, and about their adult jobs ranging from wilderness guide to merchant seaman and soldier, and from roofer to truck driver, and teacher. At the opposite end of the career spectrum, when we asked Michelle Magorian for a "People Behind the Books" statement, she asked us to try again in a year or so because she was busy caring for her 6-year-old and 18-month-old children, plus her elderly father. Besides writing fiction, she gives talks and does one-woman shows—her first career was as an actress.

Moving from this encouraging kaleidoscope of authors and going back to less happy interpretations, there have always been critics who questioned the value of books written for teenagers. An article in the *Louisville Courier-Journal* in 1951 described young adult books as "Flabby in content, mediocre in style, narrowly directed at the most trivial of adolescent interests." The writer went on to say, "Like a diet of cheap candies, they vitiate the appetite for sturdier food—for that bracing, ennobling and refining experience, immersion in the great stream of the English classics."[3]

Fourteen years later, J. Donald Adams, editor of the "Speaking of Books" page in *The New York Times Book Review,* pointed to adolescent literature as a symptom of what is wrong with American education and American culture:

> The teen-age book, it seems to me, is a phenomenon which belongs properly only to a society of morons. I have nothing but respect for the writers of good books for children; they perform one of the most admirable functions of which a writer is capable. One proof of their value is the fact that the greatest books which children can enjoy are read with equal delight by their elders. But what person of mature years and reasonably mature understanding (for there is often a wide disparity) can read without impatience a book written for adolescents.[4]

In 1977, John Goldthwaite, writing in *Harper's,* gave as one of his nine suggestions for improving literature for young readers in particular and the world in general the termination of teenage fiction. His reasoning was that any literate 12-year-old could understand most science fiction and fantasy, and "As for all that novelized stuff about alienation, drugs, and pregnancy, the great bulk of it might be more enjoyable presented in comic books."[5]

Even people who are known to be committed to the concept of adolescent literature sometimes question its authenticity. For example, in a call for papers for the April 1992 issue of the *English Journal* celebrating the fiftieth anniversary of Maureen Daly's *Seventeenth Summer* and the twenty-fifth anniversary of S. E. Hinton's *The Outsiders,* editor Ben Nelms asked, "Is the adolescent (or YA) novel simply a marketing device, or does it represent a legitimate literary genre?"[6]

Those of us who have positive attitudes about teenage books of course argue for its being a literary genre, and we think that the critics quoted earlier were not talking about the good adolescent literature published today. We can also conjecture that they were making observations based on a biased or inadequate sampling.

Teenage books were never as hopelessly bad as some people claim. Criticism of any field, young adult literature or ornithology or submarine designing, begins with firsthand experience of the subject. Critics who decide to do a cursory piece on young adult literature once a year or so seldom have the reading background necessary to choose representative titles. People who generalize about an entire field of writing based on reading only five or ten books are not merely unreliable sources, but intellectual frauds. Wide knowledge surely implies a background of at least several hundred books selected from a variety of types and styles.

Although we have grounds for rejecting the kind of negative criticism quoted previously, we need to be aware that it exists. Such a pessimistic view of teenage books is an unfortunate literary heritage that may well influence the attitudes of school boards, library directors, parents, teachers, and anyone else who has had no particular reason to read and examine the best of the new young adult literature. Besides, so many new books for young readers appear each year (approximately 2000, with about one-fourth of these aimed at teenagers) that people who have already made up their minds about adolescent literature can probably find titles to support their beliefs no matter what they are. In an area as new as young adult literature, we can look at much of the disagreement and the conflicting views as inevitable. They are signs of a lively and interesting field.

Characteristics of the Best Young Adult Literature

We did some research to come up with a selection of books that would be representative of what both young adults and professionals working in the field consider the best books. We should caution, however, that books are selected as "the best" on the basis of many different criteria, and one person's best will not necessarily be yours or that of the young people with whom you work. We hope that you will read many books, so that you can recommend them not because you saw them on a list, but because you enjoyed them and believe they will appeal to a particular student.

In drawing up our list of "best books," we started with 1967 because this seemed to be a milestone year, when writers and publishers turned in new directions. We have compiled this list from several other "Best Book" lists, including yearly lists from the editors of *School Library Journal, Booklist,* and *Horn Book* and from such committees as those who choose the Newbery Awards and the *Boston Globe–Horn Book Awards* as well as the units of the American Library Association that put together such lists as "Best Books for Young Adults," "Recommended Books for the Reluctant Young Adult Reader," and "Notable Children's Books."

We have also used our own judgment and that of our colleagues and taken into consideration any special lists that have appeared, such as the "Top One Hundred Countdown: Best of the Best Books for Young Adults" selected from the past 25 years by young adult librarians during the American Library Association 1994 Annual Conference. We have labeled the results of our research our Honor List, but we make no claim that it includes all the good books or even the best books published each year. We guarantee, however, that a number of knowledgeable people—professionals as well as young readers—were favorably impressed with each book that appears on the Honor List.

As the years have gone by, the number of books has made the list so unwieldy that for this edition we deleted most books that are out of print and moved the biographies and nonfiction, as well as collections of poetry and short stories, to Focus Boxes in appropriate chapters. On the Honor List, asterisks indicate that a book has been produced in a film version. "J" stands for the juvenile division of a publishing house, while "A" stands for the adult division. In recent years as young adult literature became big business more of the books have come from juvenile divisions. Also over the years, the number of pages has decreased as has the number of publishing houses involved, especially now that the same companies often handle both the hardback and paperback editions.

HONOR LIST

Title and Author	Hardbound Publishers	Publishing Division	Paperback Publisher	Genre	Protagonist Sex	Age	Number of Pages	Ethnic Group or Unusual Setting
1995								
The Eagle Kite Paula Fox	Orchard	J		Realistic Death	M	13	127	
Ironman Chris Crutcher	Greenwillow	J		Realistic Sports	M	16	181	
Like Sisters on the Homefront Rita Williams-Garcia	Lodestar/ Dutton	J		Realistic	F	14	165	African American
The Midwife's Apprentice Karen Cushman	Clarion	J		Historical	F	13	122	Medieval
The Squared Circle James Bennett	Scholastic	J		Realistic Sports	M	18	165	
The War of Jenkin's Ear Michael Morpurgo	Philomel	J		Realistic/ Religious	M	14	171	1951 England
1994								
Deliver Us from Evie M. E. Kerr	Harper-Collins	J		Realistic Lesbianism	F	17	177	
Driver's Ed. Caroline Cooney	Delacorte	J		Suspense	M/F	teens	184	

Iceman Chris Lynch	Harper-Collins	J		Realistic Sports	M	14	181	
Letters from the Inside John Marsden	Houghton Mifflin	J		Realistic	F	teens	146	Australia
When She Hollers Cynthia Voigt	Scholastic	J		Realistic Abuse	F	17	177	
1993								
Charms for the Easy Life Kaye Gibbons	Putnam's	A	Avon	Historical Romance	F	mixed	254	Southern U. S.
The Giver Lois Lowry	Houghton Mifflin	J	Dell	Science Fiction	M	mixed	180	Futuristic Dystopia
Harris and Me Gary Paulsen	Harcourt Brace	J		Realistic Humorous	M	young teens	157	Rural
Make Lemonade Virginia Euwer Wolff	Holt	J	Scholastic	Realistic Single parent	F	14/17	200	Inner City
Missing Angel Juan Francesca Lia Block	Harper-Collins	J	Harper-Collins	Problem Occult	F	teens	138	Los Angeles New York
Shadow Boxer Chris Lynch	Harper-Collins	J		Realistic Sports	M	young teens	215	
1992								
Dear Nobody Berlie Doherty	Orchard	J	Morrow	Realistic Pregnancy	M/F	older teens	192	England
The Harmony Arms Ron Koertge	Little	J	Avon	Realistic Humorous	M	14	182	Los Angeles
Missing May Cynthia Rylant	Orchard	J		Realistic Death	M/F	mixed	89	
Somewhere in the Darkness Walter Dean Myers.	Scholastic	J	Scholastic	Realistic Family	M	14	224	African American
1991								
The Brave Robert Lipsyte	Harper-Collins	J	Harper-Collins	Realistic Sports	M	18	195	Native American
Castle in the Air Diana Wynne Jones	Greenwillow	J		Fantasy	M/F	teens	199	Middle East
Lyddie Katherine Paterson	Lodestar	J	Puffin	Historical mid-1800s	F	13	183	U.S. Northeast

The Man from the Other Side Uri Orlev	Houghton Mifflin	J	Puffin	Historical	M	14	186	Poland WW II
Nothing But the Truth Avi	Orchard	J	Avon	Realistic	M	14	177	
1990								
The Shining Company Rosemary Sutcliff	Farrar	J	Farrar	Historical 7th century	M	mixed	296	England
The Silver Kiss Annette Curtis Klause	Bradbury	J	Dell	Occult Romance	F	teens	198	
The True Confessions of Charlotte Doyle Avi	Orchard	J	Avon	Historical Adventure	F	13	215	1800s trans-Atlantic
White Peak Farm Berlie Doherty	Orchard	J	Morrow	Realistic Family	F	older teens	86	England
1989								
Blitzcat Robert Westall	Scholastic	J	Scholastic	Animal	M		230	England WW II
Celine Brock Cole	Farrar	J	Farrar	Realistic	F	16	216	
Eva Peter Dickinson	Delacorte	J	Dell	Science Fiction	F	13	219	Dystopian Future
No Kidding Bruce Brooks	Harper-Collins	J	Harper-Collins	Science Fiction	M	14	207	Dystopian Future
Shabanu: Daughter of the Wind Suzanne Fisher Staples	Knopf	J		Realistic Problem	F	12	140	Pakistan Desert
Sweetgrass Jan Hudson	Philomel	J	Scholastic	Historical 1830s	F	15	159	Blackfoot Indians
Weetzie Bat Francesca Lia Block	Harper	J	Harper-Collins	Realistic Spoof	M/F	teens	88	Hollywood
1988								
Fade Robert Cormier	Delacorte	J	Dell	Occult	M/F	mixed	320	
Fallen Angels Walter Dean Myers	Scholastic	J	Scholastic	Realistic	M	older teens	309	Vietnam War/ethnic mix
A Kindness Cynthia Rylant	Orchard	J	Dell	Realistic Family	M	15	117	

Memory Margaret Mahy	Macmillan	J	Dell	Realistic Disability	M/F	19 80+	240	New Zealand
Probably Still *Nick Swanson* Virginia Euwer Wolff	Holt	J	Scholastic	Realistic Disability	M	teens	144	
Scorpions Walter Dean Myers	Harper- Collins	J	Harper- Collins	Realistic Crime	M	teens	167	ethnic mix
Sex Education Jenny Davis	Orchard	J		Realistic Death	F	teens	150	
1987								
After the Rain Norma Fox Mazer	Morrow	J	Avon	Realistic Death	F	mid- teens	290	
The Crazy Horse *Electric Game* Chris Crutcher	Greenwillow	J	Dell	Realistic Sports Disability	M	teens	224	ethnic mix
The Goats Brock Cole	Farrar	J	Farrar	Realistic	M/F	teens	184	
*Hatchet Gary Paulsen	Bradbury	J	Puffin	Adventure Survival	M	12	195	
Permanent *Connections* Sue Ellen Bridgers	Harper- Collins	J	Harper- Collins	Realistic Family	M/F	teens	164	
Sons from Afar Cynthia Voigt	Atheneum	J	Fawcett	Realistic	M	mid- teens	224	
The Tricksters Margaret Mahy	Macmillan	J		Occult	F	17	266	New Zealand
1986								
Cat Herself Mollie Hunter	Harper- Collins	J		Historical	F	teen	279	British nomads
The Catalogue of *the Universe* Margaret Mahy	Macmillan	J		Realistic	F	17	185	New Zealand
Izzy, Willy-Nilly Cynthia Voigt	Atheneum	J	Fawcett	Realistic Disability	F	15	288	
Midnight Hour Encores Bruce Brooks	Harper- Collins	J	Harper- Collins	Realistic	F	16	288	mixed ethnic

1985

Beyond the Chocolate War Robert Cormier	Knopf	J	Dell	Realistic	M	17	234	
Dogsong Gary Paulsen	Bradbury	J		Adventure Occult	M	13	177	Alaska Inuit
Ender's Game Orson Scott Card	Tor	A	Tor	Science Fiction	M	young teens	357	
*In Country Bobbie Ann Mason	Harper-Collins	A	Harper-Collins	Realistic	F	teens	247	
The Moonlight Man Paula Fox	Bradbury	J	Dell	Realistic Alcoholism	F	teens	192	Nova Scotia
Remembering the Good Times Richard Peck	Delacorte	J	Dell	Realistic Suicide	M/F	teens	192	

1984

The Changeover: A Supernatural Romance Margaret Mahy	Macmillan	J	Puffin	Fantasy	M/F	teens	214	New Zealand
*Cold Sassy Tree Olive Ann Burns	Ticknor & Fields	A	Dell	Realistic	M/F	mixed	391	1906 rural Georgia
Downtown Norma Fox Mazer	Morrow	J	Avon	Realistic	M/F	young teen	216	
Interstellar Pig William Sleator	Dutton	J	Bantam	Science Fiction	M	16	197	
The Moves Make the Man Bruce Brooks	Harper-Collins	J	Harper-Collins	Realistic	M	young teens	280	ethnic mix
One-Eyed Cat Paula Fox	Bradbury	J	Dell	Realistic	M	young teens	216	

1983

Beyond the Divide Kathryn Lasky	Macmillan	J	Dell	Historical Fiction	F	teens	254	1800s American West
The Bumblebee Flies Anyway Robert Cormier	Pantheon	J	Dell	Futuristic	M	teens	211	
*A Gathering of Old Men Ernest J. Gaines	Knopf	A	Random	Realistic	M	elderly	214	Depression South, African-American

A Solitary Blue Cynthia Voigt	Atheneum	J	Scholastic	Realistic Family	M	early teens	182	

1982

Annie on My Mind Nancy Garden	Farrar	J	Farrar	Realistic Lesbianism	F	teens	233	
The Blue Sword Robin McKinley	Greenwillow	J	Ace	Fantasy	F	late teens	272	
A Formal Feeling Zibby Oneal	Viking	J	Viking Puffin	Realistic Death	F	teens	162	
*A Midnight Clear William Wharton	Knopf	A	Ballantine	Realistic	M	early 20s	241	World War II
Sweet Whispers, Brother Rush Virginia Hamilton	Philomel	J	Avon	Occult	F	teens	224	African-American

1981

Let the Circle Be Unbroken Mildred D. Taylor	Dial	J	Bantam	Historical U.S. South	F	early teens	166	African American
Notes for Another Life Sue Ellen Bridgers	Knopf	J	Bantam	Realistic Family	M/F	teens	252	
Rainbow Jordan Alice Childress	Coward McCann	J	Avon	Realistic	F	14	142	African American
Stranger with My Face Lois Duncan	Little	J	Dell	Occult	F	17	250	
Tiger Eyes Judy Blume	Bradbury	J	Dell	Realistic	F	15	206	New Mexico ethnic mix
Westmark Lloyd Alexander	Dutton	J	Dell	Historical Fiction	M	16	184	England

1980

The Beginning Place Ursula K. Le Guin	Harper-Collins	J	Harper-Collins	Fantasy	M/F	early 20s	183	
The Hitchhiker's Guide to the Galaxy Douglas Adams	Crown	A	Pocket Books	Science Fiction	M	adults	224	
Jacob Have I Loved Katherine Paterson	Crowell	J	Harper-Collins	Realistic Family	F	teens	216	Chesapeake Bay WW II

1979

After the First Death Robert Cormier	Pantheon	J	Dell	Realistic Suspense	M/F	teens	233	
All Together Now Sue Ellen Bridgers	Knopf	J	Bantam	Realistic Familly	M/F	teens	238	
*Birdy William Wharton	Knopf Random	A		Realistic Insanity	M	early 20s	310	
The Last Mission Harry Mazer	Delacorte	J	Dell	Realistic	M	late teens	182	World War II
*Tex S. E. Hinton	Delacorte	J	Dell	Realistic	M	teens	194	
Words by Heart Ouida Sebestyen	Little, Brown	J	Bantam	Realistic 1920s West	F	young teen	162	African-American

1978

Beauty: A Retelling . . . Robin McKinley	Harper-Collins	J	Harper-Collins	Fantasy	F	teens	247	
The Book of the Dun Cow Walter Wangerin, Jr.	Harper-Collins	J	Harper-Collins	Animal Fantasy	—	—	255	
Gentlehands M. E. Kerr	Harper-Collins	J	Harper-Collins	Realistic	M	teens	283	
Killing Mr. Griffin Lois Duncan	Little, Brown	J	Dell	Realistic Suspense	M/F	teens	166	

1977

Dragonsinger Anne McCaffrey	Atheneum	J	Bantam	Fantasy	F	teens	256	
*I Am the Cheese Robert Cormier	Knopf	J	Dell	Realistic Suspense	M	teens	233	
One Fat Summer Robert Lipsyte	Harper-Collins	J	Bantam	Realistic	M	teens	150	
Winning Robin Brancato	Knopf	J	Bantam	Realistic Disability	M	teens	211	

1976

*Are You in the House Alone? Richard Peck	Viking	J	Dell	Realistic Rape	F	teens	156	

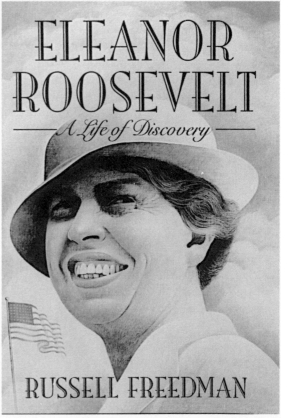

See Focus Box 7.5 (p. 206) for biographies, Focus Box 11.2 (p. 330) for collections of short stories, and Focus Box 11.4 (p. 349) for collections of poetry chosen for the Honor List.

Home Before Dark Sue Ellen Bridgers	Knopf	J	Bantam	Realistic	F	teens	176	migrant workers
*Ordinary People Judith Guest	Viking	A	Viking Penguin	Realistic Family	M	teens	263	
1975								
Dragonwings Laurence Yep	Harper-Collins	J	Harper-Collins	Historical Fiction	M	young teens	248	Chinese-American
Forever Judy Blume	Bradbury	A		Realistic	F	17	216	
*Rumble Fish S. E. Hinton	Delacorte	J	Dell	Realistic	M	teens	122	

Title / Author	Publisher	J/A	Paperback	Genre	M/F	Age	Pages	Setting/Theme
Z for Zachariah Robert C. O'Brien	Atheneum	J	Collier	Science Fiction	F	16	249	Post-nuclear
1974								
*The Chocolate War Robert Cormier	Pantheon	J	Dell	Realistic	M	14	253	
*Carrie Stephen King	Doubleday	A	NAL Dutton	Occult	F	pre-teen	199	
House of Stairs William Sleator	Dutton	J	Puffin	Science Fiction	M/F	teens	166	
If Beale Street Could Talk James Baldwin	Dial	A	Dell	Realistic	F	19	197	African-American
M. C. Higgins, the Great Virginia Hamilton	Macmillan	J	Dell	Realistic	M	13	278	African-American
1973								
A Day No Pigs Would Die Robert Newton Peck	Knopf	J	Dell Random	Historical 1920s	M	13	159	Rural Vermont
The Friends Rosa Guy	Holt	J	Bantam	Realistic	F	early teens	203	West Indians in New York
A Hero Ain't Nothin' But a Sandwich Alice Childress	Coward McCann	J	Avon	Realistic Drugs	M	early teens	126	African American
The Slave Dancer Paula Fox	Bradbury	J	Dell	Historical 1800s	M	13	176	ethnic mix
*Summer of My German Soldier Bette Greene	Dial	J	Dell Bantam	Historical WW II	F	14	199	U.S. South Jewish
1972								
*Deathwatch Robb White	Doubleday	A	Dell	Realistic Suspense	M	early 20s	228	
*Dinky Hocker Shoots Smack! M. E. Kerr	Harper-Collins	J	Dell Harper-Collins	Realistic Family	F	14	198	
*The Man Without a Face Isabelle Holland	Lippincott	J	Harper-Collins	Realistic Homosexuality	M	16	248	

Title / Author								
My Name Is Asher Lev Chaim Potok	Knopf	A	Fawcett	Realistic Family	M	teens	369	Hasidic Jews
A Teacup Full of Roses Sharon Bell Mathis	Viking Peter Smith	J	Puffin	Realistic Drugs	M	17	125	African-American
1971								
*The Autobiography of Miss Jane Pittman Ernest Gaines	Dial	A	Bantam	Historical U.S. South	F	life-time	245	African-American
*The Bell Jar Sylvia Plath	Harper-Collins	A	Bantam	Realistic Suicide	F	19	196	
1970								
*Bless the Beasts and Children Glendon Swarthout	Doubleday	A	Simon & Schuster	Realistic	M	early teens	205	American Southwest
1969								
My Darling, My Hamburger Paul Zindel	Harper-Collins	J	Bantam	Realistic Abortion	M/F	17/18	168	
*Sounder William Armstrong	Harper-Collins	J	Harper-Collins	Historical U.S. South	M	14	116	African-American
Where the Lilies Bloom Vera and Bill Cleaver	Lippincott	J	Dell HarperCollins	Realistic	F	14	174	Rural Isolated
1968								
The Pigman Paul Zindel	Harper-Collins	J	Bantam	Realistic Death	M/F	16	182	
*Red Sky at Morning Richard Bradford	Lippincott	A	Harper-Collins	Realistic	M	17	256	New Mexico ethnic mix
1967								
*The Chosen Chaim Potok	Simon & Schuster	A	Fawcett	Realistic	M	teens	284	Hasidic Jews
The Contender Robert Lipsyte	Harper-Collins	J	Harper-Collins	Realistic	M	17	167	African-American
*Mr. and Mrs. Bo Jo Jones Ann Head	Putnam	A	NAL Dutton	Realistic Pregnancy	M/F	18	253	
*The Outsiders S. E. Hinton	Viking	J	Dell	Realistic	M	14	156	

If a book is included on this Honor List, obviously it is outstanding in some way, but the reasons might differ considerably. One book may be here because of its originality, another for its popularity, and another for its literary quality. We should warn that just because a book has not found its way to this list, it should not be dismissed as mediocre. The list covers nearly 30 years during which there were many more outstanding books published than the ones included here. Whenever such lists are drawn up, a degree of chance is involved.

Many of these books are described in more detail in the following chapters. Here they are simply cited as the evidence we use to illustrate the following generalizations about the best of modern young adult literature.

Characteristic 1: Young Adult Authors Write from the Viewpoint of Young People

A prerequisite to attracting young readers is to write through the eyes of a young person. The most consistent characteristic of the books on the Honor List is the ages of the protagonists. We can count on one hand those in which the protagonist is under 12, and there are fewer than a dozen in which the protagonist is over 20.

With those over 20, the book was most likely published for an adult audience but "found" by mature young adults because the characters are involved in the kinds of activities with which young people identify, such as beginning to live on one's own, finding someone to love, earning a living, and deciding whether earning money is more important than doing what one wants to do. We used to say that in the eyes of teenagers, the big dividing line—the final rite of passage—between childhood and adulthood was having children of one's own so that stories about parenting seldom, if ever, appeared in young adult fiction. With the public acknowledgment of a soaring birthrate to teenaged mothers, however, this is no longer true, as shown by the success of Virginia Euwer Wolff's *Make Lemonade,* the story of 14-year-old Verna LaVaughn who answers a baby-sitting ad and is surprised to find that it was put up by Jolly, the teenaged mother of 2-year-old Jeremy and a younger "gooey baby" named Jilly.

When adult characters play important roles in fictional stories written for young readers, young adult authors take steps to guarantee a youthful viewpoint. For example, in *Fade,* Robert Cormier tells the life story of a man, Paul Moreaux, who inherited his family's blessing/curse of being able to make himself invisible. Cormier makes the first half of the book autobiographical, with Paul Moreaux telling about growing up in the 1930s. Then, to tell about Moreaux's adult years when he has become a successful author, Cormier switches narrators and speaks through the voice of a young female cousin who aspires to be a writer herself.

In general, authors don't have to plot so carefully if the adult characters they write about are a generation removed from teenagers (i.e., are the age of grandparents rather than parents). Perhaps because they are both on the edge of—close but not central to—the mainstream of power, young people seem able to relate more comfortably with elderly than with middle-aged adults (see Focus Box 1.2). Margaret Mahy's *Memory* lets readers get to know both 19-year-old Jonny Dart and 80-plus Sophie West. In Berlie Doherty's *White Peak Farm,* the narrator of a three-generation family story set in England chooses to start the book with her grand-mother's story, "Gran was a gentle soul who'd once had wild and willful ways and who had made my mother the way she is—a cut above the rest, my father says." Other Honor List books that show characters relating to elderly adults include Francesca Block's *Weetzie Bat,* Norma Fox Mazer's *After the Rain,* and Sue Ellen Bridgers *Notes for Another Life.*

Characteristic 2: "Please, Mother, I Would Rather Do It Myself!"

With formula fiction for young readers, one of the first things an author does is to figure out how to get rid of the parents so that the young person will be free to take credit for his or her own accomplishments. Although the Honor List is not made up of formula fiction, there is evidence of the "Please, Mother, I would rather do it

FOCUS BOX 1.2

Across Generations

After the Rain by Norma Fox Mazer. Morrow, 1987.   Getting to know and love a cantanker-ous old man just before he dies is hard, espe-cially when he's your grandfather.

Checking on the Moon by Jenny Davis. Or-chard, 1991. Cab, named after the taxi she was born in, lived all her 13 years in Blue Cloud, Texas, until she and her older brother are shipped off to spend the summer in Pittsburgh with their grandmother.

Like Sisters on the Homefront by Rita Williams-Garcia.   Lodestar/Dutton,   1995. Against her wishes, 14-year-old Gayle and her seven-month-old baby are sent from her "homefront" in Jamaica, New York, to relatives in rural Georgia where she develops a surpris-ing relationship with her dying grandmother.

Memory by Margaret Mahy. Macmillan, 1988. Nineteen-year-old Jonny Dart and 80-plus So-phie West, an Alzheimer's victim, both struggle with problems of time and memory.

Missing May by Cynthia Rylant. Orchard, 1992.   Twelve-year-old Summer has lived with her beloved Aunt May and Uncle Ob since she was 6. When Aunt May dies, Uncle Ob is so devastated that Summer almost loses him too.

Notes for Another Life by Sue Ellen Bridgers. Knopf, 1981.   Wren and Kevin live with Bliss

and Bill, a couple of really nice people who happen to be their grandparents. Their father is in a mental institution, and their mother is off building a career.

Phoenix Rising by Karen Hesse. Holt, 1994. Thirteen-year-old Nyle Sumner lives with her grandmother on a Vermont sheep farm that has been poisoned by an accident at a nearby nuclear-power plant. As Nyle follows the ex-ample of her grandmother, she sees love and hope rise from death and destruction.

Tiger, Tiger, Burning Bright: A Novel by Ron Koertge. Orchard/Kroupa, 1994.   The subject is grim but the approach humorous in this story of 13-year-old Jesse covering up for his cowboy grandfather's problems with symptoms of Alzheimer's.

Walk Two Moons by Sharon Creech. Harper-Collins, 1994. In this unusual Newbery Award winner, 13-year-old Sal takes a car trip—a gift of genuine love—from Ohio to Idaho with her grandparents.

Western Wind by Paula Fox. Orchard Books, 1993.   Elizabeth thinks it's because of a new baby in the family that she has been sent to her grandmother's, but life isn't quite that simple.

myself!" syndrome, as shown by the missing parents in Avi's *The True Confessions of Charlotte Doyle,* Francesca Block's *Weetzie Bat,* Brock Cole's *Celine,* Chris Crutcher's *The Crazy Horse Electric Game,* Norma Fox Mazer's *Downtown,* and all of S. E. Hinton's books.

A different twist to this same idea is for an author to show that the young person is smarter than the parent(s). In Cynthia Rylant's *A Kindness,* 15-year-old Chip Becker has been raised by his single mother, Anne. Rylant sets the stage for the story by explaining that

> Chip was brighter than his mother. His was a logical and quick mind. . . . He was a computermaestro . . . in a word, handy. He had assembled all his own Christmas toys as a child, reading lengthy directions in small print on thin paper as his mother stared helplessly at bags of colored pieces of plastic. At eleven he fixed the Hoover vacuum, and at thirteen he filled out Anne's income tax form. And for the last two years, every Sunday night he had price-compared in the Acme, making a deal with Anne that if she cooked whatever he bought, he would save her twenty dollars a week. It worked.

The conflict in the story begins on the day that Anne confides to Chip that she is pregnant and steadfastly refuses to tell him who the father is. Chip goes through some bad times feeling left out of this momentous event in their lives, but at the end of the story it's his wisdom and his speaking out that bring about a best-case ending.

Obviously the characterization of Chip in this story is meant to appeal more to his than to his mother's generation of readers. In keeping with the variety that exists in the Honor List, other books give more credit to parents and even call into question the idea that the teenager is always right. For example, Bruce Brooks' futuristic *No Kidding* has a protagonist, Sam, who is much like Chip in that at age 8 he balanced the checkbook, at 9 he bought the groceries, and at 10 he conducted his own parent-teacher conferences. Now that he's 14 he thinks he has the duty and the smarts to make all the decisions for his alcoholic mother and his 10-year-old brother, Ollie. Ollie has been placed with foster parents who hope to adopt him, and to the couple's amazement and sometimes irritation Sam takes it upon himself to be their supervisor. But by the end of the book he realizes that there are some things that he can't—and in fact, doesn't even want to—be in charge of.

One of the strengths of the kind of high-quality writing that appears in the Honor List is that good writers gradually lead their readers to look more realistically at themselves and at parent-child relationships. Books that feature at least one capable parent playing a strong, supportive role for a young protagonist include Berlie Doherty's *White Peak Farm,* Peter Dickinson's *Eva,* Jan Hudson's *Sweetgrass,* Virginia Euwer Wolff's *Probably Still Nick Swanson,* Bruce Brooks' *The Moves Make the Man,* Mollie Hunter's *Cat, Herself,* William Armstrong's *Sounder,* Alice Childress' *A Hero Ain't Nothin' But a Sandwich,* Kathryn Lasky's *Beyond the Divide,* and Virginia Hamilton's *M. C. Higgins, the Great.* In Robert Newton Peck's *A Day No Pigs Would Die,* the boy desperately loves his father, and in Bobbie Ann Mason's *In Country* and

Bruce Brooks' *Midnight Hour Encores,* the young protagonists place great importance on learning about an unknown parent.

Characteristic 3: Young Adult Writers Avoid Speechifying

Time magazine described a 1991 off-Broadway play as "MTV drama . . . told in montage, in short riffs of scenes and crosscuts and simultaneous action instead of symphonic arcs of speechifying."[7] We're borrowing the *Time* reporter's description and applying it to young adult books because nearly all young adult authors avoid "symphonic arcs of speechifying," and many of them tell their stories at the same frantic pace and with the same emphasis on powerful images as viewers have come to expect from MTV. Postindustrial countries have become hurry-up societies, and people want their stories to be presented in that same fashion.

The book from the Honor List that comes the closest to being an MTV story is Francesca Block's *Weetzie Bat,* which is 88 pages long. It is a controversial book be-

Two authors whose experiments with literary techniques have contributed to the variety and quality now found in young adult books are Francesca Lia Block and Virgina Euwer Wolff.

cause people who read it under the expectation that it is a realistic story that provides role models for teens come away shocked. But those who read it as an MTV story—a fairytale spoof of Hollywood and reality—come away amused with some vivid images of unforgettable teenage characters. Weetzie hangs out with homosexual Dirk, who is much admired by all the girls. Dirk prefers Weetzie's company, however, not only because, "Under the pink Harlequin sunglasses, strawberry lipstick, earrings, dangling charms, and sugar-frosted eye shadow she was almost beautiful," but because she's different. On the day he meets her, she's wearing her feathered headdress and her moccasins and a pink, fringed mini-dress. "I'm into Indians," she explains. "They were here first and we treated them like shit."

We're not saying that all young adult books are going to have the disjointed punch of music videos or that MTV is responsible for changing teenagers' expectations for leisure entertainment. But there is probably a circular effect in that modern mass media entertainers appeal to the same powerful emotions of adolescence—love, romance, sex, horror, and fear—as young adult authors do. As the mass media provides access to such dramatic material more quickly and more easily, writers may feel pressure to compete.

Evidence from the Honor List shows, however, that long before MTV, teenagers liked their stories to be short and to the point. They preferred a limited number of characters and narrative events and language that flows naturally while still presenting dramatic images that can transfer easily from words in a book to pictures in the mind or on a screen. For example, William Armstrong's 1969 *Sounder* has only 116 pages, Alice Childress' 1973 *A Hero Ain't Nothin' But a Sandwich* has 126 pages, and S. E. Hinton's 1975 *Rumble Fish* has 122 pages.

In 1964, when British author Leon Garfield submitted his first novel to a publishing house, it was turned down "after three or four agonizing months, when they said they couldn't quite decide whether it was adult or junior." He next submitted it to an editor who was just beginning to develop a juvenile line. Garfield said, "She suggested that, if I would be willing to cut it, then she'd publish it as a juvenile book. And of course, though I'd vowed I'd never alter a word, once the possibility of its being published became real, I cut it in about a week."[8]

The assumption that publishers start with is that teenagers have shorter attention spans than adults and less ability to hold one strand of a plot in mind while reading about another strand. There is a tremendous difference, however, in the reading abilities of young people between the ages of 12 and 20. As students mature and become better readers, they are able to stick with longer, more complex books. Approximately a half-dozen of the Honor List books have more than 300 pages. None of Robert Cormier's books is simple and straightforward. Gary Paulsen's *Dogsong* blends the past and the future with the present, whereas with Ernest Gaines' *A Gathering of Old Men*, William Wharton's *Birdy*, and Alice Childress' *A Hero Ain't Nothin' But a Sandwich*, readers must draw together and sort out alternating viewpoints and chronologies. And it is obvious from reading Judith Guest's *Ordinary People*, Rosemary Sutcliff's *The Shining Company*, and James Baldwin's *If Beale Street Could Talk* that their appeal is based on something other than easy reading.

Characteristic 4: Young Adult Literature Includes a Variety of Genres and Subjects

Because the *raison d'être* for adolescent literature is to tell a story about making the passage from childhood to adulthood, some people assume that books for teenagers are all alike. People who say this are revealing more about their reading patterns than about the field of adolescent literature. The Honor List reveals a tremendous variety of subjects, themes, and genres. Although we have moved our Honor List poetry books and short story collections to Chapter Eleven, and such personal narratives as Gary Paulsen's *Woodsong,* Jean Fritz's *Homesick,* and Maya Angelou's *I Know Why the Caged Bird Sings* and *All God's Children Need Traveling Shoes* to Chapter Seven, there is still plenty of variety. Examples of historical fiction in the Honor List include Kaye Gibbons' romantic *Charms for the Easy Life,* Olive Ann Burns' romantic *Cold Sassy Tree,* Kathryn Lasky's pioneer story *Beyond the Divide,* and Rosemary Sutcliff's *The Shining Company,* set in England in 600 A.D. Elements of fantasy and science fiction are as old as the oldest folktales (Walter Wangerin's *The Book of the Dun Cow* and Robin McKinley's *Beauty : A Retelling of Beauty and the Beast*) and as new as nuclear war and the latest board game (Robert C. O'Briens' *Z for Zachariah* and William Sleator's *Interstellar Pig*). Occult fiction is filled with romance (Annette Curtis Klause's *The Silver Kiss* and Virginia Hamilton's *Sweet Whispers, Brother Rush*), whereas futuristic stories thrive on high-tech intrigue (Peter Dickinson's *Eva* and Robert Cormier's *The Bumblebee Flies Anyway*).

Although about half the books are contemporary realistic fiction, even these are far from identical. They range from tightly plotted suspense stories as in Margaret Mahy's *The Tricksters* and John Marsden's *Letters from the Inside* to serious introspection as in Paula Fox's *One-Eyed Cat.* The theme of alienation and loneliness is seen in William Wharton's *Birdy,* whereas the need for a hero is seen in Robert Newton Peck's *A Day No Pigs Would Die* and Glendon Swarthout's *Bless the Beasts and Children.* Threats to the social order are explored in William Sleator's *House of Stairs* and *Interstellar Pig* and in Lois Lowry's *The Giver.* A search for values is shown in Richard Bradford's *Red Sky at Morning* and Chris Crutcher's *The Crazy Horse Electric Game.* What it means to care for others is examined in Norma Fox Mazer's *Downtown,* Isabelle Holland's *The Man Without a Face,* Francesca Lia Block's *Missing Angel Juan,* and Gary Paulsen's *Harris and Me.*

Characteristic 5: The Body of Work Includes Stories About Characters from Many Different Ethnic and Cultural Groups

Thirty years ago, the novels written specifically for teenagers and sold to schools and public libraries presented the same kind of middle-class, white, picket-fence neighborhoods as the one featured in the *Dick and Jane* readers from which most American children were taught to read. But the mid-1960s witnessed a striking change in attitudes. One by one, taboos on profanity, divorce, sexuality, drinking, racial unrest, abortion, pregnancy, and drugs disappeared. With this change, writers were freed to set their stories in realistic rather than romanticized neighborhoods and to explore the experiences of characters whose stories had not been told before.

This freedom was a primary factor in the coming of age of adolescent literature. Probably because there was such a lack of good books about non-middle-class protagonists and because this was where interesting things were happening, many writers during the late 1960s and the 1970s focused on minorities and on the kinds of kids that S. E. Hinton called *The Outsiders.* With the conservative swing that the United States took in the 1980s, not as much attention has been paid to minority experiences; nevertheless, several of the most appealing of the new books feature minority characters and will probably be read by large numbers of teenagers of all races. It's also encouraging that we are seeing books with main characters from different ethnic groups relating to each other (see Focus Box 10.1, p. 309). In Virginia Euwer Wolff's *Make Lemonade,* there is no overt mention of skin color, but as one reviewer stated, Jolly and LaVaughn are held together by "the race of poverty."

Although most schools and libraries are making a concerted effort to stock and teach books reflecting minority cultures (see Focus Boxes 1.3 and 1.4, pp. 30 and 31, as well as Focus Boxes 2.2 and 2.3, pp. 52 and 53), educators worry that publishers who are now marketing books directly to teenagers will not work as hard to include books about minority characters because less affluent kids, many of whom are from minorities, are not as likely to spend money on books as are white, middle-class teenagers. Also, as publishers try to make their books more wish-fulfilling, they tend to return to the romanticized beautiful-people view that was characteristic of the old adolescent literature.

Another fear is that as with most television programming, everything will be watered down to suit mass tastes. But there are some crucial differences, for one person at a time reads a book, whereas television is usually viewed by a group. Even with cable television, the number of channels from which a viewer can choose is limited, but books offer a vast choice. Moreover, advertisers pay for most television programs, whereas readers pay the production costs of books.

Book watchers are encouraged that world events are helping teenagers to become less parochial in their reading. *Shabanu: Daughter of the Wind,* set in present-day Pakistan, was written by Suzanne Fisher Staples, a UPI news correspondent. She uses the story of a young woman's betrothal to introduce English readers to a culture very different from their own. Mollie Hunter's *Cat, Herself* is a romantic story of a Scottish gypsy; Gary Paulsen's *Dogsong* is about a young Inuit; John Marsden's *Letters from the Inside* is set in Australia; Margaret Mahy's books *Memory* and *The Tricksters* are set in New Zealand; and Berlie Doherty's *White Peak Farm* grew out of her work preparing a BBC documentary in Sheffield, England.

Characteristic 6: Young Adults Books Are Basically Optimistic, with Characters Making Worthy Accomplishments

Ensuring that teenage characters are as smart as or smarter than their parents is only one of the devices that authors use to appeal to young readers. They also involve young characters in accomplishments that are challenging enough to earn the reader's respect. In the 1970s, when realism became the vogue and books were written with painful honesty about the frequently cruel world that teenagers face,

FOCUS BOX 1.3

Being African-American

(Other titles featuring African-American characters are presented throughout this text. Especially see Chapter Ten, p. 296, for a discussion.)
Beloved by Toni Morrison. Knopf, 1987. Beloved is the ghost of a girl murdered by her mother to keep her from slavery. Mature young adults could also appreciate the Nobel Prize winner's 1992 *Jazz,* 1972 *The Bluest Eye,* 1973 *Sula,* and 1982 *Tar Baby* (all Knopf).
Betsey Brown by Ntozake Shange. St. Martin's, 1985.   Thirteen-year-old Betsey lives in a loving, middle-class family, but this doesn't take away the pain when in 1959 she enters one of the first integrated schools in St. Louis.
The Color Purple by Alice Walker. Harcourt, 1982.   This powerful story of friendship among women was helped along by the success of Steven Spielberg's movie, which introduced Whoopi Goldberg and Oprah Winfrey to their first mass audiences.
Fast Talk on a Slow Track by Rita Williams-Garcia. Dutton/Lodestar, 1991.   Smart Denzel Watson was class president and valedictorian, but when he gets to Princeton for a six-week summer program he's shocked to find that "winging it" is no longer enough.
Freedom's Children: **Young Civil Rights Activists Tell Their Own Stories** (nonfiction) by Ellen Levine. Putnam, 1993.   In straightforward but moving language, Levine presents 30 first-person accounts collected through interviewing adults who as children or teenagers in the South participated in the civil rights protests of the 1950s and 1960s.
The Glory Field by Walter Dean Myers. Scholastic, 1994.   One reviewer called this a

Roots for teenagers because of the way it focuses on a strong young adult in each generation of the same family starting in Sierra Leone in 1753 and ending in New York City in the 1990s.
If Beale Street Could Talk by James Baldwin. Doubleday, 1974.   In this mature story told in frank, black English, pregnant Tish loves Fonny, who has been jailed on a false charge. Mature teens can also appreciate Baldwin's autobiographical 1953 *Go Tell It on the Mountain.*
Many Thousand Gone: African Americans from Slavery to Freedom by Virginia Hamilton. Knopf, 1993.   This book is especially appealing both because of Leo and Diane Dillon's illustrations and because of Hamilton's writing skill in using many of the actual words of the more than thirty escaped slaves whose stories she tells.
Roll of Thunder, Hear My Cry by Mildred Taylor. Dial, 1976.   In this Newbery Award winner and its sequel *Let the Circle Be Unbroken* (Dial, 1981), the Logan family stands together against the hard times and the prejudice they encounter in Depression-era Mississippi.
Toning the Sweep by Angela Johnson. Orchard, 1993.   Emily knows this will be the last cross-country trip she and her mother make to visit her grandmother, who is dying of cancer. The title comes from an African-American variation on ringing the dead to heaven, a ceremony that symbolizes Emily and her mother's coming to terms with each other and with Grandma Ola's illness.

some critics worried that modern young adult literature had become too pessimistic and cynical. Even in so-called downer books, however, authors created characters that readers could admire for the way they faced up to their challenges.

A comparison of E. B. White's beloved *Charlotte's Web* and Robert Newton Peck's *A Day No Pigs Would Die* illustrates one of the differences between children's and adolescent literature. In White's classic children's book, a beloved but useless

FOCUS BOX 1.4

Being Asian-American

(Other books featuring Asian-American characters are presented throughout this text. Especially see Chapter Ten, p. 296, for a discussion.)

American Eyes: New Asian-American Short Stories for Young Adults edited by Lori M. Carlson. Holt, 1994. These well written stories about immigrants from Japan, China, Vietnam, Korea, and the Philippines are an antidote to readers viewing all Asians as the same.

Children of the River by Linda Crew. Delacorte, 1989. One of the first young adult novels to come to grips with the tremendous adjustments that today's refugees must make, Crew's story is about 17-year-old Sundara's life in Oregon after fleeing the Khmer Rouge in Cambodia.

China Boy by Gus Lee. Dutton, 1991. In this autobiographical novel, American-born Kai Ting shocks his aristocratic Mandarin family by learning to get along on the streets of San Francisco.

Gathering of Pearls by Sook Nyul Choi. Houghton, 1994. Sookan Bak comes from Korea to attend college in New York City, where she struggles not only with the English language, but also with inner conflicts about her family and her future.

The Joy Luck Club by Amy Tan. Putnam, 1989. Jing-Mei, the daughter of an immigrant mother who had lost everything in China, feels the pressure of fulfilling her mother's dreams for America. The story is continued in *The Kitchen God's Wife* (Putnam, 1991).

Shadow of the Dragon by Sherry Garland. Harcourt, 1993. Danny Vo wants to get on with his life in a Houston, Texas, high school, but his plans are upset when he's called on to help Sang Le, a cousin newly arrived from a Vietnamese prison camp.

The Sunita Experiment by Mitali Perkins. Little, Brown, 1993. Thirteen-year-old Sunita thinks she is doing just fine until her grandparents from India arrive for a year-long visit and she comes face-to-face with her Indian heritage. It's some comfort when she discovers that adjustments aren't easy for her mother either.

Tales from Gold Mountain: Stories of the Chinese in the New World by Paul Yee. Macmillan, 1990. Yee's stories show how Chinese immigrants to North America mixed their folklore traditions and beliefs with their new working and living conditions.

Under the Blood-Red Sun by Graham Salisbury. Delacorte, 1994. Thirteen-year old Tomi Nakaji lives on the island of Oahu, Hawaii, and witnesses from a distance the horrific attack on Pearl Harbor. His family's life is forever changed when his grandfather and father are arrested because of their Japanese ancestry.

The Woman Warrior: Memoirs of a Girlhood Among Ghosts by Maxine Hong Kingston. Knopf, 1976. Older teens relate to the author's account of growing up in California surrounded by parents and other relatives who emigrated from China.

pig wins a ribbon at the County Fair and is allowed to live a long and happy life, whereas in Peck's young adult book a beloved but useless pig wins a ribbon at the County Fair but must be slaughtered anyway. Nevertheless, rather than being devastated by the death of the pig, readers identify with the boy and take pride in his ability to do what had to be done.

This kind of change and growth is the most common theme appearing in young adult literature, regardless of format. It suggests, either directly or symbolically, the gaining of maturity (i.e., the loss of innocence as part of the passage from

BERLIE DOHERTY
On a Shared Experience

This statement is in celebration of readers.

When I was eight or nine my mother gave me a book for Christmas. I discovered that she had given a copy of the same book to her friend's son. That was the first time I realized that there could be more than one copy of the same book, and that when I wandered in the secret garden that the writer had created for me I was not alone.

Now as a writer, I invite people to share the garden of my imagination with me. Without the reader there can be no story.

One of the most rewarding things that can happen to a writer is to meet the people she writes for. Writing involves a lot of daydreaming. A boy once described it to me as thinking on purpose, and this is perfectly true. Somewhere between the thoughts that swim about in my head and the scrawly handwriting that skitters across my page the random images take shape and turn into words. All of that is a private and necessarily solitary experience. Then comes the crafting, and the to-ing and fro-ing of manuscripts between myself and my publisher, and at last comes the finished book. It goes on my shelf, and I don't read it again. I didn't write it for myself, or for my editor, or for the booksellers or librarians who stock it. But it's sometimes easy to forget exactly who the book is written for in the first place. So when I meet a group of children and read to them, talk about the idea that the book came from, and answer their questions, it reminds me and reassures me that the book is really for them.

From time to time I need the reassurance long before a book is finished; occasionally, before it is even started. I need to know that the idea is going to work before I embark on the huge process of writing it down. Some of my books would never have been written unless I had chosen to talk to children about them first. *Tough Luck* and *Spellhorn* were both written alongside groups of children who shared the writing process with me. I would discuss a chapter with them and then encourage them to write their own versions while I was writing mine. We would compare notes, reading to each other and seeing how each of us had developed our ideas from the same starting point. Our ideas often overlapped and were like electric currents, sparking off each other. It was a very exciting process, and we all learned something from it. They would learn how to sustain and control an idea, and I would learn from the energy of their writing and the enthusiasm of their response. What we all experienced was a shared joy in writing. It is a thrill to create something out of nothing, and the best reward is to have an immediate audience for it, to know that you are writing for somebody in particular.

Later, when I was redrafting *Tough Luck* and *Spellhorn* in the quiet of my own writing-room, I would hear the voices of those children in every word I wrote, and see their faces. I had no doubt who I was writing for then.

I spoke to many young people before I started to write *Dear Nobody,* which is a story about love and young parenthood. I needed to know how teenagers feel about love and friendship, parents and parenthood, loyalty to others and loyalty to themselves. I think it was the most difficult book I have ever written and there is no way I could have embarked on it without having a sense of the young people who might choose to read it.

Another book, *Street Child,* is set in another century, on the streets of London. I read it out as I wrote each chapter, to a class of eleven-year-olds. I needed to know whether a story that was set in the past would work for children of today. Within a few weeks of meeting that class I knew I was writing the book for them.

I am pleased that I have the opportunity now to acknowledge the role all these young people play in helping to identify my readers, and to celebrate the great sharing that the novel is all about. Writers and readers inhabit the same imaginary world for a time, and the contribution the reader makes is every bit as important as that of the writer.

Berlie Doherty's books for teenagers include *Dear Nobody,* Orchard, 1992; *White Peak Farm,* Orchard, 1990; *Granny Was a Buffer Girl,* Orchard, 1988; and *The Snake-Stone,* Orchard, 1996.

childhood to adulthood). Such stories communicate a sense of time and change, a sense of becoming and catching glimpses of possibilities—some that are fearful and others that are awesome, odd, funny, perplexing, or wondrous.

One of the most popular ways to show change and growth is through a quest story (see Chapter Four for discussion). Avi's *The True Confessions of Charlotte Doyle* is an almost pure example of a quest story camouflaged as a rollicking historical adventure. The intrepid narrator explains on page 1:

> . . . before I begin relating what happened, you must know something about me as I was in the year 1832—when these events transpired. At the time my name *was* Charlotte Doyle. And though I have kept the name, I am not—for reasons you will soon discover—the *same* Charlotte Doyle.

This captures the psychologically satisfying essence of quest stories, which is that over the course of the story, the protagonist will learn something and will change significantly as do the protagonists in Chris Lynch's *Iceman* and *Shadow Boxer,* Cynthia Voigt's *Izzy, Willy-Nilly,* Katherine Paterson's *Lyddie,* Brock Cole's *The Goats,* Bruce Brooks' *Midnight Hour Encores,* and Bobbie Ann Mason's *In Country.* Quest stories with varying degrees of fantasy include Peter Dickinson's *Eva,* Annette Curtis Klause's *The Silver Kiss,* Mollie Hunter's *Cat, Herself,* Lloyd Alexander's *Westmark,* and Robin McKinley's *The Blue Sword.*

Characteristic 7: Successful Young Adult Novels Deal with Emotions That Are Important to Young Adults

Often the difference in the life span between two books that are equally well written from a literary standpoint is that the ephemeral book fails to touch kids where they live, whereas the long-lasting book treats experiences that are psychologically important to young people. Good authors do not peruse psychology books searching for case histories or symptoms of teenage problems they can envision making into good stories. This would be as unlikely—and as unproductive—as it would be for a writer to study a book on literary devices and make a list: "First, I will use a metaphor, and then a bit of alliteration and some imagery, followed by personification."

The psychological aspects of well-written novels are a natural part of the story as protagonists face the same kinds of challenges readers are experiencing, such as the developmental tasks outlined a generation ago by Robert J. Havighurst:

1. Acquiring more mature social skills.
2. Achieving a masculine or feminine sex role.
3. Accepting the changes in one's body, using the body effectively, and accepting one's physique.
4. Achieving emotional independence from parents and other adults.
5. Preparing for sex, marriage, and parenthood.
6. Selecting and preparing for an occupation.
7. Developing a personal ideology and ethical standards.
8. Assuming membership in the larger community. [9]

Some psychologists gather all developmental tasks under the umbrella heading of achieving an identity, which they describe as *the* task of adolescence. In any year, dozens of young adult books touch on the problem of finding one's identity. One of the ways authors show in concrete terms how young people struggle to develop their own identities is to give their characters multiple names, as Ursula K. LeGuin does in her *Earthsea* books, in which she gives her characters a birth name, a use name, and finally a "true" name, each with different meanings and connotations.

In Bruce Brooks' *Midnight Hour Encores*, after considerable soul—and dictionary—searching, the gifted young musician changes her flower-child name of *Esalen Starness Blue* to *Sibilance T. Spooner*, whereas in Katherine Paterson's *Jacob Have I Loved* the protagonist is called *Wheeze*, the nickname given her at age two by her twin who couldn't pronounce *Sara Louise*. Her beloved Captain, however, without seeming to give the matter much thought calls her by her full name, and she writes, "Strange how much that meant to me."

Robert Cormier's *I Am the Cheese* is a multifaceted exploration of Adam Farmer's search for identity as explored through the "reidentification" that his family underwent when Adam was a toddler. He has no memory of being Paul Delmonte, but now that he is an orphaned teenager in a psychiatric institution he wakes in a cold sweat thinking:

But Adam Farmer was only a name, words, a lesson he had learned here in the cold room and in that other room with the questions and answers. Who is Adam Farmer? He didn't know. His name might as well have been Kitchen Chair. Or Cellar Steps. Adam Farmer was nothing—the void yawned ahead of him and behind him, with no constant to guide himself by. Who am I? Adam Farmer. Two words, that's all.

Authors use hundreds of other techniques to hint at the matter of adolescent identity, but they also explore it directly as shown through the following quotes:

I was beginning to develop, at least physically, but nothing seemed to be the right size. Every morning I woke up, I had to check me out to see who was there. Some mornings I was a kid. Some mornings I was a maniac. Some mornings I didn't wake up at all: I just sleepwalked through the day. (From Richard Peck's *Remembering the Good Times*)

Laura picked up her hair brush, looking into the mirror in her room. . . . She stared at herself intently. . . . Sometimes small alterations are more alarming than big ones. If Laura had been asked how she knew this reflection was not hers she could not have pointed out any alien feature. The hair was hers, and the eyes were hers, hedged around with the sooty lashes of which she was particularly proud. However, for all that, the face was not her face, for it knew something that she did not. It looked back at her from some mysterious place alive with fears and pleasures she could not entirely recognize. There was no doubt about it. The future was not only warning her, but enticing her as it did so. (From Margaret Mahy's *The Changeover: A Supernatural Romance*)

"Father, something is bothering me."
He replied around the meat. "I know. I have seen it."
"But I don't know what it is."
"I know that, too. It is part that you are fourteen and have thirteen winters and there are things that happen then which are hard to understand. But the other part that is bothering you I cannot say because I lack knowledge. You must get help from some other place. . . . I think you should go and talk to Oogruk. He is old and sometimes wise and he also tells good stories." (From Gary Paulsen's *Dogsong*)

Close connections exist between adolescent literature and adolescent psychology, with psychology providing the overall picture and adolescent literature providing individual portraits. Because space in this text is too limited to include more than a hint of what you need to know about adolescent psychology, we suggest reading a good text on adolescent psychology such as *Adolescence* by L. Steinberg or *At the Threshold: The Developing Adolescent* edited by S. S. Feldman and G. R. Eliot. Understanding the psychology of young people will help adults

- Judge the soundness of the books they read.
- Decide which ones are worthy of promotion.
- Predict which ones will last and which will be transitory.
- Make better recommendations to individuals.
- Discuss books with students from their viewpoints.
- Gain more understanding and pleasure from personal reading.

Notes

. . . .

[1]David Van Biema, "The Loneliest—and Purest—Rite of Passage: Adolescence and Initiation," *The Journey of Our Lives, Life* magazine (October 1991): 31.

[2]Robert Cormier's acceptance speech for the 1991 Margaret A. Edwards Award, American Library Association Annual Conference in Atlanta, Georgia, June 30, 1991. Printed in *School Library Journal,* 37 (September 1991): 184–86.

[3]"Trash for Teen-Agers: Or Escape from Thackeray, the Brontés, and the Incomparable Jane," *Louisville Courier-Journal,* June 17, 1951. Quoted in Stephen Dunning, "Junior Book Roundup," *English Journal* 53 (December 1964): 702–703.

[4]J. Donald Adams, *Speaking of Books—and Life* (Holt, Rinehart and Winston, 1965), pp. 250–52.

[5]John Goldthwaite, "Notes on the Children's Book Trade," *Harper's* 254 (January 1977): 76, 78, 80, 84–86.

[6]Ben Nelms, "Call for Manuscripts," *English Journal* 80 (October 1991): 7.

[7]William A. Henry III, "MTV Drama: *Unidentified Human Remains and the True Nature of Love,*" *Time* (September 30, 1991): 81.

[8]Justin Wintle and Emma Fisher, eds., *The Pied Pipers: Interviews with the Influential Creators of Children's Literature* (Paddington Press, 1974), p. 194.

[9]Robert Havighurst, *Developmental Tasks and Education* (McKay, 1972).

Titles Mentioned in the Text of Chapter One

. . . .

(in addition to the Honor List and Focus Boxes)

Alcott, Louisa May. *Little Women: or Meg, Jo, Beth, and Amy. The Story of Their Lives. A Girl's Book.* 1868.

Feldman, S. S. and G. R. Eliot, editors. *At the Threshold: The Developing Adolescent.* Harvard University Press, 1993.

Gallo, Donald R., editor. *Speaking for Ourselves: Autobiographical Sketches by Notable Authors of Books for Young Adults.* National Council of Teachers of English, 1990.

Gallo, Donald R., editor. *Speaking for Ourselves, Too: More Autobiographical Sketches by Notable Authors of Books for Young Adults.* National Council of Teachers of English, 1993.

Hipple, Theodore, editor. *Writers for Young Adults.* Charles Scribner's, 1996.

Steinberg, L. *Adolescence,* 3rd edition. McGraw Hill, 1992.

Twentieth-Century Young Adult Writers. St. James Press, 1994.

Zindel, Paul. *The Effect of Gamma Rays on Man-in-the-Moon-Marigolds.* Dramatists, 1970.

Chapter 2

Literary Aspects of Young Adult Books

. . . .

Writers of books for young readers work in much the same way as writers of other sorts of books. They have the same tools and largely the same intent: to evoke a response in a reader through words on a page. In this chapter, we look at some of the tools and techniques that writers use and at the typical ways that young readers respond. For some of you, this may be an introduction to the basics of literary criticism and appreciation, whereas for others it may be simply a review. Even students well versed in literary concepts and terminology, however, may not have thought about them in relation to young adult literature. We hope that the illustrations in this chapter lay a foundation for the way you approach the reading you will do throughout this course.

Stages of Literary Appreciation

Table 2.1 on the stages of literary appreciation outlines one view of how individuals develop reading skills and an appreciation of literature. Read the chart from the bottom up because each level is built on the one below it. People do not go *through* these stages of development; instead they *add on* so that at each level they have all that they had before, plus a new way to gain pleasure and understanding (see also the discussion of teaching literature in Chapter Eleven).

Level 1: Understanding That Pleasure and Profit Come from Printed Words

Lucky children who have bedtime stories and make frequent visits to the library for story hour and for borrowing books and who also have songs, nursery rhymes, and jingles woven into the fabric of everyday life are fortunate enough to develop this first stage of appreciation before they enter school. Jim Trelease, in his highly acclaimed *Read-Aloud Handbook,* explained that he was not writing a book to help parents teach their children to read but to help them teach their children to *want to read.* His interest is in building a firm foundation for the development to follow.

TABLE 2.1

STAGES OF LITERARY APPRECIATION

Read this chart from the bottom up to trace the stages of development most commonly found in reading the autobiographies of adults who love to read.

Level	Optimal Age	Stage	Sample Reading Materials	Sample Actions
7	Adulthood to death	Aesthetic appreciation	Classics Significant contemporary books	Reads constantly Dreams of writing the great American novel Enjoys literary criticism Reads fifty books a year Buys house with built-in bookshelves Rereads favorites
6	College	Reading widely	Best-sellers Acclaimed novels, poems, plays, magazines	Talks about books with friends Joins a book club Gathers a stack of books to take on vacation
5	High school	Venturing beyond self	Science fiction Social issues fiction Forbidden materials "Different" stories	Begins buying own books Gets reading suggestions from friends Reads beyond school assignments
4	Jr. high	Finding oneself in books	Realistic fiction Contemporary problem novels Wish-fulfilling stories	Hides novels inside textbooks to read during classes Stays up at night reading Uses reading as an escape from social pressures
3	Late elementary	Losing oneself in books	Series books Fantasies Animal stories Anything one can disappear into	Reads while doing chores Reads while traveling Makes friends with a librarian Checks books out regularly Gets "into" reading a particular genre or author
2	Primary grades	Learning to decode	School reading texts Easy-to-read books Signs and other real-world messages	Takes pride in reading to parents or others Enjoys reading alone Has favorite authors
1	Birth to kindergarten	Understanding of pleasure and profit from printed words	Nursery rhymes Folktales Picture books	Has favorite books for reading aloud "Reads" signs for certain restaurants and foods Memorizes favorite stories and pretends to read Enjoys listening to adults read

Fortunate children start on the long road to developing literary appreciation even before they learn to talk.

If children are to put forth the intellectual energy required in learning to read, they need to be convinced that it is worthwhile—that pleasure awaits them—or that there are concrete benefits to be gained. In U.S. metropolitan areas, there's hardly a 4-year-old who doesn't recognize the golden arches of a McDonald's restaurant. Toddlers too young to walk around grocery stores reach out from their seats in grocery carts to grab favorite brands of cereal. We know one child who by the time he entered first grade had taught himself to read from *TV Guide*. The format of *TV Guide* breaks almost every rule any good textbook writer would follow in designing a primer for clear and easy reading, but it had one overpowering advantage. The child could get immediate feedback. If he made a correct guess, he was rewarded by getting to watch the program he wanted. If he made a mistake, he knew immediately that he had to return to the printed page to try again.

Level 2: Learning to Read

Learning to decode (i.e., to turn the squiggles on a page into meaningful sounds) is the second stage of development. It gets maximum attention during the primary grades, where as much as 70 percent of the school day is devoted to language arts. But developing literacy is more than just decoding; it is a never-ending task for anyone who is intellectually active. Even at a mundane level, adults continue working to develop their reading skills. The owner of a new VCR trying to tape a television program, the person trying to get a new printer to "handshake" with the computer, and the person who rereads several tax guides in preparation for an audit exhibit the same symptoms of concentrated effort as do children first learning to read. They point with their fingers, move their lips, return to reread difficult parts, and in frustration slam the offending booklet to the floor. But in each case they are motivated by a vision of some benefit to be gained, and so they increase their efforts.

Those of us who learned to read with ease may lack empathy for children who must struggle to master reading skills. In our impatience, we may forget to help them find pleasure and enjoyment. Children who learn to read easily—the girl who sits in the backseat of the car and reads all through the family vacation and the boy who reads a book while delivering the neighborhood newspapers—find their own rewards for reading. For these children, the years between 7 and 12 are golden. They can read the great body of literature that the world has saved for them: *Charlotte's Web;* The Little House books; *The Borrowers; The Chronicles of Narnia; The Wizard of Oz; Where the Red Fern Grows;* and books by Beverly Cleary, William Steig, Dr. Seuss, and hundreds of other good writers.

At this stage, children are undemanding. They are in what Margaret Early has described as a stage of unconscious enjoyment.[1] With help, they may enjoy such classics as *Alice in Wonderland, The Wind in the Willows, Treasure Island,* and *Little Women,* but by themselves they are far more likely to turn to less challenging material. Parents worry that their children are wasting time, but nearly 100 percent of our college students who say they love to read went through childhood stages of being addicted for months to one particular kind of book. Apparently, readers find comfort in knowing the characters in a book and what to expect. They develop speed and skill that stand them in good stead when they tire of a particular kind of book (they always do, sooner or later) and go on to reading some of the books parents and teachers wished they had been reading all along.

Level 3: Losing Oneself in a Story

Those children who read only during the time set aside in school may never get to the third stage of reading development, which is losing oneself in a book. If they do, it is likely to happen much later than in the third or fourth grades, which is typical of good readers. In this segment from *The Car Thief* by Theodore Weesner, Alex Housman, who is being kept in a detention home, is 17 years old when he first experiences losing himself in a story (i.e., finding what we refer to as "a good read"). Someone has donated a box of books to the detention home and because there's nothing else to do

> Alex started to read a book called *Gunner Asch,* starting it mainly because he knew how to read, although he was intimidated by the mass of words. He had never read anything but the lessons in schoolbooks—assignments in history or science spaced with water colors of Washington crossing the Delaware or Thomas Edison working under candlelight. But the novel was simply written and fairly easy to understand, and he soon became interested enough in what

was happening to stop reminding himself page after page that he was reading a book, to turn the pages to see what was going to happen next.

He sat on the floor reading until he grew sleepy. When his eyelids began to slide down and his head began to cloud, he lay over on his side on the floor to sleep awhile, pulling up his knees, resting his head on his arm. When he woke he got up and carried the book with him to the bathroom . . . reading the book again, he became so involved in the story that his legs fell asleep. He kept reading, intending to get up at the end of this page, then at the end of this page, if only because he would feel more comfortable with his pants up and buttoned, but he read on. He rose finally at the end of a chapter, although he read a little into the next chapter before he made himself stop. His legs were buoyant with saws and needles as he buttoned up, and he had to hold a hand against the wall not to sway from balance. Then he checked the thickness of pages he had read between his fingers, and experienced something he had never experienced before. Some of it was pride—he was reading a book—and some of it was a preciousness the book had assumed. Feeling relaxed, un-threatened, he wanted to keep the book in his hands for what it offered. He did not want to turn the pages, for then they would be gone and spent; nor did he want to do anything but turn the pages.

He stepped over legs again and sat down to read, as far from anyone as he could get, some fifteen feet, to be alone with the book. He read on. Something was happening to him, something as pleasantly strange as the feeling he had had for Irene Scheaffer. By now, if he knew a way, he would prolong the book the distance his mind could see, and he rose again, quietly, to sustain the pleasant sensation, the escape he seemed already to have made from the scarred and unlighted corridor. Within this shadowed space there were now other things—war and food and worry over cigarettes and rations, leaving and returning, dying and escaping. The corridor itself, and his own life, was less present.[2]

Level 4: Finding Oneself in a Story

The more experience children have with reading, the more discriminating they be-come. To receive pleasure they have to respect the book. In reminiscing about his childhood fondness for both *The Hardy Boys* and motorcycles, the late John Gard-ner remarked that his development as a literary critic took a step forward when he lost patience with the leisurely conversations that the Hardy boys were supposed to have as they roared down country roads side by side on their motorcycles.

Good readers begin developing this critical sense in literature at about the same time they develop it in real life—at the end of childhood and the beginning of their teen years. They move away from a simple interest in what happened in a story to ask *why*. They want logical development and are no longer satisfied with stereotypes. They want characters controlled by believable human motives because now their reading has a real purpose to it. They are reading to find out about them-selves, not simply to escape into someone else's experiences for a few pleasurable hours. They may read dozens of contemporary teenage novels, looking for lives as much like their own as possible. They read about real people in biographies, personal essays, and journalistic stories. They are also curious about other sides of life, and so they seek out books that present lives totally different from their own. They look for anything bizarre, unbelievable, weird, or grotesque: stories of occult happenings, trivia books, and horror stories. And, of course, for their leisure-time reading they may revert to level 3 of escaping into a good story. But when they are reading at the highest level of their capability, their purpose is largely one of finding themselves and their places in society.

Level 5: Venturing Beyond Themselves

The next stage in reading development comes when people go beyond their egocentrism and look at the larger circle of society. Senior high school English teachers have some of their best teaching experiences with books and stories by such writers as Ernest Hemingway, John Steinbeck, Harper Lee, F. Scott Fitzgerald, Carson McCullers, William Faulkner, Arthur Miller, and Flannery O'Connor. Students respond to the way these books raise questions about conformity, social pressures, justice, and other aspects of human frailties and strengths. Book discussions at this level can have real meat to them because readers make different interpretations as they bring their own experiences into play against those in the books.

Obviously, getting to this level of literary appreciation is more than a matter of developing an advanced set of decoding skills. It is closely tied in with intellectual, physical, and emotional development. Teenagers face the tremendous responsibility of assessing the world around them and deciding where they will fit in. Reading at this level allows teenagers to focus on their own psychological needs in relation to society. The more directly they can do this, the more efficient they feel, which probably explains the popularity of contemporary problem novels featuring young protagonists, as in the books by Will Hobbs, Bruce Brooks, M. E. Kerr, Robert Cormier, Jacqueline Woodson, Alice Childress, Paula Fox, Sue Ellen Bridgers, Chris Lynch, Richard Peck, and Virginia Euwer Wolff.

Although many people read fantasy and science fiction at the level of losing themselves in a good story, others may read such books as William Sleator's *House of Stairs;* Virginia Hamilton's *Sweet Whispers, Brother Rush;* and Robin McKinley's *The Blue Sword* at a higher level of reflection. They come back from spending a few hours in the imagined society with new ideas about their own society.

Levels 6 and 7: Reading Widely and for Aesthetic Appreciation

When people have developed the skills and attitudes necessary to read at all the levels described so far, they are ready to embark on a lifetime of reading both fiction and nonfiction. They not only read for all the purposes described at earlier levels, but also they read for literary or aesthetic appreciation. This is the level at which authors, critics, and literary scholars concentrate their efforts. But even they don't work at this level all the time because it is as demanding as it is rewarding. The professor who teaches Shakespeare goes home at night and loses himself in a televised rerun of "L. A. Law" or "Cheers," and the author who writes for hours in the morning might read herself to sleep that night with an Agatha Christie mystery. Reading at this highest level is an active endeavor because the reader is doing half the work in identifying with the author and figuring out how he or she brought about a certain effect. Additional pleasure comes in knowing facts about the author's life and how the author's books have grown out of personal experiences and beliefs (see Focus Box 2.1).

Summary of Stages

The important points to learn from this discussion of stages of literary development are

- The ages given are the ideal; many people come to the later stages much later or not at all.
- People do not go through these stages but instead add each one onto the foundation below. This means that those who miss a stage are disadvantaged for all subsequent stages.
- Teachers, librarians, and parents should meet young readers where they are and help them feel comfortable at that stage before trying to move them on.
- Moving up to a new level takes not only improved reading skills, but also increased intellectual, physical, and psychological maturity.
- With an adult's help, young people can read at a higher level than they can by themselves; nevertheless, we should not push young people always to work at the highest level of their ability.
- We need to continue to provide for all the levels below the one on which we are focusing; for example, readers at any stage need to experience pleasure and profit from their reading, or they may grow discouraged and join the millions of adults who have dropped off this chart and read only when they are forced to.

Becoming a Literary Critic

The top level is not something a reader reaches effortlessly or that once reached requires no further effort. Reaching that level as a reader means becoming a literary critic, not necessarily for other people but at least for oneself. The difference between being a critic and a reviewer is that a reviewer evaluates and makes recommendations about who would most like to read which book. Critics do more. Besides evaluating and recommending books, they give guidance. They explain. The good critic makes observations that, when shared, help others to read with understanding and insight.

FOCUS BOX 2.1

Memoirs from Contemporary Authors

Bill Peet, an Autobiography by Bill Peet. Houghton, 1989. The many teenagers who have fond memories of Bill Peet's picture books will enjoy this autobiography, which is supplemented with typical Peet drawings.

Boston Boy by Nat Hentoff, Knopf, 1986. Although written as an adult book, Hentoff's story of his Jewish boyhood in the anti-Semitic world of 1930s Boston will be interesting to older teens.

A Girl from Yamhill: A Memoir by Beverly Cleary. Morrow, 1988. Cleary tells the story of her life as a child and a teenager, first on a farm and later in Portland.

I Was a Teenage Professional Wrestler by Ted Lewin. Orchard, 1993. In the 1950s, Ted Lewin went to art school on the money he earned from wrestling. In this unusual memoir, his interest in the sport is lovingly, and sometimes humorously, portrayed through words, photographs, and paintings.

The Ink-Keeper's Apprentice by Allen Say. Houghton, 1994 reissue of a 1979 HarperCollins book, with a new foreword. Allen Say is a noted author and artist, who won the 1994 Caldecott Award. In this autobiographical novel, he tells about his teenage years in postwar Japan when he was apprenticed to a cartoonist.

ME, ME, ME, ME, ME, Not a Novel by M. E. Kerr. HarperCollins, 1983. Although this col-lection of eleven short stories is just as much fun to read as most of Kerr's novel, she says that this one is a true account of the young life of Marijane Meaker, which is Kerr's real name.

Oddballs by William Sleator. Dutton, 1993. Kids who dream of getting even with family members by telling the world how strange they are can use Sleator's nine funny stories as a model.

The Pigman & Me by Paul Zindel. Harper-Collins, 1992. Readers will both laugh and cry at this true account of a year in the teenage life of Paul Zindel.

Speaking for Ourselves: Autobiographical Sketches by Notable Authors of Books for Young Adults and Speaking for Ourselves, Too: More Autobiographical Sketches . . . compiled and edited by Donald R. Gallo. National Council of Teachers of English, 1990 and 1993, respectively. Lively one- or two-page statements, accompanied by photos and lists of their books, make these two volumes wonderful introductions to nearly 150 contemporary authors.

Starting from Home: A Writer's Beginnings by Milton Meltzer. Viking, 1988. Meltzer has brought different periods of history alive for thousands of young readers, and now he does the same thing for the early 1900s, as he tells about his family and childhood.

Developing into the kind of reader able to derive nourishment at the highest level of literary response is a lifelong task, one that challenges all of us. The information presented in this chapter is basic to identifying with a story through the eyes of the author as well as those of the characters. It will help you:

- Sharpen your insights into authors' working methods, so that you will get more out of your reading.
- Give you terminology and techniques to use in sharing your insights with young readers.
- Evaluate books and assist readers in moving up in developing their skills.
- Read reviews, articles, and critical analyses with greater understanding.

Some people speak of literature with a capital *L* to identify the kind of literature that is set apart from, or has a degree of excellence not found in, the masses of printed material that daily roll from the presses. This literature rewards study, not only because of its content, but also because of its style; the techniques used; and the universality, permanence, and congeniality of the ideas expressed.

It is on the question of universality and permanence that some critics have asked whether stories written specifically for young readers can be considered Literature. Their feeling is that if a story speaks only to readers of a certain age, it cannot really have the kind of universality required in true literature. Every adult has lived through an adolescence, however, and continues to experience many of the doubts, leave-takings, embarkings on new roles, and sudden flashes of joy and wonder that can be found in books with protagonists between the ages of 12 and 25. Books that show the uniqueness and at the same time the universality of such experiences—*Adventures of Huckleberry Finn, The Catcher in the Rye, Little Women,* and *Lord of the Flies,* for example—are often referred to as classics. They have proven themselves with different readers across different time periods. Also, they are the books that readers return to for a second and third reading, each time feeling rewarded.

In contrast to literature with a capital *L,* there is formula literature and escape literature. In truth, all stories consist of variations on a limited number of plots and themes, but the difference between what is referred to simply as literature and what is referred to as formula literature is one of degree. Formula literature is almost entirely predictable. Many of the situation comedies, crime shows, and adventure shows on television are formula pieces. So are many of the books that young people—and adults—enjoy reading.

Because formula literature is highly predictable, the reader can relax and enjoy a story while expending a minimum of intellectual energy. For this reason, formula literature is often used as escape literature—something people read only for entertainment and relaxation with little or no hope of gaining insights or learning new information.

Although some significant literature has a plot exciting enough to be read at the level of escapism and fun, the reverse isn't true. There simply is not enough content in formula fiction to make it worthy of the kind of reading done at the upper levels. When viewed in perspective as only part of the world's literature, there is nothing wrong with young people enjoying formula or escape literature either in books or on film.

It is understandable, however, that the goal of most educators who work with young readers is to help them develop enough skill that they are not limited to this kind of reading. We want them to be able to receive pleasure from all kinds of literature, including that which offers much more than escape or amusement.

As is seen in the following chapters, literary techniques can be discussed in many different ways. Two approaches that have proven useful, however, to nearly all considerations of literature include classification by genre and the analysis of

GARY PAULSEN
On Writing

If there were more space and time I would like to tell you how writing came to be for me, about the start of writing, of leaving all things secure—a job as an electronics engineer working in satellite tracking (part of what Tom Wolfe would call the right stuff but what was really the wrong stuff)—of throwing that life over, completely, to be a writer.

Madness.

A writer.

I would tell of the first tries, the first attempts to put words down and have them make sense, show a story, *be* a story and how dismal it was, how sad the first times. Feeble pawing, scratches at the door . . .

And the rejections.

If there were time and more time I would tell of all the rejections, every single one because every one became important, became the thing that kept me going more than anything. Dear author: you do not fit our format. Dear author, in the interests of brevity . . . Dear author, unfortunately at this time we are a bit overstocked on just about anything and everything you want to write about for the rest of your life and on and on . . . And then the pearls, the true saviors, the editors' letters. Dear Author, you show some promise. Dear Author, while we can't use this we would like to see other projects you may be working on . . .

And in the absence of acceptance the rejections, the rejection letters become the reason for writing; the knowledge that somebody out there is actually reading the work, evaluating it, judging it becomes important, must become important enough to take you through all the rough jobs, the dishwashing, the construction, the janitorial services, the grunt labor doing hot tar and gravel roofing in August in Denver, the truck driving, the replacing septic systems and demolitions work in the mountains. Writing through all of that, every night, studying and writing and the only pay a letter, a word.

An editorial comment. God, in the dark of failure, in the pit of it to get that, just that saving time spent by an editor who really read, who really understood, who really cared, who really wanted to help.

If there were time I would tell you of the editors, the ones who saved and the ones who hurt, the letters saved and read and reread, folded and refolded and finally taped to the wall so that when it was bad, when it was grinding down and bad and it didn't seem possible to sell work, to live as a writer, there would be the letter. Editorial comments. The only pay for long work, for life work.

If there were time and more time I would tell you of other writers. Every one, every single one I asked for help willingly gave it, helped with work, helped with salve for wounds, helped sometimes with small money and food and advice just as I try to help now and when you see that old cliché, see that bit of silliness that says writing is a lonely profession it is perhaps wise to remember the editors and other writers and wives and husbands and families and friends and publishers and sales people and book stores and libraries who all are part of it. Writing is a lonely profession as running the Iditarod is lonely—without the help of others, the support, the writer and dog runner cannot be alone.

And still more, if there were more time I would tell you of acceptance.

Acceptance.

What a small word to mean so much, no, to mean everything. All of it comes down to that, to that one word:

Acceptance.

It finally becomes something that cannot be, cannot ever come; so many rejections, so many letters and comments and failures that it becomes a grail, something never achieved, something dreamed for, longed for, lusted for and never, never there and one day it comes.

The same kind of letter. So similar that at first it is thrown down as another rejection but a word catches, a different word jumps from the paper and there will never be another first like this one; not first love nor first hope nor first time never, no never one like this.

Dear author, we have decided to publish your book.

Can you *imagine?* Your life, your work, your hopes and thoughts and songs and breath—we have decided to publish your book. We have decided to publish *you*— God it thunders, burns into your mind, your soul.

I remember thinking that it didn't matter if I died right then. That nothing would be better, sweeter than that moment. Nothing. And nothing has been better.

If there were yet more time I would tell you of other moments and acceptances and failures that were not quite as big but close, close, and I would, finally, tell you stories . . .

Stories of love and death and cold and heat and ice and flame, stories sad and stories happy and stories of laughter and tears and places soft and hard, of dogs and the white-blink of arctic ice, stories of great men and beautiful women and souls and devils and gods, stories of lost dreams and found joys and aches and torture and great rolling hills and towering storms and things quick and hot and slow and dull, stories of graves and horses, pigs and kings, war and the times between wars, stories of childrens' cheeks and the soft hair at a woman's temple when it is moist, stories of rage and spirit and spit and blood and bodies on fences and hay so sweet you could eat the grass, oh God yes, stories of all things there are I would tell you, to make the hair go up on the back of the neck and stop the breath and bring life—stories that are everything, all of everything there is, these stories.

All these things I would try to do if there were only time.

But there is not. There is, sadly, only time to thank you for all you have done for me and to offer a hope that you will continue with me in this wonderful dance.

Thank you.

Gary Paulsen's books include *Woodsong,* Bradbury, 1990; *Hatchet,* Bradbury, 1985; *Voyage of the Frog,* Orchard, 1989, and *Harris and Me,* Harcourt Brace, 1993.

such essential literary elements as plot, theme, character, point of view, tone, setting, and style.

Plot

When friends tell each other about "good" books, they usually begin by recounting the plot. Plots are the skeletons on which all other aspects of a story hang. Plot is what happens; that is, the sequence of events in which the characters play out their roles in some kind of conflict.

Elements of Plot

For most young readers, there needs to be a promise within the first few pages that something exciting is going to happen, that there is going to be a believable conflict. Authors use various techniques to get this message across to their readers, or to "hook" them. Notice how Bruce Brooks arouses the curiosity of his readers in the first two paragraphs in *The Moves Make the Man:*

> Now, Bix Rivers has disappeared, and who do you think is going to tell his story but me? Maybe his stepfather? Man, that dude does not know Bix deep and now he never will, will he? Only thing he could say is he's probably secretly happy Bix ran away and got out of his life, but he won't tell you even that on account of he's busy getting sympathy dumped on him all over town as the poor deserted guardian.
>
> How about Bix's momma? Can she tell you? I reckon not—she is crazy in the hospital. And you can believe, they don't let crazies have anything sharp like a pencil, else she poke out her eye or worse. So she won't be writing any stories for a long time. But me—I have plenty of pencils, number threes all sharp and dark green enamel on the outside, and I have four black and white marble composition books. . . .

Other authors use catchy titles as narrative hooks; for example, Jerry Spinelli's *There's a Girl in My Hammerlock,* Paula Fox's *The Moonlight Man,* Douglas Adams' *The Hitchhiker's Guide to the Galaxy,* and Olive Ann Burns's *Cold Sassy Tree.* Titles that are questions, such as Richard Peck's *Are You in the House Alone?* and M. E. Kerr's *If I Love You, Am I Trapped Forever?* trigger other questions in readers' minds and make them pick up the book to find the answers.

Asking questions like this works much the same as *in media res* (Latin for "in the midst of things"). It's a technique that authors use to bring the reader directly into the middle of the story. This is usually followed by a flashback to fill in the missing details. Paul Zindel does this in *The Pigman.* Few readers put the book down after they get acquainted with two likable teenagers and then read John's statement:

Now Lorraine can blame all the other things on me, but she was the one who picked out the Pigman's phone number. If you ask me, I think he would have died anyway. Maybe we speeded things up a little, but you really can't say we murdered him.

Not murdered him.

The most exciting plots are the ones in which the action is continually rising, building suspense, and finally leading to some sort of climax. In most books, the climax will be followed by a *denouement*. The purpose may be to wrap up the details, as when Bruce Brooks ends *The Moves Make the Man* by showing that it was really Jerome's (the narrator's) story, as much as Bix's, which was being told. Jerome makes the transition to his own story with, "Then it was summer and no sign of Bix and I decided to write this book. Now it is fall and you have the story." The remaining six paragraphs reassure the reader that although Bix is gone, Jerome is going to make it.

In emotional stories, the denouement serves to let readers down gently, as when Orson Scott Card uses a family's nicknames to soften the ending of *The Lost Boys: A Novel.* The oldest son is abducted and murdered, but the grief is assuaged by the narrator's belief in an afterlife. Early in the story, Card explained how Step Fletcher and his wife Deanne called each other *Junkman* and *Fishlady*. The children had nicknames too. The oldest, Stevie, was *Doorman*, Robbie was *Robot* or *Roadbug,* Elizabeth was *Betsy* and sometimes *Betsy Wetsy,* and the new baby, Jeremy, was *Zap.* After Stevie's abduction and murder was discovered on a traumatic Christmas Eve, Card concluded his story by saying that one other thing was lost on that Christmas Eve. The children lost their nicknames and all memory of their parents calling each other *Junkman* and *Fishlady.* No one made a conscious decision about the names; it was just that they were part of a set, and it didn't seem right to use only some of them. "But someday they would use all those names when *Doorman* met them on the other side."

In contrast to plots with rising action are those that are episodic. Writers of nonfiction use many of the literary techniques discussed here so that as they describe incidents and quote dialogue, the paragraphs they write differ little from fiction. Rather than developing an overall plot, however, they are more likely to present a series of episodes. This is typical of memoirs such as James Herriot's *All Creatures Great and Small,* Maya Angelou's *I Know Why the Caged Bird Sings,* and Milton Meltzer's *The American Revolutionaries: A History in Their Own Words.*

The more unusual a plot is, the greater is the need for foreshadowing, in which the author drops hints that prepare readers for what is ahead. In *Cat, Herself,* Mollie Hunter does it through fortune-telling and the vision that Cat sees of herself. Robert Cormier did it in *We All Fall Down* by naming the handyman, who turns out to be a psychopath, Mickey Looney. Anyone familiar with Cormier's writing would know better than to dismiss Jane's explanation:

"His name is Mickey Stallings but everybody calls him Mickey Looney," she said. "Behind his back of course." Needing to explain: "Because he looks like that old movie star, Mickey Rooney. But, Looney because he is sort of odd."

Jane feels she's betrayed the neighborhood by confiding Mickey's name because the "nickname Mickey Looney was used affectionately for this gentle man who patted dogs, tousled the hair of small kids, nodded respectfully to the men and tipped his faded baseball cap to the ladies." Cormier establishes tension by having Jane's friends say he gives them the creeps, and when Jane goes on to explain how smart he is, she is setting up an explanation that will make credible what happens 150 pages later.

In fantasy and science fiction, foreshadowing may be what identifies the genre. For example, in William Sleator's *Interstellar Pig,* the foreshadowing starts with the first sentence, "I'm telling you, there's more history to this house than any other place on Indian Neck, and that's the truth." On page 5, the landlord says about the new neighbors, "This here's the place they wanted, but they were too late. Already rented it to you folks. Man, were they ever disappointed. Never heard anybody get so upset about a summer rental."

The effect of foreshadowing is not to give away the ending, but to increase excitement and suspense and prepare the reader for the outcome. If authors fail to prepare readers—at least on a subconscious level—their stories may lack verisimilitude or believability. Readers want interesting and exciting plots, but they do not want to feel manipulated.

Traditionally, readers have expected to know all the answers by the end of the book, to have the plot come to a tidy close. With some stories, however, authors think this is an unrealistic expectation, and so they leave it up to the reader to imagine the ending. In *A Hero Ain't Nothin' But a Sandwich,* Alice Childress didn't think it fair to predict either that Benjie would become a confirmed drug addict or that he would go straight. Boys in his situation turn either way, and Childress wanted readers to think about this.

To have an interesting plot, a story must have a problem of some sort. In adult books, several problems may be treated simultaneously, but in most of the books written specifically for young adults as well as in those that they respond to from the adult list, the focus is generally on one problem. Authors may include a secondary or minor problem, however, to appeal to specific readers. For example, Paul Zindel usually focuses on personal growth and development, but he also tucks in unobtrusive elements of love that bring satisfaction to romantically inclined readers without being bothersome to the rest of his audience.

Types of Plots

Basically the problems around which plots are developed are of four types: protagonist against self, protagonist against society, protagonist against another person, and protagonist against nature.

PROTAGONIST AGAINST SELF

Many rites-of-passage stories are of the protagonist-against-self type, in which the protagonist comes to some new understanding or level of maturity. In Paula Fox's *One-Eyed Cat,* much of the conflict takes place in the mind of 11-year-old Ned. An uncle gives him a Daisy air rifle for his birthday, which his father puts in the attic and forbids him to use. But when Ned goes to the attic he finds "it almost at once, as though it had a voice which had called to him." He takes the gun outside and convinces himself that if he tries it just once, he will "be able to do what his father had told him to do—take his mind away from it."

Events do not turn out as Ned anticipated. It's true that after he fires the gun, he no longer has an interest in shooting, but this is because he is tortured by his memory:

> As he blinked and opened his right eye wide, he saw a dark shadow against the stones which the moon's light had turned the color of ashes. For a split second, it looked alive. Before he could think, his finger had pressed the trigger. There was a quick *whoosh,* the sound a bobwhite makes when it bursts out of under-brush, then silence. He was sure there hadn't been any loud report that would have waked anyone in the house, yet he had heard something, a kind of thin disturbance in the air. He walked over to the barn. There was no shadow now. There was nothing. He might have only dreamed that he had fired the rifle.

But within a few days when Ned is visiting the old man who lives next door, he sees a gaunt-looking cat and notices that the cat has dried blood on its face and a little hole where its left eye should be. "A thought was buzzing and circling inside his head, a thought that stung like a wasp could sting. . . . He had disobeyed his father and he had shot at something that was alive. He knew it was that cat."

The rest of the book is the story of Ned's internal anguish, his keeping the terrible secret to himself at the same time he attempts to make up for his action, and finally his coming to terms with the event and his sharing of it with his mother.

PROTAGONIST AGAINST SOCIETY

Protagonist-against-self stories are often, in part, protagonist-against-society stories. For example, in Sylvia Plath's *The Bell Jar,* Esther Greenwood is struggling to understand herself, but the depression and the fears and doubts that she feels are brought on by her experience in New York as a college intern on a fashion magazine. Getting accepted for this position had been an important goal of hers, and she is disappointed because, when she achieves this goal, she finds that the work and the life that go with it seem frivolous and hollow.

Books about members of minority groups (see Focus Boxes 1.3, p. 30; 1.4, p. 31; 2.2, p. 52; and 2.3, p. 53) frequently include themes of protagonist-against-society because of the tensions that exist when members of the smaller group face choices about how much they want to try fitting into the norms of the larger group. In such books, the individuals' self-concepts as well as the problems they face are directly related to the society around them, as with the Hasidic Jews in Chaim Potok's *My Name Is Asher Lev* and *The Chosen,* the Hispanic characters in Gary Soto's *Baseball in April* and *Local News,* and the Native American characters in Louise Erdrich's *Love Medicine.* In Marie Lee's *Finding My Voice,* the father illustrates society's effects on his behavior when he explains to the daughter who wonders why he never talks about Korea, "When you leave a country it is like an animal caught in a trap that gnaws a limb off to free itself. You can't dwell on what you've lost—if you want to survive. You have to go on with what you have."

PROTAGONIST AGAINST ANOTHER

Sometimes there is a combination in which the protagonist struggles with self and

FOCUS BOX 2.2

Being Latin American

(Other books featuring Hispanic or Latin-American characters are presented throughout this text. Especially see Chapter Ten, p. 296, for a discussion.)

An Island Like You by Judith Ortiz Cofer. Orchard, 1995. The kids who narrate these interconnected short stories live in a tenement in Paterson, New Jersey, called *El Building*. Their families are Puerto Rican immigrants, and many of the conflicts revolve around balancing family values with those of the new culture.

Barrio Boy by Ernesto Galarza. University of Notre Dame Press, 1977. Written in the style of a biography, this traces a boy's journey from a small village in northern Mexico to a barrio in Sacramento.

Famous All Over Town by Danny Santiago. Simon & Schuster, 1983. In this family story set in East Los Angeles, Chato stands up against pressure not only from the neighborhood gang but also from his father.

Hunger of Memory: The Education of Richard Rodriguez an autobiography by Richard Rodriguez. Godine, 1982. When Richard Rodriguez earned his Ph.D. from the University of California at Berkeley, the honor symbolized Rodriguez's assimilation into mainstream culture but alienation from his roots.

The House on Mango Street by Sandra Cisneros. Arte Publico, 1984. Although published for adults, these vignettes about Esperanza and her friends coming of age in a Chicago neighborhood speak to many teenagers as do the more mature stories in her 1991 *Woman Hollering Creek and Other Stories* (Random House).

Jesse by Gary Soto. Harcourt, 1994. Judging from the authentic voice of 17-year-old Jesse, a Mexican-American living in Fresno, California, in the late 1960s, the young Gary Soto probably faced many of the same challenges met by his protagonist. Lighter stories for younger readers are in Soto's short story collections, including his 1993 *Local News* (Harcourt), 1991 *Taking Sides* (Harcourt), 1991 *A Summer Life* (Dell), and 1990 *Baseball in April and Other Stories* (Harcourt).

Journey of the Sparrows by Fran Leeper Buss and Daisy Cubias. Dutton/Lodestar, 1991. This dramatic story of an illegal immigrant family begins with 15-year-old Maria and her family being nailed into a wooden crate in the back of a truck to be driven across the Mexican border into the United States.

Latino Voices edited by Frances R. Aparicio. Millbrook, 1994. This collection of poetry, fiction, and biography is good for illustrating the variety that exists among and within the groups that make up this fast-growing minority.

Nilda by Nicholasa Mohr. HarperCollins, 1973. *Nilda* and its sequels *El Bronx Remembered* (HarperCollins, 1975), *In Nueva York* (Dial, 1977), and *Going Home* (Dial, 1986) show what it was like for the author to be a Puerto Rican and a New Yorker.

Pocho by Jose Antonio Villarreal. Doubleday, 1959. Set during the Depression in California, Villarreal's story was one of the first to show the frustration and pain of trying to be part of two worlds.

with another person or persons. For example, in Judith Guest's *Ordinary People,* Conrad is struggling to gain his mental health after he attempts suicide, but this struggle is tied to the sibling rivalry that he felt with his older brother who was killed accidentally. And the sibling rivalry is tied to the relationship that exists between him and his parents. Because nearly everyone has experienced conflicts with family members, they can identify with the sibling rivalry in Katherine Paterson's

FOCUS BOX 2.3

Being Native American

(Other books featuring Native American characters are presented throughout this text. Especially see Chapter Ten, p. 296, for a discussion.)

Bearstone by Will Hobbs. Atheneum, 1989. Cloyd, whose mother is dead and whose father is kept alive only by machines, resents being sent to spend the summer as a helper to an elderly farmer whose wife recently died.

The Brave by Robert Lipsyte. HarperCollins, 1991. Sonny Bear, an up-and-coming young boxer, leaves the Moscondaga reservation and ends up in Harlem, where, fortunately, not all the people he meets are as devious as his self-appointed welcoming committee.

Ceremony by Leslie Marmon Silko. Viking/Penguin, 1977. Mature readers appreciate this story of a young Native American soldier coming home to search for meaning in his life.

Love Medicine by Louise Erdrich. Holt, 1984. In *Love Medicine* and its sequels *The Beet Queen* (Holt, 1986) and *Tracks* (Holt, 1988), Erdrich tells interrelated stories set on a North Dakota reservation. They are written for adults and focus on mature subject matter; however, powerful and poetic language makes for good reading aloud of some of the stories.

Navajo Visions and Voices Across the Mesa written and illustrated by Shonto Begay. Scholastic, 1995. Begay's paintings and free verse explanations celebrate this Arizona artist's native culture.

Skinwalkers by Tony Hillerman. HarperCollins, 1987. Hillerman writes intriguing mysteries set on a Navajo reservation in Arizona. Other titles about his Navajo detectives Lieutenant Joe Leaphorn and Officer Jim Chee include *The Dance Hall of the Dead, The Listening Woman, People of Darkness, The Dark Wind,* and *The Blessing Way.*

Talking Leaves: Contemporary Native American Short Stories edited by Craig Lesley and Katheryn Stavrakis. Laurel, 1991. Although designed as a textbook for college literature classes, many of the stories are fine for high school readers.

When the Legends Die by Hal Borland. HarperCollins, 1963. One of the first young adult books to treat the problem of growing up in two cultures, Borland's book is the story of a Ute boy raised by whites after the death of his parents.

Winter in the Blood by James Welch. Penguin, 1974. In this most accessible of Welch's novels, a young man recounts the death of his brother and other memories of his family's life on a western reservation.

A Yellow Raft in Blue Water by Michael Dorris. Holt, Rinehart & Winston, 1987. Three generations of women tell their stories in this engrossing novel that centers around 15-year-old Rayona, who is half-Native American, half African American.

Jacob Have I Loved, the tenuousness of the father-daughter relationship in Paula Fox's *The Moonlight Man,* and the intergenerational conflicts between the three women in Michael Dorris' *A Yellow Raft in Blue Water.*

Adventure stories, for example, the *Rambo* movies based on David Morrell's *First Blood,* epitomize the person-against-person plot, as does Robb White's *Deathwatch,* in which the hunting guide becomes the hunting target.

Fantasy and science fiction often have person- (or creature-) against-person plots because it is easier to personify evil when the subjects are not real people, as with the aliens in William Sleator's *Interstellar Pig,* the twin in Lois Duncan's occult *Stranger with My Face,* and the evil Arawn in Lloyd Alexander's *The Black Cauldron.*

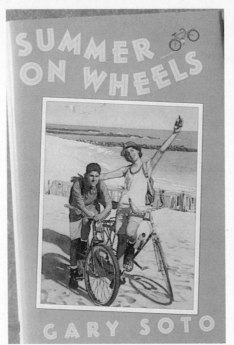

A welcome trend is for books by and about members of minority groups to show characters participating in mainstream activities.

PROTAGONIST AGAINST NATURE

Among the most exciting of the protagonist-against-nature stories are accounts of true adventures, such as Piers Paul Read's *Alive: The Story of the Andes Survivors,* Thor Heyerdahl's *The "RA" Expeditions,* and Dougal Robertson's *Survive the Savage Sea.* The stories of contemporary young adults challenging the seas include Steven Callahan's *Adrift: Seventy-Six Days Lost at Sea* and Robin Graham's *Dove.*

Within recent years, several authors have done a reverse twist on the person-against-nature plot and have made nature the protagonist and people the antagonists. This is the beginning situation in Richard Adams' *Watership Down* and in Robert C. O'Brien's post-nuclear-war *Z for Zachariah.*

Theme and Mode

Closely related to plot is theme. Theme in a book is what ties it all together and answers the questions: What does the story mean? What is it about? Theme should not be confused with a didactic moral tagged on at the end of a story, and it should not be confused with plot. Instead, it is something that pervades the story and stays with the reader long after details of plot, setting, and even character have faded.

Sometimes an author is explicit in developing a theme, even expressing part of it in the title, as with Maya Angelou's *All God's Children Need Traveling Shoes,* John Knowles's *A Separate Peace,* and Virginia Euwer Wolff's *Make Lemonade.* At other times, the theme is almost hidden so that young readers need help in finding it through discussion of the book with others who have read it. A book can have more than one theme, but usually the secondary themes are less important to the story. Because of the experiences that a reader brings to a book, however, it may be a secondary theme that happens to impress a particular reader. A theme must be discovered by the reader. It cannot simply be told or else it is reduced to a moral.

The kinds of themes treated in stories are closely correlated with the mode in which they are written. Northrop Frye divided mode into comedy, romance, irony/satire, and tragedy. Together these make up the story of everyone's life, and in literature as in life they are interrelated, flowing one into the other. Comedy might be compared to spring, childhood, innocence, and happiness. Romance also connotes happiness and is often associated with summer, the teen years, young love, and growth. Irony and satire correlate symbolically with fall, middle age, the existence of problems, and unhappiness. Tragedy is correlated with winter, old age, suffering, and sadness.[3]

Books for children and young people have most often been written in the comic and romantic modes because, as Annie Gottlieb pointed out in "A New Cycle in 'YA' Books," "An unwritten commandment of YA fiction had always been, 'Thou shalt leave the young reader with hope.'" She credited Robert Cormier with shattering this rule in 1974, when he published *The Chocolate War,* and "The American Library Association's *Booklist* gave it a black-bordered review, suggesting an obituary for youthful optimism."[4] Throughout the 1970s, the problem novels that got the most attention from teachers, librarians, reviewers, and young readers were books in the darker modes of irony/satire and even tragedy. These included such books as the anonymous (really Beatrice Sparks')[5] *Go Ask Alice,* John Donovan's *Wild in the World,* and Jean Renvoize's *A Wild Thing.* The protagonists in these books are helpless to change the forces of the world that gather against them.

The reader of a tragedy is usually filled with pity and fear—pity for the hero and fear for oneself that the same thing might happen. The intensity of this involvement causes the reader to undergo an emotional release or catharsis that drains away subconscious fears, leaving the reader filled with pride in what the human spirit is able to undergo and still survive. Robert Cormier's books stand out as being among a small number of young adult books that come close to being tragedies. As shown in Chapter Three, however, many problem stories are written in the ironic mode.

Today it is easier to find examples of books written in the happier modes, those of comedy and romance. In these optimistic books, there are challenges to be met, but the stories have happy endings. Chapter Four explores the romantic mode, which is characterized by not only happy endings, but also exaggeration and wish fulfillment.

In popular culture, the term *comedy* most often refers to something funny, something that makes people laugh. In literary criticism, *comedy* or *the comic mode* are terms that can be used as descriptors for stories that are mostly serious or even grim. What is necessary is that the events in the story move from ironic chaos to a renewal of human hope and spirit. An example is Felice Holman's *The Wild Children,* set in the postrevolutionary Russia of the 1920s. Twelve-year-old Alex comes downstairs from his attic bedroom to find that his family has been taken away. He is alone in the world, as are thousands of young Russians who make up the *bezprizorni*—the unsheltered ones. Most of the story is about Alex's terrible fear, his loneliness, and the hardships endured by these children of war. He becomes part of a gang of children who aid each other in the hard business of survival and at the end of the book escape to Finland. The closing line is a brief sentence that is almost a literal fulfillment of the definition of the comic mode, "Once again, life began." It is important to the symbolic nature of the story that it is not only Alex's life, but also the lives of the ten children who escaped with him, that can begin again. Hope for the future is made even greater by the decision of the gang's leader, 14-year-old Peter, to stay behind as a helper in the underground, bringing more of the orphans to freedom.

Character

The popularity of many books that do not have exciting or even interesting plots is a testament to the power of good characterization. When, through a writer's skill, readers identify closely with the protagonist, they feel as if they are living the experience. They become more interested in what is going on in the character's mind than they may be in what is happening to the character. Young adult authors who do an especially good job of developing memorable characters include Virginia Hamilton, Sue Ellen Bridgers, Chris Crutcher, Cynthia Voigt, Katherine Paterson, Francesca Lia Block, Robert Cormier, Lois Lowry, Cynthia Rylant, and Brock Cole.

Character Development and Types

Because of the short length of most adolescent books, the author does not have space to develop fully more than a small cast of characters. There is usually a protagonist, an antagonist, and various supporting characters. The protagonist is usually the central character, the one with whom the reader identifies. Most commonly, this is a young adult, perhaps a bit older than the reader but not always. After reading a book with a fully developed protagonist, readers should know the character so well that if a situation outside of the book were described, they could predict how this character would feel and act in the new situation. They could do this because the author has developed a round character. Many sides—many different aspects—of the character have been shown. A major character can undergo changes in personality in ways a minor character cannot. Such changes are often the heart of the story, but if the character is not well developed, the changes have no meaning. Readers cannot rejoice in the arrival of a character unless they know where the character started.

A character who undergoes changes is said to be dynamic, whereas a character who stays basically the same is static. Chances are that if the focus of a story is characterization, the protagonist will be dynamic. Readers will be led to understand how and why the protagonist has changed. Background characters are usually static. In many books in which the focus is on an exciting plot or the protagonist is telling someone else's story, the main character may also be static, having much the same goals and attitudes at the end as at the beginning. Many static characters are flat or stereotyped. As books (not just those for teenagers but for all ages) have gotten shorter and shorter, the literary element most affected has been characterization. For efficiency, authors have begun to rely more heavily on character types than on unique individuals.

Of course, this is not entirely new. Since the beginning of literature, there have been archetypes that appear again and again. The hero who leaves home on a danger-fraught mission and returns as a stronger and better person is an archetype seen in stories as divergent as the biblical story of Joseph, Steven Callahan's nonfiction *Adrift: Seventy-Six Days Lost at Sea,* Robin McKinley's fantasy *The Blue Sword,* and Sharon Creech's realistic *Walk Two Moons.* It is because this particular archetype is a part of most readers' backgrounds that they have a good feeling at the end of Robert C. O'Brien's *Z for Zachariah.* As Ann Burden leaves the "safety" of Hidden Valley and ventures out into the radioactive world, readers feel confident that she will complete her quest and find other people with whom she can live and build a new society.

A reviewer is probably making a negative comment in saying that an author's characters are stereotypes, but, in reality, it is necessary that at least some characters in nearly every story be stereotyped. (The word *stereotyped* comes from the printer's world, where it used to refer to the process by which an image is created over and over again.) It would be impossible for an author to build a unique personality for every background character, and it would be too demanding for a reader to respond to a large number of fully developed characters.

The use of stock characters was always accepted as part of the act of storytelling, but in the late 1960s and 1970s, as people's social consciousness grew, so did their dislike for stereotyping. Minority groups complained that their members were stereotyped in menial roles, feminists complained that women and girls always took a back seat to men and boys, and parents complained that they were presented as unimportant or even damaging to their children's lives. Justified as these complaints were (or are), it does not mean that writers can get along without relying on stock characters or stereotypes. But they can feature as main characters members of those groups who have previously been ignored or relegated to stereotypes. Doing this well is always a challenge, especially when the character is someone that most young readers are not accustomed to identifying with, for example, a boy with cerebral palsy as in Jan Slepian's *The Alfred Summer,* a lesbian as in M. E. Kerr's *Deliver Us From Evie,* and a despondent Vietnam veteran as in Bobbie Ann Mason's *In Country.*

Communicating Character

We focus on Katherine Paterson's 1940s story set on Rass Island in the Chesapeake Bay, *Jacob Have I Loved,* to illustrate techniques authors use to help readers know and understand their characters. Characterization is crucial in this book because the problem in the story—that of sibling rivalry between the competent and practical Sara Louise and her beautiful and talented twin sister Caroline—takes place inside Sara Louise's mind. If readers don't have empathy for Sara Louise, they won't identify with her or appreciate the story.

Paterson explained in her Newbery Award acceptance speech that the conflict at the core of the book

> . . . began east of Eden, in the earliest stories of my heritage. "Cain was jealous of his brother and slew him." If, in our Freudian orientation, we speak of the basic conflict as that between parent and child, the Bible—which is the earth from which I spring—is much more concerned with the relationships among brothers and sisters. "A friend loveth at all times," says the writer of Proverbs, "but a brother is born for adversity." They never taught us the second half of that verse in Sunday School.[6]

She went on to cite the numerous fairy tales in which the youngest brother or sister must surpass the supposedly more clever elders or outwit the wicked ones, and she argued with Bruno Bettelheim's suggestion that the rivalry between brothers and sisters is actually an Oedipal conflict or is about the split self. "I do not think," she said, "we can avoid the most obvious meaning of the stories, which is that among children who grow up together in a family there run depths of feeling that will permeate their souls for both good and ill as long as they live."

Authors develop characters by telling readers what the characters do, what they say, what others say about them, what they think, and how they feel. *Jacob Have I Loved* is written in the first person, so it's easy and natural for Sara Louise to describe herself and her feelings, but notice how efficiently in this brief quote Paterson introduces Sara Louise and the secondary character McCall Purnell and also through the dialogue presents some foreshadowing that gives readers a peek at how others relate to Sara.

> Call and I made quite a pair. At thirteen I was tall and large boned, with delusions of beauty and romance. He, at fourteen, was pudgy, bespectacled, and totally unsentimental.
>
> "Call," I would say, watching dawn break crimson over the Chesapeake Bay, "I hope I have a sky like this the day I get married."
>
> "Who would marry you?" Call would ask, not meanly, just facing facts.

Readers learn more about Sara Louise a few pages later when she tells Call a joke about a "p-sychiatrist," who gets into heaven because as St. Peter explains, "We got this problem. God thinks he's Franklin D. Roosevelt." Call questions Sara's use of the word "p-sychiatrist," and she explains in hindsight:

> I was an avid reader of *Time* magazine, which, besides the day-old Baltimore *Sun,* was our porthole on the world in those days, so although psychiatry was not yet a popular pastime, I was quite aware of the word, if not the fact that

the p was silent. Call's response to the actual joke is, "How can it be a joke? There ain't neither funny about it."

Paterson's inclusion of these two linguistic "errors" was an efficient way to show not only how isolated these children were, but also how Call looks inward at the Island identifying with the watermen, whereas Sara Louise looks outward at the world. Call and Sara are both dynamic characters, who undergo change, whereas Sara's sister, Caroline, is a static character, remaining much the same from beginning to end. She's almost a stereotype of the beautiful and adored child, "the kind of person other people sacrifice for as a matter of course" and the kind of person who tells other people's stories, snatching their "rights without even thinking." But Caroline sings so beautifully that on the Saturday night before Christmas, Sara Louise felt surely that she would shatter when Caroline "went up effortlessly, sweetly, and oh, so softly, to the high G, holding it just a few seconds longer than humanly possible and then returning to the last few notes and to silence."

Paterson walked a fine line in creating Caroline, who had to be irritating enough to make Sara's resentment credible, but at the same time typical enough that readers would understand the problem as representative rather than unique. One of the ways that Paterson did this was to filter everything through Sara's eyes, as on the summer day that Sara had earned extra money, and as a result her mother was making her and her father's favorite dinner. Sara was relaxed:

> [bathing her] sister and grandmother in kindly feelings that neither deserved, when Caroline said, "I haven't got anything to do but practice this summer, so I've decided to write a book about my life. Once you're known," she explained carefully as though some of us were dim-witted, "once you're famous information like that is very valuable. If I don't get it down now, I may forget."

The worst thing about this statement is that Caroline said it "in that voice of hers that made me feel slightly nauseated."

By the last quarter of the book, readers know Sara so well that they suffer along with her when the Captain, whom she adores, shares his idea of sending Caroline to music school and ironically announces that "I have Sara Louise to thank for the idea." And they react right along with Sara Louise's body when after the war Call returns home and before announcing his engagement remarks that he stopped in New York to see Caroline. "My body understood long before my mind did. First it chilled, then it began to burn, with my heart thumping overtime in alarm."

One of the advantages of books over movies and plays is that an author can more easily get inside the characters' minds and tell what they are thinking. Paterson often uses this technique, having Sara Louise carry on a continual interior monologue. In one of them she acknowledges her lack of generosity in not wanting to share Call with the Captain. "He didn't remember his own father, and if any boy needed a father, it was Call." But "Call was my only friend. If I gave him to the Captain, I'd have no one."

Authors commonly use physical attributes as a concrete substitute for less easily described abstractions. Throughout *Jacob Have I Loved,* Paterson uses descriptions of hands in this way as when Caroline would make Sara Louise "fly into a wounded rage" because of a comment about dirty fingernails. Sara Louise thought Caroline "was using my fingernails to indict my soul."

Midway in the book when the Captain's house is washed out to sea, readers are shown how much Sara Louise loves the Captain. She hugs him and suddenly hears voices inside her head, one saying "Let go, stupid," while the other urges her to hold him tighter. She is terribly embarrassed and dares to look only at his hands.

> I had never noticed how long his fingers were. His nails were large, rounded at the bottom and blunt and neat at the tips. He had the cleanest fingernails of any man I'd ever seen—it was the male hand in the ad reaching to put the diamond on the Ponds-caressed female hand. Why had I never noticed before how beautiful his hands were?

In another incident, Sara Louise overreacts when Caroline borrows her hand lotion, and that fall Sara Louise studies all the hands in the classroom. "It was my current theory that hands were the most revealing part of the human body—far more significant than eyes."

Sara's mother and father are important background characters, but because they act much like readers expect good parents to act, Paterson does not have to devote extensive space to their development but instead relies on a few crucial details.

The Captain and Sara's grandmother are almost archetypes. The Captain is the foolish young man who left home on a quest only to return many years later kinder and wiser than anyone dared to hope for. The grandmother is the wicked old witch, who mumbles incantations and makes dire predictions. When Sara's heart is already broken because Caroline is going to be sent to the wonderful music academy in Baltimore, the grandmother stands close behind her and whispers, "Romans nine thirteen, 'As it is written, Jacob have I loved, but Esau have I hated.'"

Some readers and critics have objected to these contrasting archetypes, the positive portrayal of the elderly man and the negative portrayal of the elderly woman. But the archetypes are as old as the world's literature, and at least Paterson reveals some of the reasons behind the grandmother's bad behavior. At the end of the book, actually in the denouement, new characters appear, including the man Sara Louise marries and the twins whose birth she attends. These characters are foils. They are there as background for the simple purpose of making Sara Louise shine. There was no need for Paterson to develop them any further than to give readers a vaguely positive feeling toward them.

This discussion has pointed out several techniques Paterson used to develop the full range of characters in *Jacob Have I Loved.* She had the narrator describe minor characters, whereas major characters were not only described, but also shown in action. Readers were allowed to listen in on their conversations and to hear what they said as well as how they said it and how others responded to them and talked about them. Readers were privy to the thoughts and daydreams of the protagonist.

Paterson also used Biblical allusion, foreshadowing, and descriptions of physical attributes as symbols for abstract ideas. Examples of each technique have been given, but careful readers can find other equally interesting examples.

Point of View

A story needs to be told from a consistent viewpoint. The storyteller has to decide just how far from the characters to stand, from which direction to illuminate their actions with sympathy, and when and if it is time to speak from inside one of them. The viewpoint that gives the storyteller the most freedom is the one called omniscient, or "all knowing." With this viewpoint, it is as if the writer is present in all the characters, knowing what is inside their minds. This was the viewpoint that Joanne Greenberg, writing under the pseudonym Hannah Green, used when she wrote *I Never Promised You a Rose Garden.* It would hardly have been believable for the girl Deborah to tell the story because throughout most of the book she is psychotic. Yet it is necessary that the readers be told what she is thinking because the real story takes place in her mind. Also, by using the third-person omniscient viewpoint, Green could share the thoughts of the other patients, Deborah's psychiatrist, and her parents.

Writers have much less freedom if they decide to enter into the mind and body of one of the characters and stay there, that is, to write the book in the first person. First-person narrators can describe other characters in an objective manner; that is, they can tell about whatever can be seen from the outside, but they cannot tell what is going on inside the minds of the other characters. One way to get around the limitations of a first-person book is to have the first-person chapters come alternately from different people. M. E. Kerr used this technique in *I'll Love You When You're More Like Me,* and so did Alice Childress in *A Hero Ain't Nothin' But a Sandwich.* William Wharton began *Birdy* by having Birdy's friend Al visit him in a veteran's hospital, where he alternates between talking to the unresponsive Birdy and thinking his own thoughts. Birdy's thoughts—at first just fragments and pieces—are given in a slightly different style of type. By the end of the book, Birdy's thoughts have grown to whole chapters.

In a similar way to how William Wharton told most of Birdy's story through the eyes of his best friend, authors may use a relatively minor character to tell the story. Richard Peck has explained that he chooses to do this because the interesting stories are at the extreme ends of the normal curve. The exciting things are happening to the brilliant and successful students, such as the girl that Bruce Brooks wrote about in *Midnight Hour Encores.* Or they are happening to the kids at the other end of the scale as in Chris Lynch's *Shadow Boxer* and S. E. Hinton's *That Was Then, This Is Now.* Peck says that these extreme characters are wonderful to write about, but they aren't the ones who will read his books. The kids at one end probably don't have the reading skill and at the other end are too busy, too involved in their own lives. Readers are most likely to come from the large group of students in between whose lives aren't full of such highs and lows.

GARY SOTO
On the Particulars of the World

I am new to children's writing and am only now getting to know some of the books in the field. What has struck me, now that I am reading YA novels, is that despite their other literary merits, the writing has so little that is obviously regional, obviously bent on nailing down a life that is wholly particular. Seldom are real rivers mentioned, or mountains, gangs, streets, cars; in short, the particulars of the world. Seldom do place names matter, names ringing of the familiar, such as Avocado Lake, Pinedale, Academy Cemetery, Francher's Creek, real names that might give rise to a reader's dreaming state of mind and curiosity for a faraway place. For the most part, the novels I have been reading are homogenous and widespread in their feelings and cast of characters. They lack a sense of place. The stories could happen anywhere. And they often happen in a way that doesn't exclude anyone by race, thus, in a way, satisfying the book market, but also, in a way, dissatisfying any reader who knows what the real world is like. The characters are interchangeable, racially, that is.

I suppose because I was first trained as a poet and was told repeatedly to go to the particular—your block, your family, your friends, some dirt pile in the backyard—that I wrote about my hometown, Fresno, California. And then, more particularly, I looked to the southeast area of Fresno—the Roosevelt High area—the industrial area of south Fresno, where I grew up. My characters are Mexican-American, mostly playground kids, mostly the children of people whose parents work for Color Tile or a Safeway distribution center. I'm beginning to think that children's writing could learn to see regionality and particularity as underexplored territory. I'm beginning to think we don't have to satisfy everyone. We can remember the adult writers—Flannery O'Connor, Mark Twain, Sherwood Anderson, William Saroyan, Bernard Malamud—who had tenderness and longing toward place, even if that place scared the hell out of them when they were young.

Gary Soto's books include *Summer on Wheels,* Scholastic, 1995; *Chato's Kitchen,* Putnam, 1995; *Baseball in April,* Harcourt Brace Jovanovich, 1990; *A Summer Life,* Dell, 1991; and *The Skirt,* Delacorte, 1992.

Tone

The tone of a book is determined by the author's attitude toward subject, characters, and readers. It is difficult to pick out the exact elements that contribute to the tone of a book because many times the author is not even aware of them. If an author were speaking directly to you, tone would simply be communicated through the lilt of the voice, the lifting of an eyebrow, a twinkle in the eye, or a crease in the forehead. When tone has to be communicated exclusively through the written word, it is more complex.

Sometimes language reminiscent of church hymns or the Bible is used to lend weight and dignity to a book, as in the titles *All Creatures Great and Small* by James Herriot, *Jacob Have I Loved* by Katherine Paterson, and *Manchild in the Promised Land* by Claude Brown.

The tone in these books contrasts sharply with the humorous and irreverent tone that appears in many popular new books. Americans have always been fond of exaggeration or hyperbole, and its use is one way of establishing a light, humorous tone. When writers use hyperbole, readers know that what they say is not true, but they nevertheless enjoy the farfetched overstatement, as in Ellen Conford's title, *If This Is Love, I'll Take Spaghetti* and Ron Koertge's *Where the Kissing Never Stops.*

Euphemisms also set a tone. In general, modern writers think it better to speak directly than to make the vague kinds of circumlocutions that used to be fashionable in writing, but some euphemisms have literary impact. For example, Margaret Craven's title *I Heard the Owl Call My Name* is more intriguing than a bald statement such as "I knew I was going to die." And Hemingway's title *For Whom the Bell Tolls* is both more euphemistic and more euphonious than "the one who has died."

A challenge for young adult authors is to avoid an overly didactic tone. Certainly it is the goal—conscious or unconscious—of most adults to teach worthwhile values to young people. Nevertheless, in literary criticism, calling a work "didactic" usually implies that the tone comes across as preachy. The story has been created around a message instead of having a message or a theme grow naturally out of the story.

Great literature always leaves the reader with something to think about. Lessons are taught, but they are subtle lessons, and the reader is left with the responsibility of analyzing what the writer has presented and of coming to a conclusion. William Golding's *Lord of the Flies* is a book from which people learn a great deal, but it is not usually considered a didactic book because the author, William Golding, does not spell out the lesson for the reader. We might contrast Golding's nondidactic tone with the didactic message that appears in an introduction written by E. M. Forster to a 1962 edition of the same book:

> It is certainly not a comforting book. But it may help a few grownups to be less complacent and more compassionate, to support Ralph, respect Piggy, control Jack, and lighten a little the darkness of man's heart. At the present moment (if I may speak personally) it is respect for Piggy that seems needed most. I do not find it in our leaders.

Forster's comments could also be described as editorializing. Notice how he asked permission to express his personal opinion. Sometimes authors editorialize, or give their own opinions, through the voice of a character, as S. E. Hinton did in *The Outsiders* when Ponyboy explains why he wrote his story.

> I could see boys going down under street lights because they were mean and tough and hated the world, and it was too late to tell them that there was still

good in it, and they wouldn't believe you if you did. It was too vast a problem to be just a personal thing. There should be some help. Someone should tell their side of the story, and maybe people would understand then and wouldn't be so quick to judge a boy by the amount of hair oil he wore.

In reality, it is probably not so much that we dislike a didactic tone as that we dislike that tone when the message is something with which we do not agree. If the message is reaffirming one of our beliefs, we identify with it and enjoy the feeling that other people are going to be convinced of the "truth."

A nostalgic tone is a potential problem in much young adult literature. Nearly all books with teenage protagonists are of potential interest to young adult readers. But one of the things that keeps some of them from reaching a large young adult audience is that the authors have looked back at their own adolescence and have romanticized it. Most 16-year-olds interpret such a tone as condescension, which is unappealing to readers of any age.

Setting

The creation of setting varies tremendously from author to author. When Virginia Euwer Wolff wrote *Make Lemonade* about a poverty-stricken teenage mother, she started with little more than a dirty high chair.

When I was a young mother, I had to put my babies in an old plastic-upholstered high chair from the Salvation Army that I could never get clean. It completely overwhelmed me at the time—even now I could pick it out from a million others. Jolly, Jilly, and Jeremy came straight out of that dirty high chair.

In contrast, when Lois Lowry wrote *The Giver,* she imagined a whole society clear down to the rows of gleaming bicycles and identical hair ribbons, deserted streets after curfew, scraps of food on the doorsteps to be picked up each night, and special rooms for "releasing" the unwanted—all of which could be seen only in black and white.

Setting—the context of time and place—is more important in some genres than in others. For example, it is often the setting, a time in the future or the far past or some place where people now living on this earth have never actually been, that lets readers know they are embarking on reading a fantasy. The special quality in J. R. R. Tolkien's *The Lord of the Rings* would not be possible were it not set in the mythical world of Middle Earth. Nor would many popular pieces of science fiction be possible without their outer space or futuristic settings.

In historical fiction, the setting is of central interest. Bette Greene's *Summer of My German Soldier* could not have happened at any time other than during World War II. Without the war, there would not have been German prisoners in Patty Bergan's hometown, nor would there have been the peculiar combination of public and private hysteria that worked on Patty's southern Christian community and her Jewish family. All of this makes it easy to think of *Summer of My German Soldier* as a historical novel. In contrast, Maureen Daly's *Seventeenth Summer* was set in approximately the same time period, but the crux of the story centers around a young girl's feelings toward the adult role that she is growing into and toward her first experience with love. Readers of *Seventeenth Summer* are likely to come away feeling that they have read a slightly old-fashioned, but not historical, novel. This is because the setting in *Seventeenth Summer* is little more than a *backdrop,* whereas the setting in *Summer of My German Soldier* is *integral* to the plot.

Among the stories that have integral settings are those in which the plot or problem is person against nature. In accounts of mountain climbing, survival, exploring, and other sorts of adventuring, the setting is actually the antagonist. It is interesting in and of itself, just as a character would be. Regional stories also have integral settings as in Hal Borland's *When the Legends Die* and Frank Herbert's *Soul Catcher.* These are both stories about young Native American men whose searches for their own identities cannot be separated from the regions in which they grew up.

Traditionally, most regional stories have had rural settings in which the protagonists are close to nature, but as the United States has changed to an urban society and realism has become more fashionable, cities appear as important background settings, as in Nicholasa Mohr's *El Bronx Remembered* and *In Nueva York.* These collections of short stories about Puerto Ricans living in New York are held together by their common setting, which Mohr illustrates through the touch of Spanish in the titles.

Books with backdrop settings are usually set in a small town, an inner-city neighborhood, a modern suburb, or a high school. Authors want to give enough details to bring the story alive while still being vague enough that readers can imagine the story happening in their own town or at least in one they know.

A good book to read and study as an illustration of how an author uses what might at first appear to be a backdrop setting for various purposes is Sue Ellen Bridger's *Permanent Connections.* Her descriptions of the southern Appalachians where Rob, a boy from Monmouth, New Jersey, finds himself spending several months make the story come alive for readers. They also serve as foreshadowing while establishing tone and mood. They allow Bridgers to be efficient in communicating the passage of time, while revealing information about the personalities of her various protagonists. Both Rob and his girlfriend Ellery blame their unhappiness on being forced to leave their city homes and live in the mountains. Also, outside of this particular setting, Rob couldn't have gotten the homegrown marijuana that causes him to wreck his uncle's truck. More important than these contributions to the plot, however, is the skilled way that Bridgers uses her descriptions metaphorically to show what is happening inside people's minds.

The most common backdrop setting in young adult literature is that of a high school because school is the business—the everyday life—of teenagers. The fact that there are only so many ways to describe stairways, restrooms, lockers, cafeterias, classrooms, and parking lots is one of the things that gives a sameness to books for this age group.

A refreshing change occurs in books set outside the United States (see Focus Box 2.4). Having been selected as worthy of translation or reprinting in American versions, these are often among the best books published. Educators should en-

Contemporary Teens in the World Around Us

Chain of Fire by Beverley Naidoo. Harper-Collins, 1990. Teenagers Naledi and Taolo help to lead a resistance movement against the forced relocation of the people in their South African village.

Grab Hands and Run by Frances Temple. Orchard, 1993. When Felipe's father, a political activist in El Salvador, is killed, the 12-year-old boy, his younger sister, and their mother "grab hands and run," finally making their way to Canada.

Haveli by Suzanne Fisher Staples. Knopf, 1993. In this sequel to the well-received *Shabanu: Daughter of the Wind* (Knopf, 1989), Staples continues the story of the strong-willed young woman who because of custom and family needs becomes the fourth wife of a powerful landowner in the Cholistan desert of Pakistan.

Over the Water by Maude Casey. Holt, 1994. A bonus to this coming-of-age story about a young woman whose Irish family has moved to London but returns every summer to Ireland is that readers get a glimpse into Irish/English differences that is less political than what is shown in the daily news.

The Real Plato Jones by Nina Bawden. Clarion, 1993. Set in a suburb of London, this is the story of a 13-year-old boy trying to come to terms with his heritage—a Welsh grandfather considered a World War II hero and a Greek grandfather considered a World War II traitor.

Rice Without Rain by Minfong Ho. Lothrop Lee & Shepard, 1990. Seventeen-year-old Jinda falls in love with Ned, who comes from a university to help her Thai village adapt to drought and poverty.

The Secret Diary of Adrian Mole, Aged 13 3/4 by Sue Townsend. U. S. printing by Avon, 1984. "The biggest British sensation since the Beatles" is the way the publishers describe this popular and truly funny book, along with its sequel *The Growing Pains of Adrian Mole* (Avon, 1987).

Shizuko's Daughter by Kyoko Mori. Henry Holt, 1993. The Japanese setting adds dignity and interest to Yuki's story of her mother's suicide, her father's marriage to the woman who has been his mistress, and finally Yuki's leaving for art school and coming to terms with her mother's decision.

The Song of Be by Lesley Beake. Holt, 1993. The voice in this unusual story is that of a young woman dying from a self-inflicted wound. Her name is *Be,* and as she tells her story through flashbacks readers get glimpses into what is happening to the San (the Bushmen) of Nambia.

Truth to Tell by Nancy Bond. McElderry, 1994. Fourteen-year-old Alice undergoes more than the usual discomfort caused by moving when she and her mother move from England to New Zealand.

courage the reading of such books because whether the setting is integral or backdrop, readers are likely to come away feeling a little more comfortable and knowledgeable about the country where the book is set—an outcome surely to be encouraged in today's shrinking world.

Style

Style is the way a story is written as contrasted to what the story is about. It is the result or effect of combining the literary aspects we have already talked about.

An Individual Matter

No two authors have exactly the same style because with writing, just as with appearance, behavior, and personal belongings, style consists of the unique blending of all the choices each individual makes. From situation to situation, these choices may differ, but they are enough alike that the styles of particular authors, such as Kurt Vonnegut, Jr., Richard Brautigan, and E. L. Doctorow, are recognizable from book to book. Style is also influenced by the nature of the story being told. For example, Ursula K. Le Guin used a different style when she wrote the realistic *Very Far Away from Anywhere Else* from the one she used when she wrote her fantasy *A Wizard of Earthsea.* Nevertheless, in both books she relied on the particular writing techniques that she likes and is skilled at using.

Virginia Hamilton is another author whose sense of style is evident throughout her writing, which ranges from the realistic *M. C. Higgins, the Great* to the romantic *A Little Love,* the occult *Sweet Whispers, Brother Rush,* and the science fiction Justice trilogy beginning with *Justice and Her Brothers.* Authors' styles are influenced by such factors as their intended audience and their purpose in writing. For example, a general-information book has a different style from that of an informative book written to persuade readers to a belief or an action. Even after an author has made the decision to write a persuasive book, the style is affected by whether the author chooses to persuade through humor, dramatic fiction, or a logical display of evidence.

Probably the book that has had the greatest influence on the style of writing about young protagonists is J. D. Salinger's *The Catcher in the Rye.* Nearly every year, promotional materials or reviews compare five or six new books to *Catcher.* Some of these comparisons are made on the basis of the subject matter, but the theme of a boy wavering between the innocence of childhood and acceptance of the adult world—imperfect as it is—is not all that unusual. It is the style of the writing that makes Salinger's book so memorable, indeed such a milestone, and has inspired other authors to imitate the colloquial speech, the candid revelations of feelings, the short snappy dialogue, the instant judgments, and the emotional extremes ranging from hostility to great tenderness.

One of the most memorable scenes in the book is the one in which the young prostitute comes to Holden's hotel room, and he is so touched by her youth and innocence that he gives up the whole idea:

> She was very nervous, for a prostitute. She really was. I think it was because she was young as hell. She was around my age. I sat down in the big chair, next to her, and offered her a cigarette. "I don't smoke," she said. She had a tiny little wheeny-whiny voice. You could hardly hear her. She never said thank you, either, when you offered her something. She just didn't know any better.
>
> "Allow me to introduce myself. My name is Jim Steele," I said.
>
> "Ya got a watch on ya?" she said. She didn't care what the hell my name was, naturally. "Hey how old are you, anyways?"
>
> "Me? Twenty-two."

"Like fun you are."

It was a funny thing to say. It sounded like a real kid. You'd think a prostitute and all would say, "Like hell you are" or "Cut the crap" instead of "Like fun you are."

As the girl gets ready to leave, Holden observes, "If she'd been a big old prostitute, with a lot of makeup on her face and all, she wouldn't have been half as spooky."

Teenage readers are more likely than adults to appreciate hyperbole and exaggeration, and with their shorter attention spans they like succinctness, as when the two protagonists in M. E. Kerr's *Night Kites* are swimming and Erick writes, "Somehow we got down to the shallow end, where we could touch, and that was what we did. We touched." Richard Peck was equally succinct in communicating the living situation of his protagonist, Buck Mendenhall, in *Remembering the Good Times.* Buck explains that what his father got out of the divorce was a "full-time trailer and a part-time kid."

Writing in dialect is an effective stylistic device to set a character apart as different from mainstream speakers, but difficulties in spelling, printing, and reading mean that most authors use this device sparingly and for the benefit of young readers may offer an explanation as Gary Paulsen did in *Dogsong.* The Inuit boy, Russel, is camping in a snow-covered wilderness and he finds an ancient lamp.

"See what a man has been given," he said. "By the dogs who brought me. By the night. See what a man has been given." He had dropped into the third person usage without thinking, though it was no longer used very much. He had heard the old people talk that way sometimes out of politeness.

No explanation is needed if the usage is easy to understand as in Hal Borland's *When the Legends Die,* "The Ute people have lived many generations, many grandmothers, in that land." The same can be said for most uses of black dialect, which is commonly included in the writings of June Jordan, Brenda Wilkinson, Maya Angelou, Virginia Hamilton, Ntozake Shange, Walter Dean Myers, and others. They use it not only for characterization, but also to communicate pride in being African-Americans.

It is possible to describe the literary techniques that are the basic ingredients of an author's style, but there is more to literary style than various devices. To have a unique style, an author has to be brave enough to go beyond the tried and true. In addition, something has to click so that the devices blend together into a unified whole.

Figurative Language

Much of what determines writers' styles is how they use figurative language to set a mood, surprise the reader, create imagery, make a passage memorable, and sometimes show off their skill. Words used figuratively have different, or at least additional, meanings from those they have in standard usage. One type of figurative language—metaphors, symbols, allegories, and similes—stimulates the reader's mind to make comparisons. A second type appeals to the sense of sight or hearing. Examples include alliteration, assonance, rhyme, euphony, rhythm, and cadence. In the following sentence from Harold Brodkey's story, "Sentimental Education," both kinds of figurative language occur:

> Dimitri had a car, which Elgin borrowed—an old, weak-lunged Ford—and they could wheeze up to Marblehead and rent a dinghy and be blown around the bay, with the sunlight bright on Caroline's hair and the salt air making them hungry and the wind whipping up small whitecaps to make the day exciting.

The personification of the "weak-lunged Ford" that "wheezes" up to Marblehead helps the reader visualize the old car while the alliteration in "be blown around the bay" and "wind whipping up small whitecaps" and the rhyme in "sunlight bright" and "Caroline's hair and the salt air" affect the reader more subtly in establishing mood. The word "wheeze" is also an example of onomatopoeia, in which the sound of a word hints at its meaning.

Poetry, of course, is filled with figurative language because poets have so little space that they have to make their words do double duty. But as Maya Angelou shows in her autobiographical writing, figurative language is not limited to any one genre. She begins her *All God's Children Need Traveling Shoes* with euphonious personification:

> The breezes of the West African night were intimate and shy, licking the hair, sweeping through cotton dresses with unseemly intimacy, then disappearing into the utter blackness. Daylight was equally insistent, but much more bold and thoughtless.

And a page later:

> July and August of 1962 stretched out like fat men yawning after a sumptuous dinner. They had every right to gloat, for they had eaten me up. Gobbled me down. Consumed my spirit, not in a wild rush, but slowly, with the obscene patience of certain victors.

Metaphors are among the most common kinds of figurative language. In a metaphor, basically dissimilar things are likened to one another to give the reader a new insight. A fresh metaphor can be an effective device for making readers active instead of passive participants. Readers have to become mentally involved to make associations that they have not thought of before. A metaphor can be simple, consisting of only a word or a phrase, or it can be a series of interwoven ideas running through an entire book. In at least fourteen places in the Vietnam War story *Fallen Angels,* author Walter Dean Myers makes comparisons to movies or television.

For example, Richie observes that the stopping and starting of firing in a jungle battle "was as if somebody had changed channels and then switched back to the war." Ten pages later:

> The shadows moved, Peewee moved. He was getting up. I didn't want to get up. I wanted to sit there forever. Where the hell was the popcorn machine? Couldn't I just watch the rest of this f_____ war? Couldn't I just be out of it for a few hours, a few minutes?

The fact that the Vietnam War was in many ways the first war fought in front of television cameras makes Myers' metaphor especially appropriate.

A technical distinction is sometimes made between metaphors and similes. Similes, like metaphors, make comparisons between basically dissimilar things, but they are literally true, whereas metaphors are only figuratively true. The creator of a simile hedges by putting in such words as *like, as, similar to,* or *resembles* to indicate that a comparison is being made. In Bruce Brooks' *Midnight Hour Encores,* Sib was glad when her father told her she could choose a new name, because "I had been thrashing around inside that name like it was a wet wool coat worn inside out against my skin." A more fully developed simile appears in Zibby Oneal's *A Formal Feeling.* Sixteen-year-old Anne Cameron must let go of the dream of perfection in which she had wrapped the memories of her deceased mother. Near the end of the book, she was able at last to form the question that had bothered her since she was 8 years old and her mother temporarily left the family, "If she loved me, why did she leave me?"

> That was one of the questions, but it was only one. Beneath it there was another. It had been swimming at the edges of her mind for days, darting away as a fish does, startled by a movement that comes too close. She thought she could not avoid it any more, and so she pushed herself down one more time, like a diver. She knew the question had always been there, unspeakable, at the bottom of all she remembered and had chosen to forget. And she made herself ask: Did I ever love my mother at all?

Being able to ask this question is in effect the climax of the book, but without the interesting simile readers would have been less likely to recognize its importance. Also, since it was something that occurred in Anne's mind, the only way to make readers visualize it was through some sort of figurative language.

Allegories are extended comparisons or metaphors. They can be enjoyed on at least two levels. One is the literal or surface level on which the story is enjoyed simply for itself. On the second or deeper level, we can interpret and extend the meaning of the story, and it thereby becomes more interesting. It is in part the challenge of interpreting the allegory in William Golding's *Lord of the Flies* that makes it a good piece to read and discuss in a group.

An allegorical device that authors sometimes use is giving their characters symbolic names as Robert C. O'Brien did in *Z for Zachariah.* The title is taken from a Bible ABC book in which the first letter of the alphabet stands for Adam and the last for Zachariah. The symbolism suggests that if Adam was the first man on earth, Zachariah must be the last. The girl in the book who carries a tremendous responsibility and at the end is left with the task of rebuilding a civilization is symbolically named Ann Burden. These names may influence readers' attitudes and enhance their pleasure without their being aware of it. In a similar way, many young readers of Paula Fox's *One-Eyed Cat* probably didn't notice that when Ned confessed to shooting the cat he and his mother were sitting on the front porch of the Makepeace mansion.

Allusions work in the same way. They are an efficient way to communicate a great deal of information because one reference in a word or a phrase triggers the readers' minds to think of the whole story or idea behind the allusion. Robert Cormier's title *I Am the Cheese* is an allusion to the old nursery song and game, "The Farmer in the Dell." Besides being efficient, allusions, similar to metaphors, are effective in forcing readers to become actively involved in making connections. A lazy or uninterested reader might not see any allusion in Cormier's title. Someone else, especially when discovering that the family's name is Farmer, would connect the title to the nursery rhyme and perhaps think of the last line, "And the cheese stands alone!" An even more thoughtful reader might carry it back one more step and think of the next to last line, "The rat takes the cheese."

The concepts and the terminology from this discussion reappear throughout the rest of this textbook as well as in much of whatever else you read about literature. We placed this discussion early in the text, first, because we wanted to make it clear that authors for young adults use the same literary techniques as those used by all good writers, and, second, we wanted to lay a foundation for the way you approach the reading you will do throughout this course. We want you to lose yourselves—and also find yourselves—in some good stories. But at the same time we want to encourage you to keep a part of your mind open for looking at literature from the pleasure-giving viewpoint of the literary critic.

Notes

. . . .

[1]Margaret Early, "Stages of Growth in Literary Appreciation," *English Journal* 49 (March 1960): 163–66.

[2]First cited by G. Robert Carlsen in an article exploring stages of reading development, "Literature Is," *English Journal* 63 (February 1974): 23–27.

[3]Glenna Davis Sloan, *The Child as Critic* (Teachers College Press, 1975).

[4]Annie Gottlieb, "A New Cycle in 'YA' Books," *New York Times Book Review,* June 17, 1984, pp. 24–25.

[5]Alleen Pace Nilsen, "The House That Alice Built: An Interview with the Author Who Brought You *Go Ask Alice,*" *School Library Journal* 26 (October 1979): 109–112.

[6]Katherine Paterson, "Newbery Medal Acceptance," *Horn Book Magazine* 57 (August 1981): 385–393.

Titles Mentioned in the Text of Chapter Two

. . . .

Adams, Douglas. *The Hitchhiker's Guide to the Galaxy.* Harmony, 1979.

Adams, Richard. *Watership Down.* Macmillan, 1974.

Alcott, Louisa May. *Little Women,* 1868.

Alexander, Lloyd. *The Black Cauldron.* Holt, Rinehart & Winston, 1965.

Angelou, Maya. *All God's Children Need Traveling Shoes,* Random House, 1986.

Angelou, Maya. *I Know Why the Caged Bird Sings*. Random House, 1970.

Anonymous. *Go Ask Alice*. Prentice-Hall, 1969.

Borland, Hal. *When the Legends Die*. HarperCollins, 1963.

Bridgers, Sue Ellen. *Permanent Connections*. HarperCollins, 1987.

Brodkey, H. "Sentimental Education." In *First Love and Other Sorrows*. Dial Press, 1957.

Brooks, Bruce. *Midnight Hour Encores*. HarperCollins, 1986.

Brooks, Bruce. *The Moves Make the Man*. HarperCollins, 1984.

Brown, Claude. *Manchild in the Promised Land*. Macmillan, 1965.

Burns, Olive Ann. *Cold Sassy Tree*. Ticknor & Fields, 1984.

Callahan, Steven. *Adrift: Seventy-Six Days Lost at Sea*. Houghton Mifflin, 1986.

Card, Orson Scott. *The Lost Boys: A Novel*. HarperCollins, 1992.

Childress, Alice. *A Hero Ain't Nothin' But a Sandwich*. Coward, McCann, 1973.

Conford, Ellen. *If This Is Love, I'll Take Spaghetti*. Four Winds, 1983.

Cormier, Robert. *The Chocolate War*. Pantheon, 1974.

Cormier, Robert. *We All Fall Down*. Delacorte, 1991.

Craven, Margaret. *I Heard the Owl Call My Name*. Doubleday, 1973.

Creech, Sharon. *Walk Two Moons*. HarperCollins, 1994.

Daly, Maureen. *Seventeenth Summer*. Dodd, 1942.

Donovan, John. *Family*. HarperCollins, 1976.

Dorris, Michael. *A Yellow Raft in Blue Water*. Holt, 1987.

Duncan, Lois. *Stranger with My Face*. Little, Brown, 1981.

Erdrich, Louise. *Love Medicine*. Holt, 1984.

Fox, Paula. *One-Eyed Cat*. Bradbury, 1985.

Fox, Paula. *The Moonlight Man*. Bradbury, 1985.

Golding, William. *Lord of the Flies*. Coward, McCann & Geoghegan, 1955.

Graham, Robin. *Dove*. HarperCollins, 1972.

Greene, Bette. *Summer of My German Soldier*. Dial, 1973.

Guest, Judith. *Ordinary People*. Viking, 1976.

Hamilton, Virginia. *Justice and Her Brothers*, Greenwillow, 1978.

Hamilton, Virginia. *A Little Love*. Philomel, 1984.

Hamilton, Virginia. *M. C. Higgins, the Great*. Macmillan, 1974.

Hamilton, Virginia. *Sweet Whispers, Brother Rush*. Philomel, 1982.

Hemingway, Ernest. *For Whom the Bell Tolls*. Scribner, 1940.

Herbert, Frank. *Soul Catcher*. Putnam, 1972.

Herriot, James. *All Creatures Great and Small*. St. Martin, 1972.

Heyerdahl, Thor. *The "RA" Expeditions*. New American Library, 1972.

Hinton, S. E. *The Outsiders*. Viking, 1967.

Holman, Felice. *The Wild Children*. Scribner, 1983.

Hunter, Mollie. *Cat, Herself*. HarperCollins, 1986.

Kerr, M. E. *Deliver Us from Evie*. HarperCollins, 1994.

Kerr, M. E. *If I Love You, Am I Trapped Forever?* HarperCollins, 1973.

Kerr, M. E. *I'll Love You When You're More Like Me*. HarperCollins, 1977.

Kerr, M. E. *Night Kites*. HarperCollins, 1986.

Knowles, John. *A Separate Peace*. Macmillan, 1960.

Koertge, Ron. *Where the Kissing Never Stops*. Little, Brown, 1987.

Lee, Marie. *Finding My Voice*. Houghton, 1992.

Le Guin, Ursula K. *Very Far Away from Anywhere Else*. Atheneum, 1976.

Le Guin, Ursula K. *A Wizard of Earthsea*. Parnassus, 1968.

Lowry, Lois. *The Giver*. Houghton Mifflin, 1993.

Mason, Bobbie Ann. *In Country*. HarperCollins, 1985.

McKinley, Robin. *The Blue Sword*. Greenwillow, 1982.

Meltzer, Milton. *The American Revolutionaries: A History in Their Own Words*. Crowell, 1987.

Mohr, Nicholasa. *El Bronx Remembered*. HarperCollins, 1975.

Mohr, Nicholasa. *In Nueva York*. Dial, 1977.

Morrell, David. *First Blood*. M. Evans, 1972.

Myers, Walter Dean. *Fallen Angels*. Scholastic, 1988.

O'Brien, Robert C. *Z for Zachariah*. Atheneum, 1975.

Oneal, Zibby. *A Formal Feeling*. Viking, 1982.

Paterson, Katherine. *Jacob Have I Loved*. HarperCollins, 1980.

Paulsen, Gary. *Dogsong*. Bradbury, 1985.

Peck, Richard. *Are You in the House Alone?* Viking, 1976.

Peck, Richard. *Remembering the Good Times*. Delacorte, 1985.

Plath, Sylvia. *The Bell Jar*. HarperCollins, 1971.

Potok, Chaim. *The Chosen*. Simon & Schuster, 1967.

Potok, Chaim. *My Name Is Asher Lev*. Knopf, 1972.

Read, Piers Paul. *Alive: The Story of the Andes Survivors*. HarperCollins, 1974.

Renvoize, Jean. *A Wild Thing*. Little, Brown, 1971.

Robertson, Dougal. *Survive the Savage Sea*. G. K. Hall, 1974.

Salinger, J. D. *The Catcher in the Rye*. Little, Brown, 1951.

Sleator, William. *House of Stairs*. Dutton, 1974.

Sleator, William. *Interstellar Pig*. Dutton, 1984.

Slepian, Jan. *The Alfred Summer*. Macmillan, 1980.

Soto, Gary. *Baseball in April*. Harcourt Brace, 1990.

Soto, Gary. *Local News*. Harcourt, 1993.

Spinelli, Jerry. *There's A Girl in My Hammerlock.* Simon & Schuster, 1991.

Tolkien, J. R. R. *The Lord of the Rings.* Houghton Mifflin, 1974.

Trelease, Jim. *Read-Aloud Handbook,* Penguin, 1982.

Twain, Mark. *Adventures of Huckleberry Finn.* 1884.

Weesner, Theodore. *The Car Thief.* Random House, 1972.

Wharton, William. *Birdy.* Knopf, 1978.

White, Rob. *Deathwatch.* Doubleday, 1972.

Wolff, Virginia Euwer. *Make Lemonade.* Holt, 1993.

Zindel, Paul. *The Pigman.* HarperCollins, 1968.

Part Two

Modern Young Adult Reading

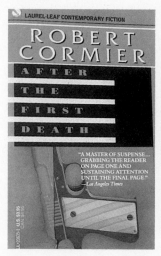

Chapter 3

The New Realism
Of Life and Problems

· ·

With fantasy, folklore, humor, informative nonfiction, memoirs, poetry, and science fiction, age-level distinctions among readers are fairly fluid, but because stories about rites of passage from childhood to adulthood naturally have young people as their protagonists, in readers' minds they have become closely affiliated with young adults.

In standard literary criticism, such books are known as *Bildungsroman*, or less commonly, *apprenticeship novels*, based on Goethe's 1795 *Wilhelm Meister's Apprenticeship*. Classic examples from British literature include Samuel Butler's 1903 *The Way of All Flesh*, James Joyce's 1914 *A Portrait of the Artist as a Young Man*, and Somerset Maugham's 1915 *Of Human Bondage*.

Contemporary books of this type published in the United States for a general adult audience but read and appreciated by sophisticated young adults include William Golding's *Lord of the Flies*, Harper Lee's *To Kill a Mockingbird*, Sylvia Plath's *The Bell Jar*, Chaim Potok's *The Chosen*, and, most famous of all, J. D. Salinger's *The Catcher in the Rye*.

In the late 1960s, societal, education, and business values had changed enough that publishers felt comfortable in encouraging writers to create serious coming-of-age stories to be read by teenagers themselves as they made that treacherous journey from childhood to adulthood. The books were wisely identified as *new realism* (as opposed to the romanticized stories that had been considered appropriate for children) or *problem novels* rather than as *bildungsroman*. Publishers were surprisingly successful in creating appealing formats and in marketing them to teen readers through libraries and schools.

In real life, the steps that a young person takes toward maturity may be so small as to be almost invisible, but the nature of the literary craft demands that authors find some concrete way to show the growth and so most such stories focus on an unfortunate event or life experience, such as an accident or grave illness, having serious troubles in one's family, being a victim of physical harm or violence, suffering from extreme forms of social pressure, or becoming addicted to drugs or alcohol.

The Ground-Breaking Books

If we were to pinpoint the birth of this new genre for young readers, the year would be 1967, which is why we chose that year as the place to begin our Honor List (see pp. 13–22) The early books include S. E. Hinton's *The Outsiders,* about the Socs (the society kids) and the Greasers, and it's the Greasers' story she tells. Robert Lipsyte's *The Contender* is about an African-American boy hoping to use boxing as his ticket out of the slums. In Paul Zindel's *The Pigman,* an alienated boy and girl make friends with a lonely old man who can't admit that his wife has died. The three of them share feelings of love and carefree playfulness, but in the end the old man dies tragically, and the boy and girl are left to ponder their role in his death and what it all means. In Richard Bradford's *Red Sky at Morning,* Southerner Josh Arnold and his mother go to a little town in New Mexico, where they are to wait out World War II. While living there, Josh gains at least a partial understanding of his Mexican-American neighbors and of himself. William Armstrong's *Sounder* is a grim historical piece about a poverty-stricken African-American family of tenant farmers.

These books exemplify several of the characteristics that during the 1970s came to be associated with the realistic problem novel for young adults. In addition to their candor and the selection of subject matter, they differ from earlier books in four basic ways. The first difference lies in the choice of *characters.* These protagonists come mostly from lower-class families, which ties in with the second major difference, *setting.* Instead of living in idyllic, pleasant suburban homes, the characters in these books come from settings that are harsh, difficult places to live. To get the point across about the characters and where and how they live, authors used colloquial *language,* which is the third major difference. Authors began to write the way people really talked (e.g., in dialogue using profanity and ungrammatical constructions). That the general public allowed this change in language shows that people were drawing away from the idea that the main purpose of fictional books for young readers is to set an example of proper middle-class behavior.

The fourth difference also relates to this change in attitude, and that is the change in *mode.* As people began to think that the educational value of fiction is to provide readers with more vicarious experiences than would be either desirable or possible in real life, the mode of stories for young adults changed. It used to be that most of the books—at least most of the books approved of by parents and educators—were written in the comic and romantic modes. These were the books with upbeat, happy endings. As long as people believed that children would model their lives after what they read, of course they wanted young people to read happy stories because a happy life is what all of us want for our children.

The problem novel, however, is based on a different philosophy. The idea is that young people have a better chance to be happy if they have realistic expectations and if they know both the bad and the good about the society in which they live. This changed attitude opened the door to writers of irony and even tragedy for young people.

Irony differs from tragedy in that it may be less intense; similarly, instead of having heroic qualities, the protagonist is an ordinary person, much like the reader. Irony is a "tennis serve that you can't return." You can admire its perfection, its appropriateness, and even the inevitability of the outcome, but you just can't cope with it. There is a refreshing honesty to stories that show readers they are not the only ones who get served that kind of ball and that the human spirit, although totally devastated in this particular set, may rise again to play another match. Brock Cole's *Celine,* Cynthia Rylant's *Missing May,* and M. E. Kerr's *Night Kites* are books of this sort.

Several of Robert Cormier's books come closer to being tragedies. In traditional literary criticism, tragedies have three distinct elements. First, there is a noble character who, no matter what happens, maintains the qualities that the society considers praiseworthy; second, there is an inevitable force that works against the character; third, there is a struggle and an outcome. The reader of a tragedy is usually filled with pity and fear—pity for the hero and fear for oneself that the same thing might happen. The intensity of this involvement causes the reader to undergo an emotional release as the outcome of the story unfolds. This release, or catharsis, has the effect of draining away dangerous human emotions and filling the reader with a sense of exaltation or amazed pride in what the human spirit is called on to undergo.[1]

The Chocolate War as a Problem Novel

Robert Cormier's *The Chocolate War* is our favorite example of a modern bildungsroman for young adults. It contains the kind of realism that many other books had been leading up to, and its message about conformity and human manipulation is all the more powerful because the young protagonist is so vulnerable. The religious symbolism serves as a contrasting backdrop to the terrible evil that pervades Trinity High School, where the protagonist is a freshman. The opening paragraph is the following simple line: "They murdered him." *Him* is 14-year-old Jerry Renault, who is being "tested" to see if he has enough guts to be on the football team.

The story begins and ends on the athletic field, where the shadows of the goal posts resemble a "network of crosses, empty crucifixes." On Jerry's third play at Trinity High, he is "hit simultaneously by three of them." He blinks himself back to consciousness and jumps to his feet:

> . . . intact, bobbing like one of those toy novelties dangling from car windows, but erect.
> "For Christ's sake," the coach bellowed, his voice juicy with contempt. A spurt of saliva hit Jerry's cheek.
> Hey coach, you spit on me, Jerry protested. Stop the spitting, coach. What he said aloud was, "I'm all right, coach," because he was a coward about stuff like that, thinking one thing and saying another, planning one thing and doing another—he had been Peter a thousand times and a thousand cocks had crowed in his lifetime.

Over the course of the book, Jerry gets the courage to think and do the same thing. He refuses to sell 50 boxes of chocolate that the corrupt teacher, Brother Leon, has assigned to each student. For the first ten days of the candy campaign, he

Through his own writing as well as what has been written about his work, Robert Cormier has brought adolescent literature a step closer to literary respectability. (Photo by Beth Bergman, Sentinel/Enterprise.)

---

simply follows the orders of the Vigils, a gang whose members, in the words of their head man, Archie Costello, "were the school." But when the ten days are up and the Vigils order Jerry to do a reversal and participate in the selling campaign, he dares to say, "No."

At first Jerry is a hero, but because this threatens the power of the Vigils, Archie uses his full potential in people management to turn the student body against Jerry. When all the chocolates except Jerry's are sold, Archie arranges a boxing match between Jerry and a bully who is trying to work his way into the Vigils. It is supposed to be set up "with rules. Fair and square," but what Archie really masterminds is a physical and psychological battering much worse than anything Jerry underwent at football practice.

The last chapter of the book could have begun with the same line as the first chapter—"They murdered him"—except that this time it would have been less of a metaphor. Although Jerry may recover physically from a fractured jaw and internal injuries, his spirit has been murdered. In the midst of the fight:

> A new sickness invaded Jerry, the sickness of knowing what he had become, another animal, another beast, another violent person in a violent world, inflicting damage, not disturbing the universe but damaging it. He had allowed Archie to do this to him.

After the fight, when the pain—"Jesus, the pain"—brings Jerry back to consciousness, the reader sees how changed he is because of what he tries to tell his friend Goober:

> They don't want you to do your thing, not unless it happens to be their thing, too. It's a laugh, Goober, a fake. Don't disturb the universe, Goober, no matter what the posters say.

In selecting *The Chocolate War* as a touchstone example, we asked ourselves several questions about the book. These same or similar questions could be asked when evaluating almost any problem novel (Table 3.1). First, does the book make a distinctive contribution? Does it say something new, or does it convey something old in a new way? And if so, is it something of value? Robert Cormier was praised

TABLE 3.1

SUGGESTIONS FOR EVALUATING THE PROBLEM NOVEL

A good problem novel usually has:	A poor problem novel may have:
A strong, interesting, and believable plot centering around a problem that a young person might really have.	A totally predictable plot with nothing new and interesting to entice the reader.
The power to transport the reader into another person's thoughts and feelings.	Characters who are cardboardlike exaggerations of people and are too good or too bad to be believed.
Rich characterization. The characters "come alive" as believable with a balance of good and negative qualities.	More characters than the reader can keep straight comfortably.
A setting that enhances the story and is described so that the reader can get the intended picture.	Many stereotypes.
	Lengthy chapters or descriptive paragraphs that add bulk but not substance to the book.
A worthwhile theme. The reader is left with something to think about.	A preachy message. The author spells out the attitudes and conclusions with which he or she wants each reader to leave the book.
A smoothness of style that flows steadily and easily, carrying the reader along.	Nothing that stays with the reader after the book has been put down.
A universal appeal so that it speaks to more than a single group of readers.	A subject that is of interest only because it is topical or trendy.
A subtlety that stimulates the reader to think about the various aspects of the story.	Inconsistent points of view. The author's sympathies change with no justification.
A way of dealing with the problems so that the reader is left with insights into either society or individuals or both.	Dialogue that sounds forced or inappropriate to the characters.
	"Facts" that do not jibe with those of the real world.
	Unlikely coincidences or changes in characters' personalities for the sake of the plot.
	Exaggerations that result in sensationalism.

by *The Kirkus Reviews* because with *The Chocolate War* he dared to "disturb the up-beat universe of juvenile books." He did not compromise by providing a falsely hopeful conclusion, nor did he sidestep the issue by leaving it open for readers to imagine their own happy ending. Until Cormier, most writers for young readers had chosen one of these two approaches. Yet Cormier was not being "difficult" just for the sake of being different. When he was questioned at a National Council of Teachers of English convention about his motives in writing such a pessimistic book for young readers, he answered that he had written three other novels and numerous short stories, all with upbeat endings, and that in *The Chocolate War* he was simply providing a balance. He then went on to say that today's young readers are a television generation. They have grown up thinking that every problem can be solved within a half-hour or an hour at the most, with time out for commercials. It is important for people to realize that all problems are not that easily solved. In real life, some problems may never be solved, and the solutions to others demand the utmost efforts of the most capable people in the world.

The plot of a book must be examined to see how closely it grows out of the characters' actions and attitudes. Is it an idea that could easily have been dropped into another setting or onto other characters? With Cormier's book, there wouldn't have been a story without the unique but believable personalities of both Jerry and Archie as well as of Brother Leon. The problem was not so bizarre or unusual that it overshadowed the characters, and the characters were not so unusual that readers could not identify with them or imagine themselves having to deal with people like them. It is because the characters at first appear to be such ordinary people that readers are drawn into the story. The theme is similar to that in Golding's *Lord of the Flies,* but because Golding's book is set on a deserted island in the midst of a war it could be dismissed as unrealistic. Cormier's book has an immediacy that is hard to deny. The problem is a real one that teenagers can identify with on the first or literal level, yet it has implications far beyond one beaten-up 14-year-old and 20,000 boxes of leftover Mother's Day candy.

In looking at the setting, we might ask, is it just there or does it contribute something to the mood or the action or to revealing characterization? In *The Chocolate War,* the story would not have been nearly so chilling without the religious setting, which provided contrast. In some ways the evil in Archie, is less hideous than that in Brother Leon, the corrupt teacher who enlists Archie's help in making his unauthorized investment pay off. The Brother hides behind his clerical collar and his role of teacher and assistant headmaster, whereas Archie only identifies himself as a nonbeliever in the so-called Christian ethic. When his stooge Obie asks him how he can do the things he does and still take Communion, he responds, "When you march down to the rail, you're receiving the Body, man. Me, I'm just chewing a wafer they buy by the pound in Worcester."

Another relevant question is the respect the author has for the intended audience. Cormier showed a great deal of respect for his readers: Nowhere did he write down to them. The proof of his respect is in some of the subtle symbolization that he worked into the story and the care with which he developed his style. For example, the irony of the whole situation is exemplified in the gang's name, the Vigils. He chose the name as a shortened form of *vigilante,* an accurate description of the way the gang worked. But in response to an interview question about whether or not the name was an ironic reference to vigil lights, the candles placed devotionally before a shrine or image, he agreed that the religious connotation, the image of the boys in the gang standing like vigil lights before Archie, who basked in the glow of their admiration, "was also very much a part of my choice."[2] Another example of Cormier's subtlety is the fact that Archie's name has such meanings as "principal or chief," as in *archvillain,* and "at the extreme, that is, someone or something most fully embodying the qualities of its kind," as in *archrival.*

A question that has to be asked somewhere in the evaluation process is how many people a particular book attracts as readers. *The Chocolate War* has gone through innumerable reprintings, so it's obviously being read, although many of those who read it are doing it as a class assignment either in a college young adult literature class or in a high school English class. It is ideal for class reading and discussion because there is more in the book than any one student sees at a first reading.

The Value of Problem Novels in Today's World

In the late 1960s, when the problem novel was first developing as *the* genre in young adult literature, it played a relatively unique role in openly acknowledging that many young people lived lives far removed from the happy-go-lucky images shown in television commercials and sit-coms. The books on the Honor List from the 1960s and 1970s were new and interesting because they vividly demonstrated that young people worried about sex, drugs, money, peer pressure, and health problems. They also showed that not all teenagers had parents as kindly as Wally and June Cleaver or as cute and competent as the caregivers portrayed on "The Brady Bunch."

Such information does not come as news today, which means that teenagers do not need to read young adult novels to learn they are not the only ones with problems. The mass media does a thorough job of communicating that message because reporters for both print and broadcast media have discovered that teenagers are at a stage in their lives when they have more than their share of decisions to make as shown by such recent news headlines as:

Exchange students find gun; 1 slain
Police say coed lied about rape
School a dangerous place for teenagers, survey says
Teen moms live in different world
Teen found safe in San Francisco after online-aided disappearance
Juvenile detention sites face crowding crisis
Teen held in bogus AIDS calls
Little wars' little victims: Tally of slain kids tops 1.5 million
Teen's death likely due to speeding ticket
Teen-age homicide rate has soared
Third bullied pupil hangs self in Japan
Teen health in the age of AIDS

Because of today's mass media, teenagers are well aware that they are not the only ones with problems.

Considering the sheer numbers of young people and the decisions they are called on to make, it is to be expected that some of their decisions will go disastrously wrong and bring horrific problems to the individuals as well as to their families and associates. What is different today is the increased role of the media in telling the world about such problems. *Time* magazine headlined an article on the 1995 Cannes film festival (June 5, 1995) "Festival of Lost Children." Reporter Richard Corliss wrote:

> You couldn't swing a cat—or kick one, as the main character in *Kids* does—without hitting a movie about troubled teens in heat and on the rampage. Between frantically perfunctory bouts of sexmaking, the rich kids in the Spanish film *Stories of the Kronen* hang recklessly from a bridge over a busy highway. The teenage girls in the Thai film *Daughters* sniff glue as a break from their stealing and prostitution. In *La Haine* denizens of the bleak projects outside Paris rip off Chinese grocers and face off in grudge matches with the police. For the drug-dealing Arab pre-teens in *Bye-Bye* set in Marseilles, the only moral imperative is to stay alive. . . .

In more optimistic movies and on television, beautiful young adults add visual appeal to romances and situation comedies as well as to the amazingly popular talk shows in which participants, including many young adults, share their intimate secrets with millions of viewers. These shows have helped to create what Ellen Goodman has labeled "a cultural climate of true confession," where silence is not golden but instead "is considered a taboo to be broken."[3] Kurt Anderson, writing for *Time* magazine, credited the success of talk shows to a literal response to Andy Warhol's quip about each of us being allotted 15 minutes of fame. Of all the ways to become momentarily famous, he wrote, public mortification is by far the easiest.[4]

Anderson's observation may partially explain why people participate on the shows, but it does not say why so many viewers, including young adults, watch them. A scene in Chris Lynch's *Iceman* serves as a clue by showing how lonely and isolated some people feel. Eric is at a funeral parlor with his older friend McLaughlin who lets him peek, unseen, through a crack in the wood paneling where he watches three old friends come to say goodbye to a World War I comrade. As he watches, Eric suddenly understands why McLaughlin works there.

> Like a ghoul, he fed on it. Like a vampire sucking the life, the blood, he found that this was where to find it, the place where people *said* they were sad, they were hurt, said they didn't want to be alone. Where people let it rip and didn't give a damn who knew about it. I saw—and stole—more emotion raw and real in that room in twenty minutes than I'd gotten from my family in fourteen years.

The need that Eric expresses to "feel" some emotion is endemic to our culture. Living in what Marshall McLuhan so aptly labeled a "global village" means that we are privy to so many people's problems that we simply do not have the energy to empathize with all those we hear about. We shrug our shoulders and turn off our tear ducts, which leaves us feeling alienated and dehumanized.

Ameliorating such feelings is a role that well-written problem novels can fill in ways that the mass media cannot. Although fiction writers can hardly compete with the real-life problems of such singular young adults as Timothy McVeigh, the teenage victims of Jeffrey Dahmer, the Menendez brothers, the late River Phoenix, Olympic ice skaters Nancy Kerrigan and Tonya Harding, or the teenage mistresses of Joey Buttafuoco and of the former national director of the United Way, they can explore the motivations and the feelings that lie beneath surface descriptions of their characters.

Another reason that books can succeed where the news media cannot is the simple matter of how much time is involved. For example, on television talk shows, suffering individuals are shuffled through their paces in less than an hour and then sent on their respective ways. In contrast, readers usually spend several hours with a book. Also, because few kids finish a book in a single sitting, they have time between readings to ponder the characters' problems and solutions.

From the production standpoint, authors of the best books spend several months or even years figuring out how best to communicate the crucial details that will help readers understand the heart of their story. They seek a balance between stories that are different enough to be interesting while common enough that readers can relate to them. In contrast, reporters and producers compete with each

CYNTHIA VOIGT
On Learning and Knowing

I have a theory that the real difference between kids and adults is that kids expect themselves to be learning and adults expect themselves to know. This seems to me to be both a central and an essential difference.

If I expect myself to be learning, my attitude towards experiences, people, the whole side show, is characterized by questions and curiosity; probably more important, my understanding of who I am, myself, is that I am changing, growing, adding to myself. If I expect myself to know, then I stand before the world as a completed creature—and I am bound to be a disappointment to everybody concerned in the encounter. If I must know, in order to be a self I recognize and respect, the possibility for change diminishes. If I require the adults around me to know, I diminish them.

This may just be the difference between growing up and grown-up. Kids have it easy because there is no question that they are in process. Adults stand under the danger, or the temptation, of thinking that process ought to have been completed, or has been completed—which is, of course, a fool's paradise. I don't know about the rest of the adults out there, but it seems to me I spend my time perpetually growing up, with no end in sight to the arduous and uneasy occupation—which strikes me, on the whole, as a good thing, and a beneficial thing. I don't envy kids, the young, and I don't regret the years I've got on them, but one of the things I cherish about teaching is that constant reminder, unspoken but clear, that learning, not knowing, is what it's about.

Cynthia Voigt's books include *When She Hollers,* Scholastic, 1994; *Izzy, Willy-Nilly,* Atheneum, 1986; *A Solitary Blue,* Atheneum, 1983; and *Homecoming,* Atheneum, 1981.

other to find something new and so look for stories further and further removed from people's ordinary experiences.

Certainly the shouting matches that make for high ratings on television talk shows do not serve as a good model for the development of oral skills in problem solving. But when a novel is read by one or more students and discussed under the leadership of a knowledgeable adult, students can be led to think deeply about issues and problem solving (see Focus Box 10.1, p. 309). Thoughtful discussions can counteract the tendency of people to make superficial decisions based on first impressions and emotions rather than through gathering and weighing solid information. One of the marks of emotional and intellectual maturity is understanding that there may be many viewpoints from which to judge the actions and beliefs of others, whereas another worthwhile lesson is recognizing the distance between knowing something is wrong and being able to do something about it.

Cynthia Voigt's *When She Hollers*—a title readers are to complete in their own minds with "make him pay"—does a superb job of illustrating how hard it is for Tish to confront the stepfather who has been abusing her. Even after she has sought out the help of an attorney and has a plan that gives her a chance, "Maybe even a pretty good chance," she turns down the offer of a ride home by telling the aptly named *Mr. Battle,* the attorney who is helping her,

> that she wanted to walk so she'd have time to get ready, but she wasn't sure that was true. She thought maybe it was to give herself time to change her mind. She didn't have to tell Tonnie [her stepfather] about the paper, and the lawyer. She could get rid of the card in her pocket, with Mr. Battle's office phone number on it, and his home phone number. . . .
>
> Fear grew in her belly, like some speeded-up pregnancy, and shoved up against her heart and vibrated along her bones until she almost couldn't find the leg muscles to keep on walking, clump, clump, back to Tonnie's house.

But having come this far, Tish knows she can't turn back, and when she gets to her own front door "bulging out with all the fury behind it," she rings the doorbell and then steps back so that she can confront Tonnie and say what she has to say outside in the open, rather than in Tonnie's house. She gets an image of how big the world is:

> . . . round—like a picture in a book, with the Australians hanging off by their feet and smiling, and the Japanese sticking out of one side, smiling. She pictured how little a dot Tonnie's home made on that globe. Everything except for that tiny little dot *wasn't* his.

Wrapping her mind around this image and holding "it out in front of her, like a knife" gives her the courage to do what she has to do.

This powerful story of a girl taking steps to save herself also illustrates another advantage that well-written problem novels have over superficial media treatments. Because most such treatments present a one-shot portrait, chosen to tug at the emotions of viewers or readers, they make a virtue of suffering and pain by portraying people as victims unable to move beyond their pain. In contrast, the best of the problem novels help young readers develop an internal locus of control through which they assume that their own actions and characteristics will shape their lives. They ask the question, "What am I going to do with my life?", whereas people with an external locus of control depend on luck, chance, or what others do. Their major life question is "What will happen to me?"

Although we all know adults who blame others for whatever happens to them and take little responsibility for making their own decisions, most of us would agree that we want to help young people feel responsible for their own lives. Books cannot substitute for real-life experiences, and one or two books, no matter how well written, are not enough to change a teenager's view of life. Skilled authors, however, can show what's going on in characters' minds, whereas cameras can show only what is externally visible. Also, authors of the problem novels have the space to develop various strands of their stories and to show characters making progress. This differs from television sit-coms as well as most series books, which preserve the status quo.

In the problem novels, young protagonists take steps toward maturity so that at the end of the book they are different in some significant way. Most importantly, the protagonists are shown solving the problem, as illustrated by the previous discussion of Cynthia Voigt's *When She Hollers*. Instead of sitting by waiting for something to happen, they take responsibility. As one of our graduate students, Diana Kraus, wrote in her justification for wanting to teach Virginia Euwer Wolff's *Make Lemonade:*

> LaVaughn has a goal to go to college from which she never deviates. When her desperate friend asks for a loan (impossible to repay) of her college money, LaVaughn feels no ambivalence about saying, "No." She has enormous sympathy for her friend, she helps in every way she can, even side-stepping the truth to her mom, yet she does not jeopardize her own agenda. I think this is something many young adults, and especially girls, need to learn. It's okay, even good, to say "No," to put yourself first.

Hundreds of books present variations on this theme of taking responsibility for oneself. It isn't hard to devise plots that include such incidents, but for authors to make them believable and bring enough life to the characters so that readers care is challenging.

What Are the Problems?

Good young adult authors treat candidly and with respect problems that belong specifically to young adults in today's world. As we pointed out in Chapter One, adolescence as a unique period of life is a fairly recent development coinciding with the growth of complex industrial societies. Many of the problems that go along with modern adolescence did not exist in the nineteenth century, so, of course, they were not written about. At least in this one area, there is ample justification for books directed specifically to a youthful audience because there is a difference in the kinds of real-life problems that concern children, teenagers, and adults.

"Teens Face Whirlwind of Worries" read the headline of a newspaper story summarizing a recent convention of the American Psychological Association.[5] Conference sessions focused on the following topics:

- *Fears:* Researchers at McGill University in Montreal reported that the teens in their study who live in a safe, clean suburb "with parks everywhere" feared globe-threatening environmental disasters, unemployment, World War III, drugs, and violence. They found some teenagers so troubled by the fear of AIDS that they won't eat in restaurants.
- *Dating and Sex:* Other researchers found that kids, bombarded by MTV and other sex-obsessed media, are dating and having sex almost as soon as their ages hit double digits. One-on-one dating at a tender age (fifth through eighth grades) was more likely to occur with children from broken homes. Also,

young teens paired off with a boyfriend or girlfriend were not as happy as those who socialized in groups.

- *Alcohol and Drugs:* The National Institute on Drug Abuse was criticized for touting the fact that drug use among teenagers has dropped 18 percent since the early 1980s without explaining that the statistics are only for teenagers in school, and once kids are addicted to drugs they are likely to drop out.
- *Money:* As the economy worsens, more kids are going to work. Two-thirds of all teens in junior and senior high have jobs. Most go to work right after school and come home too tired to read or think about homework.
- *Academics:* In this first generation growing up in a high number of single-parent families, parents probably haven't had as much time and energy to help their children with schoolwork or to serve as career models, especially in science and math, which are chosen as college majors by only 7% of incoming students.
- *Independence:* Although rebellion and freedom were the code words of many teenagers in the 1950s and 1960s, today "there's been a revision of the model that says teenagers need to cut themselves off from their families. Now kids are saying, 'I wish there was someone I could be close to.'"
- *Mental Illness:* College counseling centers no longer treat mainly developmental issues and boyfriend/girlfriend problems. Maureen Kenny of Boston College reported that they are now dealing on a regular basis with serious mental illness and that the "kids [of divorce] suffer more than previously we had given them credit for."

Today's teenagers are not the first in history with difficult decisions to make, but certainly few of us will argue against the idea that they have a special set of problems unique to their age and to today's world. Parents, writers, and educators are eager to help young people in these decisions, and one of the ways we believe we can help is to provide books that honestly explore problems and present alternative solutions.

Family Relationships

A look at mythology, folklore, and classical and religious literature shows that the subject of family relationships is not what's new about the problem novel (see Focus Box 3.1, for example). Stories featuring inadequate or absent parents appeal to young readers because they provide opportunities for young people to assert their independence and prove that they can take care of themselves, as in Thelma Hatch Wyss's *Here at the Scenic-Vu Motel*. The school board in Bear Flats, Idaho, decides to quit bussing seven kids into town for high school. The solution is for the teenage children to live Monday through Friday in a motel.

Wyss's story is fairly light and could probably fit in the next chapter just as well as here. Cynthia Voigt's Newbery Award–winning *Dicey's Song* is clearly heavy enough to be classified as a problem novel. It begins:

And They Lived Happily Ever After

FOCUS BOX 3.1

Parents and Kids

Celine by Brock Cole. Farrar, 1989. Celine, a 16-year-old artist, is left to make friends with her new, and almost embarrassingly young, stepmother when her father takes off on a European lecture tour.

A Day No Pigs Would Die by Robert Newton Peck. Knopf, 1973. The love that the boy Robert feels for his Pa is only one of the themes in this powerful story of a Vermont farm family from the 1920s.

Dinky Hocker Shoots Smack by M. E. Kerr. HarperCollins, 1972. The first of M. E. Kerr's young adult books was inspired by her watching a do-gooder mother solving everyone's problems except those of her own daughter.

The Great Gilly Hopkins by Katherine Paterson. Crowell, 1979. Gilly manipulates her caregivers until she gets the wise and wonderful Trotter as a foster mother. But when Gilly's attempts to find her flower-child birth mother backfire, not even Trotter can help.

Gypsy Davey by Chris Lynch. HarperCollins, 1994. A lifetime of parental neglect makes Davey all the more determined to make things better for his older sister's baby, but it isn't to be.

Hannah in Between by Colby Rodowsky. Farrar, 1994. Hannah, the teenaged daughter of an alcoholic mother, tries her best to "fix" her mother's problem.

Ice by Phyllis Reynolds Naylor. Atheneum, 1995. When Chrissa's father disappears, she is sent to live with her grandmother in the country. Time, nature, and new friends help heal old wounds.

Missing Pieces by Norma Fox Mazer. Morrow, 1995. Fourteen-year-old Jessie goes looking for "the disappearing dude" who is her father and who she imagines to be a prince of a fellow.

The Moonlight Man by Paula Fox. Bradbury, 1986. In a memorable summer visit, Catherine ends up playing the role of the grown-up when she discovers that her father is a "falling-down-drunk."

Somewhere in the Darkness by Walter Dean Myers. Scholastic, 1992. Jimmy arrives home from school to find a tall, thin man waiting to introduce himself as the father who's been gone so long that Jimmy has to look at a photograph to verify the truth of what the man says.

Not the Tillermans, Dicey thought. That wasn't the way things went for the Tillermans, ever. She wasn't about to let that get her down. She couldn't let it get her down—that was what had happened to Momma.

Dicey's view that when parents are weak the children have to be that much stronger is a theme often illustrated through the way brothers and sisters pull together to close gaps in the family circle, as in Betsy Byars's *The Night Swimmers*, Vera and Bill Cleaver's *Where the Lilies Bloom* and *Trial Valley*, and S. E. Hinton's *Tex*. Other stories exploring sibling relationships include Judy Blume's *Here's To You, Rachel Robinson*, M. E. Kerr's *Linger*, Chris Lynch's *Iceman*, and Jan Slepian's *Risk n'Roses*, which explores Skip's apprehensions over her retarded sister as Skip tries to fit into her new Bronx neighborhood.

Jamaica Kincaid's *Annie John*, set on the Caribbean Island of Antigua, is a powerful exploration of a daughter's painful gaining of emotional independence from her mother. In Paula Fox's *A Place Apart* and in Judy Blume's *Tiger Eyes*, the fathers of the families die unexpectedly (a heart attack and a shooting, respectively), and the mothers and daughters move to new locales, almost as if they are embarking on dual quests in search of a way to put their lives back together. In neither book is it easy, as shown by the climax of *Tiger Eyes,* when Davey's mother invites her out to a special dinner.

> "This is nice," I say. What I mean is that it is nice to be alone with my mother. This is the first time since we came to Los Alamos that it is just the two of us.
>
> "Yes," Mom says. "It's very nice."
>
> "It's been a long time."
>
> "Yes," Mom says. "And I've wanted to explain that to you, Davey."
>
> She is arranging and rearranging her silverware, moving the spoon into the fork's place, then the fork into the spoon's. "Up until now, I've been afraid to be alone with you."
>
> "Afraid?"
>
> "Yes."
>
> "But why?"
>
> "I was afraid you'd ask me questions and I wouldn't have any answers. I've been afraid you'd want to talk about Daddy . . . and the night he was killed . . . and the pain would be too much for me."
>
> "I did want to talk about it," I tell her. "For a long time . . . and it hurt me that you wouldn't."
>
> "I know," she says, reaching across the table and touching my hand. "But I had to come to terms with it myself, first. Now I think I'm ready . . . now I can talk about it with you."
>
> "But now I don't need to," I say.

The impending death of John Rodgers' father from leukemia gives a double meaning to the title of David Klass's *California Blue,* about a young biologist finding a previously unknown species of butterfly. Although the book raises questions about ecology, for many readers the most memorable part is the progress of the father-son relationship. Seventeen-year-old John is five years younger than any of his brothers and sisters, and he figures he was an accident that his parents decided to keep. He feels like something "between a nerd and a wimp," especially when compared to his athletic older brothers who followed in his father's footsteps. John runs, but as he says about himself, "a middle-distance runner without a sprint kick is a scared animal." What happens to change this "scared animal" makes for a good story.

Friends and Society

Peer groups become increasingly important to teenagers as they move beyond social and emotional dependence on their parents. By becoming part of a group, clique, or gang, teenagers take a step toward emotional independence. Even though they are not making truly independent decisions about such social conventions as clothing, language, and entertainment, it's no longer their parents who are deciding on and enforcing their behavior. As part of a group, they try out various roles ranging from conformist to nonconformist, from follower to leader. These roles can be acted out by individuals within the group or they can be acted out by the group as a whole, as, for example, when one gang challenges another gang. Group members in such a situation are caught up in a kind of emotional commitment that they would seldom feel as individuals.

It is not automatic that all teenagers find groups to belong to, and even if they do, they are still curious about other groups. This is where young adult literature comes in. It extends the peer group, giving teenagers a chance to participate vicariously in many more personal relationships than are possible for most youngsters in the relatively short time that they spend in high school. When they were children, making friends was a simple matter of playing with whoever happened to be nearby. Parents were responsible for locating in the "right" neighborhood near "good schools," so that children had no reason to give particular thought to differences in social and economic classes or ethnic backgrounds. Then quite suddenly their environments are expanded not only through larger, more diverse schools, but also through jobs, extracurricular activities, public entertainment, shopping in malls, and church or community activities.

Tradition says that the United States is a democracy and that we do not have a caste system. Anyone can grow up to be president. But real-life observations do not support this, and that may be why books exploring differences in social classes are especially popular with young adults.

Naturally, school is a common topic for teenage books because this is what young people are involved in on a daily basis. Compassionate teachers include Ann Treer in Robin Brancato's *Winning,* Nigeria Greene and Bernard Cohen in Alice Childress's *A Hero Ain't Nothin' But a Sandwich,* Miss Stevenson and Miss Widmer in Nancy Garden's *Annie on My Mind,* the school nurse in Phyllis Reynolds Naylor's *The Keeper,* and Miss Merrill in David Klass's *California Blue,* but these are the exceptions. Society forces young people to treat authority figures—teachers, librarians, ministers, housemothers, coaches, parole officers, and so on—with respect. Because young people are not allowed to discuss differences of opinion or "quarrel" with these adults as they might with their parents, hostilities undoubtedly build up. It's therefore fairly common for authors to tap into this reservoir of resentment to bring smiles to young readers, as when in Paul Zindel's *Confessions of a Teenage Baboon,* fatherless Chris relates his conversation with a solicitous police officer:

> "What you need is the PAL or a Big Brother," he advised, squeezing my shoulder. "If you were my kid you'd be playing football." "If I were your kid I'd be playing horse," I said. "Horse?" he said, looking a little puzzled as he opened the patrol-car door. "You know," I clarified. "I'd be the front end—and you could just be yourself."

Although this kind of humor is both unfair and irritating to adults, it serves as a respite and a refreshing change of pace that is necessary to keep some problem novels from becoming too depressing.

Problems of group identification are a part of all of S. E. Hinton's books, especially *The Outsiders,* in which the *greasers* (i.e., the dirt heads) are in conflict with the *socs* (i.e., the society kids). Myron Levoy's *A Shadow Like a Leopard* is a grim, but at the same time upbeat, story of 14-year-old Ramon Santiago, who makes friends with an old man who is a painter. Ramon is a Puerto Rican living in the slums of New York, and in one scene, when people stare at him as he walks through a hotel lobby, he feels ashamed "of his clothing, of his face, of his very bones. Ashamed to be Puerto Rican."

It is a mark of maturity in the field of young adult literature that no longer are just the big group distinctions being made. In *Tiger Eyes*, Judy Blume includes many subtle observations, which lead readers to see and judge inductively various status symbols in the high-tech, scientific community of Los Alamos (e.g., Bathtub Row, gun racks in pickup trucks, and tell-tale comments about Native Americans and Chicanos). In *Remembering the Good Times*, Richard Peck's narrator has fun describing the various groups in his new school:

> There were suburbanites still maintaining their position and their Izod-and-L.L. Bean image . . . a few authentic Slos, the polyester people . . . punk . . . funk . . . New Wave . . . Spaces . . . people at the top of the line looked a lot like the Pine Hill Slos down at the bottom who'd been having to wear this type gear all along except with different labels.

In *The Friends*, Rosa Guy does a masterful job of leading her readers to see how Phyllisia is taught that she's too good for the neighborhood. Her family has immigrated to Harlem from the West Indies, and her overly strict, restaurant-owner father constantly instills in her a feeling of superiority. He is horrified when Phyllisia brings home poor "ragamuffin" Edith, with her ragged coat, holey socks, turned-over shoes, and matted hair.

Body and Self

Books that treat problems related to accepting and effectively using one's physical body are treated in several sections of this text. When the physical problem is relatively minor, or is at least one that can be corrected, it might be treated as an accomplishment-romance, discussed in Chapter Four. Also, many nonfiction books as well as sports stories focus on the physical body, and in many realistic novels physical problems serve as a concrete or visible symbol for mental growth, which is harder to show.

It is almost obligatory in realistic fiction for young protagonists to express dissatisfaction with their appearance. Part of this is because hardly anyone has a perfect body or hasn't envied others for their appearance or physical skill. A bigger part is that adolescent bodies are changing so fast that their owners have not yet had time to adjust. The reason they spend so much time looking in mirrors is to reassure themselves, "Yes, this is me!"

In 1970, Judy Blume surprised the world of juvenile fiction by writing a book that gave major attention to physical aspects of growing up. In *Are You There, God? It's Me, Margaret*, Margaret Simon worries because her breasts are small and because she's afraid she will be the last one in her crowd to begin menstruating. A later Blume book, *Then Again, Maybe I Won't,* features Tony Miglione and his newly affluent family. He too worries about his developing body. In fact, he carries a jacket even on the warmest days so that he will have something to hide behind in case he has an erection. These books are read mostly by younger adolescents. But both junior and senior high students read Blume's *Deenie.* It is about a pretty teenager whose mother wants her to be a model, but then it's discovered that she has scoliosis and must wear an unsightly back brace. A minor point that goes unnoticed by some readers (but not by censors) is Deenie's worry that her back problems might be related to the fact that she masturbates. Because Blume ties physical development in with emotional and social development, her books are more fun to read (and more controversial) than are factual books about the development of the human body.

The problem novel does not stop with treating the more or less typical problems of growing up. See Focus Box 3.2 for recommended books that treat mental and physical disabilities. Alden Carter's *Up Country* and Gary Paulsen's *Harris and Me* explore various aspects of parental alcoholism, whereas Robert Cormier's *We All Fall Down* explores teenage alcoholism.

Some of the most powerful problem novels are those that deal with death (see Focus Box 3.3 for examples). In Gunnel Beckman's *Admission to the Feast,* 19-year-old Annika Hallin accidentally learns from a substitute doctor that she has leukemia. She flees by herself to her family's summer cottage, where she tries to sort out her reactions:

> I don't think I understood it until last night . . . that I, Annika, . . . will just be put away, wiped out, obliterated. . . . And here on earth everything will just go on. . . . I shall never have more than this little scrap of life.

Although Katherine Paterson's *Bridge to Terabithia* is considered a children's book because it's about two fifth-graders, we know several young adults who have read it and wept, as have many adults. Jean Ferris's *Invincible Summer* is a restrained but sad love story about two teenagers with leukemia. The boy, Rick, dies, but the book ends with readers and the girl, Robin, still uncertain about her prognosis and her future. Of course, she wants to live, but she consoles herself by thinking that if the treatments are unsuccessful, as Rick's were, if it were truly going to be "lights out, the end, eternal sleep, then what was there to worry about?" but if she were going to be someplace, then Rick would be there too.

Fran Arrick's *Tunnel Vision* shows what suicide does to a devastated family left vainly trying to figure out why bright and popular Anthony chose to take his own life. Richard Peck's *Remembering the Good Times* is no more comforting even though it is easier to understand Trav's motivation. For older readers, Anne Tyler's *Saint Maybe* is a powerful story of what happens to a family after a brother's suicide.

One of the values of books about disabilities and death is that they illustrate relationships between physical and emotional problems. It would be hard to say whether Nancy Werlin's *Are You Alone on Purpose?* is about physical or mental problems. It begins when the Shandling family hears about the death of great-uncle Simon.

FOCUS BOX 3.2

Disabilities—Physical and Mental

The Alfred Summer by Jan Slepian. Macmillan, 1980. Once readers get to know Alfred, they will think differently about people with cerebral palsy.

All Together Now by Sue Ellen Bridgers. Knopf, 1979. When Casey Flanagan goes to spend the summer with her grandparents, she makes friends with 33-year-old Dwayne Pickens, who is retarded and thinks that Casey is a boy.

Black Water by Rachel Anderson. Holt, 1995. One of the interesting details in this story of a nineteenth-century English boy with epilepsy is his meeting with Edward Lear, an epileptic who went to extraodinary lengths to keep his condition secret.

Freak the Mighty by Rodman Philbrick. Scholastic, 1993. Kevin and Max are drawn together because they are both shunned by classmates, Max for being learning disabled and Kevin for being small and crippled. Their short but extraordinary friendship will stick in readers' minds.

I Never Promised You a Rose Garden by Hannah Green. Holt, 1964. Teenager Deborah Blau is being treated in a mental institution. The book's title comes from the warning her psychiatrist gives that once she is released she will still have problems.

Little Little by M. E. Kerr. HarperCollins, 1981. Little Little is a PF (Perfectly Formed) dwarf whose mother wants her to marry an-other PF, Lionel Knox (also known as Opportunity Knox). Little Little prefers Sidney Applebaum, whose spine is crooked but whose morals are straight.

Probably Still Nick Swansen by Virginia Euwer Wolff. Holt, 1988. Nick has "minimal brain damage" and at school is doomed to being in Room 19, home of the "droolers" and other misfits. Shana is on her way back to regular classes when she accepts Nick's invitation for a star-crossed date to the junior prom.

Not the End of the World by Rebecca Stowe. Pantheon, 1992. Maggie's grandmother jovially explains to her tittering bridge friends that Maggie's crazy. All the way through, readers—along with Maggie—wonder about the truth of the "joke."

The Silent Storm by Sherry Garland. Harcourt, 1993. Thirteen-year-old Alyssa is so devastated by the death of her parents in a hurricane that for three years she does not speak—not until another hurricane threatens her brother and grandfather and their Galveston Island home.

Staying Fat for Sarah Byrnes by Chris Crutcher. Greenwillow, 1993. Eric and Sarah are drawn together because of their "terminal uglies." Eric is overweight and Sarah is horribly scarred, both inside and outside, from burns inflicted on her when she was 3 years old.

If you believed in fate, and Alison did, then with hindsight it was clear that this was the first event in some capricious cosmic conspiracy to upset her life, which she kept in precarious balance as it was.

The reason Alison's life was only precariously balanced is that her autistic twin brother has necessarily received most of their parents' attention. No one, including Alison, knew how much she resented this until her family seeks out a Jewish synagogue so her father can say Kaddish (the Jewish prayer for the dead). Alison and her family get much more involved than they had ever dreamed in the lives of

FOCUS BOX 3.3

Dying Is Easy—Surviving Is Hard

The Bell Jar by Sylvia Plath. HarperCollins, 1971. Mature teens are still fascinated by this story of a young woman who does more than flirt with suicide.

The Eagle Kite by Paula Fox. Orchard, 1995. As a high school freshman, Liam learns that his father is dying of AIDS. His grief is complicated by anger as well as by the frustrations of change when his father moves out of the family apartment.

Earthshine by Theresa Nelson. Orchard, 1994. Even though the author gets a little heavy-handed about homophobia, readers will be touched by this story of Slim and her desperate search for help as she watches her father come closer and closer to death from AIDS.

In Country by Bobbie Ann Mason. HarperCollins, 1985. A teenage girl's acceptance and partial understanding of her father's death comes through a trip that she takes with her uncle and her grandmother to the Vietnam War Memorial in Washington.

My Brother Stealing Second by Jim Naughton. HarperCollins, 1989. While star athlete and favorite son Billy is drunk, he kills himself as well as a couple celebrating their wedding anniversary. His parents and brother, along with

the daughter of the couple, suffer but survive.

Remembering Mog by Colby Rodowsky. Farrar, 1996. It is Annie's high school graduation, but neither she nor her family can celebrate because the event is a grim reminder of her older sister's murder two years earlier.

Say Goodnight, Gracie by Julie Reece Deaver. HarperCollins, 1988. When Jimmy is killed by a drunk driver, Morgan realizes how much he meant to her, then and now.

Soulfire by Lorri Hewett. Dutton, 1996. Sixteen-year-old Todd Williams, an African American living in Denver, shares his anguish over the gang-related death of his cousin, Tommy.

A Summer to Die by Lois Lowry. Houghton Mifflin, 1977. While her older sister is dying of leukemia, Meg finds comfort and solace in the help that comes from 70-year-old Will Banks, landlord, handyman, and photographer.

Tell Me Everything by Caroline Coman. Farrar, 1993. Twelve-year-old Roz and her mother, Ellie, have an exceptionally close and spiritual relationship in their secluded mountain home. When Ellie is killed while trying to rescue a hiker, Roz must face her loss while also making a new life.

the rabbi and his angry son, who over the course of the story suffers a crippling accident.

Sex-Related Problems

Here we will give some examples of different kinds of sexual relationships treated in problem novels (see Focus Box 3.4), but lest we leave the impression that we look at sex only as a problem, we hasten to add that discussions of the matter also appear in Chapter Four under "The Love Romances" and in Chapter Eight under "Informational Books."

In trying to satisfy their curiosity, teenagers seek out and read the vivid descriptions of sexual activity in such books as Scott Spencer's *Endless Love* and William Hogan's *The Quartzsite Trip*, both published for adults but featuring young protagonists. Male and female readers have also been intrigued by Don Bredes's *Hard Feelings*, Terry Davis's *Vision Quest*, Jay Daly's *Walls*, and Aidan Chambers's

FOCUS BOX 3.4

Sex-Related Problems

Am I Blue: Coming Out from the Silence edited by Marion Dane Bauer. HarperCollins, 1994.   Several of the most popular writers for young adults have contributed stories to this well-received collection that centers on coming to terms with homosexuality.

Baby Be-Bop by Francesca Lia Block. HarperCollins, 1995.   Block uses her unusual style to explore homosexuality through telling the life story of Dirk McDonald, the gay young man who first appeared in *Weetzie Bat.*

Dear Nobody by Berlie Doherty. Orchard, 1992.   Pregnant Helen writes longer and longer letters to the child she is carrying who over the course of the book becomes less and less of a nobody.

Don't Think Twice by Ruth Pennebaker. Holt, 1996.   The setting is 1967 in a group home for pregnant teenagers. The story is told through the eyes of 17-year-old Anne Harper, but readers also get acquainted with some of the other residents.

The Hanged Man by Francesca Lia Block. HarperCollins, 1994.   Seventeen-year-old Laurel spins dangerously close to a breakdown as she tries purging herself of years of sexual abuse from her now deceased father.

I Hadn't Meant to Tell You This by Jacqueline Woodson. Delacorte, 1994.   In a starred review, *School Library Journal* defined Woodson's book not as a diatribe on child abuse, but as an exploration of "the complex and often contradictory responses of individuals—and society—to the plight of abused children."

Jack by A. M. Homes. Macmillan, 1989.   Fifteen-year-old Jack is devastated when after his parents' divorce he learns that his father is gay. Shame and bewilderment are gradually replaced with respect and a realization that people's lives come with problems.

The Man without a Face by Isabelle Holland. HarperCollins, 1972.   The high-powered movie starring Mel Gibson gave a new burst of popularity to Holland's story of 14-year-old Charles trying to find a way out of his female-dominated life.

Out of Control by Norma Fox Mazer. Morrow, 1993.   When Valerie Michon is molested by school mates, "everyone" conspires to hide what happened, but Valerie chooses to "go public" by writing a letter to the editor of the local newspaper.

Peter by Kate Walker. Houghton, 1993.   *Peter* was the only young adult book included on the *Boston Book Review's* "The Ten Best" of the year list. It's the emotional story of a 15-year-old Australian boy trying to sort out the differences between the reality and the stereotypes of being gay.

Breaktime, all coming-of-age stories that focus on young men's sexual desires. Books that are intended primarily for young female audiences are more likely to focus on romantic elements of a story, while only hinting at the characters' sexuality.

In the first edition of this textbook, we wrote that the three sexual issues treated in young adult problem novels were rape, homosexuality, and premarital sex resulting in pregnancy. For the next two editions we added disease, incest, and child abuse, and for this edition we also need to add teenagers as parents. Although in the earlier books, pregnant girls had an abortion as in Paul Zindel's *My Darling, My Hamburger,* the baby died as in Ann Head's *Mr. and Mrs. Bo Jo Jones,* or the baby was given up for adoption as in Richard Peck's *Don't Look and It Won't Hurt,* today the babies actually appear as in the highly acclaimed *Make Lemonade* by Virginia Euwer Wolff, *Gypsy Davey* by Chris Lynch, and *David & Della* by Paul Zindel.

Michael Borich's *A Different Kind of Love* is about a 14-year-old girl's ambivalence about her affection for the 25-year-old rock star uncle who has come to live with her and her mother. Fran Arrick's *Steffie Can't Come Out to Play* is a sympathetic portrayal of a teenage prostitute, and Richard Peck's *Are You in the House Alone?* and Patricia Dizenso's *Why Me?* treat the physical, emotional, and societal aspects of rape.

One of the early criticisms of the new realism was that the whole area of sexuality was treated so negatively. For example, in 1975, when W. Keith Kraus analyzed several books about premarital pregnancy—including Ann Head's *Mr. and Mrs. Bo Jo Jones,* Zoa Sherburne's *Too Bad About the Haines Girl,* Jean Thompson's *House of Tomorrow,* Margaret Maze Craig's *It Could Happen to Anyone,* Nora Stirling's *You Would if You Loved Me,* Jeannette Eyerly's *A Girl Like Me,* Paul Zindel's *My Darling, My Hamburger,* and John Neufeld's *For All the Wrong Reasons*—he concluded that the "old double standard is reinforced by the so-called new realism." He compared the stories to the old romances in which the girl is at the beginning an outsider who is discovered by a popular athlete. As she begins to date, a whole new social world opens up to her. But the dating leads to petting, and then to sex, and finally pregnancy and unhappiness. He lamented that the "sexual act itself is never depicted as joyful, and any show of intimacy carries a warning of future danger."[6] Many of the authors whose books will be treated in the next chapter under "The Love Romance" purposely set out to counterbalance the negative images that Kraus and other critics noted.

While the physical aspects of sex-related problems are important parts of the stories, it's really the emotional aspects that interest most readers. When Paul Zindel was speaking in Arizona in the late 1970s, he commented on the fact that next to *The Pigman,* his most popular book was *My Darling, My Hamburger,* which is about pregnancy and abortion. Soon after the book was published in 1969, a Supreme Court decision made most abortions legal, and Zindel thought that would be the end of all sales because his book would seem terribly old-fashioned. It didn't turn out this way, however, because rather than settling the issue, the legalization of abortions increased interest in the moral and psychological aspects of the problem. Decision making was passed from the courts to every woman with an unwanted pregnancy. And it is not only just the woman herself who is involved, but also the father, the grandparents, and the friends.

Even in books in which the main focus is not on whether someone is going to have an abortion, it may be mentioned as a possibility. For example, in Judy Blume's *Forever,* one of Katherine's friends has an abortion. In *Love Is One of the Choices,* Norma Klein told the story of two close friends and their first sexual loves. One of them chooses to marry and become pregnant right away, but the other gets pregnant, refuses to marry, and has an abortion.

Three landmark books opened the door to the treatment of homosexuality in books for young readers. They were John Donovan's *I'll Get There. It Better Be Worth the Trip* in 1969, Isabelle Holland's *The Man Without a Face,* and Lynn Hall's *Sticks and Stones,* both in 1972. The protagonists are male, and in all three books an important character dies. In none can a direct cause-and-effect relationship be charted between the death and the homosexual behavior, but possibilities for blame are there. And because the three books were all published within a relatively short period, critics were quick to object to the cumulative implications that homosexual behavior will be punished with some dreadful event. Despite this criticism, Sandra Scoppettone's *Trying Hard to Hear You,* published in 1974, was surprisingly similar, ending in an automobile accident that killed one of the teenage male lovers.

Books featuring female homosexuals were almost a decade behind the ones about males. In 1976, Rosa Guy published *Ruby,* which was a sequel to *The Friends.* Ruby is Phyllisia's older sister, and in the book she has a lesbian relationship with a beautiful classmate. *Publishers Weekly* described the homosexuality in the book as "perhaps just a way-step toward maturity." This relaxed attitude toward female homosexuality was reflected in Deborah Hautzig's 1978 *Hey Dollface* and in Nancy Garden's 1982 *Annie on My Mind,* which was praised for its strong characterization and tender love story.

One of the strengths of M. E. Kerr's *Deliver Us from Evie* is that although it is an issues book intended to make readers give second thoughts to various aspects of lesbianism, it is not limited to the one issue. The narrator is Parr Burrman, who is almost 16 and tells the story in what one reviewer described as a voice "perfectly pitched between wit and melancholy."[7] It is the story of one year in the life of a Missouri farm family when they lose much of their farm to a flood and also come close to losing Parr's sister, 18-year-old Evie, to community prejudices and family bad feelings. Kerr touches on the complications of friendships that cross socioeconomic and religious lines and, more importantly, on family dynamics when one player in a carefully structured pyramid pulls out.

In actuality, the big sex-related problems—rape, abuse, disease, homosexuality, and unwanted pregnancy—are experienced by few teenagers, but nearly all young people wonder abut the moral and social implications of experimenting with sexual activity, whether or not it leads to intercourse. Todd Strasser's *A Very Touchy Subject* and Norma Fox Mazer's *Up in Seth's Room* do a good job of showing the magnitude of teenagers' concerns. As Jean Fritz said when she reviewed Mazer's book for the *New York Times Book Review:*

> The questions we follow relentlessly from beginning to end are the perennial ones of adolescence: Will she or won't she? And what's it like? . . . Everyone should be pleased with the outcome. Finn sticks to her guns, although the fact that she "doesn't" is hardly more than a technicality. There are enough explicit scenes to give young readers, who don't know, a good idea of "what it's like."[8]

Mazer said she wrote the book as an antidote to all the "realistic" books implying that having sexual relationships is the norm for high school kids. Half of the kids in high school are not sexually intimate,[9] and even the half that are have dozens of unanswered questions and worries.

To get direct answers to their questions, young readers can turn to the informational books discussed in Chapter Eight. But because the questions they are most concerned with involve moral, emotional, and psychological issues, the fuller kinds of fictional treatments described here will continue to be popular.

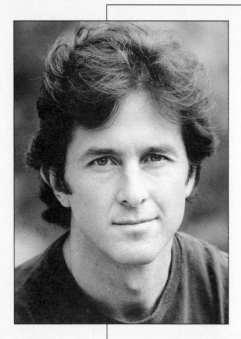

CHRIS LYNCH
On a Constituency

I don't know for sure. A writer is not supposed to say this, but I should. There are some days when I doubt what I'm doing. I doubt the value, doubt the effect, doubt the sense and the meaning of writing fiction for a living. Fortunately, those demons come, blast away at the psyche, then go on their way to assault the next unfortunate writer.

By the next morning I see it again, the real stuff, and I know why I do it. And I do it.

But this much I know, and I know it every day: It is *not* worth less to create work for a 15-year-old than for a 40-year-old. If you do not agree (and I've met so many who do not) it says as much about how we treat our young people as it does about our literary taste.

Our attitude toward the teenage reader seems to parallel our attitude toward teens in general: "God, I wish they'd just grow up. Or stay small." It's that godawful messy in-between period of adolescence that gives everybody such problems. This group, this constituency, has got a set of concerns and interests as serious and complex as any other population. So why doesn't it feel exactly like they have a literature all to themselves?

Check the mainstream book reviews. Should *The Giver* really be vying for space with *The Stupids?* Is there a book editor somewhere asking himself, "Should I give this column on Sunday to Deepak Chopra's new self-help, or should I bump it for Bruce Brooks's latest work?" Of course not, because Brooks does not write self-help books.

But he also does not write picture books. Picture books are written for children, and like it or not (I think we do not) *15-year-olds are not children!* So, bravo for the full page dedicated to children's book reviews. But would it throw the balance of things so far off if we gave another page to adolescent literature? As they are not children, adolescents are also not adults. They are Young Adults.

Writers, of course, have an even greater obligation to acknowledge their readers' integrity. Writing about the great lurch from childhood to adulthood is just as frightening, exhilarating, complicated and dangerous as living it was (remember that?). If you talk down to your audience it does not matter if you get ten pages of glowing press. They will reject you. Soft-pedal your message, and they will reject you. Think for one moment that younger readers will accept dishonest or half-hearted work, and see what happens to you. Anyone who thinks that writing for younger readers is an easy way of breaking into the game, should just stay on the bench.

I doubt that, if treated right, there could be a more passionate, intense constituency than adolescent readers. Treated less than right, however, they have one more reason for apathy. One more reason to point at the adult establishment and say, "See, told ya so," and turn their backs.

Chris Lynch's books include *Shadow Boxer,* 1993; *Iceman,* 1994; *Gypsy Davey,* 1994, and an original paperback series, *Blue-Eyed Son,* 1996, all HarperCollins.

Living in a Multicultural World

The demographic makeup of the United States is undergoing considerable change with both long-term and short-term effects; for example:

- Declining birth rates mean that the United States would have a net loss in population growth if it were not for rapidly increasing numbers of immigrants.
- In 1970, 4.7 percent of Americans were foreign born; in 1990, the figure was 8.6 percent, and in 2040, it is predicted to be 14.2 percent.[10]
- Today's immigrants are bringing in different family values, religion, and attitudes toward education. More than 80 percent of today's immigrants are Hispanic or Asian, as compared with the "old days," when most immigrants came from Europe.
- The United States is becoming one of the oldest populations in the world. By the year 2020, the fastest-growing segment of the population will be the very old—those over age 80.
- In 1990, 24 percent of all new births occurred outside of marriage, many to teenage mothers. Nineteen percent of new births were to women in the lowest income range.
- In 1990, 66 percent of women with children under age 18 were working outside the home.
- The population is being divided into extremes with the middle class shrinking and the numbers of those in "permanent" poverty and in "permanent" affluence growing. This is especially true for African-Americans; there are now large numbers of well-educated professionals whose lives are in sharp contrast with large numbers of people living under conditions as painful as anything known since the days of slavery.[11]

Although few people have these specific facts at hand, almost everyone realizes that changes are occurring, and to many people these changes are threatening, especially when coupled with bad economic conditions. One of the results has been an increase in incidents of racism on high school and college campuses. Even more frightening is the hostility expressed by disaffected young people who have dropped out from society and are expressing their rebellion through acts of aggression against minorities or against the U.S. government or other symbols of authority.

Among the most critically acclaimed books of the 1960s and early 1970s that young adults responded to were Eldridge Cleaver's *Soul on Ice,* William H. Armstrong's *Sounder,* Maya Angelou's *I Know Why the Caged Bird Sings,* Sharon Bell Mathis's *Teacup Full of Roses,* Alice Childress's *A Hero Ain't Nothin' But a Sandwich,* and Rosa Guy's *The Friends.* As powerful as these books were, they had a grimness and a sameness to them, and it's refreshing today to have them supplemented by books in which a variety of characters from different backgrounds face problems by working together; see Focus Box 10.2, p. 318 for examples.

We aren't saying that reading one book or even a dozen books will change a skinhead into someone who would rather sit home and read books, but we are saying that for the majority of young readers, books can be one way of focusing needed attention on the matter of hostility related to racial, ethnic, and class differences.

Today, as shown in Focus Boxes 1.2 (p. 24), 1.3 (p. 30), 2.2 (p. 52), and 2.3 (p. 53), we have a visible cadre of stars writing consistently fine books featuring characters from different ethnic groups. These focus boxes should be viewed as samplings, however, rather than as comprehensive lists. We pulled them together simply because we were so frequently asked to provide lists of books about members of minority groups. We have both philosophical and pedagogical reasons, however, for not wanting to lump together all the books about minorities. Although some of them focus on interracial relationships or problems connected with being a minority, others focus on the same kinds of problems that are treated in nonminority books. In addition, there's a welcome trend for "differentness" not to be treated as just a matter of skin color. Hazel Rochman's professional book, *Against Borders: Promoting Books for a Multicultural World,* is a good illustration of diverse cultures coming together in that before she goes to the expected treatments of racial oppression and ethnic differences she has chapters treating such themes as "The Perilous Journey," "The Hero and the Monster," "Lovers and Strangers," "Family Matters," and "Finding the Way Home."

Also, we need to realize that some authors prefer to focus on the similarities among all people rather than on differences between particular groups. For example, African-American author Lorenz Graham is quoted in Anne Commire's *Something About the Author* as saying:

> My personal problem with publishers has been the difference between my image and theirs. Publishers have told me that my characters, African and Negro, are "too much like white people." And I say, "If you look closely you will see that people are people."[12]

Jamake Highwater expresses a counterbalancing view:

> In the process of trying to unify the world we must be exceedingly careful not to destroy the diversity of the many cultures of man that give human life meaning, focus, and vitality. . . .
>
> Today we are beginning to look into the ideas of groups outside the dominant culture, and we are finding different kinds of "truth" that make the world we live in far bigger than we ever dreamed it could be—for the greatest distance between people is not geographical space but culture.[13]

Something that probably wouldn't have been in a young adult book 25 years ago is the following line from Barbara Ann Porte's *I Only Made Up the Roses:* "Like everybody else in the room of relatives, except mother and me, Perley is black. . . . " This line is indicative of one of the biggest changes that has occurred in young adult books treating ethnic minorities. Most of the early books were clearly segregated. Characters came from a single race. When authors chose to write about characters from outside their own groups, they were met with hostility. Fortunately, that kind of parochialism is lessening, and the result has been more books that include characters from different groups interacting with each other in a variety of ways.

By having characters from different groups involved in the same activities, authors can show a wide spectrum of actions and attitudes. Bruce Brooks's *The Moves Make the Man* is basically a quest story of accomplishment, and it almost doesn't matter that with the two best friends, one is African-American and the other is white. But when white Bix comes to dinner at African-American Jerome's house, big brother and future psychologist Maurice is disappointed that they are going to have a white guest because he had hoped for some "in-house observation." The rest of Jerome's family laughs at Maurice's disappointment and his pretentious pronouncement that, "Counseling across the color line is notoriously fruitless, due to preconditions of mistrust." But when Bix arrives, Jerome is surprised to see that his old friend has equally strange expectations. When he is introduced to younger brother Henri, Bix gives Henri an awkward high-five and says, "Dig it."

> Now, dig it is a very stupid thing to say when being introduced. Henri did not notice, but I did, and I thought it was queer. But when Maurice was there and I introduced him and he peered at Bix like to see if there was any chance of busting the color line with a little counseling anyway, and Bix grinned right into his stare and held out his hand and said, What be happening, Maurice my man?
>
> Maurice, who does not know jive talk from bird song, just looked confused and said Fine thank you and shook hands, but I was nearabout flipped. What be happening, Maurice my man? Where did Bix get this jive talking junk? It was ridiculous.

This light-hearted treatment of stereotypes is possible because today's young readers are more sophisticated about ethnic and racial differences. A generation ago, many white, middle-class readers had been so isolated from other racial groups that learning the generalities—what some would call the stereotypes—was a kind of progress. Today most teenagers are ready to go beyond those stereotypes.

In her novels about white, middle-class kids, M. E. Kerr often includes shrewd observations about prejudice. For example, in *If I Love You, Am I Trapped Forever?* Alan's grandfather teaches him not to call anyone a Jew. Instead he is to describe people as being "of the Jewish persuasion." Once a year in Cayuta, Rabbi Goldman gives the Sunday sermon at the Second Presbyterian Church while Reverend Gosnell speaks to the Saturday congregation at Temple Emmanuel. Still Jews do not belong to the Cayuta North Country Club and "No one's exactly pushing for intermarriage. . . . "

In *Little Little,* African-American Calpurnia Dove and white Little Little are in the same English class, where they compete as writers. When Miss Grossman reads aloud one of Calpurnia's essays, Little Little thinks that the teacher is only being nice to Calpurnia because she's African-American. In her heart, Little Little recognizes the ridiculousness of her assumption and conjectures that Calpurnia probably "decides Miss Grossman is only being nice to me because I'm a dwarf." Little Little goes on to explain that most of the African-American teenagers in town go to Commercial High to learn business skills or trades. Of the few who do go to her high school, "one is always elected to some office, unanimously. But that high honor rarely gets one of them a seat saved at noon in the cafeteria among the whites, or even a particularly warm hello."

One of the advantages of authors including racism as a secondary, as opposed to a primary, theme is that more readers are exposed to the issue and are led to think about it. Both adults and young readers tend to color-code books, thinking that books about African-Americans or Hispanics, for example, are only for African-American or Latin-American readers. Walter Dean Myers has pointed out the ridiculousness of such a notion by asking why those librarians in white, middle-class neighborhoods who refuse to buy books about minority characters keep purchasing Dickens's novels even though they have no nineteenth-century English children in their schools.

Another damaging tendency is for teachers, librarians, and reviewers to present books and discuss them as if they represent *the* African-American point of view or *the* Asian-American point of view. Adults need to help young readers realize that people are individuals first and members of particular groups second. In John Patrick's play *The Teahouse of the August Moon,* one of the lines that gets a big laugh from the white middle-class American audiences is about all Americans looking alike. The audience laughs because the tables are turned on an old joke, and a glimpse is provided of how ridiculous it is to think of any group of individuals as carbon copies of one another.

Perhaps for the sake of efficiency, history and social studies textbooks have to lump people together and talk about them according to the characteristics of the majority in the group, but good literature can counterbalance these generalizations and show individual perspectives. When students have read enough to go beyond the stereotypes of at least one group, they will be more aware that the study of people as groups needs to be filled in with individual portrayals.

The Future of the Problem Novel—From Realism to Postmodernism

We are willing to predict that for all the reasons discussed previously, authors will continue to write problem novels and young adults will continue to read them. Adolescent literature, however, does not exist in a vacuum separate from the literature of the rest of the world. It is more than a coincidence that when the problem novel appeared in the late 1960s, great changes were also taking place in American society and literature as a whole. The world was a new and scary place, with the imaginative fallout from the atomic bomb being a recognition that human extinction was quite possible.

In literature, belief in an ordered universe was gradually being replaced with theories about reader response and deconstructionism. The idea of deconstructionism is that what seems to be an event in a piece of literature is really a construct created through language. As a linguistic construct, it can also be undone or deconstructed through language. In an interview with CNN's Larry King (November 4, 1991), Norman Mailer illustrated the difference between how structuralists and deconstructionists' might approach the same piece of literature. In structural terminology, a piece that is experientially true and is an author's honest attempt to de-pict people in ordinary situations without sentimentalizing or glossing over any-thing would probably be described as *realism*. In contrast, Mailer, representing the deconstructionist viewpoint, claims that as soon as a character—whether real or imagined—is written about, fiction results because the character now lives as imagined in people's minds rather than as a real person who can be talked to and touched. This is why in *Anatomy of Criticism,* Northrop Frye puts quotes around the term *realism* and why G. Robert Carlsen has written that

> If we evaluate literature by its realism alone, we should be forced to abandon most of the truly great literature of the world: certainly most of tragedy, much of comedy, and all of romance. We would be forced to discard the Greek plays, the great epics, Shakespeare, Molière. They succeed because they go beyond the externals of living and instead reach out and touch that imaginative life deep down inside where we live.[14]

As writers in the 1960s began searching for new ways to "touch that imagina-tive life," they experimented with postmodernism (a literary term invented as an almost joking corollary to the art term of *postimpressionism*) and with black humor, in which authors distorted their observations of people and events by exaggerating the negatives and minimizing the positives. Although bright and sophisticated teenagers were quick to appreciate some of these writings, including Ken Kesey's *One Flew Over the Cuckoo's Nest,* Kurt Vonnegut's *Slaughterhouse-Five,* and Joseph Heller's *Catch–22,* it is doubtful that authors for young people are ever going to be comfortable with the idea of writing about antiheroes suffering from alienation or with simply holding up life's absurdities.

Nevertheless, as authors of problem novels try not to repeat themselves and also try to pluck psychic strings that remain untouched by superficial media sto-ries, they are going to be pulled in the same directions as writers for adults. Among the reasons that Kesey's, Vonnegut's, and Heller's writing is so appealing is that they juxtapose humor and pathos for the purpose of creating emotional tension or frus-tration. As Terry Heller has observed:

> By repeatedly calling upon the reader to shift his interpretations of the inci-dent, to laugh only to weep only to laugh only to weep again, [the author] sus-pends the reader between two poles.[15]

Paul Zindel does this in his 1993 *David & Della.* The story of alcoholic Della and her friendship with lonely David frightens and threatens readers at the same time it amuses them. Della, who pretends to be a blind writing coach and promises to get David over his writer's block by "oiling his neck," makes readers laugh when they see that her real goal is to steal his parents' liquor. In another part she makes readers cry when she talks about the baby daughter that her now-absent boyfriend convinced her to give up for adoption so that he and Della "would have a chance for a life together!"

Another characteristic of black humorists is that they reject boundaries be-tween realism and fantasy. Also, their writing exhibits what Bruce Friedman has described as "a nervousness, an upbeat tempo, a near hysteria or frenzy."[16] Some thirty years after Friedman observed this about the writing of such fellow authors as Thomas Pynchon, J. P. Donleavy, Vladimir Nabokov, Edward Albee, John Barth, Terry Southern, and James Purdy, it is almost a perfect description of Francesca Lia Block's books for young adults. While she focuses on the same kinds of problems as do other young adult writers of problem novels, including loneliness, alienation, sexual problems, and love, she accepts wholeheartedly the deconstructionist idea of creating her own world and then working within it. Readers who are puzzled or troubled by her books are usually those accustomed to looking for a kind of "realism" that can be tested against their own observations or against statistics of probability.

Virginia Hamilton was one of the first writers to mix a fantasy element in a problem novel when in her 1982 *Sweet Whispers, Brother Rush* she had the ghost of Teresa's uncle help the troubled 14-year-old understand her family's history and its relationship to her dearly beloved, retarded brother. In her 1990 *The Silver Kiss*, Annette Curtis Klause created a vampire ghost to help Zoë adjust to her mother's death, while Robert Cormier's 1988 *Fade* is about the struggles of young Paul Moreaux, who through his inherited ability to be invisible begins to understand the difference between good and evil. In Bruce Brooks's 1989 *No Kidding,* Sam is struggling with problems caused by his mother's alcoholism and his feeling of responsibility for his younger brother. The story is all the more interesting because it is set in a dystopian future society, a technique that Lois Lowry also used for her 1993 Newbery Award–winning *The Giver.* Perhaps the most stunning of all the problem novels in which the author makes use of a fading line between fantasy and reality is Peter Dickinson's 1989 *Eva.* It pursues the major question faced by teenagers and treated in many problem novels: "Who am I?" But what makes this story so fascinating is the originality of the plot in which after a serious automobile accident, Eva's life "is saved" through having her brain transferred into the body of a chimpanzee.

The point we are making by citing these various examples of imaginative stories, which are further discussed in later chapters, is that although we see a continuing interest in writing about the physical and emotional problems that are unique to adolescents, we also see that the genre is changing. While we, along with many readers, continue to appreciate well-done problem novels of the kind that were considered such an innovation in the late 1960s and the 1970s, we are at the same time pleased to realize that the field is not standing still and that many of today's writers are finding new ways to treat old problems.

Notes

[1]Glenna Davis Sloan, *The Child as Critic* (Teachers College Press, 1975), pp. 19–21.

[2]Alleen Pace Nilsen, "The Poetry of Naming in Young Adult Books," *ALAN Review* 7 (Spring 1980): 3–4, 31.

[3]Ellen Goodman, syndicated column, printed in *The Arizona Republic,* November 9, 1993.

[4]Kurt Anderson, "Oprah and Jo-Jo the Dog-Faced Boy," *Time* magazine, October 11, 1993.

[5] Bernard Bauer, *San Jose Mercury News,* reprinted in *The Arizona Republic,* August 23, 1991.

[6] W. Keith Kraus, "Cinderella in Trouble: Still Dreaming and Losing," *School Library Journal* 21 (January 1975): 18–22.

[7] Annotation of *Deliver Us from Evie,* "Editors' Choice '94" *Booklist* 91 (January 15, 1995): 859.

[8] Jean Fritz, review of *Up in Seth's Room, New York Times Book Review* (January 20, 1980), p. 30.

[9] The Federal Center for Disease Control conducted a 1990 study released January 3, 1992, and reported in various news media the following day. Findings were that 54 percent of high school students have had sexual experiences, 39 percent within the last three months. The percentage climbed from 40 percent of ninth graders to 72 percent of twelfth graders. One in 25 students reported having a sexually transmitted disease, and 78 percent of the students reporting intercourse said they had recently used some form of contraception.

[10] "Immigrant Impact Grows on U.S. Population," *Wall Street Journal,* March 16, 1992.

[11] George Keller, Director of Strategic Planning for the University of Pennsylvania outlined these changes in a workshop at Arizona State University, February 14, 1992.

[12] Anne Commire, *Something about the Author,* Vol. 2 (Gale Research, 1971), pp. 122–23.

[13] Jamake Highwater, *Many Smokes, Many Moons* (Lippincott, 1978), pp. 13–14.

[14] G. Robert Carlsen, "Bait/Rebait: Literature Isn't Supposed to Be Realistic," *English Journal* 70 (January 1981): 8.

[15] Terry Heller, "Notes on Technique in Black Humor," *Thalia: Studies in Literary Humor* 2.3 (Winter 1979–80): 16.

[16] Bruce J. Freidman, ed. *Black Humor.* New York: Bantam, 1965.

Titles Mentioned in the Text of Chapter Three

Angelou, Maya. *I Know Why the Caged Bird Sings.* Random House, 1976.

Armstrong, William. *Sounder.* HarperCollins, 1969.

Arrick, Fran. *Steffie Can't Come Out to Play.* Bradbury, 1978.

Arrick, Fran. *Tunnel Vision.* Bradbury, 1980.

Beckman, Gunnel. *Admission to the Feast.* Holt, 1972.

Blume, Judy. *Are You There God? It's Me, Margaret.* Bradbury, 1970.

Blume, Judy. *Deenie.* Bradbury, 1973.

Blume, Judy. *Forever.* Bradbury, 1975.

Blume, Judy. *Here's to You, Rachel Robinson.* Orchard, 1993.

Blume, Judy. *Then Again, Maybe I Won't.* Bradbury, 1971.

Blume, Judy. *Tiger Eyes.* Bradbury, 1981.

Borich, Michael. *A Different Kind of Love.* Holt, 1985.

Bradford, Richard. *Red Sky at Morning.* Lippincott, 1968.

Brancato, Robin. *Winning.* Knopf, 1977.

Bredes, Don. *Hard Feelings.* Atheneum, 1977.

Brooks, Bruce. *The Moves Make the Man.* HarperCollins, 1986.

Brooks, Bruce. *No Kidding.* HarperCollins, 1989.

Butler, Samuel. *The Way of All Flesh.* 1835.

Byars, Betsy. *The Night Swimmers.* Delacorte, 1980.

Carter, Alden. *Up Country.* Putnam, 1989.

Chambers, Aidan. *Breaktime.* HarperCollins, 1979.

Childress, Alice. *A Hero Ain't Nothin' But a Sandwich.* Coward, McCann, 1973.

Cleaver, Eldridge. *Soul on Ice.* McGraw-Hill, 1968.

Cleaver, Vera and Bill. *Trial Valley.* Lippincott, 1977.

Cleaver, Vera and Bill. *Where the Lilies Bloom.* HarperCollins, 1969.

Cole, Brock. *Celine.* Farrar, Straus & Giroux, 1989.

Cormier, Robert. *The Chocolate War.* Pantheon, 1974.

Cormier, Robert. *Fade.* Delacorte, 1988.

Cormier, Robert. *We All Fall Down.* Delacorte, 1991.

Craig, Margaret Maze. *It Could Happen to Anyone.* Berkeley, 1970.

Daly, Jay. *Walls.* HarperCollins, 1980.

Davis, Terry. *Vision Quest.* Viking, 1979.

Dickinson, Peter. *Eva.* Delacorte, 1989.

Dizenzo, Patricia. *Why Me? The Story of Jenny.* Avon, 1976.

Donovan, John. *I'll Get There. It Better Be Worth the Trip.* HarperCollins, 1969.

Eyerly, Jeannette. *A Girl Like Me.* Lippincott, 1966.

Ferris, Jean. *Invincible Summer.* Farrar, Straus & Giroux, 1987.

Fox, Paula. *A Place Apart.* Farrar, Straus & Giroux, 1982.

Frye, Northrop. *Anatomy of Criticism.* Princeton University Press, 1957.

Garden, Nancy. *Annie on My Mind.* Farrar, Straus & Giroux, 1982.

Goethe, Johann Wolfgang von. *Wilhelm Meister's Apprenticeship*, 1795–96.

Golding William. *Lord of the Flies*. Putnam, 1955.

Guy, Rosa. *The Friends*. Holt, 1973.

Guy, Rosa. *Ruby*. Viking, 1976.

Hall, Lynn. *Sticks and Stones*. Follett, 1972.

Hamilton, Virginia, *Sweet Whispers, Brother Rush*. Philomel, 1982.

Hautzig, Deborah. *Hey Dollface*. Morrow, 1978.

Head, Ann. *Mr. and Mrs. Bo Jo Jones*. Putnam, 1967.

Hinton, S. E. *The Outsiders*. Viking, 1967.

Hinton, S. E. *Tex*. Delacorte, 1979.

Hogan, William. *The Quartzsite Trip*. Atheneum, 1980.

Holland, Isabelle. *The Man Without a Face*. Lippincott, 1972.

Joyce, James. *A Portrait of the Artist as a Young Man*. 1914.

Kerr, M. E. *Deliver Us from Evie*. HarperCollins, 1994.

Kerr, M. E. *If I Love You, Am I Trapped Forever?* HarperCollins, 1973.

Kerr, M. E. *Linger*. HarperCollins, 1993.

Kerr, M. E. *Little Little*. HarperCollins, 1981.

Kerr, M. E. *Night Kites*. HarperCollins, 1986.

Kesey, Ken. *One Flew Over the Cuckoo's Nest*. Viking, 1962.

Kincaid, Jamaica. *Annie John*. Farrar, Straus & Giroux, 1985.

Klass, David. *California Blue*. Scholastic, 1994.

Klein, Norma. *Love Is One of the Choices*. Dial, 1979.

Lee, Harper. *To Kill a Mockingbird*. Lippincott, 1960.

Levoy, Myron. *A Shadow Like a Leopard*. HarperCollins, 1981.

Lipsyte, Robert. *The Contender*. HarperCollins, 1967.

Lowry, Lois. *The Giver*. Houghton Mifflin, 1993.

Lynch, Chris. *Gypsy Davey*. HarperCollins, 1994.

Lynch, Chris. *Iceman*. HarperCollins, 1994.

Mathis, Sharon Bell. *Teacup Full of Roses*. Viking, 1975.

Maugham, Somerset. *Of Human Bondage*, 1915.

Mazer, Norma Fox. *Up in Seth's Room*. Delacorte, 1979.

Naylor, Phyllis Reynolds. *The Keeper*. Atheneum, 1986.

Neufeld, John. *For All the Wrong Reasons*. NAL Penguin, 1980.

Paterson, Katherine. *Bridge to Terabithia*. Crowell, 1977.

Patrick, John. *The Teahouse of the August Moon*. Dramatists, 1953.

Paulsen, Gary. *Harris and Me*. Harcourt, 1993.

Peck, Richard. *Are You in the House Alone?* Viking, 1976.

Peck, Richard. *Don't Look and It Won't Hurt*. Holt, 1972.

Peck, Richard. *Remembering the Good Times*. Delacorte, 1985.

Plath, Sylvia. *The Bell Jar*. HarperCollins, 1971.

Porte, Barbara Ann. *I Only Made Up the Roses*. Greenwillow, 1987.

Potok, Chaim. *The Chosen*. Simon & Schuster, 1967.

Rochman, Hazel. *Against Borders: Promoting Books for a Multicultural World*. American Library Association, 1993.

Rylant, Cynthia. *Missing May*. Orchard, 1992.

Salinger, J. D. *The Catcher in the Rye*. Little Brown, 1951.

Scoppettone, Sandra. *Trying Hard to Hear You*. HarperCollins, 1974.

Sherburne, Zoa. *Too Bad About the Haines Girl*. Morrow, 1967.

Slepian, Jan. *Risk n'Roses*. Philomel, 1990.

Spencer, Scott. *Endless Love*. Knopf, 1979.

Stirling, Nora. *You Would If You Loved Me*. Evans, 1969.

Strasser, Todd. *A Very Touchy Subject*. Delacorte, 1985.

Thompson, Jean. *House of Tomorrow*. HarperCollins, 1967.

Tyler, Anne. *Saint Maybe*. Knopf, 1991.

Voigt, Cynthia. *Dicey's Song*. Atheneum, 1982.

Voigt, Cynthia. *When She Hollers*. Scholastic, 1994.

Vonnegut, Kurt, Jr. *Slaughterhouse-Five*. Delacorte, 1969.

Werlin, Nancy. *Are You Alone on Purpose?* Houghton, 1994.

Wolff, Virginia Euwer. *Make Lemonade*. Holt, 1993.

Wyss, Thelma Hatch. *Here at the Scenic-Vu Motel*. HarperCollins, 1988.

Zindel, Paul. *Confessions of a Teenage Baboon*. HarperCollins, 1977.

Zindel, Paul. *David & Della*. HarperCollins, 1993.

Zindel, Paul. *My Darling, My Hamburger*. HarperCollins, 1969.

Zindel, Paul. *The Pigman*. HarperCollins, 1968.

For information on the availability of paperback editions of these titles, please consult the most recent edition of *Paperbound Books in Print,* published annually by R. R. Bowker Company.

Chapter 4

The Old Romanticism
Of Wishing and Winning

· ·

Romances serve as a counterbalance to the depressing realism of the problem novel. They have happy endings, and their tellers can exaggerate just enough to make the stories more interesting than real life. There is usually a quest of some sort in which the protagonist experiences doubts and undergoes severe trials, but he or she is successful in the end. This success is all the more appreciated because of the difficulties the protagonist has suffered. In bad moments, the extremes of suffering resemble a nightmare, but in good times the successes are like happy daydreams.

The word *romance* comes from the Latin adverb *romanice,* which means "in the Roman, [i.e., the Latin] manner." It is with this meaning that Latin, Italian, Spanish, and French are described as romance languages. The literary meaning of *romance* grew out of its use by English speakers to refer to French dialects, which were much closer to Latin than was their own Germanic language of English. Later, it was used to refer to Old French and finally to anything written in French.

Many of the French stories read by English speakers were tales about knights who set out on bold adventures, slaying dragons, rescuing princesses from ogres, and defeating the wicked enemies of a righteous king. Love was often an element in these stories because the knight was striving to win the hand of a beloved maiden. Today, when a literary piece is referred to as a romance, it usually contains adventure or love, or both.

The romance is appealing to teenagers because many romantic symbols relate to youthfulness and hope, and many of the protagonists even in traditional and classic tales are in their teens. They have reached the age at which they leave home or anticipate leaving to embark on a new way of life. This is more likely to be called "moving out" than "going on a romantic quest," but the results are much the same. Also, seeking and securing a "true love" usually—but not always—takes up a greater proportion of the time and energy of young adults than of middle-aged adults. The exaggeration that is part of the romantic mode is quite honestly felt by teenagers. Robert Cormier once said that he began writing about young protagonists when he observed that in one afternoon at the beach his own children could go through what to an adult would be a whole month of emotional experiences.

This range of emotions sometimes makes it difficult to decide whether a book is a realistic problem novel or a romance. Author Richard Peck has observed that teenage readers really want romanticism masked as realism; they want both the happy ending and the assurance that it is realistic to expect such an ending. This truism encourages authors of problem novels to incorporate at least some elements of romanticism in their problem novels, which makes for an overlap. Some of the "heavier" books talked about in this chapter and some of the "lighter" books talked about in Chapter Three might be one and the same.

Deciding whether to label a book a "problem novel" or a "romantic quest" could depend on which aspects of the book most strongly touched the reader's emotions. Because young people are characteristically viewed as optimists, a writer working with basically the same plot in a story to be published for a general adult audience might be inclined to present the adult story in an ironic mode but the young adult story in a romantic mode. For example, three popular quest stories about young protagonists that were published as somber adult novels are J. D. Salinger's *The Catcher in the Rye,* Hannah Green's *I Never Promised You a Rose Garden,* and Judith Guest's *Ordinary People.* In all three, worthy young heroes set out to find wisdom and understanding. They make physical sacrifices, including suicide attempts, and even though they receive help from wise and kindly psychiatrists (today's counterpart to the white witches, the wizards, and the helpful gods and goddesses of traditional romances), they must prove their worthiness through hard, painstaking work. This is what Deborah Blau's psychiatrist communicates in the phrase used for the book's title, *I Never Promised You a Rose Garden.* If Green's book had been a romance, there would have been no such reminder of life's difficulties. Readers could have imagined Deborah leaving the mental institution and living "happily ever after."

In contrast, *It Happened to Nancy* is a grim story that is nevertheless written in the romantic mode. It is advertised as a true story taken from the diary of an anonymous girl who "thought she'd found love but instead lost her life to AIDS." The editor is Beatrice Sparks, the same author who back in the late 1960s did *Go Ask Alice* about a young drug addict. Like Alice, Nancy dies at the end of the book, which is certainly a chilling touch of realism, but there are several other elements of the story that made Frances Bradburn ask questions similar to the ones which critics asked about *Go Ask Alice:* "Is this really a teen's diary, or is it Sparks's attempt to convey the reality of adolescent susceptibility to HIV/AIDS in a format that will impact [young adult] readers?"[1]

Among the romanticized elements that made Bradburn question the book's authenticity was the extreme vulnerability of 14-year-old Nancy, who because she's asthmatic already had a weakened immune system. Aside from the announcement on the cover of the book, there was little foreshadowing that Nancy's gentle and caring 18-year-old boyfriend would date-rape her or that he would be a carrier of HIV. The rape, followed by the horror of the diagnosis of AIDS, truly fills the "nightmare" part of the definition of a romance, whereas the loving support she receives in her last months of life fills the "daydream" part of the definition. As Bradburn implied, young readers pick up the book because of the horror of the situation and they keep reading because of its poignancy.

Although no one wants to have Nancy's experience, the story is nevertheless wish-fulfilling in the way Nancy's friends, including a new boyfriend, stay close to her and lend support throughout her illness and in the way her divorced parents put aside their differences to care for her. People who work with such real-life tragedies say that neither of these situations is very likely. The strain of a gravely ill child is often the last straw in a fragile marriage relationship, and, as illustrated in Robin Brancato's *Winning* and Cynthia Voigt's *Izzy, Willy-Nilly* old friends are likely to flee when they are made uncomfortable by a drastically changed situation.

The Adventure/Accomplishment Romance

The great satisfaction of the adventure or the accomplishment romance lies in its wish fulfillment, as when David slays Goliath, when Cinderella is united with the noble prince and given the fitting role of queen, and when Dorothy and Toto find their way back to Kansas. In every culture, there are legends, myths, and folk and fairy tales that follow the pattern of the adventure/accomplishment romance. In the Judeo-Christian culture, the biblical story of Joseph is a prime example. Early in life, Joseph was chosen and marked as a special person. When his brothers sold him as a slave to the Egyptian traders, he embarked on his quest for wisdom and knowledge. Just when all seemed lost, he received divine help—being blessed with the ability to interpret dreams. This got him out of prison and into the pharaoh's court. The climax of the story came years later, during the famine that brought his brothers to Egypt and the royal palace. Without recognizing Joseph, they begged for food. His forgiveness and his generosity were final proofs of his worthiness.

A distinguishing feature of such romances is the happy ending, achieved only after the hero's worth is proved through a crisis or an ordeal. Usually as part of the ordeal the hero must make a sacrifice, be wounded, or leave some part of his or her body, even if it is only sweat or tears. The real loss is that of innocence, but it is usually symbolized by a physical loss, as in Norse mythology, when Odin gave one of his eyes to pay for knowledge, or in J. R. R. Tolkien's *The Lord of the Rings,* when Frodo, who has already suffered many wounds, found that he could not throw the ring back and so must let Gollum take his finger along with the ring. The suffering of the hero nearly always purchases some kind of wisdom, even though wisdom is not what the hero set out to find.

The adventure/accomplishment romance has elements applicable to the task of entering the adult world, which all young people anticipate. The story pattern includes the three stages of formal initiation as practiced in many cultures. First, the young and innocent person is separated both physically and spiritually from the nurturing love of most or all friends and family. This is one of the reasons that so many accomplishment stories include a trip (see Focus Box 4.1). Another reason for the trip is that the new environment provides new challenges and learning experiences. During the separation, the hero, who embodies noble qualities, undergoes a test of courage and stamina that may be mental, psychological, or physical. In the final stage, the young person is reunited with former friends and family in a new role of increased status.

FOCUS BOX 4.1

Literal Trips: Figurative Quests

Chicago Blues by Julie Reece Deaver. Scholastic, 1995. "I've just kidnapped my 11-year-old sister," begins this story of scholarship art student Lissa and the months they spend together while their mother begins her recovery from alcoholism.

The Cuckoo's Child by Suzanne Freeman. Greenwillow, 1996. It is 1962 and Mia and her two older half-sisters are happily living in Beirut. Everything changes when their parents disappear while on a sailing vacation and the girls come "home" to relatives in the states.

The Harmony Arms by Ron Koertge. Little, 1992. Fourteen-year-old Gabriel and his puppeteer father from Bradleyville, mid-America, go to Los Angeles for the summer, where Gabriel learns to be more accepting of people's differences—including his father's.

Moon Dancer by Margaret I. Rostkowski. Harcourt, 1995. Two sisters, a cousin, and the cousin's boyfriend embark on a backpacking trip through southern Utah in search of Anasazi rock art.

One Fat Summer by Robert Lipsyte. HarperCollins, 1977. Bobby's story shows that a heroic quest does not have to take a person far from home. He goes only to the other side of the island where he works for Dr. Kahn. Sequels include *The Summer Boy* (1982) and *Summer Rules* (1981), both HarperCollins.

Out of Nowhere by Ouida Sebestyen. Orchard, 1994. When 13-year-old Harley is left at a desert campground by his mother and her boyfriend, he first clings for comfort to an equally deserted pit bull. In a heartwarming story, he and the dog join three other "rejects" and make a new kind of family.

Rats Saw God by Rob Thomas. Simon & Schuster, 1996. Older teens will relate to this story of gifted but troubled Steve York, who moves from Houston to live with his mother and her new husband in San Diego.

Rear-View Mirror by Paul Fleischman. HarperCollins, 1986. Seventeen-year-old Olivia Tate sets out on a commemorative bike trip in remembrance of the father she learned to love only a few months before his death.

3 NBs of Julian Drew by James M. Deem. Houghton Mifflin, 1994. A young boy, so troubled that he writes in code, keeps his thoughts in three notebooks, which in the course of his travels from Tempe, Arizona, to Wheeling, West Virginia, gradually, get more readable.

The True Confessions of Charlotte Doyle by Avi. Orchard, 1990. The difference between this and most historical sailing adventures is that the heroine is a 12-year-old girl who happens to be crossing the Atlantic on a ship with a villainous captain and crew.

Izzy, Willy-Nilly *as an Adventure/Accomplishment Romance*

Authors often dramatize mental accomplishments as physical ones because it is extremely hard to show something occurring inside someone's head. The physical challenge serves as a symbol for the mental one. The effect of this has been that adventure romances are more likely to feature males than females because males' lifestyles usually include more physically challenging activities (e.g., athletic competition, war, physical labor, and surviving on one's own). Today's authors, however, are consciously trying to write adventure/accomplishment stories about females.

Cynthia Voigt's *Izzy, Willy-Nilly* is a good illustration of how traditional arche-typal initiation rites can be translated into a modern and appealing story. Tenth-grader-cheerleader-nice-girl Izzy has been in a serious automobile accident, and before she is really conscious, her leg is being amputated. Chapter Two is a flash-back to before the accident. The author uses this chapter to set the background and to show readers that Izzy Lingard is a special person worthy of the challenge she will face. Izzy is the first of her group to be asked out by a senior, and she is strong enough not to succumb to the boy's teasing her because she has to ask her parents' permission before she accepts.

Because a romance is essentially the story of one person's achievement and de-velopment, everything else is a condensation. For the sake of efficiency, the person-alities of the supporting characters are shown through symbols, metaphors, and significant details, all of which highlight the qualities that are important to the story. It is not really the villain the hero must ultimately defeat, but the villain stands in the way of the true accomplishment and gives the hero an enemy upon whom to focus. Without some scary, nightmarish, and usually life-threatening inci-dent, the happy ending could not be appreciated.

The boy who asked Izzy for a date is the villain of the story. He is a "notorious flirt," who at the party gets so drunk that although he isn't hurt when he plows his car into a tree, he does nothing to help Izzy. Then he lies to the police about Izzy doing the driving, and instead of apologizing for what happened, he manipulates Izzy's friend, hoping to influence what Izzy will tell the police.

Izzy faces the physical loss of her leg and the challenge of learning to walk with a prosthesis, but the real challenge is the emotional one of acceptance. In the daytime, at least in front of other people, Izzy is cheerful. The first day that she dares to look down at the blanket covering her "leg-and-a-half" she begins her quest for emotional peace. Heroes in traditional romances often had visions or vis-its from divine beings. Izzie's "vision" comes through her mental image of a tiny lit-tle Izzy doll:

> My brain wasn't working. It was as if the little Izzy was running around and around in circles, some frantic wind-up Izzy, screeching *No, no, no.*
>> But it was *Yes, yes, yes.*
>> And I knew it.
>> I knew it, but I couldn't believe it.

Izzy lays her head on the formica hospital table over her bed, and although she is not asleep, she has a nightmare:

> I felt as if a huge long slide was slipping up past me, and I was going down it. I couldn't stop myself, and I didn't even want to. . . . Something heavy and wet and cold and gray was making me go down, pushing at the back of my bent neck and at my shoulders. At the bottom, wherever that was, something heavy and wet and cold and gray waited for me. It was softer than the ground when I hit it. I went flying off the end of the slide and fell into the gray. The gray reached up around me and closed itself over me and swallowed me up.

When a nurse comes in, Izzy wishes she would leave because she is afraid she might cry, and, "We didn't cry, not the Lingards. We were brave and made jokes about things hurting. . . . " The nurse is a physical therapist who gives Izzy painful massages to toughen up her skin and muscles so she will be ready for the prosthesis. Izzy is hurt that the woman concentrates on her work and doesn't look at Izzy's face or talk with her. In her depressed mood, Izzy decides that it is because she is no longer a whole person. "I guessed if you'd finished working on the pizza dough, you wouldn't bend over and say goodbye to it. You don't talk to *things*. And that's what I was, a thing, a messed-up body."

The worst times for Izzy are at night, when she wakes up alone and can't keep her "mind from going down that slide thinking of all the things that I managed not

KATHERINE PATERSON
On Comfort and Calm

During the period when my youngest was sweating out the wait for college acceptance, I came upon her in the living room reading. Now that was not in itself extraordinary. Mary has been a reader since she was 5. But the book my intelligent 18-year-old was absorbed in was *Charlotte's Web,* which she first met when she was about 3. She looked up at me, her eyes shining, "This is a great book," she said.

When adults talk about books for young adults, I wish they'd remember how hard it is to be an adolescent — how many life-shaping decisions must be made at a time when most people are not ready to make them. Parents and teachers may try to encourage and reassure, but I have found that my children often return to the stories they loved when they were young to help them get through rough periods.

Books for young adults should include mind and heart stretchers like the classics. Can I ever forget what *Tale of Two Cities* and *Cry the Beloved Country* meant to me as a teenager? Surely they will include books like those of Sue Ellen Bridgers and Robert Cormier with which young people will more readily identify. But for comfort, for reassembling the identities that seemed to have come unstuck, what about a fresh look at *Charlotte's Web, Where the Wild Things Are,* or *Tuck Everlasting?*

It might be fun, as well as instructive, to have students write about or discuss their favorite childhood book. A lot can be learned about story structure by examining children's books, and a side benefit for the students may be a few hours of calm amidst the general turbulence of their lives.

Katherine Paterson's books include *Lyddie,* Lodestar, 1991; *Jacob Have I Loved,* Crowell, 1980, *Bridge to Terabithia,* Crowell, 1977; and *The Great Gilly Hopkins,* Crowell, 1978.

to think about during the days." She never knew until then, never even suspected, how it felt to be depressed.

> I'd been miserable. I'd been blue. But depressed, no, I hadn't been that. I never knew how it felt to sigh out a breath so sad you could almost see tears in it. I never knew the way tears would ooze and ooze out of your eyes. I never knew the way something could hang like a gray cloud over all of your mind and you could never get away from it, never forget it.

Help comes to Izzy, not from her old friends, who are too involved in their own lives and too uncomfortable with her misfortune to stay long, but from the strange misfit Rosamunde—"not at all like Lisa and the rest"—who arrives to decorate Izzy's hospital room; and to play Yahtze; and to bring fruit, good conversation, homemade turnovers, and piroshki.

When Izzy is released from the hospital, she doesn't go back to her old room on the second floor. Instead she is given her parents' bedroom on the first floor, and it's here in the middle of the nights that Izzy, isolated from her family and in a strange and lonely place, undergoes the suffering that makes her eventual victory that much sweeter.

During a particularly bad time, Izzy sees the little doll in her head "standing there waving her detached leg at a crowd of people, like a safety monitor waving her stop sign." In contrast, the first day that someone at school forgets about Izzy's crutches, the little doll "gathered herself up and did an impossible back-flip, and then another and another." The book ends with Izzy seeing the little doll:

> . . . standing alone, without crutches. . . . Her arms were spread out slightly. She looked like she was about to dance, but really her arms were out for balance. . . . The little Izzy balanced there briefly and then took a hesitant step forward—ready to fall, ready not to fall.

Other Quest Stories of Accomplishment

The motif of a worthy young hero embarking on a quest of wisdom appears in many more good books than those mentioned in this chapter because it fits well in biographies, adventure stories, historical fiction, fantasy, science fiction, and problem novels. Even when the quest is not the main part of a story, motifs that fit the quest romance are incorporated. For example, in traditional romances, the protagonist usually receives the vision or insight in a "high or isolated place like a mountain top, an island, or a tower."[2] In Virginia Hamilton's *M. C. Higgins, the Great*, the boy, M. C., comes to his realizations about his family and his role while he contemplates the surrounding countryside from a special bicycle seat affixed to the top of a tall steel pole standing in the yard of his mountain home. The pole is unique and intriguing, and M. C. earned it as a reward from his father for swimming across the Ohio River.

Robert Lipsyte's *The Contender* opens with Mr. Donatelli, the manager of a boxing gym, listening to the confident sound of young, African American Alfred Brooks climbing the steps to his gym. Mr. Donatelli says he can tell who has what it takes to be a contender (readers are to interpret this as meaning a contender in life as well as in the boxing ring) by how they climb those stairs. A generation later, in another quest story, *The Brave,* this same Alfred Brooks helps Sonny Bear, a 17-year-old boxer from the Moscondaga Indian reservation, change the monster he feels inside himself into the dignified Hawk spirit of his people.

A railroad lantern named Spin Light that Jerome wins with his basketball skill is an intriguing symbol in Bruce Brooks's *The Moves Make the Man.* It enables him to go to a hidden, lonely court and play basketball after dark, but by the end of the book, readers share in Jerome's optimism that Spin Light will enable him to see more than his way around the basketball court.

In Chris Crutcher's *The Crazy Horse Electric Game,* pitching star Willie Weaver is seriously injured in a water-skiing accident. He runs away when it appears that on top of losing his athletic and speaking abilities, he is also losing his girlfriend. At first, he is concerned only with surviving, but then he gets involved with other people and attends an alternative school where, with help, he recovers many of his motor skills. He returns home strong enough to cope with all the changes that have occurred.

Some critics fear that when authors use such physical changes as Willie Weaver's almost miraculous recovery as a tangible or metaphorical way to communicate emotional or mental accomplishment, young readers interpret the physical achievement literally rather than figuratively. Teenagers are already overly concerned about their bodies and any defects they might have. Many physical challenges, including the common motif of obesity, cannot be totally overcome, so these critics prefer stories in which the protagonist comes to terms with the problem as does Izzy in *Izzy, Willy-Nilly* and the young Native American boy in Anne Eliot Crompton's historical *The Sorcerer.* The boy is named Lefthand because he was injured by a bear and cannot hunt. In his tribe, this is a serious problem, because hunting is what the men do. There is no miraculous cure for his disability, but he gains both his own and his tribe's respect when he develops enough skill as an artist to draw the pictures of animals needed for the tribe's hunting rituals.

The acceptance of the compromised dream is an element of the romance pattern that is particularly meaningful to young adults. Many of them are just beginning to achieve some of their lifelong goals, and they are discovering the illusory nature of the end of the rainbow, which is a symbolic way of saying such things as, "When I graduate," "When we get married," "When I'm 18," or "When I have my own apartment." Like the characters in the romances, they are not sorry they have ventured, for they have indeed found something worthwhile, but it is seldom the pot of gold they had imagined.

Because the pattern of the romance has been outlined so clearly by critics, and because its popularity has passed the test of time with honors, it would seem to be an easy story to write. The plot has already been worked out. An author needs only to develop a likable protagonist, determine a quest, fill in the supporting roles with stock characters, and supply a few interesting details. It is far from being this simple, however. Sometimes, as in dance, the things that look the simplest are the hardest to execute. The plot must not be so obvious that the reader recognizes it as the same old thing. The good author develops a unique situation that on the surface appears to be simply a good story. Its appeal as a romantic quest should be at a deep, almost subconscious level, with readers experiencing a sense of *déjà vu*. It is as if their own life story is being told because the romantic quest is everyone's story.

Animal and Nature Stories

Many children come to high school already familiar with the pattern of the accomplishment romance, which they met in such stories as Francis Hodgson Burnett's *The Secret Garden* and Kenneth Grahame's *The Wind in the Willows*. Animals play major roles in Allan Eckert's *Incident at Hawk's Hill*, Fred Gipson's *Old Yeller*, Sterling North's *Rascal*, Marjorie Rawlings's *The Yearling*, and Wilson Rawls's *Where the Red Fern Grows*. In many such stories, the animals are sacrificed as a symbol of the loss the young person undergoes in exchange for wisdom, but fortunately not all animals in such stories are sacrificed. Some of them live long, happy lives, providing companionship and even inspiration to the humans with whom they share the planet (see Focus Box 4.2).

Jean George's *Julie of the Wolves* shows Julie separated from her Eskimo foster family when she runs away from the retarded Daniel, who plans to make her his wife in fact as well as name. She sets out with the vague, unrealistic goal of finding her pen pal in San Francisco. As she gains wisdom and confidence, she decides to live in the old ways. Amaroq, the great wolf, lends "miraculous" help to her struggle for survival on the Arctic tundra. The climax comes when Julie learns that her father still lives and that she has arrived at his village. When she learns that he has married a "gussack" and now pilots planes for hunters, the disillusioned Julie grieves for the wolves and the other hunted animals and vows to return and live on the tundra. The temperature falls far below zero and the "ice thundered and boomed, roaring like drumbeats across the Arctic." Despite all that Julie does to save him, Tornait, Julie's golden plover, who has been her faithful companion, dies from the cold. Tornait is the last symbol of Julie's innocence, and as she mourns his death, she comes to accept the fact that the lives of both the wolf and the Eskimo are changing, and she points her boots toward her father and the life he now leads.

Through her quest, Julie comes to understand that her life must change, but, unexpectedly, she also learns a great deal about her native land and the animals who live there. Readers are optimistic that Julie will not forget what she has experienced and that she will have some part in protecting the land and animals, although perhaps not to the degree that she desires.

Twenty years after *Julie of the Wolves* won the Newbery Award, Jean Craighead George wrote a sequel entitled *Julie*. Although it lacks the surprising originality of the earlier book, junior high readers are likely to enjoy reading more about Julie's continuing quest to save "her" wolves.

Of all the authors writing for young adults, Gary Paulsen is the one who most often uses nature as he explores the theme of a young person poised on the brink of a new stage of development or understanding. His books are further discussed in

FOCUS BOX 4.2

Accomplishment Stories Involving Animals

Bill by Chap Reaver. Delacorte, 1994. The only companion that Jess Gates, the mother-less daughter of a moonshiner, has is her loyal dog Bill. When her father is sent to jail, Jess and Bill have to decide where to put their trust.

Black Star, Bright Dawn by Scott O'Dell. Houghton Mifflin, 1988. Bright Dawn helps her father train his dogs for the Iditarod sled race and ends up running in it herself.

Call of the Wild by Jack London. Macmillan, 1903. This coming-of-age story is set in the excitement of the Alaskan gold rush, where both dogs and men were severely tested.

Dawn Rider by Jan Hudson. Philomel, 1990. A young Native American girl finds a special place in her tribe by proving the worth of the horse that her tribe has stolen from the Snake Indians.

Every Living Thing by Cynthia Rylant. Bradbury, 1985. In these 12 short stories, people's lives are changed by their relationships with animals.

Mariposa Blues by Ron Koertge. Avon/Flare, 1993. Graham's dad is a horse trainer, but Graham decides to make his own decision about when a special horse is ready for competition.

To Race a Dream by Deborah Savage. Houghton Mifflin, 1994. The setting is the early 1900s in a small town in Minnesota where 15-year-old Theodora Stevenson wants to be a driver in harness racing. Savage's *A Rumour of Otters* (Houghton Mifflin, 1986), set on a sheep ranch in New Zealand, is also recommended.

Sniper by Theodore Taylor. Harcourt Brace Jovanovich, 1989. When Ben's parents go on a trip, they leave him in charge of their wild animal preserve, never dreaming of the challenges he will face.

A Solitary Blue by Cynthia Voigt. Atheneum, 1983. Jeff Greene, whose mother has left him and his father, feels as alone in the world as a beautiful blue heron that he observes in a Carolina marsh.

Taming the Star Runner by S. E. Hinton. Delacorte, 1988. Fifteen-year-old Travis moves from a detention center to his uncle's horse ranch, where everyone hopes he will be rehabilitated.

Chapter Five, but in relation to the genre of the accomplishment romance, it is interesting to see how he puts his characters at the right spot at the right time to receive inspiration and insight. In combination with the characters' own efforts, these insights bring them to a new level of maturity. One of our students, Laurie Platt, wrote her Honors College thesis on Paulsen's books and on what she called "catalysts for change," which she defined as the individuals, events, or settings that triggered emotional or intellectual growth.

With all three kinds of catalysts, nature plays a major part. In *The Monument*, when Rocky Turner follows and watches the artist who has been commissioned to create the Vietnam War memorial for the town of Bolton, Kansas, part of her learning comes from his desire to build a monument that would interrelate the natural aspects of the setting with the beliefs and emotions of the townspeople. In *Harris and Me*, the young narrator takes on the task of initiating his city cousin into "the nature" of farm life. In *Dogsong*, the catalyst is the mystical, fortune-telling dreams that come to Russel "like heavy fog and steam rising from the ocean" as he journeys alone on a dogsled. In *Canyons*, Brennan Cole finds a skull and through a variety of dreams and voices understands that he needs to take the skull to its proper resting place, which turns out to be no easy task. When he finally gets there, Brennan stood:

> And saw the world.
>   That was the only way he could think of it—he saw the world. The desert lay below him. He stood on a flat almost-table of rock that jutted out, formed one side of the canyon, and below and away lay all the world he knew.

In this symbolically appropriate high place, Brennan feels a oneness with the Apache boy whose skull he is caring for and who a hundred years ago had stood at this same place and seen this same world.

In several of Paulsen's most popular books (e.g., *Hatchet, The Voyage of the Frog, The Island,* and *The Haymeadow*), he isolates his characters so that they are in fictional situations similar to the real-life one he wrote about in *Woodsong,* in which he and his dogs were totally dependent on each other during the two-and-a-half weeks it took to run the 1000-mile Iditarod dogsled race in Alaska. In *Tracker,* 13-year-old John Borne follows a doe for two days. He is so moved by the doe's tenacity that when he finally returns home, he explains to his worried grandparents, "A thing changed. A thing changed in hunting, in everything, and I walked after her but didn't shoot her." John's experience was the beginning of his understanding that

> his grandfather was going to die. He would die and there was nothing John could do about it—nothing touching the doe could do about it. Death would come.
>   And the second thing was that death was a part of it all, a part of living. It was awful, a taking of life, but it happened to all things, as his grandfather said, would happen to John someday. Dying was just as much a part of Clay Borne [his grandfather] as living.

Westerns

The conquering of the American West is one of the great romantic quests of all time. As such, it caught the imagination of not only the United States but also the entire world. Dime novelists of the 1870s and 1880s glorified the wildness and vitality of miners, cowboys, mountain men, soldiers, and outlaws. In 1902, Owen Wister's *The Virginian: A Horseman of the Plains* established the genre of the quiet and noble hero, the schoolmarm heroine, the hero's weak friend, and villains galore. Wister set up the archetypal showdown between good guys and bad guys. Jack Shaeffer's 1949 *Shane,* helped along by the Alan Ladd movie, added to the myth of the western loner-hero. All through the first third of the twentieth century, Zane Grey published his romanticized and highly popular westerns, a tradition carried on more recently by Louis L'Amour, but with more skill and attention to historical detail.

Literally hundreds of writers have published westerns (stories set roughly between 1880 and 1895). Equally important in establishing the genre of the West have been movies and television. In 1990, Kevin Costner's *Dances with Wolves* surprised moviemakers and critics when it became the most successful film of the year. Expectations were that people had seen, heard, or read so many westerns that they wouldn't come to see another one. Costner's story, however, had a new plot plus all the elements of the adventure/accomplishment romance, one of the oldest stories in the world. Its popularity shows that readers and viewers do not want a new story as much as they want a variation on a familiar theme.

In *Dances with Wolves,* a young soldier decides to volunteer for duty on the western frontier because he wants to see buffalos. He embarks on a more difficult task than anything he could have imagined. He arrives at the North Dakota post to find it abandoned, which results in the traditional period of isolation and contemplation necessary for the development of a hero. The fact that he works hard to salvage the abandoned post and do his duty as a completely unsupervised soldier shows viewers that he's a special person worthy of the friendships that develop, first with the wolf who plays with him and then with the Sioux Indians who are supposed to be his enemies.

By the time the other soldiers arrive and accuse the hero of treason because he has become friends with the Native Americans, viewers have no doubt who is the hero and who are the villains. They suffer with the hero when the villains shoot his wolf, and by the end they are clearly on his side when they see him riding off with the young woman whose life he has saved. It is appropriate that he looks different and that he is called by a new name because the ordeal he endured transformed him from a curious young soldier into a wise and caring man.

Of course, not all westerns follow the pattern of the romantic quest as closely as does *Dances with Wolves,* but most of them have some aspects of the adventure romance (e.g., the embarking on a literal journey that carries over into an intellectual and psychological journey, the exaggerated differences between the good guys and the bad guys, the taking of risks, the existence of life-threatening dangers, and the winning of someone's love).

Most writers of westerns are aiming for a popular culture audience and therefore use a straightforward style that is easy to read. It is endemic to the genre that the heroes are involved in the same kinds of tasks as today's young adults—they are unencumbered individuals setting forth to find themselves a place to live, a way to earn their keep, and suitable companions. This means that teenagers can and do read many of the westerns written for a general adult audience (see Focus Box 4.3). In fact, the first book officially published as a "junior novel" was a western. See the discussion in Chapter Thirteen of Rose Wilder Lane's *Let the Hurricane Roar.*

Although some of the westerns published specifically for young readers do not fit quite so clearly into the pattern of the romantic quest, most of them are easy reading filled with lots of action, and some provide readers with insights into lesser-known aspects of western history. For example, Kathryn Lasky's *The Bone Wars* is about teams of scientists competing for dinosaur fossils in the American West in the 1800s. Her powerful *Beyond the Divide,* told in journal form, is the story of Meribah Simon and her father, who in 1849 head west after Meribah's father is shunned for attending the funeral of a friend who had failed to observe Amish customs.

FOCUS BOX 4.3

Western Novels That'll Stick to Your Ribs

Borderlands by Peter Carter. Farrar, Straus & Giroux, 1990.   Ben Curtis joins a cattle drive in 1871, meets an African American man he learns to respect, and loses his brother in a gunfight in this epic novel.

The Brave Cowboy by Edward Abbey. Dodd, Mead, 1956.   A cowboy, an anachronism in our modern world, tries to help a friend break out of jail. Failing that, the cowboy flees, pursued by a lawman who won't give up.

Fire on the Mountain by Edward Abbey. Dial, 1962.   When the government takes over his property to use as a missile range, an old rancher fights back.

The Last Picture Show by Larry McMurtry. Dial, 1966.   The end of the West comes to dusty and drying-up Thalia, Texas, and the movie theatre shuts down as well.

The Man Who Killed the Deer by Frank Waters. Farrar, Straus & Giroux, 1942.   A young Indian is caught between two cultures.

The Ox-Bow Incident by Walter Van Tilburg Clark. Random House, 1940.   This is the prototypical western about lynching and mob justice.

Promised Lands: A Novel of the Texas Rebellion by Elizabeth Crook. Doubleday, 1994. There's little glamour but lots of empathy shown for all sides in this 1830s story of the battle for Texas independence.

The Road to Many a Wonder by David Wagoner. Farrar, Straus & Giroux, 1974.   A young couple set off for the West and all that they've ever dreamed of. A funny and accurate vision of the West, too, in its own way.

Walking Up a Rainbow by Theodore Taylor. Harcourt Brace, 1994 (an earlier version was published by Delacorte in 1986).   In the 1850s, 14-year-old Susan Darden Carlisle is left an orphan in Kanesville, Iowa. To save her family home, she sets out with the help of her elderly guardian and "the first American cowboy" to drive several thousand sheep from Iowa to California.

The White Man's Road by Benjamin Capps. HarperCollins, 1969.   Young Native American men break loose from a stifling reservation to prove their manhood.

Young people growing up in single-parent or newly formed families may be interested in such books as Joan Lowry Nixon's *The Orphan Train Quartet,* which includes *A Family Apart, Caught in the Act, In the Face of Danger,* and *A Place to Belong.* The four stories are based on true accounts of homeless New York children sent to the frontier West for adoption. Isabelle Holland's *The Journey Home* is about two orphaned sisters, 12-year-old Maggie and 7-year-old Annie, who are taken to Kansas and adopted. Annie adjusts and likes the new life, but Maggie feels resentful partly because she's behind her classmates in school and she fears the farm animals. Patricia MacLachlan's *Sarah, Plain and Tall* is also about the forming of a new family. It's a children's story (a Newbery Award winner) of a mail-order bride who comes west to be the mother of Caleb and Anna. The 1991 television special starring Glenn Close was powerful enough to attract readers of all ages to the book.

Another appealing young adult western is Pam Conrad's *Prairie Songs,* about a young doctor and his beautiful wife who are welcomed as newcomers to a Nebraska prairie town. Their joy turns to sorrow, however, as the young wife slips into madness. Liza K. Murrow's *West Against the Wind* is set during gold rush times.

Abigail Parker and her family set out for California, in search not for gold but for her missing father.

Gary Paulsen's first book for young adults was *Mr. Tucket,* published in 1969 and described in *Publishers Weekly* as a "real rock 'em sock 'em ripsnorter." Fourteen-year-old Francis Tucket is kidnapped by Pawnee Indians from an Oregon-bound wagon train. He escapes with help from a one-armed mountain man who over the course of a year teaches Francis how to live in the wilderness. In a 1995 sequel, *Call Me Francis Tucket,* the boy leaves his benefactor and sets off west to find his family. Of course, complications ensue.

Avi's *The Barn,* set in Oregon Territory during the 1850s, is a powerful yet simple story of three pioneer children and their dying father. The youngest child, Ben, is obsessed with the idea that they must build the barn that his now-paralyzed father has always wanted. The other children disagree, and in frustration Ben tries to enlist his father's support by asking him if he wants the barn built and then screaming, "If you mean *yes,* you *must* close your eyes!" The father closes his eyes, but it is never clear whether it was an accident or a purposeful communication. Nevertheless, the children begin work on an amazingly difficult task, all carefully detailed in the book. As they work, they prop their father in a wheelbarrow and bring him outside to watch, but in this sparse and moving story the higher the barn rises, the lower the father sinks.

Accomplishment Stories with Religious Themes

A different kind of accomplishment story is the one in which a young person is helped through a religious experience. In many ways, Cynthia Rylant's *A Fine White Dust* exemplifies this subgenre. The book's title comes from the chalklike dust that gets on Pete's fingers when he handles the "little bitty pieces of broken ceramic" that used to be a cross he had painted in Vacation Bible School—back before he got so old that it wasn't cool to go anymore. His best friend is a confirmed atheist, and he has "half-washed Christians for parents." Nevertheless, the summer that Preacher Man comes to town, "something religious" begins itching Pete, something that going to church couldn't cure.

Rylant's skill in developing Pete's character and revealing the depths of his emotions when he is saved and wooed and then betrayed by the Preacher Man won for her a well-deserved Newbery Honor Award. The 12 short chapters are almost an outline for a quest story beginning with "Dust" and a sense of ennui, moving through "The Joy," "The Wait," and "Hell," and ending with "The Light" and "Amen." In the end, Pete decides that, "The Preacher Man is behind me. But God is still right there, in front."

Books that unabashedly explore religious themes are relatively rare, partly because schools and libraries fear mixing church and state through spending tax dollars for religious books. Also, mainstream publishers fear cutting into potential sales by printing books with protagonists whose religious beliefs may offend some readers and make others uncomfortable. It has been easier for schools to include religious books with historical settings, such as Lloyd Douglas's *The Robe,* Scott O'Dell's *The Hawk That Dare Not Hunt by Day,* Elizabeth George Speare's *The Bronze Bow,* and Jessamyn West's *Friendly Persuasion.* Also accepted are books with contemporary settings that have proven themselves with adult readers, for example, Margaret Craven's *I Heard the Owl Call My Name,* Catherine Marshall's *A Man Called Peter,* and William Barrett's *Lilies of the Field.*

In lamenting the shortage of young adult books treating religious themes author Dean Hughes wrote:

> We need to be careful that, in effect, we do not say to young people that they *should* be most concerned about pimples and clothes and dates and football games—or even sex. Part of being human is addressing oneself to questions about justice, creation, morality, and the existence of divinity.[3]

Patty Campbell made a similar point when she wrote that although nearly 60% of Americans attend some type of religious services, young adult fiction presents a world almost devoid of either personal or corporate religious practices. "Where," she asks, "are the church youth groups, the Hebrew or confirmation classes, the Bible study meetings that are so much a part of middle-class teenage American life? Where, too, is the mainstream liberal Protestant or Catholic practice and sensibility?" Practically the only religious characters developed in young adult books are villains who are "presented as despicable in direct proportion to the degree of their religious involvement."[4]

Examples of the "despicable" characters she was thinking about include the fanatical and unbending parents who make life miserable for their kids in Suzanne Newton's *I Will Call it Georgie's Blues,* Norma Howe's *God, The Universe, and Hot Fudge Sundaes,* and Kathryn Lasky's *Memoirs of a Bookbat.* In Stephanie Tolan's *A Good Courage,* Tie-Dye's hippie mother ends up in a religious commune which forces Tie-Dye to take control of his own future, whereas in M. E. Kerr's *Is That You, Miss Blue?* the hypocritical attitudes of the faculty members at a religious school inspire the students to come to the aid of a teacher who is fired because she "believes." In Bette Greene's *The Drowning of Stephan Jones,* homophobic ministers are at the heart of the evil treatment of two gay men, whereas in Lois Ruby's *Miriam's Well,* religious leaders do not let Miriam receive medical help.

In many ways, the negative portrayal of religion in books for teenagers is similar to the negative portrayal of parents and other authority figures. Such presentations serve as a foil to make the good qualities of the young protagonists shine all the brighter. Authors rely on the general assumption that religious people are good to provide contrast, as when the evil in Robert Cormier's *The Chocolate War* (see Chapter Three) is all the heavier because of the book's setting in a religious school.

Another reason that books for teenagers appear to have so many religious characters portrayed in a negative light is that the good characters go unnoticed. For example, in M. E. Kerr's *Little Little* one of Little Little's suitors is a dishonest evangelical preacher. When Kerr was criticized for this negative portrayal, she pointed out that Little Little's grandfather—the only person in the whole book who approached Little Little's dwarfism with common sense—was also a minister, but few readers noticed because he did his work in the manner expected from a competent clergyman in a mainstream church.

Although there are some good books focusing on broad religious themes and questions about whether there is a God and an afterlife (e.g., Aidan Chambers's

RON KOERTGE
On Failure as Opportunity

I never wanted to be a Young Adult writer; I never really wanted to be anything. It got on my nerves when grown-ups would nag me about planning for my future. When I was younger, I had a kind of pinball philosophy: I'd just bounce around and see what happened.

I did, though, think that words were interesting. And I liked the feel of a book in my hand. But it would never have occurred to me to say, "I want to be a writer." My parents were modest, blue collar folks and so was I. No one from Collinsville, Illinois, crowed about being an author; lots of kids never went to college; some didn't finish high school.

Looking back, though, from the rickety pinnacle of 55, it sure looks like writing was inevitable. It was about the only thing I was good at and, like most people, I wanted to be good at something.

In 1958, I went to the University of Illinois. When I found out that I could be an English major, get college credits for reading and writing, and graduate with a B.A., I was thrilled. I was reading and writing, anyway. It was like getting paid to work in the chocolate factory. Or the Y.W.C.A.

Like a lot of young guys with a library card, I thought about the novel. So when I got out of graduate school and was teaching at the city college in Pasadena, I wrote one. It took a while, but it was published (*The Boogeyman*, W. W. Norton) and that's when my career as YA novelist began—with the failure of my next two novels for adults.

The idea of failure-as-opportunity rather than failure-as-tragedy interests me a lot. My first marriage failed, but my second is a marvel. My health once failed but finding alternative ways to be well has made me healthier than I've ever been. And by turning those two rejected novels-for-adults into YA's, I met interesting people, got reviewed well, and—in a sense—burst on the YA scene because my books were funnier and sexier than the standard issue book for teens.

I also get to travel, and it's much more fun to talk to kids than it is to adults. Kids never ask the soul-bleaching questions about writing that adults feel compelled to ask. Kids want to know how much money I make, why I don't have children of my own, and why I love to bet on horses. They don't peddle the popular resentments, and they don't take the obvious for granted.

All this sure makes me wonder—What door marked FAILURE will I find next, and what room, criss-crossed by light and shadow, will that door open onto.

Ron Koertge's books include *Tiger, Tiger, Burning Bright*, Orchard, 1994; *The Harmony Arms*, Little, 1992; and *The Arizona Kid*, Little, 1988.

NIK: *Now I Know,* Iris Rosofsky's *Miriam,* and Phyllis Reynolds Naylor's *A String of Chances),* what is more common is for an author to bring in religion as a small part of a bigger story. In Jim Naughton's *My Brother Stealing Second,* Bobby reminisces about his family's church experiences before his brother was killed, and in Sue Ellen Bridgers's *Permanent Connections,* Rob finds comfort by visiting a little country church. Katherine Paterson, who has attended theological school and served as a missionary in China, includes both implicit and explicit religious references in her books, most directly in *Jacob Have I Loved* and *Bridge to Terabithia.* Madeleine L'Engle is devout, and along with some other writers of fantasy and science fiction, she includes religious overtones in her books (e.g., the struggle between good and evil in *A Wrinkle in Time*). Other books that include references to religious people and beliefs are Alice Childress's *Rainbow Jordan,* J. D. Salinger's *Franny & Zooey: Two Novellas,* Mary Stolz's *Land's End,* and Jill Paton-Walsh's *Unleaving.* Chaim Potok's *The Chosen, My Name Is Asher Lev,* and *In the Beginning* show what it is to come of age in a Hasidic Jewish community. Cynthia Voigt's *David and Jonathan* asks questions about religious and cultural differences; Marc Talbert's *A Sunburned Prayer* is about 11-year-old Eloy making a 17-mile pilgrimage on Good Friday to pray for his grandmother who is dying of cancer.

Of course, religious publishing houses provide books focusing on religious themes, but these are seldom useful in schools because they are aimed so directly at believers of a particular faith, and sometimes in their zeal to convert potential believers, the authors write polemics against other groups. Nevertheless, teachers and librarians are advised to visit local religious bookstores to see what is offered because some students may prefer to fill their independent reading assignments with books from these sources. Today's religious books range from biblical and western romances and adventures to self-help books and inspirational biographies. People who haven't taken a look at religious books over the past few years will probably be surprised at the slick covers and the upscale marketing techniques.

In relation to the accomplishment romance, an especially troublesome group consists of books in which a misguided life is set right by an end-of-the-book conversion. Teachers hesitate to discuss the credibility of such stories because they fear that in the process of building up literary sophistication, they may be tearing down religious faith. Nevertheless, teachers and librarians need to seek out and support those authors and publishers who treat religious motifs with honesty as well as with respect for literary quality. They also need to help parents and other critics realize that strong religious feelings, including doubts, are part of the maturation process and that reading about the doubts that others have or about imperfections in organized religion does not necessarily destroy one's own faith.

The Love Romance

The love romance is slightly different from the accomplishment romance or the adventure romance, but it shares many of their characteristics. Love stories are symbolically associated with youth and springtime. An ordeal or a problem must be overcome, which is followed by a happy ending. The "problem" is invariably the successful pairing of a likable young couple. An old definition of the love-romance pattern is, "Boy meets girl, boy loses girl, boy wins girl." This is a fairly accurate summary except that with teenage literature it is the other way around. Most of the romances are told from the girl's point of view. She is the one who meets, loses, and finally wins a boy.

The tone of the love romance is lighter than that of the adventure romance. In a love story, the protagonist neither risks nor gains as much as in an adventure. Notwithstanding *Romeo and Juliet,* people seldom die, emotionally or physically, because of young love. For this reason, the love romance tends to be less serious in its message. Its power lies in its wish fulfillment. Women of all ages enjoy reading romances for the same reasons that people have always enjoyed either hearing or reading wish-fulfilling fantasies. The "Open Sesame" door to prosperity and the transformation of a cindermaid into a queen, a frog into a prince, and a Scrooge into a kindly old man are all examples of the same satisfying theme that is the key to the appeal of love romances. In the teen romances, an ugly duckling girl is transformed by the love of a boy into a swan. In her new role as swan, she is not only popular and successful, but also happy.

For the writer of a love story, probably no talent is more important than the ability to create believable characters. If readers do not feel that they know the boy and girl or the man and woman as individuals, they cannot identify with them and consequently won't care whether they make it or not. Another characteristic of the good love story is that it provides something beyond the simple pairing of two individuals. This something extra may be interesting historical details, introduction to a social issue, glimpses into the complexity of human nature, or any of the un-

Many educators hesitate to promote love romances because of feeling that commercial interests already do enough such promotion.

FOCUS BOX 4.4

Love Stories with Something Extra

Charms for the Easy Life by Kaye Gibbons. Putnam, 1993. The three generations of southern women in this lively story are characterized by "grace and gumption." Despite their being feminists, the author makes sure that each gets her man—in one way or the other.

Cold Sassy Tree by Olive Ann Burns. Ticknor & Fields, 1984. Although this is the story of Will Tweedy growing up, it's also his grandfather's love story.

Daniel and Esther by Patrick Raymond. Macmillan, 1990. In 1936, Esther's anti-Fascist parents send her to a boarding school in England, hoping that she will be safe. There she and Daniel fall in love with each other, but when the war starts she returns to Vienna and Daniel is evacuated to the United States.

Forever by Judy Blume. Bradbury, 1975. Katherine and Michael become sexually involved, and although nobody gets punished, their love does not last forever.

If Beale Street Could Talk by James Baldwin. Doubleday, 1974. In this mature story told in frank, black English, pregnant Tish loves Fonny, who has been jailed on a false charge.

I Am Wings: Poems about Love by Ralph Fletcher. Photos by Joe Baker. Bradbury, 1994. In 33 free-verse poems, Fletcher takes readers through a high school romance that moves in the clear, fresh voice of the boy from "Falling In" to "Falling Out."

A Knot in the Grain and Other Stories by Robin McKinley. Greenwillow, 1994. The first of these five love stories about seemingly incompatible lovers is contemporary, whereas the other four share the setting of McKinley's fantasies *The Blue Sword* (1982) and *The Hero and the Crown* (1984), both Greenwood.

Orfe by Cynthia Voigt. Atheneum, 1992. In this modern telling of the myth about Orpheus and the Underworld, a young rock singer tries using her talent to entice the man she loves from a house of drug addicts.

The Unlikely Romance of Kate Bjorkman by Louise Plummer. Delacorte, 1995. The six-foot-tall narrator is much too smart and much too funny to write a typical romance, but that's what makes this one refreshing.

We All Fall Down by Robert Cormier. Delacorte, 1991. Readers familiar with Robert Cormier's books wouldn't expect him to write a typical love story, and he doesn't.

---

derstandings and concepts that might be found in quality books or movies (see Focus Box 4.4).

Although most formula romances are aimed exclusively at a female audience, comparable to the way that most pornography is aimed at a male audience, some writers are trying to write romances that are also read by boys, even though they are not sports, adventure, or mystery stories. Hazel Rochman described such books as "domestic novels about boys in which heroes stay home and struggle with their feelings and their conscience rather than with tumultuous external events." Many such books are love stories, and as Rochman observed:

The theme of so many girls' books—finding that you love the boy next door after all—has a new vitality from the male perspective, as in [Harry] Mazer's *I Love You, Stupid!* Sex is treated with honesty: in [Chris] Crutcher's *Running Loose,* after a long romantic buildup in which the couple drive and then ski to an isolated cabin for a weekend of lovemaking, the jock hero finds that he cannot perform. In [Richard] Peck's *Father Figure* and [Katie Letcher] Lyle's *Dark But Full of Diamonds,* the love for an older woman, in rivalry with the boy's own father, is movingly handled. . . . in *The Course of True Love Never Did Run Smooth,* [Marilyn] Singer's heroine finds strong and sexy a boy who is short, funny, and vulnerable.[5]

The most obvious difference between these boy-oriented romances and the larger body of love stories written from a girl's point of view is that their authors, who are mostly men, tend to put less emphasis on courtship and romance and more on sexuality. Rather than relying on discreet fade-outs, they allow their readers to know what happens, which sometimes means sexual intercourse. For the most part, the descriptions are neither pornographic nor lovingly romantic, but in such books as Chris Crutcher's *Running Loose,* Robert Lehrman's *Juggling,* Terry Davis's *Vision Quest,* and Aidan Chambers' *The Toll Bridge,* there is little doubt about the abundance of sexual feelings that the characters experience.

As an antidote to the lopsidedness of books that are either overly romantic or overly sexy, some adult critics suggest offering books in which boys and girls are as much friends as lovers. This is especially true in lighter books read by 11-, 12- and 13-year olds (see Focus Box 4.5). The romantic relationship is only part of a bigger story, and there is no indication of either partner exploiting or manipulating the other, as often happens in exaggerated romances or in pornographic or sex-oriented stories. As a ploy to attract male readers, since authors already feel confident that girls will read love stories, the narrator may be the boy, or there may be a mix with alternate chapters coming from the boy and the girl, as in Paul Zindel's *The Pigman* and M. E. Kerr's *I'll Love You When You're More Like Me.*

An example of a combination love and friendship story is Harry Mazer's *The Girl of His Dreams.* Willis Pierce, the boy Mazer wrote about in his first book, *The War on Villa Street,* has graduated from high school and is living by himself. He is a runner but too shy to compete or to make friends. On his long, solitary runs, he dreams about the girl he is sure to meet one day. When he meets Sophie, who takes care of the newsstand by the factory where he works, she doesn't look or act like the girl of his dreams. Nevertheless, Mazer has done such a good job of character development that readers understand why the two are attracted to each other, and they end the book feeling like Sophie does: "She's happy, but the little bit of worry is always there, the little bit of uncertainty."

The runaway popularity of formula love romances written especially for teenagers and published as original paperbacks was the big marketing surprise of the early 1980s. Formula romances most often feature girls 15, 16, or 17 years old with boyfriends who are slightly older. The target audience is supposedly girls between the ages of 12 and 16, although some 10- and 11-year-olds are also finding them. The typical setting is a small town or suburb. There is no explicit sex or profanity. As one editor told us, "If there are problems, they have to be normal ones—no drugs, no sex, no alcohol, no bad parents, etc."

The kinds of problems featured are wish-fulfilling ones that most girls dream of coping with. For example, in Jill Ross Klevin's *That's My Girl,* ice skater Becky has to fight off getting ulcers while worrying about the upcoming Nationals, her

FOCUS BOX 4.5

Love and Laughs for Junior High/Middle Schoolers

All but Alice by Phyllis Reynolds Naylor. Atheneum, 1992. Alice McKinley does not have a mother and she's overly optimistic in the way she goes looking for friendship and guidance from any females who happen to be around. Part of a series, this book fits in between *Reluctantly Alice* (1991) and *Alice the Brave* (1995), both Atheneum.

The Best School Year Ever by Barbara Robinson. HarperCollins, 1994. In this sequel to *The Best Christmas Pageant Ever* (Harper-Collins, 1972), the Herdmans continue to make life interesting for their classmates.

Bingo Brown and the Language of Love by Betsy Byars. Viking, 1989. Sandwiched between *The Burning Questions of Bingo Brown* and *Bingo Brown, Gypsy Lover,* this book shows Melissa moving to Bixby, Oklahoma. Poor Bingo has to cook 36 dinners for his parents to pay his long-distance phone bills.

Captain Hawaii by Anthony Dana Arkin. HarperCollins, 1994. Fifteen-year-old Arron wants to do more than sit around a hotel swimming pool when his family takes a vacation in Hawaii. For better or for worse, he gets his wish and as part of the adventure gets acquainted with Kate.

Flour Babies by Anne Fine. Little Brown, 1994. When the boys in Room 8 are assigned to "experience parenthood" by taking care of a six-pound sack of flour for three weeks, Simon learns more than he thinks he will. Fine is also the author of *Alias Madame Doubtfire* (Little, Brown, 1988), the source of the popular movie starring Robin Williams.

Frankenlouse by Mary James (a.k.a. M. E. Kerr). Scholastic, 1994. Nick Reber attends a military school run by his father—and therein lies at least part of his problem. Readers get to see how he copes through an evolving comic strip that he draws about characters who are book lice.

I Love You. I Hate You. Get Lost: A Collection of Short Stories by Ellen Conford. Scholastic, 1994. Conford's witty writing and on-target dialogue make her a favorite. Among her many other titles are *If This Is Love, I'll Take Spaghetti* (Four Winds, 1983) and *The Genie with the Light Blue Hair* (Bantam, 1989).

Remember Me to Harold Square by Paula Danziger. Delacorte, 1987. Kendra Kaye, her little brother, and Frank Lee, a boy she has a crush on, embark on a parent-designed scavenger hunt for facts about New York City. In a sequel, *Thames Doesn't Rhyme with James* (Putnam, 1994), the same group is joined by two other kids for an adventure in London.

Space Station Seventh Grade by Jerry Spinelli. Little Brown, 1982. Spinelli was one of the first writers to zero in on the hilarity of junior high. Other recommended titles include *Dump Days* (Little Brown, 1988) and Newbery Award winner *Maniac McGee* (Little Brown, 1990).

Squashed by Joan Bauer. Delacorte, 1992. Ellie Morgan wants to lose 20 pounds for herself and gain 20 pounds for Max, the giant pumpkin she's growing for the Rock River Pumpkin Weigh-In. There's laughs all around when Max goes up against Big Daddy, raised by the obnoxious Cyril Pool.

chance at the Olympics. Her biggest worry is whether she will lose her boyfriend, who feels ignored. Janet Quin-Harkin's *California Girl* has an almost identical plot except that Jennie is competing for the Olympics as a swimmer. In Rosemary Vernon's *The Popularity Plan*, Frannie is too shy to talk to boys, but her friends draw up a plan in which she is assigned certain ways to relate to a boy each day. Sure enough, she is soon asked for so many dates she has to buy a wall calendar to keep

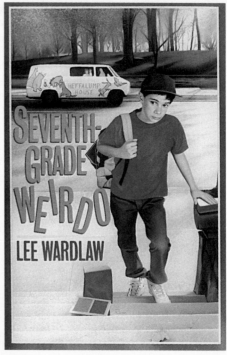

See Focus Box 4.5 for other books showing that, for pre-teens, surviving school can sometimes be its own accomplishment romance.

---

from getting mixed up. But by the end of the story she is happy to "give it all up" and settle for Ronnie, the boy she really liked all along.

Formula romances have many of the same qualities that publishers have developed for high-interest, low-vocabulary books. They are short books divided into short chapters. They have quick beginnings, more action than description, considerable use of dialogue, a straightforward point of view, and a reading level not much above fifth grade. Perhaps most important of all, the books are clearly labeled, so that readers know what they will be getting. As shown by the popularity of movie sequels, television serials and reruns, and continuing columns in newspapers, although viewers and readers do not want to see or read precisely the same thing over and over again, they are comforted by knowing that a particular piece is going to be similar to something they have previously enjoyed.

Some adults worry that teenage readers take the books seriously, that they fail to recognize them as fantasy, and that they therefore model their behavior and attitudes—and, more important, their expectations—after those portrayed in the romances. A sampling of published quotations from critics illustrates a range of concern:

> Playing on the insecurities and self-doubt which plague most teenaged girls, the Wildfire [a Scholastic imprint] romances come just close enough to real life to be convincing to young readers. But implicit in these hygienic stories

are the old, damaging and limiting stereotypes from which we've struggled so hard to free ourselves and our children: that the real world is white and middle-class; that motherhood is women's only work; that a man is the ultimate prize and a woman is incomplete without one; and that in the battle for that prize, the weapons are good looks and charm, intelligence is a liability, and the enemy is the other woman.[6]

Absence is, in fact, at the heart of the criticism of these books. Third World people are absent, disabled people are absent, lesbians and gay men are absent, poor people are absent, elderly people are absent. . . . [7]

There is an eternal paradox here. We read such romantic stories as an escape from reality and yet they form our ideals of what reality should be. Hence that frustration, that vague sense of failure and disappointment when a night out at the disco doesn't turn out the way it does in the magazines.[8]

In an attempt to appear wholesome enough to be mass marketed to girls in their early teens, many authors of formula romances encourage a kind of wish fulfillment that relates to the psychological ambivalence that young females feel about sexuality. On the one hand, girls want to be loved, not only because it is emotionally satisfying, but also because dating and courtship are glamorous and exciting. On the other hand, many of them are not yet ready for a sexual relationship and would be happy to have the dating and the cuddling without the complications of sex. This makes authors gloss over the part that sex plays in male-female relationships. In many of the books, it's love at first sight, which must imply a physical attraction (i.e., a sexual attraction), yet the boys are portrayed as being almost platonically interested in the girl's thoughts and feelings rather than in her body. When Rainbow Jordan, the protagonist in Alice Childress's realistic book of the same name, learned that this wasn't the way it was in real life, she complained:

True love is mostly featured in fairy tales. Sleepin' Beauty put off sex for a hundred years. When a prince finally did find her . . . he kiss her gently, then they gallop off on a pretty horse so they could enjoy the happy-ever-after. They never mentioned sex.

Defenders of formula romances most often focus on their popularity and the fact that they are recreational reading freely chosen by young girls who otherwise would most likely be watching TV. Vermont Royster, writing in the *Wall Street Journal,* compared the romances to the reading of books his mother considered trash— Tom Swift, the Rover Boys, Detective Nick Carter, and Wild Bill Hickok. He acknowledged that the plotting was banal and monotonous and that writers could probably turn them out wholesale, but at least, "The spelling is correct and they do manage mostly to abide by the rules of English grammar." He welcomed the books as an aid in helping a generation of television-oriented kids acquire the habit of reading. Once they are hooked, "Call it an addiction if you will . . . young people can be led by good teachers to enlarge their reach."[9]

Teachers and librarians need to be especially careful in criticizing students' enjoyment of romances because young readers are as sensitive as anyone else to hints that they are gullible and lacking in taste and sophistication. So rather than making fun of love romances, it is better to approach them from a positive angle, offering readers a wide variety of books, including ones that treat boy-girl relationships not as the only thing of importance, but as part of a bigger picture.

The various types of accomplishment and adventure stories, including love romances, are psychologically satisfying. More than any other genre, these stories match the particular stage of life that is young adulthood. Because of this match, and because the plots are straightforward and the reading levels are generally comfortable, these books are likely to remain among the most popular for young adult leisure time reading.

Notes

[1] Frances Bradburn, "Focus: Dear Diary," *Booklist* 90 (June 1 & 15, 1994): 1791.

[2] Glenna Davis Sloan, *The Child as Critic* (Teachers College Press, 1975), p. 33.

[3] Dean Hughes, "Bait/Rebait: Books with Religious Themes," *English Journal* 70 (December 1981): 14–17.

[4] Patty Campbell, "The Sand in the Oyster," *The Horn Book Magazine,* (September/October 1994): 619.

[5] Hazel Rochman, "Bringing Boys' Books Home," *School Library Journal* 29 (August 1983): 26–27.

[6] Brett Harvey, "Wildfire: Tame but Deadly," *Interracial Books for Children Bulletin* 12 (1981).

[7] Sharon Wigutoff, "First Love: Morality Tales Thinly Veiled," *Interracial Books for Children Bulletin* 12:4 and 12:5 (1981): 17.

[8] Mary Harron, "Oh Boy! My Guy," (London) *Times Educational Supplement* (July 1, 1983): 22.

[9] Vermont Royster, "Thinking Things Over: The Reading Addiction," *Wall Street Journal* (June 24, 1981): 30.

Titles Mentioned in the Text of Chapter Four

Anonymous. *Go Ask Alice.* Prentice-Hall, 1969.

Avi. *The Barn.* Orchard, 1993.

Barrett, William. *Lilies of the Field.* Doubleday, 1962.

Brancato, Robin. *Winning.* Knopf, 1977.

Bridgers, Sue Ellen. *Permanent Connections.* HarperCollins, 1987.

Brooks, Bruce. *The Moves Make the Man.* HarperCollins, 1984.

Burnett, Francis Hodgson. *The Secret Garden.* 1911.

Chambers, Aiden. *NIK: Now I Know.* HarperCollins, 1988.

Chambers, Aiden. *The Toll Bridge.* HarperCollins, 1995.

Childress, Alice. *Rainbow Jordan.* Putnam, 1981.

Conrad, Pam. *Prairie Songs.* HarperCollins, 1985.

Cormier, Robert. *The Chocolate War.* Pantheon, 1974.

Craven, Margaret. *I Heard the Owl Call My Name.* Doubleday, 1973.

Crompton, Anne Eliot. *The Sorcerer.* Second Chance, 1982.

Crutcher, Chris. *The Crazy Horse Electric Game.* Greenwillow, 1987.

Crutcher, Chris. *Running Loose.* Greenwillow, 1983.

Davis, Terry. *Vision Quest.* Viking, 1979.

Douglas, Lloyd. *The Robe.* Houghton Mifflin, 1942.

Eckert, Allan W. *Incident at Hawk's Hill.* Little, Brown, 1971.

George, Jean. *Julie.* HarperCollins, 1994.

George, Jean. *Julie of the Wolves.* HarperCollins, 1972.

Gipson, Fred. *Old Yeller.* HarperCollins, 1964.

Grahame, Kenneth. *Wind in the Willows.* 1908.

Green, Hannah. *I Never Promised You a Rose Garden.* Holt, 1964.

Greene, Bette. *The Drowning of Stephan Jones.* Bantam, 1991.

Guest, Judith. *Ordinary People.* Viking, 1976.

Hamilton, Virginia. *M. C. Higgins, the Great*. Macmillan, 1974.

Holland, Isabelle. *The Journey Home*. Scholastic, 1990.

Howe, Norma. *God, the Universe, and Hot Fudge Sundaes*. Houghton Mifflin, 1984.

Kerr, M. E. *I'll Love You When You're More Like Me*. HarperCollins, 1977.

Kerr, M. E. *Is That You, Miss Blue?* HarperCollins, 1975.

Kerr, M. E. *Little Little*. HarperCollins, 1981.

Klevin, Jill Ross. *That's My Girl*. Scholastic, 1981.

Lane, Rose Wilder. *Let the Hurricane Roar*. 1933.

Lasky, Kathryn. *Beyond the Divide*. Macmillan, 1983.

Lasky, Kathryn. *The Bone Wars*. Morrow, 1988.

Lasky, Kathryn. *Memoirs of a Book Bat*. Harcourt, 1994.

Lehrman, Robert. *Juggling*. HarperCollins, 1982.

L'Engle, Madeleine. *A Wrinkle in Time*. Farrar, Straus & Giroux, 1962.

Lipsyte, Robert. *The Brave*. HarperCollins, 1991.

Lipsyte, Robert. *The Contender*. HarperCollins, 1967.

Lyle, Katie Letcher. *Dark But Full of Diamonds*. Putnam, 1981.

MacLachlan, Patricia. *Sarah, Plain and Tall*. HarperCollins, 1985.

Marshall, Catherine. *A Man Called Peter*. McGraw-Hill, 1951.

Mazer, Harry. *I Love You, Stupid!* HarperCollins, 1981.

Mazer, Harry. *The Girl of His Dreams*. HarperCollins, 1987.

Mazer, Harry. *The War on Villa Street*. Delacorte, 1978.

Murrow, Liza K. *West Against the Wind*. Holiday House, 1987.

Naughton, Jim. *My Brother Stealing Second*. HarperCollins, 1989.

Naylor, Phyllis R. *A String of Chances*. Atheneum, 1982.

Newton, Suzanne. *I Will Call It Georgie's Blues*. Viking, 1983.

Nixon, Joan Lowry. *The Orphan Train Quartet (A Family Apart, Caught in the Act, In the Face of Danger, and A Place to Belong)*. Bantam, late 1980s.

North, Sterling, *Rascal: A Memoir of a Better Era*. E. P. Dutton, 1963.

O'Dell, Scott, *The Hawk That Dare Not Hunt by Day*. Houghton Mifflin, 1975.

Paterson, Katherine. *Jacob Have I Loved*. Crowell, 1980.

Paulsen, Gary. *Call Me Francis Tucket*. Delacorte, 1995.

Paulsen, Gary. *Canyons*. Delacorte, 1990.

Paulsen, Gary. *Dogsong*. Bradbury, 1985.

Paulsen, Gary. *Harris and Me*. Harcourt Brace, 1993.

Paulsen, Gary. *Hatchet*. Bradbury, 1987.

Paulsen, Gary. *The Haymeadow*. Doubleday, 1992.

Paulsen, Gary. *The Island*. Orchard, 1988.

Paulsen, Gary. *The Monument*. Delacorte, 1991.

Paulsen, Gary. *Mr. Tucket*. Funk & Wagnalls, 1969.

Paulsen, Gary. *Tracker*. Bradbury, 1984.

Paulsen, Gary. *The Voyage of the Frog*. Orchard, 1989.

Paulsen, Gary. *Woodsong*. Bradbury, 1990.

Peck, Richard. *Father Figure*. Viking, 1978.

Potok, Chaim. *The Chosen*. Simon & Schuster, 1967.

Potok, Chaim. *In the Beginning*. Knopf, 1975.

Potok, Chaim. *My Name Is Asher Lev*. Knopf, 1972.

Quin-Harkin, Janet. *California Girl*. Bantam, 1981.

Rawlings, Marjorie Kinnan. *The Yearling*. Scribner's, 1938.

Rawls, Wilson. *Where the Red Fern Grows*. Doubleday, 1961.

Rosofsky, Iris. *Miriam*. HarperCollins, 1988.

Ruby, Lois. *Miriam's Well*. Scholastic, 1993.

Rylant, Cynthia. *A Fine White Dust*. Bradbury, 1986.

Salinger, J. D. *The Catcher in the Rye*. Little, Brown, 1951.

Salinger, J. D. *Franny & Zooey: Two Novellas*. Little, Brown, 1961.

Shaeffer, Jack. *Shane*. Houghton Mifflin, 1949.

Singer, Marilyn. *The Course of True Love Never Did Run Smooth*. HarperCollins, 1983.

Sparks, Beatrice, ed. *It Happened to Nancy*. Avon/Flare, 1994.

Speare, Elizabeth George. *The Bronze Bow*. Houghton Mifflin, 1973.

Stolz, Mary. *Land's End*. HarperCollins, 1973.

Tolan, Stephanie. *A Good Courage*. Morrow, 1988.

Tolkien, J. R. R. *The Lord of the Rings*. Houghton Mifflin, 1974.

Vernon, Rosemary. *The Popularity Plan*. Bantam, 1981.

Voigt, Cynthia. *David and Jonathan*. Scholastic, 1992.

Voigt, Cynthia. *Izzy, Willy-Nilly*. Atheneum, 1986.

Walsh, Jill Paton. *Unleaving*. Farrar, Straus & Giroux, 1976.

West, Jessamyn. *Friendly Persuasion*. Harcourt Brace Jovanovich, 1956.

Wister, Owen. *The Virginian: A Horseman of the Plains*. Macmillan, 1902.

Zindel, Paul. *The Pigman*. HarperCollins, 1968.

For information on the availability of paperback editions of these titles, please consult the most recent edition of *Paperbound Books in Print,* published annually by R. R. Bowker Company.

Chapter 5

Adventure, Mysteries, and the Supernatural
Of Excitement and Suspense

. . . .

Almost all of us occasionally need to dream old and new dreams about living in the fast lane or even on the edge. We need to dream about the strange and impossible so that we can return refreshed to the mundane and ordinary. The books discussed in this chapter—adventures, mysteries, and the supernatural—provide the challenges and the vicarious thrills and danger we crave.

These genres are usually considered to provide pleasure reading rather than reading that develops the intellect. We recently heard, for example, an argument against a faculty member's promotion to full professor because "She reads mysteries," the words said with the utmost disdain. Presumably if the woman read mysteries, she was intellectually incapable of doing real research.

Betty Rosenberg wrote, "Rosenberg's First Law of Reading: never apologize for your reading tastes."[1] Sensible as this advice is, most of us worry when we're caught reading something that someone, someplace might not find intellectually acceptable. That does not mean that we don't get goose bumps from a supernatural thriller or read ourselves to a satisfying sleep with a good mystery. Defensively, we make claims that are hard to substantiate—for example, we claim that mysteries are psychologically helpful to our inner-well being, or we claim that horror stories are a substitute for aggression. Those claims may have some truth, but they are hard to prove.

We are on safer ground if we accept the simple truth that reading for pleasure is a worthy activity and goal, in and of itself. If we, or our students, get more than pleasure, serendipity is working for us. Why some English teachers and some librarians insist that virtually all reading have an intellectual justification is one of life's great mysteries. Real English teachers and real librarians know that pleasure reading is worthwhile without any other defense.

Adventure Stories

"Once upon a time" is a magical phrase. Stated directly or implied, it opens every adventure tale and suggests action and excitement to follow. We may care about the

young adults

The books discussed in this chapter have enticed a whole new group of kids into becoming regular visitors to public libraries.

people in these adventures, but we care equally—or more—about the actions that follow. The greatest of these actions is implied violence, things we fear will happen. The pace and tempo force the action to move faster and faster and to speed us into the tale.

The most common story of pure adventure, almost devoid of characterization, pits one human being against another. Richard Connell's "The Most Dangerous Game," perhaps *the* classic adventure short story, reduces the cast to two people, the big game hunter Sanger Rainsford and General Zaroff, in a simple setting, on an apparently deserted island. Before being accidentally cast ashore, Rainsford and a friend had talked about the nature of hunting and debated whether an animal can feel fear or impending death. Rainsford had said, "Be a realist. The world is made up of two classes—the hunter and the huntee," words he regrets when he meets the apparently highly civilized Zaroff. Rainsford soon suspects that Zaroff is nearly mad. Once Zaroff makes clear that only one animal—a human—is worth hunting, few readers can stop reading, and we're off into a frightening tale of adventure.

The better adventure stories demand more than mere excitement and action (Table 5.1). Good writers must provide believable characters, at least a likable and imperfect (and probably young) protagonist and a wily and dangerous antagonist (or villain), but because we are primarily interested in the action, we're likely to be irritated by long descriptive or meditative passages. Writers must reveal characterization through the plot—what could happen, what might happen, and how do all the incidents tie together.

TABLE 5.1

SUGGESTIONS FOR EVALUATING ADVENTURE STORIES

A good adventure story has most of the positive qualities generally associated with good fiction. In addition it usually has:	A poor adventure story may have the negative qualities generally associated with poor fiction. It is particularly prone to have:
A likable protagonist with whom young readers can identify	A protagonist who is too exaggerated or too stereotyped to be believeable
An adventure that readers can imagine happening to themselves	Nothing really exciting about the adventure
Efficient characterization	Only stereotyped characters
An interesting setting that enhances the story without getting in the way of the plot	A long drawn-out conclusion after the climax has been reached
Action that draws readers into the plot within the first page or so of the story	

We want surprises and turns of the screw. Heroes become trapped and the only way to safety is through even greater jeopardy. Of the three basic conflicts, adventure tales usually focus on person against person, although person against nature and person against self may become important as the tale unfolds and the protagonist faces frustration and possible failure. Readers of adventure tales feel much the same way about taking a chance with adventure as did Susan Hiscock. For 50 years she and her husband sailed the globe, Hiscock never letting loose of her wanderlust. She was a fan of Arthur Ransome's books, and she and her husband painted a motto from Ransome over their cabin door: "Grab a chance and you won't be sorry for a might-have-been."[2] That's a great motto for reading or living.

The most important literary device found in adventure stories is verisimilitude. With so much emphasis on danger, writers must provide realistic details galore to assure us, despite some inner misgivings, that the tale is possible and believable. We must believe that whatever the hero's frustrations, the cliffhanging scenes are possible.

Robb White's *Deathwatch* epitomizes the elements of adventure novels—person versus person, person versus nature, person versus self, conflicts, tension, thrills, chills, and a hero frustrated at every turn by an inventive, devious, and cruel villain. The first paragraph forces us into the action and introduces the two actors:

> "There he is!" Madec whispered. "Keep still!" There had been a movement up on the ridge of the mountain. For a moment something had appeared between the two rock outcrops.
> "I didn't see any horns," Ben said.
> "Keep quiet!" Madec whispered fiercely.

We know from those few words that *Deathwatch* has something to do with hunting, although we have no reason yet to suspect that hunting will become an ominous metaphor. We recognize that the name *Madec* sounds harsh and seems vaguely related to the word *mad,* again without recognizing how prescient we are. Within the next few pages, we learn how carefully White has placed the clues before us. Ben crouches with his little .22 Hornet and watches Madec with his "beautifully made .385 Magnum Mauser action on a Winchester 70 stock with enough power to knock down an elephant—or turn a sleeping Gila monster into a splatter" and remembers that Madec had been willing to shoot anything that moved.

> Madec huddled over his gun. There was an intensity in his eyes far beyond that of just hunting a sheep. It was the look of murder.

And murder is present. Before long, Madec takes a shot at a bighorn sheep, which turns out to be an old desert prospector—now quite dead—and he asks Ben to quash the incident and forget it ever happened. Ben refuses, and the book is off and running. So is Ben, running for his life, without gun, water, or food, amid hostile desert mountains and sand and a killing gun.

Madec personifies the maddened but crafty villain, able to read Ben's mind and forestall his attempts to get clothes, weapons, or water. We are almost certain Ben will win, but we wonder because Madec is an extraordinary opponent. At each of Madec's devious turns to stop Ben from escaping, we doubt that sanity and virtue will win, just as we should in a good adventure novel. Ben changes from a calm, rational young man to a frightened, desperate animal and then into a cold, dangerous person who must think as Madec thinks to win out over the villain. Madec begins with all the power on his side—guns, water, food, and wealth. Given reality, we know that Madec must win, but given our sense of rightness and justice, we believe that he cannot be allowed to win. Ben has little interest in right or wrong after the first few pages. His interest is more elemental and believable—simple survival until he can escape.

Adventure stories are popular because boredom chafes at our souls and crowds out of our minds such practical concerns as safety and caution. But the human body—at least our own—reminds us all too quickly of risk. This may be why we prefer our adventures to come through books or, even better, through movies, in which trick photography and special effects can make it easier for viewers to forget that losing is more common than winning.

Because the theme of going up against incredible odds and winning is so appealing, it is not surprising that adventure and survival stories appear in many different genres. Steven Callahan's *Adrift: Seventy-six Days Lost at Sea* is a fine book about a true personal experience, but it is also a book of adventure. Robert C. O'Brien's *Z for Zachariah* is a dystopian look at the future, but it is also an adventure novel. Kathryn Lasky's *Beyond the Divide* is a fine novel about moving west, but it is also a story of many adventures. Avi's *The True Confessions of Charlotte Doyle* is a story of a young girl traveling by ship to America in 1832, but it is also one of the most frightening and thrilling adventure stories of our time. What all these stories have in common is a young protagonist who goes against incredible odds and comes out a survivor.

WILL HOBBS
On Kids and the Natural World

I believe there is a part of the human heart that longs for wild places. We yearn for the connection to nature that helped form our consciousness over the millennia. Our sense of beauty derives from natural forms; our sense of adventure and discovery, in books and in real life, finds ready fulfillment on the grandest stage of them all, the outdoors.

The letters I get from kids, no matter the postmark, almost always mention some of the wild places I've drawn as pictures for their imaginations. The Window and the Rio Grande Pyramid in *Bearstone* and *Beardance,* the Grand Canyon's "River of Blue" (the Little Colorado) in *Downriver,* the red-walled canyon of the Escalante in *The Big Wander.* Although the human drama is central in all my books, the connection of the characters to place is nearly as important.

I've always felt that our connection to the American earth is the great subject of American literature, and it has been and will continue to be one of the major subjects of American young adult literature as well. My first hope for my novels is that they tell a good story, that the reader will keep turning the pages and will hate to see the story end. Beyond that, I try to weave lore about the natural world and these special places that I know and love into the fabric of my stories. I believe that if kids come to care about and identify with the characters, they will also learn more about and ultimately care more about preserving the treasures of our natural world—the wellsprings of our sense of wonder.

It's joy and hope I'm wishing for kids. A connection to nature has a healing power for a young person and offers the possibility of journeys, challenges, and personal growth. I wish they could all raft a river or climb a mountain or milk a goat or watch seeds sprout that they have planted in the earth. It's gratifying to hear from kids that my stories have led them to their own adventures in the outdoors. In *Kokopelli's Flute,* I've attempted to glorify gardening. If I get letters from kids telling me that they've planted some seeds after reading my book, I'll be a happy man.

Will Hobbs's books include *Kokopelli's Flute,* 1995; *Beardance,* 1993; *The Big Wonder,* 1992; *Downriver,* 1991; and *Bearstone,* 1989, all Atheneum.

One of the most dramatic ways that people challenge themselves *and* nature is through mountain climbing. Recommended accounts include Sir Edmund Hillary's *Nothing Venture, Nothing Win* and Arlene Blum's *Annapurna: A Woman's Place,* which tells the story of 13 women climbers, two of whom reached the top while two died. Elaine Brook and Julie Donnelly's *The Windhorse* shows how a mountaineer taught a blind woman to climb. Julie Tullis's *Clouds from Both Sides* is the biography of a woman who at 47 conquered K2 and died two days later. David Roberts's *Deborah: A Wilderness Narrative* tells of an attempted two-person climb of Mount Deborah in Alaska; Tom Holzol and Audrey Salkeld's *First on Everest: The Mystery of Mallory and Irvine* explores the disappearance of George Mallory and Andrew Irvine, who in June of 1924 were seen for the last time 800 feet from the top of Mt. Everest.

Person-against-person stories include spy thrillers such as John Le Carré's *The Spy Who Came in from the Cold,* James Lehrer's *Blue Hearts: A Novel,* William F. Buckley, Jr.'s *A Very Private Plot*, and Len Deighton's *Faith.* The murder mysteries discussed later in this chapter also fall into this category, and so do some of our oldest legends (e.g., that of Robin Hood) and our newest science fiction (e.g., *Star Trek)*. With either of these types of conflict, the satisfaction comes because the protagonist is able to win through overcoming his or her fears and weaknesses, which makes the stories also person against self.

Adventure Writers for Young Adults

Gary Paulsen is one of the best writers for young readers in the last decade. *Canyons* and *The River* are relatively quiet adventure stories, but in *Hatchet* Paulsen has written one of the better adventure stories of our times. Thirteen-year-old Brian Robeson is the only passenger in a small plane when the pilot suddenly dies from a heart attack; the plane goes down far off course in the Canadian wilderness and the boy must save himself from starvation as well as a multitude of other dangers with only the help of a hatchet and his wits. One of our students, Julie Resner, commented, "Not only does Paulsen write an exciting adventure story, he writes it in a sensitive, almost poetic style. His terse, staccato rhythms enhanced the atmosphere and mood." Then she cites an early passage from *Hatchet.*

> He tried to move, but pain hammered into him and made his breath shorten into gasps and he stopped, his legs still in the water.
> Pain.
> Memory.
> He turned again and the sun came across the water, late sun, cut into his eyes and made him turn away.
> It was over then. The crash.
> He was alive (Hatchet 33).

Will Hobbs is another talented writer whose books reflect his interest in hiking, whitewater rafting, archaeology, and natural history. *Bearstone,* about a Native American boy sent to live with an old rancher whose wife has died, combines adventure with a story of growth and friendship. *Downriver,* the story of a group of boys and girls sent to an outdoor program designed to help troubled teenagers, comes closer to being a pure adventure. Jesse and her companions steal the counselor's van and rafts and drive to the Grand Canyon for whitewater rafting on their own.

One of the strangest adventure stories of recent years is Julian F. Thompson's *The Grounding of Group Six*. Some admittedly misfit teenagers, despised by their parents, who have paid to have them killed, survive the special school where they have been sent. Thompson's novel works because he makes us care about these young people, because the novel is genuinely thrilling, and mostly because Thompson has a delightful, and sometimes morbid, sense of humor that makes the book often extraordinarily funny.

Two gifted English writers for young adults may be missed when we search for good adventure stories. Gillian Cross's *On the Edge* is about a young son of a well-known London journalist who is kidnapped by a terrorist group. It is a story of adventure and mind games and the psychology of terrorism. Peter Dickinson's *The Seventh Raven* also concerns terrorism, this time about a radical group who planned to kidnap the young son of an ambassador to England. Dickinson's novel has more tension per page as the terrorists come closer and closer to their aim.

Harry Mazer's *The Island Keeper* is one of the most effective, yet quiet, adventure stories, here a story of person versus self. Cleo Murphy, fat and rich and lonely, has recently lost her mother and sister to death, her father is rich and cold and distant, and her grandmother is rich and cold and arrogant. On a flight from Chicago to New York to attend summer camp, Cleo decides on a whim to spend the summer by herself on Duck Island in Clear Lake near her father's property.

She learns early on that the cabin she had expected to live in has burned down so she desperately finds a tiny cave for temporary shelter. Naive about camping and nature, Cleo leaves her food exposed and animals take all her supplies.

That is when Cleo begins to realize that she is alone and this is no longer a bit of whimsy. She learns to catch and eat raw fish, she learns to eat off the land, and she acquires a pet, of sorts, a small owl with a bad wing. She learns that the land can betray her as she becomes desperately ill from a careless choice of roots, she decides to leave only to discover that in a storm a tree had fallen on her canoe, and then she recognizes she is truly alone and truly in control of her own life. By this time ice has begun to form on the water and fish become less and less likely as food, and Cleo knows she that must kill a doe or she will die. Not too long before, Cleo could never have snared the deer, much less killed it, but by this time Cleo is ready.

> Where Cleo had spread the twigs across the trap, the big doe stopped, sniffed, turned aside. The second deer followed, but the one with the bad leg hesitated, sniffed, then began browsing. It found one of the apples and searched for more.
>
> The deer was standing directly over the snare. Cleo leaned forward. The sapling whipped into the air. The deer recoiled, one of its hind legs caught by the rope. Cleo darted forward. The deer leaped up. A hoof caught Cleo in the shoulder as she drove the knife into its body. The animal cried out. She drove the knife in again. The deer grunted, sighed quietly, died. Cleo looked around. She was acutely aware of every single thing, of the silence, of her aloneness.
>
> The two other deer had disappeared. She shuddered. A black smear spread across the velvet fur. Nearby, a woodpecker hammered at a rotten apple limb.

Mysteries

Why are mysteries so enduringly popular? Basically, they are unrealistic and, as mystery writers cheerfully admit, usually have almost nothing to do with real-life detection by police or private agents. They demand that we suspend most of our disbelief, and the faithful gladly do so. Mysteries are mere games, but we love games. Some of us claim that we want to beat the detective to the murderer, but we rarely do, and when we do succeed, we feel cheated.

The popularity of mystery movies (see Focus Box 5.1) and the number of hotels, ships, and individuals who sponsor parties in which a mock murder takes

FOCUS BOX 5.1

Movies with Real Mysteries

And Then There Were None (1945, 98 min., black and white; Director: René Clair; with Walter Huston and Louis Hayward) Ten people, all guilty of crimes but never convicted, are invited to a lonely island and murdered one by one.

The Big Sleep (1946, 114 min., black and white; Director: Howard Hawks; with Humphrey Bogart and Lauren Bacall) Mix Philip Marlowe with a wealthy family and you may get murder. From Raymond Chandler's novel.

Charlie Chan in London (1934, 79 min., black and white; Director: Eugene Forde; with Warner Oland) The detective saves a condemned man. Other fans believe *Charlie Chan in Panama* (1940, 67 min., black and white; Director: Norman Foster; with Sidney Toler) is the best Chan mystery.

Chinatown (1974, 131 min., color; Director: Roman Polanski; with Jack Nicholson, Faye Dunaway, and John Huston) Set in the 1930s and influenced by Chandler, an enigmatic detective falls for a femme fatale and finds murder.

Laura (1944, 85 min., black and white; Director: Otto Preminger; with Gene Tierney, Dana Andrews, and Clifton Webb) Vera Caspary's novel about a detective who falls in love with a corpse who doesn't stay dead.

The Maltese Falcon (1941, 100 min., black and white; Director: John Huston; with Humphrey Bogart, Mary Astor, Sydney Greenstreet, and Peter Lorre) The search for the fabulous statue and the killer of Bogart's partner. From Dashiell Hammett's novel.

Murder, My Sweet (1944, 95 min., black and white; Director: Edward Dmytryk; with Dick Powell and Claire Trevor) Philip Marlowe tries to find an ex-con's old girlfriend and finds murder. From Raymond Chandler's *Farewell, My Lovely*. The 1975 film of Chandler's novel under the same name (97 min., color; Director: Dick Richards; with Robert Mitchum and Charlotte Rampling) is also worth seeing.

Narrow Margin (1952, 70 min., black and white; Director: Richard Fleischer; with Charles McGraw and Marie Winsor) A cop accompanies a gangster's wife on a train trip to a trial. Much better than the 1990 movie version.

The Spiral Staircase (1946, 83 min., black and white; Director: Robert Siodmak; with Dorothy McGuire, George Brent, and Ethel Barrymore) A madman kills those who are handicapped; McGuire plays a maid who is mute.

The Thin Man (1934, 93 min., black and white; Director: W. S. Van Dyke; with William Powell and Myrna Loy) The death of an inventor working on a secret sets off the first of the "Thin Man" series. Great mystery-comedy.

place, with the partygoers playing detectives, shows the entertainment value of mayhem, murder, and suspense. Because of the high entertainment value of mysteries and their sometimes easy reading level, many mysteries published for a general audience find their way into the hands of young adults.

Daniel's detection of the guilty Elders in "The Story of Susanna" in the *Apocrypha* may be the world's first detective story. Critics generally agree, however, that the modern mystery begins with Edgar Allan Poe's "The Murders in the Rue Morgue," although "The Purloined Letter" is more satisfying today. Poe's detective, C. Auguste Dupin, is unquestionably the first criminal investigator.

Dime novel imitations of Poe soon appeared, notably Old Sleuth, Young Sleuth, Old King Brady, Cap Collier, and—best of them all—Nick Carter. What is usually said to be the first detective novel was published in 1868—Wilkie Collins's *The Moonstone*. The world's greatest fictional detective appeared only a few years later when Sherlock Holmes (and his ever-faithful and often befuddled Dr. Watson) moved out of Arthur Conan Doyle's *A Study in Scarlet* and into the affections of thousands of readers.

Holmes was followed by other distinctive detectives—brilliant and cocky, like Jacques Futrelle's Professor S. F. X. Van Deusen, or brilliant and humble, like G. K. Chesterton's Father Brown. Others followed and won their fans—Agatha Christie's Miss Marple and Hercule Poirot, Erle Stanley Gardner's Perry Mason, Dashiell Hammett's Sam Spade, and Raymond Chandler's Philip Marlowe. Where they left off, contemporary writers and detectives have picked up.

Writer and critic Hillary Waugh has said that the skeletons on which mysteries hang are "nothing more nor less than a series of ironclad rules." The rules are essential to present the puzzle properly and to ensure fair play. He lists them as follows:

Rule One: All clues discovered by the detective must be made available to the reader.
Rule Two: The murderer must be introduced early.
Rule Three: The crime must be significant.
Rule Four: There must be detection.
Rule Five: The number of suspects must be known, and the murderer must be among them.
Rule Six: The reader, as part of the game of fair play, has the right to expect that nothing will be included in the book that does not relate to or in some way bear on the puzzle.[3]

Herbert Resnicow provides an intriguing list of 15 rules for the classic, or golden-age, mystery.[4]

Types of Mysteries

The characteristics of the traditional murder mystery are well-known and relatively fixed, although devotees are always interested in variations on the theme of murder. A mystery short story may settle for theft, but a novel, of course, demands murder. Accompanying crimes such as blackmail or embezzlement may add to the delights of murder, but they never replace murder. The ultimate crime normally takes place a few chapters into the book, after readers have been introduced to major and minor characters, including the victim and those who might long for his death. The detective appears, clues are scattered, the investigation proceeds, the detective solves the case, the guilty are punished, the innocent are restored to their rightful place, and the world becomes right again.

Shannon Ocork classifies mysteries into these six types.[5]

1. *The amateur detective:* At least in the older stories, the amateur detective was male (e.g., C. August Dupin or Sherlock Holmes and later Rex Stout's Nero Wolfe). These detectives are altruistic and usually optimistic. They are bright and see what others do not. Sometimes called traditional, golden-age, or classic mysteries (see some of them included in Focus Box 5.2), these flourished from the 1920s through the 1940s.

2. *The cozy mystery:* These stories are close to the amateur detective stories. They are usually set in a small English village, although New England is increasingly popular. Agatha Christie, who began writing in the 1920s, is the most obvious writer of cozies. She scattered her best books throughout her life. Her 1939 *And Then There Were None* is her best book without a detective. Others

---

 FOCUS BOX 5.2

Mostly Old Mysteries Too Good to Miss

And Then There Were None by Agatha Christie. Dodd, Mead, 1939. Guilty people who escaped punishment are isolated and killed off one by one.

Buried for Pleasure by Edmund Crispin (Bruce Montgomery). Lippincott, 1949. A professor in England takes a holiday to run for political office, only to learn that death is easier to find than votes.

Eye of the Storm by Marcia Muller. Mysterious Press, 1989. Sharon McCone, private investigator for a law firm, visits her sister, who's getting a bed-and-breakfast ready for business in the Sacramento delta. Then death comes visiting.

The Greek Coffin Mystery by Ellery Queen (Frederic Dannay and Manfred B. Lee). Little, Brown, 1932. An art dealer dies, as does a forger, and a great painting is stolen. Ellery Queen challenges the reader to solve the case before he does.

The Maltese Falcon by Dashiell Hammett. Knopf, 1930. Sam Spade and others search for a statue of a black bird worth $2 million.

A Murder Is Announced by Agatha Christie. Dodd, Mead, 1950. The best of all the Miss Marple mysteries. A murder is announced in an English village newspaper and the murder happens on schedule.

Murder on the Yellow Brick Road by Stuart Kaminsky. St. Martin's, 1977. The first Toby Peters story about a private investigator in the 1930s and 1940s. Here he investigates a killing on the set of *The Wizard of Oz*.

The Old Contemptibles by Martha Grimes. Little, Brown, 1991. Melrose Plant and Scotland Yard's Richard Jury work on a case in the Lake District in England involving a family with a history of unnatural deaths.

Phantom Lady by William Irish (Cornell Woolrich). Simon & Schuster, 1942. An innocent man is convicted of murder, and the woman who loves him sets out to find the murderer.

An Unsuitable Job for a Woman by P. D. James. Scribner's, 1972. Cordelia Gray investigates a case officially called a suicide, but the victim's father believes it is murder.

include her 1950 *A Murder Is Announced,* a Miss Marple book, and her 1968 *By the Pricking of My Thumbs,* in which the usually tiresome Tommy and Tuppence Beresford stumble into a believable mystery.

3. *The puzzle:* These stories are exercises in ingenuity as we are led into an intricate murder, with the detective daring us to figure out the end of the story. Ellery Queen's early mysteries had a "Challenge to the Reader" about three or four chapters from the end, when the writer announced that we had all the clues Queen had and should be able to solve the mystery. Luckily, we rarely succeeded.

4. *The private detective:* These hard-boiled mysteries differ from other mysteries in significant ways. Private detectives lack altruistic motives. They enter cases for pay rather than for love of the chase or intellectual fondness for the puzzle. Working out of a cheerless office and around even less cheerful people, they are tired and cynical about the courts, the police, class distinctions, and life in general. Many are former police officers who left the force under a cloud. They have seen too much of the seamy world to feel hope for anything or anyone, and they know that detective work is hard and mostly routine and dull. With patience, any bright person could do what they do. Not only does violence come with the territory, it is the territory. Moreover, we are surprised, even disappointed, if the violence isn't there.

5. *The police procedural:* Police procedurals are often the most believable mysteries because the central characters are officers doing their mundane jobs and tracking down murderers with scientific methods and machines available only to the police. The books of Ed McBain are probably the most popular police procedurals today.

6. *The thriller:* These are usually spy thrillers. They may have bits of mystery tucked into them, but as in Ian Fleming's James Bond series, the mystery involves not so much who did it as how our hero can escape his latest impossible situation with even more than his usual derring-do.

Today's Popular Writers

Some of today's mystery writers (see Focus Box 5.2) defy neat classifications, but their books may share the same characteristics. Sue Grafton is one of the hottest new writers, and her detective, Kinsey Millhone, is a great creation. Grafton's alphabetical series (e.g., *"A" Is for Alibi* currently through *"L" Is for Lawless*) shows Millhone working as an insurance investigator in Santa Teresa (the name Ross Macdonald gave Santa Barbara in his mysteries). Readers meet Kinsey Millhone in *"A" Is for Alibi:*

My name is Kinsey Millhone. I'm a private investigator, licensed by the state of California. I'm 32 years old, twice divorced, no kids. The day before yesterday I killed someone and the fact weighs heavily on my mind. I'm a nice person and I have a lot of friends. My apartment is small but I like living in a cramped space. I've lived in trailers most of my life, but lately they've been getting too elaborate for my taste, so now I live in one room, a "bachelorette." I don't have houseplants. I spend a lot of time on the road and I don't like leaving things behind. Aside from the hazards of my profession, my life has always been ordinary, uneventful, and good. Killing someone feels odd to me and I haven't quite sorted it through. I've already given a statement to the police, which I initialed page by page and then signed. I filled out a similar report for the office files. The language in both documents is neutral, the terminology oblique, and neither says quite enough.

In this relatively short paragraph, Grafton lets us know who Kinsey Millhone is, not merely the obvious information but details that tell us about the real Millhone—her taste in apartments, her dislike for stuff she'll have to leave behind, the effect of her killing another human being, and her pawky wit ("The day before yesterday I killed someone and the fact weighs heavily on my mind").

In beginning her story this way, Grafton was following the advice of the Roman poet and critic Horace, who urged writers to begin *in medias res*. In his brilliant police procedural series, the 87th Precinct, Ed McBain (Evan Hunter) uses a similar technique in *Widows*. But notice how he gets more quickly into the plot because readers already know detective Steve Carella from earlier books:

She'd been brutally stabbed and slashed more times than Carella chose to imagine. The knife seemed to have been a weapon of convenience, a small paring knife that evidently had been taken from the bartop where a bottle opener with a matching wooden handle sat beside a half-full pitcher of martinis, an ice bucket, and a whole lemon from which a narrow sliver of skin was missing.

No one writes police procedurals like McBain. His books are fiction, but they describe a real world inhabited by policemen of the 87th Precinct in Isola (presumably New York City). Although they often feature detective Steve Carella, they are mostly about the plodding, lackluster grind of police officers sifting through this and blundering through that to find out who has done what to whom. *Kiss* is about betrayal and bitterness, focusing on Carella, who attends the trial of the man who killed his father. *Romance* is about interracial love tinged with the irony of the title in any police procedural.

Patricia Cornwell has written several police procedurals featuring Virginia Chief Medical Examiner Kay Scarpetta. *From Potter's Field* shows the mind and actions of a psychopathic murderer and the problems Scarpetta faces in understanding that mind and those actions. As with many other police matters, humor and irony are hard to find in this book, although Scarpetta's friend, Capt. Pete Marino, has a nicely balanced view of life. Janwillem van de Wetering has written many tales of the Amsterdam police, particularly Adjutant Henk Grijpstra and Sgt. Rinus de Gier. *Just a Corpse at Twilight* is a recent entry into an impressive series of books. Michael Connelly's *The Concrete Blonde* is both a police procedural and a courtroom drama.

Sarah Paretsky is another hot mystery writer. *Indemnity Only* introduces us to her V.I. Warshawski, private investigator, who is tough and drinks Johnny Walker

Black Label. Proof that Warshawski is not typical of most private eyes comes in the first few lines of *Guardian Angel:*

> Hot kisses covered my face, dragging me from deep sleep to the rim of consciousness. I groaned and slid deeper under the covers, hoping to sink back into the well of dreams.

But it's not male passion that bothers V. I.; it's her dog, Peppy, wanting to be taken on a walk. Peppy is also due for puppies, and the old woman whose male dog impregnated Peppy has irritated many of her neighbors with her free-roaming canines. When the old woman winds up in the hospital with a broken hip, some neighbors take her dogs to be destroyed. V. I. is outraged at this nasty trick and sets out to right the wrong. When another person who lives in her building hires her to find a lost friend, Warshawski is off and running on the best of her cases thus far.

In the February 1992 *English Journal,* the editors published responses to the question, "Who is your favorite writer of detective fiction?" Tony Hillerman won by a margin of ten to one. One of the reasons for Hillerman's popularity is that he does such a good job of establishing atmosphere. He does what the fine mystery writer P. D. James[6] argues all writers must do—give a sense of place. For example, Hillerman begins *The Listening Woman* by letting us see, hear, and feel the world of the Indian Reservation:

> The southwest wind picked up turbulence around the San Francisco Peak, howled across the emptiness of the Moenkopi plateau, and made a thousand strange sounds in windows of the old Hopi villages at Shongopovi and Second Mesa. Two hundred vacant miles to the north and east, it sand-blasted the stone sculptures of Monument Valley Navajo Tribal park and whistled eastward across the maze of canyons on the Utah-Arizona border. Over the arid immensity of the Nokaito Bench it filled the blank blue sky with a rushing sound. At the hogan of Hosteen Tso, at 3:17 P.M., it gusted and eddied, and formed a dust devil, which crossed the wagon track and raced with a swirling roar across Margaret Cigaret's old Dodge pickup truck and past the Tso brush arbor.

Hillerman's place may not be our place, or a place we know, but it is a place we can recognize, and it is a place we will soon know. Hillerman has come close to breaking the boundary of mystery writers and being accepted as a fine novelist without regard to a specific genre. His Navajo police novels began appearing in 1970 with *The Blessing Way,* in which we meet officer Joe Leaphorn's detection and the villain who uses Navajo religion to protect himself. The Indian lore and the religious aspects of the book are accurate, just as they are in later Hillerman novels, including *The Dance Hall of the Dead, The Listening Woman, The Ghostway, The Skinwalkers, Coyote Waits,* and *Sacred Clowns.* Joe Leaphorn and Jim Chee, Hillerman's detectives, have the best of two worlds, the Anglo and the Native American. Although they are often confused about who and what they are, they always find that ultimately they are Native American.

[handwritten margin note: in winter mysteries is such a good setting description anyone can picture it]

Two writers who have established themselves as benchmark writers against whom others are judged are Robert B. Parker and Dick Francis. In *Double Deuce,* Parker has his one-name Boston detective, Spenser, and his sidekick, Hawk, searching for the killer of a 14-year-old girl and her 3-year-old daughter in a Boston housing project. And in *Walking Shadow* Spenser is bored being part of an experimental drama theater, but his interest rises when there's murder. In his *Wild Horses,* Francis' thirty-third novel, a movie is being made about a 20-year-old death when more death follows. Francis is one of the rare writers of mystery to write his own autobiography, and *The Sport of Queens: The Autobiography of Francis* is great fun, although there is far more about his horse racing days than his writing.

Several English writers besides Francis deserve readers among young adults. Robert Barnard is a prolific writer of quality books. In *A Hovering of Vultures,* Barnard spoofs Brontë fans who have traveled to Yorkshire to honor the author only to find murder. *The Masters of the House*, Barnard's best book in years, is about two young children who have to take control of a household when their mother dies in childbirth and their out-of-work father falls apart. Everything might have worked out if a nosy woman had not been found dead on their property.

Several American authors also deserve readers. Nevada Barr began with *Track of the Cat*, a novel set in the Guadalupe Mountains Park in Texas and featuring a National Park Service ranger, Anna Pigeon. It is a delightful book, and it was followed by *A Superior Death*, this time locating Anna Pigeon in Isle Royale National Park in Michigan. A third, *Ill Wind*, features Anna in Mesa Verde National Park. All three books are great fun, beautifully plotted, and more humorous than most mysteries.

Alaska may have been slow in picking up detectives and private eyes, but in the last few years Alaska has done quite well. Sue Henry's *Murder on the Iditarod Trail* was soon followed by an even better writer, Dana Stabenow, and her Alaskan Native American investigator, Kate Shugak. *A Cold Day for Murder, A Fatal Flaw, Dead in the Water, A Cold-Blooded Business,* and *Play With Fire* are five enjoyable, offbeat, and soundly constructed mysteries. Scott Young's *The Shaman's Knife* features Matteesie, a native detective for a mystery set in northern Canada. If the mystery tails off a bit near the end, it conveys a sense of time and place about a real people existing in extreme cold.

Mysteries Written for Teenagers

Mysteries written specifically for teenagers are usually shorter than books described in the previous section. Protagonists (i.e., those who solve the crime) are bright young people who see what others do not. Violence is more likely to be on the edges, or outside, of the story, and usually the person killed is connected to the protagonist (e.g., a parent or other relative, a boyfriend or girlfriend, or perhaps an adult that the young person liked or admired). The young person recovers from the grief through doing the detective work.

Of mystery writers for young adults, three authors, Patricia Windsor, Jay Bennett, and Joan Lowery Nixon, stand out. *The Christmas Killer* is not Windsor's first book, but it is her finest atmospheric thriller. A Connecticut town is terrorized by a killer who begins with Nancy Emerson before Thanksgiving. Rose Potter starts having dreams in which the murdered girl appears and hints where her body can be found. The police question Rose's honesty and sanity, wonder if she's not involved in the killing, and finally realize that Rose may be in danger herself. Sections dealing with Rose's story and the murders of more young girls alternate with sections in which the deranged killer speaks about his lust for blood. He says:

> Killing is not a bad thing. Death is easeful, death is kind. I am friends with death. It cools the boiling blood. Blood is as red as a Christmas ribbon. Blood ties a body like a Christmas package. Blood is the color of Christmas berries, baubles, all things of joy. Why shouldn't I find joy in blood?

And he does. But in the last two paragraphs of the book, imprisoned as the killer is, we realize the story may not be over. He writes:

> Let a little time pass. I will send her a letter, tied up in my own blood and sealing wax. She will know me from my work. And she will think of me again.
> And, before long, I will escape this place, and I will be seeing her again.

Here's an eerie and scary book, just right for the night when a reader is home alone with the wind blowing and the house creaking.

Jay Bennett's novels rarely disappoint. *Deathman, Do Not Follow Me,* his first book, is less a mystery than a fascinating story of a loner. Later books have added to Bennett's reputation and brought him many young readers. *Say Hello to the Hit Man* is a marvelously suspenseful book about a young man who gets threatening phone calls from a gangland hit man. *Sing Me a Death Song* is a cliffhanger in which a young man is the only person who can save his mother's life.

Joan Lowery Nixon's thrillers are even more popular with young adults. *Whispers From the Dead* is about a near-death drowning and a spirit that seems to shadow the protagonist thereafter. *The Dark and Deadly Pool* concerns a young girl who discovers a body floating in a pool, a typical ploy for Nixon that pushes a young adult into a sudden crisis. *Shadow Maker* is about going to a new school and investigative reporting and environmental problems. Cody Garnett's friend in *Spirit Seeker* is accused of murder, and Cody sets out to find the truth.

A few other writers deserve our attention and readership from young adults. M. E. Kerr's books about John Fell are mysterious and always fun to read. Walter Dean Myers's *The Mouse Rap* is one of those rare mysteries, lighthearted and happy, yet telling a mystery that is unusually entertaining. Avi's *Wolf Rider* may not be Avi at his best, but the eerie phone calls Andy Zadinski gets would be a real worry to any of us. Chap Reaver's *Mote* is a fast-moving and increasingly intriguing book about Mote, the protagonist's friend accused of murder. *The Man in the Woods* by Rosemary Wells is an atmospheric thriller about a young girl who is in danger because she knows more than she should about a murder.

Stories of the Supernatural

The supernatural has been an important part of our conscious fascination and our subconscious fear ever since humanity learned to communicate. That ambivalence may go back to prehistoric times, when shadows in a cave and light and dark mystified and frightened humans. We have demanded answers to the unknown but have rarely found them, and so we have settled on myths and legends about superior and unseen beings. Such explanations are satisfying because when we are fighting the inexplicable, they make winning more pleasing and losing more acceptable.

Amidst all our modern knowledge and sophistication, we hold onto our fascination with the unknowable. We delight in chambers of horrors, tunnels of terror, and haunted houses. We claim to be rational beings, yet we read astrology charts. We mock the superstitions of others yet hold as pets one or two of our own, joking all the time when we toss salt over our shoulder, refuse to walk under a ladder, avoid black cats, and knock on wood. We follow customs without wondering why they came about. Black is assumed to be the appropriate dress for funerals because it is dark and gloomy and demonstrates solemnity. We may not know that black was worn at a time lost in history because spirits, sometimes malignant or perhaps indignant, were thought to linger near a corpse for a year. Wearing black made it more difficult for these evil spirits to see the living. As long as spirits were around, danger lurked. Hence, long mourning periods in black dress.

Greek and Roman literature abounds with supernatural elements, but so does Elizabethan literature. Whether Shakespeare believed in ghosts or witches is anyone's guess. Certainly, his audiences often did, and they apparently delighted in or were frightened by incidents in plays such as *Macbeth, Hamlet,* and *The Tempest.*

The Gothic novel of unexplained terror and horror began with Horace Walpole's *The Castle of Otranto* in 1764. Success bred imitators, and Clara Reeves's *The Old English Baron* appeared in 1780; William Beckford's *Vathek* was published in 1786. The two greatest of the Gothics appeared in the 1790s: Ann Radcliffe's *The Mysteries of Udolpho* and Matthew Gregory Lewis's *The Monk.* Although Jane Austen did much to demolish the fad with *Northanger Abbey* in 1818, that posthumously published novel did not prevent Mary Shelley's 1818 *Frankenstein, or the Modern Prometheus,* the apotheosis of the genre, from winning admirers. The Romantic poets and prose writers continued to be half in love with the dark and the unknown, as much of Coleridge and Keats and the novels of the Brontë sisters illustrate.

Some radio shows capitalized on our fears, as anyone old enough to have enjoyed "Inner Sanctum" or "The Whistler" will testify. The supernatural never worked as well on television, perhaps because it is too literal a medium. But horror movies (see Focus Box 5.3) have almost always been popular with the masses, and they have sometimes produced masterpieces of our internal struggles against evil or the unknown (e.g., the episode with Michael Redgrave playing a schizophrenic ventriloquist in *Dead of Night*).

Supernatural novels have well-established ground rules. Settings are usually in an eerie or haunted house or in a place where a mysterious event occurred years

FOCUS BOX 5.3

Movies to Give You the Delights of Terror, Suspense, and the Supernatural

The Abominable Dr. Phibes (1971, 94 min., color; Director: Robert Fuest; with Vincent Price)   Scarred in a car crash that killed his wife, a mad doctor sets out to revenge his wife's death in a series of macabre murders.

The Body Snatchers (1945, 77 min., black and white, Director: Robert Wise; with Boris Karloff and Bela Lugosi)   From Robert Louis Stevenson's story, a doctor must work with evil men to get bodies for medical experiments.

The Bride of Frankenstein (1935, 75 min., black and white; Director: James Whale; with Boris Karloff and Elsa Lanchester)   The Monster gets a wife, which makes him more understandable and somehow more believable and almost human. Surprisingly funny, a true movie classic.

The Cat People (1942, 73 min., black and white; Director: Jacques Tourneur; with Simone Simon)   A shy woman lives in fear that an ancient curse will turn her into a killer. The sequel, *The Curse of the Cat People* (1944, 70 min., black and white; Director: Guthrie von Fritsch), is equally good. Both are superior to the 1982 version.

Ghost Breakers (1940, 82 min., black and white; Director: George Marshall; with Bob Hope and Paulette Goddard)   Goddard inherits a Cuban mansion filled with zombies and other spooky stuff. Better than most Hope films and genuinely scary.

The Haunting (1963, 112 min., black and white; Director: Robert Wise; with Julie Harris and Clare Bloom)   A group find the supernatural they're seeking in a 90-year-old house. Based on Shirley Jackson's *The Haunting of Hill House*.

The Innocents (1961, 100 min., black and white; Director: Jack Clayton; with Deborah Kerr)   A governess, hired to take care of two children, is haunted by ghosts in a truly terrifying movie. Based on Henry James's *Turn of the Screw*. Kerr and the children are superb. A great movie on several levels.

The Mummy's Hand (1940, 67 min., black and white; Director: Christy Cabanne; with Dick Foran and Peggy Moran)   Archaeologists find that an ancient princess they're searching for is guarded by a living mummy, Kharis.

Night of the Living Dead (1968, 96 min., black and white; Director: George A. Romero)   Made on less than a shoestring budget and with no actors that anyone would recognize, the story of flesh-eating zombies out to kill and eat seven people barricaded in a house is still terrifying.

Nosferatu (1922, 63 min., black and white; Director: F. W. Murnau)   The classic German silent film about Dracula. It's scary and eerie and has lost little of its power to shock and give viewers the shakes and the willies.

ago. Some thrillers occur in more mundane places, perhaps a brownstone in New York City or a hotel shut down for the season, but readers know the mundane will remain calm only for a short time before frightening events begin and strange people come out to play. Darkness is usually essential, but not always physical darkness. The protagonist is oblivious to evil for a time but ultimately recognizes the pervasive power of the darkness of the soul. Sometimes the wife or husband sells out to evil and entices the spouse to join in a black mass. Rituals or ceremonies are essential. Family curses or pacts with the Devil have become commonplaces of the genre.

A master of suspense, Alfred Hitchcock, reminds us over and over that the most terrifying things can happen in the most commonplace settings. On a lovely day in the middle of a South Dakota cornfield, Cary Grant is suddenly attacked by a crop-dusting airplane in *North by Northwest*. In *Birds*, a placid setting alongside the ocean suddenly turns to terror when sweet little birds begin to tear into human flesh.

In the 1989 edition of this textbook, Robert Westall observed that supernatural books break quite naturally into horror stories and ghost stories. The horror stories make the point that "the human organism is a frail thing of flesh subject to an infinity of abuse, and that it is painful and undignified for the human spirit to have to dwell in it." Such a depressing fact may be well worth saying, but not over and over again. Even the books by such ingenious and powerful writers as Poe and Lovecraft aren't something you would want to read if you were "on the way to build the Taj Mahal, or paint the Sistine Chapel ceiling, or even have a happy love affair."

> On the other hand, the ghost story is about the undying spirit, not the dying flesh. . . . [Ghosts] add an exciting fifth dimension to the often-boring four dimensions of real life. They make it possible for us to escape into the land of the impossible where, delightfully, anything can happen. They are also a comfort; a reassurance of our own immortality. I would adore to spend my first few years of death as a ghost, drifting round the world painlessly in the company of other friendly ghosts, seeing all the things I never got round to seeing in life because there were other boring earthbound things to be done.

He went on to explain that we need ghost stories:

> In terms of love and the passing of time, we are all haunted houses, full of rooms we have shut off because of loss, or fear, or regret. To spend all our time wandering through such rooms would lead to madness. But to wander sometimes can be agonizingly sweet and rich. And never to dare to wander through them can make life a dusty boring hell.[7]

Annette Curtis Klause's *The Silver Kiss* is a good illustration of the genre. Nearly every night Zoë comes home to a dark and empty house. Her mother is in the hospital dying of cancer, and as early as page 2 readers get clues about supernatural elements. Zoë is almost as thin as her mother—"a sympathy death perhaps, she wondered half seriously. . . . Wouldn't it be ironic if she died, too, fading out suddenly when her look-alike went?" On page 3, Zoë remembers happier times with her mother, but even here there's a shadow: "'You're a dark one,' her mother said sometimes with amused wonder. 'You're a mystery.'"

Zoë likes to walk in the neighborhood park and sit in front of the old-fashioned gazebo, where one night "a shadow crept inside, independent of natural shades." Then she saw his face:

> He was young, more boy than man, slight and pale, made elfin by the moon. He noticed her and froze like a deer before the gun. They were trapped in each other's gaze. His eyes were dark, full of wilderness and stars. But his face was ashen. Almost as pale as his silver hair.

With a sudden ache she realized he was beautiful. The tears that prickled her eyes broke his bonds, and he fled, while she sat and cried for all things lost.

This was Zoë's first meeting with Simon, a 200-year-old vampire from Bristol, England. The story within a story, in which Simon explains how he became a vampire, is a gem in its own right and so is the end of the book when Zoë and Simon bid each other farewell.

As the popularity of books with supernatural themes has grown, more well-established authors include supernatural elements in their books or focus largely on the supernatural. For example, Robert Cormier stepped away from the harsh realism that supposedly is his trademark when he wrote *Fade,* a book that was inspired by an old family picture. Both the *Horn Book Magazine* and *Publishers Weekly* quoted Cormier as explaining that he had been fascinated by a photo in which one of his uncles didn't appear. "It always haunted me—why didn't my uncle appear? So I wrote a story to see what might have happened."

Fade begins in 1938, when a young French Canadian, Paul Moreaux, discovers that he has inherited a family gift/curse that comes to only one person in each generation, the ability to fade, to become invisible. At first, Paul is understandably intrigued by his new ability, but he learns soon enough that the power is more tragedy than blessing. Once after meeting a friend's sister and being smitten with love, Paul gives in to his own urges, becomes invisible, enters his friend's house, and watches horrified as his friend and the sister engage in incestuous lovemaking. Later, as he trembles from the cold of the night and the horror of what he has seen, Paul remembers a time when he had asked his Uncle Adelard about the fade.

> "If the fade is a gift, then why are you so sad all the time?"
> "Did I ever say it was a gift?" he replied.
> I thought a moment. "I guess not."
> "What's the opposite of gift, Paul?"
> "I don't know."
> But now I knew. Or thought I knew.

The best of the humorous ghost stories are Richard Peck's Blossom Culp books, including *The Ghost Belonged to Me* and *Ghosts I Have Been.* Peck also relied on ghosts in *Voices After Midnight,* in which a family from California rents a 100-year-old townhouse for a short stay in New York. Chad, Luke, and their sister, Heidi, seek to find the truth about mysterious voices they hear and are drawn back to the great blizzard of 1888.

Among young adult novelists specializing in supernatural themes, Lois Duncan has proved consistently popular. In *Summer of Fear,* Rachael Bryant's family is notified that relatives have died in a car crash, leaving a 17-year-old daughter, Julia, behind. The girl, who looks surprisingly mature, soon arrives and changes the lives of everyone around her. Rachael, the narrator, realizes, without knowing quite how or why, that Julia is different, somehow sinister, particularly because Julia has "the strangest eyes." The family dog Trickle clearly distrusts Julia (according to legend, animals have insight about the forces of evil). Trickle does not last long, but then neither does anyone who gets in Julia's way. Duncan's *Stranger with My Face* and *The Third Eye* were enjoyable, although not as powerful as *Summer of Fear* and the more recent *Locked in Time.*

Other young adult novels that emphasize the supernatural include Avi's *Devil's Race,* with the protagonist believing that the ghost of his great-great-great grandfather has come to claim his soul. Margaret Buffie's *The Warnings* is about ghosts and psychics and ESP. In Meredith Ann Pierce's *The Darkangel*, a servant girl tries to save her vampire master from his evil deeds.

Without question and despite the objections of numerous parents and teachers and librarians, the most popular reading for many young people today are books of horror manufactured for them. For example, Scholastic Inc. published six in its "Nightmare Hall" series during 1995. Number 19 was *The Coffin* followed in turn by *Deadly Visions, Student Body, The Vampire Kiss, Dark Moon,* and *The Biker.* All six covers suggest frightening thoughts—a hand sticks out of a coffin; a young woman in bed is clearly terrified; a person is wrapped in bandages that look like a shroud; a young woman is kissed by a young man in dark clothing and the young woman is apparently either terrified or passionate; a young woman gazes out of a window into a dark night; a biker sets out for the night dressed to conceal himself. All six are set at Salem University at or near Nightingale Hall, which the students have appropriately nicknamed Nightmare Hall. The descriptive material on the back of the books is loaded with words like *coffin, terrorizing, horror, death, wolves, vampire, deadly images, grisly visions,* and more.

British writer Robert Westall was one of the superior writers in the field, but he is undeservedly little known by young people in the United States, mostly because too few of his books have appeared in paperback in this country. Violence in *The Wind Eye* is powerfully implied as three youngsters find an old boat with strange designs, which they learn can take them back to St. Cuthbert's time and place. *The Watch House* carries on the theme of time shifts. A young girl's imagination is captured by an old crumbling watch house on the coast. *The Devil on the Road* is the best of Westall's supernatural tales. A university student on a holiday travels north and finds temporary employment as a caretaker of an old barn, once the home of a witch hanged 300 years before. *Break of Dark* is a fine series of chilling short stories, as is *The Haunting of Chas McGill and Other Stories. Rachel and the Angel and Other Stories* is particularly interesting for young writers because one story, "Urn Burial," was later developed into a full-scale novel under the same title. *In Camera and Other Stories* is another collection of short stories.

New Zealand's Margaret Mahy is certain to become better known as readers sample her offbeat fare: *The Tricksters, The Changeover,* and *The Haunting.* Mahy makes her readers care about her characters, no mean achievement given the inherent strangeness of her plots.

Teenagers make up a goodly number of the readers of tales of exorcism and devil worship published for general adult audiences. William Blatty's *The Exorcist* and Ira Levin's *Rosemary's Baby* are standards. V. C. Andrews' books defy rational explanation, and their popularity is even more difficult to explain. Her tales of incest and general family ghoulishness and foolishness in *If There Be Thorns, Flowers in the Attic,* and *My Sweet Audrina* are mawkish and badly written, but no one can question their popularity.

CAROLINE B. COONEY
On Why Kids Read Horror Books

So many books don't speak to boys. I want books out there that boys love. Horror does it. Back when Stephen King was the only horror writer around, his books transcended the judgment boys often make against the whole concept of reading. No matter what scumbags you hung out with (or were), you were proud to carry a Stephen King. Now that cachet passes on to any book with a terrifying cover. Boys who would never have been caught with a book are now reading routinely—for horror's sake. Those covers are so important: Reading is no longer for the squeamish and pathetic; it's for tough guys, too.

I like to pose a moral question in my horror novels, and I'm not subtle. The question is: Will you join Good or Evil? I don't want my readers ignorant of physics, math, grammar, or the choice of where to stand. We need only glance at Yugoslavia or Rwanda to know that Evil is always waiting its chance. The moral of the horror story is: You represent Good; fight back.

(Of course . . . not always. I shouldn't be a Pollyanna about this genre. Some teen horror books have no moral and are heavy on grotesque violence: Good guys lose; bad guys come back again and again to triumph. Evil has assets Good never dreamed of. I am in the minority because I skip violence; atmosphere is more horrific.)

In school visits, I ask kids why they read so much horror.

Are they sick and twisted? Are the books sick and twisted? Is society sick and twisted? Or are they just books; for heaven's sake—lighten up. Of course, junior high kids adore being called sick and twisted, but when they pause to think, here's the unvarying answer—"You can't put a horror book down."

Isn't that what we're here for? Books they cannot put down?

My writing is predicated on the fact that one of my three children found reading an exhausting and unconquerable burden. Those are the readers I aim for: kids who for the first time discover that reading is a delight. Here's my simplistic conclusion on the values of reading horror: I want kids to read eagerly; they love horror; they are reading; therefore I love horror.

Caroline Cooney's horror books include *The Cheerleader,* 1991, and *The Return of the Vampire,* 1992, both from Scholastic; her suspense novels include *The Face on the Milk Carton* 1990, and *Whatever Happened to Janie?,* 1993, both from Delacorte.

The queen of supernatural writers, certainly the best-seller of the bunch, is Anne Rice. Her *Memnoch, the Devil* is a recent entry in Rice's "Vampire Chronicles," focusing on the struggle between God and the Devil in which the vampire Lestat is wooed by the Devil and taken on a trip of heaven and hell.

Leading all the writers in the field is Stephen King, a former high school English teacher who frequently includes likable young people among his characters. The fact that he writes about them without condescension is not lost on the audience. "The Langoliers" (from *Four Past Midnight*) is the story of a late-night flight from Los Angeles to Boston. The plane goes through a time rip, and the only passengers who survive are the ten who happened to be sleeping. Fortunately, one of them is a pilot; otherwise there wouldn't have been much of a story to tell. There is also the blind Dinah, a young girl on her way to Boston for an operation on her eyes. She has such a superdeveloped sense of hearing that she is mistaken by the mad Craig Toomy, the ultimate Yuppie gone awry, as the chief Langolier. The character most closely filling the role of a young adult hero on a romantic quest is Albert Kaussner, a gifted violinist on his way to enroll in a Boston music conservatory. In his own mind, he's not Albert or Al, but Ace Kaussner, "The Arizona Jew" and "The Fastest Hebrew West of the Mississippi." The journey turns out to be much more difficult than anything faced by Ace's mythical heroes of the Old West, and it even requires him to sacrifice his beloved violin. At the end of the trip, he is rewarded with his first love and the feeling of growth and confidence that comes with having passed a difficult test.

Stephen King's first book, *Carrie,* appeared in 1974 and sold well for a then unknown writer. From that point on, King maintained his place as *the* writer of the genre. Carrie is a young outsider, the daughter of religious fanatics, and the brunt of cruel jokes. She possesses the power of telekinesis, and she uses it to destroy the school, the students, and the town in a fit of justified rage. *Salem's Lot,* although better characterized, is something of a letdown after *Carrie,* as are *The Stand* and *The Shining,* which is possibly better known through its film version than as a novel. *Firestarter* is far better, with its portrait of an 8-year-old girl with the power to start fires merely by looking at an object. A government agency, "The Shop," learns about the child and launches a search for her. King effectively indicts this bureaucracy become evil. *Firestarter* may not be King's best book, but it is his most penetrating study of character and the United States. King's later books include *Different Seasons,* a collection of four novelettes; *Cujo,* a messy and disappointingly obvious horror tale of the lovable St. Bernard dog gone mad; and *Christine,* the story of a 1958 Plymouth Fury gone equally mad. *Pet Sematary* is an acknowledged variation of W. W. Jacobs' 1904 "The Monkey's Paw," which has a power that cannot be ignored, although it remains something of a prolonged ghastly joke. *The Tommyknockers* and *It* added a chill or two to King's repertoire, but little more. Two recent books, *Gerald's Game* and *Insomnia,* indicate that King is back on track.

The most literate addition to the field comes from Joyce Carol Oates. Her *Haunted: Tales of the Grotesque* is a set of 16 stories about our relation to our own psyches. "The Model" is about a questionable artist who wants to sketch an adolescent, a seemingly unsophisticated young girl, but the girl is able to protect herself very well. "Haunted," the title story, is about a haunted house and an old woman who thinks back about something terrible that happened when she was a child. Years later those memories haunt her and her community.

Because young adults are curious and relatively open about exploring new ideas, the supernatural appeals to them. Treading on spooky ground is a social experience—one not always approved of by censorious parents—and teenagers delight in rounding up friends to see a scary movie or discuss the possibilities of ghosts and goblins and worse horrors. This means that with or without approval from adults, supernatural stories are likely to remain popular with young readers.

Notes

[1] Betty Rosenberg, *Genreflecting: A Guide to the Reading Interests in Genre Fiction.* (Libraries Unlimited, 1982), in place of a dedication page.

[2] London *Independent,* June 30, 1995, p. 18.

[3] Hillary Waugh, "What Is a Mystery?" *The Basics of Writing and Selling Mysteries and Suspense: A Writer's Guide* 10 (1991): 6–8.

[4] Herbert Resnicow, "'Rules' for the Classic Whodunit." *Writer* 107 (August 1994): 18–20, 46.

[5] Shannon Ocork, "What Type of Mystery Are You Writing?" *The Basics of Writing and Selling Mysteries and Suspense: A Writer's Digest Guide* 10 (1991): 10–12.

[6] P. D. James, in Sylvia Burack, ed., *Writing Mystery and Crime Fiction* (Fiction, Inc., 1985), p. 93.

[7] Robert Westall, "On Nightmares for Money," *Literature for Today's Young Adults* (Scott, Foresman, 1989), pp. 166–167.

Titles Mentioned in the Text of Chapter Five

Andrews, V. C. *Flowers in the Attic.* Simon & Schuster, 1979.

Andrews, V. C. *If There Be Thorns.* Simon & Schuster, 1981.

Andrews, V. C. *My Sweet Audrina.* Simon & Schuster, 1982.

Avi. *Devil's Race.* Lippincott, 1984.

Avi. *The True Confessions of Charlotte Doyle.* Orchard, 1990.

Avi. *Wolf Rider.* Macmillan, 1986.

Barnard, Robert. *A Hovering of Vultures.* Scribner, 1993.

Barnard, Robert. *The Masters of the House.* Scribner, 1994.

Barr, Nevada. *Ill Wind.* Putnam, 1995.

Barr, Nevada. *A Superior Death.* Putnam, 1994.

Barr, Nevada. *Track of the Cat.* Putnam, 1993.

Bennett, Jay. *Deathman, Do Not Follow Me.* Hawthorne, 1968.

Bennett, Jay. *Say Hello to the Hit Man.* Delacorte, 1976.

Bennett, Jay. *Sing Me a Death Song.* Watts, 1990.

Bishop, Paul. *Chapel of the Ravens.* Tor, 1991.

Black, Veronia. *A Vow of Silence.* St. Martin's, 1990.

Blatty, William. *The Exorcist.* HarperCollins, 1971.

Blum, Arlene. *Annapurna: A Woman's Place.* Sierra Club Books, 1980.

Brook, Elaine, and Julie Donnelly. *The Windhorse.* Dodd, Mead, 1987.

Buckley, William F. *A Very Private Plot.* Morrow, 1994.

Buffie, Margaret. *The Warnings.* Scholastic, 1989.

Callahan, Steven. *Adrift: Seventy-six Days Lost at Sea.* Houghton Mifflin, 1986.

Christie, Agatha. *And Then There Were None.* Dodd, Mead, 1939.

Christie, Agatha. *By the Pricking of My Thumbs.* Dodd, Mead, 1968.

Christie, Agatha. *A Murder Is Announced.* Dodd, Mead, 1950.

Connelly, Michael. *The Concrete Blonde.* Little, Brown, 1994.

Cormier, Robert. *Fade.* Delacorte, 1988.

Cornwell, Patricia. *From Potter's Field.* Scribner, 1995.

Cross, Gillian. *On the Edge.* Holiday House, 1985.

Deighton, Len. *Faith.* HarperCollins, 1995.

Dickinson, Peter. *The Seventh Raven.* Dutton, 1981.

Duncan, Lois. *Don't Look Behind You.* Delacorte, 1989.

Duncan, Lois. *Locked in Time.* Little, Brown, 1985.

Duncan, Lois. *Summer of Fear.* Little, Brown, 1976.

Duncan, Lois. *The Third Eye.* Little, Brown, 1984.

Duncan, Lois. *Stranger with My Face.* Little, Brown, 1981.

Francis, Dick. *The Sport of Queens: The Autobiography of Dick Francis.* Macmillan, 1994.

Francis, Dick. *Wild Horses,* Putman, 1994.

Grafton, Sue. *"A" Is for Alibi.* Holt, 1982.

Grafton, Sue. *"L" Is for Lawless.* Holt, 1995.

Henry, Sue. *Murder on the Iditarod Trail.* Atlantic Monthly, dist. by Little, Brown, 1991.

Hillary, Sir Edmund. *Nothing Venture, Nothing Win.* Coward McCann Geoghegan, 1975.

Hillerman, Tony. *The Blessing Way.* HarperCollins, 1970.

Hillerman, Tony. *Coyote Waits.* HarperCollins, 1990.

Hillerman, Tony. *The Dance Hall of the Dead.* Harper-Collins, 1973.

Hillerman, Tony. *The Ghostway.* HarperCollins, 1985.

Hillerman, Tony. *The Listening Woman.* HarperCollins, 1978.

Hillerman, Tony. *Sacred Clowns.* HarperCollins, 1993.

Hillerman, Tony. *The Skinwalkers.* HarperCollins, 1987.

Hobbs, Will. *Bearstone.* Atheneum, 1989.

Hobbs, Will. *Downriver.* Atheneum, 1991.

Holzol, Tom and Audrey Salkeld. *First on Everest: The Mystery of Mallory and Irvine.* Henry Holt, 1986.

Kerr, M.E. *Fell.* HarperCollins, 1987.

Kerr, M.E. *Fell Back.* HarperCollins, 1989.

Kerr, M.E. *Fell Down.* HarperCollins, 1991.

King Stephen. *Carrie.* Doubleday, 1974.

King Stephen. *Christine.* Viking, 1983.

King Stephen. *Cujo.* Viking, 1981.

King Stephen. *Different Seasons.* Viking, 1982.

King Stephen. *Firestarter.* Viking, 1980.

King Stephen. *Four Past Midnight.* Viking, 1990.

King Stephen. *Gerald's Game.* Viking, 1992.

King Stephen. *Insomnia.* Viking, 1994.

King Stephen. *It.* Viking, 1986.

King Stephen. *Pet Sematary.* Doubleday, 1983.

King Stephen. *Salem's Lot.* Doubleday, 1975.

King Stephen. *The Shining.* Doubleday, 1977.

King Stephen. *The Stand.* Doubleday, 1978.

King Stephen. *The Tommyknockers.* Putnam, 1987.

Klause, Annette Curtis. *The Silver Kiss.* Delacorte, 1990.

Lasky, Kathryn. *Beyond the Divide.* Macmillan, 1983.

Le Carré *The Spy Who Came in from the Cold.* Coward, McCann, 1963.

Lehrer, James. *Blue Hearts: A Novel.* Random House, 1993.

Levin, Ira. *Rosemary's Baby.* Random House, 1967.

Lewis, Matthew Gregory. *The Monk.* Grove Weiden-feld, 1952 (originally published in 1797).

Mahy, Margaret. *The Changeover.* Atheneum, 1984.

Mahy, Margaret. *The Haunting.* Atheneum, 1982.

Mahy, Margaret. *The Tricksters.* McElderry, 1987.

Mazer, Harry. *The Island Keeper.* Delacourte, 1981.

McBain, Ed (Evan Hunter). *Kiss.* Morrow, 1992.

McBain, Ed (Evan Hunter). *Romance.* Warner, 1995.

McBain, Ed (Evan Hunter). *Widows.* Morrow, 1991.

Myers, Walter Dean. *The Mouse Rap.* Harper & Row, 1990.

Nixon, Joan Lowery. *The Dark and Deadly Pool.* Dela-corte, 1987.

Nixon, Joan Lowery. *Shadow Maker.* Delacorte, 1994.

Nixon, Joan Lowery. *Spirit Seeker.* Delacorte, 1995.

Nixon, Joan Lowery. *Whispers From the Dead.* Dela-corte, 1989.

O'Brien, Robert C. *Z for Zachariah.* Atheneum, 1975.

Oates, Joyce Carol. *Haunted: Tales of the Grotesque.* Dutton, 1994.

Paretsky, Sara. *Guardian Angel.* Delacorte, 1992.

Paretsky, Sara. *Indemnity Only.* Delacorte, 1982.

Parker, Robert B. *Double Deuce.* Putnam, 1992.

Parker, Robert B. *Walking Shadow.* Putnam, 1994.

Paulsen, Gary. *Canyons.* Delacorte, 1990.

Paulsen, Gary. *Hatchet.* Bradbury, 1987.

Paulsen, Gary. *The River.* Doubleday, 1991.

Peck, Richard. *The Ghost Belonged to Me.* Viking, 1975.

Peck, Richard. *Ghosts I Have Been.* Viking, 1977.

Peck, Richard. *Voices After Midnight.* Delacorte, 1989.

Pierce, Meredith Ann. *The Darkangel.* Little, Brown, 1982.

Rever, Chap. *Mote.* Delacorte, 1990.

Rice, Anne. *Memnoch, the Devil.* Knopf, 1995.

Roberts, David. *Deborah: A Wilderness Narrative.* Van-guard, 1970.

Stabenow, Dana. *A Cold-Blooded Business.* Berkley, 1994.

Stabenow, Dana. *A Cold Day for Murder.* Berkley, 1992.

Stabenow, Dana. *Dead in the Water.* Berkley, 1993.

Stabenow, Dana. *A Fatal Flaw.* Berkley, 1993.

Stabenow, Dana. *Play With Fire.* Berkley, 1995.

Thompson, Julian F. *The Grounding of Group Six.* Avon, 1983.

Tullis, Julie. *Clouds from Both Sides.* Sierra Club Books, 1987.

van de, Wetering, Janwillem. *Just a Corpse at Twilight.* Soho, 1994.

Wells, Rosemary. *The Man in the Woods.* Dutton, 1984.

Westall, Robert. *Break of Dark.* Greenwillow, 1982.

Westall, Robert. *The Devil on the Road.* Greenwillow, 1979.

Westall, Robert. *The Haunting of Chas McGill and Other Stories.* Greenwillow, 1983.

Westall, Robert. *In Camera and Other Stories.* Scholas-tic, 1992.

Westall, Robert. *Rachel and the Angel and Other Stories.* Greenwillow, 1988.

Westall, Robert. *The Watch House.* Greenwillow, 1978.

Westall, Robert. *The Wind Eye.* Greenwillow, 1977.

White, Rob, *Deathwatch.* Doubleday, 1972.

Windsor, Patricia. *The Christmas Killer.* Scholastic, 1991.

Young, Scott. *The Shaman's Knife.* Viking Penguin, 1993.

For information on the availability of paperback editions of these titles, please consult the most recent edition of *Paperbound Books in Print,* published annually by R. R. Bowker Company.

Chapter 6

Fantasy, Science Fiction, Utopias, and Dystopias

· ·

Fantasy and science fiction are related to each other and to humankind's deepest desires, but it is not always easy to draw a clear-cut line between the two. Ursula LeGuin offered this distinction:

> The basic concept of fantasy, of course, is this; you get to make up the rules, but then you've got to follow them. Science fiction refines the canon: you get to make up the rules, but within limits. A science-fiction story must not flout the evidence of science, must not, as Chip Delaney puts it, deny what is known to be known.[1]

Or, as Walter Wangerin, Jr., said in a lecture to a college audience:

> Fantasy deals with the "immeasurable" while science fiction deals with the "measurable."[2]

No matter what the definitions or distinctions, the boundaries between science fiction and fantasy are fuzzy, so that more often than not the two genres are treated together (witness two important journals about these areas—*Science Fiction Chronicle: The Monthly Science Fiction and Fantasy Newsmagazine* and *The Magazine of Fantasy and Science Fiction*). Advertisements for the Science Fiction Book Club often mix choices of science fiction and fantasy with horror, the supernatural, mythology, folklore, and some selections that seem impossible to pigeonhole. Anyone who teaches or is around young people knows that in this area books cross genre lines and age lines. Young adults read what adults read, and books that may have been published for young readers (e.g., Robin McKinley's *Beauty* or Lloyd Alexander's *Prydain* series) are now also read by adults.[3]

· ·

What Is Fantasy?

Fantasy comes from a Greek word meaning "a making visible." Perhaps more than any other form of literature, fantasy refuses to accept the world as it is, so readers can see what could have been (and still might be), rather than merely what was or must be.

The appeal of fantasy may be, simply, that it is so elemental. Some see its most comparable form of communication in music, which may be why so many composers have been influenced by it. Fantasy sings of our need for heroes, for the good, and for success in our eternal fight against evil. Composers of works as dissimilar as Stravinsky's *Firebird* and Mahler's *Song of the Earth* and Strauss's *Thus Sprach Zarathustra* have sung that song. Writers sing similar songs when they tell stories of great heroes, usually of humble means and beginnings, seeking truth, finding ambiguities, and subduing evil, at least temporarily. On its lighter side, musicians sing of beauty and love and dreams and dreamers, as in Mozart's *The Magic Flute* or Ravel's *Daphnis and Chloë* and Tchaikovsky's *Swan Lake*. Writers sing their lighter tales through stories about Beauty and the Beast, the happier and younger life of Arthur, and many of the old folktales and legends that are childhood favorites.

Ray Bradbury agrees that fantasy is elemental and essential:

> The ability to "fantasize" is the ability to survive. It's wonderful to speak about this subject because there have been so many wrong-headed people dealing with it. We're going through a terrible period of art, in literature and living, in psychiatry and psychology. The so-called realists are trying to drive us insane, and I refuse to be driven insane. . . . We survive by fantasizing. Take that away from us and the whole damned human race goes down the drain.[4]

Fantasy allows us—or even forces us—to become greater than we are, greater than we could hope to be. It confronts us with the major ambiguities and dualities of life—good and evil, light and dark, innocence and guilt, reality and appearance, heroism and cowardice, hard work and indolence, determination and vacillation, and order and anarchy. Fantasy presents all these, and it provides the means through which readers can consider both the polarities and the many shadings in between.

Conventions of Fantasy

Jo-Ann Goodwin's comment about the nature of fantasy is worth repeating for its accuracy and succinctness:

> Classic fantasy is centered around quests. The quest may have any number of different motives—spiritual, political, sexual, material—but its presence in the text is essential. The quest expresses the desire to accomplish a thing fraught with difficulty and danger, and seemingly doomed to failure. It also enables fantasy writers to deal with rites of passage; the central figure grows in stature as the quest evolves. Typically, the journey will be full of magical, symbolic and allegorical happenings which allow the hero to externalize his or her internal struggles: thus Odysseus must pass through Charybdis and Scylla and

the Knight of Temperance must extricate himself from Acracia and the Bower of Bliss.

Fantasy also deals with flux. The central characters operate in a world turned upside down, amid great wars and events of a cataclysmic nature. The possible outcomes are open and endlessly variable; the responsibility carried by the hero is enormous. In fantasy, the imagined world is always a global village. No action can take place in isolation. Every decision taken by the hero affects someone else, and sometimes the fate of nations. It is a deeply social genre.[5]

Heroes must prove worthy of their quest, although early in the story they may be fumbling or unsure about both themselves and their quests.

The quest may be ordained, required, or, occasionally, self-determined. The hero may briefly confuse good and evil, but the protagonist ultimately recognizes the distinction. When the obligatory battle comes between the powers of good and evil, the struggle may be prolonged and the outcome in doubt. But eventually good prevails, although the victory is always transitory.

John Rowe Townsend, both a fine writer of young adult novels and one of the most perceptive and honored critics of the field, maintained that the quest motif is a powerful analogy of life's pattern:

Life is a long journey, in the course of which one will assuredly have one's adventures, one's sorrows and joys, one's setbacks and triumphs, and perhaps, with luck and effort, the fulfillment of some major purpose.[6]

We all begin our quest, that long journey, seeking the good and being tempted by the evil that we know we must ultimately fight. We face obstacles and barriers throughout, hoping that we will find satisfaction and meaning during and after the quest. Our quests may not be as earthshaking as those of fantasy heroes, but our emotional and intellectual wrestling can shake our own personal worlds. In the December 1971 *Horn Book Magazine,* Lloyd Alexander wrote about this kind of comparison:

The fantasy hero is not only a doer of deeds, but he also operates within a framework of morality. His compassion is as great as his courage—greater, in fact. We might consider that his humane qualities, more than any other, are really what the hero is all about. I wonder if this reminds us of the best parts of ourselves?[7]

Tamora Pierce notes an important element of the appeal of fantasy to young people.

Fantasy, more than any other genre, is a literature of empowerment. In the real world, kids have little say. This is a given; it is the nature of childhood. In fantasy, however short, fat, unbeautiful, weak, dreamy, or unlearned individuals may be, they find a realm in which those things are negated by strength. The catch—there is *always* a catch—is that empowerment brings trials. Good novels in this genre never revolve around heroes who, once they receive the "Spatula of Power," call the rains to fill dry wells, end all war, and clear up all acne. Heroes and heroines contend as much with their granted wishes as readers do in normal life.[8]

Fears of Fantasy

Attacks on fantasy are common and predictable. Fantasy is said to be childishly simple reading. It is true there are simple fantasies, but anyone who has read Walter Wangerin, Jr.'s *The Book of the Dun Cow* or Evangeline Walton's Mabinogion series knows that fantasy need not be childish or simple. Fantasies are often difficult and demand close reading, filled as they are with strange beings and even stranger lands with mystical and moral overtones and ambiguities.

Fantasy has also been labeled escapist literature, and, of course, it is in several ways. Fantasy allows readers to escape the mundane and to revel in glorious adventures. For some readers (perhaps for all readers at certain times), escape is all that's demanded. For other readers, venturing on those seemingly endless quests, encountering all those incredible obstacles, and facing all those apparently tireless antagonists to defend the good and defeat the evil lead to more than mere reading to pass time. The escape from reality sends those readers back to their own limited and literal worlds to face many of the same problems they found in fantasy.

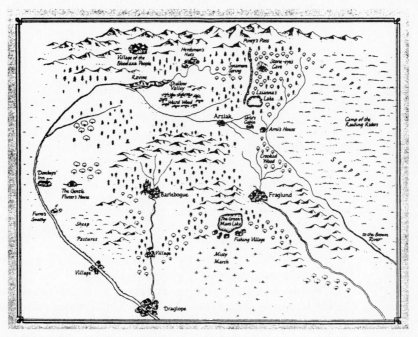

Authors of fantasies commonly provide maps to help students envision the setting of each book, as in Hans Benmann's *The Stone and the Flute* (Viking, 1986).

In the most illogical objection (and more common than we could have predicted only a few years ago), fantasy has been attacked for being unreal, untrue, and imaginative (the term *imaginative* seems to have replaced *secular humanism* as one of today's leading bogeymen). To critics who believe that using imagination leads to unwillingness to face reality, fantasy doubtless seems dangerous. But fantasy is about reality, as Ursula K. LeGuin explained nearly twenty years ago:

> For fantasy is true, of course. It isn't factual, but it is true. Children know that. Adults know it too, and that is precisely why many of them are afraid of fantasy. They know that its truth challenges, even threatens, all that is false, phony, unnecessary, and trivial in the life they have let themselves be forced into living. They are afraid of dragons because they are afraid of freedom.
>
> So I believe we should trust our children. Normal children do not confuse reality with fantasy—they confuse them much less often than we adults do (as a certain great fantasist pointed out in a story called "The Emperor's New Clothes"). Children know perfectly well that unicorns aren't real, but they also know that books about unicorns, if they are good books, are true books.[9]

Important Writers of Fantasy

Contemporary authors are producing well-written fantasies receiving critical and popular acclaim. But some continue to lead the rest. For many fantasy enthusiasts, J. R. R. Tolkien is the writer against whom all other writers in the field are measured. *The Hobbit, or There and Back Again* began in 1933 as a series of stories Tolkien told his children about the strange little being known as Bilbo, the Hobbit. Even more famous is his trilogy, *The Lord of the Rings*. His love of language led him to create the language of Elfish for his own amusement and for the book. Appendices to *The Lord of the Rings* are devoted to the history of Middle-Earth, its language, and its geography. An extension of Tolkien's work, *The Silmarillion,* led the *New York Times* bestseller list for several weeks in 1977, amazing for a fantasy, although the work disappointed some Tolkien fans. Tolkien created many of the conventions of fantasy. For that alone he would be important. But his greatest importance lies in the excellence of *The Hobbit* and *The Lord of the Rings,* which often are read again and again for delight and insight.

Ursula LeGuin continues to dominate contemporary fantasy. Her early books, *The Left Hand of Darkness* and *The Dispossessed,* were mixtures of science fiction and fantasy, but her four finest books about Earthsea are superb fantasy. The setting of *A Wizard of Earthsea* is, of course, Earthsea, a world of vast oceans and multitudinous islands. Duny demonstrates early that he is capable of becoming a wizard, is given his true name, Ged, and learns the names of all things—word magic binds the worlds of fantasy and fairy tales together. Childishly showing off in a forbidden duel of sorcery at his school on Roke Island "where all high arts are taught," he uses his powers to call a woman from the dead and accidentally releases an evil power, a shadow that follows him thereafter. That capricious and childish act causes Ged to become deaf, blind, and mute for 4 weeks in a hot summer. The Archmage Gensher comes to Ged and says:

You have greater power inborn in you, and you used that power wrongly, not knowing how that spell affects the balance of light and dark, life and death, good and evil. And you were moved to do this by pride and by hate. Is it any wonder the result was ruin?

Ged completes his training and leaves a certified wizard, but with Ged goes the shadow, of what he knows not except that it is evil.

The remaining two-thirds of the novel consist of many adventures, but always, at the center of Ged's existence, is his quest for the meaning of the shadow. Ged ultimately recognizes that his quest is not to undo what he has done but to finish what he has started. On a lonely shore, Ged meets the shadow, and as if they were one—and they are—they speak the shadow's name, "Ged," and "Light and darkness met, and joined, and were one."

Vetch, Ged's friend, believes that Ged has been overcome by his foe, and he runs to help Ged. When Vetch finds Ged safe:

[H]e began to see the truth, that Ged had neither lost nor won but, naming the shadow of his death with his own name, had made himself a whole: a man who, knowing his whole true self cannot be used or possessed by any other power other than himself, and whose life therefore is lived for life's sake and never in the service of ruin, or pain, or hatred, or the dark.

A short work less than 200 pages long, *A Wizard of Earthsea* is rich in characters and suspense and meaning. Ged's quest is an initiation rite that leads him to understand the nature of responsibility and who and what he is.

Ged reappears in *The Tombs of Atuan,* but the chief character is Tenar, dedicated from youth to the Powers of the Earth. In *The Farthest Shore,* Ged, now Archmage and the most powerful of wizards, accompanies a young man on a quest to seek out the evil that threatens to destroy the lands and the powers of the wizards. The evil is Cob, one of the living dead, who seeks the peace of death but cannot find it. Ged helps to find death for Cob, but it costs Ged dearly. Even that is not too much, for earlier Ged had told the young man:

You will die. You will not live forever. Nor will any man nor any thing. Nothing is immortal. But only to us is given to know that we must die. And that is a great gift: the gift of selfhood. For we have only what we know we must lose, what we are willing to lose.

Readers had long assumed that *The Farthest Shore* was the end. Then in 1990, *Tehanu: The Last Book of Earthsea* appeared, almost thirty years after the first Earthsea book. Characters from the previous books reappear, particularly Tenar and Ged. Many years after the last book, Tenar has married, raised two children of her own, and taken in a child, Therru, raped by her uncle who pushed her into a fire and left her emotionally and physically scarred. Soon thereafter, Tenar is summoned to the deathbed of Ogion, an ancient wizard. The ancient man tells Tenar about Therru: "teach her all; they will fear her." Tenar nurses the injured Ged back to life, and after some plot convolutions, evil is again defeated, for the time being, as Therru uses her power to call a dragon to aid her. This concluding book is in some ways the most beautiful of them all, and it pulls together all the themes of the other books—the values and dangers of power, the fear of the unknown, the need to live and to love, the need for hope, the perpetual need to fight evil. Contemporary readers find in the book other messages they want to find—the importance of feminism, the horror of child abuse (and other kinds of human abuse), proof that Therru, and others like her, can find inner strength to fight and win. *Tehanu* is a rich book, a fitting end to Earthsea.

Anne McCaffrey's fantasy world is set on Pern. In her trilogy of *Dragonsong, Dragonsinger,* and *Dragondrums,* Pern is threatened every 200 years by shimmering, threadlike spores. Inhabitants protect themselves through the great Pern dragons, who destroy the threads as they fall. In *Dragonsong,* Menolly is forced by her father to give up music and her dream of becoming a Harper, although at the book's conclusion she is known to the Master Harper and is well on her way to a life of music. In the lesser second volume, Menolly trains to become a Harper and meets the sweet-voiced young boy Piemur. *Dragondrums* gets back on track in an exciting finale to the series. McCaffrey tells fine stories of adventures of believable young people in the throes of initiation rites, but rarely does she approach the complexity of thought or the mythic qualities of LeGuin's work. Two recent books, *Freedom's Landing* and *Powers That Be* (the first by McCaffrey alone, the second with Elizabeth Ann Scarborough), indicate that McCaffrey has not lost her storytelling powers.

Several other writers have written marvelous tales of dragons and fantastic worlds. Jane Yolen's *Dragon's Blood, Heart's Blood* and *A Sending of Dragons* make up a marvelous series with two extraordinarily likable young people fighting for their lives and their dragons. Patricia C. Wrede's *Dealing With Dragons, Searching for Dragons, Calling on Dragons,* and *Talking to Dragons* are funny adventure stories about a princess/queen and her magical world. Laurence Yep's *Dragon Cauldron* is a fast-paced, intense, and highly enjoyable dragon story, one of several by Yep, all of them fun to read.

Although most fantasies follow the basic conventions, they fall into these loose categories: those set in new worlds, as with LeGuin and McCaffrey; those derived from myths from the Welsh *Mabinogion;* those celebrating Arthurian legends; those with one foot in contemporary reality and one foot in a fantasy world; those employing animals and often aiming moral barbs at humans; and those using fantasy to amuse. Obviously, some overlapping occurs in many fantasies.

Marion Zimmer Bradley's Darkover books are among the most popular fantasies set in a new world. Colonists from Earth come to the planet Darkover, with its one sun and four multicolored moons, but over 2000 years, they lose touch with their home planet and evolve new cultures and new myths alongside the psi-gifted natives. *Darkover Landfall* is a good introduction to the series, although wherever fantasy buffs enter Darkover is likely to serve equally well as a starting point. Darkover fans have written so extensively about Bradley's imaginary world that DAW books collected some of the best articles under the title *Red Sun of Darkover,* with

PAUL ZINDEL
On Behalf of Monsters

Humans have always been captivated by real and imagined monsters. Adult humans like them. Young humans adore and hunger for them. Lochness monsters have always swum. Sasquatches and Abominable Snowmen patrolled our forests for eons. Humans themselves are often the greatest monsters in fiction. Sixteenth and Seventeenth Century literature abounds with chilling struggles among families to devise the most monstrous ways to remove limbs and heads, usually royal, from torsos. Shakespeare hardly began a tragedy worth its salt without a ghost walking a parapet or a gaggle of witches stirring newts and frogs into a stew. Why do we so court monsters in our fiction? Three reasons:

First, progress inspires the creation of monsters. The mortar was hardly dry on Notre Dame before we read of a hunchback gamboling high in the sanctuary. After anatomy and autopsies came Frankenstein. Science found blood-drinking rodents and fox bats, and then Dracula flew. When Darwin told us man descended from the apes, fiction released the Wolfman. Archeology made mummies walk. The Bomb gave us Godzilla. Toxic waste dumps fomented avengers, humongous ants, and oozing, deadly blobs. Breaking the sound barrier brought spaceships, and aliens in our fiction beamed us up.

Secondly, we love a monster because it brings the most powerful tussle one can imagine. Fights, arguments, and car chases pale against monsters as a cause of magnificent conflict—the key ingredient of any story. Monsters give punch and grit. They thrust a story quickly, ferociously into a life-or-death struggle of monsters against our beloved heroes and heroines.

Thirdly, the supreme reason monsters deserve respect is that they allow us to transcend our own mortality. They scream and claw and devour and threaten and stalk. And when the human champion in our fiction survives, we, the reader, survive for the moment too.

Paul Zindel's books include *Loch,* HarperCollins, 1994; *David and Della,* HarperCollins, 1993; *The Pigman and Me,* HarperCollins, 1992; *The Pigman,* HarperCollins, 1969; and *The Effect of Gamma Rays on Man-in-the-Moon Marigolds,* Dramatists, 1970.

an introduction by Bradley along with two Bradley articles about Darkover and 13 contributions by fans elaborating on the magic and power and people of Darkover. The recent *Lady of the Trillium* and *The Best of Marion Zimmer Bradley's Fantasy Magazine,* a collection of her short fantasy along with brief prefaces, remind readers how powerfully Bradley can write.

Fantasy and the Mabinogion

The *Mabinogion* is a collection of medieval Welsh tales, first published in English in 1838–1849 by Lady Charlotte Guest. The 11 stories fall into three parts: The four branches of the Mabinogi (tales to instruct young bards) deal with Celtic legends and myths dealing with Pywll, prince of Dived; Branwen, daughter of Llyr; Manawyddan, son of Llyr; and Math, son of Mathonwy. There are also four independent tales and four Arthurian romances. Several writers have used the Mabinogi myths and legends as a basis for their books.

Lloyd Alexander's Prydain Chronicles consists of five volumes about Taran, the young Assistant Pig-Keeper. The opening book of this rich fantasy, *The Book of Three*, introduces the main characters, especially Taran, and sends him on his quest to save his land, Prydain, from evil. He seeks his own identity as well, for none know his heritage. Taran's early impatience is understandable but vexing to his master, Dalben, who counsels patience "for the time being."

> "For the time being," Taran burst out. "I think it will always be for the time being, and it will be vegetables and horseshoes all my life."
>
> "Tut," said Dalben, "there are worse things. Do you set yourself to be a glorious hero? Do you believe it is all flashing swords and galloping about on horses? As for being glorious. . . . "
>
> "What of Prince Gwydion?" cried Taran. "Yes, I wish I might be like him."
>
> "I fear," Dalben said, "that is entirely out of the question."
>
> "But why?" Taran sprang to his feet. "I know if I had the chance. . . . "
>
> "Why?" Dalben interrupted. "In some cases," he said, "we learn more by looking for the answer to a question and not finding it than we do from learning the answer itself."

Taran, youthful impetuousness and righteous indignation aglow, is bored by Dalben's thoughts and wants action, and that he finds soon enough in the books that follow: *The Black Cauldron, The Castle of Llyr, Taran Wanderer,* and *The High King.*

More difficult than Alexander and aimed at an older audience, Alan Garner's earlier books force his young protagonists to face the problem of good versus evil in *The Weirdstone of Brisingamen, The Moon of Gomrath,* and *Elidor.* Garner maintains they are less successful than his later work, but the three books have remained popular in England, although they are less widely read in the United States. His two best works are *The Owl Service* and *Red Shift,* both complex—perhaps unduly so—and rewarding. *The Owl Service* has been praised by Mary Cadogan and Patricia Craig:

> *The Owl Service* is perhaps the first really adult children's book; the first book, that is, in which childish sensibilities are not deferred to, in which the author has not felt that his audience needs, above all, to be protected.[10]

Based on the legend of Blodenweddin in "Math, son of Mathonwy" in the *Mabinogion, The Owl Service* tells of three young people who find a set of old dishes in an attic and learn that the pattern in the dishes is related to an old Welsh legend involving love and jealousy and hatred. *Red Shift* uses three parallel narratives about love—contemporary, seventeenth century, and second century—intertwining them to make connections about love and about our relationships with the past.

Evangeline Walton (real name, Evangeline Walton Ensely) stands out among writers who have used the *Mabinogion* as a basis for fantasy. Her four-part series, *The Prince of Annwn: The First Branch of the Mabinogion, The Children of Llyr: The Second Branch of the Mabinogion, The Song of Rhiannon: The Third Branch of the Mabinogion,* and *The Virgin and the Swine: The Fourth Branch of the Mabinogion* (the last volume was reprinted in 1970 as *The Island of the Mighty: The Fourth Branch of the Mabinogion*), is among the best of retellings of the old Welsh legends. Walton's quartet is both mythology and ecology, for the author makes the earth a divinity that must not be despoiled by humanity. In an afterword to the first book, Walton writes:

> When we were superstitious enough to hold the earth sacred and worship her, we did nothing to endanger our future upon her, as we do now.

King Arthur and Other Myths in Fantasy

Arthurian legends have long been staples of fantasy. T. H. White's *The Once and Future King* (a source, for which it can hardly be blamed, for that dismal musical, *Camelot*) is basic to any reading of fantasy. In four parts, *The Sword in the Stone, The Witch in the Wood, The Ill-Made Knight,* and *The Candle in the Wind,* White retells the story of Arthur—his boyhood, his prolonged education at the hands of Merlin, his seduction by Queen Morgause, his love for Guinivere and her affair with Lancelot, and Mordred's revenge and Arthur's fall. A later work, *The Book of Merlyn: The Unpublished Conclusion* to *The Once and Future King,* should, like most work left unpublished at an author's death, have been allowed to remain unpublished and largely unknown.

Among the shorter retellings of the legends, no one has surpassed the series by Rosemary Sutcliff. *The Sword and the Circle: King Arthur and the Knights of the Round Table, The Light Beyond the Forest: The Quest for the Holy Grail,* and *The Road to Camlann: The Death of King Arthur* are masterfully written by a writer who loves the legends and has a firm grasp on the materials and the meanings.

Mary Stewart, author of several fine suspense novels, focuses more on Merlin than on Arthur in *The Crystal Cave, The Hollow Hills,* and *The Last Enchantment* and more on Mordred than on Arthur in the last book, *The Wicked Day.* Even better are Gillian Bradshaw's three books. *Hawk of May, Kingdom of Summer,* and *In Winter's Shadow* may puzzle a few readers at first—the author writes about Medraut instead of Mordred, Gwynhwyfar rather than Guinivere, Gwalchmai rather than

Gawain—but readers who stay with the books find them readable and most satisfying. Marion Zimmer Bradley's deservedly popular *The Mists of Avalon* focuses on the conflict between the old religion of the Celtics, represented by Morgan Le Fay (here called Morgaine), and the new religion of Christianity, represented by Guinivere (here called Gwenhyfar).

Animal Fantasies

Animal stories aimed at instructing humans are as old as Aesop and as recent as yesterday's book review. Many students come to high school having already enjoyed books such as E. B. White's *Charlotte's Web*, Jane Langton's *The Fledgling*, Robert C. O'Brien's *Mrs. Frisby and the Rats of NIMH*, Kenneth Grahame's *The Wind in the Willows*, and Richard Adams's *Watership Down*.

They may be ready to read Walter Wangerin, Jr.,'s *The Book of the Dun Cow*, a delightfully funny theological thriller retelling the story of Chaunticleer the Rooster. Supposedly the leader for good against evil (the half-snake, half-cock—Cockatrice—and the black serpent—Wyrm), Chaunticleer is beset by doubts. He is aided by the humble dog, Mondo Cani, some hilariously pouting turkeys, and assorted other barnyard animals. Although this may sound cute, it is not, and the battle scenes are among the bloodiest, ugliest, and most realistic that readers are likely to find in fantasy. *The Book of Sorrows* was a disappointing sequel.

Readers who do not know fantasy may associate the genre with high seriousness, but readers of the genre know how funny some fantasy writers can be. Peter Beagle's fantasies stand out for their quiet wit, even in treating a serious theme. The title of *A Fine and Private Place* comes from Andrew Marvell's "To His Coy Mistress":

> The Grave's a fine and private place,
> But none, I think, do there embrace.

The grave is a lively and often funny place in Beagle's novel with a living human talking to a delightfully tough old raven. In *The Last Unicorn*, a lonely unicorn seeks the company of others of its kind, helped by the magician Schmendrick, who is incapable of telling any story without wild elaboration. Stopping at a town early in the quest, Schmendrick tells of his adventures:

> During the meal Schmendrick told stories of his life as an errant enchanter, filling it with kings and dragons and noble ladies. He was not lying, merely organizing events more sensibly.

Beagle's *The Innkeeper's Song* concerns a duel between two great magicians with a story told from multiple points of view—a black woman, a brown woman, a dead woman, a man desperately in love, the innkeeper, and others even more fantastic. As usual, Beagle's language is rich and rewarding. Speaking of the awful taste left in the mouth of using a language associated with many evils, a character says, "that tongue has been dead for five centuries, which is not nearly long enough."

One Especially Outstanding Fantasy Writer

Robin McKinley deserves special attention for several of her books. *The Blue Sword* and *The Hero and the Crown* are successful both for making use of traditional stories and for creating strong feminine heroes. Her *Beauty* is a retelling of the "Beauty and the Beast" legend, differing from earlier versions in a few significant details. McKinley's Beauty is strong and unafraid and loving. When her father tells her that he has been condemned to death by the Beast for stealing a rose, Beauty gladly agrees to change places with her father:

> "He cannot be so bad if he loves roses so much."
> "But he is a Beast," said Father helplessly.
> I saw that he was weakening, and wishing only to comfort him, I said, "Cannot a Beast be tamed?"

McKinley's version may lack the surrealistic quality of Jean Cocteau's filmed version (Focus Box 6.1), but in most important ways her novel compares favorably with any other retelling, including the recent Disney film.

What Is Science Fiction?

In 1953, Robert A. Heinlein, one of science fiction's gurus, asked the question: "But what, under rational definition, is *science fiction?*" He went on to answer the question by defining the genre as speculative fiction based on the real world, with all its "established facts and natural laws." Although the result can be extremely fantastic in content, "it is not fantasy: it is legitimate—and often very tightly reasoned—speculation about the possibilities of the real world."[11]

Science fiction must adhere to natural law. A novel can use quite different laws of another planet than Earth, but those laws must be scientifically clear and consistent. We once wrote that no dragons need apply for work in science fiction, but then Anthony Wolk pointed out that Anne McCaffrey's dragons have a biochemical foundation, arguably making Pern a science fiction world.[12]

There are other conventions, although none are as important as Heinlein's. Characters voyage into space and face all sorts of dangers. (Science fiction is, after all, more adventure than philosophy, although the latter is often present.) Other planets have intelligent or frightening life forms, although they may differ drastically from Earth's humans. Contemporary problems are projected hundreds or thousands of years into the future, and those new views of overpopulation, pollution, religious bickering, political machinations, and sexual disharmony often give readers a quite different perspective of our world and our problems today.

Prophecies are not required in science fiction; nevertheless, some of the rich-

FOCUS BOX 6.1

Fantasy Films

Beauty and the Beast (1946, 95 min., black and white;   Director: Jean Cocteau; with Jean Marais and Josette Day)   The most beautiful and splendid retelling of the legend in almost surrealistic style.

A Christmas Carol (1951, 86 min., black and white;   Director: Brian Desmond Hurst; with Alastair Sim)   The best of all possible versions.

Clash of the Titans (1981, 118 min., color; Director: Desmond Davis; with Harry Hamlin and every major British film star of the time) A host of gods help Perseus and his love through many adventures.

The Seven Faces of Dr. Lao (1946, 100 min., color;   Director: George Pal; with Tony Randall)   A mysterious circus comes to a western town.

The Ghost and Mrs. Muir (1947, 104 min, black and white; Director: Joseph L. Mankiewitz; with Gene Tierney and Rex Harrison)   A love story involving the ghost of an old sea captain and a lonely widow.

Ladyhawke (1985, 124 min, color;   Director: Richard Donner; with Michelle Pfeiffer and Rutger Hauer)   Star-crossed lovers.

The Seventh Seal (1957, 96 min., black and white;   Director: Ingmar Bergman; with Max von Sydow)   A knight returning from the crusades faces death and life.

The Thief of Bagdad (1924, 155 min., black and white;   Director: Raoel Walsh; with Douglas Fairbanks)   The Arabian Nights, a beautiful princess, a magic carpet, and adventures galore. The 1940 British remake is almost as good.

The Wizard of Oz (1939, 101 min., color; Director: Victor Fleming; with Judy Garland and Bert Lahr)   A children's classic becomes a classic for everyone.

Yellow Submarine (1968, 85 min., color; Director: George Dunning; with the Beatles) An animated feature with jokes and puns and songs and pure magic.

est books of Isaac Asimov and Arthur C. Clarke have been prophetic. (Ray Bradbury, conversely, has said, "I don't try to predict the future—I try to prevent it.")

Occasionally a scientifically untenable premise may be used. On the August 15, 1983, "Nightcap" talk show on Arts Cable Television, Isaac Asimov said, "The best kind of sci-fi involves science." Then he agreed that, "Time travel is theoretically impossible, but I wouldn't want to give it up as a plot gimmick." Essentially, he was agreeing with Heinlein but adding that plot and excitement counted even more. The internal consistency and plausibility of a postulated imaginary society creates its own reality.

Ray Bradbury argues that the appeal of science fiction is understandable because science fiction is important literature, not merely popular stuff. Opening his essay on "Science Fiction: Why Bother?" he compares himself to a fourth-rate George Bernard Shaw who makes an outrageous statement and then tries to prove it. Bradbury says, "Science fiction is the most important fiction being written today." He adds that it is not "part of the Main Stream. It *is* the Main Stream."[13]

Carl Sagan, the Cornell University astronomer/author, has added his testimony, writing that it was science fiction that brought him to science. Kurt Vonnegut, Jr., also applauded science fiction through character Eliot Rosewater in *God Bless You, Mr. Rosewater, or Pearls Before Swine.* Stumbling into a convention of science fiction writers, Rosewater drunkenly tells them that he loves them because they are the only ones who:

> . . . know that life is a space voyage, and not a short one either, but one that'll last billions of years. You're the only ones with guts enough to really care about the future, who really notice what machines do to us, what wars do to us, what cities do to us, what big, simple ideas do to us, what tremendous misunderstandings, mistakes, accidents and catastrophes do to us.

He goes on to praise them for being "zany enough to agonize over time and distances without limit, over mysteries that will never die, over the fact that we are right now determining whether the space voyage for the next billion years or so is going to be Heaven or Hell."

Science fiction writer and scientist Arthur C. Clarke agrees with Rosewater on the admittedly limited but still impressive power of science fiction to scan the future. In his introduction to *Profiles of the Future,* Clarke writes:

> A critical—the adjective is important—reading of science-fiction is essential training for anyone wishing to look more than ten years ahead. The facts of the future can hardly be imagined *ab initio* by those who are unfamiliar with the fantasies of the past.
>
> This claim may produce indignation, especially among those second-rate scientists who sometimes make fun of science-fiction (I have never known a first-rate one to do so—and I know several who write it). But the simple fact is that anyone with sufficient imagination to assess the future realistically would inevitably be attracted to this form of literature. I do not for a moment suggest that more than one percent of science-fiction readers would be reliable prophets; but I do suggest that almost a hundred percent of reliable prophets will be science-fiction readers—or writers.[14]

Why does science fiction appeal to young adults and to adults? First and probably most important, it is exciting. Science fiction may have begun with the "rah-rah-we're-off-to-Venus-with-Buck-Rogers" sensational fiction, and although it has gone far beyond that, the thrill of adventure is still there. Science fiction writers do not write down to their audience, and this is recognized and admired. Science fiction allows anyone to read imaginative fiction without feeling the material is kid stuff. Science fiction presents real heroes to readers who find their own world often devoid of anyone worth admiring, of heroes doing something brave, going to the ultimate frontiers, even pushing these frontiers further back, all important at a time when many young people wonder if any new frontiers exist.

Science fiction has a heritage of fine writers and important books. Some critics maintain that the genre began with Mary Wollstonecraft Shelley's *Frankenstein, or The Modern Prometheus* in 1818. Others argue for Swift's *Gulliver's Travels* in 1726 or the much earlier Lucian's *The True History* in the second century A.D. No matter, for nearly everyone agrees that the first major and widely read writer was Jules

Many boys like science fiction because it provides an opportunity to read romances without feeling the stigma attached to "girls' love stories."

Verne, whose *Journey to the Center of the Earth* in 1864 and *Twenty Thousand Leagues Under the Sea* in 1870 pleased readers on several continents. The first American science fiction came with Edgar Allan Poe's short story, "The Unparalleled Adventures of One Hans Pfaall," which appeared in the June 1835 issue of *Southern Literary Messenger* and was included in *Tales of the Grotesque and Arabesque* in 1840. Hans Pfaall's balloon trip to the moon in a 19-day voyage may be a hoax, but the early trappings of science fiction are there. Dime novels occasionally used science fiction, particularly in the "Frank Reade" series, as did some books from the Stratemeyer Literary Syndicate, particularly in the Tom Swift and Great Marvel series.

These books were readable and fun, and they were read over and over by many people who had no idea how good most of the stories were. But most critics were snobs about science fiction. Some fans didn't consider the genre respectable, but the fact that science fiction, or whatever it was called in the early days, was not part of mainstream writing may have made it more attractive to readers who were not seeking literary respectability so much as they were looking for books that were entertaining.

For better of worse, academic respectability came to science fiction in December 1959, when the prestigious and often stuffy Modern Language Association began its science fiction journal, *Extrapolation*. Two other journals, *Foundation* (in England) and *Science-Fiction Studies* (in Canada), began publishing in the early 1970s. Colleges and secondary schools offered courses in the genre, and major publishers and significant magazines recognized and published science fiction.

Four writers are usually regarded as being *the* fathers of science fiction—Isaac Asimov, Arthur C. Clarke, Robert Heinlein, and Ray Bradbury. One writer is often hailed as the writer most likely to become a science fiction master, Orson Scott Card.

The prolific Asimov—more than 450 books—wrote so much on so many fields that he comes the closest to being a truly renaissance figure, but whatever his contributions to the study of the Bible or Shakespeare, no one could question his contributions to science fiction. His multivolume "Foundation" series established a basis for a multidimensional society that an incredible number of readers have temporarily inhabited and accepted.

Arthur C. Clarke may be less widely read than Asimov, but few could argue that *Childhood's End* is one of classics in the field. *2001: A Space Odyssey*, the basis of the movie (Focus Box 6.2) and developed from one of Clarke's short stories, may in book and film form be the most widely cited of any work in science fiction.

After several young adult books, Robert A. Heinlein moved on to adult material and never looked back. Books for the young such as *Farmer in the Sky* and *Podkayne of Mars* may be largely forgotten, but for many young people, these books provided a vision of the future new to them. Later books, particularly *The Moon Is a Harsh Mistress* and *Stranger in a Strange Land*, are both better written and far more powerful visions of a deeply troubled universe. Heinlein may have been unable to picture a believable, strong woman, as critics often claim, but he wrote exceptionally fine science fiction.

Ray Bradbury may be less interested in the mechanics of science fiction than any other major writer, but he may have been the most sensitive of them all about humanity's ability to befoul Earth and the rest of the universe. He seemed to have almost no interest in how his characters moved from Earth to Mars, but *The Martian Chronicles* is a marvelous set of semirelated short stories about the problems of being human in a universe that does not treasure our humanity.

Almost anything by Orson Scott Card is magical, but one novel is usually cited as his best novel thus far—with other great ones to come. *Ender's Game* came out of Card's reading of Asimov's first three "Foundation" books and is set in a somewhat vague future time when humans fear another attack from the insectoid Buggers. Seventy years earlier, a military genius in Earth's army saved the world, and the military are now looking for one more military genius who can save Earth again. Peter and Valentine Wiggin have the military genius but the wrong temperament to be the proper choice, but Andrew Wiggin (who wants to be called Ender) has both the temperament and the genius, and he becomes the tactician who can understand and therefore defeat the enemy.

Ender's Game is a complicated book, as is its sequel, *Speaker for the Dead*, but unquestionably it is the most significant novel in the genre to appear in the last twenty or so years. If there are any limits to Card's ability, readers have not spotted them.

Science Fiction in the Movies

Aliens (1986, 137 min., color; Director: James Cameron; with Sigourney Weaver) A return to a planet to destroy what spawns killer life forms. Better by far than the 1979 *Alien.*

Blade Runner (1982, 118 min., color; Director: Ridley Scott; with Harrison Ford) A former cop turns bounty-hunter tracking down androids in the twenty-first century.

Forbidden Planet (1956, 98 min., color; Director: Fred McLeod Wilcox; with Walter Pigeon and Leslie Nielsen) A retelling of Shakespeare's *The Tempest* as science fiction.

Invasion of the Body Snatchers (1956, 80 min., black and white; Director: Don Siegel; with Kevin McCarthy) People begin acting strangely. Then pods with bodies suspiciously like other residents are found.

Plan 9 from Outer Space (1959, 79 min., black and white; Director: Edward D. Wood, Jr.) Aliens plan to bring the dead to life and take over Earth. Many young people, critics and ordinary viewers, believe this is the worst film ever made, but it's great fun to see if you don't take it seriously. (Who could?)

Sleeper (1973, 88 min., color; Director: Woody Allen; with Allen and Diane Keaton) A man frozen in 1973 is awakened 200 years later in a despotic world. The Miss America contest is hilarious in a wonderful sci-fi spoof. This gets better with every viewing.

Star Wars (1977, 121 min., color; Director: George Lucas; with Mark Hamill, Carrie Fisher, and Harrison Ford) The modern film that made Saturday serial science fiction films respectable again—the excitement never lets up. *The Empire Strikes Back* (1980) and *The Return of the Jedi* (1983) look just fine on the small TV screen.

The Time Machine (1960, 103 min., color; Director: George Pal; with Rod Taylor) Loosely based on H. G. Wells's social satire about the destiny of humans.

2001: A Space Odyssey (1968, 139 min., color; Director: Stanley Kubrick; with Keir Dullea) Space travel and machines and God and almost everything in between. A marvelous film that gets richer with each viewing.

Village of the Damned (1960, 78 min., black and white; Director: Wolf Rilla; with George Sanders) Residents of a small English village black out; later, the women bear eerie-eyed children. From John Wyndham's novel. A spooky and strange film deserving far more attention than it has received.

Types of Science Fiction

The most obvious type, and probably the first to be read by many later fans of science fiction, is the simple-minded but effective story of wild adventure, usually with a touch of sociological or environmental concern. Isaac Asimov's "Lucky Starr" series, written under the Paul French pseudonym, begins with *David Starr: Space Ranger* and a story of an overly populated Earth in need of food. It's a poor book, but it's better adventure than most because Asimov simply could not tell a dull story. Robert Heinlein's early juvenile books suffer from the same fate, particularly the episodic but often thrilling *The Rolling Stones.*

H. G. Wells's *The War of the Worlds* spawned many imitations as we read about this group of aliens invading Earth and that group of aliens attacking another threatened outpost of civilization. But the visits of the aliens continues to appeal to us, partly because it combines the best of two worlds—science fiction and horror.

William Sleator's *Interstellar Pig* may sound like an odd or funny book, but it is not. Sixteen-year-old Barney is intrigued to discover that three different neighbors moved next door. Soon, Barney and the three are playing a board game called Interstellar Pig, and Barney learns fast enough that he stands between the neighbors and the destruction of Earth. John Wyndham's (pseudonym of John Beynon Harris) *The Midwich Cuckoo* is set in an apparently tranquil small town in England. Suddenly and briefly, the town stops dead, and nine months later a number of children with strange eyes and even stranger attitudes are born.

Time travel has been a theme in science fiction since H. G. Wells's *The Time Machine.* Jack Finney's *Time and Again* and its recent sequel *From Time to Time* begin with Simon Morley charged with taking part in a government secret mission. He is transported back to New York City of the 1880s along with a sketch book and a camera and a clear mind for taking detailed notes. He meets the usual corrupt officials, but he also meets Julia and he falls in love, and that makes up for what he does not like. He returns to the present only to learn that the government wants him to continue his work and to change history, or as it puts it, "to correct mistakes of the past which have already affected the present for us."

From Time to Time is, in the minds of some reviewers, one of those rarities, a sequel even better than the original.

The wonder and danger of space travel is an obvious theme in much science fiction. In Larry Niven and Jerry Pourelle's *The Mote in God's Eye*, humans have colonized the galaxy. An alien society sends emissaries to work with the humans and the aliens accidentally die. The humans must send representatives dashing through space to ward off disaster and war. Ben Bova's *Mars* reminds us of the excitement of watching mortals first going into space. Gregory Benford's *Furious Gulf* focuses on the last humans alive on an old spaceship moving directly to a black hole at the center of the universe. It is also about 18-year-old Toby who is going through this disaster just as he goes through the disaster of being an adolescent.

Science frightens most of us some time or other, and the mad scientist or the threat of science gone sour or insane is another theme that runs through science fiction. In a note in Bantam's 1954 revision of Ray Bradbury's *The Martian Chronicles*, Clifton Fadiman describes Bradbury as "a moralist who has caught hold of a simple, obvious but overwhelmingly important moral idea—that we are in the grip of a psychosis, a technology-mania, the final consequences of which can only be universal murder and quite conceivably the destruction of our planet."

William Sleator's *House of Stairs* illustrates how mad psychologists can become to prove a point. Five young people are brought to an experimental house made up almost entirely of stairs madly going everywhere, and the young people learn how cruel scientists can be in attempting to find something adults think is important. Isaac Asimov's *The Ugly Little Boy* is the most touching use of this theme that we know. Scientists have trapped a young Neanderthal boy and have brought him back to our time, all in the name of science. A nurse is hired to take care of him until he is sent back to his own time. The boy is a terrified mess, and the nurse is horrified by him, but her native compassion and his normal need for a friend bring the two together.

The holocaust of a nuclear explosion is a constant fear for all humanity, just as it is for science fiction writers. Robert O'Brien's *Z for Zachariah* begins after the blast. Ann Burden believes that she is the sole survivor because the valley she lives in is protected from fallout. Then she discovers another survivor, and she learns that she is in danger. The book ends somewhat enigmatically with Ann looking for yet more survivors and the hope that decency and compassion survive somewhere out there. Louise Lawrence also writes about the final explosion, and *Andra, Children of the Dust,* and *Moonwind* are powerful stories about survivors. Vonda N. McIntyre's finest novel, *Dreamsnake*, is a mystical story of a world recovering from nuclear war and a young woman who becomes a healer.

Perhaps the gloomiest view of the future is in Philip K. Dick's *Do Androids Dream of Electric Sheep* (reissued as *The Blade Runner* in 1982 when the film adaptation came out). A cop/bounty hunter searches for human-created androids who have escaped from another planet to come back to a horribly drizzling and bleak Earth.

Jane Donawerth made some excellent points in her significant and helpful article in the March 1990 *English Journal;* she noted that between 1818 when Mary Wollstonecraft Shelley published *Frankenstein, or the Modern Prometheus* and the 1930s, women were among the most important writers dealing with technological utopias and similar topics that foreshadowed science fiction:

> But the times when such visions were welcomed did not last; at least in *Amazing Stories* and in *Wonder Stories*, the women virtually disappeared by the mid–1930s. I think that editorial policy, or simply civic pressure on the women, kept their stories from earning money that could go, instead, to a man supporting a family during the Depression.[15]

By the time women returned to science fiction in the 1940s, they used masculine-sounding pen names, for example, Andre Norton and Leigh Brackett. Today, however, science fiction readers have a number of women writers to turn to, notably Ursula K. LeGuin with *The Left Hand of Darkness* and *Dispossessed: An Ambiguous Utopia*, both studies in gender restrictions. Joanna Russ mines much the same field in her books.

Harry Turtledove's *Worldwar: In the Balance* is another type of science fiction in which the author changes history, a type of "what if" book. In *Worldwar*, the first of four projected volumes, the time is 1942, the Allies are at war with the Axis powers, and an alien force of lizardlike things invade Earth with a technology that far surpasses human knowledge. Phillip K. Dick's *The Man in the High Castle* postulates that Germany and Japan have won World War II and the Nazis have taken over most of the United States. Robert Harris's *Fatherland* is set in the 1960s, Germany has supposedly won World War II, and the Holocaust has not yet been uncovered.

Cyberpunk is one of the wildest, rampaging kinds of science fiction today. Gene LaFaille defines cyberpunk as:

> A subgenre of science fiction that incorporates our concern about the future impact of advanced technologies, especially cybernetics, bionics, genetic engineering, and the designer drug culture, upon the individual, who is competing

with the increasing power and control of the multinational corporations that are extending their stranglehold on the world's supply of information.[16]

Cyberpunk is about technology and the power of communication, particularly power used to manipulate people. Bruce Sterling's *Mirrorshades: The Cyberpunk Anthology* is 10 years old, but it still has enough variety to give readers opportunity to see what cyberpunk is and what its ramifications can be. William Gibson's *Neuromancer* was the novel that brought cyberpunk to readers' attention. The antihero of *Neuromancer* gives way to far more likable characters in *Virtual Light*. Neal Stephenson's *Snow Crash* is about a strange computer virus that does all kinds of weird and horrible things to computer hackers. David Brin's *Earth* describes the powerful implications of information technology on society at large.

Science fiction was never as popular on radio as it deserved to be, though "Dimension-X" and "X Minus One" had many fans, but science fiction was popular on television. From Rod Serling's "The Twilight Zone" on through the ever-new casts of "Star Trek," viewers seemed to find TV science fiction irresistible. A recent entry in the field, "The X-Files," seems to have been different enough that it has found an audience. N. E. Genge's *The Unofficial X-Files Companion* is a record of the plots and characters along with the serial killers, cults, werewolfs, robots, and other strangenesses that have roamed through "X-Files" episodes.

Humor is not often the strongest feature of science fiction, but Douglas Adams's *The Hitchhiker's Guide to the Galaxy* is rich in humor, a genuinely funny spoof of the genre. The books that follow in the series are not nearly as happily done, but Adams's first book began as a BBC radio script, progressed to a television script, and ultimately became a novel. When Arthur Dent's house is due for demolition to make way for a highway, he finds Ford Prefect, a strange friend, anxiously seeking a drink at a nearby pub. Ford seems totally indifferent to Arthur's plight because, as he explains, the world will soon be destroyed to make way for a new galactic freeway. Soon the pair are safe aboard a Vogon Construction Fleet Battleship, and that is the most easily explained of the many improbabilities that follow. Any reader desperate to know the meaning of life can find a simple answer in this book.

There are all sorts of scholarly, and unscholarly, books about science fiction, but one new source of information deserves mention for its detailed coverage and superb illustrations. John Clutz's *Science Fiction: The Illustrated Encyclopedia* provides an admirable history of science fiction, comments on major (and minor) authors, classic titles and graphic works, and ample words about science fiction films and international TV. It's a marvelous book and readers of the genre will find it both helpful and provocative.

Utopias and Dystopias

Utopias and dystopias are neither science fiction nor fantasy, but they share characteristics with both. Readers must suspend disbelief and buy into the author's vision, at least for the duration of the story. As with science fiction, utopian and dystopian books are usually set in the future, with technology having played a role

LOUISE LAWRENCE
On Exercising the Imagination

These days we place great emphasis on physical health, the needs of our bodies for a wholesome, nourishing diet and regular exercise. Multimillion-pound industries cater to our requirements. Sports and leisure centers spring up overnight. Extensive advertising campaigns urge and inform us—to eat brown bread and bran-flakes, plenty of fresh fruit and vegetables, not to smoke or drink too much, wear sensible training shoes, jog daily, swim, play squash or practice yoga. But what about our mental health? Who advises us on how to feed and exercise our minds?

From an early age, once past the years of basic infant learning, we are encouraged to apply our minds to a process of rational thinking, to calculate and work things out in a logical way. We are thus trained throughout our growing years, primarily to take our places in the work-job-system. Our capacity to work is, unfortunately, our main value to society and our developing minds are generally geared to this end. In factories, offices, banks, shops, and businesses, in a multitude of jobs that are automatic, mentally untaxing, uncreative, and often boring, the majority of us are destined to spend our working lives. And our main form of mental relaxation is watching television.

But the human mind has other capabilities—impulses driven by imagination—those curious, dreaming, inventive, creative faculties, that give rise to art and music, literature and poetry, great works, great ideas, boundless possibilities. Apart from writing imaginative essays at school, apart from the statutory lessons in art or literature, we are not encouraged to use these faculties or exercise them in any way. Within the work-job-system into which most of us are heading, imagination is seldom required.

Upon leaving the educational system, how and upon what we feed and nourish our minds is entirely up to us. We can binge non-stop on pornographic videos. Feast on television violence. Plug in our Walkmans and fill our heads with punk, or rap, cease to think and never exercise our imagination again.

Imagination—the power to envision images in one's head —to mentally visualize—to actively daydream—what use is it anyway? What's the point of it? We know that every cell, every blood vessel, is necessary to our well-being. We know that limbs that are never exercised atrophy, and bodies fall sick that are fed on junk. It is equally necessary, then, to attend to the health of our minds.

So don't turn on the television. Television cannot feed our imaginations—its images are already formed and in front of us. Instead, pick up a good book and read. And as you read, imagine the scenes the words describe, imagine the characters, share their feelings. And soon you will begin to imagine for yourself —beauty in place of slum dwellings, food in the bellies of starving children, the end of wars and pollution, a world that is better than the world we live in now.

Louise Lawrence's books include *The Patchwork People,* Clarion, 1994; *Keeper of the Universe,* Clarion, 1993, and *Children of the Dust,* HarperCollins, 1985.

in establishing the conditions out of which the story grows. But unlike science fiction and more like fantasy, once the situation is established, authors focus less on technology and more on sociological and psychological or emotional aspects of the story. A utopia is a place of happiness and prosperity; a dystopia is the opposite.

Three interesting young adult books are dystopias. One is Bruce Brooks's *No Kidding,* which tells a serious story of a boy realizing that he cannot, and in fact doesn't want to, make all the decisions for his alcoholic mother and his strange little brother. The story is set in a Washington, D. C., of the future, where 69 percent of the population is alcoholic and children are a treasured commodity because so many people have been made sterile by sitting in front of cathode ray tubes. The story is about two young brothers, Sam and Ollie. Sam is rehabilitating his mother at the same time he attempts to direct and control the foster parents who want to adopt the younger Ollie. Sam is shocked when he finds out that even with all his help Ollie feels a need for something he doesn't have and regularly sneaks out at night to meet with a cultlike religious group.

Despite the grim plot, *No Kidding* is filled with some wonderful kidding about schools, social workers, educational jargon, and the wishful thinking that any problem can be corrected if only we can give it a name and obtain federal funding. Sam goes to an AO (Alcoholic Offspring) school, where, in a tough moment, the counselor confesses to the school nurse that she has not been trained as a generalist counselor, only as an AO specialist:

> I have *no* certification outside AO programs. My thesis was on the doctrinal interface between quantified behavior-analysis patterns and AOCLEP. Quantified! I am trained to deal with kids who are tested every week for theoretical knowledge of specific AO doctrine *and* behavioral adjustment in AO alignments. At my previous school a kid would come in and say "I aggressed on the math teacher's car in a third-level postdenial anger/pity syndrome, and I broke the windshield." I would say, "What's your denial factor?" and he would say "Eight," and I would say "Index of control achievement?" and he would say "Six," and I would know *exactly* what to do with him. . . . Now, what am I supposed to do with a kid who knows nothing except that he threw a rock at a car?

Peter Dickinson's *Eva* is a fascinating story about the daughter of a famous scientist devoting his life to working with chimpanzees. In this futuristic world, chimpanzees are relatively important because all the big animals have vanished. The scientist, his wife, his 13-year-old daughter Eva, and a chimpanzee named Kelly are driving home from an outing when they get in a horrible wreck. Eva remembers nothing but slowly wakes to a controlled environment. Over several weeks she discovers that her mind has been planted in Kelly's body.

The rest of the book is about the next 30 years of Eva's life. The technology is intriguing to read about, but it's the psychological and the social aspects that leave readers pondering ideas about ecology, parent-child and male-female relationships, mass media advertising, medical ethics, and young adult suicide.

Of the three young adult books, Lois Lowry's *The Giver* is the most powerful and disturbing. Jonas lives in an apparently perfect society. At the Ceremony of 12 when the elders assign each young person his career, Jonas is selected to be "our next receiver of memory." Jonas discovers that this job requires him to learn everything that the society has forgotten, in effect things such as color or music or anything else his people have given up for the common good. *The Giver* is brief but gripping, and any reader will be caught up in the story of people who have willingly given up their freedom and their imagination for the supposed "good of the people."

Utopias and dystopias are never likely to be popular with the masses because they usually lack excitement and fast-moving plots. Writers of adventure or fantasy or science fiction begin with a story (the more thrilling the better) and later, if ever, add a message. Writers of utopias and dystopias think first of the message and then devise a story to carry the weight of the message.

The books are usually about dissatisfaction with contemporary society. Many people have no drive to think seriously about societal issues—or to think at all. Readers who do not share the anger or irritation of utopian writers easily miss the allusions needed to follow the story or find the message. For these reasons, utopian literature is likely to appeal only to more thoughtful and intellectual readers. Although these young adults may not share the anger of the writer, given their idealism, they probably share the writer's concerns about society and humanity.

The centuries-old fascination with utopias is suggested by the Greek origin of the word, which includes two meanings, "no place" and "good place." Most of us, in idle moments, dream of a perfect land, a perfect society, a place that would solve all our personal problems and, if we are altruistic enough, all the world's problems as well. In our nightmares, we also dream of the opposite, the dystopias, which are diseased or bad lands. But few of us do more than dream, which may explain why some people are so intrigued with authors who transfer their dreams to the printed page.

In his *Republic* in the fifth century B.C., Plato presented his vision of the ideal world, offering suggestions for educating the ruling class. With wise philosopher-kings, or so Plato maintains, the people would prosper, intellectual joys would flourish (along with censorship, for Plato would ban poets and dramatists from his perfect society), and the land would be permanently safe.

Later utopias were geared less to a ruling class and more to a society that would preserve its peace and create harmony and happiness for the people. Sir Thomas More's *Utopia* (1516) argued for mental equality of the sexes, simple laws understandable to all, and common ownership of everything. Whether More intended his book as a practical solution to society's problems is doubtful, but he probably did mean it as a criticism of contemporary English life. Utopias, after all, are personal and reflect an author's enthusiasm for (or abhorrence of) certain ideas. That was clearly true of two early utopias, Francis Bacon's *The New Atlantis* (1626) and Tommaso Campanella's *City in the Sun* (1623).

During the late 1800s, the popularity of such utopias as Samuel Butler's *Erewhon* (1872) and *Erewhon Revisited* (1901), William Dean Howell's A *Traveler from Altruia* (1894), and Edward Bellamy's *Looking Backward* (1888) paralleled the popularity of people's real-life attempts to seek better lives through various utopian schemes. In the United States, utopian communities at places such as Harmony, Pennsylvania; New Harmony, Indiana; Brook Farm, Massachusetts; Fruitlands, Massachusetts; Oneida, New York; Nauvoo, Illinois; and Corning, Iowa, were rarely more than temporarily satisfactory.

Utopian communities have been the setting for several novels. Elizabeth Howard's *Out of Step with the Dancers* shows a celibate Shaker community in 1853 through the eyes of Damaris as she accompanies her converted father to a strange new life. Religious pacifism in the face of the Civil War is the subject of Janet Hickman's *Zoar Blue,* about the German separatist community of Zoar, Ohio. Lynn Hall's excellent *Too Near the Sun* focuses on 16-year-old Armel Dupree and his Icarian community near Corning, Iowa. To the shame of his family, Armel's older brother has sought life in the outside world. Armel now wonders if he should follow his brother as he views an ideal community composed of less than ideal people.

Yearning for the simpler life, in which we dream of being part of something greater than ourselves, is natural. For some young people, however, the search has led to religious groups less like communes and more like cults. Robert Coover explored the power and madness of a cult in *The Origin of the Brunists.* In that novel, a mining explosion kills 97 people, but one survivor believes that God has saved him to proclaim the approaching end of the world. Two sound nonfiction works give insights about cults and why and how they are often so successful in attracting the most sincere young adults—Willa Appel's *Cults in America: Programmed for Paradise* and David G. Bromley and Anson D. Shupe, Jr.'s, *Strange Gods: The Great American Cult Scare.* The frightening consequences of the assault on the Branch Davidian compound in Waco, Texas, in early 1993 is the subject of Dick J. Reavis's *The Ashes of Waco: An Investigation*, not the last of the cult problems but a particularly troubling one because of the death of many children.

Dystopias are more dramatic and exaggerated than their counterparts and for that reason are more successful in attracting young adults. Dystopias warn us of society's drift toward a particularly horrifying or sick world lying just over the horizon. They are sometimes misinterpreted as prophecies alone, but books such as Aldous Huxley's *Brave New World* and George Orwell's *Nineteen Eighty-Four* and *Animal Farm* are part prophecy, part warning. Readers who get to know and care about the Savage and Winston Smith are never again able to regard a discussion of individual freedom in an abstract way.

A theme that we'll certainly see more of is that of disasters caused by ecological carelessness. Thomas Baird's *Smart Rats* is a disturbing exploration of this theme. Everything is rationed, including children (one per family); the government is all-powerful except when it comes to solving problems; contaminated areas are said to be harmless, and areas that the government does not want entered are said to be infested with killer rats, from which the book gets its title. Inspired by all the terrible things that are happening both inside and outside his family, 17-year-old Laddie Grayson connives his way into a forbidden area of the library and reads about the effects of various chemicals. In this truly depressing book, Laddie keeps his theories to himself about an insecticide that his pregnant mother encountered, but he realizes what he must do. He also enrolls in a special school to become part of the "system." The question for readers is whether Laddie can remain inside the system without becoming corrupt.

To attract young adult readers, dystopian books have to have something extra because, with a few exceptions, young adults are optimistic and imaginative. Adults might read dystopian books on the premise that misery loves company, but teenagers have not lived long enough to lose their natural curiosity, and they have not been weighed down with adult problems such as failing health, heavy family responsibilities, expenses surpassing income, and dreams gone bankrupt. So even when teenagers read dystopian books, they probably wear rose-colored glasses, feeling grateful for the world as it usually is.

David Macaulay's *Motel of the Mysteries* is a wonderful spoof of scientific arrogance unmasked as a wild guessing game. The book begins with the ominous description of the burial of the North American continent under tons of third-class and fourth-class mail (caused by an accidental reduction in postal rates). Since the year 3850, scholars have wondered about the lost civilization, but it is left to 42-year-old Howard Carson to stumble and fall into a secret chamber. There he discovers a "gleaming secret seal" (DO NOT DISTURB) and a "plant that would not die." He enters the chamber and finds a body atop a "ceremonial platform" near a statue of the "deity WATT" and a container, "ICE," designed to "preserve, at least symbolically, the major internal organs of the deceased for eternity." Later he enters the inner chamber and there finds another body "in a highly polished white sarcophagus" behind translucent curtains. Near this body is a "sacred urn" and a "sacred parchment" holder and the "sacred collar" with a headband beating a ceremonial chant, "Sanitized for Your Protection." The drawing of Howard Carson playing savant and the many artifacts recovered from the motel bedroom and bathroom add to the fun. Museum goers will particularly enjoy the concluding section of the book devoted to "Souvenirs and Quality Reproductions" from the Carson excavations now for sale.

The books we've talked about in this chapter start with life as we know it and attempt to stretch readers' imaginations. All of us need to dream, not to waste our lives but to enrich them. To dream is to recognize humanity's possibilities. In a world hardly characterized by undue optimism, the genres treated here offer us challenges and hope, not the sappy sentimentalism of "everything always works out for the best" (for it often does not) but realistic hope based on our noblest dreams of surviving. If we go down, we do it knowing that we have cared and dreamed and found something for which we are willing to struggle.

Notes

[1]Ursula LeGuin, "On Teaching Science Fiction," in Jack Williamson, ed., *Teaching Science Fiction: Education for Tomorrow* (Oswick Press, 1980), p. 22.

[2]Walter Wangerin, Jr., in a lecture, "By Faith, Fantasy," quoted in John H. Timmerman's *Other Worlds: The Fantasy Genre* (Bowling Green University Popular Press, 1983), p. 21.

[3]This point, with many more examples, is made repeatedly by Leslie E. Owen in "Children's Science Fiction and Fantasy Grow Up," *Publishers Weekly* 232 (October 30, 1987): 32–37.

[4]Mary Harrington Hall, "A Conversation with Ray Bradbury and Chuck Jones," *Psychology Today* 1 (April 1969): 28–29.

[5]Jo-Anne Goodwin, "In Defence of Fantasy," *Independent* Magazine, London, July 25, 1993, p. 32.

[6]John Rowe Townsend, "Heights of Fantasy," in Gerard J. Senick, ed., *Children's Review,* Vol. 5. (Gale Research, 1983), p. 7.

[7]Lloyd Alexander, "High Fantasy and Heroic Romance," *Horn Book Magazine* 47 (December 1971): 483.

[8]Tamora Pierce, "Fantasy: Why Kids Read it, Why Kids Need it," *School Library Journal* 39 (October 1993): 51.

[9]Ursula LeGuin, "Why Are Americans So Afraid of Dragons?" *PNLA* (Pacific Northwest Library Association) *Quarterly* 38 (Winter 1974): 18.

[10]Mary Cadogan and Patricia Craig, *You're a Brick, Angela! A New Look at Girls' Fiction from 1839 to 1975* (Gollancz, 1976), p, 371.

[11]Robert Heinlein, "Ray Guns and Rocket Ships," *Library Journal* 78 (July 1953): 1188.

[12]Anthony Wolk, "Challenge the Boundaries: An Overview of Science Fiction and Fantasy," *English Journal* 79 (March 1990): 26–31.

[13]Ray Bradbury, "Science Fiction: Why Bother?" *Teacher's Guide: Science Fiction* (Bantam, n.d.), p. 1.

[14]Arthur Clarke, *Profiles of the Future* (Holt, 1984), p. 9.

[15]Jane Donawerth, "Teaching Science Fiction by Women," *English Journal* 79 (March 1990): 39–40.

[16]Gene LaFaille. "Science Fiction: Top Guns of the 1980s," *Wilson Library Bulletin* 65 (December 1990); 34.

Titles Mentioned in the Text of Chapter Six

Adams, Douglas. *The Hitchhiker's Guide to the Galaxy.* Harmony, 1979.

Adams, Richard. *Watership Down.* Macmillan, 1974.

Alexander, Lloyd. *The Black Cauldron.* Holt, 1965.

Alexander, Lloyd. *The Book of Three.* Holt, 1964.

Alexander, Lloyd. *The Castle of Llyr.* Holt, 1966.

Alexander, Lloyd. *The High King.* Holt, 1968.

Alexander, Lloyd. *Taran Wanderer.* Holt, 1967.

Appel, Willa. *Cults in America: Programmed for Paradise.* Holt, 1983.

Asimov, Isaac. *Forward the Foundation,* Doubleday, 1993.

Asimov, Isaac. *The Ugly Little Boy.* TOR, 1958.

Bacon, Francis. *The New Atlantis.* 1627

Baird, Thomas. *Smart Rats.* HarperCollins, 1990.

Beagle, Peter. *A Fine and Private Place.* Viking, 1960.

Beagle, Peter. *The Innkeeper's Song.* Penguin, 1993.

Beagle, Peter. *The Last Unicorn.* Viking, 1968.

Bellamy, Edward. *Looking Backward.* 1887.

Benford, Gregory. *Furious Gulf.* Bantam, 1994.

Bova, Ben. *Mars.* Bantam, 1992.

Bradbury, Ray. *The Martian Chronicles.* Doubleday, 1950.

Bradley, Marion Zimmer. *The Best of Marion Zimmer Bradley's Fantasy Magazine.* Warner, 1994.

Bradley, Marion Zimmer. *Darkover Landfall.* DAW Books, 1972.

Bradley, Marion Zimmer. *Lady of the Trillium.* Bantam, 1995.

Bradley, Marion Zimmer. *The Mists of Avalon.* Knopf, 1983.

Bradley, Marion Zimmer. *Red Sun of Darkover.* DAW Books, 1987.

Bradshaw, Gillian. *Hawk of May.* Simon & Schuster, 1982.

Bradshaw, Gillian. *Kingdom of Summer.* Simon & Schuster, 1981.

Bradshaw, Gillian. *In Winter's Shadow.* Simon & Schuster, 1982.

Brin, David. *Earth.* Bantam, 1990.

Bromley, David G., and Anson D. Shupe, Jr. *Strange Gods: The Great American Cult Scare.* Beacon Press, 1982.

Brooks, Bruce. *No Kidding.* HarperCollins, 1989.

Butler, Samuel. *Erewhon,* 1872.

Butler, Samuel. *Erewhon Revisited,* 1901.

Campanella, Tommaso. *City in the Sun,* 1637.

Card, Orson Scott. *Ender's Game.* TOR, 1985.

Card, Orson Scott. *Speaker for the Dead.* TOR, 1986.

Clarke, Arthur C. *Childhood's End.* Houghton Mifflin, 1953.

Clarke, Arthur C. *Profiles of the Future.* Holt, 1984.

Clarke, Arthur C. *2001: A Space Odyssey.* New American Library, 1968.

Clute, John. *Science Fiction: The Illustrated Encyclopedia.* Dorling Kindersley, 1995.

Coover, Robert. *The Origin of the Brunists.* Viking, 1977.

Dick, Phillip K. *Do Androids Dream of Electric Sheep.* Doubleday, 1968.

Dick, Phillip K. *The Man in the High Castle.* Putnam, 1962.

Dickinson, Peter. *Eva.* Delacorte, 1989.

Finney, Jack. *From Time to Time.* Simon & Schuster, 1995.

Finney, Jack. *Time and Again*. Simon & Schuster, 1970.

Frank, Pat. *Alas, Babylon*. Lippincott, 1959.

French, Paul (Isaac Asimov). *David Starr: Space Ranger*. Doubleday, 1952.

Garner, Alan. *Elidor*. London: Collins, 1965.

Garner, Alan. *The Moon of Gomrath*. London: Collins, 1963.

Garner, Alan. *The Owl Service*. Walck, 1967.

Garner, Alan. *Red Shift*. Macmillan, 1973.

Garner, Alan. *The Weirdstone of Brisingamen*. London: Collins, 1960.

Genge, N. E. *The Unofficial X-Files Companion*. Crown, 1995.

Gibson, William. *Neuromancer*. Ace, 1984.

Gibson, William. *Virtual Light*. Bantam, 1993

Grahame, Kenneth. *The Wind in the Willows* (originally published in 1908).

Hall, Lynn. *Too Near the Sun*. Follett, 1970.

Harris, Robert. *Fatherland*. Random House, 1992.

Heinlein, Robert A. *Farmer in the Sky*. Scribner, 1950.

Heinlein, Robert A. *The Moon Is a Harsh Mistress*. Putnam, 1966.

Heinlein, Robert A. *Podkayne of Mars*. Putnam, 1963.

Heinlein, Robert A. *The Rolling Stones*. Scribner, 1952.

Heinlein, Robert A. *Stranger in a Strange Land*. Putnam, 1961.

Hickman, Janet. *Zoar Blue*. Macmillan, 1978.

Howard, Elizabeth. *Out of Step with the Dancers*. Morrow, 1978.

Howells, William Dean. *A Traveller From Altruria*. 1894.

Huxley, Aldous. *Brave New World*. HarperCollins, 1932.

Langton, Jane. *The Fledgling*. HarperCollins, 1980.

Lawrence, Louise. *Andra*. Harper & Row, 1971. First American edition, 1991.

Lawrence, Louise. *Children of the Dust*. HarperCollins, 1980.

Lawrence, Louise. *Moonwind*. HarperCollins, 1986.

LeGuin, Ursula K. *The Dispossessed: An Ambiguous Utopia*. HarperCollins, 1974.

LeGuin, Ursula K. *The Farthest Shore*. Atheneum, 1972.

LeGuin, Ursula K. *The Left Hand of Darkness*. Ace, 1969.

LeGuin, Ursula K. *Tehanu: The Last Book of Earthsea*. Macmillan, 1990.

LeGuin, Ursula K. *The Tombs of Atuan*. Atheneum, 1972.

LeGuin, Ursula K. *The Wizard of Earthsea*. Parnassus, 1963.

Lowry, Lois. *The Giver*. Houghton Mifflin, 1993.

Lucian. *The True History*. 2nd Century A.D.

Macaulay, David. *Motel of the Mysteries*. Houghton Mifflin, 1979.

McCaffrey, Anne. *Dragondrums*. Atheneum, 1979.

McCaffrey, Anne. *Dragonsinger*. Atheneum, 1977.

McCaffrey, Anne. *Dragonsong*. Atheneum, 1976.

McCaffrey, Anne. *Freedom's Landing*. Putnam, 1995.

McCaffrey, Anne, and Elizabeth Ann Scarborough. *Powers That Be*. Ballantine, 1993.

McKinley, Robin. *Beauty: A Retelling of the Story of Beauty and the Beast*. HarperCollins, 1978.

McKinley, Robin. *The Blue Sword*. Greenwillow, 1982.

McKinley, Robin. *The Hero and the Crown*. Greenwillow, 1984.

More, Thomas. *Utopia*. 1516.

Niven, Larry, and Jerry Pournell. *The Mote in God's Eye*. Simon & Schuster, 1974.

O'Brien, Robert C. *Mrs. Frisby and the Rats of NIMH*. Atheneum, 1971.

O'Brien, Robert C. *Z for Zachariah*. Atheneum, 1975.

Orwell, George. *Animal Farm*. Harcourt Brace Jovanovich, 1954.

Orwell, George. *Nineteen Eighty-Four*. Harcourt Brace Jovanovich, 1940.

Plato. *The Republic*. 5th Century B.C.

Reavis, Dick J. *The Ashes of Waco: An Investigation*. Simon & Schuster, 1995.

Shelley, Mary Wollstonecraft. *Frankenstein, or the Modern Prometheus*. 1818.

Sleator, William. *House of Stairs*. Dutton, 1974.

Sleator, William. *Interstellar Pig*. Dutton, 1984.

Stephenson, Neal. *Snow Crash*. Bantam, 1992.

Sterling, Bruce, ed. *Mirrowshades: The Cyberpunk Anthology*. Morrow, 1986.

Stewart, Mary. *The Crystal Cave*. Morrow, 1970.

Stewart, Mary. *The Hollow Hills*. Morrow, 1973.

Stewart, Mary. *The Last Enchantment*. Morrow, 1979.

Stewart, Mary. *The Wicked Day*. Morrow, 1984.

Sutcliff, Rosemary. *The Light Beyond the Forest: The Quest for the Holy Grail*. Dutton, 1979.

Sutcliff, Rosemary. *The Road to Camlann: The Death of King Arthur*. Dutton, 1982.

Sutcliff, Rosemary. *The Sword and the Circle: King Arthur and the Knights of the Round Table*. Dutton, 1981.

Swift, Jonathan. *Gulliver's Travels*. 1726.

Tolkien, J. R. R. *The Hobbit, or There and Back Again*. Houghton Mifflin, 1938.

Tolkien, J. R. R. *The Lord of the Rings*. Houghton Mifflin. Composed of three parts: *The Fellowship of the Rings*, 1954, rev. ed., 1967; *The Two Towers*, 1955, rev. ed., 1967; and *The Return of the King*, 1956, rev. ed., 1967.

Tolkien, J. R. R. *The Silmarillion*. Houghton Mifflin, 1983.

Turtledove, Harry. *Worldwar: In the Balance*. Ballantine, 1994.

Verne, Jules. *Journey to the Center of the Earth*. 1864.

Verne, Jules. *Twenty Thousand Leagues Under the Sea.* 1870.

Vonnegut, Kurt, Jr. *God Bless You, Mr. Rosewater or Pearls Before Swine.* Holt, 1965.

Walton, Evangeline. *The Children of Llyr: The Second Branch of the Mabinogion.* Ballantine, 1971.

Walton, Evangeline. *The Island of the Mighty.* Ballantine, 1970 (first printed as *The Virgin and the Swine: The Fourth Branch of the Mabinogion*).

Walton, Evangeline. *The Prince of Annwn: The First Branch of the Mabinogion.* Ballantine, 1974.

Walton, Evangeline. *The Song of Rhiannon: The Third Branch of the Mabinogion.* Ballantine, 1972.

Wangerin, Walter, Jr. *The Book of the Dun Cow.* HarperCollins, 1978.

Wangerin, Walter, Jr. *The Book of Sorrows.* HarperCollins, 1985.

Wells, H. G. *The Time Machine.* 1895.

Wells, H. G. *The War of the Worlds.* 1898.

White, E. B. *Charlotte's Web.* HarperCollins, 1952.

White, T. H. *The Book of Merlyn: The Unpublished Conclusion.* University of Texas Press, 1977.

White, T. H. *The Once and Future King.* Putnam's, 1958.

Wrede, Patricia C. *Calling on Dragons.* Harcourt Brace, 1993.

Wrede, Patricia C. *Dealing with Dragons.* Harcourt Brace, 1990.

Wrede, Patricia C. *Searching for Dragons.* Harcourt Brace, 1991.

Wrede, Patricia C. *Talking to Dragons.* Harcourt Brace, 1993.

Wyndham, John. *The Midwich Cuckoo.* M. Joseph, 1957.

Yep, Laurence. *Dragon Cauldron.* HarperCollins, 1991.

Yolen, Jane. *Dragon's Blood.* Delacorte, 1982.

Yolen, Jane. *Heart's Blood.* Delacorte, 1984.

Yolen, Jane. *A Sending of Dragons.* Delacorte, 1987.

For information on the availability of paperback editions of these titles, please consult the most recent edition of *Paperbound Books in Print,* published annually by R. R. Bowker Company.

Chapter 7

History and History Makers
Of People and Places

. . . .

The United States has always viewed history in its own way. More than a century ago, Ralph Waldo Emerson described the great American tradition as "trampling on tradition," and Abraham Lincoln said that Americans had a "perfect rage for the new." But by the beginning of the twentieth century, Americans were feeling more confident and were ready to look back. American history became a standard part of the school curriculum, thousands of towns erected statues of Abraham Lincoln and Ulysses S. Grant, and historical pageants flourished, including in the South, where Confederates began to look back with pride on their role in the Civil War.

As interested as we may be in history, we are always more concerned about the present, and we find ourselves imposing present-day values on the past. In 1927, Henry Seidel Canby wrote, "Historical fiction, like history, is more likely to register an exact truth about the writer's present than the exact truth of the past."[1] Historian Michael Kammen developed a similar point in *Mystic Chords of Memory*. *Time* magazine reviewer Richard Stengel praised Kammen for showing how "Throughout American history, facts have been transformed into myths and myths transformed into beliefs." Immigrants came to the United States to escape the past, but once they were settled here they contributed to a "kind of ethnic American syllogism: the first generation zealously preserves; the second generation zealously forgets; the third generation zealously rediscovers." Kammen wrote that after World War II, Americans were tied together by a sense of patriotism, but in the 1960s this was replaced by a decade of questioning. In the 1970s, it turned to nostalgia (i.e., "history without guilt"), which continued in the 1980s with a "selective memory and a soothing amnesia." History became a growth industry, and under Reagan "public history was privatized, so that it was Coca Cola, not the U.S. government, that brought you the centennial of the Statue of Liberty."[2]

Despite the flaws that Kammen points out, the history "growth industry" has generally been positive for the education of young people.

. . . .

Trade Books for History Study

Kammen's book focuses on people's predilection for comfortable myths (i.e., nostalgia), as opposed to factual history, but what he says is more true of popular entertainment, such as *Gunsmoke*'s portrayal of the wild west and *The Waltons*' portrayal of American life in the early twentieth century than about history-related trade books. Moreover, it is not as true of trade books as it is of textbooks. Textbook writers often rely on comfortable myths because to be adopted in a school district the books must go through so many committees and stages of approval that by the time they actually get to classrooms they are likely to be extremely bland. If a point of view is expressed, it is likely to be in support of the status quo. For example, a 1983 State of Texas mandate on textbook selection reads, "Positive aspects of the USA's history must be stressed in world history texts used in public schools." In commenting on this mandate, Betty Carter and Richard Abrahamson observed that "Those negatives—the sorry mistakes that have dotted our past and may well affect our future—are either left out, glossed over, or presented in a favorable light." For example, a history book prepared under this philosophy might present the Spanish-American War as "little more than a dramatic charge up San Juan Hill" and America's ignoring of Hitler's rise to power and his evil intentions as a "failure to communicate with Eastern Europe." Carter and Abrahamson warn that such distortions "turn the drama of history into a whitewash."[3]

Fortunately the writers of history-related trade books are freer to pursue particular points of view because their books are purchased individually or by libraries, which endorse, at least on paper, having a great variety of opinions and

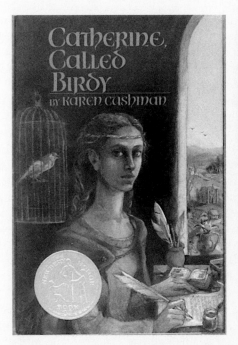

Karen Cushman's *Catherine, Called Birdy* and Art Spiegelman's *Maus* and *Maus II* are among the most original history books to appear within a decade.

points of view. Also with trade books, writers have frequent chances to incorporate new attitudes and new findings because individuals and libraries provide a steady market. Reviewers and other evaluators stand guard, so that over the last several years increasing emphasis has been given to the importance of authenticity and the use of primary sources. Nonfiction writer Brent Ashabranner, for example, has said that one of the things he's learned from reviewers is how seriously they feel about documentation. After his first few books were criticized, he has been much more careful with his bibliographies and has taken special pains to let readers know where he has gotten his information. He thinks extensive footnotes interrupt the flow of reading, and so he tries to put the information "into the text in a way that doesn't interfere with the prose but assures the reader that I didn't just make things up."[4]

Books created from letters and diaries reassure readers that they are reading authentic history, as in Barry Denenberg's *Voices from Vietnam* and Annette Tapert's *Lines of Battle: Letters from American Servicemen, 1941–1945.* Relying on primary sources goes a long way toward keeping authors and subsequently their readers from wallowing in nostalgia. Also, today it's standard practice in history books for the author to include a foreword or afterword discussing his or her methods of research and giving suggestions for further reading. Milton Meltzer uses photos, letters, diaries, and speeches of people who were there to provide a personal-experience account of the Civil War in *Voices from the Civil War: A Documentary History of the Great American Conflict.*

Interest in one area or one medium almost always feeds interest and work in related areas. For example, in 1989, *The Civil War* series broadcast by PBS generated interest in books and movies about the Civil War. An obvious follow-up was a large and expensive coffee table book, *The Civil War: An Illustrated History* by Geoffrey Ward, based on the filmscript and including many of the original letters. Dozens of other books also grew out of the project, either directly or indirectly.

The PBS series, which was broadcast a year earlier, undoubtedly increased interest in the movie *Glory,* a story of African-American Civil War soldiers. In turn, Clinton Cox, a prize-winning African-American journalist, capitalized on the interest engendered by the movie when he wrote *Undying Glory: The Story of the Massachusetts 54th Regiment,* published by Scholastic in 1991. But when a history teacher in our local high school showed *Glory,* a parent protested "because of the violence" and a major controversy erupted. The result was that the school board voted that no "R"-rated movies were to be shown. Many of the townspeople who came to the public hearing to protest the board's recommendation suspected that the original discomfort over the movie *Glory* was not because of the violence, but because of the challenge the movie posed to several comfortable myths about African-Americans.

We need to make our students aware of controversies, such as that which surrounded the showing of Oliver Stone's *JFK* or the appearance of several books about Christopher Columbus a few years ago. Kathy Pelta in *Discovering Christopher Columbus: How History Is Invented* and Milton Meltzer in *Columbus and the World Around Him* both sorted out what was factual and undisputed about Columbus from the conjectural and the contradictory.

One way we can do this is to demand that authors be careful to distinguish between what is known and what is only believed but unproven or unprovable. We need to help students develop skills to interpret the author's clues. A good book to start with, because of its format, is Dorothy and Thomas Hoobler's *The Fact or Fiction Files: Lost Civilizations.* On one side of the pages are the facts as they are known about such mysteries as Stonehenge and the carved heads on Easter Island. On the other side, the authors present hypotheses and conjectures. William Loren Katz, in his *Breaking the Chains: African-American Slave Resistance,* spends a good deal of time discussing and refuting some of the myths and historical misrepresentations about slavery that have allowed people to believe that most slaves were satisfied with their lot.

The best way to show young readers that there are different opinions and different ways of looking at history is to encourage the use of several books on the same subject. When a topic is to be studied, instead of assigning all students to read the same book, bring in individual copies of various books, so that students can choose. Encourage them to trade with one another, to skim, and to read excerpts. Then after they have immersed themselves in their topic, they can make some kind of presentation to the class or work together on a culminating activity that illustrates the different viewpoints.

By making connections, students can understand not only the *who, what,* and *when* of things, but also the *why.* For example, Malcolm C. MacPherson's *Time Bomb: Fermi, Heisenberg, and the Race for the Atomic Bomb* is a good companion book to Carl B. Feldbaum and Ronald J. Bee's *Looking the Tiger in the Eye: Confronting the Nuclear Threat.*

One of the most useful contributions of teachers and librarians is to pull together groups of related books. For example, students can better appreciate Walter Dean Myers's *Malcolm X: By Any Means Necessary* if they also have access to other books about the history of African-Americans. See Chapter Eleven on thematic units for further discussion of this point.

Historical Fact and Fiction

Most of us read historical novels because we are curious about other times, places, and peoples; we also read them because, most important, we want adventure, suspense, and mystery. Movies as old as *Captain Blood, Gone with the Wind,* or *The Scarlet Pimpernel* continue to pique our interest, however ignorant we may be of the times and places described. Historical adventures remain readable much longer than contemporary, realistic stories (e.g., Sir Walter Scott's *Ivanhoe* [1819], Alexandre Dumas's *The Count of Monte Cristo* [1844], Mary Johnston's *To Have and to Hold* [1900], Rafael Sabatini's *Scaramouche* [1921], Helen Waddell's *Peter Abelard* [1933], Elizabeth Goudge's *Green Dolphin Street* [1944], and Margaret Walker's *Jubilee* [1966]).

As with any literary form, there are standards for judging historical novels.(See Table 7.1). They should be historically accurate and steeped in the sense of time and place. We should recognize totems and taboos, food, clothing,

TABLE 7.1

SUGGESTIONS FOR EVALUATING HISTORICAL FICTION

A good historical novel usually has	A poor historical novel may have
A setting that is integral to the story	A story that could have happened any time or any place. The historical setting is for visual appeal and to compensate for a weak story
An authentic rendition of the time, place, and people being featured	
An author who is so thoroughly steeped in the history of the period that he or she can be comfortably creative without making mistakes	Anachronisms in which the author illogically mixes up people, events, speaking styles, social values, or technological developments from different time periods
Believeable characters with whom young readers can identify	Awkward narration and exposition as the author tries to teach history through characters' conversations
Evidence that even across great time spans people share similiar emotions	Oversimplification of the historical issues and a stereotyping of the "bad" and the "good" guys
References to well-known events or people, or other clues through which the reader can place the happenings in their correct historical framework	Characters who fail to come alive as individuals having something in common with the readers. They are just stereotyped representatives of a particular period
Readers who come away with the feeling that they know a time or place better. It is as if they have lived in it for at least a few hours	

vocations, leisure activities, customs, smells, religions, literature—all that goes to make one time and one place unique from another. Enthusiasts forgive no anachronism, no matter how slight. Historical novels should give a sense of history's continuity, a feeling of the flow of history from one time into another, which is, for good reason, different from the period before. But as writers allow us to feel that flow of history, they should particularize their portraits of one time and one place. Historical novels should tell a lively story with a sense of impending danger, mystery, suspense, or romance.

Historical novels allow us—at their best they force us—to make connections and to realize that despair is as old and as new as hope, that loyalty and treachery, love and hatred, compassion and cruelty were and are inherent in humanity, whether it be in ancient Greece, Elizabethan England, or post–World War I Germany. As with most writers, historical novelists may want to teach particular lessons. Christopher Collier, for example, makes no pretense about why he and his brother write about the American Revolution in their fine historical novels:

> . . . [T]he books I write with my brother are written with a didactic purpose—
> to teach about ideals and values that have been important in shaping the

course of American history. This is in no way intended to denigrate the importance of the dramatic and literary elements of historical novels. Nothing will be taught, and certainly nothing learned, if no one reads the books.[5]

Collier later added that "there is no better way to teach history than to embrace potential readers and fling them into a living past."[6] Sheila A. Egoff clearly felt happily about the historical novel when she wrote, "For most adults over fifty years of age, childhood reading is almost synonymous with historical romance."[7] But Patty Campbell in 1980 questioned whether young adults read historical novels today:

> This reviewer has long been convinced that young adults lack a sense of history to a significant degree. They will accept a good YA novel with a historical setting if the other elements of the story are appealing enough to overcome that drawback, but, in general, so-called historical fiction is sudden death on the YA shelf.[8]

Campbell's point may still be uncomfortably true today.

For years, British critics have acclaimed Rosemary Sutcliff the finest writer of British historical fiction for young people. From her finest early novel in 1954, *The Eagle of the Ninth,* through her 1990 *The Shining Company,* she clearly has no peer in writing about early Britain. We need someone now to find a way to get American kids to read her books and savor them as most adult readers do. The books need to be promoted by excited librarians to the right young readers, those who care about history and a rattling good story and who are not put off by a period of time they know little about. Her 1990 *The Shining Company* may be even harder to sell than Sutcliff's earlier books about the Normans and the Saxons (e.g., *The Shield Ring* and *Dawn Wind*) because it is set in a more obscure time, seventh-century Britain. Sutcliff knows what happened in the horrible battles in her novels, and she knows about the cries of men and the screams of stricken horses, the smell of blood and filth. Sutcliff cares about people who make history, whether knaves or villains or, in this case, naive men who trusted their king and themselves beyond common sense.

Leon Garfield's world is the eighteenth century, with an occasional detour into early nineteenth-century England. Beginning with *Jack Holborn* in 1965 and continuing with his more recent books, including *The Empty Sleeve,* Garfield set a standard for historical writing that few can match. Garfield's eighteenth century is the world of Fielding and Smollett, lusty and squalid and ugly and bustling and swollen, full of life and adventure and the certainty that being born an orphan may lead you ultimately to fame and fortune. Typically, eighteenth-century novels open with an orphan searching for identity. Garfield does not fear conventions, but his stories also play with reality versus illusion, daylight versus dreams, flesh versus fantasy. His ability to sketch out minor characters in a line or two and make them come alive is impressive. Of a man in *The Sound of Coaches,* he writes, "He was one of those gentlemen who affect great gallantry to all the fair sex except their wives."

Of a prostitute, he writes, "A full face of beauty spots, with graveyard dust between." And of the protagonist we are told, "although jealousy was ordinarily foreign to Sam's nature, they did, on occasion, talk the same language." Garfield's epigrams are often most effective—for example, "Many a man is made good by being thought so."

Wit, humor, and liveliness permeate Garfield's books. Perhaps the funniest are *The Strange Affair of Adelaide Harris* and its sequel, *The Night of the Comet*. In *Adelaide,* Bostock and Harris, two nasty pupils in Dr. Bunnion's Academy, become so entranced with stories of Spartan babies abandoned on mountaintops, there to be suckled by wolves, that they borrow Harris' baby sister to determine for themselves the truth of the old tales. Therein begins a wild comedy of errors and an even wilder series of coincidences and near duels and wild threats that hardly lets up until the last lines.

Scott O'Dell's death ended a career of excellent historical novels. *The King's Fifth* is probably his most convincing work, with its picture of sixteenth-century Spaniards and the moral strains put on anyone involved in the search for gold and fame. It is convincing, often disturbing, and, similar to most of O'Dell's historical novels, generally worth pursuing. Students coming to high school with a good reading background probably already know O'Dell from his *Island of the Blue Dolphin* and *Sing Down the Moon,* both of which present original and positive portrayals of young Native American women suffering at the hands of white settlers in the middle to late 1800s.

O'Dell was a pioneer in featuring strong young women in these two books, but within the last couple of decades several good writers have followed his lead, so that good historical books about women and minorities are much easier to find. *The True Confessions of Charlotte Doyle* by Avi is a brilliant example. This rollicking nineteenth-century sea yarn has to be read with a willing suspension of disbelief. The adventure begins in 1832, when 13-year-old Charlotte is brought to a British ship on which she is to sail to America to join her family. Her father's shipping company had called him home to Rhode Island in midwinter, and the family had gone with him while Charlotte stayed behind to finish her year at the Barrington School for Better Girls. She was to travel home during the summer on one of the company's ships. Two other families, who were to travel with her, are frightened away from the ship by something so terrible that even porters on the dock refuse to carry her luggage to the *Seahawk*. Readers who revel in adventures at sea would also like Philip McCutchan's *Apprentice to the Sea*.

Half the excitement is finding out the cause of the terror; the other half is seeing whether Charlotte can face it. Indeed she can, but not without some significant chills and thrills on the way. The story is enough to warm the hearts of feminists because, despite the accusation of murder, the trial, and the guilty verdict, Charlotte emerges as an exceptionally strong young woman ready to accept the challenge of the *Seahawk* all over again.

Ann Rinaldi has written a number of excellent historical novels using real historical figures and teaching readers about a time and a place. Four of her books are particularly fine—*Wolf by the Ears; A Break With Charity: A Story About the Salem*

PETER CARTER
On Passports

I have a British passport; handsome, stoutly bound in blue, and embossed in gold with our Royal coat of arms. It is stamped with dozens of visas which remind of my travels (and travails) and which awaken memories, mainly good but some bad—waiting for days at remote border points upon some corrupt and indolent official—and a few hair-raising, like my trip across the Sahara Desert.

This August (1995) I have to obtain a new passport. Mine, redolent of Imperial majesty, will be exchanged for a slim, limp, orange document informing the world at large that I am a citizen of the European Community.

Many Brits (including friends of mine) are outraged by this change in passports, feeling that they are being robbed of their national identity. I, on the contrary, am delighted; in fact, I wish I could have a world passport; but as it is I shall be glad to be legally as well as culturally a citizen of Europe, and without in any way losing my pride in my country's vast achievements in art, science, and democracy, to be able to live or work in Europe as I wish and to relish its dazzling variety—all available within a couple of hours from London—although I am not unmindful of the shadows of the death camps and torture chambers which still linger on.

I think that this is a good response for a writer. There are exceptions (Celine is one) but the *best* writers (I don't count myself as one) while deeply rooted in their own communities and cultures are able to reach out to people everywhere. I remember as a youth being absorbed in William Faulkner's novels, although Mississippi was as alien to me as Mars. This sounds a little odd to my ears since my own work ranges from Iron Age Britain to the Berlin of the Cold War—taking in Mao's China and the Kansas of the Old West, but while drawing on my own experiences I have tried (I put it no higher) to speak to those who, brought up in vastly different circumstances, nonetheless face, as we all do, those implacable certainties of growing up, earning a living in a tough world, getting old, and finally hearing as the great Ray Charles says, Death, "That old tom-cat scratching at the door, and you got no choice but to let him in."

But "One touch of nature makes the whole world kin," and, without being pious, kin is what we are; and even if we don't actually believe it we had better start acting as if we do or the Four Horsemen of the Apocalypse are really going to whoop it up; you might already hear them in the distance; as Jefferson said about slavery, "Like a fire-bell in the night."

This small but noble island, Britain, has a vast coastline, dangerous and littered with innumerable wrecks. Occasionally I go sailing, and as dusk falls, Trinity House, charged with the safety of our seas, switches on its illuminations and the light-houses blink out their assuring messages; and it seems to me that the best writers are somewhat like that; beams of light in a moral darkness saying, "Humans here. Human Beings. Come and join us. All you need to do is open a book."

But there are two other nautical signals which appeal to me. The first is Echo Delta (E. D.) (in Morse Code .-. .), which means, "Your distress signal understood."

(continued)

And writers may not be, as Shelley claimed, the unacknowledged legislators of the world, but at least they understand and empathize with your distress signals and can answer Echo Delta.

Having made these obvious, and no doubt tedious, points, I might add this. By a nice coincidence, the Delta of the signal has its own meaning, and looking back on my own, long life, from childhood in poverty to Oxford University (England) and from years as a rough laborer to being a professional writer, I like to think of Delta (-. .), which means, "Steer clear of me, I am not fully under control."

It's the signal for me; had I lived fully under control I might never have written a novel, or had the pleasure of addressing you.

Peter Carter's books include *Bury the Dead,* 1987; *Borderlands,* 1990; and *The Hunted, 1994;* all from Farrar, Straus & Giroux.

Witch Trials; *The Fifth of March: A Story of the Boston Massacre*; and *Finishing Becca: A Story About Peggy Shippen and Benedict Arnold.*

Rinaldi tackled a particularly ambitious subject in *Wolf by the Ears*, a fictional story of Sally Hemings' family. Sally was a mulatto slave in Thomas Jefferson's household, and some historians believe that Jefferson fathered several of her children. Rinaldi's book implies that this is true, but the question is never clearly answered, even though the protagonist, supposedly Jefferson's daughter, asks it often enough. The book's title comes from Jefferson's statement about slavery: "as it is, we have the wolf by the ears, and we can neither hold him, nor safely let him go. Justice is in one scale, and self-preservation the other." In a preface, Rinaldi cites her main source, Fawn M. Brodie's *Thomas Jefferson: An Intimate History.* She also explains that she wanted to write a book about alienation, because her own mother died when she was born, and "I never knew her family or even saw a picture of her until I was married. So there was always a part of me I could not acknowledge, a part of me I yearned to understand." This is why she was fascinated when she first heard of Sally Hemings' family, which included two boys who were thought to have run away, the young woman, Harriet, who is the protagonist of the book, and two younger brothers who apparently stayed on the plantation as slaves.

It is unlikely that Rinaldi could please all her readers, no matter how she portrayed such controversial topics as the treatment and education of slaves, mixed-bloods "passing" as white, and the commonness of slave women loving their masters and of masters impregnating slave women with or without love. Because of her audience, Rinaldi tiptoed around the issue of Jefferson's sexuality, even though it's at the heart of the plot. A common literary technique is to insert a love story as a counterbalance for whatever bad has happened to a woman. Rinaldi has an educated, white liberal architect visit Monticello from Washington, D.C. and find Harriet attractive. He is a perfect gentleman and agrees to sponsor Harriet in Washington, D.C., where she will be a teacher until she decides whether or not she wants to marry him. Granted, this romantic element may be necessary to attract readers, but it's a sugar-coating that's likely to gag historians.

Historical novels come in all times and all places. Readers interested in prehistoric times would enjoy Joan Wolf's *The Reindeer Hunters* or Peter Dickinson's *A Bone from a Dry Sea*. Even more excitement waits in medieval Europe. Karen Cushman has two brilliant works that ought to appeal to slightly younger students— *Catherine, Called Birdy* and *The Midwife's Apprentice*. The best of the bunch is Frances Temple's *The Ramsay Scallop*. Temple describes the apprehension that 13-year-old Eleanor of Ramsey feels as she awaits marriage to 22-year-old Lord Thomas of Thornham. Thomas is no happier about his upcoming marriage because he has become cynical about life and religion after fighting in the Crusades. Father Gregory sets them off on a pilgrimage to the cathedral in Santiago, Spain, and asks that they remain chaste during the trip. Temple's portraits of the people and the time and the friendships they form and the deceit and pain they meet are brilliant.

If readers want to travel to the Orient, they can do so in Malcolm Bosse's *The Examination* with its picture of two quite different brothers in sixteenth-century China and Erik Christian Haugaard's novels about the life of the Samurai. *The Samurai's Tale* tells of a captured boy who becomes the first servant of a Lord in feudal sixteenth-century Japan. More recently, Haugaard's *The Revenge of the Forty-Seven Samurai* is a tale of honor and revenge in Japan two centuries later.

Phillip Pullman's novels about Victorian England have appealed to many readers. *The Ruby in the Smoke* is about Sally Lockhart and a missing ruby and a deep-dark mystery. Two other books complete the series—*Shadow in the North* and *The Tiger in the Well*.

The United States has been the subject of a number of historical novels. Kathryn Lasky's *Beyond the Burning Time* is a fine novel focusing on the terrors of the Salem witch trials, and *Beyond the Divide* is a novel of the western movement. James Lincoln Collier and Christopher Collier's *My Brother Sam Is Dead* is only one of many excellent Collier books. Howard Fast's *April Morning* is more than 30 years old, but it is still worth reading by anybody who cares about young people and their place in the Revolutionary War. Katherine Paterson's *Lyddie* presents the manufacturing world of the 1840s and Lyddie's place therein. Irene Hunt's *No Promises in the Wind* is a brilliant picture of the Depression and the hopelessness of two small boys during the time.

Books About War

It's becoming increasingly difficult to distinguish between fiction and nonfiction, and this is especially true in the writing of memoirs and reminiscences about war (Focus Boxes 7.1 and 7.2). Struggling to survive in a war is not an adventure we would choose either for ourselves or for our children, but so many people of all ages have been forced into terrible circumstances that books on war—histories, journalistic nonfiction, autobiographic works, diaries, and collections of letters and interviews—are among our most powerful. Old war movies abound on the late show (see Focus Box 7.1). Newspapers and magazines banner the headlines of this new or that old war, and television news programs barrage us with the latest atrocities.

FOCUS BOX 7.1

Even in the Movies, War Is No Game

All Quiet on the Western Front (1930, 105 min., black and white; Director: Lewis Milestone; with Lew Ayres and Louis Wolheim) Young Germans flock to join the army to fight for glory. Based on Erich Maria Remarque's novel.

The Americanization of Emily (1964, 117 min., black and white; Director: Arthur Hiller; with James Garner and Julie Andrews) Paddy Chayefsky's cynical script about the stupidity of war versus the romanticized view that dying for one's country is good and noble.

Apocalypse Now (1979, 105 min., color; Director: Francis Coppola; with Martin Sheen and Marlon Brando) An agent travels in Vietnam to kill another officer. Based on Joseph Conrad's *Heart of Darkness.*

Attack (1956, 107 min., black and white; Director: Robert Altman; with Eddie Albert and Jack Palance) A study of cowardice and ineptness during the Battle of the Bulge in World War II.

Dr. Strangelove or: How I Learned to Stop Worrying and Love the Bomb (1964, 93 min., black and white; Director: Stanley Kubrick; with Peter Sellers, George C. Scott, and Sterling Hayden) A black comedy about a true-blue American general who decides on his own to start World War III. Hysterically funny and terrifying all at once.

The Execution of Private Slovik (1974, 120 min., color; Director: Lamont Johnson; with Martin Sheen) Based on William Bradford Huie's account of the only American executed for desertion during wartime since the Civil War.

Forbidden Games (1951, 87 min., black and white; Director: René Clement) A young girl's parents are killed in World War II, and she is taken in by a peasant family. Their son and the girl form a deep bond that is shattered by the war. One of the world's most poignant war films.

Glory (1989, 122 min., color; Director: Edward Zwick; with Denzel Washington and Matthew Broderick) The founding and fighting of the first African American unit during the Civil War.

King and Country (1964, 90 min., black and white; Director: Joseph Losey; with Dirk Bogarde and Tom Courtenay) An officer is assigned to defend a soldier accused of desertion during wartime.

Paths of Glory (1957, 86 min., black and white; Director: Stanley Kubrick; with Kirk Douglas) During World War I, the stupidity and cupidity of the French top brass cause men to die pointlessly.

We are preoccupied with war, perhaps because it is inherently frightening and evil and, in the minds of too many of us, horribly inevitable. The Bible is full of battles, but so are the *Iliad* and the *Odyssey.* War serves as background for *Antigone,* just as it does for *The Red Badge of Courage.* War has influenced artists and musicians, or it might be fairer to say that it has left its indelible mark on them.

Young adults are painfully aware of the nearness of war, although they may know little about its realities and even less about the details of past wars. Reading war literature, fiction or not, serves to acquaint young people with some of war's horrors and how easily people forget, or ignore, their humanity in the midst of war.

During World War II, Ernie Pyle was American soldiers' favorite war correspondent, mostly because he took a genuine interest in people and demanded no special favors for being shot at. *Ernie's War: The Best of Ernie Pyle's World War II Dis-*

FOCUS BOX 7.2

War's Effect on Young People

The Dreams of Mairhe Mehan by Jennifer Armstrong. Knopf, 1996.   A recent Irish immigrant to the United States tries to persuade her brother not to fight in the Civil War.

The Forty-Third War by Louise Moeri. Houghton Mifflin, 1989.   In Central America, three boys are forced to join a rebel army.

Goodnight, Mr. Tom by Michelle Magorian. HarperCollins, 1981.   Abused by a fanatic mother, young Willie Beach is evacuated from London in World War II and sent to live in the English countryside with an embittered old man. See also Magorian's *Back Home* (Harper & Row, 1984), and *Not a Swan* (HarperCollins, 1992).

Gulf by Robert Westall. Scholastic, 1996.   In this unusual story, Westall portrays the awful madness of war through a twelve-year-old boy.

Hiroshima by Laurence Yep. Scholastic, 1995. Two Japanese sisters in Hiroshima see the falling of the atomic bomb. One is killed, and the other is horribly scarred.

I Had Seen Castles by Cynthia Rylant. Harcourt Brace, 1993.   A young man is filled with John Wayne-fervor to join the army and win World War II single-handed. Then he meets and loves Ginny, devoutly against all war.

Linger by M. E. Kerr. HarperCollins, 1993. Journal entries by Robert Peele from the time he arrives in Saudi Arabia in the Iraqi war until he's badly wounded by "friendly fire."

Lisa's War by Carol Matas. Scribner, 1987.   In 1940 Denmark, Lisa is planning her fourteenth birthday when the country is invaded by Germany. See also the sequel, *Code Name Kris* (Scribner, 1990).

No Hero for the Kaiser by Rudolf Frank. Lothrop, Lee & Shepard, 1986, first published in Germany in 1931 (and publicly burned when Hitler took power in 1933).   On his fourteenth birthday, Jan Kubitzky watched as his Polish village was blown up by Russian soldiers from the east and German soldiers from the west.

So Far from the Bamboo Grove by Yoko Yawashima Watkins. Lothrop, Lee & Shepard, 1986.   Koko Yawashima Watkins lived in peaceful North Korea until the Communists attacked in 1945, and Koko's family fled south to Seoul. They hoped to return to their native Japan, but instead they learned what it meant to be refugees. See also the continuation in *My Brother, My Sister, and I* (Bradbury, 1994.)

---

patches (edited by David Nichols) collects some of the work Pyle did in Great Britain, North Africa, Sicily, France, and the Pacific from 1940 until his death in 1945. Pyle wrote honestly without the trite theatrics of many newspaper reporters. Writing about the death of Captain Henry T. Waskow, one of the most "beloved" men Pyle ever found in war, he told of Waskow's men coming in, gently, to see and honor the body, and Pyle ended the account this way:

> Then a soldier came and stood beside the officer, and bent over, and he spoke to the dead captain, not in a whisper but awfully tenderly, and he said:
> "I sure am sorry, sir."

Then the first man squatted down, and he reached down and took the dead hand, and he sat there for a full five minutes, holding the dead hand in his own and looking intently into the dead face, and he never uttered a sound all the time he sat there.

And finally he put the hand down, and then reached up and gently straightened the points of the captain's shirt collar, and then he sort of re-arranged the tattered edges of his uniform around the wound. And then he got up and walked away down the road in the moonlight, all alone.

After that the rest of us went back into the cowshed, leaving the five dead men lying in a line, end to end, in the shadow of the low stone wall. We lay down on the straw in the cowshed, and pretty soon we were all asleep.

Jack Stenbuck's *Typewriter Batallion* with its 73 dispatches from World War II conveys much of the horror that we get from Ernie Pyle's material. Annette Tapert's *Lines of Battle: Letters from American Servicemen, 1941–1945* makes the horror even more personal.

Few books about World War II, or any other war, succeed so well in creating a revulsion to the blood and messiness as does Farley Mowat's *And No Birds Sang*. Af-ter Mowat's company encountered and killed six truckloads of German soldiers, Mowat said:

It was not the dead that distressed me most—it was the German wounded. There were a great many of these, and most seemed to have been hard hit.

One ghastly vignette from that shambles haunts me still: the driver of a truck hanging over his steering wheel and hiccuping great gouts of cherry-pink foam through a smashed windscreen, to the accompaniment of a sound like a slush pump sucking air as his perforated lungs labored to expel his own heart's blood . . . in which he was slowly drowning.

Mowat's book is hardly the only honest account, but it reeks of death and lost dreams, and anyone wanting to know what war is like should not miss it.

Six novels about war, five of them about World War II, are worth reading. William Wharton's *A Midnight Clear* is about six high-I.Q. American soldiers in an intelligence and reconnaissance platoon sent to determine whether there are Ger-man troops near a French chateau. The six play bridge and chess and word games and begin to believe they have nothing to do with the war. Then the Germans show up, and instead of warfare, everyone engages in a snowball fight. They sing Christ-mas carols and set up a Christmas tree and wonderful peace reigns. Then war starts again and the killing resumes, and what had been warm is now bloody.

English novelist Robert Westall writes about young people who refuse to stay outside the war in *The Machine Gunners* and the sequel, *Fathom Five*. The first novel begins in an English coastal town during 1940–1941. Rumors of a German invasion are rife, and Chas McGill wants to help win the war. Chas and his friends locate a downed German plane, find the machine gun in working order, and hide it. When a school is hit by a German plane somewhat later, Chas steals sandbags to create a fortress, a safe place to display the machine gun. The rear gunner of the downed plane stumbles into their fortress and becomes the boys' prisoner. All this childish innocence dies when adults discover the fortress, the German is shot, and the young people are rounded up by their parents. *Fathom Five* is a rousing spy story set later in the war and the story of Chas's lost love and lost innocence. Westall has an amazing ability to portray the ambivalence of young people, the alienation they feel mixed with love and duty.

Peter Carter's *The Hunted* is set in 1943 France when Italian troops are heading home after the Italian surrender to the Allies. Corporal Vito Salvani is fleeing when he finds a young Jewish boy, Judah, and takes the boy with him. A fanatic collaborator with the Nazis, Palet believes the boy has jewels on him, and he sets out after the Italian and the boy, an example of evil hunting down good. *The Hunted* is a big book, but it stays with the reader long after it's been finished.

Harry Mazer's *The Last Mission* is set near the end of World War II. Jack Raab uses his older brother's identification to lie his way into the Air Force to destroy Hitler and to save democracy, all by himself; that dream lasts only a short time before Jack learns that the Air Force involves more training and boredom than fighting. When Jack does go to war, his first 24 bombing raids go well, but on the last mission, his plane is hit, all his buddies die, and he is captured. When he returns home, the principal at his old high school asks him to talk.

> "I'm glad we won," he said. "We couldn't let Hitler keep going. We had to stop him. But most of all, I'm glad it's over." Had he said enough? There was a silence . . . a waiting silence. There was something more he had to say.
>
> "I don't like war. I thought I'd like it before. But war is stupid. War is one stupid thing after another. I saw my best friend killed. His name was Chuckie O'Brien. My whole crew was killed." Now he was talking, it was coming out, all the things he'd thought about for so long. "A lot of people were killed. Millions of people. Ordinary people. Not only by Hitler. Not only on our side. War isn't like the movies. It's not fun and songs. It's not about heroes. It's about awful, sad things, like my friend Chuckie that I'm never going to see again." His voice faltered.
>
> "I hope war never happens again," he said after a moment. "That's all I've got to say."
>
> He sat down. He hardly heard the applause. The floor of the radio room was still slippery with Chuckie's blood. . . . Dave was still fumbling with his chute . . . the plane was still falling through the sky.

James Forman's finest work, too little known, is *Ceremony of Innocence*. Hans and Sophie Scholl, brother and sister in Nazi Germany, print and distribute literature attacking Hitler. Arrested by the Gestapo, they are urged by friends to escape. A lawyer, who Hans suspects is a Nazi, encourages them to plead insanity. They refuse, endure the mock trial, are found guilty, and are taken away to be executed. Hans is the last to die by the guillotine.

> Hans heard the sound of rollers, and at last there burst from his throat a cry, uttered in a great voice, a voice that combined anger, reproof, and an overwhelming conviction for which he was willing to die.
>
> "Long live freedom!"

Then the greased blade fell. His teeth met through his tongue, and it was over.

Readers curious about the White Rose, a German movement to end the war, can find information in Richard Hanser's *A Noble Treason: The Revolt of the Munich Students Against Hitler;* Hermann Vinke's *The Short Life of Sophie Scholl;* Annette E. Dumbach and Jud Newborn's *Shattering the German Night: The Story of the White Rose;* and Inge Jens's *At the Heart of the White Rose: Letters and Diaries of Hans and Sophie Scholl.*

A few good books about life in Germany during World War II are Bernt Engelmann's *In Hitler's Germany: Daily Life in the Third Reich* and Wendelgard von Staden's *Darkness Over the Valley.* Barbara Gehrts's *Don't Say a Word* shows life in a Berlin suburb through the eyes of a daughter of an officer in the Luftwaffe. T. Degens's *The Visit* begins after the end of the war when young Kate Hofmann reads her aunt's diary to find out exactly how her aunt died. Kate learns that her aunt had been a member of the Hitler Youth, and worse discoveries follow that.

Vietnam was the most unpopular war in American history, and for some time few novels or books about it were published. Now they abound in great numbers. Nonfiction such as Elizabeth Becker's *America's Vietnam War: A Narrative History* may help young readers unravel the strangeness that was Vietnam. What it was like to be in Vietnam from the point of view of the run-of-the-mill American soldier can be learned through Harry Maurer's *Strange Ground: Americans in Vietnam, 1945–1975, An Oral History;* Mark Baker's *Nam: The Vietnam War in the Words of the Men and Women Who Fought There;* Al Santoli's *Everything We Had: An Oral History of the Vietnam War by Thirty-Three American Soldiers Who Fought It;* and Kathryn Marshall's *In the Combat Zone: An Oral History of American Women in Vietnam.*[9]

When teacher Bill McCloud tried to decide what to tell his junior high students about Vietnam, he wrote to people involved in the war to get their advice. The result is his book *What Should We Tell Our Children About Vietnam?* Responses came from more than 100 people as different as Garry Trudeau, Jimmy Carter, Pete Seeger, Kurt Vonnegut, Alexander Haig, Henry Kissinger, and Barry Goldwater. Another unusual book on Vietnam is Laura Palmer's *Shrapnel in the Heart: Letters and Remembrances from the Vietnam Veterans Memorial.* All items left at the Vietnam Memorial are saved by the U.S. Park Service, and from these letters, notes, and personal memorabilia Palmer chose deeply moving examples.

Unhappily, war doesn't stop with Vietnam. The incredible mess that has killed hundreds of thousands of people, many of them children and innocent civilians, in Serbia and Bosnia and Croatia goes on, apparently without end. Zlata Filipovic's *Zlata's Diary: A Child's Life in Sarajevo* is precisely what the title says, a diary of the horrors and the friendship and the love and the blood that a fifth-grade girl in Sarajevo sees and feels every day.

Of all the many books on war, none has a more horrible indictment of the absurdity and cruelty of war than Roger Rosenblatt's *Children of War.* Rosenblatt circled the globe seeking out children in Belfast, Israel, Cambodia, Hong Kong, and Lebanon whom he asked about themselves and what war had done to them. A 9-year-old girl in Cambodia had made a drawing, and after a year of help by an American psychologist, she was able to explain how the instrument in the drawing worked. Rosenblatt writes:

> The children harvesting rice include Peov. She is the largest of the three. Whenever a child refused to work, he was punished with the circular device. The soldiers would place it over the child's head. Three people would hold it steady by means of ropes. . . . A fourth would grab hold of the ring at the end of the other rope. . . . When the rope with the ring was pulled . . . the child would be decapitated. A portable guillotine.
>
> But it wasn't the soldiers who worked the device. It was the children.

Literature of the Holocaust

Only a few years back, anyone wishing to read about the Holocaust would read Anne Frank's *The Diary of a Young Girl*. Advanced students might find a few other sources, mostly historical, and the most mature students might view Alain Resnais's powerful short film, "Night and Fog." Today an outpouring of books about the Holocaust means that no one can pretend not to know about the happenings and the evils that went with it. (Focus Box 7.3)

One book of that outpouring is the definitive edition in 1995 of Anne Frank's *Diary,* in which Anne becomes far more human and far less saintly. A number of passages touch on Anne's interest in sex and love, and Anne's entry for March 24, 1944, is sexual and analytical. The definitive edition should please readers who want to read about a human being with all her faults. It should almost equally please censors, who will have new reasons to find fault with a nearly perfect book. Miep Gies's *Anne Frank Remembered*, the autobiography of the woman who helped hide the Frank family, adds more detail and should be read alongside Anne's *Diary.*

Most young adults seek out books about young people caught in the Holocaust because they are better able to identify with people their own age or slightly older. A book that is similar to Anne Frank's *Diary* is Etty Hillesum's *An Interrupted Life: The Diaries of Etty Hillesum, 1941–1943*. Being 27 years old, Hillesum probably knew precisely what her fate was to be. Her diary begins, "Here goes, then," and she writes of her love affairs, her graduate study at the University of Amsterdam, and her friends and ideas. She seems to have had little interest in politics until Jews were required to wear the yellow star. That jolted her, but she never sought to escape. In her last days, she volunteered to go with a group of condemned Jews to Westerbork Camp. She must have known that Westerbork was the usual first step to Auschwitz. Her journal complements Anne's *Diary;* Etty's irony and sophistication neatly counterpoint Anne's simplicity and innocence. *An Interrupted Life* is completed in *Letters from Westerbork.*

Students continue to read and love Johanna Reiss's *The Upstairs Room* and its sequel *The Journey Back.* The first book is a true story of the author and her sister, two young Jewish girls in Holland, kept safely in hiding by a Gentile family for over two years during the Nazi occupation. The girls detest having to stay inside all the time, but when they learn from an underground newspaper what is happening to Jews across Europe, they realize how precarious is their life. The second book is

FOCUS BOX 7.3

Experiencing The Holocaust

Ghost Waltz by Ingeborg Day. Viking, 1980. The author thinks back on her childhood in Nazi Austria. As an exchange student to the United States, she sees World War II movies and realizes her father was an S.S. member and involved in the Holocaust.

The Holocaust by Martin Gilbert. Holt, 1987. An almost encyclopedic account of the Holocaust beginning in 1933.

Jack and Rochelle: A Holocaust Story of Love and Resistance by Jack and Rochelle Sutin. Graywolf Press, 1995. Jack Sutin escaped from a ghetto in eastern Poland, Rochelle Scheleiff escaped from a forced-labor camp nearby, and they became lovers fighting the Germans in 1942.

The Journey by Ida Fink. Farrar Straus & Giroux, 1992. An autobiographical novel about a group of Jewish women, farm workers, who hide their identities from the Gestapo.

In Kindling Flame: The Story of Hannah Senesh, 1921–1944 by Linda Atkinson. Lothrop, Lee & Shepard, 1985. Senesh, a Hungarian Jew, was a resistance fighter. See also *Hannah Senesh: Her Life and Diary* (Schocken, 1972).

One, by One by One: Facing the Holocaust by Judith Miller. Simon & Schuster, 1990. A disturbing book by a journalist who examined the ways West Germany, Austria, France, the Netherlands, Russia, and the United States handled its responsibility for the Holocaust.

For example, the French Resistance never tried to stop a single Jewish deportation train, and the Jewish death rate in the Netherlands was the highest in western Europe.

Playing for Time by Fania Fenelon and Marcelle Routier. Atheneum, 1977. Fenelon describes playing in a camp orchestra for the S.S. officers in 1944 Birkenau.

Return to Auschwitz by Kitty Hart. Atheneum, 1982. The author survived Auschwitz, and then in 1978, she returned to the camp to help make an English documentary.

Soldiers of Evil: The Commandants of the Nazi Concentration Camps by Tom Segev. McGraw-Hill, 1989. Fifty-five men who ran concentration camps, or in some cases their wives or children, explain why or how they excused the horrors of the Holocaust. The answers were that they were told what to do and they did it, and mostly they felt little guilt in following orders—as good soldiers should.

Stella by Peter Wyden. Simon & Schuster, 1992. After being removed from a German public school because he was Jewish, the author went to a Jewish school in Berlin and fell passionately in love with Stella Goldschlag. In 1937, Wyden and his family came to the United States. After the war, he learned to his horror that Stella had been one of the chief Jewish informants who turned in other Jews.

about their trip back to their hiding place after the war. Karen Ray's *To Cross a Line* is about Egon Katz, a 17-year-old Jewish baker's apprentice who was certain that if he followed all the rules, he'd be safe. Then the Gestapo shows up with a warrant for him. Kati David's *A Child's War: World War II Through the Eyes of Children* is an account of World War II through the eyes of 15 children, 8 girls and 7 boys. Those eyes tell stories of fear and death and every horror that war brings about.

Thomas Keneally's *Schindler's List* should be read alongside any work about the Holocaust. But then so should the accounts of inmates of the concentration camps in Sylvia Rothchild's *Voices from the Holocaust* and Milton Teichman and Sharon Leder's *Truth and Lamentations: Stories and Poems on the Holocaust*. Hazel

Rochman and Darlene Z. McCampbell's *Bearing Witness: Stories of the Holocaust* is a marvelous collection of material that will shock readers just as other selections will give them pictures of real heroes. Hanna Volavkova's *I Never Saw Another Butterfly: Children's Drawings and Poems from Terezin Concentration Camp, 1942–1944* and Chana Byers Abells's *The Children We Remember* are unquestionably the most painful reading because they detail the massacre of the innocent.

Milton Meltzer does his usual fine job of collection and reporting in *Never to Forget: The Jews of the Holocaust*. Ten years later, he wrote a book about a much smaller number of people, *Rescue: The Story of How Gentiles Saved Jews in the Holocaust*. As he explained in the introduction:

> Now I have come to realize the great importance of recording not just the evidence of evil, but also the evidence of human nobility. Love, not hatred, is what the world needs. Rescue, not destruction. The stories in the book offer reason to hope. And hope is what we need, the way plants need sunlight.

Two other books deserve to be read alongside Meltzer—Eva Fogelman's *Conscience and Courage: Rescuers of Jews During the Holocaust*, and Maxine B. Rosenberg's *Hiding to Survive: Stories of Jewish Children Rescued from the Holocaust*. Ina R. Friedman's *The Other Victims: First Person Stories of Non-Jews Persecuted by the Nazis* is a worthy addition to Holocaust literature.

Ruth Minsky Sender's three volumes on her life from 1939 Poland to today show the horrors of the time. *The Cage* has 16-year-old Riva and her brothers taken by the Nazis to a concentration camp. It's a painful book, but it's also a brave book. *To Life* deals with post–World War II and Riva searching for her family. *The Holocaust Lady* is about Riva, now Ruth, who marries and comes to the United States and starts a family and decides that she must remember the past so that others will never relive it.

Some recent books have focused on the obvious fact that bigotry endures. In Lois Ruby's *Skin Deep*, Dan comes from a fatherless home. When multiethnic quotas keep him off the swimming team and from getting a job at the University of Colorado, he turns to the local skinheads for support, adopting their dress code but never quite accepting their racism. Han Nolan's *If I Should Die Before I Wake* portrays a young girl, a Neo-Nazi initiate, who is in a coma from a motorcycle accident. In her dreams in the hospital, she becomes a young Jewish girl whose family lives in a ghetto and then Auschwitz. *The Wave* by Morton Rhue (pen name of Todd Strasser) has proven incredibly popular with many young people. In a high school history class, students wonder why the non-Nazi Germans let the Holocaust happen. The teacher responds by introducing students to a new movement, The Wave, which captures the imaginations and the hearts of students apparently longing for indoctrination and belief in certainties.

The best of all these books is Fran Arrick's *Chernowitz!* Bob Cherno, 15, looked back on his fights with Emmett Sundback, a bigot who ridiculed Bob's Jewishness. When Bob's school shows a film about the concentration camps, some students who have ridiculed Bob leave in tears because they understand the horrors of the Nazis' treatment of Jews and other minorities. To Arrick's credit, Sundback does not change and remains the horrible creep that he was.

Japanese Internment Camps in World War II

The most shameful American action during World War II began in February 1942, when President Roosevelt ordered the forced evacuation of anyone of Japanese ancestry on the West Coast into detention camps scattered in desolate places inland. More than 120,000 people were deported for the remainder of the war. Jeanne Wakatsuki Houston and James D. Houston's *Farewell to Manzanar* describes the first author's life in a camp ringed by barbed wire and guard towers and with open latrines. That 3-year ordeal destroyed the family's unity and left them with a burdening sense of personal inadequacy that took years to remove.

John Armor and Peter Wright discovered many photographs that Ansel Adams took for his ironically titled 1944 book, *Born Free and Equal*, and Armor and Wright wrote a text to go with Adams's pictures and titled the book *Manzanar*. With a commentary by John Hersey, *Manzanar* is largely a record of a people who had a right to be bitter but were instead making conditions at the camp work for them (Focus Box 7.4).

In February 1983, a Congressional committee concluded its deliberations and agreed that internment of Japanese-American citizens was a "grave injustice." The commission said that the relocation was motivated by "racial prejudices, war hysteria, and failure of political leadership," not by any military considerations.[10] Five years later, the House passed and sent on to President Reagan legislation giving apologies and $20,000 tax-free payments to Japanese-American survivors of World War II internment camps. Typical of bureaucratic bumbling, it was 1990 before the first checks were sent out. American justice may be slow—in this case 45 years—but it often may arrive.

Autobiographies and Personal Experiences

The Greeks enjoyed stories about the gods of Mount Olympus and hero tales about the moral descendants of the gods. But hero tales had an added feature that helped listeners identify with the protagonists. Unlike the gods, who live forever, heroes had one human parent, which meant that they were mortal. The most that the gods could risk in any undertaking was their pride, but heroes could lose their lives.

When we're reading modern fiction, we know that the author can always bring the protagonist out alive. But in true hero tales—biographies—protagonists risk their lives, just as readers would in the same situation (Focus Box 7.5). This adds credibility and intensity because the reader thinks, "If this happened to someone else, then it might happen to me."

Personal Experiences with Illness and Death

Death is an eternal mystery, as anyone who has read *Hamlet,* Dickinson's poetry, or Edgar Lee Masters's *Spoon River Anthology* knows full well.

Young adults sometimes complain about the "morbid" or "sick" literature adults foist on them: *Macbeth,* Romantic poetry, "Thanatopsis," *Death of a Salesman, Oedipus Rex,* and "A Rose for Emily." In reality, both adults and young adults may be preoccupied with death, but they prefer to choose their own literature.

FOCUS BOX 7.4

Life in World War II Japanese Internment Camps

Behind Barbed Wire: The Imprisonment of Japanese Americans During World War II by Daniel S. Davis. Dutton, 1982. Particularly readable for young adults. Davis points out that the United States was not alone in this ugly action—Canada was equally guilty.

Democracy on Trial: The Japanese American Evacuation and Relocation in World War II by Page Smith. Simon & Schuster, 1995. Why 10 centers were chosen to house Japanese-Americans in the West and why officials rationalized that necessity in World War II.

I Am an American: A True Story of Japanese Internment by Jerry Stanley. Crown, 1994. The life of Shi Nomura from the bombing of Pearl Harbor through the life of an internment camp through the return after the war to find continued racial prejudices through the recent official apology by the American government. Brief but good.

The Invisible Thread by Yoshiko Uchida. Simon & Schuster, 1991. Yoshiko may have felt like an American, but as the United States entered World War II, American authorities assigned her and her family to an internment camp, which she hated.

And Justice for All: An Oral History of the Japanese American Detention Camps by John Tateishi. Random House, 1984. True stories of what the camps were like.

Keeper of Concentration Camps: Dillon S. Myer and American Racism by Richard Drinnon. University of California Press, 1987. How Myer, ignorant of Japanese culture and history, was put in charge of relocation camps, and how he, again ignorant of the cultures and history of Native Americans, was named to head the Bureau of Indian Affairs in 1950.

The Moved Outers by Florence Crannell Means. Houghton Mifflin, 1945. A Japanese-American family is forced into a relocation camp during World War II. Written when the racial problem was still fresh, her message is powerful even today.

Prisoners Without Trial: Japanese-Americans in World War II by Roger Daniels. Hill & Wang, 1993. The story of 120,000 Americans of Japanese ancestry and their barbed-wire homes after 1942.

Stubborn Twig: Three Generations in the Life of a Japanese-American Family by Lauren Kessler. Random House, 1994. Nearly a century in one family's history including World War II and Tule Lake Center.

They Call Me Moses Masaoka by Mike Masaoka and Bill Hosokawa. Morrow, 1987. A veteran of both internment camp and the army works for the good of Japanese-American and Caucasian relationships.

Surely it could be argued that reading such literature helps young adults develop an appreciation of their own lives as well as a code of values to hold dear in the dread times to come.

Books about young people dying have been popular for years, including Doris Lund's *Eric,* about her son's losing battle with leukemia; John Gunther's *Death Be Not Proud,* about his son's slow death from a brain tumor; and three different versions of the story of Chicago Bears runningback Brian Piccolo and his struggle with cancer. The favorite of this last group is usually William Blinn's *Brian's Song,* created from the television movie, which is still shown in reruns. The movie plot came originally from a chapter in Gale Sayers's *I Am Third,* whereas Jeanne Morris wrote the most complete version of the story in *Brian Piccolo: A Short Season.* She and Piccolo worked together on the manuscript during his hospitalization.

FOCUS BOX 7.5

Honor List: Biographies and Personal Experiences

Abigal Adams: Witness to a Revolution by Natalie S. Bober. Atheneum, 1995. Fortunately—at least for readers of this well-written biography—Abigal Adams was often living at a distance from her husband. Quotes from her letters provide revealing glimpses into both the times and the woman.

All God's Children Need Traveling Shoes by Maya Angelou. Random House, 1986. (Random pbk.) and *I Know Why the Caged Bird Sings* by Maya Angelou. Random House, 1970. (Random pbk.) These lyrical and powerful autobiographies remain favorites of both adults and young readers.

Black Ice by Lorene Cary. Knopf, 1991. (McKay pbk.) Although written for a general adult audience, this memoir of the author's move as a scholarship student from the public schools of West Philadelphia to the prestigious St. Paul's prep school explores Cary's feelings of being an outsider.

Columbus and the World Around Him by Milton Meltzer. Franklin Watts, 1990. Meltzer brought his usual careful research and writing to this biography, which helps readers understand the controversy over the 500th anniversary of Columbus' arrival in the Americas.

Dove by Robin L. Graham. HarperCollins, 1972. (Bantam pbk.) Young readers like this true story of a 16-year-old doing something that most kids can only dream about. He set off in his own boat to sail around the world.

Eleanor Roosevelt: A Life of Discovery by Russell Freedman. Clarion, 1993. More than 120 photos, along with intriguing details and insights, make this large-format biography especially appealing.

The Long Road to Gettysburg by Jim Murphy. Clarion, 1992. Murphy used the personal journals of John Dooley, an 18-year-old Southern lieutenant, and Thomas Galway, a 17-year-old Union corporal, as the centerpiece of his retelling of the story of the Battle of Gettysburg.

The Pigman and Me by Paul Zindel. HarperCollins, 1992. (Bantam pbk.) Zindel entertains and educates readers with this memoir from his own teenage years when he was lucky enough to have Nonno Frankie (the model for Zindel's fictional *Pigman*) as a mentor.

Unconditional Surrender: U.S. Grant and the Civil War by Albert Marrin. Atheneum, 1994. Marrin nicely balances this story of a man whose life alternated between peaks of success and depths of failure.

Woodsong by Gary Paulsen. Bradbury, 1990. (Puffin pbk.) Paulsen uses the same literary techniques and nature-based metaphors to relate his training for and running in the Iditarod as he used in such fictional pieces as *Hatchet* (Bradbury, 1987), *The Island* (Orchard, 1988), and *Dogsong* (Bradbury, 1985).

It should come as no surprise that many young readers are fascinated by *Ryan White: My Own Story* by Ryan White and Ann Marie Cunningham. As a hemophiliac, Ryan received dozens of blood infusions. One of them was with AIDS-infected blood, and when he developed the disease, he became a national symbol of both American prejudice and American caring. He died at age 18, shortly after the book was written. Elaine Landau's *We Have AIDS*, in which nine teenagers tell their stories, may not be quite as dramatic, but it is equally frightening to young people. Some young adults prefer to pick up straightforward informational books focusing on death or illness, for example, Jill Krementz's *How It Feels to Fight for Your Life* and *How It Feels When a Parent Dies*. Krementz presents full-page photos of the young people whose stories she tells through their own words. Elizabeth Richter's

Losing Someone You Love: When a Brother or Sister Dies has a similar format; the book is based on 17 young people who shared their firsthand experiences and feelings on the death of a sibling.

Because readers identify with the young protagonists, it's particularly satisfying when they win their struggle against an illness or a disability. Geri Jewell's autobiography, *Geri,* is the story of a young woman with cerebral palsy who succeeded in reaching her goal of becoming an acclaimed actress and comedienne. She also succeeded in writing an upbeat book showing the "hardness and usefulness of the disabled."

Gilda Radner's long fight against cancer is retold in her *It's Always Something.* The funny star of "Saturday Night Live" proves to be just as funny and even more incredibly brave. She found a needed support group called the Wellness Community, which was an outlet for her talents as a comedienne. It's a courageous book and deliciously funny at the same time.

Two books by young cancer patients are wise and funny by turns. Although they will bring tears to their readers, that is clearly not their purpose. Matthew Lancaster's *Hang Toughf* is a solid little classic in which a 10-year-old author gives sound advice to other kids who have cancer. As he says, it's not fair, "but it happened, and you and I have to except it." And if your hair falls out, then "if your friends laugh at you, they're not very good friends." Eight-year-old Jason Gaes hated other books about kids with cancer because they always died, and he had cancer and he hadn't died, so he wrote *My Book for Kids with Cansur,* almost as good (and sometimes funnier) than *Hang Toughf.* Erma Bombeck tuned into the same theme with the help of young cancer patients for her book *I Want to Grow Hair, I Want to Grow Up, I Want to Go to Boise.*

Edie Clark's *The Place He Made* and Edith Kunhardt Davis's *I'll Love You Forever, Anyway* are two warm and wonderful books about two people who learn to survive the death of someone they deeply love. *Paula* by Isabel Allende comes from an important political person who found something far more troubling than her political battles—the slow death of her 27-year-old daughter, Paula.

Perhaps the most deeply troubling of books about death are Linda Gray Sexton's *Searching for Mercy Street: My Journey Back to My Mother* and William Wharton's *Ever After: A Father's True Story.* Sexton tries to come to terms with the suicide death of her mother, poet Anne Sexton, and all the powerful emotions that ran through her mother's existence and that permeated the mother-daughter relationship. In August 1988, a pileup of 22 cars on Highway 5 in Oregon led to seven deaths, including Wharton's daughter Kate and Kate's husband and two babies, all killed, all burned. All the deaths were senseless, but Wharton is clearly heartbroken by the death of his daughter and a quiet rage of horror and frustration and anger is essentially what the book is about.

More Upbeat Personal Experiences and Autobiographies

Most personal experience stories are not about death and illness but instead about adventures, successes, and experiences the writers feel so strongly about that they wish to share them with readers. Some are career stories, for example, Bonnie Tiburzi's *Takeoff! The Story of America's First Woman Pilot for a Major Airline* and former surgeon-general C. Everett Koop's *Koop: The Memoirs of America's Family Doctor.* Partly because of their fondness for animals, many readers appreciate Jane Goodall's *My Life with the Chimpanzees.* Other animal-related books include Diane Ackerman's *The Moon by Whale Light: And Other Adventures Among Bats, Penguins, Crocodilians and Whales;* R. D. Lawrence's *In Praise of Wolves* and *The North Runner;* and Candace Savage's *Wolves.*

Although Farley Mowat's books are not as upbeat, they make fascinating reading. In *A Whale for the Killing,* he thought he had found the perfect place to live until he discovered his neighbors were savages who took pleasure in killing a trapped whale. His angry prose also typifies *Never Cry Wolf* and *Sea of Slaughter.* He's less angry in his earlier *The Dog Who Wouldn't Be* and *Owls in the Family. Born Naked* is Mowat's childhood memories of 1920s and 1930s Canada. Given Mowat's irritation with people in most of his books, *Born Naked* is a relatively quiet and gentle book.

Some authors tell their own quite ordinary stories of growing up in ways that make young readers feel privileged to get acquainted with a new friend. Annie Dillard's *An American Childhood* tells about growing up in the 1950s and 1960s. Tobias Wolff's *This Boy's Life* is set at about the same time, but in Seattle, where he grew up longing to be a "boy of dignity."

Sometimes memories are incredibly funny to readers, although just how amusing the memories were to the writer early in his life is open to question. The first paragraph in Mark Salzman's *Lost in Place: Growing Up Absurd in Suburbia* is witty and certainly likely to grab the attention of most readers:

> When I was thirteen years old I saw my first kung fu movie, and before it ended I decided that the life of a wandering Zen monk was the life for me. I announced my willingness to leave East Ridge Junior High School immediately and give up all material things, but my parents did not share my enthusiasm. They made it clear that I was not to become a wandering Zen monk until I had finished high school. In the meantime I could practice kung fu and meditate down in the basement. So I immersed myself in the study of Chinese boxing and philosophy with the kind of dedication that is possible only when you don't yet have to make a living, when you are too young to drive and when you don't have a girlfriend.

Salzman's life is not an easy one, but one filled with melodrama and near tragedy, at least so Salzman says. About halfway through the book, he muses about the values of high school, much as we have all done during that traumatic point in our existence:

> Even with my limited knowledge of physiology at that time, I knew that teenagers were designed for humping, fighting and little else, but the modern world asks that we put all that off until after high school. Instead we must fidget in uncomfortable wooden chairs and learn how to learn. As mentioned before, you're told it will pay off one day, but between the ages of thirteen and eighteen you cannot help wondering, What if it *doesn't* pay off? What if our parents, and their parents, were all wrong about what's really important? How

YOKO KAWASHIMA WATKINS
On Living in Harmony

I know we live in a splendid country. In Chinese, it takes two characters to spell *America*. The first character is *Bi*, which means "beautiful, and the other is *Koku*, which means "country." We certainly DO live in the most beautiful country where the freedoms—the freedom of speech, press, worship, and the right to assemble—still strongly exist.

There was no such thing when I was growing up in China and North Korea, Russia, or even in Japan during the Tojo era, where martial law was strictly enforced. We did not know who were our friends or enemies. If even in a small group or at school we expressed our opinions of the government's doings, a couple of days later the Army Police would be at the front door. Without any explanation or listening to their side of the story, the Police forced people to go to their headquarters. They would throw people into a cell until they confessed . . . but confess to what? People would be threatened, beaten and tortured until they agreed to make some sort of confession that they were against the government's doings. Finally they would end up in a prison for a long time.

It is sad in the present day that many in the United States are taking advantage of their freedom and twisting it for their own greed and pleasure, turning themselves into egotistical and self-centered human beings. We as parents and teachers must not let this happen. We must take full responsibility for the rearing of our children. Again in Chinese characters, there is a lesson to learn. The character meaning "parent" is made from the character meaning "to stand" and "tree." The "standing" part of the character is placed on top of the tree showing that parents must stand on a tall tree and keep observing their children all the time.

Now in modern times we try to take care of things quickly by computers, copy machines, and telecommunications. They are all splendid. However, many parents and teachers lack teaching something important; something that people cannot see. Whenever I am invited to schools, I always introduce my culture in a simple and tranquil style which children can appreciate in this hectic and mixed-up society. For example, I make a flower arrangement showing that the Sky, the People, and the Earth are ONE. This is the splendor of living. Dad, Mom, and I are all one in harmony, forgiveness, and kindness. While believing in one's self, we trust and accept others as they are, which connects to True Beauty.

If my humble books help motivate children who suffer deeply, I am glad. Why not! Let parents and teachers cooperate and guide children of the world in the right way of humankind. We are the builders of our own children, and their happiness depends, in the end, on themselves, which will bring true PEACE to us all.

Yoko Kawashima Watkins's books include *My Brother, My Sister and I,* Bradbury, 1994; *Tales from the Bamboo Grove*, Macmillan, 1992; and *So Far from the Bamboo Grove*, Morrow, 1986.

will it ever end if no one questions it? And these are supposed to be the best years of your life.

The success of an autobiography depends largely on the quality of the writing because there usually isn't a plot for readers to get excited about, and it lacks the kinds of literary exaggeration that make for intriguing villains and heroes as in some genres. Authors of books for young people have written a particularly good set of autobiographies (see Focus Box 2.1). We placed it early in this text in hopes of encouraging you to begin developing connections with the people behind the books you would be reading.

Teachers and librarians can use authors' autobiographies to introduce students to writers who are alive and well. Although all the books are written by authors accustomed to writing for young people, they are not part of a planned series and so differ widely in reading levels and sophistication. For example, Nat Hentoff's *Boston Boy* is aimed at adult readers, whereas Richard Peck's *Anonymously Yours* is written for junior high or middle school students. With these extremes, and everything in between, students in a typically heterogeneous class can select the books that match their reading skills and levels of perseverance.

One aspect of personal experience stories that makes them attractive to young readers is that they are by people looking back on experiences they had when they were young. For example, Robin Graham, author of *Dove,* was only 16 and Steven Callahan, author of *Adrift: Seventy-six Days Lost at Sea,* was 29 when they set sail on their respective adventures. Bruce Feiler in *Under the Big Top* is an adult, but he remembers back to his childhood when he learned to juggle with a handful of oranges and when he first developed his love affair with the circus.

Some of the best autobiographies are by adults concerned with adult problems. Jill Ker Conway's two autobiographies, *The Road from Coorain* and *True North*, are among the most admired in the last decade. In her first book, Conway traces her life from a remote sheep station in Australia until the time she is ready to go to college. When her beloved father dies suddenly, her mother loses the center of her existence, and her mother attempts to take over and control Conway's life, the beginning of a long and sometimes ugly decline in their personal relationship. In *True North,* Conway is on her way to begin graduate study at Harvard. She falls in love with a Canadian professor, marries him, but learns after an idyllic honeymoon that her husband suffers from long bouts with depression. The book concludes as she is offered the job of president at Smith College, and she and her husband are ready to move once more.

We are so intrigued with the personal lives of stars and writers and such that we seem to demand intrusion into personal matters that are none of our business. Some writers give us more salacious details than we want or need. It's refreshing to see how writer Nina Bawden takes care of a love affair and a divorce in only a few sentences:

When Niki was three I had another son, Robert, and two years later left their father for another man. I met Austen on a bus; he was married, with two daughters, an ex-naval officer who was now a journalist. Our divorces went through expeditiously with the usual wailing and complaint and self-justification for bad behavior on our part. Austen's daughters went to South Africa with their mother; my sons stayed with us. Austen and I were still in our twenties when we married and the boys were young enough to accept him as a father. For Robert, Daddy was a synonym for Austen. When Niki was nine, and Robert six years old, we had a daughter, Perdita.

So much for that.

When personal experience books feature adult protagonists, the adults are likely to be unencumbered by family responsibilities. Travel books enjoyed by mature young readers include Peter Matthiessen's *African Silences,* William Least Heat Moon's *Blue Highways: A Journey into America,* Charles Kuralt's *A Life on the Road,* and Bruce Chatwin's *What Am I Doing Here?*

Whether to consider a book a personal experience or an autobiography is often up to the reader. For example, Maya Angelou's *I Know Why the Caged Bird Sings* and its three sequels are usually considered to be autobiographies because they move chronologically through Angelou's life, but it might be argued that they are personal experience stories because each book is about only a part of her life. There's also a crossover between personal experience accounts and the new journalism discussed in Chapter Eight.

Autobiography has an immediate and obvious appeal to readers. "Who," we ask ourselves, "would know more about this person than the person? Who could better tell us this person's story?"

The truth may be that almost any other good writer could have been more honest and could have written a better story. Even a tiny bit of thought might suggest to us that most people are poor witnesses of their lives. Most of us want to look good to others. Most of us might even leave out a significant piece of our lives that still embarrasses us or humiliates us or leaves us feeling unsure of ourselves and our motives. Most of us know friends who are incapable of telling us precisely, much less accurately, what happened at certain turns in their lives.

This is not to say that autobiographies are automatically untrustworthy, only that they may not tell the whole story or that certain parts may be left out, possibly for good reason, possibly not. Writers of autobiographies are not necessarily out to con us, but they may be. Worse yet, they may even con themselves.

Biographies

John Dryden introduced the word "biography" to English readers in his 1683 edition of Plutarch's *Parallel Lives.* Obviously the form was not new to readers who had long read the lives of famous generals and politicians and religious leaders.

People today remain fascinated by biographies. Where else can we see the uniqueness and authenticity of one person's life and, at the same time, emotions and problems that all humans face. Traditionally, biographies—especially those for young readers, for example, Parson Weems's biography of George Washington—were about heroic figures whose lives were models for mere mortals to emulate. Today's biographies for young adults are likely to be written more objectively, providing a balance of both strengths and weaknesses. They demonstrate how the subject

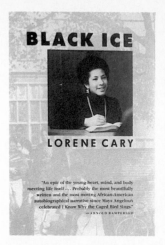
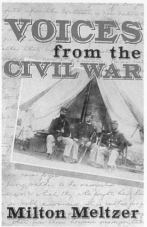

Biographies appreciated by young adults include personal memoirs of an author's youth, collective biographies based on original source material, and fully illustrated biographies of the same people adults are reading about.

---

and the reader share similar emotions. Both have fears and insecurities, and both succumb to temptations and vanities. After reading a good biography, the reader feels a kinship with the subject, not so much in spite of as because of the character's human frailties.

To say that a biography is written "objectively" does not mean that it is written without feeling. For biographies to ring true, the author must become immersed in the subject's life so that he or she can write with passion and commitment. This implies a point of view, not one imposed by an author who set out to prove a preconceived idea but a unifying force that guided the person's life and was discovered by the author through his or her research.

Just as we need to keep our wits about us as we read an autobiography, so do we in reading a biography. Biographers may have agendas not immediately clear to readers. They may want subtly to poison or to vent their spleen about any number of things, from the subject of the biography to an institution or anything at all.

Subjects of Biographies

Few of us admit to selecting the biographies we are going to purchase and promote on the basis of how we feel about the subject, but that's like one of those old clichés, such as "Never judge a book by its cover," that is honored more in word than in deed. Someone could write a Ph.D. dissertation on how Americans' values have changed over the last 30 years as reflected by whose biographies were put on the shelves of libraries.

In the early 1960s, readers at almost any library would find a predominance of biographies about white men who were inventors, statesmen, soldiers, and business leaders. During the 1970s, the imbalance became so obvious, particularly in school libraries, that educators and publishers took steps to correct the situation by preparing biographies about previously unsung heroes, including members of minority groups, women, handicapped individuals, and people whose contributions were not in military, political, or business spheres. Of course, there is still room for good books presenting new information on traditional heroes, for example, Tom D. Crouch's *The Bishop's Boys: A Life of Wilbur and Orville Wright* and Russell Freedman's *Franklin Delano Roosevelt*.

Collective biographies (i.e., one book presenting the stories of several individuals) have become increasingly popular because authors can write about individuals whose lives may not have been chronicled fully enough to provide information for an entire book. Authors usually bring together the stories of people who have something in common, such as a similarity of accomplishments or the same ethnic backgrounds, an efficient way to get information about previously ignored individuals into a library. Also, developing a unifying theme may be the best way to show a trend or connections among various subjects. For example, Russell Freedman's *Indian Chiefs,* the biographies of six western Indian chiefs during the 1800s, is a stronger condemnation of Anglo treatment of Native Americans than it would have been had he told only one of the stories. Don Gallo's *Speaking for Ourselves: Autobiographical Sketches by Notable Authors of Books for Young Adults* does an excellent job of introducing teenagers to the fact that authors tend to be individualistic. More than eighty contemporary young adult authors contributed two-page bibliographic statements—each telling a quite different story. William Drake's *The First Wave: Women Poets in America, 1915–1945* shows that many women are interested in literary endeavors through presenting accounts of 27 highly acclaimed poets, including Marianne Moore, Edna St. Vincent Millay, and Amy Lowell. Jim Haskins's *One More River to Cross: The Stories of Twelve Black Americans* counters the stereotype that African-Americans have succeeded only as entertainers and athletes by including the stories of businesswoman C. J. Walker, explorer Matthew Henson, diplomat Ralph Bunche, congresswoman Shirley Chisolm, and astronaut Ronald McNair, whereas Peter Irons's *The Courage of Their Convictions: Sixteen Americans Who Fought Their Way to the Supreme Court* shows the variety of problems the justices are asked to solve.

Ruth Ashby and Deborah Gore Ohrn's *Herstory: Women Who Changed the World* is a marvelous collection of brief comments (1–3 pages) about women from Queen Hatshepsut in the fifteenth century B.C. to Rigoberta Menchú of contemporary Guatemala. In between those women are brief comments about Jane Austen and Charlotte Perkins Gilman and Beatrix Potter and Mary Leakey and Barbara Jordan and many others, 120 in all. Studs Terkel's *Coming of Age: The Story of Our Century by Those Who've Lived It* includes the voices of more than seventy people, the youngest of whom is 70 and the oldest 99. The cast ranges from well-known people such as dancer Katherine Dunham and actress Uto Hagen to scholar John Kenneth Galbraith to the unknowns of the world. Similar to all of Terkel's collective biographies, this one ranges from charming chitchat to resounding ideas.

Two collective biographies of writers by Rebecca Carroll should attract young people. *I Know What the Red Clay Looks Like: The Voice and Vision of Black Women*

Writers has excerpts from 15 black authors, including Rita Dove, Gloria Naylor, Lorene Cary, and Nikki Giovanni. *Swing Low: Black Men Writing* has works by 16 writers, including Henry Louis Gates, Jr., Ishmael Reed, and August Wilson.

Biographies About Celebrities and Other Famous People

Celebrity biographies, the ones that get in the news and are likely to be requested from libraries, may present problems for educators. One such problem comes from Andy Warhol's statement that each of us will have "15 minutes of fame." The problem is that it takes more than 15 minutes for a book to be written, published, and purchased, so schools and libraries are usually a step behind. By the time a biography of some new celebrity has gone through a rigorous selection procedure, the subject may no longer be of interest.

A number of biographies, however, are about famous people who are likely to remain in the public eye for some time to come. For example, biographies such as Barbara Leaming's *Katharine Hepburn* and Donald Spoto's *A Passion for Life: The Biography of Elizabeth Taylor* may be read for several years to come. Helen Lepstein's *Joe Papp: An American Life* is about the man who founded the public theater in 1983 and who produced an amazing number of Shakespeare's plays in New York City. Anyone curious about the American theater should care about Joe Papp and the way he looked at many plays.

Similarly, Frances Mason's *I Remember Balanchine: Recollections of the Ballet Master by Those Who Knew Him* and Agnes de Mille's *Martha: The Life and Work of Martha Graham* are significant books valuable to anybody who cares about ballet, particularly the growth of ballet in the United States. Young adults who care about the history of the dance should recognize the name of Pavlova and should enjoy Ellen Levine's *Anna Pavlova: Genius of the Dance*.

Young readers who have particular favorite authors should enjoy biographies about those favorites. Roald Dahl's *Charlie and the Chocolate Factory* is a favorite of many children, but whether readers will enjoy Jeremy Treglown's *Roald Dahl: A Biography* and learning that he was not a nice person may be questionable. Almost certainly, fans of Dr. Seuss will love Judith Morgan and Neil Morgan's *Dr. Seuss and Mr. Geisel: A Biography*. Fans of *The Little Prince*, and they are legion, who read Stacy Schiff's *Saint-Exupery: A Biography* will get a picture of a man of action, a lover of flying, and a man who wrote some exceptional books. Whether Jay Parini's *John Steinbeck: A Biography* will convince readers that Steinbeck is a major writer is unclear, but young adults who love *Of Mice and Men* and *The Grapes of Wrath* will surely enjoy Parini's book. A biography of Willa Cather by Sharon O'Brien appeared recently. O'Brien's *Willa Cather* is part of Chelsea House's series, "Lives of Notable Gay Men and Lesbians," but the book is a solid study of Cather's life and work, not just her sex life.

There's always a place for biographies about women and men who have changed the world. Patricia C. McKissack and Fredrick McKissack's *Sojourner Truth: Ain't I a Woman?* is a compelling life of a woman who began as a slave and ultimately emerged as a powerful African-American voice in the United States. Ellen

Chesler's *Woman of Valor: Margaret Sanger and the Birth Control Movement in America* is the life of a nurse who became a militant socialist and ultimately saved many other women's lives. Carolyn G. Heilbrun's *The Education of a Woman: The Life of Gloria Steinem* portrays the woman who may have had more power in the women's movement than any other.

Two biographies of Franklin Delano Roosevelt have recently appeared. Jeoffrey C. Ward's *Closest Companion: The Unknown Story of the Intimate Friendship Between Franklin Roosevelt and Margaret Suckley* tells one side of Roosevelt's life, whereas Doris Kearns Goodwin's *No Ordinary Time: Franklin and Eleanor Roosevelt, The Homefront in World War II* is particularly exciting because it has considerable new material and it focuses on one of the most widely known women of her time. Gale E. Christianson's *Edwin Hubble: Mariner of the Nebulae* is a story of an astronomer who changed the course of his discipline but who was anything but easy to get along with.

We rarely think about young people changing the course of the world, but Ellen Levine's *Freedom's Children: Young Civil Rights Activists Tell Their Own Stories* should make young people proud of other young people. Joseph Berger's *The Young Scientists: America's Future and the Winning of the Westinghouse* tells of Berger's study of the winners of the annual national Westinghouse Science Talent Search. Berger notes one of the major problems with " . . . most science classes. Students learn scientific concepts and facts that they feed back on tests. They do not learn methods of research, and they do not perform any research." Berger becomes excited, and so will readers, as he learns how dedicated these young scientists are and how they have developed their own research.

Debunking Biographies

In the debunking biography, a popular hero or an institution or anything treasured by many people is taken down from a pedestal. Although such books are certainly "antihero," they differ from true examples of the literary meaning of the term in that the subject of a debunking biography is not written about with sympathy. Among the most famous is the recent *Nancy Reagan: The Unauthorized Biography* by Kitty Kelley. Probably few young adults have read it because politics and the Reagans are not part of their sphere of interest.

Sports heroes and movie stars are prime subjects for debunking biographies that attract young readers. For example, some young adults were attracted to the antiparent theme in Christina Crawford's *Mommie Dearest,* which debunked actress Joan Crawford for the way she played her real-life role of mother. Jim Bouton's *Ball Four: My Life and Hard Times Throwing the Knuckleball in the Big Leagues* was a debunking of professional baseball, and Samuel Wilson Fussell's *Muscle: Confessions of an Unlikely Body Builder* debunked weightlifting. Books such as these serve as antidotes for gullibility and excessive hero worship. Not to read debunking books is to miss one facet of humanity, but to read only debunking books is to produce only debunkers, and that we already have in sufficient number.

Young people may have been more attracted to the many books about Princess Diana that have appeared in the last few years. Andrew Morton's *Diana: Her True Story* and Colin Campbell's *Diana in Private: The Princess Nobody Knows* added wonderful ammunition to the soap opera Diana vs. Charles war. They provided questions that we might ponder: What is the real Diana like? Will Charles and Diana ever resume their storybook love story? Readers speeding over the first few lines of the front dust jacket of Andrew Morton's book were in danger of becoming diabetic:

Diana, Princess of Wales, is probably the best-loved and most admired woman in the world. After her marriage to Prince Charles she blossomed into one of the world's great beauties while at the same time she was raising a young family and attending to a long list of charities. Her world seemed perfect, but behind the image of perfection lay a disturbing truth: in *Diana: Her True Story* we learned that her marriage to Prince Charles has been unhappy from the very beginning.

Michiko Kakutani has commented on vicious, or fawning, contemporary biographies:

It's not surprising that a society obsessed with the Bobbitts, the Menendez brothers, Amy Fisher, and Tonya Harding should spawn a growing number of gossipy, speculative and just plain tasteless biographies. Indeed, this development is indicative, in many respects, of broader currents in our society at large, for biography writing has served, throughout its history, as a kind of mirror of the cultural Zeitgeist.

Borrowing a phrase from Freud, Joyce Carol Oates has called this disturbing new subgenre "pathography." Kakutani says, "Its motifs are dysfunction and disaster, illnesses and pratfalls, failed marriages and failed careers, alcoholism and breakdowns and outrageous conduct." "Its scenes are sensational, wallowing in squalor and foolishness; its dominant images are physical and deflating; its shrill theme is 'failed promise,' if not outright 'tragedy.'"[11]

Teachers and librarians face the obvious fact that there are questionable books out there for young adults. Wilt Chamberlain's *A View from Above* has a chapter on "On Sex and Love: What Rules the World," which makes clear that he believes he is lucky because he has had sexual relations with nearly 20,000 women. That may impress Chamberlain, but it is likely to bother most adults. Vincent Bugliosi's *Helter Skelter: The True Story of the Manson Murders* was popular several years back, but the book is still read by young people because Manson periodically pops up in the news.

With questionable books, it's usually better that teenagers have a chance to read the whole book rather than just get the smatterings of sexual or violent titillation that appear in the media. One thing we can feel confident in suggesting is that when it comes to selecting books that you are unsure about, check out your initial reaction with others. Talk to colleagues, parents, and students. Perhaps it's the last group that is most important to include in discussions about book selection because unless someone starts young people along such a line of thinking they may never understand that reading about someone's life does not necessarily mean emulating everything about that person. As librarian Mary Mueller observed:

> Our past and present are full of personages who lived outside traditional rules. They often used poor judgment or acted in a less-than-exemplary fashion. . . . How can we expect our students to really see the personality of Harry Truman without letting them see the tenacity, salty language, and temper that so characterized him?[12]

Connections Between History and Biography

We borrowed the title for this chapter from an "Up for Discussion" piece in *School Library Journal* entitled "History and History Makers: Give YAs the Whole Picture."[13] Mary Mueller, librarian at Rolla Junior High School in Missouri, was recommending biographies and histories as mutually complementary because individuals are shaped by the times and circumstances of their lives, which they, in turn, influence and shape for themselves as well as for those around them and those who will follow. In making a plea for librarians to be assertive in recommending biographies alongside history books, she pointed out how few books about the 1960s, the civil rights movement, and the Vietnam War include information about the "rich, complex character of Lyndon Johnson, a man who greatly influenced all three and who is extremely important to any understanding of these happenings and the era in which they occurred." She also argued for updating the 900s sections in our libraries, noting that in times of shrinking budgets we hesitate to weed out historical books and feel more justified in spending money for a new computer book than for a biography of someone who lived 200 years ago.

We'll end this chapter with the same plea that Mueller made; there are so many changes in attitudes and outlooks, "to say nothing of revisionists' theories," that history and biography sections need just as much loving care and attention—including weeding, replacing, and promoting—as do any other sections of a library.

Notes

[1] Henry Seidel Canby, "What Is Truth?" *Saturday Review of Literature* 4 (December 31, 1927): 481.

[2] Richard Stengel, "Books: American Myth 101," *Time*, December 23, 1991, p. 78.

[3] Betty Carter and Richard F. Abrahamson, *From Delight to Wisdom: Nonfiction for Young Adults* (Oryx Press, 1990), p. 180.

[4] Betty Carter and Richard F. Abrahamson, "A Conversation with Brent Ashabranner," in *From Delight to Wisdom: Nonfiction for Young Adults* (Oryx Press, 1990), p. 101.

[5] Christopher Collier, "Criteria for Historical Novels," *School Library Journal* 29 (August 1982): 32.

[6] Christopher Collier, "Fact, Fiction, and History: The Role of the Historian, Writer, Teacher, and Reader," *ALAN Review* 14 (Winter 1987): 5.

[7] Sheila A. Egoff, *Thursday's Child: Trends and Patterns in Contemporary Children's Fiction* (American Library Association, 1981), p. 159.

[8] Patty Campbell, "The Young Adult Perplex," *Wilson Library Bulletin* 55 (November 1980): 214.

[9] Larry R. Johannessen's *Illumination Rounds: Teaching the Literature of the Vietnam War* (NCTE, 1992) is an uncommonly helpful source of information on teaching or using material in secondary schools. So are Johannessen's article, "Young-Adult Literature

and the Vietnam War," *English Journal* 82 (September 1993): 43–49; and articles by Perry Oldham, "Some Further Thoughts on Teaching Vietnam Literature," *English Journal* 82 (December 1993): 65–67; Christie N. Bradley, "Teaching Our Longest War: Constructive Lessons from Vietnam," *English Journal* 78 (April 1989): 35–38; and Fred A. Wilcox, "Pedagogical Implications of Teaching Literature of the Vietnam War," *Social Education* 52 (January 1988): 39–40.

[10]Judith Miller, "Wartime Internment of Japanese Was 'Grave Injustice,' Panel Says." *New York Times,* February 25, 1983, p.1.

[11]Michiko Kakutani, "Biography as a Blood Sport." *New York Times,* May 20, 1994, pp. B–1, B–6.

[12]Mary E. Mueller, "Up for Discussion: History and History Makers: Give YAs the Whole Picture." *School Library Journal* 37 (November 1991): 55–56.

[13]Mueller, "Up for Discussion," pp. 55–56.

Titles Mentioned in the Text of Chapter Seven

Abells, Chana Byers. *The Children We Remember.* Greenwillow, 1986.

Ackerman, Diane. *The Moon by Whale Light: And Other Adventures Among Bats, Penguins, Crocodilians, and Whales.* Random House, 1991.

Allende, Isabel. *Paula.* HarperCollins, 1995.

Angelou, Maya. *I Know Why the Caged Bird Sings.* Random House, 1970.

Armor, John, and Peter Wright. *Manzanar.* Times Books, 1989.

Arrick, Fran. *Chernowitz!* Bradbury, 1981.

Ashby, Ruth, and Deborah Gore Ohrn, eds. *Herstory: Women Who Changed the World.* Viking, 1995.

Avi. *The True Confessions of Charlotte Doyle.* Orchard, 1990.

Baker, Mark. *Nam: The Vietnam War in the Words of the Men and Women Who Fought There.* Morrow, 1981.

Bawden, Nina. *In My Own Time: Almost an Autobiography.* Virago, 1994.

Becker, Elizabeth. *America's Vietnam War: A Narrative History.* Clarion, 1992.

Berger, Joseph. *The Young Scientists: America's Future and the Winning of the Westinghouse.* Addison-Wesley, 1994.

Blinn, William. *Brian's Song.* Bantam,1972.

Bombeck, Erma. *I Want to Grow Hair, I Want to Grow Up, I Want to Go to Boise: Children Surviving Cancer.* HarperCollins, 1989.

Bosse, Malcolm. *The Examination.* Farrar Straus & Giroux, 1994.

Bouton, Jim, edited by Leonard Shecter. *Ball Four: My Life and Hard Times Throwing the Knuckleball in the Big Leagues.* World, 1970.

Brodie, Fawn M. *Thomas Jefferson: An Intimate History.* Norton, 1974.

Bugliosi, Vincent, and Curt Gentry. *Helter Skelter: The True Story of the Manson Murders.* Norton, 1974.

Callahan, Stephen. *Adrift: Seventy-six Days Lost at Sea.* Thorndike, 1986.

Campbell, Colin. *Diana in Private: The Princess Nobody Knows.* St. Martins, 1992.

Carroll, Rebecca. *I Know What the Red Clay Looks Like: The Voice and Vision of Black Women Writers.* Crown, 1994.

Carroll, Rebecca. *Swing Low: Black Men Writing.* Crown, 1995.

Carter, Peter. *The Hunted.* Farrar Straus & Giroux, 1994.

Chamberlain, Wilt. *A View from Above.* Villard, 1991.

Chatwin, Bruce. *What Am I Doing Here?* Viking, 1989.

Chesler, Ellen. *Woman of Valor: Margaret Sanger and the Birth Control Movement in America.* Simon & Schuster, 1992.

Christianson, Gale E. *Edwin Hubble: Mariner of the Nebulae.* Farrar Straus & Giroux, 1995.

Clark, Edie. *The Place He Made.* Villard, 1995.

Collier, James Lincoln, and Christopher Collier. *My Brother Sam Is Dead.* Scholastic, 1974.

Conway, Jill Ker. *The Road from Coorain.* Kanopf, 1990.

Conway, Jill Ker. *True North.* Knopf, 1994.

Cox, Clinton. *Undying Glory: The Story of the Massachusetts 54th Regiment.* Scholastic, 1991.

Crawford, Christina. *Mommie Dearest.* Morrow, 1978.

Crouch, Tom D. *The Bishop's Boys: A Life of Wilbur and Orville Wright.* Norton, 1989.

Cushman, Karen. *Catherine, Called Birdy.* Clarion, 1994.

Cushman, Karen. *The Midwife's Apprentice.* Clarion, 1995.

David, Kati. *A Child's War: World War II Through the Eyes of Children.* Four Walls Eight Windows, 1990.

Davis, Edith Kunhardt. *I'll Love You Forever, Anyway.* Fine, 1995.

Degens, T. *The Visit.* Viking, 1982.

de Mille, Agnes. *Martha: The Life and Work of Martha Graham.* Random House, 1991.

Denenberg, Barry. *Voices from Vietnam.* Scholastic, 1995.

Dickinson, Peter. *A Bone from a Dry Sea.* Delacorte, 1992.

Dillard, Annie. *An American Childhood.* HarperCollins, 1987.

Drake, William. *The First Wave: Women Poets in America, 1915–1945.* Macmillan, 1987.

Dumbach, Annette E., and Jud Newborn. *Shattering the German Night: The Story of the White Rose.* Little, Brown, 1986.

Engelmann, Bernt. *In Hitler's Germany: Daily Life in the Third Reich.* Pantheon, 1987.

Epstein, Helen. *Joe Papp: An American Life.* Little, Brown, 1994.

Fast, Howard. *April Morning.* Crown, 1961.

Feiler, Bruce. *Under the Big Top.* Scribner, 1995.

Feldbaum, Carl B., and Ronald J. Bee. *Looking the Tiger in the Eye: Confronting the Nuclear Threat.* HarperCollins, 1988.

Filipovic, Zlata. *Zlata's Diary: A Child's Life in Sarajevo.* Penguin, 1994.

Fogelman, Eva. *Conscience and Courage: Rescuers of Jews During the Holocaust.* Anchor, 1994.

Forman, James. *Ceremony of Innocence.* Hawthorne, 1970.

Frank, Anne. *Diary of a Young Girl: The Definitive Edition.* Doubleday, 1995.

Freedman, Russell. *Indian Chiefs.* Holiday, 1986.

Freedman, Russell. *Franklin Delano Roosevelt.* Clarion, 1990.

Friedman, Ina R. *The Other Victims: First Person Stories of Non-Jews Persecuted by the Nazi.* Houghton Mifflin, 1990.

Fussell, Samuel Wilson. *Muscle: Confessions of an Unlikely Body Builder.* Poseidon, 1991.

Gaes, Jason. *My Book for Kids with Cansur.* Melius & Peterson, 1987.

Gallo, Donald R., ed. *Speaking for Ourselves: Autobiographical Sketches by Notable Authors for Books for Young Adults.* National Council of Teachers of English, 1990.

Garfield, Leon. *The Empty Sleeve.* Delacorte, 1988.

Garfield, Leon. *Jack Holborn.* Pantheon, 1965.

Garfield, Leon. *The Night of the Comet.* Delacorte, 1979.

Garfield, Leon. *The Sound of Coaches.* Viking, 1974.

Garfield, Leon. *The Strange Affair of Adelaide Harris.* Pantheon, 1971.

Gehrts, Barbara. *Don't Say a Word.* McElderry, 1986.

Gies, Miep. *Anne Frank Remembered.* Simon & Schuster, 1987.

Goodall, Jane. *My Life with the Chimpanzees.* Pocket Books, 1988.

Goodwin, Doris Kearns. *No Ordinary Time: Franklin and Eleanor Roosevelt, The Home Front in World War II.* Simon & Schuster, 1994.

Graham, Robin. *Dove.* HarperCollins, 1972.

Gunther, John. *Death Be Not Proud.* HarperCollins, 1949.

Hanser, Richard. *A Noble Treason: The Revolt of the Munich Students Against Hitler.* Putnam, 1979.

Hanser, Richard. *Which Way Freedom?* Walker, 1986.

Haskins, Jim. *One More River to Cross: The Stories of Twelve Black Americans.* Scholastic, 1992.

Haugaard, Erik Christian. *The Revenge of the Forty-Seven Samurai.* Houghton Mifflin, 1995.

Haugaard, Erik Christian. *The Samurai's Tale.* Houghton Mifflin, 1984.

Heilbrun, Carolyn G. *The Education of a Woman: The Life of Gloria Steinem.* Dial, 1995.

Hentoff, Nat. *Boston Boy.* Knopf, 1986.

Hillesum, Etty. *An Interrupted Life: The Diaries of Etty Hillesum, 1941–1943.* Pantheon, 1984.

Hillesum, Etty. *Letters from Westerbork.* Pantheon, 1986.

Hoobler, Dorothy and Thomas Hoobler. *The Fact or Fiction Files: Lost Civilizations.* Walker, 1992.

Houston, Jeanne Wakatsuki, and James D. Houston. *Farewell to Manzanar.* Houghton Mifflin, 1973.

Hunt, Irene. *No Promises in the Wind.* Follett, 1979.

Irons, Peter. *The Courage of Their Convictions: Sixteen Americans Who Fought Their Way to the Supreme Court.* Free Press, 1988.

Jens, Inge. *At the Heart of the White Rose: Letters and Diaries of Hans and Sophie Scholl.* Harper & Row, 1987.

Jewell, Geri, with Stewart Winer. *Geri.* Morrow, 1984.

Johannessen, Larry R. *Illumination Rounds: Teaching the Literature of the Vietnam War.* National Council of Teachers of English, 1992.

Kammen, Michael. *Mystic Chords of Memory.* Knopf, 1991.

Katz, William Loren. *Breaking the Chains: African-American Slave Resistance.* Atheneum, 1990.

Keen, Ann T. *Willa Cather.* Julian Messner, 1995.

Kelly, Kitty. *Nancy Reagan: The Unauthorized Biography.* Simon & Schuster, 1991.

Keneally, Thomas. *Schindler's List.* Simon & Schuster, 1982.

Koop, C. Everett. *Koop: The Memoirs of America's Family Doctor.* Random House, 1991.

Krementz, Jill. *How It Feels to Fight for Your Life.* Little, Brown, 1989.

Krementz, Jill. *How It Feels When a Parent Dies.* Knopf, 1981.

Kuralt, Charles. *A Life on the Road.* Putnam, 1985.

Lancaster, Matthew. *Hang Tough.* Paulist, 1985.

Landau, Elaine. *We Have AIDS.* Franklin Watts, 1990.

Lasky, Kathryn. *Beyond the Burning Time.* Scholastic, 1994.

Lasky, Kathryn. *Beyond the Divide.* Macmillan, 1983.

Lawrence, R. D. *In Praise of Wolves.* Holt, 1986.

Leaming, Barbara. *Katharine Hepburn*. Crown, 1995.

Least Heat Moon, William. *Blue Highways: A Journey into America*.

Little, Brown, 1982.

Levine, Ellen. *Anna Pavlova: Genius of the Dance*. Scholastic, 1995.

Levine, Ellen. *Freedom's Children: Young Civil Rights Activists Tell Their Own Stories*. Putnam, 1993.

Lund, Doris. *Eric*. Lippincott, 1974.

MacPherson, Malcolm C. *Time Bomb: Fermi, Heisenberg and the Race for the Atomic Bomb*. Dutton, 1986.

Marshall, Kathryn. *In the Combat Zone: An Oral History of American Women in Vietnam*. Little, Brown, 1987.

Mason, Frances. *I Remember Balanchine: Recollections of the Ballet Master by Those Who Knew Him*. Doubleday, 1991.

Masters, Edgar Lee. *Spoon River Anthology*. Macmillan, 1962.

Matthiessen, Peter. *African Silences*. Random House, 1991.

Mauer, Harry. *Strange Ground: Americans in Vietnam, 1945–1975, an Oral History*. Holt, 1988.

Mazer, Harry. *The Last Mission*. Delacorte, 1979.

McCloud, Bill. *What Should We Tell Our Children About Vietnam?* University of Oklahoma Press, 1989.

McCutchan, Phillip. *Apprentice to the Sea*. St. Martins, 1995.

McKissack, Patricia C., and Fredrick McKissack. *Sojourner Truth: Ain't I a Woman?* Scholastic, 1992.

Meltzer, Milton. *Columbus and the World Around Him*. Watts, 1990.

Meltzer, Milton. *Never to Forget: The Jews of the Holocaust*. HarperCollins, 1976.

Meltzer, Milton. *Rescue: The Story of How Gentiles Saved Jews in the Holocaust*. HarperCollins, 1988.

Meltzer, Milton. *Voices from the Civil War: A Documentary History of the Great American Conflict*. Crowell, 1989.

Morgan, Judith, and Neil Morgan. *Dr. Seuss and Mr. Geisel: A Biography*. Random House, 1995.

Morris, Jeannie. *Brian Piccolo: A Short Season*. Rand McNally, 1971.

Morton, Andrew. *Diana: Her True Story*. Simon & Schuster, 1992.

Mowat, Farley. *Born Naked*. Houghton Mifflin, 1994.

Mowat, Farley. *The Dog Who Wouldn't Be*. Little, Brown, 1957.

Mowat, Farley. *Never Cry Wolf*. Little, Brown, 1963.

Mowat, Farley. *And No Birds Sang*. Little, Brown, 1980.

Mowat, Farley. *Owls in the Family*. Little, Brown, 1961.

Mowat, Farley. *Sea of Slaughter*. Atlantic, 1985.

Mowat, Farley. *A Whale for the Killing*. Little, Brown, 1972.

Myers, Walter Dean. *Fallen Angels*. Scholastic, 1988.

Myers, Walter Dean. *Malcolm X: By Any Means Necessary*. Scholastic, 1993.

Nolan, Han. *If I Should Die Before I Wake*. Harcourt Brace, 1994.

O'Brien, Sharon. *Willa Cather*. Chelsea House, 1995.

O'Dell, Scott. *Island of the Blue Dolphins*. Houghton Mifflin, 1960.

O'Dell, Scott. *The King's Fifth*. Houghton Mifflin, 1966.

O'Dell, Scott. *Sing Down the Moon*. Houghton Mifflin, 1970.

Palmer, Laura. *Shrapnel in the Heart: Letters and Remembrances from the Vietnam Veterans Memorial*. Random House, 1987.

Parini, Jay. *John Steinbeck: A Biography*. Holt, 1995.

Paterson, Katherine. *Lyddie*. Dutton, 1991.

Peck, Richard. *Anonymously Yours*. Julian Messner, 1991.

Pelta, Kathy. *Discovering Christopher Columbus: How History Is Invented*. Lerner, 1991.

Pullman, Phillip. *The Ruby in the Smoke*. Knopf, 1987.

Pullman, Phillip. *Shadow in the North*. Knopf, 1988.

Pullman, Phillip. *The Tiger in the Well*. Knopf, 1990.

Pyle, Ernie. *Ernie's War: The Best of Ernie Pyle's World War II Dispatches*. David Nichols, ed. Random House, 1986.

Radner, Gilda. *It's Always Something*. Simon & Schuster, 1989.

Ray, Karen. *To Cross a Line*. Orchard, 1994.

Reiss, Johanna. *The Journey Back*. Crowell, 1976.

Reiss, Johanna. *The Upstairs Room*. Harper & Row, 1972.

Rhue, Morton (Todd Strasser). *The Wave*. Del, 1981.

Richter, Elizabeth. *Losing Someone You Love: When a Brother or Sister Dies*. Putnam, 1986.

Rinaldi, Ann. *A Break with Charity: A Story about the Salem Witch Trials*. Harcourt Brace Jovanovich, 1992.

Rinaldi, Ann. *The Fifth of March: A Story of the Boston Massacre*. Harcourt Brace Jovanovich, 1993.

Rinaldi, Ann. *Finishing Becca: A Story about Peggy Shippen and Benedict Arnold*. Harcourt Brace Jovanovich, 1994.

Rinaldi, Ann. *Wolf by the Ears*. Scholastic, 1991.

Rochman, Hazel and Darlene Z. McCampbell, eds. *Bearing Witness: Stories of the Holocaust*. Orchard, 1995.

Rosenberg, Maxine B. *Hiding to Survive: Stories of Jewish Children Rescued from the Holocaust*. Clarion, 1994.

Rosenblatt, Roger. *Children of War*. Doubleday, 1983.

Rothchild, Sylvia, ed. *Voices from the Holocaust*. New American Library, 1981.

Ruby, Lois. *Skin Deep*. Scholastic, 1994.

Salzman, Mark. *Lost in Place: Growing Up Absurd in Suburbia*. Random House, 1995.

Santoli, Al. *Everything We Had: An Oral History of the Vietnam War by Thirty-Three American Soldiers Who Fought It*. Random House, 1981.

Sayers, Gale. *I Am Third.* Viking, 1970.

Schiff, Stacy. *Saint-Exupery: A Biography.* Knopf, 1994.

Sender, Ruth Minsky. *The Cage.* Macmillan, 1986.

Sender, Ruth Minsky. *The Holocaust Lady.* Macmillan, 1992.

Sender, Ruth Minsky. *To Life.* Macmillan, 1988.

Sexton, Linda Gray. *Searching for Mercy Street: My Journey Back to My Mother, Anne Sexton.* Little, Brown, 1994.

Spoto, Donald. *A Passion for Life: The Biography of Elizabeth Taylor.* HarperCollins, 1995.

Staden, Wendelgard von. *Darkness over the Valley.* Tickner and Fields, 1981.

Stenbuck, Jack. *Typewriter Battalion.* Morrow, 1995.

Sutcliff, Rosemary. *Dawn Wind.* Walck, 1961.

Sutcliff, Rosemary. *The Eagle of the Ninth.* Walck, 1954.

Sutcliff, Rosemary. *The Shield Ring.* Oxford University Press, 1957.

Sutcliff, Rosemary. *The Shining Company.* Farrar, 1990.

Tapert, Annette, ed. *Lines of Battle: Letters from American Servicemen, 1941–1945.* Times Books, 1987.

Teichman, Milton and Sharon Leder, eds. *Truth and Lamentation: Stories and Poems on the Holocaust.* University of Illinois Press, 1994.

Temple, Frances. *The Ramsay Scallop.* Orchard, 1994.

Tiburzi, Bonnie. *Takeoff! The Story of America's First Woman Pilot for a Major Airline.* Crown, 1984.

Treglown, Jeremy. *Raold Dahl: A Biography.* Farrar Straus & Giroux, 1994.

Vinke, Hermann. *The Short Life of Sophie Scholl.* Harper & Row, 1980.

Volavkova, Hanna, ed. *I Never Saw Another Butterfly: Children's Drawings and Poems from Terezin Concentration Camp, 1941–1944.* Schocken, 1978.

Ward, Geoffrey. *The Civil War: An Illustrated History.* Knopf, 1990.

Ward, Geoffrey. *Closest Companion: The Unknown Story of the Intimate Relationship Between Franklin Roosevelt and Margaret Suckley.* Houghton Mifflin, 1995.

Westall, Robert. *Fathom Five.* Greenwillow, 1979.

Westall, Robert. *The Machine Gunners.* Greenwillow, 1976.

Wharton, William. *Ever After: A Father's True Story.* Newmarket, 1995.

Wharton, William. *A Midnight Clear.* Knopf, 1982.

White, Ryan, and Ann Marie Cunningham. *Ryan White: My Own Story.* Dial, 1991.

Wolf, Joan. *The Reindeer Hunters.* Penguin/Dutton, 1995.

Wolff, Tobias. *This Boy's Life.* Atlantic Monthly Press, 1989.

For information on the availability of paperback editions of these titles, please consult the most recent edition of *Paperbound Books in Print,* published annually by R. R. Bowker Company.

Chapter 8

Nonfiction Books
Of Interesting Information

. . . .

When the American Library Association made history by awarding its coveted 1988 Newbery Medal to Russell Freedman's *Lincoln: A Photobiography,* Milton Meltzer, who has long championed the cause of nonfiction, applauded by saying:

> It was a terrific thing to do, but it took fifty years to do it. The few books they gave prizes to before, that were called nonfiction, really were not. Instead, they were books written in the outmoded vein of biography that was highly fictionalized, had invented dialogue, and sometimes concocted scenes. That's all changed today, but it took a long time.[1]

In their 1990 *Nonfiction for Young Adults: From Delight to Wisdom,* Betty Carter and Richard F. Abrahamson cited 22 research studies. Among the reported findings:

- An interest in reading nonfiction emerges at about the fourth grade and grows during adolescence.
- Interest in reading nonfiction crosses ability levels; one study showed that nonfiction made up 34 percent of the leisure reading of academically able teenagers and 54 percent of the control group's leisure reading.
- Nonfiction makes up a much larger proportion of boys' reading than of girls' reading.
- One study categorized the seven most popular types of nonfiction as cartoon and comic books, weird but true stories, rock stars, ghosts, magic, stories about famous people, and explorations of the unknown.
- Remedial readers prefer informative nonfiction and read "primarily to learn new things."
- Students choose nonfiction for a variety of reasons often unrelated to school curricular matters, as shown by the fact that computer-related books are popular in schools with no computers and books on the Ku Klux Klan are frequently checked out in junior highs in which recent American history is not studied.
- When students gave reasons for reading particular books, it became clear that the purpose of the reading is guided more by the student than by the type of book. One boy read books on subjects he already knew about because it made

him feel smart; others preferred how-to books so that they could interact with the author while learning to draw, care for a pet, program a computer, make a paper airplane, and so on; and still others preferred *The Guinness Book of World Records.* Even here purposes differed. Some read the book to discover amazing facts, but others read it to imagine themselves undergoing strange experiences.

Narrative or Storytelling in Nonfiction

When Thomas Keneally's 1982 *Schindler's List* won a Pulitzer Prize in fiction, there was considerable controversy over whether the book was eligible because it was supposedly a journalistic account of a true event. E. L. Doctorow spoke to the same issue when he said in his acceptance speech for the National Book Critics Circle Award for *Ragtime,* "There is no more fiction or nonfiction—only narrative."

Three hundred English teachers who responded to a survey asking for 10 adolescent novels and 10 adult novels worthy of being recommended to teenagers gave further evidence that in people's minds, fiction and nonfiction are blending together. Among 20 nonfiction titles recommended as novels were Piers Paul Read's *Alive,* James Herriot's *All Creatures Great and Small,* Robin Graham's *Dove,* Peter Maas's *Serpico,* Doris Lund's *Eric,* Alvin Toffler's *Future Shock,* Maya Angelou's *I Know Why the Caged Bird Sings,* Dee Brown's *Bury My Heart at Wounded Knee,* Claude Brown's *Manchild in the Promised Land,* Eldridge Cleaver's *Soul on Ice,* and John H. Griffin's *Black Like Me.*

The blending has occurred from both directions. On one side are the nonfiction writers who use the techniques of fiction, including suspense, careful plotting and characterization, and literary devices, such as symbolism and metaphor. On the other side are the novelists who collect data as an investigative reporter would. In *Midnight Hour Encores,* Bruce Brooks acknowledged 32 individuals for talking to him "about music in relentless detail," and at the beginning of *Izzy, Willy-Nilly,* Cynthia Voigt acknowledged help from medical personnel who taught her about physical and mental aspects of amputation. When Richard Peck wrote *Are You in the House Alone?,* he gathered current statistics on rape and then fashioned his story around the most typical case—that is, a young girl in a familiar setting being raped by someone she knows, who is not prosecuted for the crime. Readers are so accustomed to writers doing this kind of research that following the popular success of Robert J. Waller's *The Bridges of Madison County, National Geographic Magazine* had a hard time convincing readers that they could not buy or even look at a historical feature on Iowa bridges because Waller's story was purely fictional.

Books such as these are fiction in the sense that fictional names are used and they combine bits and pieces of many individual stories. Nevertheless, in another sense, these stories are more real and actually present a more honest portrayal than some pieces labeled nonfiction that are true accounts of bizarre or strange happenings.

Literature—fiction and nonfiction—is more than a simple recounting or replaying of the life that surrounds the writer. It is a distillation and a crystallization. Only when an author skillfully chooses descriptive details and develops believable dialogue does an account of an actual event become real to the reader. Certainly Alex Haley's *Roots* became real to millions of television viewers as well as to millions of readers, yet the book contains many fictional elements in both subject matter and presentation. Part of Haley's success comes from his ability to select powerful incidents and details. Good writers of nonfiction do not simply record everything they know or can uncover. With Haley's book, readers' imaginations were captured by the fact that on September 29, 1967, he "stood on the dock in Annapolis where his great-great-great-great-great-grandfather was taken ashore on September 29, 1767," and sold as a slave to a Virginia plantation owner. From this point, Haley set out to trace backward the six generations that connected him to a 16-year-old "prince" newly arrived from Africa. What the public might not stop to consider as they read about this dramatic incident is that it is setting the stage for only a small portion of Haley's "roots." In the generation in which Haley started his story with the young couple, Omoro and Binta Kinte, and the birth of their first son, Kunta, there were 256 parents giving birth to 128 children, each one of whom is also a great-great-great-great-great-grandfather or grandmother to Alex Haley. The point is that even though Haley was writing nonfiction, he had an almost unlimited range of possibilities from which to choose, and he made his choices with the instinct of a storyteller rather than a clerk, who might have put together a more complete but less interesting family history. Those writers whose nonfiction books have been popular enough to earn a place on our Honor List (Focus Box 8.1) have done much the same thing. They have been storytellers first, and teachers second.

New Journalism

Roots is part of the genre sometimes labelled *new journalism*. Truman Capote called it the "most avant-garde form of writing existent today" and coined the term *nonfiction novel* for *In Cold Blood,* an account of an especially brutal murder and the subsequent trial. Other terms that are used include *creative nonfiction, literary journalism, journalistic fiction,* and *advocacy journalism.* Although its roots were growing right along with journalism in general, it did not begin to flower until the 1950s and 1960s. Part of the reason for its development is the increased educational level of the American public. Newspaper readers and television viewers, including young adults, are not satisfied with simplistic explanations. They want enough background information that they can feel confident in coming to their own conclusions.

Affluence, combined with modern technology, helps make the new journalism possible. Compare similar incidents that happened 126 years apart. In 1846, a group of travelers who came to be known as the Donner party were trapped in the high Sierras by an early snow. They had to stay there all winter without food except for the flesh of their dead companions. After they were rescued, word of their ordeal gradually trickled back east, so that for years afterward sensationalized accounts were made up by writers who had no chance to come to the scene or interview the survivors.

In 1972, a planeload of Uruguayan travelers crashed in the Andes mountains. As in the Donner party, some people knew each other before the trip, but others were strangers. During the terrible weeks of waiting to be rescued, they all got to

FOCUS BOX 8.1

Nonfiction—History, Science, and Technology

The Great Fire by Jim Murphy. Scholastic, 1995.   Murphy uses photos, paintings, woodcuts, etchings, maps, and on-the-spot descriptions gleaned from journals, news stories, and earlier books to tell the dramatic story of the 1871 Chicago fire.

Growing Up in Medieval London: The Experience of Childhood in History by Barbara Hanawalt. Oxford University Press, 1993. This child's view of a fascinating historical period is bound to be more interesting to young readers than the more common approach of focusing on court decisions, wars, and adult love affairs.

The Ingenious Mr. Peale: Painter, Patriot and Man of Science by Janet Wilson. Simon & Schuster/Atheneum, 1996. A lively biography of a lively individual, Wilson's book shows an early American balancing three careers.

The Life and Death of Crazy Horse by Russell Freedman. Holiday, 1996.   As white people flocked to the West, the Oglala Sioux leader, Crazy Horse, recognized that a fight to the death was likely. The Battle of the Little Big Horn was the result.

Maus: A Survivor's Tale by Art Spiegelman. Pantheon, 1986.   Spiegelman won a Pulitzer Prize for his original approach to telling the story of the Holocaust. *Maus II* was almost as popular (see photo on p. 187).

Rocket! How a Toy Launched the Space Age by Richard Maurer. Crown, 1995.   "Rarely has physics been this interesting and approachable," wrote *Booklist* reviewer Frances Bradburn when she advised libraries to buy copies for both their young adult and adult collections.

Shadow Catcher: The Life and Work of Edward S. Curtis by Laurie Lawlor. Walker, 1994.   Curtis spent 30 years taking pictures of Native Americans. Lawlor continues Curtis's work by documenting and bringing to people's attention the plight of Native Americans in the early 1900s.

The Way Things Work: From Levers to Lasers, Cars to Computers—A Visual Guide to the World of Machines by David Macaulay. Houghton Mifflin, 1988.   Macaulay used his wonderful drafting skills to illustrate this oversized book which is understandably popular.

A Young Patriot: The American Revolution as Experienced by One Boy by Jim Murphy. Clarion, 1996.   Murphy's own writing ties together and supplements excerpts from the diary of Joseph Plumb Martin, a 15-year-old farm boy from Connecticut who in 1776 fought in the Continental Army.

know each other and to develop intense relationships revolving around leadership roles and roles of rebellion or giving up. They endured unspeakable hardships. Many died; those who lived did so because they ate the flesh of those who died. But in this situation, the people were rescued by helicopters after two of the men made their way out of the mountains. Word of their 2 1/2-month ordeal was flashed around the world, and by the time the 16 survivors, mostly members of a rugby team, had been flown back to Uruguay, reporters from many nations were there. A press conference was held, and the journalists were told about the cannibalism.

This was the second surprise in the story. The first had been their survival. The drama of the situation naturally fired imaginations all around the world. Lippincott suggested to author Piers Paul Read that this was the kind of story that would make a good book. He went to Uruguay, where he stayed for several months interviewing survivors, rescuers, family and friends of both the deceased and the survivors, and the government officials who had been in charge of the search. More than a year later, Lippincott published *Alive: The Story of the Andes Survivors,* which was on the *New York Times* best-seller list for 7 months, was recently made into a movie, and will probably continue to be read by young adults for the next several years, both in and out of school.

The fact that the survivors were in their early twenties undoubtedly helps teenagers to identify with the story, but so do the literary techniques that Read used. He focused on certain individuals, presenting miniature character sketches of some and fully developed portraits of others. The setting was crucial to the story, and he described it vividly. He was also careful to write so that the natural suspense of the situation came through. His tone was consistent throughout the book. He admired the survivors but did not shy away from showing the negative aspects of human nature when it is sorely tried. In a foreword he said that the only liberty he allowed himself was the creation of dialogue between the characters, although, whenever possible, he relied on diaries and remembered comments and quarrels as well as his acquaintance with the speaking styles of the survivors.

"New journalism" combines factual information with emotional appeal. Such books might be classified as biography, history, drama, essay, or personal experience, but regardless of classification, they serve as a bridge between childhood and adult reading because of the straightforward, noncondescending style that is characteristic of good journalism. Table 8.1 contains suggestions for evaluating journalistic fiction.

Nonfiction best-sellers often outsell fiction best-sellers, and television producers know they can add millions of viewers if they advertise a program as "a documentary" rather than "a drama." Popular movies are done in "nonfiction" style, whereas on television more viewers watch "live" than fictionalized police work, and thanks to a big boost from the O. J. Simpson trial, the Court TV channel now has millions of regular viewers who keep up with actual court cases shown "in progress" and discussed *ad nauseum* by experts from various arenas.

Even the success of the tabloids depends on their nonfiction format. The majority of readers do not really believe all those stories about Elvis Presley still being alive or about women giving birth to aliens or apricot pits curing cancer; yet for the fun of it they're willing to give themselves over to a momentary suspension of disbelief—something we used to talk about mainly in relation to fantasy and science fiction.

Evaluation of Nonfiction

Evaluating nonfiction for young readers is more complicated than evaluating fiction because

1. People select informational books primarily on the basis of the subject matter, and because there is such a variety in subjects, people's choices vary tremendously, resulting in a lack of consensus on what is "the best."
2. Informative books on such topics as computers and car repair become dated more quickly than fiction books. Students preparing to take the SAT tests, wanting advice on handling money, or planning for a career need the most re-

TABLE 8.1

SUGGESTIONS FOR EVALUATING JOURNALISTIC FICTION

A good piece of journalistic fiction usually has:	A poor piece of journalistic fiction may have:
An authentic story that is individual and unique but also representative of human experience as a whole.	A stacking of the evidence to prove a sensational idea. The author set out not to find the truth but to collect evidence on only one side of an issue.
Information that is accurate and carefully researched. This is extremely important because, with most of these stories, readers will have heard news accounts and will lose faith in the story if there are inconsistencies.	A trite or worn subject that is not worthy of booklength attention from either writer or reader.
A central thesis that has grown out of the author's research.	Evidence of sloppy research and little or no documentation of sources.
Enough development to show the relationship between the characters' actions and what happens. People's motives are explored, and cause and effect are tied together.	Conversations and other accessory literary devices that contradict straight news accounts.
An author with all the writing skills of a good novelist so that, for example, the characters reveal themselves through their speech and actions, rather than through the author's descriptions.	Inclusion of extraneous information that does not help the story build toward a central idea or thesis.
A dramatic style of writing that draws readers into the story.	A pedestrian style of writing that lacks drama.

cent information. The constant turnover of informative books leaves us with few touchstone examples.

3. The transitory nature of informative nonfiction books discourages teachers and critics from giving them serious consideration as instructional materials. Although well-written personal experience narratives have longer life spans, people who have made up their minds that they are not interested in nonfiction find it easy to ignore all nonfiction.

4. Reviewers and prize givers may not feel competent to judge the technical or other specialized information presented in many informative books. Also, many reviewers, especially those working with educational journals, come from an English-teaching tradition, and they tend to focus on books that would be used in conjunction with literature rather than biology, home economics, social studies, industrial arts, history, or business classes.

5. In evaluating nonfiction, there is no generally agreed-upon theory of criticism or criteria for judgment.

We suggest that the evaluation situation can be improved by readers looking at fiction and nonfiction in similar ways. Replace looking at plot and characterization with looking at the intended audience and the content of the book. (What is it about? What information does it present?) Then look at the appropriateness and success with which each of the following is established. Examining a nonfiction book carefully enough to be able to describe the setting or scope and the theme, tone, and style gives you insights into how well it is written and packaged. Also, for informative books, look at the more specific suggestions in Table 8.2.

SETTING/SCOPE Informative books may be historical, or restricted to regional interests, or have a limited scope. In evaluating these, one needs to ask whether the author set realistic goals, considering the reading level of the intended audience and the amount of space and back-up graphics available.

TABLE 8.2

SUGGESTIONS FOR EVALUATING INFORMATIVE NONFICTION

A good piece of informative writing usually has:	A poor piece of informative writing may have:
A subject of interest to young readers, written about with zest. Information that is up-to-date and accurate.	Obsolete or inaccurate information or illustrations. Even one such occurrence causes the reader to lose faith in the rest of the book.
New information or information organized in such a way as to present a different point of view than in previously available books.	Evidence of cutting-and-pasting in which the author merely reorganized previously prepared material without developing anything new in content or viewpoint.
A reading level, vocabulary, and tone of writing that are at a consistent level appropriate to the intended audience.	Inconsistencies in style or content, for example, college-level vocabulary but a childish or cute style of writing.
An organization in which basic information is presented first so that chapters and sections build on each other.	An awkward mix of fiction and nonfiction techniques through which the author unsuccessfully tries to slip information in as an unnoticed part of the story.
An index and other aids to help readers look up facts if they want to return to the book for specific information or to glean ideas and facts without reading the entire book.	A reflection of out-of-date or socially unfair attitudes, for example, a history book that presents only the history of white upper-class men with a title and introduction that give the impression that it is a comprehensive history of the time period being covered.
Adequate documentation of the sources of information, including some original sources.	
Information to help interested students locate further readings on the subject.	A biased presentation in which only one side of a controversial issue is presented with little or no acknowledgment that many people hold different viewpoints.
In how-to-books, clear and accurate directions including complete lists of the equipment and supplies needed in a project.	In how-to books, frustrating directions that oversimplify or set up unrealistic expectations so that the reader is disappointed in the result.
Illustrations that add interest as well as clarity to the text.	
A competent author with expertise in the subject matter.	

ELLEN LEVINE
On a Grand Adventure

I write to engage my reader. In nonfiction the challenge is particularly great because many young people equate nonfiction with encyclopedias, which to them means cell-aching boredom. For me, however, nonfiction is a grand adventure. How, for example, do people solve daily living problems that result from the total destruction of their world, as in the great San Francisco earthquake of 1906. Well, some strapped roller skates to the feet of bathtubs in order to push their belongings to safety. This is not boring. How do veterinarians crack the mystery of a diagnosis when their patients can't speak? Or, why should anyone today care about Anna Pavlova, born in 1881, who once said, "I am haunted by the need to dance"?

For me, there can also be another concern, and that's to try to contribute to the development of an ethical being (my reader), one capable of taking moral positions even if it means standing alone against the crush of some popular belief. Such a person, adult or child, is a true hero, and each one of us has the potential to be heroic.

Young people equate the civil rights movement, to take an example, with Martin Luther King and other famous adults. And so it is important for them to know that "ordinary" folks like their parents and kids like themselves were essential to the success of the movement. They should know that before Rosa Parks, a teenager, a real person named Claudette Colvin in Montgomery, Alabama, refused to give up her bus seat when ordered by the driver. They should also know that the Supreme Court case holding that bus segregation was unconstitutional has Colvin's not Parks's name on it.

Once, before speaking to students in a Michigan school, I chatted with four fourth-grade boys, all African-American. Among other subjects, I have written about the underground railroad and the civil rights movement of the 1950s and '60s. One of the boys asked me, "Why do you write so much stuff on black people?" A good question that I tried to answer.

Some might dismiss this in today's parlance as "politically correct." Nonsense. It's about right and wrong. That's not to say there aren't complexities and subtleties in any story. But there aren't "two sides" in the moral sense to every issue. The fact that you may tell the story of white southern slave owners without caricature, doesn't for a moment take away from the evil of slavery.

How do young people learn morality? How do they choose heroes? There are bullies in the schoolyard as well as in the political arena, and it takes courage to defy them whatever the context. How do we teach that courage to act with compassion toward another?

One young white girl, after reading my book on the underground railroad, somewhat wistfully asked her parents, "Don't we have any black ancestors?" She was

(continued)

hungry to be part of that ethical as well as physical adventure. And how gloriously color-blind. One can only hope adulthood doesn't corrupt the grandness of her wish.

Ellen Levine's books include *A Fence Away from Freedom: Japanese Americans and World War II*, Putnam, 1995; *Anna Pavlova: Genius of the Dance,* Scholastic, 1995; *Freedom's Children: Young Civil Rights Activists Tell Their Own Stories,* Putnam, 1993; and *If You Traveled on the Underground Railroad,* Scholastic, 1988.

THEME   Informational books also have themes or purposes that are closely tied to the author's point of view. Authors may write in hopes of persuading someone to a particular belief or to inspire thoughtfulness, respect, or even curiosity. Some authors shout out their themes; others are more subtle. You need to consider consistency as you evaluate the theme. Did the author build on a consistent theme throughout the book?

TONE   The manner in which an author achieves a desired goal—whether it is to persuade, inform, inspire, or amuse—sets the tone of a book. Is it hard-sell, strident, one-sided, humorous, loving, sympathetic, adulatory, scholarly, pedantic, energetic, or leisurely? Authors of informative books for children used to take a leisurely approach as they tried to entice children into becoming interested in their subject. But today's young readers are just as busy as their parents and most likely go to informative books for quick information rather than leisure time entertainment. A boy or girl who wants to repair a bicycle does not want to read the history of the Wright brothers and their bicycle shop before getting to the part on slipped gears.

STYLE   The best informative books also have style. As author Jane Langton said when she was asked to serve as a judge, the good books "exude some kind of passion or love or caring . . . and they have the potential for leaving a mark on the readers, changing them in some way."[2] George A. Woods, former children's editor of the *New York Times Book Review,* said that he selected the informational books to be featured in his review mostly on his own "gut-level" reactions to what was "new or far better than what we have had before." He looked for a majesty of language and uniqueness and for books that would add to children's understanding by making them eyewitnesses to history.[3] A problem in examining an author's style is that each book must be judged according to the purpose the author had in mind. From book to book, purposes are so different that it is like the old problem of comparing apples and oranges. Some books are successful simply because they are different— more like a mango than an apple or an orange.

Contemporary Influences on the Publishing of Informational Books

Before the 1950s, what was published for young readers was in the main fiction (novels or short stories), poetry, or textbook material to be used in school. No one thought that young readers would be interested in factual books unless they were forced to study them as part of their schoolwork. But then the Russians launched Sputnik, and Americans were sincerely frightened that Russia was scientifically and technologically ahead. In 1961, Congress passed the National Defense Education Act, which gave millions of dollars to school libraries for the purchase of science and math books (later expanded to include all books). Publishers competed to create informative books that would qualify for purchase under the Act and would attract young readers.

The rise in the popularity of nonfiction has paralleled the information explosion and the rise in the power and influence of the mass media. Today there is simply more information to be shared between reader and writer. Television, radio, movies, newspapers, magazines, and now the Internet all communicate the same kinds of information as do books, but people expect more from books because the other media are limited in the amount of space and time that they can devote to any one topic. Moreover, whatever is produced by the mass media must be of interest to a *mass* audience, whereas individual readers select books. Of course, publishers want masses of individual readers to select their books. Nevertheless, there is more room for experimentation and controversial ideas in books than in the kinds of media that are supported by advertisers and that therefore must aim to attract the largest possible audience.

As the most pervasive of the media, television has a tremendous influence on book publishing. For example, the popularity of Carl Sagan's books such as his *Pale Blue Dot: A Vision of the Human Future in Space* has been increased by the fact that he is a television personality, and most of the people who bought Warner Books's *The Wild West* were interested in it as a companion volume to the television miniseries. Less obvious television tie-ins include books about current events, issues, or topics that may be introduced on television in such a way that authors are inspired to do research to answer the questions that cursory news reports do not have time or space to probe (Focus Box 8.2).

The influence of television on format and design is harder to prove, but there is an obvious difference between the majority of informative books coming out today and those that were published 20 years ago. More of the current books are illustrated with numerous photographs, many in color, and they are organized and laid out in chunks of information, so that readers can browse, skim, and take rest breaks—comparable to taking time out for commercials. The best example is provided by the Dorling Kindersley informative books that first came to widespread attention through their Eyewitness series with such titles as *Bird, Butterfly and Moth, Mammal,* and *Armor,* which were described as "museums between book covers" and as appealing alternatives to encyclopedias.

Need for Scientific Literacy

At a meeting of the Conference on College Composition and Communication in St. Louis, science writer Jon Franklin spoke on a panel entitled "Nonfiction: The Genre of a Technological Age." Formerly a science writer for the *Evening Sun* in Baltimore and now a teacher of journalism at the University of Maryland in College Park, Franklin's topic was "Literary Structure: A Growing Force in Science Journalism." He pointed out how in the past decade, more than half the winners of the

FOCUS BOX 8.2

Going Beyond the Headlines

And the Band Played On: Politics, People and the AIDS Epidemic by Randy Shilts. St. Martin's, 1987. A personable young newspaperman, who has by now died of AIDS, wrote this devastating book, which speaks forcefully to mature young adults.

Black Stars in Orbit: NASA's African American Astronauts by Khephra Burns and William Miles. Gulliver/Harcourt, 1995. The book is based on a 1990 television special but also ties in nicely with the recent movie about the Tuskegee Airmen.

Born Naked by Farley Mowat. Houghton, 1994. Mowat is a wonderful writer, and his memoir is likely to convince a goodly number of readers to follow in his footsteps as a nature lover.

Focus: Five Women Photographers by Sylvia Worth. Albert Whitman, 1994. This well-illustrated, 64-page book about Margaret Bourke-White and Julia Margaret Cameron, along with contemporary photographers Flor Garduno, Sandy Skoglund, and Lorna Simpson, is both informative and inspiring.

Freedom's Children: Young Civil Rights Activists Tell Their Own Stories by Ellen Levine. Putnam, 1993. Levine found and interviewed several of the young students who played key roles in the Civil Rights events of the 1960s. Their stories are especially interesting when viewed from a 1990s vantage point.

Hard Time: A Real Life Look at Juvenile Crime and Violence by Janet Bode and Stan Mack. Delacorte, 1996. With compassion and immediacy, Bode and Mack tell the stories of incarcerated teenagers and the adults who work with them.

Kids at Work: Lewis Hine and the Crusade Against Child Labor by Russell Freedman, photos by Lewis Hine. Clarion, 1993. In the early 1900s, Lewis Hine used photography as a tool against the work-related child abuse that was common in a newly industrialized society. Freedman uses Hine's photos to tell both stories.

The Moon by Whale Light: and Other Adventures Among Bats, Penguins, Crocodilians and Whales by Diane Ackerman. Random, 1991. Ackerman is first a storyteller and then a conservationist. From either perspective, this book written for a general adult audience is fun to read.

Rosie the Riveter: Women Working on the Home Front in World War II by Penny Colman. Crown, 1995. Colman shows some of the underlying social problems that complicated the already difficult task faced by U.S. women in the 1940s.

A Whole New Ball Game: The Story of the All-American Girls Professional Baseball League by Sue Macy. Holt, 1993. Interesting photos help to present the history of the period as well as this interesting time for women athletes.

Pulitzer Prize in nonfiction had been science books, and how the increasingly important role of scientific writing in newspapers and magazines is changing basic concepts of journalism. The upside-down pyramid, in which the key points are stated first with the details being filled in later so an editor can cut the story whenever the available space is filled, does not work for science writing because it results in oversimplification. Science stories have to be written inductively, building from the small to the large points because most scientific developments and concepts are too complex for readers to understand unless they get the supporting details first.

There's no end to the books currently being published in the hope of satisfying teenagers' curiosity.

Franklin worries about the development of a new kind of elitism based on scientific literacy. He says that if people feel uncomfortable with scientific writing, they are likely to resent and reject scientific concepts. He gives as an example the censorship battles that have developed over beliefs in creationism versus evolution. He proposes a two-pronged approach to keep the gap from widening between the scientifically literate and those who reject all science. On the one hand, science writers have to work harder to find organizational patterns and literary techniques that will make their material understandable and interesting. On the other hand, schools must bring the reading of technological and scientific information into the curriculum with the goal of preparing students to balance their lifetime reading.

Books to Support and Extend the School Curriculum

Informational books purchased by school libraries are usually referred to as "books to support the curriculum," but a more accurate description would probably be "books to extend the curriculum." These books seldom help students who are doing poorly in class. Instead, they provide challenges for successful students to go further than their classmates. They also serve as models for research, and they go beyond the obvious facts to present information that is too complicated, too detailed, too obscure, or too controversial to be included in textbooks. A legitimate complaint often voiced about history books is that they focus on war and violence and leave out life as it is lived by most people. Another complaint is that they leave out the experiences of women and minorities. Well-written and well-illustrated trade books serve as a counterbalance to these omissions.

Teenagers are especially interested in books that present the extremes of life's experiences, which is why various editions and adaptations of the *Guinness Book of World Records* remain popular. Whatever is the biggest, the best, and the most bizarre—especially the most bizarre—is of interest, which also explains why today's kids have gone on to enjoy such books as *Barlow's Guide to Extraterrestrials* and Rosemary Guiley's *The Encyclopedia of Ghosts and Spirits. School Library Journal* editors described the latter as "A miracle—a reference book that's also a terrific read" in maintaining the "enticing lure of the supernatural" while presenting both beliefs and skepticism. An additional appeal of books presenting bits and pieces of miscellaneous information is that they provide instant entertainment. Someone with only a minute or two—or with a short attention span—can open Lila Perl's *Don't Sing Before Breakfast, Don't Sleep in the Moonlight: Everyday Superstitions and How They Began* and read a complete discourse.

Succinctness and easy accessibility are also selling points when encouraging teenagers to dip into collections of essays as opposed to books that need to be read in their entirety. Students who have enjoyed Robert Cormier's fiction might look on his *I Have Words to Spend: Reflections of a Small-Town Editor* as a chance to share thoughts with the kind of uncle or grandfather they wish they had been lucky enough to have. Teenagers can also enjoy Russell Baker's, Erma Bombeck's, and Andy Rooney's collections of newspaper columns as well as journal entries written by contemporary students and published in Nancy Rubin's *Ask Me If I Care: Voices from an American High School.*

Space in this text allows us to present only a sample of the many books available as companion reading, or even replacement reading, for typical textbooks (Focus Box 8.3). In selecting such books, librarians and teachers should remember that teenagers most often pick them up to find specific information. Because young readers lack the kind of background knowledge that most adults have, it is especially important that informative books be well organized and indexed in such a way that readers can look up facts without reading the whole book. Unclear references or confusing directions are especially troublesome in how-to books, which range from something as simple as Lee Ames's *Draw 50 Creepy Crawlies* to Peter Goodwin's *More Engineering Projects for Young Scientists.* Other examples are Jason Rich's *Ultimate Unauthorized Nintendo Super NES Game Strategies,* Vicki Cobb's *Science Experiments You Can Eat,* Margaret Ryan's *How to Give a Speech,* and Sara Gilbert's *Go for It: Get Organized.*

How-to books are seldom best-sellers, simply because they are so specialized that they appeal to fairly limited audiences. The challenge for the teacher or librarian is to let students know about their availability. Once students find their way into the library to check out a book that helps them accomplish a particular goal, they are likely to return for other books. But if they are disappointed by ambiguous or hard-to-understand directions or come-on statements that make projects look easier than they are, they may lose interest in both the project and the library.

FOCUS BOX 8.3

Nonfiction—Humanities and the Arts

Anguished English by Richard Lederer. Wyrick & Co., 1987; Dell, 1989. To get the fullest pleasure from this book, teachers recommend spending a few minutes at a time reading aloud these truly funny errors that Lederer gleaned from unpublished writings.

Bibles and Beastiaries: A Guide to Illuminated Manuscripts by Elizabeth B. Wilson. Farrar, 1994. Readers are likely to gain a new appreciation for the art of book printing and illustration.

The Book of God: The Bible as a Novel by Waltern Wangerin, Jr. Zondervan, 1996. Wangerin's well-honed writing skills are evident in this marvelous retelling of the Bible.

Celebrate America: In Poetry and Art by Nora Panzer. Hyperion, 1994. This book celebrates American diversity by matching poems—some old, some new—with full-color reproductions of paintings by some of America's best artists.

Children of Promise: African-American Literature and Art for Young People edited by Charles Sullivan. Abrams, 1991. These well-selected samplings from the last 200 years provide an antidote to the mistaken notion that art has thrived only in white America.

Just Listen to This Song I'm Singing: African-American History Through Song by Jerry Silverman. Millbrook, 1996. The history, symbolization, musical scores, photos, and reproductions of related documents are attractively presented for thirteen songs important to African-Americans between 1860 and 1960.

Keeping Secrets: The Girlhood Diaries of Seven Women Writers by Mary E. Lyons. Holt, 1995. This collective biography, which contains excerpts from the youthful diaries of well-known American writers, may encourage today's aspiring writers to keep their own journals.

Lives of the Musicians: Good Times, Bad Times and What the Neighbors Thought by Kathleen Krull. Harcourt Brace Jovanovich, 1993. Although the publishers recommend "ages 8–12," we've found that teenagers and adults—even nonmusical ones—are intrigued by the brief stories of 20 musical geniuses and the full-page paintings done by Kathryn Hewitt. Companion volumes include *Lives of the Artists: Masterpieces, Messes (and What the Neighbors Thought)* and *Lives of the Writers: Comedies, Tragedies (and What the Neighbors Thought)*.

Shimmy Shimmy Shimmy Like My Sister Kate: Looking at the Harlem Renaissance through Poems by Nikki Giovanni. Holt, 1996. Giovanni, herself a poet, uses a conversational style to tell the stories behind the poems in this collection.

A Short Walk Around the Pyramids & Through the World of Art by Philip M. Isaacson. Knopf, 1994. Isaacson serves as a friendly and knowledgeable docent in a museum without walls as he discusses colors, shapes, and forms.

With sports books, obviously the first thing a reader looks for is the particular sport; consequently, authors choose titles that practically shout to potential readers. The sports books that stand out from the crowd usually have a believable and likable personality behind them, as with Dan Jansen's *Full Circle: An Olympic Champion Shares His Breakthrough Story* and the posthumously published *Arthur Ashe on Tennis.* Such books are inspirational as much as instructive, but one thing to watch for in a how-to sports book is whether costs are mentioned. It is almost cruel for an author to write a glowing account of a child star in tennis, gymnastics, skating, swimming, or dancing and leave young readers with the impression that all it takes is hard work. Those readers whose parents do not have time or money for transportation, lessons, entry fees, equipment, and clothes should be let in on the secret that there's more to how you play the game than meets the eye.

A similar warning needs to be given to young readers of such books as Gloria D. Miklowitz and Madeleine Yates's *The Young Tycoons: Ten Success Stories* and to Randi Reisfeld's *So You Want to Be a Star! A Teenager's Guide to Breaking into Show Business*. These wish-fulfilling books about such unusual successes are likely to set the stage for disappointment among the thousands of more typical kids who find themselves working in fast-food restaurants or as grocery store courtesy clerks for minimum wages. There's a need for more books about these less glamorous jobs as well as for the kind of common-sense guidance found in Lois Schmitt's *Smart Spending: A Young Consumer's Guide*.

For academically inclined high school students, it is important to bring books about college to their attention early on because the actual application process takes 18 months, and its success or failure may depend on what classes a student took as a freshman. High school libraries should have recent editions of such books as *The Fiske Guide to Colleges* and the Princeton Review's guide to *Visiting College Campuses* as well as various practice books designed to help students do well on admissions examinations. Ellen Rosenberg's *College Life: A Down-to-Earth Guide*, *The Black College Career Guide* and *America's Lowest Cost Colleges* are also useful.

Books helping students plan their future careers are equally important. As with sports-related books, the ones that are the most fun to read are biographical or personal experience accounts (see Chapter Seven) such as those written by James Herriot on his veterinary practice or by Farley Mowat on being a naturalist. For more complete information on a wider range of jobs, see the *Careers without College* series from Peterson's Guides, the *Career Horizons* books from VGM, and the *Careers and Opportunities Series* from Rosen.

Nonfiction to Help Teenagers Learn Who They Are and Where They Fit

When young adult librarian and critic Patty Campbell spoke at an American Library Association annual meeting, she pointed out that teenagers are so wrapped up in what the psychologists have labeled the "adolescent identity crisis" that they have neither the time for nor the interest in sitting down and reading about the world in general. What they are looking for are books that will help them decide on who they are and where they fit into the scheme of things. Informative books they judge to be helpful include sex education books, some physical and mental health books, selected how-to books, and biographies or true accounts of experiences teenagers can imagine themselves or their acquaintances having. Nearly all the other information books published for teenagers are read under duress—only because teachers assign reports and research papers.

Books that are of primary interest to teenagers are those that give advice on managing one's own life so as to be successful right now as well as in the future. This includes taking care of one's body (Focus Box 8.4). When kids search out

FOCUS BOX 8.4

Physical and Emotional Well-Being

Changing Bodies, Changing Lives rev. ed. by Ruth Bell et al. Random House, 1987. The people who put together *The New Our Bodies, Ourselves* (Simon & Schuster/Touchstone) worked on this successful book, which takes a holistic approach to sex education for young males and females.

Good Sports: Plain Talk About Health and Fitness for Teens by Nissa Simon. Crowell, 1990. Simon includes basic concepts of fitness and training as well as information on how to deal with risks and injuries.

Hearing Us Out: Voices from the Gay and Lesbian Community by Roger Sutton, photos by Lisa Ebright. Little, Brown, 1994. M. E. Kerr writes the foreword to this book, which is recommended for eighth-graders and up. It contains 15 short interviews in which people speak up about both their frustrations and joys. Other books with a similar purpose are Ann Heron's *Two Teenagers in Twenty* (Alyson, 1994) and Eric Marcus's *Is It a Choice?* (Harper-Collins, 1993).

How It Feels to Fight for Your Life by Jill Krementz. Little, Brown, 1989. Krementz began her career as a photographer, and a strength of the book is the quality of the pictures printed alongside interviews with young people suffering from serious illnesses. Earlier books in the same format include *How It Feels When Parents Divorce* (Knopf, 1984), *How It Feels to Be Adopted* (Knopf, 1982), and *How It Feels When a Parent Dies* (Knopf, 1981).

"I Am Who I Am": Speaking Out About Multiracial Identity by Kathlyn Gay. Watts, 1995. While being sensitive to the frustrations experienced by young people from racially mixed families, the author helps to show that one's racial background is only part of knowing "who I am."

It's Perfectly Normal: A Book About Changing Bodies, Growing Up, Sex and Sexual Health by Robie H. Harris. Candlewick, 1994. Cartoons add a light touch to this straightforward book meant to reassure young teens.

The New Teenage Body Book rev. ed. by Kathy McCoy and Charles Wibblesman. Putnam, 1992. Emotional as well as physical development (including hygiene and nutrition) are discussed for both males and females.

A Teen's Guide to Going Vegetarian by Judy Krizmanic, illustrated by Matthew Wawiorka. Viking, 1994. A lively conversational style, quotes from young vegetarians, and an attractive layout plus lots of solid information on nutrition and meal planning make this a good choice.

What's Happening to My Body? Book for Boys: A Growing Up Guide for Parents and Sons rev. ed. by Lynda Madaras and Dane Saavedra. Newmarket, 1991. **What's Happening to My Body? Book for Girls: A Growing Up Guide for Parents and Daughters** rev. ed. by Lynda Madaras and Area Madaras. Newmarket, 1987. These companion volumes were included in the list of "Top One Hundred" books of the past 25 years compiled by the Young Adult Library Services Association in 1994.

books about health, they are usually looking for an answer to a specific problem; for example:

> Can I get AIDS from French kissing?
> Do I have diabetes?
> Why do I feel like crying all the time?
> How serious is herpes?
> What's the difference between just trying a drug and becoming addicted?

If I'm pregnant, what are my options?

What's mononucleosis?

Is being fat really unhealthy?

What causes pimples?

What happens if someone has Hodgkin's disease?

My mother has breast cancer. Is she going to die?

Is anorexia nervosa just in a person's head?

Why does my grandfather say such strange things? Will I be like that when I'm old?

What will happen if I have venereal disease and don't go to the doctor?

The best books offering answers to such questions have good indexing, clear writing, suggestions for further reading, and where appropriate even lists of telephone numbers and support groups that can be contacted. Examples include Don Nardo's *Eating Disorders*, Anna Kosof's *Battered Women: Living with the Enemy*, and Jeanne Lindsay's *Teenage Couples—Coping with Reality: Dealing with Money, In-Laws, Babies and Other Details of Daily Life*.

Books exploring various drug-related issues include John Langone's *Tough Choices: A Book About Substance Abuse*, Ben Sonder's *Dangerous Legacy: The Babies of Drug-Taking Parents*, Arnold Washton and Donna Boundy's *Cocaine and Crack*, and Gilda Berger's *Crack, the New Drug Epidemic*. Back in the 1970s, Peter G. Hammond, writing in *School Library Journal*, said that after the National Coordinating Council on Drug Education, of which he was executive director, had studied some 1000 books and pamphlets and 300 drug abuse education films, they reached the following conclusion:

> You can trust most contemporary pieces of drug information to be valid and relevant about as much as you can trust the drug sold by your friendly street pusher to be potent, safe, and unadulterated. In both cases vested interests abound: scientists and drug educators can be just as irrational about the dangers and benefits of drugs as can those who promote these chemicals to the youth culture.[4]

Hammond went on to say that information and education are not the same thing. One of the problems has been that everyone wants a pat answer, a quick-and-easy solution to a complex problem. Sociologists and anthropologists know it is a temptation when studying any new culture to want to simplify matters by lumping everything together into one clear-cut picture. Such a one-dimensional presentation would make the drug culture much easier to comprehend, but the real situation is not that simple. Books illustrating some of these complexities and the interweaving of drugs with other aspects of life include Janet Bode's *Beating the Odds: Stories of Unexpected Achievers*, Barbara Lewis's *The Kid's Guide to Social Action: How to Solve the Social Problems You Choose—and Turn Creative Thinking into Positive Action*, Thomas Thompson's *Richie*, and Margaret O. Hyde's *Kids In and Out of Trouble: Juveniles and the Law*. Alex Kotlowitz's *There Are No Children Here: The Story of Two Boys Growing Up in the Other America* tells the depressing story of two young brothers facing the daily terror of living in a Chicago public housing project.

DR. MIRIAM STOPPARD

Complete Baby and Child Care

The new *illustrated* bible of child care that *explains clearly* how to raise a healthy and happy child from infancy through preschool

Within the last few years, high school libraries have begun to provide informative books for teenage mothers.

Another depressing but informative book is *Crews: Gang Members Talk to Maria Hinojosa.* She is the host of National Public Radio's *Latino USA* and as a journalist went searching for the New York gang members who in the summer of 1994 killed Brian Watkins, a young tourist from Utah who had come with his family to see the U.S. Open tennis tournament.

Mental and emotional health is just as important to kids as is physical health. Probably the mental health book most appreciated by mature young adults is Robert M. Pirsig's *Zen and the Art of Motorcycle Maintenance: An Inquiry into Values.* This is a gently persuasive book about the Zen approach to working on the "motorcycle that is yourself." The narrative that holds it all together is an account of a cross-country motorcycle trip that Pirsig took with his 11-year-old son. More recent and down-to-earth books include Renora Licata's *Everything You Need to Know About Anger,* Susan Banfield's *Ethnic Conflicts in Schools,* Debra Goldentyer's *Family Violence,* Margaret O. Hyde and Elizabeth Held Forsyth's *The Violent Mind,* Elaine Landau's *Teenage Violence* and *Parental Divorce* (part of the Hot Line Series from Steck-Vaughn), and Claire Patterson's *It's OK to Be You: A Frank and Funny Guide to Growing Up.*

Sex Education

The exploration of sexual matters in books for young readers (see Focus Box 8.4) is an especially sensitive area for the following reasons:

1. Young adults are physically mature, but they probably have had little intellectual and emotional preparation for making sex-related decisions.
2. Parents are anxious to protect their children from making sex-related decisions that might prove harmful.
3. Old restraints and patterns of behavior and attitudes are being questioned, so that there is no clear-cut model to follow.
4. Sex is such an important part of American culture and the mass media that young people are forced to think about and take stands on such controversial issues as homosexuality, premarital sex, violence in relation to sex, and the role of sex in love and family relationships.
5. Talking about sexual attitudes and beliefs with their teenage children may make parents uncomfortable, especially if the father and the mother have different views. This means that many young people must get their information outside of the home.

Although some recent books focus specifically on AIDS (Michael Thomas Ford's *100 Questions and Answers about AIDS,* Mary Kittredge's *Teens with AIDS Speak Out,* and Charles Cozic and Karin Swisher's *The AIDS Crisis*), it's more common for information about sexually transmitted diseases (STDs) to be incorporated into overall treatments that cover emotional as well as physical aspects of sexual activity. No single book can ever satisfy all readers, and this is true of those dealing with sex education. An entire collection must be evaluated and books provided for a wide range of interests, attitudes, beliefs, and lifestyles. Those who criticize libraries for including books that present teenage sexual activity as the norm have a justified complaint if the library does not also have sex education books that present, or even promote, abstinence as a normal route for young people.

Certainly the authors of sex education books do not intend to promote promiscuity, but the fact that topics are being treated "nonjudgmentally" may give some readers that impression. The authors of one sex education book felt compelled to explain that simply because they were including a chapter on abortion

WALTER DEAN MYERS
On Finding One's Identity

My earliest conscious identity was as my mother's darling boy. The memory of this period of warmth and intimacy with the woman who first gave me the gift of reading still brings me pleasure. My introduction to school changed my self-concept in important ways. I discovered that most of my classmates could not read, which surprised me. The first idea of being "bright" entered my thoughts. But I also became aware, painfully so, that the other children and my first-grade teacher had difficulty understanding me. I began speech therapy and began to layer my identity with that disability as well. Seeing my frustration in reading before a class, a teacher suggested that I write something to read instead of reading from a book. I began to write poems, which were praised by the teacher.

School, on the whole, was a joyous experience on the elementary level. I identified with the heroes we were given: George Washington, Thomas Jefferson, the wise Benjamin Franklin, and the brave Patrick Henry. We did plays in which we were colonists at Thanksgiving or threw tea into Boston Harbor. Unconscious of differences between myself and my white classmates, I was identifying as an American. But then one day I turned the page in our history books and encountered the concept of race. There was a picture of a small group of Africans, their heads down, marching from a boat. They were identified not as Africans, of course, but as "slaves."

From that day on, the identity of race—it was Negro in those days—dominated my identity. When we read *Huck Finn* I struggled against being Nigger Jim. I wanted to be the brave, adventuresome Huck. Unconsciously, I began to accept the values, or rather the lack of values, assigned to people of my race.

I began to reject the devalued race. If Negroes were physical, liked finger-popping music, and were never serious, then I would be intellectual, study classical music, and always be serious. In retrospect, I was simply looking for those human values that the school ascribed to white Americans but neglected to give to black Americans.

The logical extension of my identity as an intellectual was the continuation of my education on the college level. The revelation that my parents would not be able to send me to college was devastating. It seemed perfectly logical for me to drop out of high school.

A gang and then the army gave me acceptable macho identities over the next few years, acceptable because I did not see alternatives. It certainly doesn't take much imagination for me to understand the lure of today's gangs.

After the army and a series of menial jobs, I started writing again. I wrote about things I knew—Harlem, basketball, gangs, the army. The values that I did not find in books as a child I was now putting into the books.

A few years ago I began writing a history book. In the book I wanted to talk about the Africans—Africans, not slaves—who had helped to create the United States. The

(continued)

book was a result of all of the experiences of my life, of my turning to books, of my racial conflicts, of my need to bring value to who I am. I knew that my own family had been held on a plantation in what is now West Virginia. I delayed going to the plantation until the book was nearly finished, and I approached it with trepidation. But I did not feel the pain that I expected and soon realized that in the years of writing, I had re-created a surety of identity that could not be threatened, not even by the shadow of enslavement.

This is what I want to do with my writing, to bring value to the young people who read my books, to allow them to discover their own identities without harmful value prejudices. In so doing, I feel more value in my own existence. It's a good feeling.

Walter Dean Myers' books include *Now Is Your Time,* HarperCollins, 1991; *Somewhere in the Darkness,* Scholastic, 1992; *Scorpions,* HarperCollins, 1988; and *Fallen Angels,* Scholastic, 1988.

did not mean they were advocating it as the right, or best, or most liberated decision. Instead, they chose to give it considerable space because the information had been unavailable in past years.

Materials dealing with sex are judged quite differently from those on less controversial topics. For example, in most subject areas, books are given plus marks if they succeed in getting the reader emotionally involved, but with books about sex, many readers feel more comfortable with straightforward, "plumbing manuals"— the less emotional involvement the better. Other readers argue that it's the emotional part that young people need to learn.

Another example of how differently teachers, librarians, and critics treat sex-related materials is the way in which we ignore pornography as a reading interest of teenagers, especially boys. Most of us pretend not to know about pornography so that we do not have to analyze and evaluate it or talk with students about it. One of the few mentions of this kind of reading that has appeared in professional literature was a mid–1970s survey made by Julie Alm of the spare-time reading interests of high school students in Hawaii. In this survey, 14 students listed *The Sensuous Woman* by "J" as their favorite book. This was the same number that listed John Steinbeck's *The Pearl,* John Knowles's *A Separate Peace,* and the Bible.

Tone is especially important in books about sex because people come to such books with their own ideas about appropriateness. (When one of our graduate students looked at Peter Mayle's cartoon-style books *Where Did I Come From?, What's Happening to Me?,* and *Will I Like It?,* he was appalled and said he'd rather make fun of the American flag than of sex.) Another thing to watch for when selecting sex education books is whether sex is portrayed from only one viewpoint, either male or female. For example, Mayle's *Where Did I Come From?* reinforces the traditional active-man/passive-woman stance. Although defenders point out that Mayle's book is simplified so as to be readable by very young children, critics argue that because young children are so impressionable, it is more important than ever that readers do not come away thinking that sexual intercourse is something done *to* women *by* men.

The design and format of all books, but especially of books about such a sensitive subject as sex, send out their own messages. For example, the cover of Ruth Bell's *Changing Bodies, Changing Lives* has five snapshots on it, only one of which is of a boy and girl, and instead of looking "romantic," they look playful. The other shots are of group activities with teens not necessarily paired off but obviously enjoying each other's company. The effect is to make sexuality seem like a normal, pleasant part of growing up.

Some authors write separate books for boys and for girls, which is a debatable practice. In no other area except perhaps athletics is there such purposeful separation between boys and girls. Starting in the fourth grade, girls are taken off to see their first movie on menstruation and boys are left in the room to be given a talk by the coach. Some people believe that this kind of separation is appropriate and, in fact, has advantages similar to the check-and-balance system practiced by the separate branches of the federal government. Others believe, however, that because sex is something participated in by males and females together, they should be taught the same set of rules. The idea is that if men and women started out with the same set of rules, they would not have so much trouble communicating and establishing fulfilling lifelong relationships.

Because there are relatively few books on the subject of homosexuality and because students hesitate to read what there is, each book takes on disproportionate importance. For example, John Cunningham criticized Morton Hunt for using third-person rather than second-person pronouns in *Gay: What You Should Know About Homosexuality*. Cunningham thought the pronoun choice showed that Hunt did not intend "to put the gay reader at ease or to suggest that the book might be directed to gays."[5] Cunningham worked with Frances Hanckel to write *A Way of Love, A Way of Life: A Young Person's Introduction to What It Means to Be Gay*.

Another issue that students may hesitate to read about is that of child abuse, but they can hardly avoid being aware of the issue because of the way it is discussed on television and radio and in newspapers and magazines. A decade ago, the topic was seldom mentioned either in public or private. For example, if Beverly Cleary had published her autobiography *A Girl from Yamhill* in 1978, instead of 1988, she probably would not have included the sexual encounter with her Uncle Joe. It is probably healthy, however, for such an incident to be included as part of a larger story rather than as something that a reader would have to search out. Of course, there are books for readers who are looking for the topic (e.g., Elaine Landau's *Child Abuse: An American Epidemic*, Helen Benedict's *Safe, Strong, and Streetwise*, and Lynn B. Daugherty's *Why Me? Help for Victims of Child Sexual Abuse [Even If They Are Adults Now]*).

When helping young adults make reading decisions in this area, we need to consider the reader's purpose. If the reader wants basic information, nonfiction is far superior because it can present a wider range of information in a clear, unambiguous way. But if the reader desires to understand the emotional and physical aspects of one particular relationship, an honest piece of fiction usually does a better job; for example, see Chapter Three for discussions of Cynthia Voigt's *When She*

Hollers and M. E. Kerr's *Deliver Us from Evie* as illustrations of the rippling effects on families of sex-related problems.

The important thing for adults to remember is that they should provide both kinds of material in conjunction with a listening ear and a willingness to discuss questions. Schools and libraries need to seek community help in exchanging ideas and developing policies. Family values must be respected, but honest, accurate information must also be available for those who seek it. Charting a course along this delicate line is more than any one individual should be expected to do, which is why people need to communicate with each other. Professionals working with books are also obligated to find and study the latest, most authentic information and to bring that information to those who are helping to shape policies and practices. The general public may get away with objecting to or endorsing ideas and books that they have never explored or read. Not so for the professional charged with leading a group to consensus or compromise. The more you know about the materials, and the more you understand about individual and group differences, the better able you are to participate in book selection, discussion, and, sometimes, defense.

Authors of Nonfiction for Young Adults

Some nonfiction authors are so productive that it makes one wonder if they have something like the Stratemeyer Syndicate helping them write their books. What's more likely is that they approach the task like journalists doing research for newspaper features. They write on current topics and bring together other people's research, making it accessible to teenagers. Elaine Landau is one such writer, whose listing in *Books in Print* takes up more than a column and includes books on current issues ranging from white supremists, to chemical and biological warfare, to adolescent prostitutes, to surrogate mothers, to Nazi war criminals. Alvin and Virginia Silverstein are also extremely productive authors focusing largely on health-related topics. Daniel Cohen does books related to current events and media interests.

Not all educators appreciate the kind of journalistic work that goes into these authors' books because they think it would be better training for students to go directly to the magazine and journal articles that the authors go to for their information. The argument is similar to the one that college teachers of freshman composition have over whether it is best to use a source book when students do research papers or to have students go only to primary sources. There's something to be said for both sides. Teachers and librarians, However, should at least be aware of the issue and should help students go beyond relying on any one book when they are researching controversial issues.

As the role of nonfiction has become increasingly recognized in the young adult market, a group of significant authors has emerged. Janet Bode, Howard and Margery Facklam, Kathlyn Gay, Margaret O. Hyde, Michael Kronenwetter, and Don Nardo are writers whose names frequently appear on lists of recommended nonfiction. Patricia Lauber has long been an acclaimed science writer for children, but publishers are now labeling some of her beautifully illustrated books as "gr. 4-up" or "gr. 5-up." Among her books that we have seen teenagers relate to are *Volcano: The Eruption and Healing of Mt. St. Helens, Summer of Fire: Yellowstone, 1988,* and *Seeing Earth from Space.*

James Cross Giblin's background as an editor of children's books stands him in good stead when he writes informational books for junior high readers. He chooses unlikely topics and then does enough research and careful planning and writing so that his readers find new and interesting information. His *The Riddle of the Rosetta Stone: Key to Ancient Egypt* is a fascinating detective story about how a large stone slab covered with writing in three different languages enabled linguists to decipher one of the world's first writing systems. Giblin's *The Truth About Unicorns* serves as an excellent model for research as it traces the history of beliefs, superstitions, stories, and art about this mythical creature.

In addition to these authors, the seven described next can usually be trusted to provide that something extra that comes when a writer is truly involved in the subject and puts heart and soul into a book. We are not claiming that the following authors, introduced in alphabetical order, are the only ones about whom this could be said, but we are willing to say that they are among a growing body of nonfiction writers who prepare their books with the same kind of care and feeling that goes into the best fiction writing.

Brent Ashabranner

At the 1991 National Council of Teachers of English Convention in Seattle, it was heartwarming to see the long lines of teachers wanting Ashabranner to autograph copies of his books. He's been a writer ever since he won a *Scholastic Magazine* contest in high school, but only after he retired in 1980 did he start writing full-time for young people. Ashabranner had an international career working in several countries for the U.S. Agency for International Development. He also directed the U.S. Peace Corps in Nigeria and India and later served as Deputy Director of the Peace Corps in Washington, D.C. Upon his retirement, he had planned on becoming a full-time writer of fiction, but then a professional photographer and good friend, Paul Conklin, came to him with the idea of doing a book about the Cheyenne Indians. Ashabranner went with Conklin to talk with members of the Sweet Medicine tribe. The book *Morning Star, Black Sun: The Northern Cheyenne Indians and America's Energy Crisis* was the result of their collaboration. The most striking fact to emerge from Ashabranner's conversations with the young Native Americans was "how much they wanted to retain their culture and yet how much they wanted to succeed in the dominant culture of today."[6] Ashabranner later explored that theme in *To Live in Two Worlds: American Indian Youth Today* and in *Into a Strange Land: Unaccompanied Refugee Youth in America*. Probably because of his years of living in other countries, he's especially interested in helping young readers reach beyond their immediate horizons and develop empathy for others. His *Always to Remember: The Story of the Vietnam Veterans Memorial* is about conflict resolution as much as it is about the memorial. To varying degrees, most of his books show some kind of conflict, as in *An Ancient Heritage: The Arab-American Minority, Still a Nation of Immigrants,* and *A New Frontier: The Peace Corps in Eastern Europe.*

Russell Freedman

Nearly thirty years elapsed between the time that Russell Freedman wrote his first book *Teenagers Who Made History* in 1961 and when he won the Newbery Award in 1988 for *Lincoln: A Photobiography.* In the intervening years, he worked steadily producing an average of more than a book a year. For the first fifteen or so years, he focused mostly on books about animals for primary and middle grade readers. A turning point came in his career when he attended an exhibition of historical photographs and found himself "communicating" with the young faces that stared out at him from the old photos. He searched out these and other pictures for a book *Immigrant Kids.* Since then, he has made a specialty out of finding evocative photographs to use not as decoration but as an integral part of his books. His timing was perfect for communicating with a generation of young readers who had grown up watching television. Since winning the Newbery Award for his book on Abraham Lincoln, he has also won the Orbis Pictus Award and the Boston Globe/Honor Book award for his 1990 *Franklin Delano Roosevelt.* His 1991 *The Wright Brothers* was a Newbery Honor Book and so was his 1993 *Eleanor Roosevelt: A Life of Discovery.* In his 1994 *Kids at Work: Lewis Hine and the Crusade Against Child Labor,* he wrote directly about the power of photograpy by telling the story of an early photographer who took it upon himself to document the conditions under which U.S. children labored.

Jean Fritz

Children's literature people may be surprised at our claiming Jean Fritz as a writer for adolescents. It is true that she has written many more books for children than for adolescents, but since she wrote *Homesick: My Own Story* published by Putnam in 1982, she has done the longer kind of book considered appropriate for teenagers. Before then, she did mostly historical biographies for children. But even if she never wrote books specifically for teenagers, her influence would have been felt, because as Jim Roginski stated:

> Jean Fritz has done one thing few authors can ever hope to accomplish: she has irrefutably changed an entire style of writing for children. Up until she started writing biographies for children, the genre was, with few exceptions, essentially a dull and lifeless one. Historical scenes were re-created, often without attention to accurate detail. Dialogues were invented, sometimes in contemporary jargon, thus negating the impact of an historical biography. Facts were frequently distorted and distilled to the point of futility. It was her attention to detail, her refusal to romanticize a person or event, and her im-

peccable searching out of diaries, journals, and letters to re-create the past that has brought Jean to the forefront of biographical writing for children.[7]

Fritz's autobiographical *Homesick* was relished by both young and old readers, who had come to love the witty author for having changed their attitudes about history through such prize-winning picture books as *And Then What Happened, Paul Revere* and *Why Don't You Get a Horse, Sam Adams?* Now in her books for older readers, Fritz uses her same compelling and thorough approach. *China Homecoming* is the story of her return to China in 1984. *China's Long March: 6,000 Miles of Danger* is the story of the men and women in the Chinese Communist Red Army who in 1934–1935 marched across China to the northwest frontier to escape from Chiang Kai-shek. *Around the World in a Hundred Years: From Henry the Navigator to Magellan* is appropriate for middle school readers. She has also done several highly acclaimed biographies for middle school and junior high readers including *The Great Little Madison, Bully for You, Teddy Roosevelt,* and *Harriet Beecher Stowe and the Beecher Preachers.*

James (Jim) Haskins

As with many other authors of nonfiction, James Haskins writes both for children and for young adults. He's been a stockbroker, a high school teacher in New York, and a faculty member at several colleges, including Staten Island Community College, Manhattanville College, Indiana University, and Purdue. In 1979, he published an adult book, *Diary of a Harlem Schoolteacher.* For young adults, his main contribution has been to recognize the need for biographies and other books about minorities. But in contrast to so many of us who bemoan the lack of a particular kind of book, Haskins set out to put his pencil (more likely his word processor) where his mouth was. Since the mid–1970s, he has consistently prepared books on African-American heroes and African-American history as well as on such topics as rights for people with disabilities, the American labor movement, and women leaders in other countries (e.g., Corazon Aquino and Indira Gandhi). Among his most recent books are *Get on Board: The Story of the Underground Railroad, I Have a Dream: The Life and Words of Martin Luther King, Jr., Thurgood Marshall: A Life for Justice, I Am Somebody! A Biography of Jesse Jackson,* and *Freedom Rides: Journey for Justice.* With some of his subjects, he's done separate books for different age groups, including a children's and a young adult book on Diana Ross and a young adult and an adult book on Lena Horne.

Albert Marrin

Albert Marrin earned a Ph.D. in history from Columbia University in 1968 and shortly thereafter began publishing history-related books. We first took notice of his books in 1985 when his *1812: The War Nobody Won* was chosen as a *Boston-Globe Horn Book* Honor Book for Nonfiction. Since then, his books (e.g., *Virginia's*

General: Robert E. Lee and the Civil War and *Unconditional Surrender: U. S. Grant and the Civil War*) have consistently appeared on best-book lists and received starred reviews. *School Library Journal* praised his *The Spanish-American War* for delineating "how American jingoists, expansionists, 'big navy' advocates, yellow journalists, and filibusterers maneuvered the nation into taking part in what politicians called 'A splendid little war!'" Mary Mueller, also writing in *School Library Journal,* recommended Marrin's *Struggle for a Continent: The French and Indian Wars* and *The War for Independence* as good introductions to the early years of the United States. She said that his two biographies, *Hitler* and *Stalin,* could "add greatly to an understanding of how evil the two men actually were, and his look at their monstrous behavior is both fascinating and repelling."[8] With *The Sea King: Sir Francis Drake and His Times,* Marrin continued his interests beyond U.S. history. *School Library Journal* editors also gave starred reviews to his *America and Vietnam: The Elephant and the Tiger* and to *Cowboys, Indians, and Gunfighters: The Story of the Cattle Kingdom.*

Milton Meltzer

Of all the nonfiction writers for young adults, Milton Meltzer is the one most consistently recognized as a spokesperson and champion of the genre. He focuses on social issues and for the last edition of this textbook wrote that, "I've often used the devices of fiction to multiply the power of facts by evoking from readers their sense of concern, even of constructive anger. I've wanted to help them to see the weaknesses of our world, its inequality, its injustice that leave so many poor, so many ignored, abused, betrayed." He investigates whatever topics he finds interesting with one area of research triggering questions about another as he has moved from poverty to crime to terrorism and on to racism, slavery, war, and politics. He has pioneered an in-their-own-words technique in which he uses historical journals, diaries, letters, and news accounts to bring out the personalities of his subjects and to illustrate how their lives have been shaped by their situations. Recent examples include *Lincoln in His Own Words* and *Frederick Douglass: In His Own Words,* both illustrated by Stephen Alcorn. In trying to make issues real to readers, he says:

> I've used almost every technique fiction writers call on (except to invent the facts) in order to draw the readers in, deepen their feeling for people whose lives may be remote from their own, and enrich their understanding of forces that shape the outcome of all our lives. In the end, I believe it is not a question of what is fiction and what is fact, but of what is true and what is false. Fiction can lie about reality; so can nonfiction. And both can tell the truth.

Among his most acclaimed titles are *The Bill of Rights: How We Got It and What It Means, Columbus and the World Around Him, Voices from the Civil War, Never to Forget: The Jews of the Holocaust,* and *Rescue: The Story of How Gentiles Saved Jews in the Holocaust.* His autobiography, *Starting from Home: A Writer's Beginnings* tells not just his story but also the story of pre-World War II America.

Laurence Pringle

Laurence Pringle is a respected and prolific writer of science-related books for young readers. For an earlier edition of this text, he discussed the challenge of being "fair" when writing about decision making that involves both social and scientific knowledge and attitudes. Because idealistic young readers may be especially vulnerable to one-sided arguments, he says that writers have a responsibility to present all sides of an issue and to show the gray as well as the black and white. He quickly adds, however, that being fair is not the same as being objective "considering that everyone involved in the controversies, including Nobel laureate scientists, is being subjective and biased." He added "anyone who is well informed on an issue is not neutral," but that does not mean that he or she can't work "to help kids understand the issues so they can make their own decisions." Pringle's goal is to encourage young adults to have a healthy skepticism on controversial issues. He aims his sharpest skepticism toward economic and political interests and toward the extremists who cluster at both ends of the spectrum.

Among Pringle's recent well-received books is *Jackal Woman: Exploring the World of Jackals,* in which he introduces middle school readers to the life of a behavioral ecologist, Patricia Moehlman. She was trained by Jane Goodall and is doing for jackals what Goodall did for chimpanzees. *Chemical and Biological Warfare: The Cruelest Weapons* for older readers is on a timely topic because of recent news stories about the possibility of such weapons being used in the Gulf War. His *Oil Spills: Damage, Recovery and Prevention* tells about both natural and man-made leaks. Other ecology-related titles are *Living Treasure: Saving Earth's Threatened Biodiversity, Global Warming,* and *Rain of Trouble: The Science and Politics of Acid Rain.*

Conclusion

This chapter has only skimmed the topic of nonfiction for young adults, which in the last few years has changed and developed more than any other genre. Contributing factors to the changes include the information explosion, new publishing technologies, the introduction of fascinating topics through the mass media, and the existence of topics of worldwide interest, including ecology, health issues, and changing political structures. Nonfiction deserves a greater proportion of our attention, if only because it is receiving a greater proportion of young people's attention. Students may graduate from high school without ever reading a science fiction novel, a romance, or even a mystery, but no student graduates without coming into contact with nonfiction. If these contacts are positive ones, there's a much better chance that the student will go on as an adult to relate to books and seek them out whenever information is needed.

Notes

. . . .

[1]"A Conversation with Milton Meltzer," in *Nonfiction for Young Adults: From Delight to Wisdom* by Betty Carter and Richard F. Abrahamson (Oryx Press, 1990), pp. 53–54.

[2]Milton Meltzer, "Where Do All the Prizes Go? The Case for Nonfiction," *Horn Book Magazine* 52 (February 1975): 23.

[3]George A. Woods, personal correspondence to Alleen Pace Nilsen, Summer 1978.

[4]Peter G. Hammond, "Turning Off: The Abuse of Drug Information," *School Library Journal* 19 (April 1973): 17–21.

[5]John Cunningham, "Growing Up Gay Male," *Voice of Youth Advocates* 1 (June 1978): 11–16.

[6]"A Conversation with Brent Ashabranner" in *Nonfiction for Young Adults: From Delight to Wisdom* by Betty Carter and Richard F. Abrahamson (Oryx Press, 1990), p. 97.

[7]Jim Roginski, "Prelude to the Interview" with Jean Fritz in *Behind the Covers: Interviews with Authors and Illustrators of Books for Children and Young Adults* (Libraries Unlimited, 1985), p. 73.

[8]Mary E. Mueller, "History and History Makers: Give YAs the Whole Picture," *School Library Journal* 37 (November 1991): 55–56.

Titles Mentioned in the Text of Chapter Eight

. . . .

Alcott, Louisa May. *Little Women*, 1868.

Ames, Lee with Ray Burns. *Draw Fifty Creepy Crawlies*. Doubleday, 1991.

America's Lowest Cost Colleges. Brandon Books, Distributed by NAR Productions, P.O. box 233, Barryville, NY 12719.

Angelou, Maya. *I Know Why the Caged Bird Sings*. Random House, 1970.

Ashabranner, Brent. *Always to Remember: The Story of the Vietnam Veterans Memorial*. Putnam, 1988.

Ashabranner, Brent. *An Ancient Heritage: The Arab-American Minority*. HarperCollins, 1991.

Ashabranner, Brent. *Into a Strange Land: Unaccompanied Refugee Youth in America*. Putnam, 1989.

Ashabranner, Brent. *A New Frontier: The Peace Corps in Eastern Europe*. Dutton, 1994.

Ashabranner, Brent. *To Live in Two Worlds: American Indian Youth Today*. Dodd, Mead, 1984.

Ashabranner, Brent. *Still a Nation of Immigrants*. Dutton, 1993.

Ashe, Arthur with Alexander McNab. *Arthur Ashe on Tennis*. Knopf, 1995.

Banfield, Susan. *Ethnic Conflicts in Schools*, Enslow, 1995.

Barlow, Wayne Douglas, and Ian Summers. *Barlow's Guide to Extraterrestrials*, rev. ed. Workman, 1987.

Benedict, Helen. *Safe, Strong, and Streetwise*. Little, Brown, 1987.

Berger, Gilda. *Crack, the New Drug Epidemic*. Watts, 1987.

The Black College Career Guide. Massey-Young Communications, 33 E. 78th St., Covington, KY 41011.

Bode, Janet. *Beating the Odds: Stories of Unexpected Achievers*. Watts, 1992.

Brooks, Bruce. *Midnight Hour Encores*. HarperCollins, 1986.

Brown, Claude. *Manchild in the Promised Land*. Macmillan, 1965.

Brown, Dee. *Bury My Heart at Wounded Knee: An Indian History of the American West*. Holt, 1971.

Capote, Truman. *In Cold Blood*. Random House, 1966.

Carter, Betty, and Richard F. Abrahamson. *Nonfiction for Young Adults: From Delight to Wisdom*. Oryx Press, 1990.

Cleary, Beverly. *A Girl from Yamhill: A Memoir*. Morrow, 1988.

Cleaver, Eldridge. *Soul on Ice*. McGraw-Hill, 1968.

Cobb, Vicki. *Science Experiments You Can Eat*. HarperCollins, 1989.

Conklin, Paul, with Brent Ashabranner. *Morning Star, Black Sun: The Northern Cheyenne Indians and America's Energy Crisis*. Putnam, 1982.

Cormier, Robert. *I Have Words to Spend: Reflections of a Small-Town Editor,* edited by Constance Senay Cormier. Delacorte, 1991.

Cozic, Charles, and Karin Swisher. *The AIDS Crisis*. Greenhaven, 1991.

Daughtery, Lynn B. *Why Me? Help for Victims of Child Sexual Abuse (Even If They Are Adults Now)*. Mother Courage, 1985.

Doctorow, E. L. *Ragtime*. Random House, 1975.

Eyewitness series. Dorling Kindersley/Knopf, late 1980s to the present.

Fiske, Edward B. *The Fiske Guide to Colleges 1995.* Random House, 1994.

Ford, Michael Thomas. *100 Questions and Answers about AIDS.* New Discovery, 1992.

Freedman, Russell. *Eleanor Roosevelt: A Life of Discovery.* Clarion, 1993.

Freedman, Russell. *Franklin Delano Roosevelt.* Clarion, 1990.

Freedman, Russell. *Immigrant Kids.* Dutton, 1980.

Freedman, Russell. *Kids at Work: Lewis Hine and the Crusade Against Child Labor.* Clarion, 1994.

Freedman, Russell. *Lincoln: A Photobiography.* Clarion, 1987.

Freedman, Russell. *Teenagers Who Made History.* Holiday House, 1961.

Freedman, Russell. *The Wright Brothers.* Holiday House, 1991.

Fritz, Jean. *Around the World in a Hundred Years: From Henry the Navigator to Magellan.* Putnam, 1994.

Fritz, Jean. *Bully for You, Teddy Roosevelt.* Putnam, 1991.

Fritz, Jean. *China Homecoming.* Putnam, 1985.

Fritz, Jean. *China's Long March: 6,000 Miles of Danger.* Putnam, 1988.

Fritz, Jean. *The Great Little Madison.* Putnam, 1989.

Fritz, Jean. *Harriet Beecher Stowe and the Beecher Preachers.* Putnam, 1994.

Fritz, Jean. *Homesick: My Own Story.* Putnam, 1982.

Fritz, Jean. *And Then What Happened, Paul Revere?* Putnam, 1973.

Fritz, Jean. *Why Don't You Get a Horse, Sam Adams?* Putnam, 1982.

Graham, Robin. *Dove.* HarperCollins, 1972.

Giblin, James Cross. *The Riddle of the Rosetta Stone: Key to Ancient Egypt.* Crowell, 1990.

Giblin, James Cross. *The Truth About Unicorns.* HarperCollins, 1991.

Gilbert, Sara. *Go for It: Get Organized.* Morrow, 1990.

Goldentyer, Debra. *Family Violence.* Steck-Vaughn, 1995.

Goldentyer, Debra. *Parental Divorce.* Steck-Vaughn, 1995.

Goodwin, Peter H. *More Engineering Projects for Young Scientists.* Watts, 1995.

Griffin, John Howard. *Black Like Me.* Houghton Mifflin, 1977.

Guiley, Rosemary Ellen. *The Encyclopedia of Ghosts and Spirits.* Facts on File, 1992.

Hanckel, Frances, and John Cunningham. *A Way of Love, A Way of Life: A Young Person's Introduction to What It Means to Be Gay.* Lothrop, 1979.

Haley, Alex. *Roots.* Doubleday, 1976.

Haskins, James. *Diary of a Harlem Schoolteacher.* Grove Press, 1970.

Haskins, James. *Freedom Rides: Journey for Justice.* Hyperion, 1995.

Haskins, James. *Get on Board: The Story of the Underground Railroad.* Scholastic, 1993.

Haskins, James. *I Am Somebody! A Biography of Jesse Jackson.* Enslow, 1992.

Haskins, James. *I Have a Dream: The Life and Words of Martin Luther King, Jr.* Millbrook, 1993.

Haskins, James. *Thurgood Marshall: A Life for Justice.* Holt, 1992.

Kittredge, Mary. *Teens with AIDS Speak Out.* Messner, 1992.

Herriot, James. *All Creatures Great and Small.* St. Martin's, 1972.

Hinojosa, Maria. *Crews: Gang Members Talk to Maria Hinojosa.* Harcourt, 1995.

Hunt, Morton. *Gay: What You Should Know About Homosexuality.* Farrar, Straus & Giroux, 1977.

Hyde, Margaret O. *Kids In and Out of Trouble: Juveniles and the Law.* Cobblehill/Dutton, 1995.

Hyde, Margaret O., and Elizabeth Held Forsyth. *The Violent Mind.* Messner, 1991.

"J." *The Sensuous Woman.* Lyle Stuart, 1970.

Jansen, Dan, with Jack McCallum. *Full Circle: An Olympic Champion Shares His Breakthrough Story.* Villard Books, 1994.

Keneally, Thomas. *Schindler's List.* Simon & Schuster, 1982.

Kerr, M. E. *Deliver Us From Evie.* HarperCollins, 1994.

Knowles, John. *A Separate Peace.* Macmillan, 1960.

Kosof, Anna. *Battered Women: Living with the Enemy.* Watts, 1995.

Kotlowitz, Alex. *There Are No Children Here: The Story of Two Boys Growing Up in the Other America.* Doubleday, 1991.

Landau, Elaine. *Teenage Violence.* Messner, 1990.

Langone, John. *Tough Choices: A Book About Substance Abuse.* Little, Brown, 1995.

Lauber, Patricia. *Seeing Earth from Space.* Orchard/Watts, 1990.

Lauber, Patricia. *Summer of Fire: Yellowstone, 1988.* Orchard/Watts, 199.

Lauber, Patricia. *Volcano: The Eruption and Healing of Mt. St. Helens.* Bradbury, 1986.

Licata, Renora. *Everything You Need to Know about Anger.* Rosen, 1994.

Lindsay, Jeanne Warren. *Teenage Couples—Coping with Reality: Dealing with Money, In-Laws, Babies and Other Details of Daily Life.* Morning Glory Press, 1995.

Lund, Doris. *Eric.* HarperCollins, 1974.

Maas, Peter. *Serpico,* Viking, 1973.

Marrin, Albert. *America and Vietnam: The Elephant and the Tiger.* Viking, 1992.

Marrin, Albert. *Cowboys, Indians, and Gunfighters: The Story of the Cattle Kingdom.* Atheneum, 1993.

Marrin, Albert. *1812: The War Nobody Won.* Atheneum, 1985.

Marrin, Albert. *Hitler.* Viking, 1987.

Marrin, Albert. *The Sea King: Sir Francis Drake and His Times.* Atheneum, 1995.

Marrin, Albert. *The Spanish-American War.* Atheneum, 1991.

Marrin, Albert. *Stalin: Russia's Man of Steel.* Viking, 1988.

Marrin, Albert. *Struggle for a Continent: The French and Indian Wars.* Atheneum, 1987.

Mayle, Peter. *What's Happening to Me?* Lyle Stuart, 1975.

Mayle, Peter. *Where Did I Come From?* Lyle Stuart, 1973.

Mayle, Peter. *Will I Like It?* Corwin, 1977.

Meltzer, Milton. *The Bill of Rights: How We Got It and What It Means.* Crowell, 1990.

Meltzer, Milton. *Columbus and the World Around Him.* Watts, 1990.

Meltzer, Milton. *Frederick Douglass: In His Own Words.* Harcourt, 1995.

Meltzer, Milton. *Lincoln in His Own Words.* Harcourt, 1993.

Meltzer, Milton. *Never to Forget: The Jews of the Holocaust.* HarperCollins, 1976.

Meltzer, Milton. *Rescue: The Story of How Gentiles Saved Jews in the Holocaust.* HarperCollins, 1988.

Meltzer, Milton. *Starting from Home: A Writer's Beginnings.* Viking, 1988.

Meltzer, Milton. *Voices from the Civil War.* Crowell, 1989.

Miklowitz, Gloria D., and Madeleine Yates. *The Young Tycoons: Ten Success Stories.* Harcourt Brace Jovanovich, 1981.

Nardo, Don. *Eating Disorders.* Lucent, 1991.

Patterson, Claire. *It's OK to Be You: A Frank and Funny Guide to Growing Up.* Tricycle Press, 1994.

Peck, Richard. *Are You in the House Alone?* Viking, 1976.

Perl, Lila. *Don't Sing Before Breakfast, Don't Sleep in the Moonlight: Everyday Superstitions and How They Began.* Clarion, 1988.

Pirsig, Robert M. *Zen and the Art of Motorcycle Maintenance: An Inquiry into Values.* Morrow, 1974.

Princeton Review. *Visiting College Campuses.* Villard Books, 1995.

Pringle, Laurence. *Chemical and Biological Warfare: The Cruelest Weapons.* Enslow, 1993.

Pringle, Laurence. *Global Warming.* Arcade, 1990.

Pringle, Laurence. *Jackal Woman: Exploring the World of Jackals.* Scribner's, 1993.

Pringle, Laurence. *Living Treasure: Saving Earth's Threatened Biodiversity.* Morrow, 1991.

Pringle, Laurence. *Oil Spills: Damage, Recovery and Prevention.* Morrow, 1993.

Pringle, Laurence. *Rain of Trouble: The Science and Politics of Acid Rain.* Macmillan, 1988.

Read, Piers Paul. *Alive.* Lippincott, 1974.

Reisfeld, Randi. *So You Want To Be a Star: A Teenager's Guide to Breaking into Show Business.* Archway Paperbacks, 1990.

Rich, Jason. *Ultimate Unauthorized Nintendo SuperNES Game Strategies.* Random House, 1995.

Rosenberg, Ellen. *College Life: A Down-to-Earth Guide.* Penguin, 1992.

Ryan, Margaret. *How to Give a Speech,* rev. ed. Watts, 1995.

Sagan, Carl. *Pale Blue Dot: A Vision of the Human Future in Space.* Random House, 1994.

Sounder, Ben. *Dangerous Legacy: The Babies of Drug-Taking Parents.* Watts, 1994.

Steinbeck, John. *The Pearl.* Viking, 1947.

Thompson, Thomas. *Richie.* Saturday Review Press, 1973.

Toffler, Alvin. *Future Shock.* Random House, 1970.

Voigt, Cynthia, *Izzy, Willy-Nilly.* Macmillan, 1986.

Voigt, Cynthia, *When She Hollers.* Scholastic, 1994.

Waller, Robert J. *The Bridges of Madison County.* Warner, 1992.

Washton, Arnold and Donna Boundy. *Cocaine and Crack.* Enslow, 1989.

For information on the availability of paperback editions of these titles, please consult the most recent edition of *Paperbound Books in Print,* published annually by R. R. Bowker Company.

Chapter 9

A Hodge Podge
Sports, Humor, Movies, and Other Stuff

. . . .

Much of the material discussed in this chapter for young people is identical to that enjoyed by adults. Most sports stories, whether fiction or nonfiction, are written simply enough that young people can identify with the heroes, who are usually closer to their age than to their parents' age. Although teenagers may not always be on the same humor wavelength as adults, they often find much the same humor in a Woody Allen film or an episode of "Cheers" or "Friends." Junior high humor is an exception because it is properly appreciated—if that's the word—almost entirely by junior high kids. To be financial successes, most movies need to appeal to a reasonably large cross section of the American audience, and films as different as *Braveheart* and *True Lies* are enjoyed by both sexes and people of different age groups.

The Challenge and Appeal of Sports

Adults and young adults alike have been fascinated by sports and sports heroes as far back as the ancient olympic games. The range of our enjoyment of sports is well covered in Brandt Aymar's *Men in Sports: Great Sport Stories of all Time, from the Greek Olympic Games to the American World Series*. Anyone curious about virtually any sport from auto racing to billiards to cricket to polo to yacht racing and almost anything in between will find something of interest in Aymar's book.

Most people watch baseball or basketball or football on television. Some play in organized softball or basketball or soccer leagues sponsored by churches, city recreation departments, or private clubs. Some played at one sport or another in high school or college. Sports play an important part in our lives and in our language; witness these clichés: to be a team player, to quarterback a situation, to have the inside track, to make a close call, or to set the pace. Given our craze for sports, most of us would be shocked if the current president of Cornell University repeated what his predecessor said in 1873 about the proposed football game with the University of Michigan: "I will not permit thirty men to travel 400 miles merely to agitate a bag of wind."

Most sport books have elements in common—description of the game with its rules and expectations, the training that is needed, the role of spectators, the expected rewards, and the inevitable disappointments that make the rewards even better. Over the last decades, authors of sports fiction and non-fiction have focused on the character-changing aspects of sports rather than providing an inning-by-inning or quarter-by-quarter account. At the heart of contemporary sports books, fiction or not, is an examination of the price of fame, the worth of the game, the fleeting nature of glory, and the temptation, always doomed, to hope that temporary glory will be permanent.

Early sports writers for young people believed sincerely in the purity of sports. For example, at the turn of the last century, Ralph Henry Barbour, who devoutly believed in hard but fair play and the amateur spirit, dedicated his 1900 novel *For the Honor of the School,* "To That School, Wherever It May Be, Whose Athletics Are Purest." Dated though his fine novel now seems, Barbour was deadly serious in his belief that school spirit was inextricably coupled with athletic *and* academic excellence. He and other writers for young adults preached this doctrine until the 1940s.

In the 1950s and early 1960s, such writers as John F. Carson and H. D. Francis wrote excellent novels filled with heroes reeking of sweat. Today their kind of sports story goes for the most part unread and unwritten. Kindly old Pop Dugout, wily with his sports wisdom and remembered for his warm and genial backpatting, may never have been very real. Nevertheless, the sentimental fiction of the past had a charm that we have lost, and with it we have also lost many sports heroes for young readers.

Even as famous and prolific an author as John R. Tunis, a sportswriter for the *New York Evening Post* who published 24 novels for young people between 1938 and 1975, has been largely ignored. There's been an attempt, however, to revive some of the old sports books with attractive new editions. Harcourt reissued Tunis's *Keystone Kids* and *Rookie of the Year,* and Morrow reissued a few of Zane Grey's sports stories, *The Shortstop* and *The Young Pitcher.* Morrow also put out new editions of several Tunis books, including his basketball story *Go Team, Go!* and his baseball story *Highpockets.* Tunis's *The Kid Comes Back* is about a young baseball player returning from World War II with one leg shorter than the other. Before the war, he was the "speediest man in the National League," and now the challenge is whether he can overcome the fear that is holding him back.

Contemporary Sports Literature

Critic Jacques Barzun once said, "Whoever wants to know the heart and mind of America had better learn baseball, the rules and realities of the game."[1]

Of the making of books about sports, there apparently is no end (Focus Box 9.1). Geoffrey C. Ward and Ken Burns's *Baseball: An Illustrated History* may look like a coffee table book, but countless fans have pored over it since it was published. Philip J. Lowry's *Green Cathedrals*, a celebration of 271 major league and Negro League ballparks, is an even more delightful and nostalgic history of what people still call America's national pastime. William Brashler's *The Story of Negro League Baseball* is frequently bitter but often softened with love. The stories of stars of that league, Smokey Joe Williams, Bob Gibson, Satchel Paige, and others, still have appeal to anyone who loves baseball. Neil J. Sullivan's *The Minors: The Strug-*

FOCUS BOX 9.1

Great Sports Books for Young Women

Coaching Evelyn: Fast, Faster, Fastest Women in the World. by Pat Connolly. HarperCollins, 1991. Training Evelyn Ashford for the Olympics. What an athlete is like. Sympathetic and believable.

Forward Pass by Thomas J. Dygard. Morrow, 1989. Jill Winston, star of the girls' basketball team, agrees to become the starting receiver for the varsity football squad. See also Dygard's *Rebound Caper* (Morrow, 1983.) A cocky young male basketball player joins the girls' team for kicks.

In Lane Three, Alex Archer by Tessa Duder. Houghton Mifflin, 1989. A New Zealand swimmer sets out to become an Olympic swimmer with the help of her boyfriend and family. A truly fine novel with an almost equally fine sequel, **Alex in Rome.** (Houghton Mifflin, 1991.)

Race Across Alaska: First Woman to Win the Iditarod Tells Her Story by Libby Riddles and Tim Jones. Stackpole Books, 1988. Riddles was the first woman to win Alaska's most famous dogsled race, 1200 miles from Anchorage to Nome.

There's a Girl in My Hammerlock by Jerry Spinelli. Simon & Schuster, 1991. Eighth-grader Maisie Potter tries out and makes the boys' wrestling team. Often funny, sometimes unfunny.

Water Dancer by Jenifer Levin. Poseidon, 1982. Dorey Thomas swam the 1500 freestyle in college swimming, but she drives herself to become competitive in marathon swimming. A friend swims to beat men, but Dorey swims to compete against the water. A really fine book.

"Whatta-Gal": The Babe Didrickson Story by William Oscar Johnson and Nancy P. Williamson. Little, Brown, 1975. A biography of the all-American in track, field, golf, bowling, tennis, swimming, baseball, and even more.

When No One Was Looking by Rosemary Wells. Dial, 1980. Kathy is a superb young tennis player, but she has demanding parents and a pushy coach. She also must face the mysterious drowning death of a rival.

A Whole New Ballgame by Sue Macy. Holt, 1993. A history of the All-American Girls' Professional League in World War II.

Zanballer by R. R. Knudson. Delacorte, 1972. Zan Hagen wants to play football, not to play what a "proper" girl should do—be a cheerleader. She sets out to change the school. **Zanbanger,** Harper, 1977, is the first of several unsuccessful sequels.

---

gles and the Triumphs of Baseball's Poor Relations from 1876 to the Present* tells the story most of us do not know.

A mythical element lives in almost all sports and sports literature but no place more so than in baseball, and three writers have written extraordinarily fine novels. Bernard Malamud's *The Natural* uses the myths of the Wasteland and the Holy Grail as background for the life of Roy Hobbs, a natural pitcher and later a natural hitter. Most people know *The Natural* from the 1984 film starring Robert Redford.

Mark Harris wrote four novels about major league star pitcher and author Henry Wiggen, but, without question, *Bang the Drum Slowly* is the best of the bunch and a fine best it is. Wiggen is the star pitcher of the New York Mammoths and a friend of a third-string catcher, Bruce Pearson, who is slowly dying. It is a beautifully written novel about friendship and love and baseball, which was made into an equally fine 1973 film.

W. P. Kinsella's *Shoeless Joe* is about Iowa farmer Ray Kinsella, who hears, "If you build it, he will come," and so he builds a baseball stadium and Shoeless Joe Jackson does come. So do countless baseball fans to the baseball field in Iowa, where the story was filmed as *Field of Dreams* in 1989.

The heritage of baseball is revealed by the number of good biographies and autobiographies of major players. Mark Ribowsky's *Don't Look Back: Satchel Paige in the Shadows of Baseball* tells us about what many people think was the finest baseball pitcher of all times. Henry Aaron and Lonnie Wheeler's *I Had a Hammer* is Aaron's story from being a poor African-American kid in Alabama who is crazy about baseball and the old Negro League until the time he became a star and the man who broke Babe Ruth's record for career homers. Ira Berkau's editing of the manuscript of *Hank Greenberg: The Story of My Life* tells of the first great Jewish baseball player and one of the most decent men to play baseball. Joseph Durso's *Dimaggio: The Last American Knight* was originally intended to be Dimaggio's autobiography, but he never carried it through. And Joe Morgan and David Falkner's *Joe Morgan: A Life in Baseball* covers 22 years in the majors, most of them with the Cincinnati Reds. One book that is certain to cause disagreements is Maury Allen's *Baseball's 100: A Personal Ranking of the Best Players in Baseball History*. Allen ranks the top five players as Willie Mays, Hank Aaron, Babe Ruth, Ted Williams, and Stan Musial.

One of the most intriguing baseball players in the majors never won awards for hitting or anything else, but he may have been the only major league player ever to be a spy for the United States. Nicholas Dawidoff's *The Catcher Was a Spy: The Mysterious Life of Moe Berg* was about a third-string catcher for the Boston Red Sox immediately before World War II. He was chosen by the Office of Strategic Services (the forerunner of the CIA) to assassinate the German scientist charged by Hilter to develop the atomic bomb. Berg was also a Princeton University graduate, a lawyer, a lady's man, and amateur linguist, and likely much more. Precisely who and what he was is still not clear, and some of the legends about Berg may be more romantic fantasies than truth. He had an incredible vocabulary and impressed almost every one of his teammates with his erudition. If he remains an enigma after we read Dawidoff's biography, he likely was just that.

Without much question, basketball is today's most popular sport, and one biography that ought to appeal to fans is Glenn Rivers and Bruce Brooks's *Those Who Love the Game: Glenn "Doc" Rivers on Life in the NBA and Elsewhere*. Rivers was a veteran guard with the New York Knicks, and his comments about life on the court and his beliefs about family and education may hit home to some young readers.

The Last Shot: City Streets, Basketball Dreams by Darcy Frey may be the most powerful book about basketball in years. Frey follows four African-American teens from the projects who are stars of Abraham Lincoln High School's basketball team. All four are talented enough to grab the attention of college coaches, but three of the four lack the educational background to qualify for top-notch college basketball programs. It is a bitter book at times about poverty and education (or the lack of education) and money and what good college coaches sometimes feel called on to do to get high school talent. Walter Dean Myers's *Hoops* shows a young boy trying to escape his ghetto existence through basketball. *The Outside Shot* is a sequel.

Hoop Dreams is a 1994 documentary film by Steve James showing two Chicago inner-city young people, Arthur Agee and William Gates, who dream of becoming NBA stars, only to run into problems, notably reality.

Anyone looking for a good collection of material on high school basketball could hardly do better than read Nelson Campbell's *Grass Roots and Schoolyards: A High School Basketball Anthology*.

Perhaps the finest book about tennis, and one of the best about sports in general, is Arthur Ashe and Arnold Rampersad's *Days of Grace: A Memoir*. This story of a brilliant young tennis player who saw glory and died of AIDS-related pneumonia in 1993 has moments of sadness mixed with moments of happiness and triumph. It's a book anyone who cares about sports would enjoy.

Young Adult Sports Fiction

Similar to John R. Tunis, Robert Lipsyte is a professional sports writer who also understands young people. Lipsyte has written both nonfiction and fiction, and some intriguing comparisons can be drawn between his nonfiction *Free to be Muhammad*

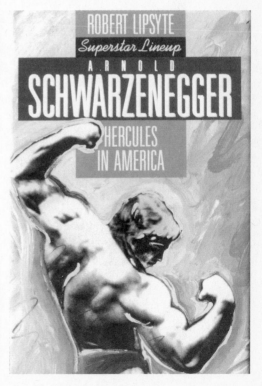

Robert Lipsyte, a professional sports writer and commentator in New York, writes sports novels as well as biographies of famous athletes.

Ali and his novel *The Contender*, about a young African-American boxer, a high school dropout named Alfred Brooks, who finds a world in the boxing ring that promises to be everything he ever wanted. The young man eventually learns that he can be a contender in many ways, not just inside the boxing ring. *The Brave* was advertised as a sequel to *The Contender*, but it's an unusual sequel because it has a new, young hero, George Harrison Bayer (named after his mother's favorite Beatle) but known as Sonny Bear. Sonny is a heavyweight boxer who runs away from his reservation in upstate New York into the arms of Alfred Brooks, now a New York City policeman. A third book, *The Chief*, continues from *The Brave*, but this is told from the point of view of an aspiring writer, and it begins as Sonny Bear's career is apparently nearly over. Then with the help of an ex-champion, Sonny gets a shot at the number-one fighter.

Chris Crutcher is one of the most talented new writers to combine sports and personal development stories. *Running Loose*, his first novel, presents one of the most intriguing protagonists in sports literature. Louie Banks wants to play football but not the way his unethical coach wants it played. He has problems with the high school principal, but he has no problems with his parents (one of the rare times when parents are sympathetic but not wimpy) or his girlfriend, at least not until she dies. It's a warm book about sports and running and love and death and caring.

Crutcher's *Stotan!* is about swimming and how a team faces up to the serious illness of one of its members. In *The Crazy Horse Electric Game,* star athlete Willie Weaver suffers brain damage from a waterskiing accident. In *Ironman,* Bo Brewster, a bitter high school athlete forced to attend anger-management classes, writes letters to Larry King because he doesn't feel anyone else will listen. The short stories in *Athletic Shorts* feature some of the characters from Crutcher's novels.

Two books by Will Weaver are about sports and far more, and both attracted the attention of critics. *Striking Out* is about Billy Baggs, who is a natural baseball player, but Billy's father, a farmer, needs Billy on the farm. It is a story of baseball and the problems of growing up and learning to live with parents who don't always stay the same. The story is continued in *Farm Team*, one of those rare sequels that is more successful than the original. When Billy's father is jailed for destroying property of an unethical businessman, Billy must run the farm. His mother comes up with a notion of developing a farm team, and the novel is off and running.

Thomas J. Dygard has produced a series of popular sports books but not with the depth of Tunis, Lipsyte, Crutcher, or Weaver. *Quarterback Walk-On* is a cliché-ridden plot about a football player desperate to play who does so only when three players ahead of him are hurt. It's also funny and almost believable. *Tournament Upstart* is one of those small-town-team-wins-out-over-impossible-odds stories, but it's also what Dygard does best: write vivid narrative that we believe in. *Backfield Package* presents a moral dilemma. A star quarterback makes a pact with three backfield mates to go to a small college where they can all play together. Then the quarterback is pursued by many big-time universities. *Game Plan* is unbelievable but fun. Beano Hatton has been the student manager in football for three years. When the coach is hurt, Beano is appointed acting head football coach. *Infield Hit* is about Hal Stevens, the son of a baseball superstar who cannot possibly live up to his father's image.

ROBERT LIPSYTE
On Books for Boys

Whenever I say that boys need more good books, people roll their eyes, "C'mon, boys got it all, even now." True. But what they've got is not necessarily in all our best interests. And books can be part of the problem in a society that conditions boys to grow up to be men who beat up smaller people, including women and children, boys who become men fearful of each other, who will fight back any attempt to socialize them out of violence.

I was lucky as a kid, although I certainly didn't think so at the time. I was very fat. I might as well have been a girl. Fat boys could read; we didn't matter.

But for normal boys, not your star athletes, just your everyday boys, reading was . . . is . . . a problem. Boys typically read about sports, about specific subjects and science, but rarely about the arts or social problems. Some experts claim this comes from the difference between the sexes: Boys want to master the world; girls want to understand it.

I think that boys don't read as much as we'd like them to because (1) current books tend not to deal with the real problems and fears of boys, and (2) there is a tendency to treat boys as a group . . . which is where males are at their absolute worst . . . instead of as individuals who have to be led into reading secretly and one at a time.

Boys are afraid of being humiliated, of being hurt, of being hit by the ball, of being made to look dumb or inadequate in front of other boys and in front of girls. Most of the sports books boys are force-fed reinforce those fears with the false values of winning as the only goal, bending mindlessly to authority, preserving the status quo, often at the cost of truth. I think I was very lucky not being a sports fan as a kid and hardly reading any sports books at all.

Boys need reassurance that their fears of violence and humiliation and competition are shared fears. Books can reassure them. But to be able to read a book properly, you have to be able to sink into a scene, to absorb characters, to care, to empathize. You have to be willing to make yourself vulnerable to a book as surely as you need to make yourself vulnerable to a person. This is not easy for a male in this society to do, particularly an adolescent male who is unsure of his own identity, his sexuality, his future.

So, you say, we have to change society first, and then boys will read good books. This is true. But if we can get just a few boys to read a few good books, we will have started the change. Cajole, *coerce,* do whatever needs to be done to get one book into one boy's hands, or back pocket. A book that he can make into a cave he can crawl into, roll around in, explore, for what's in there and what's in himself, find places of his own he never touched before, find out that a book is something you can do all by yourself, where no one can see you laughing or crying. It is the intellectual and emotional equivalent of safer sex.

Robert Lipsyte's books include *The Chief,* 1993; The Brave, 1991; *The Chemo Kid,* 1992; *The Contender,* 1967; and *One Fat Summer,* 1982, all HarperCollins.

Humor in Young Adult Literature

Rafael Sabatini began his first novel, *Scaramouche,* with a one-sentence characterization of his hero: "He was born with a gift of laughter and a sense that the world was mad." The ability to laugh at ourselves and the madness of the world is nature's gift to a perpetually beleaguered humanity. The need seems even more desperate today, although probably every previous generation could have made the same claim, so we laugh at almost everything and anything. At a time when taxes, death, and sex are serious matters indeed, they are also the staples of humor. We are pleased when we find something, anything, to laugh at. We are even more pleased when we discover someone who consistently makes us laugh. As Steve Allen reminds us:

> Without laughter, life on our planet would be intolerable. So important is laughter to us that humanity highly rewards members of one of the most unusual professions on earth, those who make a living by inducing laughter in others. This is very strange if you stop to think of it; that otherwise sane and responsible citizens should devote their professional energies to causing others to make sharp, explosive barking-like exhalations.[2]

Paula Danziger, shown here autographing a book, strikes the funny bone of junior high readers.

Given their enforced world of school and an ever-demanding society, young people need laughter every bit as much as adults, maybe even more so. What do young people find funny? Lance M. Gentile and Merna M. McMillen's article, "Humor and the Reading Program," offers a starting point. Their stages of children's and young adult's interest in humor, somewhat supplemented, are as follows:

- *Ages 10–11.* Literal humor, slapstick (e.g., "The Three Stooges"), laughing at accidents (banana-peel humor) and misbehavior, sometimes mildly lewd jokes (usually called "dirty jokes"), and grossness.
- *Ages 12–13.* Practical jokes, teasing, goofs, sarcasm, more lewd jokes, joke riddles, sick jokes, elephant jokes, grape jokes, tongue twisters, knock-knock jokes, moron jokes, TV blooper shows, and grossness piled on grossness.
- *Ages 14–15.* More and more lewd jokes (some approaching a mature recognition of the humor inherent in sex); humor aimed at schools, parents, and adults in authority; "Married with Children" and their ilk; and grossness piled on even greater grossness. Young adults may still prefer their own humor to their parents' humor, but they are increasingly catching on to adult humor and may prefer it to their own.
- *Ages 16 and up.* More subtle humor, satire and parody now acceptable and maybe even preferable, witticisms (rather than last year's half-witticisms, which they now detest in their younger brothers and sisters). Adult humor is increasingly part of their repertoire, partly because they are anxious to appear sophisticated, partly because they *are* growing up.[3]

Despite what must seem obvious truth to good teachers and librarians—that a sense of humor is essential for survival of educators and students—some deadly serious people wonder if this (or any other time, presumably) is the time for levity. The answer is, of course, yes—this is the time (and so is any other time). Many young people may be surprised to find that they laugh at the same things their parents and grandparents laughed at in the movies (Focus Box 9.2).

Ellen Conford apparently ran into one of those humorless individuals at a librarians' meeting. During a question-answer session, Conford was asked if there was any subject she felt she could not treat humorously. She answered, "Cancer and abortion. Other than those two, I can make jokes about almost anything." Another person, a man, asked about the nuclear holocaust, specifically what was Conford doing about it.

"Don't you think," he went on, "that it's your responsibility as a writer for young people to alert them about the dangers of the arms race?"

"No!" I said, horrified.

"But if their own authors don't tell them, who will?"

"Dan Rather," I said. "Peter Jennings. Tom Brokaw. Any kid with ears already knows about the possibility of being incinerated in three seconds. And they know they have no power to do anything to save themselves. You want me to scare them some more?

Not me!"[4]

FOCUS BOX 9.2

Time for the Giggles—It's Comedy Tonight

The Bank Dick (1940, 74 min., black and white; Director: Eddie Cline; with W. C. Fields) A ne'er-do-well accidentally foils a bank robbery and is made a guard. Then the real robbers appear. Maybe Fields's best movie.
Bringing Up Baby (1938, 102 min., black and white; Director: Howard Hawks; with Katharine Hepburn and Cary Grant) The epitome of screwball comedies. A wacky socialite captures a paleontologist with the help of a leopard.
The Court Jester (1956, 101 min., color; Director: Norman Panama; with Danny Kaye and Glynis Johns) Our hero pretends to be a jester to save the royal baby. Almost no let-up of laughs or derring-do. One of the great comedies.
The General (1927, 74 min., black and white; Director: Buster Keaton) Keaton's funniest film. A man anxious to enlist in the Confederate army is turned down to keep him at the switch of his railway engine. When Union forces come near, he becomes a hero. **Sherlock, Jr.** (1924, 45 min., black and white) is another Keaton film masterpiece. He plays a movie projectionist who walks into a screen and becomes part of the story.
Kind Hearts and Coronets (1949, 104 min., black and white; Director: Robert Hamer; with Dennis Price and Alec Guinness) An impoverished young man related to titled wealth sets out to kill whoever in the family stands in his way to the title. The victims are all played by Guinness. Funny black comedy.
Modern Times (1936, 83 min., black and white; Director: Charlie Chaplin) His last silent film was an attack on machines misused by greedy men and social ills of all sorts. Per-

haps his funniest film, certainly one of his best.
A Night at the Opera (1935, 92 min., black and white; Director: Sam Wood) The Marx brothers take on opera and everyone wins but the ever-present and ever-befuddled Margaret Dumont. *Duck Soup* (1933, 70 min., black and white; Director: Leo McCarey) is their other satirical masterpiece.
The Pink Panther Strikes Again (1976, 103 min., color; Director: Blake Edwards; with Peter Sellers and Herbert Lom) Inspector Clouseau's superior goes insane (all inadvertently caused by Clouseau) and sets out to conquer the world. The other funny Pink Panther film is **A Shot in the Dark** (1964).
Take the Money and Run (1969, 85 min., color; Director: Woody Allen) Not Allen at his most subtle but at his funniest. He plays an incredibly inept bank robber, always on the run, always trying, always failing.
Way Out West (1937, 65 min., black and white; Director: James W. Horne; with Stan Laurel and Oliver Hardy) The boys go west to deliver a mine deed. A gem, but their short films are funnier than most of their features. "Big Business" (1929) may be, as lots of us think, the funniest film ever made, with the boys trying to sell Christmas trees in July.
Young Frankenstein (1974, 105 min., color; Director: Mel Brooks; with Gene Wilder and Peter Boyle) Brooks's affectionate spoof of *Frankenstein* and *Bride of Frankenstein* with a much stranger housekeeper, an even stranger monster, a weird servant, and two wild and strange women who love young Frankenstein. Funny and loving and even a bit scary once in awhile.

Conford added that there are already talented young adult authors who can treat the world seriously, but there are all too few who can make young people laugh. She's right. Maybe English teachers assume that life is too serious to be treated any other way in school. Certainly there is very little humor in literary anthologies. These anthologies, especially those used in secondary schools, imply that literature is too sacred for humor. That would have seemed odd to Mark Twain, who (an oversight?) has found his way into more American literature anthologies than any other author. Maybe the problem is that high school English teachers got their training in such oh-so-serious-literature classes that they don't know where to turn for humor.

Mass Media and Humor

Actually, humor is all around us—in advertisements, television, movies, and newspapers. The comic strips might be one place to start looking. Jeff McNelly's "Shoe," Gary Larson's lamented "The Far Side," and Bill Watterson's equally lamented "Calvin and Hobbes" are imaginative and often satiric and extremely funny. If comics have to be justified, the insecure teacher could point out that McNelly has won a Pulitzer prize for editorial cartooning, and Watterson has been cited as the most admired comic strip writer/cartoonist by his fellow cartoonists. "Calvin and Hobbes" came to life on November 18, 1985, and the best of the next ten years' strips are gathered together in *The Calvin and Hobbes Tenth Anniversary Book,* a delight and an inspiration and the best use of $14.95 we can imagine. Sadly, the last "Calvin and Hobbes" strip appeared the last day of 1995.

Old-time radio, particularly the work of Paul Rhymer and "Vic and Sade," might be worth considering, especially since James Thurber thought Rhymer was a genius, but then so do Jean Shepherd and Ray Bradbury.

Newspaper columnists are another source of humor. Teenagers, along with their parents, check out the condition of the world by reading the letters written to Ann Landers and to her sister, Abigail Van Buren ("Dear Abby"). Some of them also read Erma Bombeck's, Andy Rooney's, and Art Buchwald's columns and books. They identify with the frustrations that these writers, especially Bombeck and Rooney, express about everyday events.

English teachers need to keep their eyes open for humor, particularly inadvertent humor, in newspapers. Headlines like PROSTITUTES APPEAL TO POPE (from the December 18, 1975, *Eugene Oregon Register-Guard*), FORMER MAN DIES IN CALIFORNIA (from the February 13, 1975, *Fremont County Idaho Chronicle-News*) and STATE DINNER FEATURED CAT, AMERICAN FOOD (from the February 15, 1977, *Bellingham Washington Herald*) give us the giggles partly because they reassure us that journalists are human and can make all sorts of fascinating goofs.

Sometimes a line or two buried in an otherwise dull story makes us laugh. For example, in a brief comment about the Soviet National baseball team and its return after a dismal tour of the United States—11 games, 11 lopsided defeats—the *London Times* for April 30, 1989, quoted a Russian official. "We have good players, but they are not baseball players. This is a problem."

Humor and Urban Legends

A relatively new genre in American humor is urban legends, or FOAF tales because they are told by a *Friend Of A Friend*. These stories are parodies of weird and unusual news items; in fact, many of them find their way into newspapers as serious stories. Although they are filled with fascinating details that add to their credibility, exact names and addresses are never given. This does not stop most people, however, from insisting that the stories really happened. Jan Harold Brunvand, a University of Utah folklorist and author of two of the most popular books—*The Vanishing Hitchhiker: American Urban Legends and Their Meaning* and *The Choking Doberman: And Other "New" Urban Legends*—explained that people keep asking him how he knows the stories that he collects didn't really happen. These questioners often claim that they have

> access to some indisputable evidence of the truth of one. I usually reply, "If you know that one of them is true, then please get me the proof; I'd be delighted to have it." Frequently it is some classic automobile story floating around in oral tradition, like "The Killer in the Backseat" or "The Death Car," that people are absolutely sure "really happened."

So these people try hard to remember who told them, and exactly when it was and where they were living at the time that a fine sports car was advertised for sale by a wronged wife at an extraordinarily low price; or when someone accidentally was sold an experimental car with a carburetor that got 200 miles per gallon; or when a jealous husband filled an unfamiliar new car parked in his driveway with wet cement.[5]

Brunvand said that these people "always conclude eventually that they cannot unearth any firsthand information on the stories they thought were true or locate anyone else who can vouch for them." Instead they "have for verification not personal experience, nor even a friend's own experience, but only an unnamed, elusive, but somehow readily trusted anonymous individual, a friend of a friend."

Scholars who study the tales say that the reason we are so quick to believe them and pass them on to our friends is that they speak to fears we have, which is what Alvin Schwartz capitalized on in his *Scary Stories* collections. Some of the fears are the old-fashioned, cold-blooded-murder type; others focus on technology that we aren't sure we trust (e.g., cars, computers, and microwaves). Some of them center on our fears of new immigrants and customs we don't understand or on how vulnerable we are and how dependent on big business. For example, Daniel Cohen starts his Avon Flare book *Southern Fried Rat and Other Gruesome Tales* with a story of Jim and Karen picking up a snack after a movie. The restaurant is so crowded that Jim wants to go someplace else, but Karen is so hungry that she suggests they get a carry-out order and eat in the car. Jim worries about dropping greasy crumbs on the upholstery of his car, but Karen is so hungry that she tears into the order. Pretty soon she slows down and remarks that it doesn't taste right, then she says it doesn't feel right either and asks Jim to turn on the light. To their horror, they discover that sticking out of the extra crispy coating is a 3-inch tail. Karen had been eating a fried rat.

No one likes to be preached at, but because the message in urban legends is hidden under the amusement and the irony, listeners do not recognize the stories as cautionary tales. Besides, there is something satisfying about seeing that these misfortunes are happening to someone else instead of to us. At one of the WHIM (Western Humor and Irony Membership) conferences held at Arizona State Uni-

THEODORE TAYLOR
On Books and Hollywood

Off and on, over 17 years, I worked in polluted waters where human barracudas swim and love and hate as they ride in the same canoe; where egos are stroked with verbal velvet and deceit, and money fuels it all. Hollywood, of course. Where else?

I began as a press agent, became a story editor, finally an associate producer. I'd work six months or so on a film, gather the good money and spend the next four to six months writing a book. Looking back, had I "druthers," I would have spent all 12 months pecking away on a novel.

The first television script that I sold, the lead character, a deputy sheriff, was the hero. The director said, "Make him the heavy."

The first full-length movie script that I sold (*Showdown,* for Universal) was a drama. The producer/director turned it into a comedy.

I did not script *The Cay* for television. That story hung on the racial poisoning of the white boy, Phillip, by his mother. It was a mandatory scene: the mother doing her evil, on screen, with the boy. The film version opened with Phillip on a raft, saying to James Earl Jones, "My mother doesn't like black people," or words to that effect. The whole point of the book floated away. A few minutes into the film, I took my dogs for a walk and haven't seen the rest of the travesty to this day.

More recently, I sold *The Stalker* for a full-length movie and wrote the first screenplay. The producer said it didn't have enough blood, sex, and violence and assigned three more writers. My novel was set in Orange County, California; went on to Washington, D.C.; then to Hamburg, Germany; then to Denmark; climaxing in Sweden. When I saw the HBO version, the setting was entirely in Paraguay.

My point is: Don't blame the book writer for what comes over the boob-tube or on the mulitplex screen with Dolby sound, whether for adult or young adult or purely children fare. The novelist, unless a Tom Clancy or John Grisham or Mary Higgins Clark or Anne Rice, has little or no "say."

My advice to fellow writers is to take the best money possible and run to the bank; don't look back. Don't even go see the movie until five trusted friends claim it's okay.

Over the years, there have been some distinguished films adapted from children's and young adult novels, a recent example being *Sarah, Plain and Tall.* But without the star-power and clout of actress Glenn Close, that television special made from Patricia MacLachlan's wonderful novel might well have suffered the second-rate presentation of Gary Paulsen's fine *Hatchet.*

Although I tend to write cinematically, as a result of all those years in the motion picture industry, I've never consciously thought, beginning a new book, "Hey, this one will make a good film." I've never tried to write a book as a long-version screen-

(continued)

play. In all likelihood, for me, that would be the death of both the book and the possible screen adaptation. I know that this "plan" has worked but not often.

Considering the huge number of children's books published annually, only a few reach either television or theaters. By and large, the head barracudas think in terms of star power. Sharon Stone? Demi Moore? Money is the understandable goal. Aside from the animated films, Disney category, the chances of any children's book, no matter the quality, being filmed remains relatively small.

When and if the deal is made, a stone wall usually arises. The movie folks usually don't want the book writer messing around with suggestions, visits to the set, even a reading of the rough script. There are exceptions. I understand Glenn Close and Patricia MacLachlan had a good working "Sara" relationship. Rare, indeed.

When and if the miracle happens, the writer realizes that the barracuda attorneys will make sure that the pie-slice is 99 percent producer. Between "Standard Terms and Conditions" and "Net Profits" and "Short Form Assignments" and "Deal Terms" and "Special Provisions" covering 20 to 30 pages of fine-print contracts, writers, in legal and mental disarray, discover they have had their pants removed.

I know "thereof," and "to wit."

Theodore Taylor's books include *The Cay,* Doubleday, 1969; *Timothy of the Cay,* Harcourt, 1993; *Sniper,* Harcourt, 1989; and *Tuck Triumphant,* Doubleday, 1991.

versity, Max Shulman explained that if readers are inspired by something he's written to say, "I know someone like that," they'll laugh. But if what he writes makes them say, "Oh, no, that's me!" they won't laugh. The success of urban legends illustrates his point because most of us can easily see the fatal flaw, the little mistake, that someone in the story made. We know we're too smart for that, so we laugh.

Sometimes Serious but Funny, Sometimes Just Plain Funny Young Adult Novels

If you ask teenagers for examples of humor they have enjoyed, they are much more likely to give you the names of television programs, especially sit-coms, or MTV, or movies or comedians than of young adult novels. Nevertheless, there is a fresh breeze blowing across the landscape, which Roger Sutton remarked on in the November 1990 *School Library Journal.* Under the heading "Hard Times at Sweet Valley," he showed how in *Friend Against Friend* (Sweet Valley High #69) a heavy-handed social consciousness was creeping in. He found this ironic because mainstream young adult fiction is turning to lighter treatments of serious subjects.

As an example, he compared how earnestly Sandra Scoppettone had to defend her 1974 *Trying Hard to Hear You* (a story about a girl discovering that her best friend and her boyfriend are gay) with how lightheartedly Ron Koertge could treat the subject of homosexuality in his 1988 *The Arizona Kid.* In the latter book, Billy spends the summer on an Arizona ranch and comes to terms with the fact that his uncle is gay. Sutton wrote:

Laugh at a gay person? Or at divorce?—Brock Cole's *Celine* (1989), about two children of divorce, is funny; so is Bruce Brooks's *No Kidding* (1989), a novel about children of alcoholics. All three of these books also have moments of almost unbearable pain, none of it resolved by a simple matter of "adjustment."[6]

He concluded that although these books lack the dogged explanations of the problem novel, "they more than compensate with their respect for the reader's imagination and sense of humor."

Jerry Spinelli has written a number of extraordinarily funny books, among them *Space Station Seventh Grade* and *Who Put That Hair in My Toothbrush*. Joan Bauer has written two funny books, *Squashed* and *Thwonk*, which suggest that she is going to be a force in this area for some time to come. William Sleator has written any number of exciting fantasies and science fiction books, but if readers are expecting thrills or chills when they pick up *Oddballs*, they are in for a surprise. Sleator writes about his big and strange family, all of them oddballs in one way or another.

M. E. Kerr is consistently funny, although her novels are essentially serious books about young people caught up in emotional quandaries. Kerr looks wryly at her protagonists, but she never lacks compassion for them or her readers. *Dinky Hocker Shoots Smack*, her first novel and almost the only one not told in first person, is filtered through the consciousness of 15-year-old Tucker Woolf, whose sketches remind his mother of a "depressing Bosch." After advertising for a home for his cat Nader (named after Ralph Nader), Tucker meets Dinky, whose mother suffers for all the ills of the world but ignores Dinky and Dinky's problems. He also meets Dinky's cousin Natalia, who is emotionally troubled and talks in rhymes, and P. John Knight, whose left-wing father has made P. John become right-wing with a vengeance. Kerr's humor in this and later books does not come from one-liners or obvious jokes but from the characters themselves. She drops references to Bosch, Dostoevsky, and the Bible, among other things, because she assumes young adults can think and feel and laugh.

Her best and funniest book is *If I Love You, Am I Trapped Forever?* Alan Bennett, the narrator, lives in upstate New York with a grandfather and a mother who was deserted by Alan's father years before. Early in the book, Alan describes himself as "The most popular boy at Cayuta High. Very handsome. Very cool. Dynamite." His life and his love life with Leah are perfect in every way until Duncan Stein comes to town, and slowly Alan's life and world crumble. Doomed (Alan's nickname for Duncan) is untypical. No basketball, no school clubs, no going steady, nothing that Alan understands. But Doomed gains notoriety with his underground newspaper, *Remote*, and he creates a dating fad at Cayuta High—going steady is out and one-time only dates become the in thing.

Alan is puzzled by everything that is going wrong. Doomed plays by no rules that Alan understands, and Doomed is certainly not interested in Alan's friendship. When Alan and Doomed walk together from homeroom to English class one day, they have a short and pointed conversation:

We were studying Alfred Lord Tennyson's poem "In Memoriam" that week. The poem was a tribute to his friend, Arthur Hallam, who died suddenly of influenza when he was just twenty-two. I said something to Doomed then about trying to make friends with him, and then I said, "Well, I guess we'll never be known as Tennyson and Hallam, will we, Stein?"

Stein said, "Croak and find out, why don't you?"

How hostile can you get?

Two English imports by Sue Townsend are very funny. *The Secret Diary of Adrian Mole, Aged 13 3/4* and *The Growing Pains of Adrian Mole* are, obviously, about young Adrian, who tells his life struggles in his diary, the horrors of growing up in a family in which the mother does not love the father, in which no one (especially the BBC) fully appreciates the value of his sensitive writings, in which his beloved Pandora does not long for Adrian's caresses as much as Adrian longs to caress Pandora, and in which things almost never go right and almost always go wrong.

Townsend understands and likes Adrian and young people. Adrian often sounds naive, sometimes foolish, but he is never ridiculed, although he may look ridiculous, sometimes even to himself. Adrian is an honest observer of life, but he has no objectivity and he often misreads events and people. Indeed, he may be hopefully unaware of adult duplicities at times, but his honesty is fixed and admirable. Others may not appreciate Adrian's wish to crowd all of life's experiences into the next few months. When Adrian asks Pandora to show him one of her nipples, for purely objective reasons, she is not moved to show but to write a letter terminating their relationship.

Later, we see Adrian at his most incisive and adults at their most perplexing:

My mother has decided that sugar is the cause of all the evil in the world, and has banned it from the house.

She smoked two cigarettes while she informed me of her decision.

The two funniest books in young adult literature are Robert Kaplow's *Alex Icicle: A Romance in Ten Torrid Chapters* and Gary Paulsen's *Harris and Me: A Summer Remembered.*

Alex Icicle is a delightful spoof of books and styles. Alex is filled with a passion for Amy Hart, but she does not return his passion. No one can accuse Alex of underwriting or being flat and dull in his diction or style. Here are the first two paragraphs of *Alex Icicle.*

I am a sick man. I am a diseased man. I am not even a man, merely a boy. *And yet I love her.* I am all the loathsomeness of the human condition distilled into one horrible, malignant growth and fashioned into the fourteen-year-old features of Alexander Preston Sturges Swinburne—boy monster.

Nay, when you read this line remember not the monster who writ it. Burn the wretched manuscript! Obliterate every vestige of its fetid presence from the face of humanity. The contents of this manuscript are so void of redeeming social value, so unspeakably low, so depraved and degrading, that I warn you (pray heed my warning!) to put it down. There are gentle books all around, books with pictures of gardens. There are books of sunlit poetry. Gentle reader, I implore you to read one of these other books, not the horrible document you hold before you. It is a record of humiliation and anguished self-hatred—stop, dear reader! Stop if you dare. Or, at least, hold the manuscript with long steel tongs so it cannot possibly touch you with its poison. But steel tongs may not be enough! Place the manuscript in a containment cell and reach through the walls with long neoprene gloves as your startled, trembling fingers turn each rancid page. But make sure there are no holes in your gloves! Check carefully! Even one pinprick, and the foul and pestilent vapor will creep up with long, dark, gaseous fingers to pull you down into the abyss of degradation.

Paulsen's *Harris and Me* is the funniest young adult novel we've read in years. It opens with a young boy dumped off on some relatives because his parents drink and no one else will take him in. The odd relatives consist of Glennis, a wonderful girl the narrator falls for almost immediately, a vague mother and father that the boy learns to like, and Harris who greets the narrator with a warm, "We heard your folks was puke drunks, is that right?"

From then on, it's one wild episode after another. Chapter Two closes with a broad hint of all the strange events to come as our hero follows Harris into deep cow doo-doo and then:

I was hit directly in the groin with such force that it lifted me off the ground, doubling me, I grabbed for the injured area as I started down, vaguely sensing that I was about to start puking again, and then something slammed into the top of my head and my world ended in an explosion of white light.

Immediately after this incident when our hero meets Vivian, the evil-tempered cow, he is introduced to other farm animals like Ernie, the killer rooster, Minnie, the nasty sow, and Buzzer, the dog-killing cat. Then comes the wonderful adventures with Harris, rope swinging and falling into pig-dung, horse-jumping, bull-stomping, mouse-killing, looking at "dourty peectures," peeing on electric fences, and fighting wars with corn cobs.

Harris and Me is a wonder, funny and touching and almost everything a good book ought to be.

Humor in Children's Literature

Although this text is not on children's literature, students probably remember some funny children's books., which English teachers might want to use. Shel Silverstein's *A Light in the Attic* is a wonderful collection of poems that children of all ages, 9 through 90, enjoy. Poems as funny as "Crowded Tub," "They've Put a Brassiere on the Camel," and "Spelling Bee" are inventive and magical. "If" is a great antidote to Kipling's solemn and boring poem with the same title. Best of them all is "Little Abigail and the Beautiful Pony" which has been censored as being a morbid invitation for suicide, but children know that it is simply a funny poem about a silly wish that all of us have had at one time or another.

Dr. Seuss has so many witty and delightful books it's almost a shame to list only a few. We can thank his *The Cat in the Hat* for killing all the stupid Dick and Jane stories. *How the Grinch Stole Christmas* has become a seasonal classic. If there is a funnier book in the world than *Horton Hatches the Egg,* we do not know what it would be. Our hero, Horton the elephant, desperately tries to save the egg of Maisie, the cowbird, and fights corruption and Maisie and all the other forces of evil and villainy.

Humorous Poetry

For many young people, who are hardly enamored of poetry to begin with, poetry and humor are mutually exclusive terms. Books such as Piet Hein's *Grooks* and Alvin Schwartz's *And the Green Grass Grew All Around* should help dispel that notion. Don Marquis's *archy and mehitabel* is an old standard about a giant cockroach who never uses capitals because he approaches the typewriter and dives off, hitting one key and then diving off to hit another one, until his manuscript is done. Marquis discovers archy's first literary efforts, and he follows with other poems, all of them funny—"the song of mehitabel," "the cockroach who had been to hell," "pete the parrot and shakespeare," and "freddie the rat perished."

Fritz Spiegl's *A Small Book of Grave Humor* provides us with humorous lines on gravestones. Humor about death goes way back to the Greeks. In the mammoth collection of odds-and-ends verses called *Poems from the Greek Anthology*, there are conventional and unconventional epitaphs, some bitter, some satiric and amusing.

Mark Twain made great fun of bad poetry about death. In his *Adventures of Huckleberry Finn,* he may even have been thinking of Julia Moore, "The Sweet Singer of Michigan," who never lost the opportunity to write about the dead, particularly the recent dead. Granted that she wrote in dead earnest, her poetry now can be read only as amusing, or odd, poetry of sorts. One of her major works concerned a little girl named Libbie:

> One morning in April, a short time ago,
>
> Libbie was alive and gay;
>
> Her savior called her, she had to go,
>
> Ere the close of that pleasant day,
>
> While eating dinner, this dear little child
>
> Was choked on a piece of beef.
>
> Doctors came, tried their skill awhile,
>
> But none could give relief.

A contemporary of Julia Moore, Howard Heber Clark, who tilled the same poetic field, may have helped to kill obituary verse with this tribute to little Willie

> Willie had a purple monkey climbing on a yellow stick,
>
> And when he sucked the paint all off it made him deathly sick,
>
> And in his latest hours he clasped that monkey in his hand,
>
> And bade good-bye to earth and went into a better land.

Oh! no more he'll shoot his sister with his little wooden gun;

And no more he'll twist the pussy's tail and make her yowl, for fun.

The pussy's tail now stands out straight; the gun is laid aside;

The monkey doesn't jump around since little Willie died.

Although Clark's little Willie was presumably not meant to be funny, a series of poems about another little Willie (sometimes called little Billy) was meant to make us laugh. Harry Graham, an English soldier in the Coldstream Guard who wrote under the pen name Col. D. Streamer, produced enduring and widely quoted masterpieces in 1902 with his *Ruthless Rhymes for Heartless Homes* with poems like these:

Billy, in one of his nice, new sashes,

Fell in the fire and was burned to ashes.

Now, although the room grows chilly,

I haven't the heart to poke poor Billy.

Father heard his children scream,

So he threw them in the stream,

Saying, as he drowned the third,

"Children should be seen, not heard."

So popular were these sadistic poems that papers printed new catastrophes by many imitators, most of them about Little Willie and his latest nastiness or disaster, and the form of poetry became known as "Little Willie Poems." Here are two of the imitators

Dr. Jones fell in the well,

And died without a moan.

He should have tended to the sick

And left the well alone.

Little Willie, mean as hell,

Drowned his sister in the well.

Mother said, while drawing water,

"Gee, it's hard to raise a daughter."

Parody

In recommending exercises for writing poetry, Ezra Pound recommended that students parody poems they thought were silly or pretentious.[7] Although that might sound a bit highfalutin to young people, parodies of serious poetry have resulted in some of the funniest poems in the language. It's not difficult to find collections of parodies, but among the best and certainly the most useful for secondary English teachers is Robert P. Falk's anthology, *American Literature in Parody* (when it appeared in paperback, the title was changed to *The Antic Muse: American Writers in Parody*). Within this wonderful book can be found parodies of Poe's "The Raven" and "Anabel Lee," Mark Twain's nasty attack on James Fenimore Cooper's woeful prose, mocking of Henry James's sometimes lugubrious writing, and much more.

One of the funniest and most recent books of parody is Henry Beard's *Poetry for Cats: The Definitive Anthology of Distinguished Feline Verse*. The assumption underlying the book is that many famous poets were owned by cats, and the cats wrote in much the same meter and style as the poets. For example, the poem written by John Donne's cat is entitled, "Vet, Be Not Proud." John Milton's cat wrote, "The Prologue to *Territory Lost*," Edgar Allan Poe's cat wrote, "The End of the Raven," William Butler Yeats's cat wrote, "The Dismal Isle of Innisfree," and Allen Ginsberg's cat wrote, "Meowl." The funniest of them all—and technically the most perfect—is Dylan Thomas's cat who wrote, "Do Not Go Peaceable to that Damn Vet." All in all, *Poetry for Cats* is a marvel. It should amuse teachers and students alike, and teachers who know about the intricacies of poetry will delight in it even more.

Some Gentle Satires

One of the more widely used handbooks of literature opens its definitions of satire this way:

> A work or manner that blends a censorious attitude with humor and wit for improving human institutions or humanity. Satirists attempt through laughter not so much to tear down as to inspire a remodeling. If attackers simply abuse, they are writing invective; if they are personal and splenetic, they are writing sarcasm; if they are sad and morose over the state of society, they are writing irony or a jeremiad. As a rule modern satire spares the individual and follows Addison's self-imposed rule: to "pass over a single foe to charge whole armies." Most often, satire deals less with great sinners and criminals than with a general run of fools, knaves, ninnies, oafs, codgers, and frauds.[8]

Roger Sutton asked Richard Peck how he thought kids responded to satire, and Peck answered:

> Not well. I had to write a letter back to a class who had written to me about *Secrets of the Shopping Mall* saying that they understood the first part but then it got weird. Well, it was meant to get weird, and I said to them, "Please ask your teacher to tell you what satire is." They weren't ready for it, but of course nobody's ready until he's done some reading. . . . I think maybe satirizing the

shopping mall was a problem. I could have satirized the school or the family. But the mall is their setting of choice and almost neutral ground.[9]

Some teachers and librarians assume that satire must be vicious or biting in tone and content, but some effective satires are gentle, even loving.

Jean Merrill's *The Pushcart War* is a classic among children's and young adult books, a gentle and most effective satire of war and human cupidity. Supposedly written in 1996, 10 years after the end of the brief "Pushcart War," the novel is presented as straight, factual history, allowing the reader to see the humor, nobility, and nastiness of humans as the war unfolds. The war begins as a truck driver drives over and demolishes a pushcart, propelling its owner into a pickle barrel. Soon the pushcart owners band together to fight back and the war is on. Noble figures such as General Anna (formerly Old Anna), Maxie Hammerman, Morris the Florist, and Frank the Flower walk across history, as do bad guys like Albert P. Mack (usually known as Mack, the truck driver), Big Moe, Louis Livergreen, and Mayor Emmett P. Cudd. *The Pushcart War* is funny, wise, learned, and utterly delightful for almost any reader, young adult or adult.

Several writers, all of them *New Yorker* contributors, offer young adults the chance to sample somewhat more sophisticated, although still gentle, satire. James Thurber's gentleness may be more apparent than real, but many of his sketches and short stories have proved popular to the young. Nostalgic pieces such as "The Night the Bed Fell" and "University Days" are accessible to young people, and *Fables for Our Time*—especially "The Shrike and the Chipmunk," "The Owl Who Thought He Was God," and "The Unicorn in the Garden"—are popular with sophisticated teenagers. His rewriting of history in "If Grant Had Been Drinking at Appomattox" is funny *if* readers know history, just as "The Macbeth Murder Mystery" is funny *if* readers know the play. Thurber's three best short stories are, unhappily, often beyond the emotional understanding of young adults, but if readers can handle them, "The Secret Life of Walter Mitty," "The Catbird Seat," and "The Greatest Man in the World" are among the finest and least gentle satires.

E. B. White is far more gentle and likable than Thurber, although his adult material has less immediate appeal to the young. *The Second Tree from the Corner* is, simply put, one of the great works in American literature, and why it goes largely unknown among so many teachers and librarians is one of life's great mysteries. White's poetry in that book is clever and amusing (especially "The Red Cow Is Dead" and "Song of the Queen Bee") and "The Retort Transcendental" is a wonderful parody of Thoreau taken too far. The finest short stories are "The Decline of Sport," a relatively funny satire on the inevitable decline in sports, and "The Morning of the Day They Did It," a less than amusing satire on the end of the world.

Woody Allen is a favorite of young people, although many probably have trouble following his verbal play. His movies, especially *Annie Hall* and *Take the Money and Run,* are filled with wackiness and wisdom, more often than not strangely mixed, but Allen's books are far wittier and have far better one-liners than his films. *Getting Even* is typical Allen wit, which assumes readers know Freud, Hasidic Jews, what college catalogues read like, and more. *Without Feathers* and *Side*

LENSEY NAMIOKA
On Writing About What You Don't Know

"Write about what you know!" That's what I heard in my freshman English class, and I hear that repeated by many critics today.

Several of my books are about Chinese immigrants coping with life in America. The episodes are indeed drawn from my own experiences and those of my relatives.

But I've also written a book set in ancient China. To make the background authentic, I had to do diligent research, not rely on what I already knew. Several of my books are set in Japan, my husband's country, and my material is all acquired secondhand. None of these books come from anything that has happened to me personally. Are they inferior, then, to my contemporary books about Chinese immigrants?

I'm fascinated by things that happened long ago and far away, and I think authors should write about what fascinates them. Maybe some critics think we should write only about our own experiences because that's what interests us the most. This makes authors sound very self-absorbed, and I don't think we are — not all of us.

If Shakespeare had confined himself to his own experiences, he wouldn't have written about a prince of Denmark or a pair of lovers in Verona. He would probably have described glove making in Warwickshire. No historical novels would be written, and Tolstoy's *War and Peace* would be just *Peace*.

We would have no fantasy. Wu Chengen, the author of *Journey to the West,* would write about corrupt mandarins, not the fabulous adventures of the Monkey King. Kenneth Graham's *Wind in the Willows* would be about neighborhood cats and dogs, not about Mole, Rat, and the manic Toad. Alice's adventures would be all above ground, and she would remain on this side of the looking glass.

If authors aren't allowed to go beyond what they know and let their imaginations soar, world literature would be very much poorer.

Lensey Namioka's books include *The Loyal Cat,* Harcourt, 1995; *Yang the Third and Her Impossible Family,* Little Brown, 1995; *April and the Dragon Lady,* Harcourt, 1994; and *Coming of the Bear,* HarperCollins, 1992.

Effects assume intelligent and sophisticated readers. Allen is fascinated by God and death, and his books have wisdom and some wacky wit about both.

The Ultimate in Humor

For some young adults, and for far more adults, P. G. Wodehouse is the finest of all humorists. This English writer of nearly 100 novels created a fantasy world permanently locked somewhere vaguely in the 1920s and 1930s and featuring some highly unbelievable characters. Other writers as different politically and socially as Evelyn Waugh, George Orwell, and Rudyard Kipling ardently admired Wodehouse and thought him a genius. So he is.

Wodehouse's best-known creations are the feeble-brained Bertie Wooster and his brilliant and snobbish butler, Jeeves. Readers who begin with some of the Jeeves short stories in *Very Good, Jeeves* or *Carry On, Jeeves* may be puzzled by the comic opera world they find, but they discover wit, charm, and fun in abundance. Readers may then be prepared to move on to the Jeeves novels (e.g., *The Inimitable Jeeves; The Mating Season; Jeeves and the Feudal Spirit; Stiff Upper Lip, Jeeves;* and *Much Obliged, Jeeves*).

Wodehouse enthusiasts may differ on the stories or novels they consider the funniest (some would vote for "Mulliner's Buck-U-Uppo" in *Meet Mr. Mulliner,* and others would argue for "Uncle Fred Flits By" in *Young Men in Spats),* but almost anyone who has sampled Wodehouse stays for other items on the menu.

The range of humor available to young adults is incredible. Mockery, heroism, naiveté, cynicism, stupidity, cruelty, mayhem, death, the quest, madness, nastiness, sexuality, insults, viciousness, innocence, tears, the macabre, bitterness, and laughter in abundance are easily found to meet the tastes of any reader. These smiling readers are forever grateful to whoever gave them a nudge toward what brought them happiness.

A Short Note on Films

In 1913, Robert W. Neal wrote a three-page note in the *English Journal* about a medium that was already controversial.[10] Movies had been damned from the pulpit, and librarians were understandably opposed to them, as they had been to another major time-waster, the dime novel. But Neal did not come to attack. He announced that movies were "here to stay and we shall have to make the best of them." He added that if the teacher were "to turn the moving picture to his own purposes, the teacher of course must be reasonably familiar with it." Neal suggested that teachers should read a book on the technique of the "photo-play" and read a periodical on the medium. So much for the image of the stuffy English teacher in 1913.

But English teachers proved stand-offish about the movies if Samuel Rosenkranz's 1931 comment is to be believed:

> We continue to teach our standards of evaluation in the drama and to ignore the cinema, and our pupils continue to patronize the cinema and to ignore the drama. We refuse to recognize the fact that they are going to the picture shows, and that we must adapt our literature and composition courses in such a manner that adequate recognition is given to the fact that there are some genuine needs to be met.[11]

Some teachers must have listened because eight years later, Hardy Finch could brag that English teachers kept up with the times, for "Over two hundred schools throughout the United States are now engaged in the production of films." [12]

The heyday of short and feature-length films in English classes came during the revolutionary 1960s and 1970s, when the most popular reading of many English teachers was not the *English Journal* but *Media and Methods*. Under the direction of Anthony Prete and Frank McLaughlin, *M & M* was possibly the most exciting professional magazine in our history. During those glorious days of yore, English teachers prided themselves on knowing and using short and long films.

Many of these same films are still available because they were purchased by university film cooperatives. The following are a few excellent short films that English teachers can profitably use.

"A Chairy Tale," 10 min., black and white. Norman McLaren, the genius of the National Film Board of Canada, made this symbolic and funny film using a technique he invented, pixillation (making cartoon movements with human characters) about the world of a man and his chair.

"Hangman," 12 min., color. Here is an animated version of Maurice Ogden's poem about the divide-and-conquer methods of a totalitarian regime.

"Nahanni," 19 min., color. "Nahanni" tells the true story of Albert Faille and his drive to reach the headwaters of the Nahanni River in Canada and all the gold rumored to be there.

"Neighbors," 10 min., color. McLaren uses his pixillation technique to illustrate how peace so easily becomes war.

"Night and Fog," 31 min., both black and white and color. Alain Resnais's quiet and dramatic film about German concentration camps is a must-see.

"Occurrence at Owl Creek Bridge," 27 min., black and white. Robert Enrico's film of Ambrose Bierce's Civil War story was a Cannes winner.

"Toys," 7 min. color. Kids stare at war toys in a department store, and when the toys come alive, blood flows.

In "A Revolution Reshapes Movies," an article about VCRs in the January 7, 1990, *New York Times,* Vincent Canby wrote:

Nothing that happened in the 1980s compares to the Video Cassette Revolution, sometimes known as the VCR, a term also used to designate the appliance on which cassettes are played. The VCR is turning the business of movies upside down and even affecting the kinds of movies we see. Movies will never be the same.

Doubtless Canby is right, but he missed how the VCR is changing the English classroom in many schools. Teachers can now have at their fingertips most of the great movies of the world to use in conjunction with the original source, a novel or play, or with other materials in a thematic unit. They can easily use comedies like *Singin' in the Rain, Bringing Up Baby,* and *The Court Jester* (Focus Box 9.2) and idea-films such as *Rashomon* and *The Night of the Hunter* (Focus Box 9.3).

With the VCR, teachers can use films in ways not even foreseen in the happy teaching-film world of the 1960s and 1970s. For example, teachers fascinated by what happens to a novel that is dramatized for Broadway and later filmed can now

FOCUS BOX 9.3

Ten Great Serious Films

The Conversation (1974, 113 min., color; Director: Francis Ford Coppola; with Gene Hackman and Allen Garfield) A morality tale about an electronic eavesdropper who, for the first time, gets involved in his work.

The Magnificent Ambersons (1942, 88 min., black and white; Director: Orson Welles; with Joseph Cotten, Agnes Moorehead, and Ray Collins) A family refuses to change as the industrial world comes to their lives.

My Darling Clementine (1946, 97 min., black and white; Director: John Ford with Henry Fonda and Walter Brennan) The classic version of the fight at the O.K. Corral.

Night of the Hunter (1955, 93 min., black and white; Director: Charles Laughton; with Robert Mitchum, Shelley Winters, and Lillian Gish) An allegory about evil and innocence with Mitchum playing a psychotic preacher.

Odd Man Out (1946, 115 min., black and white; Director: Carol Reed; with James Mason and Robert Newton) An IRA leader is shot during a robbery and spends the last day of his life searching for help in Dublin.

Rashomon (1950, 83 min., black and white; Director: Akira Kurosawa; with Toshiro Mifune) Four witnesses tell different versions of a sexual encounter and a death. The classic story about the nature of truth.

Ride the High Country (1962, 94 min., color; Director: Sam Peckinpah; with Joel McCrea and Randolph Scott) Two aging ex-marshals go to the high Sierra gold strike to bring the gold back to a bank.

The 39 Steps (1935, 87 min., black and white; Director: Alfred Hitchcock; with Robert Donat and Madeleine Carroll) Hitchcock's greatest spy-murder thriller.

The Treasure of the Sierra Madre (1948, 124 min., black and white; Director: John Huston with Walter Huston and Humphrey Bogart) Gold prospecting and greed in the Mexican mountains.

Wild Strawberries (1957, 90 min., black and white; Director: Ingmar Bergman with Victor Sjostrom and Ingrid Thulin) An elderly professor sets out to receive an award and relives part of his life.

---

follow those intramedia transformations with their students. One of the most interesting examples is Carson McCullers' *The Member of the Wedding*, published as a short novel in 1946. McCullers dramatized the story, which succeeded on Broadway and can be found in a Dell paperback, *Famous American Plays of the 1940s*. Later it was filmed with Ethel Waters, Julie Harris, and Brandon de Wilde.

One of the more interesting transformations occurred with a short story, "Rashomon," by a Japanese writer, Ryunosuke Akutagawa. Akira Kurosawa, the great Japanese film director, used the story, along with another by Akutagawa, "In the Grove," to make his 1950 film, *Roshomon*. Fourteen years later, Martin Ritt directed his version of Kurosawa's film, locating it in Mexico and starring Paul Newman, Claire Bloom, and Laurence Harvey. The short stories about the nature of truth are quiet and perceptive. Kurosawa's film is one of the world's greatest films, whereas Ritt's movie is usually treated as a joke. Used in conjunction with the stories and Kurosawa's film, Ritt's work may lack majesty, but it is not without interest (and it's almost certainly more immediately accessible to many of our students).

Predictably, objections have been heard to the use of films in English classes. Charlotte Larson's article in the Winter 1992 issue of *Arizona English Bulletin* summarizes her use of *The Great Santini* in a junior high unit on the family. For the several years she used the unit and the film, Larson warned parents about certain language in the film. When a parent objected, the administration followed the path of least resistance and banned the film. For once, however, there was a happy ending. Supported by many of her students and their parents, Larson appealed the decision and won her case, and the film was back in her classroom.

A more predictable end came to other teachers, as reported by Marie Hardenbrook in the same issue of the *Arizona English Bulletin*. History teachers had been using *Glory*, the brilliant film about African-American Civil War soldiers, rated "R" partly for its language and partly for its violence. At a school board meeting in which one board member alleged that some teachers were "visiting their local rental stores Sunday night for Monday morning's lesson plan," teachers and education lost when the board decided to ban all "R"-rated movies from class use.

Readers interested in learning what happens to a novel when it becomes a film would benefit from the classic statement by George Bluestone's *Novels Into Films*. Several articles in the old *Media and Methods* dealt with this topic, as do a few recent articles in the *Horn Book* and the *Top of the News*.[13]

Two books prove invaluable reading for anyone considering the use of films in classes—William V. Costanzo's *Reading the Movies: Twelve Great Films on Video and How to Teach Them* and Kenneth E. Resch and Vicki D. Schicker's *Using Film in the High School Curriculum: A Practical Guide for Teachers and Librarians*. Anyone curious about films, whether in the classroom or on television, owns Leonard Maltin's *Movie and Video Guide*, updated yearly.

There are thousands of books on film—the history of film or the making of film or the directing of film or anything about film—but a handy single volume worth having that briefly covers almost everything concerned with film is Harvey Rachlin's *The TV and Movie Business: An Encyclopedia of Careers, Technologies, and Practices*.

Notes

. . . .

[1]Jacques Barzun, *God's Country and Mine*. (Little, Brown, 1954), p. 159.

[2]Steve Allen, *Funny People* (Stein & Day, 1981), p. 1.

[3]Lance M. Gentile and Merna M. McMillan, "Humor and the Reading Program," *Journal of Reading* 21 (January 1978):343–350.

[4]Ellen Conford, "I Want to Make Them Laugh," *ALAN Review* 14 (Fall 1986):21.

[5]Jan Harold Brunvand, *The Choking Doberman and Other "New" Urban Legends* (Norton, 1984), p. 50.

[6]Roger Sutton, "In the YA Corner: Hard Times at Sweet Valley High," *School Library Journal* 35 (November 1990):50.

[7]Ezra Pound, *ABC of Reading* (1934, New Directions, 1960), p. 68.

[8]C. Hugh Holman and William Harmon, eds., *A Handbook to Literature,* 6th ed., (Macmillan, 1992), pp. 423–424.

[9]Roger Sutton, "A Conversation with Richard Peck," *School Library Journal* 35 (June 1990): 36.

[10]Robert W. Neal, "Making the Devil Useful," *English Journal* 2 (December 1913): 658–660.

[11]Samuel Rosenkranz, "English at the Cinema," *English Journal* 20 (December 1931): 824.

[12]Hardy R. Finch, "Film Production in the School—A Survey," *English Journal* 28 (May 1939): 365.

[13]For example, John Culkin's "Four Voyages of the Caine," *Media and Methods* 3 (October 1966) 222–228; Charles Suhor's "The Film/Literature Comparison," *Media and Methods* 12 (December 1975): 56–59; Fred Marcus's "From Story to Screen," *Media and Methods* 14 (December 1977): 56–58; Janet Seigel's "From Page to Screen: Where the Author Fits In," *Top of the News* 40 (Spring 1984): 277–283; and Terri Payne Butler's "Books to Films," *Horn Book Magazine* 71 (May/June 1995): 305–313.

Titles Mentioned in the Text of Chapter Nine

Aaron, Henry, and Lonnie Wheeler. *I Had a Hammer.* HarperCollins, 1991.

Allen, Maury. *Baseball's 100: A Personal Ranking of the Best Players in Baseball History.* A & W, 1981.

Allen, Woody. *Getting Even.* Random House, 1971.

Allen, Woody. *Side Effects.* Random House, 1980.

Allen, Woody. *Without Feathers.* Random House, 1975.

Ashe, Arthur, and Arnold Rampersad. *Days of Grace: A Memoir.* Knopf, 1993.

Asimov, Isaac, et al., eds. *Young Monsters.* HarperCollins, 1985.

Aymar, Brandt, ed. *Men in Sports: Great Sport Stories of all Times, from the Greek Olympic Games to the American World Series.* Crown, 1994.

Bauer, Joan. *Squashed.* Delacorte, 1992.

Bauer, Joan. *Thwonk.* Delacorte, 1995.

Beard, Henry. *Poetry for Cats: The Definitive Anthology of Distinguished Feline Verse.* Villard, 1994.

Berkow, Ira, ed. *Hank Greenberg: The Story of My Life.* Times Books, 1989.

Bluestone, George. *Novels Into Film.* University of California Press, 1957.

Brashler, William. *The Story of Negro League Baseball.* Ticknor & Fields, 1994.

Brunvand, Jan Harold. *The Choking Doberman: And Other "New" Urban Legends.* Norton, 1984.

Brunvand, Jan Harold. *The Vanishing Hitchhiker: American Urban Legends and Their Meanings.* Norton, 1981.

Campbell, Nelson, ed. *Grass Roots and Schoolyards: A High School Basketball Anthology.* Stephen Greene Press, 1988.

Costanzo, William V. *Reading the Movies: Twelve Great Films on Video and How to Teach Them.* NCTE, 1992.

Crutcher, Chris. *Athletic Shorts.* Greenwillow, 1991.

Crutcher, Chris. *The Crazy Horse Electric Game.* Greenwillow, 1987.

Crutcher, Chris. *Ironman.* Greenwillow, 1995.

Crutcher, Chris. *Running Loose.* Greenwillow, 1983.

Crutcher, Chris. *Stotan!.* Greenwillow, 1986.

Dawidoff, Nicholas. *The Catcher Was a Spy: The Mysterious Life of Moe Berg.* Pantheon, 1994.

Durso, Joseph. *Dimaggio: The Last American Knight.* Little, Brown, 1995.

Dygard, Thomas J. *Backfield Package.* Morrow, 1992.

Dygard, Thomas J. *Game Plan.* Morrow, 1993.

Dygard, Thomas J. *Infield Hit.* Morrow, 1995.

Dygard, Thomas J. *Quarterback Walk-On.* Morrow, 1982.

Dygard, Thomas J. *Tournament Upstart.* Morrow, 1984.

Falk, R. P., ed., *American Literature in Parody.* Twayne, 1955. Published in paperback as *The Antic Muse: American Writers in Parody.*

Frey, Darcy. *The Last Shot: City Streets, Basketball Dreams.* Houghton Mifflin, 1994.

Graham, Harry. *Ruthless Rhymes for Heartless Homes.* R. H. Russell, 1902.

Grey, Zane. *The Shortstop.* 1909

Grey, Zane. *The Young Pitcher.* 1911.

Harris, Mark. *Bang the Drum Slowly.* Knopf, 1956.

Hein, Piet. *Grooks.* Doubleday, 1969.

Kaplow, Robert. *Alex Icicle: A Romance in Ten Torrid Chapters.* Houghton Mifflin, 1984.

Kerr, M. E. *Dinky Hocker Shoots Smack.* HarperCollins, 1972.

Kerr, M. E. *If I Love You, Am I Trapped Forever?* HarperCollins, 1973.

Kinsella, W. P. *Shoeless Joe.* Houghlin Mifflin, 1982.

Koertge, Ron. *The Arizona Kid.* Little, Brown, 1988.

Lipsyte, Robert. *The Brave,* HarperCollins, 1991.

Lipsyte, Robert. *The Chief.* HarperCollins, 1993.

Lipsyte, Robert. *The Contender.* Harper and Row, 1967.

Lipsyte, Robert. *Free to Be Muhammed Ali.* HarperCollins, 1979.

Lowry, Phillip J. *Green Cathedrals.* Addison Wesley, 1992.

Malamud, Bernard. *The Natural.* Harcourt Brace, 1952.

Maltin, Leonard. *Movie and TV Guide.* Signet, yearly.

Marquis, Don. *archy and mehitabel.* Doubleday, 1927.

Merrill, Jean. *The Pushcart War.* W. R. Scott, 1964.

Morgan, Joe, and David Falkner. *Joe Morgan: A Life in Baseball.* Norton, 1993.

Myers, Walter Dean. *Hoops.* Delacorte, 1981.

Myers, Walter Dean. *The Outside Shot.* Delacorte, 1984.

Paulsen, Gary. *Harris and Me: A Summer Remembered.* Harcourt Brace, 1993.

Peck, Richard. *Secrets of the Shopping Mall.* Delacorte, 1979.

Rachlin, Harvey. *The TV and Movie Business: An Encyclopedia of Careers, Technologies, and Practices.* Harmony, 1991.

Resch, Kenneth E., and Vicki D. Schicker. *Using Film in the High School Curriculum: A Practical Guide for Teachers and Librarians.* McFarland, 1992.

Ribowsky, Mark. *Don't Look Back: Satchel Paige in the Shadows of Baseball.* Simon & Schuster, 1994.

Rivers, Glenn, and Bruce Brooks. *Those Who Love the Game: Glenn "Doc" Rivers on Life in the NBA and Elsewhere.* Holt, 1993

Schwartz, Alvin, collector. *And the Green Grass Grew All Around: Folk Poetry from Everyone.* HarperCollins, 1992.

Schwartz, Alvin, *Scary Stories 3: More Tales to Chill Your Bones*. HarperCollins, 1991.

Scoppettone, Sandra. *Trying Hard to Hear You*. Harper-Collins, 1974.

Seuss, Dr. (pen name of Theodor Seuss Geisel). *The Cat in the Hat*. Random House, 1957.

Seuss, Dr. (Theodor Seuss Geisel). *Horton Hatches the Egg*. Random House, 1940.

Seuss, Dr. (Theodor Seuss Geisel). *How the Grinch Stole Christmas*. Random House, 1957.

Silverstein, Shel. *A Light in the Attic*. Harper & Row, 1981.

Sleator, William. *Oddballs*. Dutton, 1993.

Spiegl, Fritz, ed. *A Small Book of Grave Humor*. Arco, 1973.

Spinelli, Jerry. *Space Station Seventh Grade*. Little, Brown, 1982.

Spinelli, Jerry. *Who Put That Hair in My Toothbrush?* Little, Brown, 1984.

Sullivan, Neil J. *The Minors: The Struggles and the Triumphs of Baseball's Poor Relations from 1876 to the Present*. St. Martins, 1990.

Thurber, James. *Fables for Our Time*. Harper & Brothers, 1940.

Townsend, Sue. *The Growing Pains of Adrian Mole*. Grove Press, 1986, first published in England in 1982.

Townsend, Sue. *The Secret Diary of Adrian Mole, Aged 13 3/4*. Grove Press, 1986, first published in England in 1982.

Tunis, John R. *Go Team Go*. Morrow, 1954.

Tunis, John R. *Highpockets*. Morrow, 1948.

Tunis, John R. *Keystone Kids*. Morrow, 1948.

Tunis, John R. *The Kid Comes Back*. Morrow, 1946.

Tunis, John R. *Rookie of the Year*. Morrow, 1944.

Ward, Geoffrey C., and Ken Burns. *Baseball: An Illustrated History*. Knopf, 1994.

Watterson, Bill. *The Calvin and Hobbes Tenth Anniversary Book*. Andrews & McMeel, 1995.

Weaver, Will. *Farm Team*. HarperCollins, 1995.

Weaver, Will. *Striking Out*. HarperCollins, 1993.

White, E. B. *The Second Tree from the Corner*. Harper-Collins, 1954.

Wodehouse, P. G. *Carry On, Jeeves*. 1925; Penguin, 1975.

Wodehouse, P. G. *The Inimitable Jeeves*. 1931; Penguin, 1975.

Wodehouse, P. G. *Jeeves and the Feudal Spirit*. 1954; Penguin, 1975.

Wodehouse, P. G. *The Mating Season*. 1949; Harper-Collins, 1983.

Wodehouse, P. G. *Meet Mr. Mulliner*. 1927; Penguin, 1981.

Wodehouse, P. G. *Much Obliged, Jeeves*. 1971; Penguin, 1982.

Wodehouse, P. G. *Stiff Upper Lip*. 1963; Harper-Collins, 1983.

Wodehouse, P. G. *Very Good, Jeeves*. 1930; Penguin, 1975.

Wodehouse, P. G. *Young Man in Spats*. 1922; Penguin, 1981.

For information on the availability of paperback editions of these titles, please consult the most recent edition of *Paperbound Books in Print,* published annually by R. R. Bowker Company.

Part Three

Adults and the Literature of Young Adults

Chapter 10

Evaluating, Promoting, and Using Young Adult Books

· ·

Chances are that you are studying adolescent literature because you expect to work, or are already working, in a situation that calls for you to bring young adults in touch with books. This chapter begins with a section on evaluation, including the evaluation of literature for and about minorities, followed by discussions centered around common professional roles for adults who work with books and young readers: librarians, reading teachers, social studies teachers, parents, and counselors or youth workers. (See Chapter Eleven for specific information for English teachers.) These areas were chosen to give focus and organization to the information, but there is considerable overlap.

Everyone working with young readers and books needs to be skilled in suggesting the right book for the right student or at least pointing someone in the right direction. When two people are talking about a book they both enjoyed, there is no way to divide the conversation into such discrete categories as literary analysis, personal feelings, sociological implications, and evaluation of potential popularity. Librarians find themselves discussing books as if they were classroom teachers. Teachers can adopt some of the promotional techniques that librarians use, and librarians can use some book discussion tactics that teachers use. In short, the organization of this chapter may make it appear that librarians work with young readers and books quite differently from teachers or counselors. In reality, nearly all adults who work with young readers and books have much the same goals and share many of the same approaches.

All of us meet wide-ranging differences in abilities and personalities, which implies great differences in interests. Those interests demand an alert and prepared adult who is aware of them, who can uncover them, and who is familiar with an enormous number of titles to meet them. To an inexperienced person, the information about books that a librarian or teacher can call forth seems magical, but developing that repertoire takes time, patience, and hard work. Reading many young adult books comes with the territory for the professional, but so does reading professional books, magazines of all sorts, several newspapers, adult books, and much, much more. The professional likes to read (or would not be working with books), so that makes the job easier and more fun, but the professional reads beyond the areas that are personally enjoyable. For example, whether a professional likes science fiction or not, he or she must know titles of new science fiction. When young adults ask a teacher or librarian for another book like *The Martian Chronicles* (or *Forever* or *The Hitchhiker's Guide to the Galaxy* or *Crossings* or *The Color Purple*), they pay that person a sublime compliment. Woe unto the teacher or librarian who says, "I'm sorry, but I don't know anything about science fiction," or "Why don't you broaden your reading background just a bit?" Such a response kills interest and will probably turn kids away from reading.

In any given group, a teacher or librarian might find students like the following (and gradations in-between): Rachel reads nothing at all (she did once, but now that she has become a woman she has put away childish things); Brenda reads nothing because her reading skills are so poor she is virtually illiterate; Candy read a book once, her first book all the way through, and she hated it; Del reads magazines and an occasional sports biography if he's in an intellectual mood; Emily reads Sweet Valley High romances; José reads all kinds of books as long as they're science fiction; George reads a few books but always classics ("He's going to college," his mother says proudly); Howie reads only religious books and has already warned the teacher about the Satanic powers in *Lord of the Flies*; Imogene reads anything that is popular—Harold Robbins, Ann Rice, best-sellers, and novelizations of movies and television specials; Jon reads classics, football stories, mysteries, and everything else and refuses to be pigeonholed; and Lynn reads all the time, perhaps too much (she's bright but socially immature). Serving the needs of such a diverse group is far from easy, but when the job is well done, it's a valuable contribution.

Evaluating Young Adult Literature

The role of the evaluator of books for young adults is more important than ever because more books are being published and publishers are opting for shorter life spans for all books. With so many ephemeral books around, there's a greater need for knowledgeable people to find and promote the excellent ones. It is ironic that when there are more books to choose from, most schools and libraries have less money to spend. Also, book prices have increased more than budgets, so that if a purchasing mistake is made, especially with a series or a set of books, a proportionately larger bite is taken out of school, library, and personal budgets.

Writing About Books

If you devote your professional life to working with young people and books, chances are that at some level you will be involved in evaluating books and helping to decide which ones will receive prizes and get starred reviews and which ones should be ignored or receive "Not Recommended" labels. Teachers and librarians working with books for young people have more opportunity to be among the decision makers than do those working with books for adults because fewer than two

ROBIN MCKINLEY
On The School Assignment Letter

I love—how could I not?—getting letters from people who have so much enjoyed or been moved by my books that they go to the trouble of writing me a letter about it. I like knowing my books are read, and I am interested in knowing *how* they are read; and while the great majority of the mail I receive is positive, the only dispraise I ignore is the sort based on the reader's annoyance that I've written some other book than the one he or she wanted. I have learned useful things about what I've gotten both right and wrong by letter-writers who tell me about the books I did write. With the exception of the very, very rare crazy or abusive letter, I answer all this book mail.

I also personally answer about 80 percent of the school assignment letters I receive. I answer them for the kids' sake. I'm sure I guess wrong sometimes about students' motives and understanding. I can't tell which letter-writers already have a pretty clear idea about the ramifications of the hierarchies they live in, with grown-ups at the top and young people at the bottom; I can't always see when a complimentary letter is insincere, composed because that's what goes down with adults. But my judgment is a bit clouded by the fact that letters which begin with any of the variations on "I am writing to you for a school assignment" instantly make my blood pressure rise; and the ones that end with "I get extra credit if you answer this" send me into orbit.

The School Assignment Letter dilemma is on my mind more than usual because of a recent round of correspondence with a librarian who took exception to the standard letter I send to the other 20 percent of school-assignment-letter-writers, which ends, having begun by saying that I like hearing from readers who have enjoyed my books, "I object to being made into a school assignment. . . . My *books* are what I'm offering to my audience, not my *self*. I'm not a homework project. I Am A HUMAN BEING. I have my own life, and more demands on my time than I can meet successfully *before* this week's book mail arrives." She wrote back that I "didn't care about anyone else's feelings," that she would never purchase another of my books for any of the libraries under her supervision ("even if you win the Newbery again"), and that she was planning on burning the ones already on her shelves. I answered that letter, too, making the same points I hope I am making in this essay, and sent copies to administrators at the school the students had written from. No one replied.

I am at a loss to understand how authors have been so dehumanized in so many teachers' and librarians' minds that blind school assignment letters to an author can appear to be a good idea. Every popular or award-winning children's book writer I've ever spoken to gets school-assignment letters. Some authors mind less than I do. Some mind more. My "I am not a homework project" letter—although it has evolved over the years—has gone out hundreds of times, and the aforementioned is the first response to it I've ever received—and it certainly wasn't to thank me for successfully communicating my point of view.

(continued)

It is not only the involuntariness of my involvement in these school assignments that is so inexplicable. How can a teacher declare that a student will receive extra credit if the author responds? The author is not under the teacher's authority. If this is not moral blackmail, what is it? Nor are circumstances under the teacher's control. What if the student wrote the most charming, perceptive letter anyone has ever written and the author has an earache and is too wretched to answer any letters? What if the letter is eaten by the Great Postal Dragon, and the author never sees it? Nor is the cost to the recipient of school-assignment letters limited to the spiritual. Perhaps ten percent of the students who write include return postage; my yearly expenditure on stamps for book mail comes to a splashy weekend holiday for my husband and me that we don't get—or, perhaps more to the point, about one-quarter of the new furnace and fittings our elderly, cold house urgently needs. Surely the myth that writers are all wealthy is not still current? Those of us who earn enough of a living to give up our day jobs are in the minority; school budgets for enrichment programs are not leaner than most writers' royalty checks. And the energy I use to answer letters is the same creative energy that I need to write my books: coherent sentence production is coherent sentence production, and I've only got a few good hours of it a day, and after that I'm an excellent washer of dishes and walker of dogs. Let me stress that the *voluntary* book mail I receive—and this includes the letters that say "I was thinking about writing to you and my teacher/librarian/parent/older-person-with-authority encouraged me"—is worth it. Absolutely. I don't in the least begrudge the price of the personal enrichment program of acknowledging the letters from readers who *want* to write to me. I am a storyteller, and the *teller* only functions if she has an audience.

What is most discouraging about the book-burning librarian's letter is that she insists on missing the crux of what both my letters to her school district were trying to convey, about the ordinary humanity of authors, and the parameters of their profession. You don't expect your car mechanic to fix your bicycle, gratis, in his spare time. Lucky you if he (or she) is willing to, but you are unlikely to boycott his gas station and write him hate mail if he isn't. And I bet at the very least you ask first and say thank-you afterward. For the several thousand school-assignment letters I have answered in the last fifteen-plus years, I can remember once that I was asked in advance and twice that I was later thanked for having responded.

Robin McKinley's books include *Beauty: A Retelling of the Story of Beauty and the Beast,* HarperCollins, 1978; *The Hero and the Crown,* Greenwillow, 1985; *The Outlaws of Sherwood,* Greenwillow, 1988; and *Deerskin,* Putnam, 1993.

dozen people in the United States are full-time reviewers of juvenile books. The bulk of the reviewing is done by teachers and librarians who evaluate books both as part of their assigned workloads and as a professionally related hobby. Whether or not you wish to be one of these reviewers, you need to know what is involved, so that you will understand how the work of these people can help you in selecting the books that are best for your purposes. The sheer number of books published each year makes it necessary that book lovers share the reading responsibilities and pool their information through written evaluations.

Evaluation underlies nearly all writing about books. Even when someone is simply making notes to serve as a reminder of the contents of a book, that person is making an evaluation and concluding that the book is worth remembering. Three concerns run throughout the evaluation of young adult literature:

1. What different types of writing meet specific needs, and how can they do it best?
2. Should reviews of young adult books be less promotional and more critical?
3. Is the writing and scholarship in the field aimed too much at the uses of literature rather than at the analysis of the literature itself?

Keeping a Record of Your Reading

The type of writing most often done by teachers and librarians is the making of note cards or, in this day of word processors, typing paragraph-length descriptions filed according to whatever organization is most helpful to the writer. This might be alphabetical or by subject matter, age level, or genre. The advantage to the computerized annotations is that they can be pulled out and reorganized for many different purposes, including booktalking, creating a display, or making a bibliography tailored to a teacher's request for books on the Holocaust, for example, or books about Native Americans. Regularly going over your write-ups jogs your memory about the books you have read and can personally recommend, and when a title or author slips your mind, you can probably find what you need by doing word searches through your write-ups.

Comments vary according to the needs of the writer, but should include at least the following:

Author's name and complete book title.
Publisher (both hardback and paperback) with original publication date.
A short summary of the story, including the characters' names and other details that make this book different.
A brief evaluation and any ideas about how you might make special use of the book.

Librarians sometimes write their descriptions in the form of a booktalk identifying a page they could read aloud, while reading teachers note the level of reading difficulty, and English teachers may mention how the book might illustrate a particular literary principle. A youth worker might make a note about the potential of the book as a catalyst to get kids talking along certain lines, whereas a teacher who anticipates that the book could be controversial is wise to note positive reviews and honors.

Writing Annotations

Annotations are similar to note cards, but they are usually written for someone else to see rather than for the writer's own use. Because they are usually part of an annotated bibliography or list in which space is at a premium, writers must make efficient use of every word. Communicating the plot and tone of a book as well as a recommendation in only one or two interesting sentences is challenging, but no one wants to read lists of characters and plot summaries all starting with "This book. . . ." That annotations can be intriguing as well as communicative is shown by the following two samples for Virginia Hamilton's *Sweet Whispers, Brother Rush*. To save space, the bibliographical information given on the lists is not reprinted here.

> Poetic, many-layered novel of 14-year-old Teresa's devotion to her retarded and doomed brother Dab. A strong story of hope and power of love.
> *School Library Journal*, December, 1982

> Fourteen-year-old Tree learns a lot about her family and the interconnections between their past and present tragedies from Brother Rush, her uncle's ghost.
> *Booklist*, March 15, 1983

Notice how both writers communicated the age of the protagonist, the fact that it was a family story, and, through the use of *doomed* and *tragedies*, that it was a fairly serious book. The writers also hinted at mystery and intrigue, the first one through "Poetic, many-layered . . . hope and the power of love" and the second one through the reference to "Brother Rush, her uncle's ghost."

Writing Reviews

A problem in reviewing juvenile books is that more books are published than can be reviewed in the media. (See Appendix A for major reviewing sources for young adult books.) In addition to these, dozens of national publications carry occasional review articles, and many library systems sponsor reviewing groups whose work is published either locally or through such nationally distributed publications as *Book Waves,* from the Bay Area (northern California) Young Adult Librarians, and *Books for the Teen Age,* from the Young Adult Services Office of the New York Public Library. Also, some teachers of children's and young adult literature work with their students to write regular review columns for local newspapers.

The field of juvenile reviewing is sometimes criticized for being too laudatory because the reviews are written by book lovers who are anxious to "sell" literature. One reason is that it's the publishers of well-established authors who can afford to send out review copies. Also, those editors who have room for only a limited number of reviews devote their space to the books they think are the best, so of course the reviews are positive.

The fact that juvenile books are reviewed mostly by librarians and teachers working on a part-time basis slows down the reviewing process, especially if they take time to incorporate the opinions of young readers. With adult books, reviews often come out before or simultaneously with the publication of the book, but with juvenile titles it is not uncommon to see reviews appearing a full year or more after the book was released. Once young adult books are launched, however, they are likely to stay afloat much longer than adult bestsellers because teachers work them into classroom units, librarians promote them, and paperback book clubs keep selling them for years. Children continue to grow older and to advance in their reading skill and taste, so that every year a whole new set of students is ready to read *A Separate Peace, The Catcher in the Rye,* and *The Outsiders.* As a result, reviews, articles, and papers continue to cover particular titles years after their original publication dates.

People generally evaluate books based on literary quality, reader interest, potential popularity, or what the book is teaching (i.e., its social and political philosophy). Evaluators should make clear their primary emphasis lest readers misunderstand them. For example, a critic may review a book positively because of its literary quality, but a reader will interpret the positive review as a prediction of popularity. The book is purchased and put on the shelf, where it is ignored by teenagers. Consequently the purchaser feels cheated and loses confidence in the reviewing source.

In an attempt to resolve that kind of conflict, when Mary K. Chelton and Dorothy M. Broderick founded *VOYA (Voice of Youth Advocates),* they devised the evaluation code shown in Table 10.1. Each review is preceded by a *Q* number, indicating *quality,* and a *P* number, indicating *popularity.* They suggest that a fringe benefit to using such a clearly outlined code is that it helps librarians analyze their buying patterns. Those who lean heavily toward either quality or popularity see their biases and are able to strike a more appropriate balance.

A quite different set of criteria from either popularity or literary quality is that of social or political values. Most reviewers—whether or not they realize it—are influenced by their personal feelings toward how a book treats social issues. For example, Sue Ellen Bridgers's *Notes for Another Life* was highly recommended and praised in *Horn Book Magazine,* the *New York Times Book Review,* and the *Bulletin of the Center for Children's Books,* but when Janet French reviewed the book for *School Library Journal* she wrote:

> The blurb suggests that this is "a family chronicle for all ages." It would have been more accurate to describe it as a propaganda vehicle for female domesticity. Good women subordinate their talents and yearnings to the home and

TABLE 10.1

VOYA EVALUATION CODE

Quality	Popularity
5Q: Hard to imagine it being better written	5P: Every young adult was dying to read it yesterday
4Q: Better than most, marred only by occasional lapses	4P: Broad general young adult interest
3Q: Readable without serious defects	3P: Will appeal without pushing
2Q: A little better editing or work by the author would have made it 3Q	2P: For the young adult reader with a special interest in the subject
1Q: Hard to understand how it got published	1P: No young adult will read unless forced to for assignments

their children; all other paths lead to havoc. For a riveting story of four deserted children, lead readers instead to Cynthia Voigt's marvelous upbeat *Homecoming.*[1]

This review was written in such a way that readers can easily recognize that the reviewer's opinion was shaped by her disagreement with the plot. For a reviewer to use this as the basis for a negative recommendation is perfectly justifiable *if* the situation is made clear. The problem comes when reviewers reject books based on such social issues but don't admit to themselves, much less to their readers, that their feelings have been influenced by whether a story sharpens or dulls whatever personal ax they happen to be grinding.

There are as many reviewing styles as there are journals and individual reviewers. Nearly all reviews contain complete bibliographical information, including number of pages and prices, perhaps a cataloguing number, the intended age level, a summary statement of the contents, and some hint of the quality of the book as evaluated by the reviewer. A few years ago, an issue of *Top of the News* (the ALA publication now called *Journal of Youth Services in Libraries*) had as its feature topic "Reviews, Reviewing, and the Review Media." Editor Audrey Eaglen solicited answers to the question, "What makes a good review?"[2] Here are excerpts from some of the responses:

> An intelligent review . . . is never obsequious, if it is favorable. It is never flip, if it is unfavorable. It never quotes from the front flap.
>
> Rosemary Wells, author

> Are there any clever devices or intriguing aspects of the book which could be used to pique the interest of a group and "sell" the book? Also I need to be alerted to potentially controversial issues, be it strong language, explicit sex, violence, or whatever, not so I can avoid buying the book, but so I can plan and prepare and thereby deal with a conflict should it arise.
>
> Katherine Haylman, school librarian

> How attractive is the cover? While we might feel that no one should judge a book by its cover, the truth is that everyone does.
>
> Dorothy Broderick, editor and educator

> I want a clear-cut commitment as to recommendation or nonrecommendation. I don't have the time to read every book published, and I'm hoping that some literate person will help me decide where to invest my reading hours.
>
> Walter Dean Myers, author

> Does the book have magic for YA's? Are there format faults, for example, does the size and shape make it look like a baby book? Is the word *children* used anywhere on the dust jacket? And if there is going to be a film or television tie-in, who are the stars and when will it be released?
>
> Patty Campbell, author and critic

Writing reviews is a skill that improves with practice and effort. A good way to begin developing this skill is to study several reviews of the same book as they appear in different publications. Note the essentials that seem to be the same in each review and then compare the information that is different. See if you can explain the differences in light of the source's reading audience.

For the person reading reviews, one of the biggest problems is that they all run together and begin to sound the same. To keep this from happening, reviewers need to approach their task with the same creative spirit with which authors write books. They need to think of new ways of putting across the point that a book is highly recommended or that it has some unique quality that readers should watch for, as in these two excerpts of reviews that were written by authors reviewing books written by other authors. Granted, authors probably have had more practice in working with words, and therefore their skill is greater than that of most reviewers, but they probably also try harder because they know how important it is to do something to make a review stand out, to give the reader something by which to remember the book.

The first excerpt is taken from a review of Alice Childress' *Rainbow Jordan*, written by Anne Tyler for the *New York Times Book Review:*

> Rainbow is so appealing that she could carry this book on her own, but she doesn't have to. There's Miss Josie, who gives us her clearer view to balance what Rainbow tells us. . . . And there's the mother herself—short-tempered, inconsistent, sometimes physically abusive, not much of a mother at all, really. Seen through Rainbow's adoring eyes, she's at least someone we can understand ("Life is complicated," Rainbow says, "I love her even now while I'm putting her down.") In fact, Rainbow's story moves us not because of her random beatings or financial hardships, but because Rainbow needs her mother so desperately that she will endlessly rationalize, condone, overlook, forgive. She is a heartbreakingly sturdy character, and *Rainbow Jordan* is a beautiful book.[3]

Katherine Paterson made these comments about Virginia Hamilton's *Sweet Whispers, Brother Rush* as part of an article she wrote for the *New York Times Book Review:*

> There are those who say that Virginia Hamilton is a great writer but that her books are hard to get into. This one is not. It fairly reaches off the first page to grab you, and once it's got you, it sets you spinning deeper into its story. Needless to say, this is not a conventional ghost story. In fact, the function of the ghost in this book is to provide 14-year-old Tree Pratt with a place from which to view her world. . . . In this book everyone we meet, including the ghost, is wonderfully human. . . . The language too is of Miss Hamilton's own special kind, which uses the speech forms of the young to enhance rather than restrict the music of the book.[4]

Writing Scholarly and Pedagogical Articles

A fourth kind of writing about young adult books is made up of articles or papers that go into more depth than is possible in reviews. Because most reviewers of juvenile books have little hope of coming out with a "scoop" or of being the first one to pass judgment on a new book, they focus on deeper treatments or on tying several books together. Dorothy Matthews analyzed the writing about adolescent literature that appeared in professional journals over a five-year period.[5] She categorized the writing into three types. First were those articles that focus on the subjective responses of readers to particular books, such as reader surveys, lists of popular titles, and reviews written from the point of view of how the book is likely to affect young readers. Articles of this kind are primarily descriptive.

The second type was also descriptive and consisted of pedagogical articles giving teachers lists of books that fit together for teaching units; ideas for book promotion; and techniques for teaching reading, social studies, or English. They may include brief comments on the literary qualities of the novels, but, again, the writer's primary intention is to be informative.

The third kind of writing was that restricted to the books themselves. It is in this group that Matthews thinks hope lies for developing a body of lasting scholarly knowledge that will be taken seriously by the academic community. These papers include discussions of adolescent literature as a genre, historical background of the field, relationships between authors and their work, patterns that appear in young adult novels, and themes and underlying issues. More of this kind of literary analysis is being done as authors write books serious enough to support it. Examples of some of these articles are included in Appendix B, "Some Outstanding Books and Articles About Young Adult Literature."

Twayne Publishers paved the way for some serious extended criticism of young adult literature when they inaugurated a Young Adult Authors subset in their United States Authors series. More than a dozen books have been completed under such titles as *Presenting Judy Blume, Presenting Sue Ellen Bridgers, Presenting Robert Cormier,* and so on. Rosa Guy, S. E. Hinton, M. E. Kerr, Norma Klein, Norma Fox Mazer, Walter Dean Myers, Zibby Oneal, Richard Peck, William Sleator, and Paul Zindel are among the authors so far written about. The same company has also begun to examine specific genres, with the first title being *Presenting Young Adult Horror Fiction* by Cosette Kies.

Also, a look into a recent edition of *Dissertation Abstracts International* shows an increasing number of dissertations being written on young adult literature. The majority of topics, however, deal more with social or pedagogical issues than with literary ones.

Writing about young adult books falls into four categories: descriptions for personal use, annotations, reviews, and scholarly or pedagogical writing. Most of you will be involved in the first kind, that is, making note cards for your own use. But some of you will also be making annotations, writing reviews, and doing scholarly or pedagogical analyses. This latter kind of writing and critiquing can be especially intriguing because significant changes have occurred within recent years and relatively few scholars have worked with young adult literature. This means there is ample opportunity for original research and observation, whether from the viewpoint of a literary scholar, a teacher, a librarian, or a counselor or youth worker. The field as a whole will grow strong as a result of serious and competent criticism and analysis.

Deciding on the Literary Canon

Educators are finding themselves in the midst of a lively debate over what books should be taught in U.S. classrooms. An oversimplification of the issue is to say that on one side are those who believe in acculturation or assimilation. They think that if we all read approximately the same books, we will come away with similar values and attitudes and hence be a more united society. On the other side are those who believe in diversity and want individuals and groups to find their own values, attitudes, and ways of life reflected in the literature they read. This latter group views the traditional literary canon as racist and sexist, with its promotion in schools serving to keep minorities and women "in their place."

Katha Pollitt, contributing editor of *The Nation,* made some interesting observations when she wrote that, "In a country of real readers a debate like the current one over the canon would not be taking place." She described an imaginary country where children grow up watching their parents read and going with them to well-supported public libraries where they all borrow books and read and read and read. At the heart of every school is an attractive and well-used library, and in classrooms children have lively discussions about books they have read together, but they also read lots of books on their own, so that years later they don't remember whether "they read *Jane Eyre* at home and Judy Blume in class, or the other way around."[6]

Pollitt wrote that in her imaginary country of "real readers—voluntary, active, self-determined readers," a discussion of which books should be studied in school would be nothing more than a parlor game. It might even add to the aura of writers not to be included on school-assigned reading lists because this would mean that their books were "in one way or another too heady, too daring, too exciting to be ground up into institutional fodder for teenagers." The alternative would be millions of readers freely choosing millions of books, each book becoming just a tiny part of a lifetime of reading. Pollitt concluded her piece with the sad statement that at the root of the current debate over the canon is the assumption that the only books that will be read are those that are assigned in school: "Becoming a textbook is a book's only chance: all sides take that for granted." She wonders why those educated scholars and critics who are currently debating this issue and must be readers themselves have conspired to keep secret two facts that they surely must know:

> . . . if you read only twenty-five, or fifty, or a hundred books, you can't understand them, however well chosen they are. And . . . if you don't have an independent reading life—and very few students do—you won't *like* reading the books on the list and will forget them the minute you finish them.[6]

Pollitt's argument puts even more of a burden on those of us who have as our professional responsibility the development of lifelong readers. We are the ones who should be raising our voices to explain the limitations of expecting children to read just what is assigned in class. We are also the ones with the responsibility of helping students develop into the kinds of committed and enthusiastic readers that Pollitt described in her imaginary country.

In the meantime, we also have an obligation to become knowledgeable about the issues that underlie the current debate over the literary canon and to assist schools and libraries in making informed choices with the resources they have. We, as authors of this textbook, have already committed ourselves to the idea of an expanded canon. Some of the harshest critics of adolescent literature are those in favor of promoting only the traditional canon; others tolerate adolescent literature only because they view it as a means to the desired end of leading students to appreciate "real" literature.

At the 1991 National Council of Teachers of English convention in Seattle, Washington, Rudolfo Anaya, author of *Bless Me, Ultima* and a professor of creative writing at the University of New Mexico, predicted that the biggest literary change that will occur in the 1990s will be the incorporation of minority literature into the mainstream. He did not mean just the inclusion on booklists of the names of authors who are members of minority groups, but also the incorporation of new styles and ideas into the writing of nonminority authors.

Anaya explained that Mexican-Americans have a different world view. When he was in college, he loved literature and read the standard literary canon with enthusiasm and respect, but when he went to write his own stories he couldn't use Hemingway or Milton as models. He could create plots like theirs, but then he was at a standstill because nowhere in the literary canon did he find people like the ones he knew. His Spanish-speaking family has lived in eastern New Mexico for more than 100 years. The harsh but strangely beautiful landscape and the spirit of the Pecos River had permeated his life, as had stories of *La Grande,* the wise old woman who had safely pulled him from his mother's body even though the umbilical cord was wrapped around his neck. There were also stories of *La Llorona,* a woman who had gone insane and murdered her children and whose tortured cries traveled on the wind around the corners of his childhood home. All his life, such dramatic dreams and stories were woven in and out of reality, but nowhere in the literature that he studied in school did he find such stories.

Anaya worked on *Bless Me, Ultima* for seven years, during which he felt he was "writing in a vacuum. I had no Chicano models to read and follow, no fellow writers to turn to for help. Even Faulkner, with his penchant for the fantastic world of the South, could not help me in Mexican/Indian New Mexico. I would have to build from what I knew best." He went on to explain:

> I began to discover that the lyric talent I possessed, as the poet I once aspired to be, could be used in writing fiction. The oral tradition which so enriched my imagination as a child could lend its rhythm to my narrative. Plot techniques learned in Saturday afternoon movies and comic books could help as

much as the grand design of the classics I had read. Everything was valuable, nothing was lost.[8]

Anaya's observations about not having models to follow and being forced to create a new narrative style to tell a story coming from his own experience relates to the frustration that teachers and librarians often express when they go to look for young adult novels about minority characters. They look for the same kinds of coming-of-age stories that are typical in mainstream young adult literature except they want the characters to have brown skin and "different" names. The absence of such books, especially such books written by Native American authors, is in itself part of the cultural difference. We've noticed that the more closely a book with a Native American protagonist resembles what we described in Chapter One as a typical young adult book, the greater the chance that the author is not a Native American and that the protagonist is of mixed parentage or is living apart from the native culture.

Young adult books containing mystical elements tied in with Native American themes are an interesting example of how Anaya's prediction that ethnic writing will become incorporated into the mainstream is already coming true. Not everyone, however, will be pleased to see this kind of incorporation because they will view the books as contaminated or impure. The authors have used old legends and beliefs for their own purposes, interweaving them with contemporary situations and ideas. Also, several of the authors are not Native Americans.

Being in the blood line of a particular group, however, does not guarantee acceptance by the group. For example, most high school teachers think they are contributing to an awareness of cultural diversity and the enlargement of the literary canon by leading students to read Maxine Hong Kingston's *Woman Warrior.* But noted Chinese writer Frank Chin criticizes Kingston, along with Amy Tan for *The Joy Luck Club* and David Henry Hwang for his plays, *F. O. B.* and *M. Butterfly.* He accuses these writers of "boldly faking" Chinese fairy tales and childhood literature. Then he goes on to ask and answer the question of why the most popular "Chinese" works in the United States are consistent with each other but inconsistent with Chinese culture and beliefs:

> That's easy: (1) all the authors are Christian, (2) the only form of literature written by Chinese Americans that major publishers will publish (other than the cookbook) is autobiography, an exclusively Christian form [based on confession]; and (3) they all write to the specifications of the Christian stereotype of Asia being as opposite morally from the West as it is geographically.[8]

Chin's comments are in an essay, "Come All Ye Asian American Writers," that is used as an introduction to an anthology entitled *The Big Aiiieeeee!,* apparently put together for use in college classes. The 619-page book is too intimidating for most high school students, but they could appreciate many of the individual stories, poems, and essays. The book's title comes from the sound in movies, television, radio, and comic books assigned to "the yellow man" who "when wounded, sad, or angry, or swearing, or wondering" either "whined, shouted, or screamed, 'Aiieeeee!' "

Chin's introductory essay illustrates the complexities involved in the whole matter of ethnic differences. As Chin goes on to state his case, he brings in religion and gender differences as well as differences caused by race, history, social class, and politics. In answer to the kind of criticism he offers, Kingston has explained:

> Sinologists have criticized me for not knowing myths and for distorting them; pirates [those who illegally translate her books for publication in Taiwan and China] correct my myths, revising them to make them conform to some traditional Chinese version. They don't understand that myths have to change, be useful or be forgotten. Like the people who carry them across oceans, the myths become American. The myths I write are new, American. That's why they often appear as cartoons and Kung Fu movies. I take the power I need from whatever myth. Thus Fa Mu Lan has the words cut into her back; in traditional story, it is the man, Ngak Fei the Patriot, whose parents cut vows on his back. I mean to take his power for women. [9]

Knowledge of these opposing viewpoints should not frighten teachers back into the comforts of the established canon; instead, it should help teachers prepare for meeting the challenges involved in going beyond the "tried and true."

Teaching Ethnic Literature

Most educators feel a duty to bring ethnic-based literature to young people in hopes of increasing general understanding (see Focus Boxes 1.3, 1.4, 2.2, and 2.3). Besides that lofty goal, here are some additional reasons for making special efforts to bring ethnic books to young people:

- Young readers can identify with characters who straddle two worlds because they have similar experiences in going between the worlds of adulthood and childhood.
- Motifs that commonly appear in ethnic-based stories—including loneliness, fear of rejection, generational differences, and troubles in fitting into the larger society—are meaningful to teenagers.
- Nearly all teenagers feel that their families are somehow different, and so they can identify with young protagonists from minority families.
- Living in harmony with nature is a common theme, especially in Native American literature, which appeals to today's ecology-minded youth.
- As movies, television programs, mass media books, and magazines inundate teens with stories and photos of people who are "all alike," readers find it refreshing to read about people who are different and in some ways exotic.
- Myths and legends that are often brought into ethnic-based literature satisfy some deep-down psychological and aesthetic needs that are not met with con-

temporary realism or with the romanticism masked as realism that currently makes up the body of fiction provided for young adults.

As pointed out by Alecia Baker and Randee Brown, who talked about several of the above-listed points at a National Council of Teachers of English convention, the role of adults is more important in relation to ethnic than to mainstream literature for young people because ethnic literature needs to be "taught," whereas with many of the books mentioned in other sections of this text it is enough just to make students aware of their existence. Doing this for ethnic books is harder because many are published by small presses, which means they are not advertised in glossy catalogs or reviewed in as many professional journals. If a library subscribes to an ordering service, ethnic books from small presses will probably not be among the ones preselected by the service.

One of the most important concepts that needs to be taught is that there are large differences among people typically identified as a group. When Europeans first came to the American continent, there were more than thirty distinct nations speaking perhaps 1000 different languages. During the past 500 years, these people have had such common experiences as losing their lands, being forced to move to reservations, and having to adapt their beliefs and lifestyles to a technological society. These experiences may have affected their attitudes in similar ways, but still it is a gross overgeneralization to write about Native Americans as if they were one people holding the same religious and cultural views. Although in a single class it would be impossible to study dozens of different Native American tribes, a compromise solution might be to study the history and folklore of those tribes who lived, or are living, in the same geographical area as the students. With this approach, it is important for students to realize that they are looking at only one small part of a bigger group, and that if they studied a different group they would learn equally interesting but different facts.

A similar point could be made about the thoughtlessness of lumping all Asian-Americans together. The Chinese and Japanese, the two groups who have been in the United States the longest, come from countries with a long history of hostility toward each other. A refugee from Vietnam or Cambodia has very little in common with someone whose ancestors came to California in the 1850s. Likewise, Puerto Ricans in New York have quite a different background from southwestern Mexican-Americans. Even in the Southwest, people whose families have lived there from the days before Anglo settlers arrived resent being grouped with people who just came over the border from Mexico.

We need to teach about the histories of groups whose literature is being read to help readers understand the bitterness that finds its way into some ethnic literature. Readers who get impatient with Hispanic authors for including words and phrases in Spanish will probably be a little more tolerant if they realize that today's generation of Mexican-American authors went to school in the days before bilingual education. In their childhoods, many of them heard nothing but Spanish and were amazed to arrive at English-speaking schools where they would be punished for speaking the only language they had ever known.

While Rudolfo Anaya broke new literary ground with his *Bless Me, Ultima,* many other minority writers are breaking new ground by changing the format of stories and translating them from an oral tradition into a written form. Before printing presses, typewriters, word processors, movies, radio, and television, people had more of an incentive to remember and tell the stories that communicated the traditions and values of a society. Even today, oral traditions play an important role, as seen on television talk shows as well as with kids telling stories at slumber parties and summer camp and workers and travelers whiling away long, boring hours. Many minority writers are experimenting in translating oral stories into written and printed formats, which means that some of the first publications to come from particular groups are more likely to be poetry and short stories than novels.

Young adult literature has more well-known books by and about African-Americans than any of the other minority groups. This is partly because English is the native language of most African-Americans and because a generation ago the ice was broken for African-Americans writers by such luminaries as Langston Hughes and Ralph Ellison. Also, the civil rights movement of the 1960s brought to publishers' attention the obvious inequity of such large school districts as Detroit, Chicago, and Harlem using textbooks and other school materials that focus almost exclusively on whites while the majority of the students belong to minority groups. A similar awareness is now developing for Asians, Hispanics, Native Americans, and to a lesser extent immigrants from the Middle East.

We'll conclude this section with a plea for all those working with books and young adults to continue seeking out and promoting the use of minority literature. Educators have shied away from working with minority literature because:

1. They didn't study it when they were in school and so they feel less prepared than when teaching mainstream literature.
2. They fear censorship both because of prejudice against minorities and because of the fact that some minority writers use language considered inappropriate for schoolbooks.
3. Minority literature is harder to find, especially minority literature that has been given a "seal of approval" by the education establishment (i.e., positive reviews and suggestions for teaching).
4. Ethnic identification is such a sensitive topic that teachers fear that when they are discussing a piece of literature either they or their students may say something that will offend some students or hurt their feelings.

Being a professional means that you do not shy away from responsibilities just because they are challenging. Instead, you prepare, so that you can be successful—at least most of the time—in the work you have chosen for your career.

Using Young Adult Literature in the Library

When discussing public libraries, we used to assume that every library has a young adult librarian and a special section serving teenagers. Although this may be the ideal arrangement, there are certainly many libraries where this has never been the practice and many others where shrinking budgets are making young adult librarians an endangered species. A fairly common approach is for libraries to enlarge their children's sections to "Youth Sections" serving readers up to age 15 or 16 while sending everyone else to the adult division. Some of the problems with such an arrangement, cited in a *Voice of Youth Advocates* article ("Whose Job Is It Anyway?"[10]), are the following:

- Teenagers enter a children's section reluctantly, and their size, voices, and active natures intimidate the children who are there.
- The purpose of young adult services is to provide a transition from the children's collection to the resources of the total library, and when a librarian accompanies a teenager looking for something into the larger adult collection there's no one left to serve the children.
- It is difficult for the same person who runs programs for preschoolers, prepares story hours for older children, and reviews hundreds of children's books to switch gears to the fads and multiple interests of teenagers.
- Young adult librarians deal not only with "safe" young adult books, but also with adult materials of interest to young adults. These are often controversial and are likely to prove more problematic to a children's librarian whose training has engendered different perceptions and attitudes.
- Without "sponsorship" by knowledgeable young adult librarians, there may not be enough circulation for serious, high-quality books, which results in a greater reliance on popular taste (e.g., formula romances and series books).

Certainly these worries are valid, and we all need to do what we can to persuade decision makers that young adult librarians serve an important role. If the choice is between having a library open only four days a week and having separate librarians for children and teenagers, however, most library boards vote to keep the library open. This dictates more flexibility and more challenge for the librarian who serves both age groups. Parents who have both teenagers and young children will vouch for the differences between the two, yet they manage somehow. Many librarians will have to do the same. We hope this textbook will help.

Matching Books with Readers

Most people working with books and young readers have come to accept the idea that there is no such thing as one sacred list of books that every student should read. The best that can be hoped for are agreeable matches between particular books and particular students. To bring such matches about, adults need to be acquainted with a wide range of books and with individual students. A commonly used technique in getting to know students is to ask them what books they have previously enjoyed and then to suggest something similar or something by the same author. An alternative is to ask young readers to describe the book they would most like if an author were going to write just for them and then to suggest three or four books that contain elements they have mentioned.

Other people use written forms or reader interest surveys in which students write down their hobbies, the kinds of classes they are taking, what they want to do for a career, what books they have read, and the kinds of stories they most enjoy. The problem with such forms is that they are usually filled out and then stored in a drawer. No one has time to interpret them. One of our students who is a junior high librarian, however, designed a reader interest survey for her students. She added their reading test scores and programmed her library computer with 100 of the best books she had read. All her students received individual computer printouts suggesting six books that they would probably like and that would be within their reading level.

Similar commercial programs are becoming available, but what made this program successful was that the librarian had read and personally reacted to each book that she listed in the program. The individualized printouts served as conversation starters from which one-to-one relationships developed. Although she worked hard to initiate the project, she considered it worth the effort because once the machinery was set in order, it could be done for hundreds of students almost as easily as for thirty, and she could continue to update it with the new books she was reading.

Some librarians have programmed their computers to present information pages about selected authors along with annotations of their books. Another way that librarians and teachers use their computers to find suggestions for books or other resources is to communicate with colleagues through Internet or commercial e-mail accounts. The following list of such sources, prepared by Chris Crowe, Professor of English at Brigham Young University, was up-to-date in the fall of 1995, but some may have dropped off and others may have been added. If you manage to get on one such list, you will probably see references to other active lists. Most of the listserves provide interactive dialogue with others who have interest or expertise in the field, whereas the Web Sites are static "bulletin boards" that contain a variety of information. The basic description is followed by the e-mail message you should send (leave the "Subject" space blank) if you wish to join the group.

INTERNET LISTSERVES

BR_Match: A "matchmaking" service for K–12 classrooms who wish to exchange e-mail about books they're reading. Subscription message:
To: mailserv@wcu.edu
Message: subscribe BR_Match (type in your own name)

CHILDLIT: Children's Literature: Criticism and Theory. A discussion group for scholars, teachers, authors, and anyone else interested in books for children and young adults. To subscribe to CHILDLIT, send an e-mail message to the listserver that looks like this:
To: majordomo@email.rutgers.edu
Message: subscribe child_lit (type in your own name)
          end

HarperCollins Childrenslibrary Digest: An electronic news subscription dedicated to serving teachers and librarians for children K–12. Features awards news, interviews with authors, information on author visits, and other useful information. Subscription message:
To: lists@harpercollins.com
Message: subscribe childrenslibrary-digest

KIDLIT-L: An international forum for teachers, librarians, authors, and students interested in the study and teaching of literature for children and young adults. Subscription message:

To: listserv@bingvmb.cc.binghamton.edu
Message: subscribe Kidlit-L (type in your own name)

Notes from the Windowsill: An electronic journal of reviews of children's and young adult books. To subscribe, send an e-mail message to Wendy E. Betts at web@armory.com telling her that you want to subscribe to her book review column.

PUBYAC: The discussion forum for Children's and Young Adult Services in public libraries. Subscription message:

To: listserv@nysernet.org
Message: subscribe PUBYAC (type in your own name)

WORLD-WIDE WEB SITES

The American Library Association Home Page: Features a variety of information, including news, award-winning books, information for librarians, booklists, and links to related sites. The URL address is http://ala.org

Children's Literature Authors & Illustrators: Provides access to more than 50 links to biographical home pages from Cormier to Stine, Alcott to Zolotow. The URL address is
http://www.ucet.ufl.edu/~jbrown/chauth.html

The Children's Literature Web Guide: Provides access to children's/young adult literature announcements and award lists, lists of recommended books, topical bibliographies, lesson plans, information about authors, and much more. Direct your Web finder to
http://www.ucalgary.ca/~dkbrown/index.html.

Fairrosa Cyber Library: Contains a reference section, author information, articles, booklists, links to other sites, and more. The URL address is
http://www.users.interport.net/~fairrosa

New Mexico State University Library Gopher: Contains recent material about teaching materials, resources, syllabi, and other information pertaining to children's and young adult literature. Direct your Web finder to
gopher://lib.nmsu.edu/11/.subjects/Education/.childlit

Utah State Library Children's Services Web Site and Booklist: A monthly review of new books for children and young adults; connections to other Web Sites of interest to teachers and students of young adult literature. Point your Web Browser to http://www.state.lib.ut.us/children.htm

The Young Adult Librarian's Help/Homepage: Contains links/lists for serving young adults in libraries, including author information, booklists, award winners, and related sites. The URL address is
http://www.acpl.lib.in.us/young_adult_lib_ass/yaweb.html

Electronic aids are wonderful, but nothing can substitute for a large and varied reading background and the ability to draw relationships between what students tell or ask and what the librarian remembers about particular books. Experience sharpens this skill, and those librarians who make a consistent effort to read a few new books every month rapidly increase their repertoire of books.

Booktalks

With all their other responsibilities, few librarians have as much opportunity as they would like to guide individual reading on a one-to-one basis. The next best thing is to give presentations or booktalks to groups. A booktalk is a short introduction to a book, which usually includes one or two paragraphs read from the book. Booktalks are comparable to movie previews or teasers in presenting the characters and a hint of the plot, but they never reveal the ending. Joni Bodart has described booktalking as a kind of storytelling that resembles an unfinished murder mystery in being "enticing. It is a come-on. It is entertaining. And it is fun, for both the listener and the booktalker."[11]

The simplest kind of booktalk may last only 60 seconds. In giving it, the booktalker must let listeners know what to expect. For example, it would be unfair to present only the funniest moments in a serious book—a reader might check it out expecting a comedy. If a book is a love story, some clue should be given, but care needs to be taken because emotional scenes read out loud and out of context can sound silly. The cover of a book often reveals its tone, which is one of the reasons for holding up a book while it is being discussed or for showing slides if a presentation is being given to a large audience.

Booktalks need to be carefully prepared ahead of time. It takes both concentration and skill to select the "heart" of a story. People who try to ad-lib have the advantage of sounding spontaneous, but they also run the risk of using up all their time telling about one or two books or of getting bogged down in telling the whole story, which would defeat the purpose. Most young readers do not want to hear a 10- or 15-minute talk on one book, unless it is dramatic and used as a change of pace along with several shorter booktalks. Even with short booktalks, people's minds begin to wander after they've listened for 10 or 15 minutes. The ideal approach is for the teacher or librarian to give booktalks frequently but in short chunks.

This may not be practical, however, if the person giving the booktalk is a visitor (e.g., a public librarian coming to a school to encourage students to sign up for library cards and begin to use the public library). In situations such as this, the librarian can arrive in class with a cart full of books ready to be checked out. A half-hour or so can be devoted to the booktalks, with the rest of the time saved for questions and answers, browsing, sign-up, and check-out. In cases like this, it's good to have a printed bibliography or bookmark to leave with students for later use in the library.

This kind of group presentation has the advantage of introducing students to the librarian, which is especially important for helping students feel at ease in public libraries. Students who already feel acquainted are more likely to initiate a one-to-one relationship, a valuable part of reading guidance. Group presentations also give students more freedom in choosing books that appeal to them. When a student asks a librarian to recommend a good book, the librarian will have time to tell the student about only two or three titles, and the student will probably feel obligated to take one of these books whether or not it sounds appealing. But when the librarian presents 10 to 15 different titles, students can choose from a much larger offering. This also enables students to learn about and to select books that might cause them embarrassment if they were recommended on a personal basis. For example, if a girl is suspected of having lesbian leanings, it may not help the situation for the librarian to hand her Nancy Garden's *Annie on My Mind*. But if this were included among several books introduced to the class and the student chose it herself, it might fill a real need. The fact that the librarian talks about it, showing that she has read it, opens the door for the girl to initiate a conversation if she so desires.

Another advantage to group presentations is that they are efficient. If a social studies class is beginning a unit on World War II in which everyone in the class is required to read a novel having something to do with the war and also write a small research paper, it makes sense for the librarian to give the basic information in one group presentation. Being efficient in the beginning enables the librarian to spend time with individual students who have specific questions rather than making an almost identical presentation to 30 individuals. Table 10.2 gives some suggestions taken from an article by Mary K. Chelton, "Booktalking: You Can Do It" (*School Library Journal*, April, 1976). Other sources of information include an American Library Association book and videotape featuring Hazel Rochman and entitled "Tales of Love and Terror: Booktalking the Classics, Old and New," and Joni Richard Bodart's *Booktalk! Booktalking and School Visiting for Young Adult Audiences* supplemented by Bodart's *The BookTalker,* a semiannual bound journal containing prepared talks on current young adult books. It is available from BookHooks Publishing, Box 370688, Denver, CO 80237–0688.

Displays

Making displays is another effective way to promote books. Most young adults have some common needs, although they might not admit them or even be aware of them. The sensitive adult who knows books can quietly alert students to titles and authors that might prove worthwhile. It can be done simply; indeed, the simpler and less obvious, the better—perhaps nothing more than a sign that says "Like to watch Oprah Winfrey?—You'll Love These" (personal experiences and social issues books, although not identified in just that way), or "Did You Cry Over *Gone with the Wind?*" (books about love problems and divorce). None of these simple gimmicks involves much work, but what's more important is that they do their job without the librarian seeming pushy or nosy. No book report is required and no one will know whether John checks out Howard Fast's *April Morning* because his father recently died or because he likes American history.

When it comes to promoting books, librarians should not be ashamed to borrow ideas from the world of commerce. After all, we are competing directly for students' time and interest and indirectly for a share of the library budget and the taxpayers' dollars. Attractive, professional-looking displays and bulletin boards give

TABLE 10.2

DO'S AND DON'TS FOR BOOKTALKING

Do	Don't
1. Prepare well. Either memorize your talks or practice them so much that you can easily maintain eye contact. 2. Organize your books so that you can show them as you talk. To keep from getting confused, you might clip a note card with your talk on it to the back of each book. 3. When presenting excerpts, make sure they are representative of the tone and style of the book. 4. Even though you might sometimes like to focus on one or two themes, be sure, over the months you meet with any group, that you present a wide variety of books. Include informative books that young readers would probably like to know about but might be too embarrassed to ask for. 5. Experiment with different formats, for example, a short movie, some poetry, or one longer presentation along with your regular booktalks. 6. Keep a record of which books you have introduced to which groups. This can be part of your evaluation when you compare before and after circulation figures on the titles you have talked about. Also, good record keeping helps you not repeat yourself with a group. 7. Be assertive in letting teachers know what you will and will not do. Perhaps distribute a printed policy statement explaining such things as how much lead time you need, the fact that the teacher is to remain with the group, and how willing you are to make the necessary preparation to do booktalks on requested themes or topics.	1. Don't introduce books that you haven't read or books that you wouldn't personally recommend to a good friend as interesting 2. Don't "gush" over a book. If it's a good book and you have done an adequate job of selecting what to tell, it will sell itself. 3. Don't tell the whole story. When listeners beg for the ending, hand them the book. Your purpose is to get them to read. 4. Don't categorize books as to who should read them, for example, "This is a book you girls will like"; or show by the books you have brought to a particular school that you expect only Asian-Americans to read about Asian-Americans and only Native Americans to read about Native Americans, and so forth. 5. Don't give literary criticisms. You have already evaluated the books for your own purposes, and if you do not think they are good, do not present them.

evidence that things are happening in the library (or the classroom), and they help patrons develop positive attitudes toward books and reading. Even if there is no artwork connected with a display, it can encourage reading simply by showing the front covers.

Preparing displays can bring the same kind of personal satisfaction that comes from creatively decorating a room or painting a picture. People who have negative feelings about making displays have probably had experiences in which the results did not adequately compensate for the amount of time and effort expended. One way to correct this imbalance is to follow some general principles that help to increase the returns on a display while cutting down on the work.

1. Go window shopping in the best stores—the ones that appeal to the young adults that you are wooing—and when you see a display that you like, adapt its features to your own purposes.
2. Promote more than one book and have multiple copies available. Enthusiasm wanes if people have to put their names on a list and wait. Use color photocopies of the book jackets, so that as the books are checked out, your display won't look skimpy.
3. Tie the displays into current happenings. Connect them with popular movies, the school play, a neighborhood controversy, or various anniversary celebrations.
4. Use displays to get people into the library. Offer free bibliographies and announce their availability through local media.
5. Put your displays in high-traffic areas where everyone, not just those who already use the young adult collection, will see them.
6. Use interchangeable parts, so that it isn't necessary to start from scratch each time. To get variety and height into a display, use wood-stained fruit baskets and crates, leaning boards with screwed-in hooks for holding books, or cardboard boxes covered with drapes. To focus attention on the books, plain backgrounds are better than figured ones.
7. Take advantage of modern technology. Buy stick-on letters and use your computer and your desk-top publishing skills to prepare attractive bibliographies and signs.

The changing location of portable displays is in itself an attention getter. A portable display can be as small as a foot-square board set in the middle of a table or as large as a camper's tent set up in the middle of a room and surrounded by books about camping, hiking, backpacking, ecology, and nature foods. If space is a problem, small bulletin boards can be hung from the ceiling or stood against pillars or walls. They can do double duty (e.g., dividing the children's section from the young adult section or separating a reading corner with its casual furniture from the desks and tables set aside for study). Give students a sense of ownership over the displays by involving them as much as possible. Art teachers are usually happy to work with librarians to have a place where student work can be attractively displayed alongside such art-related books as Louise Plummer's *My Name is Sus5an Smith. The 5 Is Silent;* Gary Paulsen's *The Monument;* Brock Cole's *Celine;* and Zibby Oneal's *In Summer Light.* When you do a display of books about animals, include snapshots of students under the headings of "The Comforts and Delights of Owning a Dog," or "The Comforts and Delights of Being Owned by a Cat."

Occasionally, students working as library interns or helpers enjoy the challenge of doing displays all by themselves. Whatever is interesting and different is the key to tying books in with real life. An ordinary object—a kitchen sink, a pan full of dirty dishes, or a torn and dirty football jersey—is out of the ordinary when it appears as part of a display. Also, don't overlook the possibility of putting up posters such as those offered by the American Library Association or tying commercial posters in with books. Remember the part that the poster message, "Don't disturb the universe," played in Cormier's *The Chocolate War.*

Using real items in displays is an easy and effective way to attract attention.

Programs

Stores have special sales and events to get people into the marketplace, where they will be tempted to buy something. In the same way, ambitious librarians put on young adult programs to do something special for those who regularly use the library and, at the same time, to bring nonusers into the library. Advice from people whose libraries have been especially active in arranging programs includes:

1. Take a survey, or better, talk with your teenage clientele to see what their interests and desires are.
2. Avoid duplicating the kinds of activities that students do in school and in conjunction with other community agencies.
3. Include young adults in planning and putting on programs so that the library can be a showcase for young adult talent.

I have just recently read a book which has really impacted me as a teacher/coach. This book, <u>Friday Night Lights</u>, is about coaches, a town, and some teachers who would do anything to win a football game on Friday night. It taught me about the truth, as well as the dishonesty, that goes on in high school athletics and how important a person's integrity is. Also, this book shows the dark side of racism, and how, unfortunately, it is still alive and well in our country.

Reggie Childress
Athletics/Physical Education

Librarian Lois Buckman at Moorhead Junior High in Conroe, Texas, makes her own "READ" posters by enlarging pictures of local heroes—this one basketball coach Reggie Childress—and asking them to write a short piece about the book they are reading.

4. Work with existing youth service agencies to cosponsor events, or plan them in conjunction with school programs so as to have the beginning of an audience and the nucleus of a support group.
5. Do a good job of publicizing the event. The publicity may influence people unable to come so they will feel more inclined to visit the library at some other time.
6. Have a casual setting planned for a relatively small group, with extra chairs available in case more people come than you expect. Bustling around at the last minute to set up extra chairs gives an aura of success that is more desirable than having row on row of empty chairs.

Program possibilities include outdoor music concerts featuring local teenage bands, talent shows in a coffeehouse setting, chess tournaments, and showings of original movies or videos. Workshops are held in computer programming, photography, creative writing, bicycle repair, and crafts. Guest speakers are often invited to discuss subjects that schools tend to shy away from, such as self-defense and rape prevention, drug and birth control information, and introductions to various hotlines and other agencies that help young adults.

Large-scale workshops are sometimes held in libraries to which various schools bring their students. For example, in a town with three high schools, one big day on choosing careers may be planned at the community library. Guest speakers who could not give up three days of their time may be willing to make a single appearance, and special exhibits and displays can be set up once rather than three times.

Regardless of the topic or format of a program, librarians should view programs as opportunities to encourage library visitors to become regular book users. The following practices help:

1. Hold the program so that it is in or near the young adult book section. If this is impractical, try routing traffic past the young adult area or past displays of young adult books.
2. Pass out miniature bibliographies, perhaps printed on a bookmark or in some other easy-to-carry format.
3. Schedule the program to end at least a half-hour before the library closes, so that participants can browse and sign up for library cards.
4. Place paperback book racks where they are as tempting as the displays that grocery and discount stores crowd into checkout areas.
5. For ten minutes at the start of the program, while waiting for latecomers to straggle in, do a welcome and warm-up by giving a few booktalks related to the subject of the evening.

Some libraries have had success with book discussion groups in which teenagers serve as readers and critics. These usually work best if their evaluations can be shared, for example, on a bulletin board, in a teen opinion magazine, through a display of recommended books, in a monthly column in a local newspaper, or through the periodic printing and distribution of annotated lists of favorites.

When an author is invited to speak, the host librarian needs to begin publicity several weeks in advance to be sure that people are reading the author's books. English and reading teachers should be notified so that they can devote some class time to the author's work. A panel of students who especially enjoyed the author's work might be set up to interact with the author at the end of the formal presentation. Another way to involve students, and perhaps teachers, would be to invite three or four to have lunch or dinner with the guest author. (Check this out first because some speakers prefer to be left alone to gather their thoughts before making a presentation.) If you are setting up an author's visit, it is usually best that you first write the publisher of the author's most recent book. State how much money, if any, you have available. Sometimes publishers pay for an author's transportation, but you will usually need to pay at least for food and housing and, if possible, to offer an honorarium. If you have no money, say so immediately, and then be patient, flexible, and grateful for whomever you get. An author might be scheduled to speak in or near your area and might then come to you as an extra. Also, it is highly possible that there are young adult authors living in your own state. The Children's Book Council (568 Broadway, Suite 404, New York, NY 10012) has a brochure *Inviting Children's Book Authors and Illustrators to Your Community*, which can be requested for a fee of $2.00 plus stamps totalling 78 cents.

Magazines

Magazines and their place in school and library collections have changed considerably since the days when girls read *Seventeen* and boys read the joke page in *Boy's Life* and looked at the pictures in *National Geographic.* Popular adult magazines such as *People, U.S. News and World Report, Sports Illustrated, Cosmopolitan,* and *Life* are staples in teenagers' reading habits, but there are also several dozen magazines devoted specifically to teenagers. See Focus Box 10.1 for recommendations by Diane Tucillo, young adult librarian for the Mesa, Arizona Public Library.

FOCUS BOX 10.1

Magazines Popular with Young Adults

Prepared by Diane Tuccillo, Young Adult Librarian, Mesa (Arizona) Public Library

Dirt Bike. A top magazine for motorcycle buffs containing the hottest information on riding, racing, and equipment. ISSN 0364–1546. $18.98 per year. Order from Hi-Torque Publications, 25233 Anza Dr., Valencia, CA 91355.

Dragons. Beautiful illustrations, gaming tips, and news are featured in this favorite choice of Dungeons and Dragons fans. ISSN 0279–6848. $30.00 per year. Order from TSR, Inc., P.O. Box 5695, Boston, MA 02206.

Gamepro. The number one source for learning about the newest video games, equipment, and hints to improve skills. ISSN 1042–8658. $24.95 per year. Order from Infotainment World, Inc. 951 Mariner's Island Blvd., Ste. 700, San Mateo, CA 94404.

Mad. The classic magazine of wacky, offbeat humor. ISSN 0024–9319. $15.50 for eight issues. Order from E. C. Publications, Inc., 1700 Broadway, New York, NY 10019.

Merlyn's Pen. This is a highly regarded publication of original young adult writing showcasing "manuscripts that grip the readers' interest and stir the heart or mind." ISSN 0882–2050. $21.00 for four issues during the school year. Order from Merlyn's Pen, Inc., P.O. Box 1058, East Greenwich, RI 02818.

Right On! Written particularly for African-American teens, this is a high-interest look at currently popular entertainment personalities. ISSN 0048–8305. $15.95 per year. Order from Sterling/Macfadden Partnership, 233 Park Ave. S., New York, NY 10003.

Sassy. In the same league as *Teen, Seventeen,* and *YM (Young Miss),* this is filled with articles and features for mostly female contemporary teens. ISSN 0899–9953. $14.97 per year. Order from Peterson Publishing Co., 6420 Wilshire Blvd., Los Angeles, CA 90048.

Starlog. Articles and reviews along with lots of full-color photos make this appeal to fans of science fiction films and other media. ISSN 0191–4626. $39.97 per year. Order from Starlog Group, Inc., 475 Park Ave. S., New York, NY 10016.

Transworld Skateboarding. Loaded with action photos, this magazine contains relevant articles and biographies for skateboarding aficionados; also includes alternative music reviews. ISSN 0748–7401. $19.95 per year. Order from Imprimatur, Inc., 353 Airport Rd., Oceanside, CA 92054.

Youth. A non-preachy, upbeat magazine for Christian youth "dedicated to showing that God's way of life is relevant, interesting and helpful to today's teens." ISSN 0279–6651. $9.95 for six issues. Order from the Worldwide Church of God, 300 W. Green St., Pasadena, CA 91123.

As with adult magazines, there are now magazines for every taste—even a few that will please teachers—but what is important for educators to realize is that many students who won't pick up books are eager to read the latest magazines in their areas of interest. With many of the teen magazines, poor readers can feel their first success with the printed word because much of the information is communicated through easy-to-read layouts and photographs. Also, the material, which is presented in short, digestible chunks, is of prime interest to teens. Some of the magazines are read by both boys and girls, but because of the abundance of advertising money for cosmetics and fashions, many magazines are purposely designed to appeal only to girls. Others are financed by advertisements for products usually purchased by boys.

There's no limit to the challenges that good students can find in magazines. A much higher percentage of adult Americans read magazines rather than books, and yet in school we give people little help in introducing them to magazines or in picking out the ones they will get the most from. It is almost as if kids find magazines despite teachers, not because of them. We would do well to change our attitudes and look on magazines as taking up where books leave off in presenting up-to-date information on a wide variety of topics chosen to be especially interesting to young adults. We need to make special efforts to teach the skills necessary to do research in all kinds of modern periodicals. As pointed out in Chapter Eight, many contemporary writers of informative books for teenagers get most of their information from magazines and journals. If teenagers can learn to get such information themselves, then they won't be limited to reading only about those topics and viewpoints chosen by someone else as "appropriate" for teens.

Using Young Adult Books in the Reading Classroom

Now that many teachers, schools, and school districts have adopted a whole-language approach to teaching reading, writing, and speaking skills to children, the role of trade books as opposed to textbooks and exercise sheets has become much more acceptable in teaching reading. Under the best circumstances, students come to high school having read many books and being eager to read many more. Under the worst circumstances (i.e., when students arrive in high school unable to read or not wanting to read), the idea of teaching them with genuine literature instead of with workbooks and exercises is at least familiar.

Including a section on reading in this text is in some sense superfluous because this whole book is devoted to teaching and promoting reading, but the interests and responsibilities of teachers of reading differ in some ways from those of English teachers or of librarians. One difference is that except for remedial programs teaching reading as an academic discipline in the high schools is a fairly recent development. The assumption used to be that normal students had received enough formal instruction in reading by the time they completed elementary school. They were then turned over to English teachers who taught mostly literature, grammar, and composition. Certainly English teachers worked with reading skills, but they were not the primary focus. Today more and more states are passing laws setting minimal reading standards for high school graduation, and this has meant that reading has become almost a regular part of the high school curriculum. In some schools, all ninth-graders now take a reading class; in other schools, such a class is reserved for those who test one or two years below grade level. Depending on how long it takes them to pass the test, students may take basic reading classes for several semesters.

In the teaching profession, the reluctant reader is nearly always stereotyped as a boy from the wrong side of town, someone S. E. Hinton would describe as an outsider, a greaser. Actually, reluctant readers come in both male and female varieties and from all social and I.Q. levels. Many of them have fairly good reading skills; they simply don't like to read. Others are poor readers partly because they get so little practice. What these students have in common is that they have been disappointed in their past reading. The rewards of reading—what they received either emotionally or intellectually—have not come up to their expectations, which were based on how hard they worked to read the material. They have therefore come away feeling cheated. The reading profession has recognized this problem and has attempted to solve it by lowering the price the student has to pay (i.e., by devising reading materials that demand less effort from the student). These are the controlled vocabulary books commonly known as "high-low books," meaning high interest, low vocabulary. They are only moderately successful because the authors are rarely creative artists; they are educators who have many priorities that come before telling a good story. An alternative approach is making the rewards greater rather than reducing the effort. This is where the best adolescent literature comes into the picture. It has a good chance of succeeding with reluctant readers for the following reasons:

1. It is written specifically to be interesting to teenagers. It is geared to their age level and their interests.
2. It is usually shorter and more simply written than adult material, yet it has no stigma attached to it. It isn't written down to anyone, nor does it look like a reading textbook.
3. There is so much of it (almost 800 new books published every year) that individual readers have a good chance of finding books that appeal to them.
4. As would be expected, because the best young adult books are the creations of some good contemporary authors, the stories are more dramatic, better written, and easier to get involved in than the controlled vocabulary books.
5. The language used in good adolescent literature is more like the language that students are accustomed to hearing. In this day of mass media communication, a student who does not read widely may still have a fairly high degree of literary and language sophistication gained from watching television and movies.

Taking all this into account, some types of adolescent literature will still be enjoyed more than others by reluctant readers. In general, reluctant readers want the same things from the books they read that the rest of us want, but they want them faster and in less space. If it's information they are looking for, they want it to be right there. If they are reading a book for thrills and chills, they want it to be really scary. If they're reading for humor, they want it to be really funny. And if they're not sure about committing themselves for a large chunk of time, they want books in which they can get a feeling of accomplishment from reading short sections, paragraphs, or even sentences, as with various kinds of trivia books.

Booklist publishes an annual list "Quick Picks for Reluctant Young Adult Readers" compiled by a Young Adult Library Services Association committee. Single copies in leaflet format can be obtained by sending a self-addressed stamped envelope to *Booklist* (American Library Association; 50 E. Huron St., Chicago, IL 60611). Quantities of 100 for $24.00 can also be ordered from ALA Editions, Order Dept., American Library Association, 155 N. Wacker Drive, Chicago, IL 60606–1719. (Phone ALA at (312) 944–6780 for further information about camera-ready sheets or multiple orders of this and other brochures designed for teenagers.) Selection criteria for the "Quick Picks" list includes short sentences, short paragraphs, simplicity of plot, uncomplicated dialogue, a sense of timeliness, maturity of format, and appeal of content. Fiction must include "believability of character and plot as well as realistic dialogue." Also, look at the February 15, 1992, *Booklist* for Frances A. Miller's "Books to Read When You Hate to Read: Recommended by Reluctant YA Readers in Grades 7–12."

Guided Reading Classes

The push for higher reading scores has opened the high school curriculum to reading classes for all students, not just those with low reading scores. Most high schools offer study skills courses in which skimming, speed reading, and selecting main ideas are taught. Some high schools also offer classes in what used to be called "free reading," but with the back-to-the-basics swing that occurred in the 1980s today are called *individualized* or *guided reading*. Rather than being a semester-long course, such programs are more likely to be incorporated into a six-week unit or a twice-a-week program as part of regular English or reading classes.

One of the chief reasons for providing kids time to read in class is to prevent the drop-off in reading that usually occurs when students begin high school and their social and work schedules leave little time for reading. A classroom library is provided containing multiple copies of popular young adult and adult titles from which students make their own selections. It is wise for teachers to send a note of explanation to parents that includes the statement that the choice of books is up to the student and his or her parents. It helps at the beginning for either the teacher or the librarian to give booktalks; once the class is started, students can recommend "good books" to each other.

When students finish a book, they hold a conference with the teacher, who preferably has also read the book. The purpose is not to test the student as much as it is to encourage thinking about the book and the author's intentions and to give teachers an opportunity to suggest other books that will help the student progress. Teachers need to show that they respect the reading of popular young adult books by being familiar with many of them and by being genuinely interested in what students have to say about them. The class is doomed to failure if teachers view it as a kind of focused study hall in which their job is to do little more than keep control and keep kids reading. It's also doomed to failure if students view it as a "cake" class, and for this reason successful teachers are fairly stringent as they devise various systems for giving credit. Students keep records of the number of books (or number of pages) read, they assist the teacher in judging the difficulty of the material, they mark their improvement over the semester (perhaps shown by a test score or by the number of pages the student reads in a class period), and they receive grades on their preparation for the individual conferences.

Various studies summarized by Dick Abrahamson and Eleanor Tyson in "What Every English Teacher Should Know About Free Reading"[12] have shown:

- Free reading is enjoyed by both students and teachers.
- Over a semester, students pick a variety of books, ranging from easy to difficult and from recent to classic.
- Reading skills improve, with some of this improvement undoubtedly related to attitude change.
- Students taught through free-reading are more likely to read as adults and to foster reading activities with their children.
- Individual conferences help literature come alive for students.
- The conferences also help to break down barriers between students and teachers.
- Good teachers employ the concept of reading ladders (e.g., helping a girl move from a Sweet Dreams romance to a Norma Fox Mazer or an M. E. Kerr book and on to *Gone with the Wind* and *Jane Eyre*).

With so many benefits, why isn't the course taught more often? Part of the reason is an image problem. *Free reading* smacks of "free love" and the permissiveness of the 1970s. Although the connotations of such a course title might attract students, these same connotations fly in the face of those who believe "You get what you pay for." Besides, the course is already suspect because of its avowal of quantity over quality; i.e., "reading by the pound," and its emphasis on pleasure for students. More people than we care to think about are sure that if students are having a good time they can't also be learning.

Another problem is that the teacher's role is practically invisible. Being able to listen to students while working ever so subtly to suggest books that will raise levels of reading and improve skills without discouraging young readers takes a knowledge of hundreds of books plus tact and considerable talent in communication. Yet this teaching occurs in private sessions between two people. One of our favorite graduate students is a high school reading teacher who teaches an individualized reading class along with some of the more traditional remedial reading classes. She laughs in frustration about her principal's visits to her individualized reading class. After popping his head into her room on several different occasions and seeing the kids reading and her talking with a student at her desk, he sent her a note requesting that she let him know "when you are going to be teaching," so that he could come and observe.

She's still trying to educate him about the type of class she's teaching. It is not for the dysfunctional or disabled reader. It is for the average, or above-average, student who simply needs a chance to read and discuss books. In effect, it is one last

RICHARD PECK
On Writing and Rewriting

"Tell them," the teacher implores while we wait in the wings, or rather out in the hall just as I am to stagger into a classroom. "Tell them how many times you rewrite, how many drafts you do. They need to hear that."

One teacher or another in almost any school where I am Visiting Author prompts me on this point, at least in the schools where students are assigned any writing at all. Down through the years I've worked up a line of patter to expand on the truism that The Only Writing Is Rewriting.

"I write each of my novels six times," I've been telling two generations of the pubescent and adolescent, holding up my latest bound book. "I'm just like you. I never get anything right in the first five tries either."

Without more than a ripple of response down the rows, I'd expand. "I write from Chapter One to the last page, and when I get stuck, I go back and rework an earlier scene. It keeps my motor running. It gives me ideas about how to proceed."

Eyes glaze now, all over the room.

"Then when I come to the end of the novel, I throw out the first chapter, no matter how often I've rewritten it. Now that I know how the story ends, I can write a new first chapter that points in the direction of the conclusion. A novel is an expanded form of a classroom composition: you say what you're going to say, then you say it, then you say what you've said."

Except that nobody has ever told them this is the essay format. Still, I get a small rise out of them. The idea that you'd throw out anything you've written is not only mildly outrageous, it's out of the question.

I have more for them in this vein. "Sometimes I reread a page I'm satisfied with. But then I go over it, seeing if I can take out ten unnecessary words."

This is met with chilling silence. The young don't want to know how short they can make their writing; they want to know how long it has to be.

"Never show anybody your rough draft," I'd say, pressing on regardless. "Letting somebody read your rough draft is like going out in public in your underwear. It shows all the wrong things about you."

They chuckle briefly as they return to private concerns. Then I throw them a freebie: "And by the way, the phrase 'a lot' is spelled as two words."

Sometimes I'd get to my punch line, sometimes not: "In the real world, spelling counts."

This has been my patter over many a semester, but I'm not married to it. Nowadays when teachers approach with that "Tell them" line about rewriting, I respond while we're still waiting in the wings.

"I'll cut you a deal," I say. "I'll urge rewriting on your students if you promise never to give any one of them another grade on a rough draft."

Some teachers look as if I've just slapped them on the way to the podium. But why should I be just one more adult telling the young the truth when they don't have to know it?

Richard Peck's books include *Lost in Cyberspace,* Dial/Penguin, 1995; *The Last Safe Place on Earth,* Delacorte, 1995; *Bel-Air Bambi and the Mall Rats,* Delacorte, 1993; and for teachers and librarians *Love and Death at the Mall, Teaching and Writing for the Literate Young,* Delacorte, 1994.

try on the part of the school to instill in young people the habit of reading for pleasure. The student who lacks the skills for this kind of self-selected and self-paced reading needs expert help from a professional reading teacher. Preparing teachers for such a challenging role is beyond the scope of this book.

Using Young Adult Books in the Social Studies Class

Turning facts into believable stories that touch readers' emotions is the biggest contribution of fiction to the social studies class. It is important for readers to realize, however, that many different books need to be read because each book presents a limited perspective. Stereotypes exist in people's minds for two reasons. One is that the same attitudes are repeated over and over, so that they become a predominant image. Another is that an individual may have had only one exposure to a particular race, group, or country. For example, readers of Chaim Potok's *The Chosen* don't learn everything about Hasidic Jews, but they know a lot more than they did before they read the book, and their interest may have been piqued, so that they will continue to watch for information and to read other books.

Nearly everyone agrees that by reading widely and sharing their findings, social studies class members can lead each other to go beyond stereotypes. For this to happen on more than an ad hoc or serendipitous basis, however, the teacher needs to identify clear-cut goals and then seek help from professional sources and other teachers and librarians in drawing up a selective list of books to be offered to students.

Social studies teachers have always recognized the importance of biographies and of the kind of historical books featured in Chapter Seven, but they may not be as aware of the many books, both fiction and nonfiction, that are available to help them teach students about contemporary social issues. See Chapter Eight for nonfiction books treating topics of interest to teenagers, such as ecology; the sex-related issues of pornography, rape, abuse, abortion, and prostitution; and medicine and health care, including questions about transplants, surrogate parenting, euthanasia, animal rights, and experiments on humans. Books on government ask questions about individual rights as opposed to the welfare of the group. Such questions range from whether the state has a right to require motorcycle helmets and seat belts to whether it should legislate drugs and sexual preference.

Social studies teachers also miss a powerful resource if they fail to bring the kind of fiction discussed in Chapter Three and in Focus Box 10.2 into their classes when they talk about current social problems. When they are talking about other countries, they need to remember that one of the great values and pleasures of literature is that it frees us to travel vicariously to other times and places. Movies, television, and photographs allow people to see other places, but literature has the added dimension of allowing the reader to share the thoughts of another person. One never feels like a stranger in a country whose literature one has read, and as today's jet age shrinks the distances between countries and cultures, it is more important than ever that people realize that members of the human race, regardless of where or how they live, have more similarities than differences.

Parents and Young Adult Literature

"Tell me a story."

"Read just one more!"

"Can we go to the library today?"

Such requests are among the pleasant memories that parents have of their young children. These memories become even more cherished when parents look at these same children, now teenagers rushing off to part-time jobs or after-school sports or spending so much time with friends that they no longer seem to have time to do required school assignments, much less read a book. When parents ask us what they can do to encourage their teenage children to read, we find it easier to tell them what *not* to do because we've observed at least three clear-cut roads to failure.

1. Don't nag. There's simply no way to force young adults to read, much less to enjoy it.
2. If you choose to read the books your teenagers are reading, don't do it as a censor or with the intent of checking up on your child or your child's school.
3. Don't suggest books to your teenager with the only purpose being to teach moral lessons.

Lest we appear unduly pessimistic, we hasten to add that we have also seen some genuinely rewarding reading partnerships between teenagers and their parents. These successful partnerships have resembled the kind of reading-based friendships that adults have with each other. Mutual respect is involved, and the partners take turns making suggestions of what will be good to read. Conversations about characters, plots, authors, and subject matter come up naturally, with no one asking teacher-type questions and no one feeling pressured to talk about what he or she has just read.

Teenagers enjoy being in a helping role (i.e., being experts whose opinions are valued). Some of the best partnerships we've seen have been between our students whose teenage children have volunteered to read and share their opinions on the books they've seen their mothers reading (sorry we can't remember any fathers in this role, although we have known fathers who do read and serve as examples). A key to enticing young people to read is simply to have lots of books and magazines available. But they need to be available for genuine browsing and reading by everyone in the family, not purchased and planted in a manner that will appear phoney to the teenager. A teenager who has never seen his or her parents read for pleasure will surely be suspicious when parents suddenly become avid readers on the day after parent-teacher conferences.

Perhaps a more important benefit than modeling behavior is that when parents read some of the best new books (the Honor List is a good starting place), they gain an understanding of what is involved in being a teenager today. Parents who have read some of the realistic problem novels have things to discuss with their children whether or not the children have read the books. Even when children are not interested in heart-to-heart discussions, parents are more understanding if they've read about the kinds of turmoil that teenagers face in struggling to become emotionally independent. In our own classes, and we understand the same is true for others teaching young adult literature, we are getting an increasing number of adult students who are there simply because they enjoy reading and talking about the young adult fiction that was not being written when they were teenagers. Those who are parents of teenagers consider it serendipitous if their teenagers also get interested and begin reading the same books.

A more structured approach is for parents to work with youth groups and church groups or to volunteer as a friend of either the public library or the school library. These kinds of activities provide parents with extra opportunities to involve young people in sharing reading experiences. In such situations, it is often a benefit to have other young people involved and for parents to trade off, so that they aren't always the leader for the particular group in which their child is a member.

Clarifying Human Relations and Values

Workers with church and civic youth groups, teachers of classes in human relations, and professional counselors working with young adults have all found that reading and discussing the kinds of books listed in Focus Box 10.2 can be useful. When we talk about using books to help students understand their own and other people's feelings and behavior, we sometimes use the term *bibliotherapy*. It is a word that goes in and out of fashion, at least in reference to the informal kind of work that most teachers and librarians do with young adults. Its technical meaning is the use of books by professionally trained psychologists and psychiatrists in working with people who are mentally ill. Because of this association with illness, many "book" people reject the term. They reason that if a young adult is mentally ill and in need of some kind of therapy, the therapy should come from someone trained in that field rather than from someone trained in the book business or in teaching and guiding normal and healthy young adults.

Most people agree, however, that normal and healthy young adults can benefit psychologically from reading and talking about the problems of fictional characters. All teenagers have problems of one type or another, and simply finding out that other people have them too provides some comfort. We are reassured to know

FOCUS BOX 10.2

Discussion Time

After the First Death by Robert Cormier. Pantheon, 1979.   Two boys are sacrificed by their fathers, one a Middle East terrorist and one a U. S. government official. Other Cormier books that force hard thinking and discussion are *The Bumblebee Flies Anyway* (Pantheon, 1974), *I Am the Cheese* (Pantheon, 1977), *We All Fall Down* (Delacorte, 1991), and *Tunes for Bears to Dance To* (Delacorte, 1992).

Bless the Beasts and Children by Glendon Swarthout. Doubleday, 1970.   A group of "losers" at a summer camp choose to align themselves with a herd of buffalo doomed by animal management practices, which were changed shortly after the author presented the first copy of the book to the then-governor of Arizona.

California Blue by David Klass. Scholastic, 1994.   When high school junior John Rodgers finds a new species of butterfly in a northern California old-growth forest, he is pulled into a savage controversy between environmentalists and the people in his hometown, including his own family.

Driver's Ed by Caroline B. Cooney. Delacorte, 1994.   A young mother is killed because of a missing STOP sign that Remy and Morgan swiped as a prank. The two young people, along with their driver's ed teacher, face both horror and guilt.

The Goats by Brock Cole. Farrar, Straus & Giroux, 1987.   The other campers strip Laura and Howie of their clothes and leave them on an island, where, to their surprise, they manage to survive both physically and emotionally.

Keeping Christina by Sue Ellen Bridgers. HarperCollins, 1993.   In an unusual book for young adults, Bridgers tells a story showing that being a friend to someone cannot always solve the person's problems and in fact may cause problems for the one doing the befriending.

The Man from the Other Side by Uri Orlev, translated from the Hebrew by Hillel Halkin. Houghton Mifflin, 1991.   A young Polish boy growing up in Warsaw during World War II participates in his neighborhood's anti-Jewish practices and then is told by his broken-hearted mother that his late father was Jewish.

Nothing but the Truth: A Documentary Novel by Avi. Orchard, 1991.   No one dreams that what starts out as a fairly simply teacher/student confrontation will give both Miss Narwin and ninth-grader Philip Malloy their 15 minutes of fame.

Scorpions by Walter Dean Myers. HarperCollins, 1988.   Jamal's brother is in jail, and an old gang leader brings word to Jamal that he's to take over as leader of the Scorpions. He also brings Jamal a gun.

Skin Deep by Lois Ruby. Scholastic, 1994.   As a *Booklist* reviewer observed, this complex novel is more than "skin deep." Ruby tells the story of Dan and Laurel and what happens to their relationship when Dan joins a neo-Nazi skinhead group.

that our fears and doubts have been experienced by others. David A. Williams, a communications professor at the University of Arizona, said in a newspaper interview that he would die happy if he could "prove that a positive correlation exists between the rise in anxiety in the country and the decline of pleasure reading." Research done during the 1950s and 1960s showed that anxiety is directly related to a poor concept of oneself. "It seems to me," he said, "that the human being's major concern in life is to determine what it means to be a human being." The paradox is that before people can see themselves, they have to get outside of themselves and look at the whole spectrum of human experience to see where they fit in. "When we are feeling anxious it is usually because we have a narrow perspective which sees only what it wants to see." Someone who is anxiety-ridden, paranoiac, or resentful selects experiences from life to validate those feelings. For people like this, reading can put things back into perspective. "When we read about others who have suffered similar anxieties, we don't feel so cut off and, although the world doesn't change, we change the way we look at it."[13]

As books put things back into perspective, they open up avenues of communication that successful discussion leaders tap into. It is important, however, for adults to be careful in guiding students to read and talk about personal problems. No one should be forced to participate in such a discussion, and a special effort should not be made to relate stories to the exact problem that a group member is having. In fact, it would probably be best to avoid matching up particular problems with particular students. When someone is in the midst of a crisis, chances are that he or she does not want to read and talk about someone else in a similar predicament. As a general rule, one would probably get the most from such a discussion before or after—rather than during—a time of actual crisis.

Such discussions are usually held in clubs, church groups, classes on preparation for marriage and human relations, and counseling and support group meetings at crisis centers and various institutions to which young people are sent. Because membership in these groups changes from meeting to meeting and there are no pressures for participants to do outside reading as "homework," a leader will probably be disappointed or frustrated if the discussion is planned around the expectation that everyone will have read the book. A more realistic plan is for the leader to give a summary of the book and a 10- to 20-minute prepared reading of the part that best delineates the problem or the topic for discussion. Using fairly well-known books, including ones that have been made into movies, increases the chances of participation. Using popular books also makes it easier for students whose appetites have been whetted to find the book and read it on their own.

In an adult group of professionals, the same purpose would be accomplished by reading a case study that would then be discussed. But case studies are written for trained adults who know how to fill in the missing details and how to interpret the symptoms. Teenagers are not psychologists, and they are not social workers or philosophers. Literature may be as close as they will ever come to discussing the kinds of problems dealt with in these fields. What follows the oral presentation can be extremely varied, depending on the nature of the group, the leader's personality, and what the purpose or the goal of the discussion is. The literature provides the group—both teenagers and adults—with a common experience that can serve as the focus for discussion. Pressures and tensions are relieved because everyone is talking in the third person about the characters in the book, although in reality many of the comments will be about first-person problems.

Reading and discussing books can in no way cure mental illness, but reading widely about all kinds of problems and all kinds of solutions helps keep young people involved in thinking about moral issues. As shown in Table 10.3, about what young adult literature can and cannot do when it is used as a tool to teach about human relations and values, the positives outweigh the negatives.

This chapter has shown that using and promoting books with young readers is a shared opportunity and responsibility. It belongs not only to librarians and English

TABLE 10.3

THE POWERS AND LIMITATIONS OF YOUNG ADULT LITERATURE

What literature can do:	What literature cannot do:
1. It can provide a common experience or a way in which a teenager and an adult can focus their attention on the same subject.	1. It cannot cure someone's emotional illness.
2. It can serve as a discussion topic and a way to relieve embarrassment by enabling people to talk in the third person about problems with which they are concerned.	2. It cannot guarantee that readers will behave in socially approved ways.
3. It can give young readers confidence that, should they meet particular problems, they will be able to solve them.	3. It cannot directly solve readers' problems.
4. It can increase a young person's understanding of the world and the many ways that individuals find their places in it.	
5. It can comfort and reassure young adult readers by showing them that they are not the only ones who have fears and doubts.	
6. It can give adults as well as teenagers insights into adolescent psychology and values.	

and reading teachers, but also to everyone who works closely with young people and wants to understand them better. It can serve as a medium through which to open communication with young adults about their concerns.

Notes

[1] Janet French, "Review of *Homecoming*," *School Library Journal* 28 (September 1981): 133.

[2] Audrey Eaglen, "What Makes a Good Review," *Top of the News* 35 (Winter 1979): 146–152.

[3] Anne Tyler, "Looking for Mom," *New York Times Book Review*, April 26, 1981, p. 52.

[4] Katherine Paterson, "Family Visons," *New York Times Book Review*, November 14, 1982, p. 41.

[5] Dorothy Mathews, "Writing about Adolescent Literature: Current Approaches and Future Directions," *Arizona English Bulletin* 18 (April 1976): 216–19.

[6] Katha Pollitt, "Why We Read: Canon to the Right of Me . . .," *The Nation*, September 23, 1991, reprinted in *The Chronicle of Higher Education*, October 23, 1991.

[7] *Rudolfo Anaya Autobiography as Written in 1985.* Copyright 1991 Rudolfo Anaya (TQS Publications; P.O. Box 9275; Berkeley, CA 94709), pp. 16–17.

[8] *The Big Aiiieeeee!: An Anthology of Chinese American and Japanese American Literature,* edited by Jeffery Paul Chan, Frank Chin, Lawson Fusao Inada, and Shawn Wong (New American Library, 1991), p. 8.

[9] Maxine Hong Kingston, "Personal Statement," in *Approaches to Teaching Kingston's THE WOMAN WARRIOR,* edited by Shirley Geok-lin Lim (Modern Language Association, 1991), p. 24.

[10] Dorothy M. Broderick, "Whose Job Is It Anyway?" *VOYA* 6 (February 1984): 320–26.

[11] Joni Bodart, *Booktalk! Booktalking and School Visiting for Young Adult Audiences* (H. W. Wilson, 1980), p. 2–3.

[12] Dick Abrahamson and Eleanor Tyson, "What Every English Teacher Should Know About Free Reading," *The ALAN Review* 14 (Fall 1986): 54–58, 69.

[13] "Feeling Uptight, Anxious? Try Reading, UA Prof Says," *Tempe Daily News*, December 15, 1977.

Titles Mentioned In the Text of Chapter Ten

Adams, Douglas. *The Hitchhiker's Guide to the Galaxy.* Crown, 1980.

Anaya, Rudolfo. *Bless Me, Ultima.* TQS Publications, 1972.

Blume, Judy. *Forever.* Bradbury, 1975.

Bodart, Joni Richard. *Booktalk! Booktalking and School Visiting for Young Adult Audiences.* H. W. Wilson, 1980.

Bradbury, Ray. *The Martian Chronicles.* Doubleday, 1958.

Bridgers, Sue Ellen. *Notes for Another Life.* Knopf, 1981.

Bronte, Charlotte. *Jane Eyre,* 1847.

Campbell, Patricia J. *Presenting Robert Cormier, Updated Edition.* G. K. Hall/Twayne, 1989.

Chan, Jeffery Paul, Frank Chin, Lawson Fusao Inada, and Shawn Wong, eds. *The Big Aiiieeeee!: An Anthology of Chinese American and Japanese American Literature.* Meridian, 1991.

Cole, Brock. *Celine.* Farrar, Straus & Giroux, 1989.

Childress, Alice. *Rainbow Jordan.* Putnam, 1981.

Fast, Howard. *April Morning.* Crown, 1961.

Garden, Nancy. *Annie on My Mind.* Farrar, Straus & Giroux, 1982.

Golding, William. *Lord of the Flies.* Putnam, 1955.

Hamilton, Virginia. *Sweet Whispers, Brother Rush.* Putnam, 1982.

Hinton, S. E. *The Outsiders.* Viking, 1967.

Hipple, Theodore. *Presenting Sue Ellen Bridgers.* G. K. Hall/Twayne, 1990.

Kies, Cosette. *Presenting Young Adult Horror Fiction.* Twayne, 1991.

Kingston, Maxine Hong. *The Woman Warrior: Memoirs of a Girlhood Among Ghosts.* Knopf, 1976.

Knowles, John. *A Separate Peace.* Macmillan, 1960.

Mitchell, Margaret. *Gone with the Wind.* Macmillan, 1936.

Oneal, Zibby. *In Summer Light.* Viking, 1985.

Paulsen, Gary. *The Monument.* Delacorte, 1991.

Potok, Chaim. *The Chosen.* Simon & Schuster, 1967.

Plummer, Louise. *My Name Is Sus5an Smith. The 5 is Silent.* Delacorte, 1991.

Salinger, J. D. *The Catcher in the Rye.* Little, Brown, 1951.

Steele, Danielle. *Crossings.* Delacorte, 1982.

Tan, Amy. *The Joy Luck Club.* Putnam, 1989.

Voigt, Cynthia. *Homecoming.* Atheneum, 1981.

Walker, Alice. *The Color Purple.* Harcourt Brace Jovanovich, 1982.

Weidt, Maryann N. *Presenting Judy Blume.* G. K. Hall/Twayne, 1989.

Zindel, Paul. *The Pigman.* HarperCollins, 1968.

For information on the availability of paperback editions of these titles, please consult the most recent edition of *Paperbound Books in Print,* published annually by R. R. Bowker Company.

Chapter 11

Literature In The English Class:
Short Stories, Novels, Poetry, Drama, and Thematic Units

· ·

In response to requests from previous users of this textbook, we devote this chapter to a discussion of standard approaches to the teaching of literature in high school. Although we recognize that there is no single best way to teach and that schools, classes, students, and goals vary from school to school, from teacher to teacher, and from parent to parent, the methods of teaching literature to young people discussed here have proven their worth for large numbers of teachers and their students.

· ·

Principles of Teaching English

We believe in five principles about English teachers and the teaching of literature. We have developed these principles from our own experiences as well as from the writings and thoughts of many others (Focus Box 11.1).

1. *English teachers must never forget that literature should be both entertaining and challenging.* Teachers need to alert students to literature that the students will find challenging and satisfying through talking about individual works in many genres, perhaps in a genre unit, a thematic unit, or free reading. Is this easy to do? No, not always, but it might convince a few students that teachers care about reading and kids. If the literature doesn't provide entertainment and challenge, English teachers have failed.

2. *English teachers must know a wide range of literature.* Teachers should know classics of English and American literature, of course; they should also know American popular literature and young adult literature and something about Asian and European literature (e.g., Asian folktales, Norwegian drama, French short stories, or Russian novels). They should know women writers and ethnic writers, especially, but not exclusively from the United States, and what

FOCUS BOX 11.1

Using Literature in Secondary Schools

(See also Appendix B, "English Classrooms and Young Adult Literature.")

Authors' Insights: Turning Teenagers into Readers and Writers, edited by Don R. Gallo. Boynton/Cook, 1992. Authors of adolescent literature wrote these articles aimed at English teachers.

Crossing the Mainstream: Multicultural Perspectives in Teaching Literature by Eileen Iscoff Oliver. National Council of Teachers of English 1994. One of the best sources of help for suggestions and reading lists.

Enhancing Aesthetic Reading and Response by Richard M. Anderson and Gregory Rubano. National Council of Teachers of English, 1991. This is good on theory, excellent on practice.

Literature in the Secondary School: Studies of Curriculum and Instruction in the United States. National Council of Teachers of English, 1993. A scholarly and comprehensive account of what goes into the English curriculum.

Literature is . . . : Collected Essays by G. Robert Carlson. Sabre Printers, 1994. Essays on literature and the curriculum.

Readers, Texts, Teachers, edited by Bill Corcoran and Emrys Evans. Boynton/Cook, 1987.

An excellent collection of articles on using literature.

Researching Response to Literature and the Teaching of Literature: Points of Departure, edited by Charles R. Cooper. Ablex, 1985. Cooper gathered research on literature and teaching literature.

Teaching Literature for Examinations by Robert Protherough. Open University Press, 1986. A case study by Terry Gifford, "Teaching Garner's *Red Shift* for an Alternative A-Level," is a model of how to prepare to use a tough book. See also Protherough's *Developing Response to Fiction* (Open University Press, 1983).

Teaching Literature in Middle and Secondary Grades by John S. Simmons and H. Edward Deluzain. Allyn & Bacon, 1992. Down-to-earth and highly recommended.

Understanding Unreliable Narrators: Reading Between the Lines in the Literature Classroom by Michael W. Smith. National Council of Teachers of English, 1991. Smith shows how students learn better when they are encouraged to bring their own real-world values and beliefs to their reading.

---

they don't know about literature, they should learn. That demands that English teachers read all sorts of literature—the great, the new, the popular, the demanding, and the puzzling. Why do they read? Because they are readers themselves and because they are always looking for books that might work with students. One of life's joys for English teachers, and maybe its greatest annoyance, is that they view every poem, every film, every newspaper article, every football game, every everything for its potential use in class.

3. *English teachers ought to know enough about dramatic techniques and oral interpretation to be comfortable reading aloud to students.* We need teachers eager and able to read material to students that just might interest, intrigue, amuse, or excite them, material that might make young people aware of new or old books or writers or techniques or ideas. Outside of speech or drama classes, no classes require so much oral performance from teachers as English classes. Poetry must be read aloud. So must drama. Reading fiction aloud is half the

fun of teaching short stories. If students are to learn how to read poetry or drama, it will come from English teachers comfortable with their own oral reading. One added benefit is that common devices in literature, such as metaphor or irony or ambiguity, are often more apparent when heard rather than read. Obviously, the availability of poetry or fiction on tapes or CDs means other voices can be heard, but that does not mean the teacher's voice should be silent. Granted, Ian McKellen's reading of Shakespeare exceeds the grasp of us mortals, but McKellen isn't there to explain why he read a passage from *Richard III* or *Macbeth* or *Othello* as he did. English teachers are there to explain why they chose to read a particular passage and why they read it as they did.

4. *English teachers need to remember the distance in education and sophistication between them and their students.* No matter what the rapport between them, it is almost equally easy for teachers to overestimate as to underestimate their students, although experienced teachers would surely prefer the first error to the second. Choosing material for an entire class is never easy and often seems impossible. Some materials—say a *New Yorker* short story or a T. S. Eliot poem or a Harold Pinter play—assume a sophistication that high school students often do not have, although sometimes their glibness in class temporarily fools a neophyte. On some occasions, a class is ready for the Pinter, but while waiting for that class, it's tempting for teachers to choose material that challenges no one and that no one greatly enjoys. Selecting literature for 15, 35, or 45 students is almost inevitably an exercise in frustration and failure. That comes with the territory, but it is no excuse for not trying to meet all students' needs with that one fabulous, never-to-be-forgotten classroom novel, poem, short story, or play. Experienced English teachers know this, but most parents and other citizens do not. Teachers should try to let others in on the secret.

5. *Finally, English teachers should teach and use only literature they enjoy.* Teachers should not be expected to fake enthusiasm or interest. If a teacher doesn't like Robert Frost's poetry or Stephen Crane's *The Red Badge of Courage,* the teacher has no business using Frost or Crane. It is permissible for both teachers and young people not to like a work or an author, assuming, of course, the teacher has read and responsibly considered the author or work in question (we can be a bit more charitable toward students on this point). If teachers do not like highly regarded modern works such as Raymond Carver's short stories or Athol Fugard's *"Master Harold"* . . . *and the Boys* or May Swenson's poetry, they shouldn't teach them. There are too many stories and plays and poems out there that teachers will presumably be enthusiastic about. (Obviously, this point follows our second point, that teachers are incurable, wide readers.)

None of this implies that teachers cannot change their minds about literature or writers, just as teachers know that occasionally it is great fun and profitable to work with literature about which they feel ambivalent. Nor does this imply that students should be discouraged from reading and talking about works for which the teacher has no great enthusiasm.

Our five principles for teaching literature extend to works in the curriculum guide as well as the literary canon of great books. It is not being unduly critical of the manner in which many literature curriculum guides are developed to note that they are created by human beings with certain strengths and weaknesses, and they are fallible. As long as they are taken as guides, teachers may be helped, particularly beginning teachers, but when curriculum guides are taken as biblical edicts, absurdity reigns, and any value disappears.

Assuming teachers have a wide knowledge of literature, they can find a variety of works of equal quality to teach. What is gained from a bored teacher presenting Poe's poetry to an equally bored class? It is much better to assume that in the four years of high school these students will have one English teacher who likes Poe. And if it doesn't happen? There are worse disasters. What if no teacher wants to teach Shakespeare? We cannot imagine an English department so devoid of taste or ability, but if one exists, it is surely preferable that students leave school ignorant of Shakespeare than that they be bored by him.

Forcing teachers to teach something they do not like encourages classroom dishonesty. Teachers spout trite and obvious interpretations of literature taken from the teacher's guide, and students regurgitate on tests what they neither care about nor understand. Such dishonesty inevitably breeds boredom with literature and contempt for learning.

Literature that a teacher thinks worth teaching, however defined, ought to encourage honest teaching and honest responses from kids. As Louise Rosenblatt has pointed out again and again:

> No one else can read a literary work for us. The benefits of literature can emerge only from creative activity on the part of the reader himself. He responds to the little black marks on the page, or to the sounds of the words in his ear, and he "makes something of them." The verbal symbols enable him to draw on his past experiences with what the words point to in life and literature.[1]

Allowing young people to respond to literature slows down the teacher and the lesson because thinking takes time and brainpower. Time is required to build trust, especially for students accustomed to memorizing and spitting back whatever the teacher has said. Some students simply do not believe that a teacher wants their opinions, sometimes for good reason. Students have to be convinced that responding honestly to literature is worth the trouble and hard work. An invitation to what appears to be an intellectual coup d'état does not come easily from a teacher, and the acceptance doesn't come easily from students.

Using Young Adult Literature in English Classes

One of the reasons we endorse young adult literature for English classes is that students can believe a teacher who asks for their honest response to a book that features a contemporary young person facing a problem that students have been more likely to face than has their teacher. Young adult literature is often recommended as a bridge to appreciating literary techniques, but its role in developing the trust needed for a response-centered approach to literature may be even more important.

Teachers who believe in the value of young adult literature for either of these purposes sometimes forget that many English teachers still make fun of young adult books. To us, the criticisms often seem irrational and defensive, almost as if the books threatened teachers and their worlds. Nevertheless, young adult converts need to be aware of the following protestations. We could not resist offering some counterarguments, even though we realize we're preaching to the choir.

1. *No one around here knows anything about it. If it was really worth knowing, we'd have heard about it.* It's been around quite a long time now, and since the publication of books by S. E. Hinton, Paul Zindel, Robert Lipsyte, Norma Fox Mazer, Harry Mazer, Robert Cormier, Rosa Guy, Gary Paulsen, and many more, lots of people have heard about it. In any case, the statement is a rationalization for learning nothing new. Ignorance isn't an impressive justification for anything.

2. *Adolescent literature has no heritage and no respectability.* It has a heritage going back more than 130 years. Some people respect it, but few respect anything they haven't read.

3. *We teach only the greatest of literature, and that automatically eliminates adolescent literature from our consideration. Why should we demean ourselves or our students—and their parents—by stooping to something inferior?* We wonder how the greatest of literature was chosen for this curriculum. Were these great books chosen from a list supplied by a college teacher or by some independent body? How great are they for high school students? How long has it been since the teacher read any adolescent books? Some students—and not just the slowest—get little pleasure from reading. We believe it is the English teacher's responsibility to help students find pleasure in reading. We wonder whether only the greatest will do that.

4. *We can't afford thirty or forty copies of something we don't know. That's why we don't use adolescent books.* Maybe you ought to read some of the books. That may tell you whether you'd want to use a class set, and it might suggest that individual titles are better than a set of anything.

5. *Kids have to grow up and take themselves and their work seriously. I do. We expect them to. That takes care of adolescent literature as far as my school is concerned.* We take our work and our kids seriously, too. We'd also like them to enjoy some of their reading. Bruce Brooks's and Sue Ellen Bridgers's books contain plenty of serious stuff, but they also provide the joy of discovering similarities between readers and characters.

6. *Adolescent literature has no permanence. Something is popular today, and something else is popular tomorrow. Great literature is timeless and unchanging. How can we be expected to keep track of ephemera?* What a wonderful justification for reading nothing new. Yes, new books come out all the time. Some new books have a chance to escape the dustheap. Some don't. Most adolescent books don't last, but Alcott's *Little Women* and Twain's *Huckleberry Finn* have been around a long time. Also, consider that S. E. Hinton's *The Outsiders*, Robert Lipsyte's *The Contender*, and Paul Zindel's *The Pigman* are nearly thirty years old. Will they last? That's anyone's guess. We would put money on a bet

that some of Robert Cormier's and Katherine Paterson's books will last. For that matter, we can think of a dozen other young adult writers who seem likely to last.

7. *Why have kids spend time in class reading something they can easily read on their own? Shouldn't class time be spent on books that are challenging, books that kids won't find on their own, books that will make kids stretch intellectually?* Some of those kids may not find those books as challenging as Cormier's *After the First Death* or Alan Garner's *The Owl Service* or Alice Childress's *A Hero Ain't Nothin' But a Sandwich,* and those three titles, among many more, are challenging emotionally and intellectually. Besides, what is there about *The Pearl* or *Silas Marner* or *The Old Man and the Sea* that makes their difficulties worth stretching for? The painful truth is that many young people don't find reading enjoyable, and even though they may not find *Silas Marner* on their own, they also won't find Lowry's *The Giver* or Voigt's *Homecoming,* which might come closer to reaching them.

8. *Isn't adolescent literature formula literature?* Yes, sometimes, but not always. *Formula* is a dirty word—*archetype* has more positive connotations. We are impressed to hear someone talk about Dostoevsky's grand inevitability in *Crime and Punishment.* We are not impressed to hear someone talk about the total predictability of a Nancy Drew mystery. There's nevertheless an uncomfortable similarity between the two comments, if not the two books. Then we mustn't forget that there's young adult literature and young adult literature. Surely a teacher could be justified in using Cormier's *I Am the Cheese* or Paula Fox's *One-Eyed Cat* in a discussion of archetypes.

9. *Isn't it silly and simple-minded stuff about dating and trivia like that?* Sometimes, yes. Most of the time, no. How long has it been since you read Virginia Hamilton, Jill Paton-Walsh, Cynthia Voigt, or Zibby Oneal?

10. *Isn't it mostly about depressing problems—like suicide, death, abortion, pregnancy? Hasn't it been censored a lot?* Yes, it can be serious, and some of it has been censored, but see the thoughtful comment on this that follows.

Observations by Elaine Simpson and Dorothy Broderick speak more effectively than we can to the last three objections.

Simpson addresses her remarks to those librarians and others who for years criticized junior novels for their innocence and their pat answers that instilled false conceptions and failed to deal with fundamental problems:

> Then juvenile authors and editors began giving us such books as *Go Ask Alice; Run Softly, Go Fast; Admission to the Feast; Run, Shelley, Run; The Chocolate War.* I could go on and on naming both fiction and nonfiction.
>
> And what happened? All too many of these same people who had been asking for an honest story about serious teenage problems began protesting: language like *that* in a book for young people? Are rape, abortion, homosexuality, unwed mothers, suicide, drugs, unsympathetic portrayals of parents, and violence appropriate for junior novels? Are young people ready for such explicit realism? Would you want your daughter to read one?[2]

Dorothy Broderick focused on the charge most often expressed by ultraconservatives, "namely, that young adult books are not uplifting. Why, oh why, cry these critics, do the authors have to deal with such depressing subjects. Why can't we go back to the good old days?" Broderick's answer:

> As one who has spent six decades on this planet, let me tell you an important fact: *there were no good old days.* Every problem confronted in a young adult novel today not only existed during my childhood and adolescence, but was known to most of us. There were drunks in families, there were wife abusers, there were child molesters, divorce, certainly death and dying, mental illness, pre-marital pregnancy, and, yes, abortions if you were among the elite. In high school, one of my classmates went home one day to find his father had hung himself in the garage; a couple of weeks later he went home to find his mother had done the same thing.[3]

Adolescent literature has a place in the literature program because it appeals to young people. Why? Young adult novels are short or at least shorter than most modern novels or classics studied in schools. It is easy for teachers to dismiss that point, but it's not a point that young people ignore. Young adult books are easier to read (or so they seem at first reading) than most adult or classic novels. They're about young people the age of the readers and concerned with real issues and problems facing adolescents, particularly the readers (and that's often not true of adult books or classics). They look like they might be fun to read. The dust jackets may bother some adults, but they may also appeal to the young. The photos or paintings on young adult paperbacks are calculated to grab readers just as are the photos and paintings on adult novels. With young adult books, there is also a blurb showing, for example, that the book is about a kid who has this wonderful brother who's dying of AIDS, or it is about a girl whose grandmother is senile, or it is about a boy and a girl enmeshed in a love affair against their parents' wishes. With such come-ons, who is surprised when young people grab young adult titles. The last reason for their popularity with many young people is that the books are often perceived to be unacceptable to traditional teachers; that is, they're forbidden fruit.

What makes young adult books so unattractive to some teachers? Besides the reasons listed earlier, Robert C. Small, Jr., adds an unpleasant final reason. He writes that the goal of most literature programs is to designate the teacher as literary expert and translator of books to lowly students who seem to have no role at all, other than to be recipients of the largesse of the expert-translator-teacher.[4] When young people read adolescent books, they are the experts, and they may need to serve as translators to adults who wish to understand the adolescent books.

What makes young adult books so attractive to other English teachers is the fact that for an imaginative teacher, young adult books have so many uses. An individual title can be studied by the whole class, although that's comparatively rare. They can be paired with adult books, classics or not, as Patricia Lee Gauch suggested.[5] They work beautifully in free reading and thematic units. Their possibilities extend as far as the teachers' imaginations because they provide what other good novels do along with an almost guaranteed adolescent interest. Richard Jackson, editor-in-chief at Bradbury Press, explained that:

YA literature should illuminate rather than educate, raise questions rather than trot out answers. And it should entertain. Though society changes from one generation to another, its rites of passage remain quite fixed. Literature for young adults will endure because the impulse to record and reconsider those rites strikes us all. We can't resist it—and though they may not admit the fact, adolescents do hear us.[6]

One aspect of older and less sophisticated young adult novels was the temptation of authors to answer questions that had been raised. In too many of these superficial novels, the questions were simple, the answers simplistic, and an education in middle-class morality was provided:

Q: What happens if I give in to my boyfriend?

A: You get pregnant or you feel gobs of guilt.

Q: Is sex pleasurable?

A: Not unless you're married.

Q: Will my mother forgive me if I go to the senior all-night dance?

A: Yes, it will hurt her, but she will forgive you. But would you want your daughter in twenty years to do that to you?

Judy Blume, easily the most popular writer for young women, retains her popularity for several reasons, but one is that she doesn't provide neat, easy answers. Sex doesn't solve all problems. Death isn't easily forgotten. Love doesn't last, but then nothing necessarily does. These lessons may not be as warm and comforting as the old trite answers of earlier young adult novels, but readers recognize and respect honesty, and that is the hallmark of Blume—and the mass of young adult writers today.

Using Short Stories in English Class

Short stories may seem to fit into today's penchant for condensations and instant gratification. A short story is more than a *Readers' Digest* version of a novel, however, because from the beginning it is planned to fit into less space. Short stories are uniquely appropriate to young readers because:

1. They have a limited number of characters.
2. Their plots are usually straightforward.
3. The development is most often direct and to the point.
4. In a classroom, students can read 15 short stories in the time it takes to read one or two novels. Through reading the larger number of short stories, they can meet a greater variety of viewpoints and representatives of different ethnic groups and cultures.
5. The best of modern American authors have written short stories, which means that students can experience high-quality writing in pieces that are short enough for comfortable reading.

FOCUS BOX 11.2

Short Story Collections for Independent Reading
(*Denotes an Honor List book)

Athletic Shorts: Six Short Stories by Chris Crutcher. Greenwillow, 1991. The athletes in these stories may attract readers to Crutcher's sports novels since several of the protagonists are the same.

Badger on the Barge and Other Stories by Janni Howker. Greenwillow, 1984. Five masterful short stories by a writer that most bright young adults will enjoy, and envy.

Baseball in April and Other Stories by Gary Soto. Harcourt Brace Jovanovich, 1990. These eleven fairly simple stories are about everyday events in lives of Mexican American kids living in the Fresno, California, neighborhood where Soto grew up.

Funny You Should Ask: The Delacorte Book of Original Humorous Short Stories, edited by David Gale. Delacorte, 1992. Funny stuff by Marion Dane Bauer, Joyce Hansen, Walter Dean Myers, and Gary Soto.

Heartbeats and Other Stories by Peter D. Sieruta. HarperCollins, 1989. A mix of the romantic and funny, several from boys' viewpoints.

A Haunt of Ghosts, edited by Aidan Chambers. HarperCollins, 1987. Ghost stories by contemporary writers such as Jan Mark and

John Gordon and an old standard by Edward Bulwer-Lytton.

The Leaving by Budge Wilson. Philomel, 1992. Winner of the 1991 Canadian Young Adult Book Award, these nine coming-of-age stories are written in the first person from the point of view of young women. Wilson's 1995 collection, *The Dandelion Garden* (Philomel), was also well received.

Sixteen: Short Stories by Outstanding Writers for Young Adults, edited by Don Gallo. Delacorte, 1984. Gallo's first collection in which he invited YA authors to contribute short stories was followed by several others including *Visions* (Delacorte, 1989), *Connections* (Delacorte, 1989), and *Join In: Multiethnic Short Stories . . .* (Delacorte, 1993).

Traveling On into the Light and Other Stories by Martha Brooks. Orchard, 1994. Each story presents a moment that matters, a time that stands out from the "insane jumble" of life experiences.

Ultimate Sports: Short Stories by Outstanding Writers for Young Adults, edited by Donald R. Gallo. Delacorte, 1995. Sports stories from people such as Will Weaver, Todd Strasser, Tessa Duder, Harry Mazer, Robert Lipsyte, Norma Fox Mazer, and Chris Crutcher.

English teachers want students to enjoy and even profit from reading short stories (Focus Box 11.2), but some preparation is necessary. Kids are not born with genes labeled "How to Read Short Stories Perceptively." Teachers need to help students develop the skills to enter imaginative works. Tempting as simple solutions have been to curriculum designers, students should not be required to master a vocabulary list of "Thirty Magic Literary Terms That Will Change Your Life and Make You the Reader You Have Always Longed to Be." There's a place for learning about *verisimilitude, point of view, unreliable narrator, sprung rhythm, synecdoche, foreshadowing, Petrarchan sonnet,* and *carpe diem* if and when the terms enlighten students but never as a series of terms in a pedagogical vacuum.

Finding out about the codes that make one piece of literature succeed while another one fails forces teachers to consider how they went about getting into a short story, for example, and how they get into a story that's new to them. There is

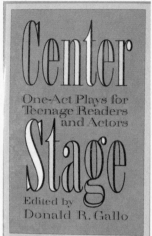

Although teenagers can and do read widely from short story collections, drama, and poetry distributed to general adult audiences, they also appreciate books designed especially for them.

no single way of getting at any literary work, and several approaches may need to be tried. Students may come to class having already learned to listen, to take assiduous notes on what the teacher says is important, and to play all this back at test time, but none of that has much to do with reading. In many ways, a careful reading of a work by student A produces a different work from an equally careful reading by student B or student C. The words in John Updike's "A & P" (in Robert S. Gold's *Point of Departure*) do not change from reader to reader, but the feelings of the readers based on past experience and present morality yield a slightly different story with each reader, and sometimes a greatly different story. One adolescent literature class suggested these steps as ways of helping ninth-graders break the code in reading a short story:

1. Speed-read the story to get some sense of what it's about and who the characters are (probably the only part that can be done outside of class).
2. Read the first sentence carefully (and the first paragraph). What do they tell you about the setting, characters, or tension?
3. Predict from the first paragraph what's likely to follow.
4. Isolate the problems in reading the story (e.g., dialect, structure, conflicting characters).
5. Reread the story, doing parts, or all, of it aloud. Going through this with students should help them learn how literary codes can be broken through careful reading. What can we safely say to our classes about virtually all short stories? We can tell students that all fiction is based on conflict, and we might begin by exploring with them different kinds of conflict. We can say, with some confidence, that the title of the story usually is significant. One of the problems young readers have with Updike's "A & P," once they're willing to get beyond the usual remark that "nothing happens," is understanding what

the title means, since many A & P (the name of the Great Atlantic and Pacific Tea Company) grocery stores seem to have gone the way of all flesh. Students rarely have a clear idea of what this store symbolized in many communities, which was something quite different from a Safeway or a Vons, for example. Students may not be incredibly richer for knowing about the A & P and its place in Updike's fictional community, but it's essential for understanding the community aspects of the story and who the characters are.

We can tell students that first-person narrators are similar to readers in many ways—fallible mortals likely to make mistakes in judging people or letting their emotions get in the way. Students are sometimes puzzled when we raise this point, but it's essential because readers tend to take the narrator's word for almost anything. In "A & P," Sammy quits his cashiering job when his boss (a family friend) tells some young women that they are inappropriately dressed. Sammy makes the grand gesture at least in part to impress the girls, who leave without witnessing Sammy's nobility. He describes the act as, "The sad part of the story, at least my family says it's sad, but I don't think it's so sad myself." A few seconds after Sammy's spur-of-the-moment gallantry, the store manager tells Sammy that he (Sammy) doesn't want to do this. And Sammy says something presumably profound about himself and other young romantics, "it seems to me that once you begin a gesture it's fatal not to go through with it." The manager tells Sammy, "You'll feel this the rest of your life," and Sammy adds, "I know that's true, too." More mature students who enjoy talking about the story—and it is slow moving and meditative and unlikely to appeal to younger students—see an eternal romantic doomed to gestures all his life. Readers may put different amounts of faith in Sammy's words, concluding that he doesn't lie, but he may not recognize the truth.

We can also tell students how important those first words are in most short stories. It's the author's opportunity to grab the audience, and some readers (at least outside school) may decide to drop the story and the author based on those words. Most students rush through the first lines. In class we can force them to slow down by reading aloud the first lines over and over.

William Saroyan begins "Seventeen" (again in Gold) with these words:

Sam Wolinsky was seventeen, and a month had passed since he had begun to shave; now he was in love. And he wanted to do something. A feeling of violence was in him, and he was thinking of himself as something enormous in the world. He felt drunk with strength that had accumulated from the first moment of his life to the moment he was now living, and he felt almost insane because of the strength. Death was nothing. It could not matter if he died; feeling as he did, it could not matter. All that mattered was this moment, Wolinsky in love, alive, walking down Ventura Avenue, in America, Wolinsky of the universe, the Crazy Polak with the broken nose.

What do these words tell, literally? We know the age of a character, and although we can't be sure he's the central character, common sense and the brevity of short stories make it likely that he is. He's developing facial hair (or he wants it to appear and he shaves to make that happen). He's in love, but he feels violent (are those emotions connected? Should they be?). Note all those tough, ugly words—*violence, enormous* (or is that sexual?), *drunk with strength, insane, death, died, the crazy Polak,* and *broken nose.* It's the juxtaposition of *in love* and *alive* and *death* that disturbs us as we read. One paragraph does not a short story make, and there's more to follow, but much can often be found in those first few lines. This story and Updike's "A & P" are published in Robert Gold's fine collection, *Point of Departure,* one of many excellent paperback anthologies designed for teaching short stories (see Focus Box 11.2). Sometimes (the most obvious example is Shirley Jackson's "The Lottery"), the first line lulls readers into a mood that proves totally wrong, and as the words roll by we begin to suspect something is amiss. If the writer has played fair, as Jackson has, and the readers later discover that they misread the clues, a surprisingly fine story can emerge. If the writer has played false and deliberately misled the reader, as O. Henry sometimes did and as many romance writers do, then we have a story providing no more than momentary amusement.

The questions English teachers pose for students should be carefully thought out and played with. Beginning teachers need to develop and practice the questions before class, whereas more experienced teachers can rely on mental notes of what will make the discussion worthwhile rather than mere chitchat to take up 55 minutes of class.

Many teachers ask students to keep journals and to respond to a question or a comment on the board for the first five or ten minutes of class. This activity serves several purposes, including quieting students, turning their attention to the story, and focusing on an issue in the story (probably a key aspect). It allows or forces students to consider what they will say later in class when the question or comment is posed again. Journals also provide an opportunity for students to outline preliminary ideas for papers that may be developed later.

The first few moments of class discussion are often taken up with simple recall questions, reassuring to students and setting up details in the story that may have significance later on. One schema developed and recommended by Edward J. Gordon and Dwight L. Burton[7] suggests how teachers can move from concrete to abstract, as in the following example based on questions our students devised for teaching Nadine Gordimer's "A Company of Laughing Faces" (again in Gold's *Point of Departure*). (Gordimer's short story is set at a beach resort in South Africa. A young girl has been brought there by her demanding mother to spend Christmas holidays with "nice" people. The girl is almost raped, finds the nice people dull and not all that nice, and finds a friend in a little boy who later drowns.)

1. *Questions requiring students to remember facts:*
   A. Describe the setting of the story.
   B. Describe the protagonist and the other major characters.
   C. What new things had Kathy's mother bought for her?
   D. List the major events in the story.
2. *Questions requiring students to prove or disprove a generalization made by someone else:*

A. Although the story is set in a South African resort, I think it could have happened at any resort frequented by the upper middle class. Do you agree or disagree? What differences were there between this holiday and that of American college students going to Florida beaches during spring break? Are these differences crucial to the story?

B. Some readers have interpreted this story as saying that Kathy was a conformist. Do you agree? In what ways was she a conformist? In what ways was she different?

C. One interpretation is that the nameless young man in the story represents the anonymous crowds of young people at the resort. Do you agree or disagree? On what evidence?

D. When Kathy put on her new clothes, the author said that the "disguise worked perfectly." Was Kathy in "disguise" any more than the others? Support your answer with evidence from the story as well as from your own experiences.

3. *Questions requiring students to derive their own generalizations:*
    A. What kind of relationship did Mrs. Hack and Kathy have?
    B. What is Kathy's perception of being young? Who has shaped that perception? Do the events in the story change her perception?
    C. Why doesn't the author give the "young man" a name?
    D. Why does the author contrast the constant activity of the other young people with Kathy's stillness?

4. *Questions requiring students to generalize about the relation of the total work to human experience:*
    A. What did Kathy mean when she said that the sight in the lagoon was the "one truth and the one beauty" in her holiday?
    B. Compare Kathy's relationship with the nameless young man to that of the Bute boy. What is the author saying by showing these two different relationships?
    C. Relate the different parts of the story to Kathy's development in life.
    D. What is the significance of the statement, "The only need she [Kathy] had these days, it seemed, was to be where the gang was; then the question of what to do and how to feel solved itself." Is Kathy satisfied with the answer the gang provides for her? Why or why not?

5. *Questions requiring students to carry generalizations derived from the work into their own lives:*
    A. Have you been in a situation similar to the one experienced by Kathy? How did it make you feel?
    B. What kinds of security do you get from a group? How hard is it to break away?
    C. Have you seen parents like Kathy's mother? What are some ways that young people defend themselves from well-meaning parents who don't understand the situation?

Probably the most important part of a discussion—and unfortunately the most often ignored—is the summing up. In too many classes, the bell rings in the midst of a discussion and students rush away without gathering their thoughts. Such "fly-away" endings cause students to lose respect for class discussions. If they think the teacher is just filling in time until the bell rings, they won't put forth their best efforts. The successful teacher keeps an eye on the clock and saves at least a couple of minutes to draw things together before students are distracted from the topic at hand. Good teachers continually work to develop skill in summarizing throughout a discussion. They draw attention to those points that the class basically agrees on, they praise insightful comments that help the rest of the class see something they might have missed, they search out reasons for disagreement, and they lead students to see connections between the present discussion and previous ones about similar themes or topics.

Determining what short stories (or poems or plays) belong in what grades is one of life's little puzzlements, probably of interest only to English teachers. Updike's "A & P" has been taught as early as ninth grade, but that seems a bit premature. Gordimer's "A Company of Laughing Faces" has been taught as early as tenth grade and possibly earlier. Both are frequently taught in college, sometimes in the freshmen year, sometimes in graduate school.

We provide here our guesses of where a few favorite short stories belong in secondary school. Information about the cited anthologies is given in Focus Box 11.2 or 11.3.

Seventh Grade

James Agee's "A Mother's Tale." 1952. A youngster tries to convince his mother and others that danger awaits. (Found in Crane's *Fifty Great American Short Stories*.)

Stephen Vincent Benet's "By the Waters of Babylon." 1937. The end of civilization is upon us with a frightening twist at the end. (Found in Crane's *Fifty Great American Short Stories*.)

Norma Fox Mazer's "I Hungry Hannah Cassandra Glen . . . " 1984. Being hungry is powerful motivation for going to a funeral. (Found in Gallo's *Sixteen*.)

Todd Strasser's "On the Bridge." 1987. A boy learns the truth, and it hurts. (Found in Gallo's *Visions*.)

Eighth Grade

Robert Cormier's "In the Heat." 1984. In the midst of anything, there is death. (Found in Gallo's *Sixteen*.)

William Melvin Kelley's "A Good Long Sidewalk." 1964. A young African American shovels a snowy sidewalk and finds out about racial prejudice. (Found in Gold' s *Point of Departure*.)

Daniel Keye's "Flowers for Algernon." 1959. An experiment changes a retarded man into a genius and back. (Found in Moffett's *Points of View*.)

Richard Peck's "Priscilla and the Wimps." 1984. A bully tyrannizes the school until Priscilla appears. (Found in Gallo's *Sixteen*.)

FOCUS BOX 11.3

Paperback Anthologies of Teachable Short Stories

American Short Story Masterpieces, edited by Raymond Carver and Tom Jenks. Dell, 1987. Included are Flannery O'Connor's "A Good Man Is Hard to Find," Bernard Malamud's "The Magic Barrell," and Joyce Carol Oates's "Where Are You Going, Where Have You Been?"

Do You Like It Here? edited by Robert Benard. Dell, 1989. Stories about school by Sue Kaufman, Maureen Daly, John O'Hara, Tobias Wolff, and Gore Vidal.

Fifty Great American Short Stories, edited by Milton Crane. Bantam, 1980. Included are Mary E. Freeman's "A New England Nun," Conrad Aiken's "Silent Snow, Secret Snow," James Agee's "A Mother's Tale," William Carlos Williams's "The Use of Force," Jack London's "To Build a Fire," Ambrose Bierce's "The Damned Thing," and Stephen Vincent Benet's "By the Waters of Babylon." Crane has also done *Fifty Great Short Stories* (Bantam, 1981).

Great American Short Stories, edited by Wallace and Mary Stegner. Dell, 1957. This fine and safe collection includes William Daniel Steele's "The Man Who Saw Through Heaven," Henry James's "The Real Thing," and Walter van Tilburg Clark's "The Wind and the Snow of Winter."

Mid-Century: An Anthology of Distinguished Contemporary American Short Stories, edited by Orville Prescott. Pocket Books, 1958. Included are Frank Rooney's "Cyclists' Raid," Shirley Jackson's "The Lottery," and Joseph Whitehill's "The Day of the Last Rock Fight."

Point of Departure: 19 Stories of Youth and Discovery, edited by Robert S. Gold. Dell, 1967. Included are John Updike's "A & P" and "Tomorrow and Tomorrow and So Forth," Bernard Malamud's "A Summer's Reading," William Saroyan's "Seventeen," John Bell Clayton's "The White Circle," Allan Sillitoe's "The Bike," William Melvin Kelley's "A Good Long Sidewalk," and Nadine Gordimer's "A Company of Laughing Faces."

Points of View, edited by James Moffett and Kenneth R. McElheny. Mentor/NAL, 1965. Included are William Carlos Williams's "The Use of Force," Nikolai Gogol's "The Diary of a Madman," Joseph Conrad's "The Idiots," Daniel Keyes's "Flowers for Algernon," John Updike's "A & P," and Anton Chekhov's "Enemies."

Short Story Masterpieces, edited by Robert Penn Warren and Albert Erskine. Dell, 1954. Included are Joseph Conrad's "An Outpost of Progress," F. Scott Fitzgerald's "Winter Dreams," D. H. Lawrence's "The Horse Dealer's Daughter," Saki's "The Open Window," Somerset Maugham's "The Outstation," Sherwood Anderson's "The Egg," and William Faulkner's "Barn Burning."

Ninth Grade

Jack London's "To Build a Fire." 1908. A man learns that the Yukon is unforgiving. (Found in Crane's *Fifty Great American Short Stories*.)

Saki's "The Open Window." 1930. A nervous man learns about ghosts. (Found in Warren's *Short Story Masterpieces*.)

John Steinbeck's "Flight." 1938. A boy accidently kills a man and must flee. (Found in Warren's *Short Story Masterpieces*.)

Joseph Whitehill's "The Day of the Last Rock Fight." 1954. A school tradition becomes a tragedy. (Found in Prescott's *Mid-Century*.)

Tenth Grade

William Faulkner's "Barn Burning." 1939. A boy's father is tried as a barn burner. (Found in Warren's *Short Story Masterpieces*.)

Bernard Malamud's "A Summer's Reading." 1958. A boy who's hardly been noticed makes a grand gesture. (Found in Gold's *Point of Departure*.).

Mauro Senesi's "A Dog for Rock." 1966. The leader of a pack of boys finds affection and loses power. (Found in *Atlantic* for November 1966. More difficult to find than the other stories but worth the effort.)

William Carlos Williams's "The Use of Force." 1933. What force can do to both people, the user and the one used. (Found in Warren's *Short Story Masterpieces*.)

Eleventh Grade

F. Scott Fitzgerald's "Winter Dreams." 1926. The prototypical Fitzgerald hero falls desperately in love with the prototypical Fitzgerald heroine. (Found in Warren's *Short Story Masterpieces*.)

Katherine Mansfield's "The Garden Party." 1922. In the midst of parties there is death. (Found in Crane's *Fifty Great American Short Stories*.)

Joyce Carol Oates's "Where Are You Going, Where Have You Been?" 1970. A flame comes to the moth's door. (Found in Carver's *American Short Story Masterpieces*.)

Irwin Shaw's "The Eighty Yard Run." 1942. A football hero marries a cheerleader, and she grows up. (Found in Warren's *Short Story Masterpieces*.)

Twelfth Grade

John Collier's "The Chaser." 1940. A young man desperately in love gets what he asks for, then. . . . (Found in Crane's *50 Great Short Stories*.)

Nadine Gordimer's "A Company of Laughing Faces." 1960. A girl who doesn't fit in finds a dead boy and chooses not to tell anyone. (Found in Gold's *Point of Departure*.)

Henry James's "The Real Thing." 1893. Appearance versus reality. (Found in Stegners's *Great American Short Stories*.)

John Updike's "A & P." 1962. A young man makes a gesture, but the right audience doesn't see him. (Found in Gold's *Point of Departure*.)

Useful reference tools for finding publication information about particular short stories are the *Chicorel Index to Short Stories in Anthologies and Collections*, which includes information on publications up until 1977, and the *Short Story Index*, published at frequent intervals by the H. W. Wilson Company. The *Index* includes information on magazine publications from 1953 to the present.

Within the last decade, publishers have produced several attractive collections of short stories designed for independent reading by teenagers. (Focus Box 11.2) Other recent and well-received anthologies include *Rites of Passage* edited by Tonya Bolden and focusing on stories about growing up by African-American writers from around the world, and *American Dragons* edited by Laurence Yep and including stories by 25 Asian American writers.

Don Gallo, as much as anyone, deserves credit for promoting short story anthologies designed for teenagers. He invited such well-known young adult authors as Sue Ellen Bridgers, Richard Peck, Bette Greene, Robert Lipsyte, Kevin Major, Ouida Sebestyen, and Rosa Guy to contribute unpublished short stories to a collection that Delacorte published in 1984 under the title of *Sixteen.* Several similar books have followed. He had a good idea because young adult novels and short stories share many characteristics. In fact, 30 years ago, many of the stories now published as young adult novels would have appeared in magazines as long short stories. M. E. Kerr began her career writing short stories about teenagers for *Compact* and *Ladies Home Journal,* and at least two of the other contributors to Gallo's collections (Norma Fox Mazer and Robert Cormier) had already published their own collections of short stories.

At a session on "The Resurgence of the Short Story" at a recent National Council of Teachers of English convention, teacher Bob Seney from Houston, Texas, recommended more than two dozen collections of short stories and showed how they represented realistic fiction, science fiction, fantasy, humor, animal stories, folklore, and myth. Students who are hung up on a particular kind of book can usually be enticed to try at least a short story in another genre. Within the same genre, they can be encouraged to select more challenging books. While warning teachers not to overanalyze short stories, he suggested reading them aloud in class to introduce a topic for discussion or writing, illustrate a point, fill out a thematic unit, provide material for readers' theater and dramatization, and give students enough experience with literary concepts that they can learn the meanings of literary terms from actual experience rather than from memorizing definitions.

Using Novels in English Class

Assigning one novel to be read by an entire class is a popular practice with teachers, partly because it is reassuring to know what's on the agenda for the next few days or, in some classes, even the next few weeks. After struggling with grammar and composition, where class members' abilities are obviously at great distances from each other, it should be a treat for teachers and the students all to join in reading the same book.

Although many teachers assume that having specific novels read by the entire class has always been a standard part of the English curriculum, the practice is not universally accepted. Some teachers argue that whatever can be learned by studying a common novel can be just as easily learned by studying several short stories. Others say that short stories neither allow for a long-term immersion in a created world nor provide complex character development taking place over a period of a character's lifetime.

One of the problems in using novels is the expense of acquiring a set of novels of your choice (e.g., Bernard Malamud's *The Assistant,* Robin McKinley's *The Hero and the Crown,* or Mary Shelley's *Frankenstein or the Modern Prometheus*) rather than inheriting whatever is left in the English department closet. Another problem is the length of time it takes for students to read the novel (rarely less than a week and more likely two or more). Adults have been known to stop reading when boredom sets in, but no such benediction comes to kids when they're reading a book for a class. More than sixty years ago, Howard Francis Seely wondered about our attraction to novels:

> Just why is it deemed imperative that a whole class read the same novels at the same time, anyway? I haven't heard a sound answer yet. . . . The burden of most of these answers can be recapitulated briefly. A frequent one is that reading one book permits class discussion (which discussion, however, more often than not turns out to be the answering of factual questions chiefly of a trifling nature). . . . A third answer indicates reading this one particular book in this particular class will enlighten the pupils to the structure of the novel as a literary form (which it won't, and which would be of doubtful immediate or ultimate value even if it did). . . . Perhaps the most frequent (and likely the most futile) argument of all is this: If Johnny hasn't read *The Talisman* in the ninth grade with his group, what will happen to him when he comes to *The Spy* in the tenth? That question is generally hurled at me with an air of utter, crushing finality. I can only faintly ask, "Well, just what *would?*" With that I'm given up as hopeless.[8]

A few years later, a teacher from England worried about teaching the novel on other grounds:

> Once the novelty has worn off a book, the child's interest in it can very easily flag. . . . Even the best novel rarely occupies us more than a few evenings. It is curious that teachers . . . should so often expect the restless mind of the child to possess a greater staying power in this respect than they possess themselves.[9]

English teachers who wish to use novels for common reading obviously need to choose books they believe will appeal to young people. Never choose something because it is reputedly a classic and therefore will somehow be magically good for students. Do not choose a book solely because it has won an award. Some teachers and librarians assume that an award-winning book is quality literature, and generally there's merit in that, but winners are chosen by humans, not gods, and humans make mistakes, some of them wondrous to behold. Anyone who has been part of a committee charged with choosing a book award knows that books are removed from final consideration for reasons having nothing to do with literary merit or adolescent appeal. Controversial books, such as those with more than marginal profanity or mild sex, frighten committees, and compromise is inevitable.[10] This is as true of awards for adults as for young people; Pulitzer and Nobel winners have frequently been controversial and debated for years.

Some teachers do not have to worry about selection because choices are established by school or district curricula. Among the most widely used titles are John

Steinbeck's *Of Mice and Men,* Harper Lee's *To Kill a Mockingbird,* Mark Twain's *Adventures of Huckleberry Finn,* William Golding's *Lord of the Flies,* and Robert Cormier's *The Chocolate War.* All five are understandably popular with teachers and students, and all five are among the most widely censored books in public schools.

Those interested in finding suggestions on what novels work well in classrooms should skim through back issues of the *English Journal* or their state NCTE affiliate journals, such as New York's *English Record,* the *Arizona English Bulletin,* *California English,* the *Connecticut English Journal,* and the *Virginia English Bulletin.* Successful English teachers understandably love to tell about the ones that didn't get away. Exceptionally helpful questions and ideas about using novels can be found in articles by Geoff Fox[11] and Richard Peck.[12]

A practice that appeals to some English teachers is to divide a class of thirty or forty students into small groups of five to seven people and select five to ten titles with closely related themes. The members of each group read one or more of the books and talk with each other about how the theme was developed in their books. Later in a class discussion each small group presents its theme, why the theme was significant, and what their books had to say about that theme.

The National Council of Teachers of English and its related organizations have always been supportive of adolescent literature. See Appendices A and B for details.

An obvious advantage is that while in a class of thirty to forty, students rarely have enough time to get across their ideas, small groups provide time and encouragement even for students fearful of talking in class. Teachers need to remember that young people do not automatically know how to take part in a small group. Worthwhile discussions occur only when teachers give guidance and set up specific tasks.

Some other advantages of reading in small groups deserve mention. It is often easier to find five or ten copies of a book than thirty copies, and it may be wise to try a novel in a small group before you consider it for an entire class. The procedure also allows students to choose books that match their individual abilities and maturity levels. Books that might cause public relations problems or attempted censorship if they are required reading for an entire class can be examined and studied by small groups whose members can decide for themselves whether or not they wish to read a particular title.

Also, when students have read different books, class members are more interested in hearing about the other books, especially if the teacher encourages a variety of creative activities. Listed below are some of those we have seen some kids enjoy:

1. Do a costumed presentation of your book. Dress either as the author or one of the characters.
2. Write a letter from one character to another character.
3. Outline a sequel.
4. Write a new conclusion or a new beginning.
5. If a journey was involved, draw a map with explanatory notes of significant places.
6. Make a diorama and explain what it shows.
7. Write a book review for a class publication.
8. Make and laminate a new book jacket with an original blurb.
9. Use e-mail to tell a reading pen pal about the book.
10. Participate with three or four classmates in a television talk show about the book.
11. With another student, do a pretend interview with the author or with one of the characters.
12. Use a journalistic style and write a news story about something that happened to one of the characters.
13. For fun, exaggerate either characteristics or events and write a tabloid-style news story related to your book.
14. Cut out magazine pictures to make a collage or a poster illustrating the idea of the book.
15. Draft a letter to a television or movie producer suggesting that your book be considered for a mass media production. (*Note:* S. E. Hinton's *The Outsiders* was made into a movie as the result of a letter written to Francis Ford Coppola by students at the Lone Star school in Fresno, California.)
16. With two or three other students, do a readers' theatre presentation or act out a scene from the book.

See pp. 341 for other alternatives to book reports. These photos were taken at Osborn Middle School in Phoenix, Arizona.

17. Lead a small group discussion with other readers of the same book. Focus on a specific topic and report your group's conclusions to the class.
18. Keep a reading journal and record your thoughts at the end of each period of reading.
19. Find a song or a poem that relates to the theme of your book. Explain the similarities.
20. Draw a comic-book page complete with bubble-style conversations showing an incident in your book.

Using Poetry in English Class

When we talk about poetry in our college classes, our students usually begin by telling us how significant poetry is, how many great poets they have read, and how much they enjoyed poetry when they were children, especially Dr. Seuss. A few tack on Shel Silverstein's work, which they read to their children. But when we ask students to write down the titles of a few poems they have enjoyed as adults, they glance upward, presumably to supplicate the almighty, or they stare out the windows, where life is real.

Then we begin talking about what happened to the fondness for poetry they felt as children and the discomfort they now feel as adults. The following five comments pop up over and over, semester after semester. We realize the statements are slanted because they come from students searching their memories for bad experiences to explain their negative feelings toward poetry, but despite the lack of objectivity, we repeat them since they may have instructional value for teachers hoping to be more successful:

1. Their high school teachers seemed unenthusiastic about poetry, "just going through the motions." Some teachers taught a unit on poetry to "get rid of it all at once." Others seemed afraid of poetry or at least uncertain of what to do with it.
2. Some teachers substituted a flood of technical terms for the poetry they might have taught. They inundated students, who had to memorize the terms but saw no connection between the terms and poetry or anything else. One teacher reportedly said, "Until you understand these terms, you won't be able to understand the poetry we'll read later." The student who reported this could not remember that they ever got around to reading poetry. Another student remembers being required to write a poem with one metaphor, at least two similes, and one example of personification. That exercise and two or three poems was the poetry unit for the entire year.
3. Some of our students' teachers talked about how terribly compressed poetry is, how terribly slow-moving it is, and how terribly significant it is. They did not seem to talk about how terribly interesting it can be.
4. Many teachers worried about the difficult language and the allusions in poetry and took great delight in expounding and expanding on these, often referring to graduate seminars they had taken that had made clear these arcane matters.
5. Students remembered playing constant guessing games on the meaning or morals of various poems. Teachers asked students for their ideas but took little

interest in what students said. Occasionally a student would guess the right answer, but more often, the teacher would be the one to announce the right meaning or moral.

To be fair, we must also report that a number of our students, although always a minority, remember their teachers with affection and their teaching of poetry with respect and admiration. Those teachers clearly honored their students and got respect by giving it. They listened to students, even when they disagreed, and they did not force their reading of a poem down anyone's throat. They chose poetry for adolescent appeal *and* literary merit, the former always outweighing the latter. These uncommon teachers were exactly what we hope our students will become—teachers who love poetry, who choose poetry they believe kids will enjoy, who are excited about poetry of many kinds, and who recognize that successful literature in class is literature that works for students today, not at some vague time in the future.

Readers' appreciation for poetry develops in much the same way as their appreciation for prose. They begin with an unconscious delight in sounds—the repetition and rhythm of nursery rhymes, songs, and television commercials. Then they go on to the fun of riddles, puns, playground chants, and autograph rhymes. Soon they get involved in such simple plots as those found in limericks and the humorous verses of Jack Prelutsky and Shel Silverstein. By the time children are in the middle grades, their favorite poems are those that tell stories, for example, Robert Browning's "The Pied Piper of Hamelin," Henry Wadsworth Longfellow's "Hiawatha's Childhood" and "The Midnight Ride of Paul Revere," Robert Service's "The Cremation of Sam McGee," James Whitcomb Riley's "The Gobble-Uns'll Get You if You Don't Watch Out," and Edgar Allan Poe's "The Raven."

Capitalizing on this interest in story, publishers continue to produce new editions of story poems in beautifully designed books that attract junior and senior high school readers. Modern writers tell stories in ways that kids hardly realize they are poetry, as in Cynthia Rylant's *Soda Jerk* and Virginia Euwer Wolff's *Make Lemonade.*

Over the years, teachers enthusiastic about and successful in teaching poetry have evolved principles for teaching poetry. Stephen Dunning developed eight such principles in 1966:

> Principle One: The teacher who is not himself a reader of poetry must not pretend to teach poetry. . . . two: The teacher of poetry must teach only those poems for which he can engender real enthusiasm. . . . three: The teacher must keep experience with poetry itself at the center of his teaching. . . . four: The teacher must teach the mechanics of poetry inductively. . . . five: Teachers must stop overexplaining poems. . . . six: the poetry unit must give way to the occasional teaching of poetry. . . . seven: Students must often have the chance to choose what poetry they will read, study, and discuss. . . . eight: Students who are asked to read and study poetry must sometimes be asked to say something poetically.[13]

Two British teachers a few years later listed six principles.

PAUL JANECZKO
On Collecting Poems

If you've ever read a book of poetry and noticed poems that touched you more than others, you've taken the first step toward creating a poetry anthology. I look for poems that strike me. These are the ones I save, copying and filing in subject/topic folders. After the poems have sat in the folders for a time, I read through them again to refresh my memory of the poems I've saved. It also helps me make connections, to see similarities and differences in the poems that may help me place them with other poems.

An anthologist must break ground, so I need to go beyond the poems that I discover in journals and books. One new source I found is the poets themselves. Since I worked on *Poetspeak: In Their Work, About Their Work,* I've stayed in touch with a long list of poets who are eager to send me new poems and spread the word to other poets. Now, when I'm thinking about a new anthology, I can generate computer postcards stating my needs and mail them to all the poets on my mailing list.

Stacks of poems, however, do not an anthology make. Poems must connect with other poems. Some associations are obvious, but I look for connections that may not be apparent at first reading. I want readers to think about why poems are where they are. I want to bring order to the collection, an order that will give the timid, inexperienced reader of poetry a gentle nudge in a helpful direction. I discovered while working on *Dont Forget to Fly* that groups of two to six poems work better for me than larger groups. Small groupings, however, make the anthology more difficult to organize because I must not only connect the poems in each section, but I must also connect the sections.

When I've decided on the poems for a new collection, I let them rest for a few months. Then I tinker with the book, fine-tune it by cutting out some poems, changing the order, perhaps adding a poem or two to make the book flow more effortlessly. Even though I realize that few people read an anthology from cover to cover as they would a novel, I try to make sure that my collections are carefully "plotted" from first poem to last.

Why collect poems? Long before I created my first anthology in 1977, I was hooked on poetry, believing the words of James Dickey, "What you have to realize . . . , if you love poetry, is that poetry is just naturally the greatest goddamn thing that ever was in the whole universe. If you love it, there's no substitute for it." And if you love it, you have to pass it on.

Paul Janeczko's edited collections include *Wherever Home Begins,* Orchard, 1995, *Looking for Your Name,* Orchard, 1993; *Preposterous: Poems of Youth,* Orchard, 1991; and *The Place My Words Are Looking For: What Poets Say About and Through Their Work,* Bradbury, 1990.

A. Poetry is to be experienced before it is to be analysed.
B. The enjoyment of a poem is often deepened by analysis, though such close study can be carried out obliquely, not only through line by line study.
C. Any classroom activity in teaching a poem should bring reader and text closer together, not come between them.
D. We need to discourage any message implicit or explicit, that poems are really puzzles in need of solutions.
E. A poem rarely "belongs" to its readers on one or two readings, particularly when such readings are immediately followed by an all class discussion of an evaluative kind; in fact, "Do you like it?" questions about the whole poem or its diction, rhythm, rhyme, etc. are best deferred as long as possible or not asked at all.
F. Whether a poem is finally valued or rejected, we need to provide means for reflection upon it, the opportunity for readers and listeners to work in and out of the text.[14]

Richard W. Beach and James D. Marshall reiterate a point or two and then urge a certain recklessness for the teacher of poetry:

> Never teach a poem you don't like.
> Do teach poems that you're not certain you understand. Teach poems about which you may have some real doubt.
> Teach poems that are new to you as well as your store of "old standards."
> Become a daily reader of poems, a habitue of used book-stores, a scavenger of old *New Yorkers* and other magazines that contain poetry.
> Give students the freedom to dislike great poetry.[15]

Teachers must—not *should* but *must*—be enthusiastic about poetry. We don't mean that teachers should fake enthusiasm or substitute gushiness for honesty. English teachers who cannot be enthusiastic about some poems should either never teach poetry or, perhaps the better alternative, leave the profession.

Teachers need to perform poetry. Samuel Thurber, one of the great fathers of English-Education, wrote in 1897:

> Not poetry analyzed, but poetry relished, enjoyed, repeated with gusto, declaimed with abandon, acted with energy, felt as a heat melting to hard natures, seen as picture with the eye of the imagination,—poetry received in the spirit in which it was offered by the artists who made it.[16]

Other teachers and writers have made much the same point:

> Poetry is first and foremost a performer's art. Its life is in the spoken language, in the application of normal speech sounds and rhythms to gain varied and subtle ends. To enjoy it you must speak and hear it—either out loud or in your head—and this is, fortunately, a skill that can be learned.[17]

> Poetry teachers, especially at the high school and undergraduate levels, should spend less time on analysis and more on performance. . . . Poems should be memorized, recited, and performed. The sheer joy of the art must be

emphasized. The pleasure of performance is what first attracts children to poetry, the sensual excitement of speaking and hearing the words of the poem. Performance was also the teaching technique that kept poetry vital for centuries. Maybe it also holds the key to poetry's future.[18]

We should spend more time reading poems aloud and allowing students to read some poems that have moved them. We can ask for a reaction, a comment, or a question on the poem that may lead to a discussion. When that doesn't happen, however, we need not feel defeated. It's important to give students a chance to hear the music of poetry.[19]

A few other bits of advice: Teachers should avoid units on poetry. Poems deserve to be used frequently but not en masse. Thematic units that use poems in conjunction with short stories or drama work well. Dropping a funny poem into class just for the fun of it—or a monster poem—works if the poems are within the grasp of kids. Teachers worthy of the name know how to choose poems that stand the best chance of getting poetry into kids. Also, students should occasionally, or regularly, help to select some poems for reading and discussion.

Poetry exists for one reason in a class, to be read by an enthusiastic teacher to kids who might respond. That demands time for the teacher to consider and wonder and revisit the poems. Time is essential, not to see how many poems can be knocked off in one class, but to allow us to hear poems again and again in our minds. (We saw one teacher who obviously hated poetry and who set at least a local record by killing 36 Emily Dickinson poems in less than one class period.)

After learning to appreciate story-poems, young readers go on to take pleasure in recognizing kinship with a poet, finding someone who expresses a feeling or makes an observation that the reader has come close to but hasn't quite been able to put into words. Much of the "Pop" poetry that English teachers consider trite or overdone is appreciated by young readers in this stage. We know a creative writing teacher who criticized a student-written poem as being overly sentimental by writing on the paper, "This sounds like Rod McKuen." The student was thrilled at being compared to McKuen, and the teacher didn't have the heart to explain that she had not intended the remark as a compliment.

Understanding and appreciating the skill with which a poet has achieved the desired effect brings extra pleasure. This is why English teachers are interested in helping students arrive at this level of poetic appreciation, but the teacher who tries to get there too fast runs the risk of leaving students behind. Fortunately, many teachers now provide students with a variety of poems and let them start where they are in their appreciation of poetry.

We did not include poetry in the first edition of this book because we didn't think that people wrote poetry specifically for teenagers. Such poets as David McCord and Aileen Fisher search for topics especially appealing to and appropriate for children, but we didn't know anyone who did this for young adults. Then in 1982, Mel Glenn published *Class Dismissed! High School Poems,* which, along with its sequels, was chosen for several best-book lists. Young protagonists from a variety of racial and socioeconomic backgrounds use candid, first-person speech to discuss intense situations, ranging from having a crush on a teacher to quitting school, getting caught shoplifting, and being stabbed. The titles of the poems are kids' names, and most poems are illustrated with a photograph. Although Glenn wrote the poems himself, the design of the book gives the impression that the kids in the photographs are the poets.

Although writing poetry specifically for a young adult audience is a recent development, collecting poems with special appeal to teenagers and packaging them for the high school market has a much longer history. A book that thirty years ago proved the potential success of this kind of venture was *Reflections on a Gift of Watermelon Pickle,* published first by Scott, Foresman in 1966, later reprinted in various formats and issued on a record, and then reprinted once more in 1995. Editors Steve Dunning, Edward Lueders, and Hugh L. Smith selected the poems by getting the reactions of teenagers to both well-known and new poems gleaned from hundreds of poetry magazines. There was more to their success than just the individual poems. The title, taken from the concluding poem, is intriguing, and the spacious design and watermelon green cover and reddish-pink endpapers make the book memorable.

Over the past twenty years, Paul Janeczko, a high school English teacher in Auburn, Maine, has consistently edited well-received anthologies with many of the same characteristics as the *Watermelon Pickle* book, that is, an intriguing title, spacious and attractive designs, poems that have been tested for their appeal to young readers, and an organization that leads readers from one poem to the next. (See Focus Box 11.4 for several of Janeczko's anthologies and other anthologies worth reading and using.)

Janeczko's books have a cyclical organization with between two and five poems on similar subjects. For example, in *Dont Forget to Fly,* Constance Sharp's "I Show the Daffodils to the Retarded Kids" is grouped with Joyce Carol Oates's "Children Not Kept at Home" and Theodore Roethke's "My Dim Wit Cousin." In all, there are forty groupings with subjects ranging from suicide to dressmaker's dummies, swimming, and Sunday.

Because readers come to poetry not so much for information as for a change of pace, a bit of pleasure through wordplay, a sudden recognition or insight, a recollection from childhood, or a time of emotional intensity, the design of the book needs to invite readers in. Even though the age range that can read and enjoy poetry is usually much wider than that for prose, there is still a subtle dividing line between children's and young adult poetry. Teenagers may be amused by humorous poetry prepared for children (see Chapter Nine for some examples), but they are likely to feel slightly insulted if offered serious children's poetry.

Many young adults are ready to read and enjoy the same poetry that educated adults enjoy, especially if teachers smooth the way by first providing access to poets whose allusions they are likely to understand and then gradually leading them into poetry representing cultures and times different from their own. It may help to ease students into appreciating the work of some poets by first offering various kinds of biographical reading as with Neil Baldwin's *To All Gentleness, William Carlos Williams: The Doctor Poet;* Jean Gould's *American Women Poets: Pioneers of Modern Poetry;* or Paul Janeczko's *Poetspeak: In Their Work, About Their Work.* In a similar way, someone who has read Alice Walker's *The Color Purple* will probably be ready to appreciate the poems in her *Good Night Willie Lee, I'll See You in the Morning.*

FOCUS BOX 11.4

Recommended Poetry Anthologies
(*Denotes an Honor List Book)

*American Sports Poems, edited by R. R. Knudson and May Swenson. Orchard, 1988. Poets as good as Grace Butcher, Tess Gallagher, John Updike, Anne Sexton, and Robert Francis treat both common and unusual sports.

*Class Dismissed! High School Poems by Mel Glenn, photographs by Michael J. Bernstein. Clarion, 1982. Glenn adapted the subjects and mode of the realistic problem novel to poetry and made his story-poems seem even more realistic by illustrating them with photographs. Sequels include *Class Dismissed II: More High School Poems* (Clarion, 1986), *Back to Class* (Clarion, 1988), and *My Friend's Got This Problem, Mr. Candler: High School Poems* (Clarion, 1991).

*Cool Salsa: Bilingual Poems on Growing Up Latino in the United States, edited by Lori M. Carlson. Holt, 1994. Poems by Sandra Cisneros, Pat Mora, and Gary Soto, as well as by less well-known Latino poets, treat such everyday subjects as parties, school, memories, hard times, and the future.

I Wouldn't Thank You for a Valentine: Poems for Young Feminists, edited by Carol Ann Duffy. Holt, 1992. Poems from many cultures ranging from sad to funny. See also *Waltzing on Water*, edited by Norma Fox Mazer and Marjorie Lewis (Dell, 1989). Poets include Sharon Olds, May Swenson, Linda Pastan, Marge Piercy, and Muriel Rukeyser.

The Inner City Mother Goose by Eve Merriam. Simon & Schuster, 1996. Unfortunately, this new edition of Merriam's poems still speaks loudly about the fears, violence, and drugs that are part of inner city life.

Mindscapes: Poems for the Real World, edited by Richard Peck. Dell, 1990. Before Richard Peck became a young adult writer, he was an English teacher with a wide and fine taste in poetry. His *Sounds and Silences* (Dell, 1990) is also a good collection.

Now Sheba Sings the Song by Maya Angelou. Dial, 1987. Beautifully done portraits of African American women accompany Angelou's poems. Other not-to-be-missed Angelou books include *And Still I Rise* (1978), *Oh Pray My Wings Are Gonna Fit Me Well* (1975), *Just Give Me a Cool Drink of Water 'fore I Die* (1971), and *I Shall Not Be Moved* (1990), all Random House.

Pierced by a Ray of Sun edited by Ruth Gordon. HarperCollins, 1995. The 73 poems in this collection are tied together in exploring human loneliness. Gordon's earlier collections *Time Is the Longest Distance* (1991), *Under All Silences* (1987), and *Peeling the Onion* (1993), all HarperCollins, are also recommended.

*Pocket Poems: Selected for a Journey, edited by Paul Janeczko. Bradbury, 1985. Buy, rent, borrow, or steal any book edited by Janeczko. He's an American treasure. Additional titles from Orchard include *Wherever Home Begins* (1995), *Looking for Your Name: A Collection of Contemporary Poems* (1993), *Preposterous Poems of Youth* (1991), and *The Music of What Happens: Poems That Tell Stories* (1988). With Bradbury he has published *Postcard Poems: A Collection of Poetry for Sharing* (1979), *Strings: A Gathering of Family Poems* (1984), and *Dont Forget to Fly* (1981).

*Reflections on a Gift of Watermelon Pickle, edited by Stephen Dunning and others. Scott, Foresman, 1967. A landmark book re-issued in 1994, this collection proved that young readers could enjoy modern poetry without the help (or hindrance) of teachers. Its sequel, *Some Haystacks Don't Even Have Any Needle: And Other Complete Modern Poems* (Lothrop, 1969), is almost as good.

Readers of Ray Bradbury's science fiction may want to read his fifty-plus poems in *When Elephants Last in the Dooryard Bloomed*. Students who have read Maya Angelou's autobiographical *I Know Why the Caged Bird Sings* will probably be interested in her poetry.

The Writing and Reading Connection

Today hundreds of small poetry magazines are published in the United States, and many of these include poems written by high school and college students. A class assignment that we have given for several years is to ask our college students to collect examples they like of ten different kinds of poems. One of the categories is an original, unpublished poem written by either the student or a roommate, friend, or family member. No student has ever complained about not being able to find a friendly poet willing to share.

Poets are looking for audiences. After a poetry reading on our campus by a nationally known poet, a man in the audience stood up to complain that he had been told by the editor of the local newspaper, who kept rejecting his poems, that there were too many people writing poems today. The poet looked thoughtful for a moment and then responded, "No, there just aren't enough people reading poems."

Poetry lovers all over are working to change this state of affairs, and among these poetry lovers are teachers and librarians who sponsor writing groups and subscribe to and display both large and small poetry magazines as well as publications from neighboring schools and poetry anthologies from national presses. Such groups serve as a support and confidence builder for teachers who themselves have not had good experiences with poetry and so are hesitant to venture beyond whatever comes in their prescribed textbooks.

Books about teaching literature inevitably give suggestions on teaching this or that genre, but readers can almost palpably sense the urgency of suggestions for teaching poetry. Recommended books include Louise Rosenblatt's seminal *The Reader, the Text, the Poem: The Transactional Theory of the Literary Work;* Patrick Dias and Michael Hayhoe's *Developing Response to Poetry;* and Stephen Dunning's *Teaching Literature to Adolescents: Poetry.* (see Focus Box 11.5 for other helpful books.)

Young people sometimes maintain that they don't like love poems, but that usually means they don't care for love poems by writers of the Romantic period or love poems outside the ken of the young. Anyone who's been around a school corridor for a few minutes knows full well that young people care about love. Another claim is that teenagers don't like nature poems. This can usually be translated to mean they didn't care for Emerson's feeble efforts or, again, the Romantic writers. Kids care about nature. They love going on hikes and picnics and hunting and fishing, and there's lots of good poetry that taps into those interests.

Although there's no such thing as a surefire poem for every occasion and all teachers, some poems come close to being successful more often than not. For example, many young people go through an Edgar Allan Poe phase and go around reciting "Annabel Lee" or "The Raven" or that most esoteric poem for the young, "Ulalume." Robert Frost's narrative poetry usually works well, especially "Home Burial."

FOCUS BOX 11.5

Books to Help Students and Teachers with Poetry

50 Contemporary Poets: The Creative Process, edited by Alberta T. Turner. David McKay, 1977. Turner asked many poets to talk in print about the creative process of one of their poems. Among the poets are Linda Pastan, Donald Justice, Nancy Willard, Norman Dubie, Robert Francis, and Maxine Kumin.

Getting the Knack: 20 Poetry Writing Exercises, by Stephen Dunning and William Stafford. National Council of Teachers of English, 1992. The book does exactly what it sets out to do, to give young writers specific details about different ways to write poems.

Gonna Bake Me a Rainbow Poem: A Student Guide to Writing Poetry by Peter Sears. Scholastic, 1990. The poems used for illustrating the points made in this entertaining guidebook came from winners in the Scholastic Writing Awards program.

The List Poem: A Guide to Teaching and Writing Catalog Verse by Larry Fagin. Teachers & Writers Collaborative, 1991. Fagin explains the concept and the history of creating poetry that begins with making lists. A 30-minute audiocassette comes with the book that includes 200 examples of list poems.

Listening to the Bells: Learning to Read Poetry by Writing Poetry by Florence Grossman. Boynton/Cook, 1991. Aimed at middle school kids, Grossman explores honesty in reading and writing poetry.

Patterns: The How-to-Write-a-Poem Program, by Jesse Hise. Interaction Publishers, 1995. In spiral ring format, Hise tells young poets and teachers how to go about writing all sorts of poems with particular patterns. One of the most effective and readable books on the market.

The Place My Words Are Looking For, edited by Paul Janeczko. Bradbury, 1990. Thirty-nine American poets talk about what they think poetry is and how to get started writing it. They use their own poems to illustrate the pleasures of expressing thoughts and feelings through words. Janeczko's *Poetspeak: In Their Work, About Their Work* (Bradbury, 1983) has more than sixty poets who contributed notes about the writing of poetry or about why and how they wrote the particular poem published in this collection.

Poem-Making: Ways to Begin Writing Poetry by Myra Cohn Livingston. Harper-Collins, 1991. Written for junior high students, Livingston's book could be used by teachers of students of any age to get ideas and examples of voice, sound, rhythm, figurative language, and special forms of poetry.

Teaching Poetry Writing to Adolescents by Joseph I. Tsujimoto. National Council of Teachers of English, 1988. Excellent examples of student poetry are included in this book about getting kids to write better poetry and become better readers of poetry.

Wishes, Lies, and Dreams: Teaching Children to Write Poetry, second edition, by Kenneth Koch. Chelsea House, 1980. In this book, and in *Rose, Where Did You Get That Red?* (Random House, 1974), Koch presents poetry ideas and patterns along with samples of poems written by students in the New York Public Schools, where Koch has been a poet in residence.

See Focus Box 11.4 for some recommended anthologies of poems. With these books, plus poems gleaned from teachers' reading in *Harpers*, the *New Yorker, Atlantic*, and, to the surprise of some, recent issues of *English Journal*, any teacher can easily have several hundred poems worth reading and using in class.

One of the delights and challenges of working with modern poetry is that students (and teachers) have no source to turn to for determining the meaning or worth of the poems. Comments on a T. S. Eliot poem are easy to come by, and a glance at criticism tells us whether this poem is major Eliot or minor Eliot. We hardly need to read the poem to comment on it, to determine its place in the canon, or to chase down all those wonderful symbols and allusions. In fact, we need not think at all. Without a critic-god, a journal article, or *Cliffs Notes* to determine the worth or meaning of a modern poem, teachers and students must fall back on honest responses to the poem. Years ago, Luella Cook, one of the great people in English education, warned teachers about the dishonesty of canned responses to literature, and although she referred to students alone, her warning might be extended to teachers as well:

> The problem of teaching literature realistically faced, then, becomes one of widening the range of responses to literature, of guiding reading experience so that reaction to books will be vivid, sharp, compelling, provocative. The great tragedy of the English classroom is not that students may have the "wrong" reactions—that is, veer from accepted judgment—but that they will have no original reaction at all, or only the most obvious ones, or that they will mimic the accepted evaluations of criticism.[20]

More than fifty years later, a Texas high school teacher wrote that he wanted his students to reject:

> . . . [T]he possibility of responding to a piece of literature by repeating what they have heard a teacher or someone else say about that piece of literature. I want to stress to students that responding to poetry is not repeating a response that someone else has made.[21]

Instead, it is the meaning that the poem has for the individual responding. The problem lies first in finding literature that students will want to respond to and second in listening to the students when they do respond. It sounds simple, doesn't it?

Using Drama in English Class

Most of the plays currently produced on high school stages had their beginnings on Broadway several decades ago and were brought into the schools within a few years after their New York successes (e.g., Moss Hart and George S. Kaufman's 1936 *You Can't Take It with You*, Thornton Wilder's 1938 *Our Town*, Joseph Kesselring's 1941 *Arsenic and Old Lace*, Rodgers and Hammerstein's 1943 *Oklahoma!*, and Jay Thompson et al.'s 1959 *Once Upon a Mattress*). These plays are still being produced because as one critic observed, the seven words you can't say on the radio have now become the seven words you must say on Broadway. Lowell Swortzell agreed that today's Broadway scripts "scarcely can be made required reading for high school students." He explains:

> David Mamet's *American Buffalo* (called by the *New York Times* the best American play of the decade) and his Pulitzer Prize winning *Glengarry Glen Ross* together present the moral corruption of contemporary life in what one critic described as a "violent vision of the dog-eat-dog jungle of urban American

capitalism." Mamet is the master of demythologizing the American dream of success through characters doomed by self-hatred and paranoia who sputter the stage's most nervous and scatological language. Sam Shepard is another Pulitzer Prize winner whose *Fool for Love* deals with a possible incestuous love affair between a half brother and half sister who literally bounce off the walls in a violent physical struggle for power over one another. Harvey Fierstein's 1983 Tony Award winning *Torch Song Trilogy* depicts a drag queen, the world of gay bars, and the complexity of homosexual relationships.[22]

Not all Broadway plays are this grim (see Focus Box 11.6), and Swortzell did recommend recent plays for high school reading, including August Wilson's *Fences,* about the loss of dreams by an African-Amercian family in the 1950s, and Neil Simon's trilogy: *Brighton Beach Memoirs, Biloxi Blues,* and *Broadway Bound.* He also suggested that commercial success does not necessarily correlate with a good reading experience. Three plays that had short runs are still good for reading: Woody Allen's autobiographical *The Floating Lightbulb;* William Gibson's *Monday After the Miracle,* a continuation of the story of Annie Sullivan and Helen Keller; and Ted Talley's *Terry Nova* about British explorer Captain Robert Scott's ill-fated exploration of the South Pole (all available from the Drama Book Shop, Inc.; 723 Seventh Avenue; New York, NY 10019).

On the good-news side of this story is the fact that within the last ten years or so a significant cadre of plays written specifically for young adult audiences has been developing. In a previous edition of this textbook, we said that one of the reasons there were not many plays written for teenagers was that they weren't the ones buying tickets to Broadway plays or flying to London on theater tours; hence, playwrights were not motivated to write for teenagers.

It is still true that young people don't have the money to go on theater tours, but they make up a healthy portion of television and movie audiences, so that most of us have grown accustomed to seeing teenagers as the main characters on both big and little screens. The carryover effect is that talented writers are now writing serious plays designed for young people either to read or to perform. But be warned that these are not the kinds of nondescript plays that were found in books for high school students a generation ago. In an *English Journal* article, "Toward a Young Adult Drama," Rick E. Amidon described them as "works which question fitting in, popularity, sex, drugs, making choices, taking chances." He labeled Jerome McDonough the "father of young adult drama" because of his dozen "powerful, practical-to-produce, and effective plays for the young adult stage." His plays differ from those typically produced at high schools in that they are shorter (50 to 70 minutes long); they deal with topics dear to the hearts of teenagers; most of the casts are flexible, so the plays can be adapted to how many actors are available; and they have contemporary settings. One of his plays, *Faugh* (pronounced "Fawg"), gets its name from the *Fine Arts Under-Graduate Housing.* As described by Amidon, the residents of F.A.U.G.H. are:

[A] mismatched group of teens and former teens: Nikky has been a student for nine years and still has no intentions of ordering graduation invitations; Herbert believes his computer has fallen in love with him because love notes keep

A Few Excellent Paperbacks on Drama

The Bedford Introduction to Drama, edited by Lee A Jacobs. Gedford Press, 1989. This extraordinary college drama anthology includes 31 plays, ranging from Aristophanes's *Lysistrata* to Henrik Ibsen's *Hedda Gabler,* Bertolt Brecht's *Mother Courage* and Athol Fugard's *"Master Harold" . . . And the Boys;* in addition, it has valuable material on history and criticism for teachers' use.

Eight Great Comedies, edited by Sylvan Barnet et al. Mentor/NAL, 1958. Included are classics such as Aristophanes's *Clouds,* Shakespeare's *Twelfth Night,* and Gay's *The Beggar's Opera.*

Eight Great Tragedies, edited by Sylvan Barnet et al., Mentor/NAL, 1957. Among the classics are Sophocles's *Oedipus the King,* Shakespeare's *King Lear,* and O'Neill's *Desire Under the Elms.*

Famous American Plays of the 1920s, edited by Kenneth Macgowan. Dell, 1959. Six plays include Philip Barry's *Holiday* and Elmer Rice's *Street Scene.* See also *Famous American Plays* of the 1930s (John Steinbeck's *Of Mice and Men* and Clifford Odets' *Awake and Sing*); the 1940s (Maxwell Anderson's *Lost in the Stars* and Arthur Miller's *All My Sons*); the 1950s (Tennessee Williams's *Camino Real* and Edward Albee's *The Zoo Story*; the 1960s (Joseph Heller's *We Bombed in New Haven* and Robert Lowell's *Benito Cereno*); the 1970s (Sam Shepard's *Buried Child* and David Rabe's *The Basic Training of Pavlo Hummel*); and the 1980s (Sam Shepard's *Fool for Love* and August Wilson's *Ma Rainey's Black Bottom*).

Greek Drama, edited by Moses Hadas. Bantam, 1965. Nine classic plays include Sophocles's *Antigone* and Euripedes's *Medea.*

Plays By and About Women by Victoria Sullivan and James Hatch. Vintage, 1973. Eight plays include Clare Boothe's *The Women,* Doris Lessing's *Play with a Tiger,* and Alice Childress's *Wine in the Wilderness.*

Plays from the Contemporary American Theatre, edited by Brooks McNamara. Mentor/NAL, 1988. Eight plays include August Wilson's *Ma Rainey's Black Bottom,* Benth Henley's *Crimes of the Heart,* and David Rabe's *Streamers.*

Stages of Drama: Classical to Contemporary Masterpieces of the Theatre, second edition. St. Martin's Press, 1991. Although planned for college classes, high school teachers will find much that they can use in addition to the 33 plays that range from Euripedes's *The Bacchae* to Henrik Ibsen's *A Doll's House,* Bertolt Brecht's *Life of Galileo,* and Vaclav Havel's *Temptation.*

Understanding Drama, edited by Cleanth Brooks and Robert B. Heilman. Holt, Rinehart & Winston, 1948. One of three anthologies to illustrate the new criticism in action, but also a good, traditional anthology of 12 plays, including Plautus's *The Twin Menaechmi,* Henrik Ibsen's *Rosmersholm,* Marlowe's *Dr. Faustus,* and Oscar Wilde's *Lady Windermere's Fan.*

Shakespeare A to Z: The Essential Reference to His Plays, His Poems, His Life and Times, and More by Charles Boyce. Roundtable Press/Dell, 1990. Not a collection of Shakespeare's plays but the handiest help for secondary teachers on anything about Shakespeare's plays or poems—plot summaries, comments on characters, history of plays, texts of plays, criticism of plays, and anything else you could hope to find or use.

---

appearing on his monitor; and a menagerie of others provide the type of complex, yet comic educational environment young adults (and not so young adults) praised in such films as *The Big Chill, The Breakfast Club,* and *Pretty in Pink.*[23]

Another McDonough play, *Juvie,* is about young suspects brought to a juvenile detention center and acting out their crime so that the audience sees both their aggression and their guilt and remorse. McDonough has also written *Addict, Limbo, Plots,* and *Stages.*

Hindi Brooks, who has been a writer for television's "Fame" and "Eight Is Enough," has written a play entitled *Wising Up!* set in a group home for teenagers. The characters in another of his plays, *Making It!,* attend a performing arts high school, where the idea of "making it" as a performer is an analogy for making it in the world. Amidon concluded about McDonough and Brooks that, "Their passion to communicate through these young adult plays, recording the conflicts with drugs, crime, family, relationships, school, race, and peer-pressure, and consciously to offer promise and reconciliation, rather than continual chaos, makes these plays significant." (McDonough's and Brooks's plays are available from I. E. Clark in Schulenberg, Texas.)

In an *English Journal* article, Anthony L. Manna complained that for English teachers and librarians, drama is the "hidden genre." He had examined several recent best-of-the-year lists compiled by such publications as *Booklist, School Library Journal,* and the *New York Times Book Review* and found only one play listed, Paul Zindel's *Let Me Hear You Whisper.* To prove that the exclusion was not because good drama isn't being written, he went on to recommend more than a dozen contemporary plays that would be excellent for reading in either junior or senior high school classrooms.[24]

In thinking about Manna's point and trying to figure out why drama has been the "hidden genre" for young adults, we came up with the following reasons:

1. Students often have trouble visualizing what they'd see if the play were being performed. Plays are meant to be seen, not read silently or even aloud in class. Settings need to be visualized. Stage directions are often puzzling and distracting.
2. Characters are revealed through dialogue. It is the way students learn about the feelings and personalities of the characters. That slows down the reading and makes drama into drudgery for many students. The list of characters before the opening of the text requires kids to look back and forth, first to the text, then to the dramatis personae, and finally back to the text to find out who's talking.
3. Plays require active reading, giving the characters voices and personalities. In contrast to fiction or narrative poems, there's no narrator to give opinions or insights or a point of view.
4. Kids are not used to reading plays aloud, and they often sound silly (usually deliberately so) when they're assigned parts. They need to read the entire play first to determine motivations and the play's mood or point. The best way to get any class ready to do a play would be to see it first, preferably done by a first-rate cast. That's unlikely, although teachers near a big city with a repertory might just be lucky one year. If not that, most high schools have drama clubs or classes eager to show off before other students. They might illustrate an act or two of a play the class will read. There are always videotapes of plays that have been filmed. Leonard Maltin's *TV Movies and Video Guide* is published yearly by Signet/New American Library, and it indicates after plot summaries whether the film is available in video.

5. It is difficult to keep kids awake when only a few kids are reading in class and no one is really listening, not even those reading parts. How can we do plays and keep our kids' interest—or ours, for that matter?

These complications mean that without help and encouragement from their teachers, few teenagers read drama. One of our graduate students, Alison Babusci, who came to study in Arizona State University's well-known program in Children's Theatre did not agree with our reference to drama as a "hidden genre." She believed that our words did more harm than good, and she offered the following five points:

1. *Make students feel like they are "on the inside" of the theatrical world.* To help them visualize the world of the play, bring in books or photocopies of reproductions of sets and costume designs from previous productions. Teach students what stage directions *mean.* It is a simple concept and it isn't difficult to obtain a stage diagram from any drama textbook. The more students understand about drama, the more interested and excited they will be.

2. *Become "friends" with the cast.* Suggest that students copy down the cast list (dramatis personae) from the beginning of the play, but instead of relying on the dramatist's descriptions of the characters and their relationships, encourage students to write their own. How would *they* describe the character? Jotting down their own observations will help them remain active readers and will add to their visualization of the action and characters.

3. *Convince yourself and students that drama is fun.* Half the excitement of reading dramatic literature is that readers have to form their own opinions and images.

4. *Let students see the play.* Contact theatre groups in your area. Almost everyone will have an outreach program designed to include children and the community and to make drama more accesible and affordable. Theaters pick their seasons about a year in advance, so contact them early and see if there will be an appropriate show in their upcoming season for you to teach. Or use the many plays available on video.

5. *Rely on improvisation and storytelling.* Instead of always having students read parts aloud, try using improvisation. Start with either a line of dialogue or a situation and let students say what they think they would say if they were one of the characters. You can also use games, storytelling, and interdisciplinary activities that combine drama with music, fine arts, or even dance or other physical activities. No one can fall asleep when their body is active.

Her concluding advice was that the real key is that teachers have to be excited by drama. Students will quickly identify and adopt the teacher's attitude; if the teacher is bored, students will be bored, but if the teacher sees drama as exciting, then the teacher can help students develop their imaginations. Drama invites *all* the senses to be involved.

The criteria for choosing plays for reading aloud are different from those for performing. When we were editing the *English Journal,* we invited teachers to tell us about plays they had successfully used for classroom reading. (See "Our Readers Write," October, 1984). Four out of the 24 teachers who responded suggested Reginald Rose's three-act television play *Twelve Angry Men,* the story of a jury making a decision on the future of a 19-year-old boy charged with murder. Three out of the four teachers commented to the effect that they and their students affectionately called the play "Twelve Angry People" because girls as well as boys were assigned parts. The following excerpts taken from the teachers' descriptions not only show why this particular play is successful in class, but also can serve as guides when predicting the potential of other scripts for reading either in classes or in interest groups sponsored by libraries or drama departments:

- It calls for 12 continual parts, enough to satisfy all students who like to read aloud.
- It teaches practical lessons of value to students' lives.
- It may serve as a springboard for research and further discussion on how the judicial system works.
- It creates a forum for students to prove the psychology of group dynamics and peer behavior.
- It sparks student excitement from the beginning and sustains it throughout.
- It can be read in two and a half class sessions.
- The "business" is minimal and can be easily carried out as students read from scripts.
- Pertinent questions can be asked when the jury recesses after Acts I and II.
- The setting is a hot, stuffy jury room—just like our classroom at the end of the year.
- Students are attracted to the realism, and they can relate to a motherless slum youth of 19.
- The excellent characterization allows students to discover a kaleidoscope of lifelike personalities.

Some of the other suggestions and the teachers' reasons follow, supplemented by suggestions from the December 1990 *English Journal* "Booksearch" column that was devoted to "Drama of the '80s":

> Robert Bolt's *A Man for All Seasons.* Baker (also French), 1960. It's good for its portrayal of one of the most famous periods of English history and for its exploration of a hero. Interesting comparisons can be drawn to works treating heroes of noble birth, as in *Antigone* and *Hamlet,* and heroes of ordinary birth, as in *Death of a Salesman* and *The Stranger.*
>
> Lucille Fletcher's *Sorry, Wrong Number* in *Fifteen American One-Act Plays,* edited by Paul Kozelka. Pocket Books, 1971. Because it is a radio play written to be heard and not seen, it is ideal for reading aloud.
>
> Athol Fugard's *"Master Harold" . . . and the Boys.* Penguin, 1982. This powerful one-act play asks students to examine the psychological effects of racism on whites.
>
> William Gibson's *The Miracle Worker.* Baker (also French), 1951. Students love the poignancy of the story of Helen Keller and Annie Sullivan, but it is also a good illustration of flashbacks, foreshadowing, symbolism, and dramatic license when compared to such biographies as Nella Braddy's *Annie Sullivan Macy* and Helen Keller's *The Story of My Life.*

A. R. Gurney, Jr.'s *What I Did Last Summer.* Dramatists, 1983. As Anna tells 14-year-old Charlie in this play about the last summer of World War II, "All choices are important. They tell you who you are."

Tim Kelly's *Les Misèrables.* Dramatists, 1987. With eleventh and twelfth graders, the boys like action, the girls like romance, and they all like music. So here's a play that answers everyone's needs.

Jerome Lawrence and Robert E. Lee's *Inherit the Wind.* Dramatists, 1955. Based on the Scopes trial, this play is especially interesting in relation to current controversies over creationism versus evolution. The lines are easy to read aloud, and there is a good balance between sharp wit and high drama.

Mark Medoff's *Children of a Lesser God.* Dramatists, 1980. Especially since the success of the movie, students appreciate this Tony Award–winning play about a deaf young woman and her relationship with a hearing teacher.

John Patrick's *The Teahouse of the August Moon.* Dramatists, 1953. The way it lightheartedly pokes fun at American customs and values is refreshing.

Rod Serling's *A Storm in Summer* in *Great Television Plays, Vol. 2,* edited by Ned E. Hoopes and Patricia Neale Gordon. Dell, 1975. Students like the way it relates an encounter between a 10-year-old Harlem boy and a bitter, sarcastic Jewish delicatessen owner in upstate New York.

Alfred Uhry's *Driving Miss Daisy.* Dramatists, 1988. The impressive film serves as a backdrop for reading this play that helps students learn what is involved in a lasting friendship.

Gore Vidal's *Visit to a Small Planet,* in *Visit to a Small Planet and Other Television Plays* by Gore Vidal. Little, Brown, 1956. Because this play was written for television, the action is easy to visualize and the stage directions simple enough to discuss as an important aspect of the drama itself.

Paul Zindel's *The Effect of Gamma Rays on Man-in-the-Moon Marigolds.* Dramatists, 1970. This moving story of the damaging forms that parent-child love can take brought Paul Zindel to the attention of the literary world.

Play scripts are sold through distributors; most of whom will happily send free catalogues to teachers who request them. A typical script price for a full-length play is $5.00, whereas a typical royalty charge is $50 for the initial production and $25 for each subsequent production. Teachers wanting scripts for in-class reading rather than for production should so note at the time of ordering so that no royalty is charged. If the play is to be produced, whether admission is charged or not, the producer should pay the fee when the scripts are ordered. A royalty contract is mailed along with the scripts. Two of the largest distributors are Samuel French (7623 Sunset Blvd.; Hollywood, CA 90046) and Dramatists Play Service, Inc. (440 Park Avenue S.; New York, NY 10016). Anchorage Press (P.O. Box 8067; New Orleans, LA 70182) is recommended for children's and teenage drama, and Contemporary Drama Service (Box 7710–5; Colorado Springs, CO 80933) is good for spoofs and for television scripts.

Three guides are especially useful. *The Crown Guide to the World's Great Plays, from Ancient Greece to Modern Times,* second edition, edited by Joseph T. Shipley, has the most detailed plot summaries (e.g., the one for *Waiting for Godot* runs to slightly more than three lengthy pages). Theodore J. Shank's *A Digest of 500 Plays:*

Student Alison Babusci made these posters to illustrate her commitment to the idea that teachers have to demonstrate their own enthusiasm for drama.

Plot Outlines and Production Notes has briefer summaries (e.g., *Godot* is about one-third of a page), but the book is excellent on production matters. The third edition of the National Council of Teachers of English *Guide to Play Selection* has even briefer summaries (*Godot* gets eight lines) but includes many more plays.

Books that are helpful in introducing students to performance with something less daunting than a whole play include *The Actor's Book of Contemporary Stage Monologues* edited by Nina Shengold, *100 Monologues: An Audition Sourcebook for New Dramatists* edited by Laura Harrington, *Scenes and Monologues from the New American Theatre* edited by Frank Pike and Thomas G. Dunn, and *Sometimes I Wake Up in the Middle of the Night*, monologues written by students of the Walden Theatre Conservatory.

Using Thematic Units in the English Class

Part of the reason that thematic units have become popular in English classes is that they provide a way to bind together a number of apparently dissimilar elements, including literature, language, media, and popular culture. But first we need to distinguish the *thematic unit* from two other kinds of units. The *project unit* has a clear end product, with all the steps that lead up to that end. For example, the production of a class play ends when the play is put on, a class-published slang dictionary ends when the booklet is put together and handed out, and reading and talking about a novel ends with the last discussion and the test. A *subject-centered* unit consists of a body of information the teacher feels is important for the class. For example, units on the history of the language, the rise of drama to Shakespeare's time, or "Our Friend, the Introductory Adverbial Clause" (the last is not made up—we saw it in action, if that's the right word). These units have no clear-cut ending, barring a test, but they do have generally clear limits of what is to be included.

The *thematic unit* is different in that it binds together many elements of English while centering on a theme or motif that runs through a body of literature. For example, a question most of us have asked ourselves is, "Why do some people want to manipulate others?" This question is also asked in Aldous Huxley's *Brave New World*, George Orwell's *1984*, Shakespeare's *Othello* and *King Lear*, F. Scott Fitzgerald's *The Great Gatsby*, Henrik Ibsen's *An Enemy of the People*, Robert Cormier's *Fade*, M. E. Kerr's *If I Love You, Am I Trapped Forever?* and Sophocles' *Antigone*. Is this a theme deserving the four or five weeks' time that the usual thematic unit takes? Here are four criteria against which to stack such a question:

1. The theme needs to appeal to kids. If it is too easy or too hard or too boring, the teacher will lose the students' interest and attention.
2. The theme needs to be worth doing—in other words, intellectually and emotionally respectable for these particular kids at this particular time of their development and at this particular time of the year.
3. There must be lots of easily located literature on the theme.
4. The theme needs to appeal to the teacher; if the teacher is not excited about it, the kids won't be either.

Assuming that the theme meets these four requirements, the teacher must begin a search for literature on the theme that students will enjoy and be challenged by, composition topics (written and spoken) worth using and related to the theme, films (short and feature-length) related to the theme and worth viewing, and spelling and vocabulary lists related to the theme. That means the teacher will need to determine the following:

1. A list of sensible objectives (or learning outcomes, if you prefer) for this *specific* unit (not English classwork in general) that both kids and their parents will understand.
2. A work of some length (usually a short novel or a play) to open the unit and make clear to students what the unit aims at. Such a work is not essential, but it's customary and usually helpful.
3. A body of short works (poetry and short stories and essays) to be used throughout the unit because they are related to the theme.
4. A series of composition assignments (usually two or three written assignments and two or three oral assignments) on the theme.
5. A list of vocabulary words related to the unit topic, perhaps twenty to thirty or so, to be talked about and tested five at a time.

6. A list of spelling words related to the unit topic, perhaps twenty to thirty or so, to be talked about and tested about five at a time.

7. A way of beginning the unit that will grab students' attention and interest while focusing on the theme. Obviously, teachers can (and do) begin thematic units with a "Hey, kids, how would you like to talk about _____?" or a "Hey, kids, we're going to turn to something entirely different now, a unit on _____," but surely there's a slightly more fascinating way. A short film or the teacher reading aloud a short story (or a recent news clipping) might work.

8. A way of wrapping up the unit that will tie all the strands together. Tests, the all-American way to wrap anything up, are always possible. Some classes find panel discussions useful, some might profit from a student evaluation of the unit and the literature read, and others might benefit from some creative art project or a dramatization.

9. The problems that the unit—and students—may encounter and how the teacher will work through them. Perhaps it's time to incorporate peer editing into the class, and if this unit is as good a time as any other to introduce kids to peer evaluation and editing, the teacher needs to plan on preparing class members to work in small groups. Perhaps the short book chosen to get the unit started (e.g., Monica Hughes's *Hunter in the Dark*) has some vocabulary problems, or Nathaniel Hawthorne's short story "Young Goodman Brown" may present problems getting the kids to understand colonial life and religion. These and similar problems need to be worked through and solutions found.

Two exceptionally helpful articles on developing thematic units are Richard S. Alm's "What Is a Good Unit?"[25] and John H. Bushman and Sandra K. Jones's "Getting It All Together . . . Thematically."[26] Thematic units can range from complex and sophisticated topics for college-bound kids to simple topics that are appropriate for junior high. For example, a thematic unit on "Our Ability to Endure," which centers on the theme of survival and power, is a topic of immediate interest to eighth- and ninth-graders. It could open with words from William Faulkner's much-anthologized Nobel Award speech and move to one of these as common reading and the remainder as supplementary reading: Avi's *The True Confessions of Charlotte Doyle,* Alice Childress's *Rainbow Jordan,* Robert Cormier's *After the First Death,* James Forman's *Ceremony of Innocence,* Anne Frank's *The Diary of a Young Girl,* Harry Mazer's *The Last Mission,* or Robb White's *Deathwatch.*

A more intellectually and emotionally complex thematic unit on "Redemption" might begin with reading and discussing Katherine Mansfield's "The Garden Party" in Crane's *Fifty Great Short Stories* or Nadine Gordimer's "A Company of Laughing Faces" in Gold's *Point of Departure* (see Focus Box 11.3). This might be followed by the entire class reading Bernard Malamud's *The Assistant,* and sometime during the unit each student might be asked to read at least one supplementary work on some phase of redemption, for example, classics such as Dante's *The Divine Comedy,* Dostoevsky's *Crime and Punishment,* Goethe's *Faust,* Shakespeare's *King Lear* or *Hamlet,* Sophocles's *Oedipus Rex* or *Antigone,* and almost any other Greek drama or major work of Joseph Conrad, Thomas Hardy, Nathaniel Hawthorne, and Herman Melville. Modern fiction applicable to the same theme includes Hal Borland's *When the Legends Die,* F. Scott Fitzgerald's *The Great Gatsby,*

AIDAN CHAMBERS
On the Best Way I Know How

As a writer of novels and stories about people in their late teens, I make three assumptions about my readers.

The main one is that whatever their age they are as capable as I am at dealing with every aspect of life, however serious or disturbing or lighthearted or trivial. So I set no restrictions on what my stories can include, on the subject matter, the incidents they describe, the thoughts and feelings and emotions their characters experience. This is how I think of it: If the main character in the story, the young protagonist, could actually know something, do something, or observe it happening in "real life," then it is okay to include it in the book.

The next follows on from the first. I assume they enjoy the English language as much as I do myself, that they take pleasure in playing with it and in adding more of it to what they already know. So no concessions, no limitations in the language I use and the way I use it. What the story and its characters need is the language that they get.

And here's the third: I assume that people in their teens want to grow up and want to be grown-up, just as I did myself at that age. Older people sometimes complain that "teenagers" are only interested in themselves and their own lives. I don't find that to be true. Most of the young people I know are just as interested in other, quite different people, and in how the world "works"—how life is lived, and how it can be lived. So my stories are about growing up and how you become the full-grown self you most want to be.

Something else: There was a time when I thought that what you had to do as a writer was give your readers what they say they want. I used to go to great lengths to find this out and then to try to write stories of that kind. Then I discovered two things. First of all, readers often do know what they want, but they don't know what they might like that's different from that because they haven't found it yet. So they can't tell you about it. Second, as it turned out, I'm not very good at writing the kind of story people told me they wanted. I'm only any good at writing the kind of story I want for myself. When I realized this, I gave up trying to write the stories readers told me they wanted and wrote one of the kind I wanted. It's called *Breaktime,* and it's still in print 20 years after it was written, whereas the other, earlier, reader-requested stories are dead and gone.

Since *Breaktime,* all my books have been of my kind. And book by book I've discovered that the more I demand of myself as a writer, and the more I demand of my readers, the more my books are read and reread closely and talked about passionately and published in other countries and other languages. It seems the more I make my stories my own, the more my readers like them and want to live inside them.

Don't misunderstand me. I'm not saying that by making books that are all my own I've achieved bigger sales than I did before. Not at all. To tell the truth, I'm not very interested in the size of my sales. Naturally, I need a readership big enough to keep my books in print, otherwise they won't be available for anyone to read. But more than anything I want readers who give themselves, not to me as a writer, but to the books, to the stories, to the language, and who give themselves thoughtfully as much as passionately.

So quite deliberately I make books for readers who are prepared to read carefully, not looking only for quick one-read thrills, but who are prepared to read again, this passage and that, and maybe the whole book, knowing that each time they'll find something more than they first set out to find. And something that will make them think and feel differently—even if only a little differently—from what they've ever thought and felt so consciously before.

It takes about five years to write a novel. I try to put the best of myself into each one. And I put as much as I can of what I know of life into them too. Having packed so much in, it isn't surprising, I suppose, that they take quite a bit of a reader's time and thought to unpack. What I hope is that those who spend the time will be rewarded with the same richness of pleasure and lasting satisfaction that I gain from writing them.

You see, to put it another way, if I want quick pastime thrills, easy entertainment, I watch a film. If I want instant reaction, here-now-and-gone-the-next-second-observation of the world, I watch television. Writing and reading (two sides of the same coin) of novels, stories, and poems are the opposite of these. They are about looking at the past and holding on to the present and digging deep into both then and now in such a way that I can discover something of what they mean—of what life itself means. They allow me to be my own interpreter. And allow me to do it at my own pace, as and when I want to. All other forms of communication show time passing, are about the instant that is gone. Writing and reading of literature are the only forms of communication that are about the permanent, the eternal, the ever-present. Only literature makes time timeless.

Aidan Chambers's books include *The Toll Bridge,* HarperCollins, 1995; *NIK: Now I Know,* HarperCollins, 1988; *Dance on My Grave,* HarperCollins, 1983; *Breaktime,* HarperCollins, 1979.

Ursula K. Le Guin's *Wizard of Earthsea,* Peter Matthiessen's *At Play in the Fields of the Lord,* John Steinbeck's *Of Mice and Men,* Frank Waters's *The Man Who Killed the Deer,* and major works of Arthur Miller, Graham Greene, and Thornton Wilder. Young adult fiction that could fit into the unit includes Fran Arrick's *Tunnel Vision,* Judy Blume's *Tiger Eyes,* Robert Cormier's *After the First Death,* Robert Lipsyte's *The Contender,* Margaret Mahy's *Memory,* Paul Zindel's *The Pigman,* and the novels of S. E. Hinton.

We once had a student come to our office and announce that he wanted to learn everything that a good high school English teacher needed to know. He wondered where he should begin, and we suggested he start with literature. He agreed and wondered yet again where he should begin. We mentioned that good English teachers know the classics. After we cleared up the confusion that we weren't talking about Steinbeck, not yet, we turned to Aeschylus, Sophocles, Euripedes, and Aristophanes, none of whom he knew. Because he begged that we move on to the eighteenth century, where he claimed he knew the novel, we moved onward and upward only to hear his complaint when we brought up writers like John Gay, William Blake, or Richard Brinsley Sheridan. A day or so later, we pointed out that good English teachers not only know English and American literature, of course, but also know Third World literature and German, Japanese, Norwegian, and Russian literature, and more.

Somewhere as we rounded Russian literature, our earnest student gave up. After this catalogue of what he needed to know, he asked one last question before he disappeared from the office, "How can anyone learn all that?"

The answer, which he obviously did not want to hear, was that thousands of good people do it all the time, not in a few hasty weeks but in a lifetime. They are called English teachers.

Notes

1Louise M. Rosenblatt. *Literature As Exploration,* 4th ed. (Modern Language Association, 1983), pp. 278–279.

2Elaine Simpson, "Reason, Not Emotion," *Top of the News* 31 (April 1975): 302.

3Dorothy Broderick, "Serving Young Adults: Why We Do What We Do," *Voice of Youth Advocates* 12 (October 1989): 204.

4Robert C. Small, "Teaching the Junior Novel," *English Journal* 61 (February 1972): 222.

5Patricia Lee Gauch, 'Good Stuff' in Adolescent Literature," *Top of the News* 40 (Winter 1984): 129.

6Richard W. Jackson, *CBC Features* 39 (October 1984–July 1985): 5. A publication of the Children's Book Council.

7Edward J. Gordon, "Levels of Teaching and Testing," *English Journal* 44 (September 1955): 330–334; Dwight L. Burton, "Well, Where Are We in Teaching Literature?" *English Journal* 63 (February 1974): 28–33.

8Howard Francis Seely, "Our Novel Stock-in-Trade," *English Journal* 18 (November 1929): 724–725.

9G. F. Lamb, "The Reading Habit," *Tomorrow* (England) 2 (July 1934): 10.

10Three informative articles that comment on books that didn't win awards (or weren't nominated), although the books are popular today and deserve careful attention: Joni Bodart's "The Also-Rans; or 'What Happened to the Ones That Didn't Get Eight Votes?'" *Top of the News* 38 (Fall 1981): 70–73; and Pam Spencer's "Winners in Their Own Right," *School Library Journal* 36 (July 1990): 23–27, and "Part II," *School Library Journal* 38 (March 1992): 163–167.

11Geoff Fox, "Twenty-four Things to Do with a Book," in Anthony Adams, ed., *New Directions in English Teaching* (Palmer Press, 1982), pp. 219–222.

12Richard Peck, "Ten Questions to Ask About a Novel," ALAN *Newsletter* 5 (Spring 1978): 1, 7.

13Stephen Dunning, *Teaching Literature to Adolescents: Poetry* (Scott, Foresman, 1966), pp.12–34.

14Geoff Fox and Brian Merrick, "Thirty-six Things to Do with a Poem," *Children's Literature in Education* 12 (Spring 1981): 51.

15Richard W. Beach and James D. Marshall, *Teaching Literature in the Secondary School* (Harcourt Brace Jovanovich, 1991), p. 384.

16Samuel Thurber, "Five Axioms of Composition Teaching," *School Review* 5 (January 1897): 10-ll.

17From the "Introduction" to Robert W. Boynton and Maynard Mack, eds. *Introduction to the Poem* (Boynton/Cook, 1985).

18Dana Gioia, "Can Poetry Matter?" *Atlantic* 267 (May 1991): 106.

19Paul Janeczko, "The Possibilities of Poetry" in Donald R. Gallo, ed., *Author's Insights: Turning Teenagers into Readers and Writers* (Boynton/Cook, 1992), p.60.

20Luella B. Cook, "Reading for Experience," *English Journal* 25 (April 1936): 280.

21Bill Martin, "Response to Poetry: Making Use of Differences," *English Record* 42 (1992): 23.

22Lowell Swortzell, "Broadway Bound? Or Beyond?" *English Journal* 76 (September 1987): 52.

23Rick E. Amidon, "Toward a Young Adult Drama," *English Journal* 76 (September 1987): 59.

24Anthony L. Manna, "Curtains Up on Contemporary Plays," *English Journal* 73 (October 1984): 51–54.

25Richard S. Alm, "What Is a Good Unit in English?" *English Journal* 49 (September 1960): 395–399.

26John H. Bushman and Sandra K. Jones, "Getting It All Together . . . Thematically," *English Journal* 64 (May 1975): 54–60.

Titles Mentioned in the Text of Chapter Eleven

Alcott, Louisa May. *Little Women*. 1868.

Angelou, Maya. *I Know Why the Caged Bird Sings*. Random House, 1970.

Arrick, Fran. *Tunnel Vision*. Bradbury, 1980.

Avi. *The True Confessions of Charlotte Doyle*, Orchard, 1990.

Baldwin, Neil. *To All Gentleness, William Carlos Williams, The Doctor Poet*. Atheneum, 1984.

Beach, Richard W., and James D. Marshall. *Teaching Literature in the Secondary School*. Harcourt Brace Jovanovich, 1991.

Beckman Gunnel. *Admission to the Feast*. Holt, 1972.

Blume, Judy. *Tiger Eyes*. Bradbury, 1981.

Bolden, Tonya. *Rites of Passage: Stories about Growing Up by Black Writers from Around the World*. Hyperion: 1994

Borland, Hal. *When the Legends Die*. Lippincott, 1963.

Boynton, Robert W., and Maynard Mack. *Introduction to the Poem*. Boynton/Cook, 1985.

Bradbury, Ray. *When Elephants Last in the Dooryard Bloomed*. Knopf, 1973.

Childress, Alice. *A Hero Ain't Nothin' But a Sandwich*. Coward, McCann, 1973.

Childress, Alice. *Rainbow Jordan*. Putnam, 1981.

Cormier, Robert. *After the First Death*. Pantheon, 1979.

Cormier, Robert. *The Chocolate War*. Pantheon, 1974.

Cormier, Robert. *Fade*. Delacorte, 1988.

Cormier, Robert. *I Am the Cheese*. Knopf, 1977.

Crane, Stephen. *The Red Badge of Courage*. 1895.

Dias, Patrick, and Michael Hayhoe. *Developing Response to Poetry*. Open University Press, 1988.

Dostoevsky, Fyodor. *Crime and Punishment*. 1866.

Dunning, Stephen. *Teaching Literature to Adolescents: Poetry*. Scott, Foresman, 1966.

Dunning, Stephen, et. al. *Reflections on a Gift of Watermelon Pickle*. Scott, Foresman, 1967.

Eliot, George, *Silas Marner*. 1861.

Fitzgerald, F. Scott. *The Great Gatsby*. Scribner, 1925.

Forman, James. *Ceremony of Innocence*. Hawthorn, 1970.

Fox, Paula. *One-Eyed Cat*. Bradbury, 1984.

Frank, Anne. *The Diary of a Young Girl*. Doubleday, 1952.

Fugard, Athol. *"Master Harold"* . . . *and the Boys*. Knopf, 1982.

Gallo, Donald R., ed., *Sixteen*. Delacorte, 1984.

Gallo, Donald R., ed., *Visions*. Delacorte, 1988.

Garner, Alan. *The Owl Service*. William Collins, 1967.

Glenn, Mel. *Class Dismissed: High School Poems*. Clarion, 1986.

Go Ask Alice. Prentice-Hall, 1971.

Goethe, Johann Wolfgang von. *Faust*. 1808, 1832.

Gold, Robert S., ed., *Point of Departure: 19 Stories of Youth and Discovery*. Dell, 1967.

Golding, William. *Lord of the Flies*. Coward, McCann, 1954.

Gould, Jean. *American Women Poets: Pioneers of Modern Poetry*. Dodd, Mead, 1980.

Harrington, Laura. *100 Monologues: An Audition Sourcebook for New Dramatists*. Mentor, 1989.

Hemingway, Ernest. *The Old Man and the Sea*. Scribner, 1952.

Hinton, S. E. *The Outsiders*. Viking, 1967.

Hughes, Monica. *Hunter in the Dark*. Atheneum, 1982.

Huxley, Aldous. *Brave New World*. HarperCollins, 1932.

Ibsen, Henrik. *An Enemy of the People*. 1882.

Janeczko, Paul, ed. *Dont Forget to Fly*. Bradbury, 1981.

Janeczko, Paul, ed. *Poetspeak: In Their Work, About Their Work*. Bradbury, 1983.

Kerr, M. E. *If I Love You, Am I Trapped Forever?* HarperCollins, 1973.

Lee, Harper. *To Kill a Mockingbird*. Lippincott, 1960.

Le Guin, Ursula K. *Wizard of Earthsea*. Parnassus, 1968.

Lipsyte, Robert. *The Contender*. HarperCollins, 1967.

Lowry, Lois. *The Giver*. Houghton Mifflin, 1992.

Mahy, Margaret. *Memory*. McElderry, 1988.

Malamud, Bernard. *The Assistant*. Farrar, Strauss & Giroux, 1957.

Maltin, Leonard. *Movie and Video Guide*. Signet, published yearly.

Matthiessen, Peter. *At Play in the Fields of the Lord*. Random House, 1965.

Mazer, Harry. *The Last Mission*. Delacorte, 1979.

McKinley Robin. *The Hero and the Crown*. Greenwillow, 1984.

Orwell, George. *1984*. Harcourt Brace Jovanovich, 1940.

Pike, Frank, and Thomas G. Dunn. *Scenes and Monologues from the New American Theatre*. Mentor, 1980.

Rosenblatt, Louise. *The Reader, the Text, the Poem: The Transactional Theory of the Literary Work*. Southern Illinois University Press, 1978.

Rylant, Cynthia. *Soda Jerk*. Orchard, 1990.

Samuels, Gertrude. *Run, Shelley, Run!* Crowell, 1974.

Shakespeare, William. *Hamlet*. c. 1601.

Shakespeare, William. *King Lear*. c. 1605.

Shelley, Mary. *Frankenstein or the Modern Prometheus*. 1818.

Shengold, Nina, ed. *The Actor's Book of Contemporary Stage Monologues*. Penguin, 1987.

Sometimes I Wake Up in the Middle of the Night. Dramatic Publishing, 1986. Monologues written by students of the Walden Theatre Conservatory.

Sophocles. *Antigone*. Fifth century B.C.

Sophocles. *Oedipus Rex*. Fifth century B.C.

Steinbeck, John. *The Pearl*. Viking, 1948.

Steinbeck, John. *Of Mice and Men*. Viking, 1937.

Twain, Mark. *Adventures of Huckleberry Finn*. 1884.

Voigt, Cynthia. *Homecoming*. Macmillan, 1981.

Waters, Frank. *The Man Who Killed the Deer*. Farrar, Straus & Giroux, 1942.

Walker, Alice. *The Color Purple*. Harcourt Brace Jovanovich, 1982.

Walker, Alice. *Good Night Willie Lee, I'll See You in the Morning*. Dial, 1979.

Wersba, Barbara. *Run Softly, Go Fast*. Atheneum, 1970.

White, Robb. *Deathwatch*. Doubleday, 1972.

Wolff, Virginia Euwer. *Make Lemonade*. Holt, 1993.

Yep, Laurence, ed. *American Dragons: Twenty-Five Asian American Voices*. HarperCollins, 1993.

Zindel, Paul. *The Pigman*. HarperCollins, 1968.

For information on the availability of paperback editions of these titles, please consult the most recent edition of *Paperbound Books in Print,* published annually by R. R. Bowker Company.

Chapter 12

Censorship
Of Worrying and Wondering

. . . .

Most teachers and librarians are aware that stories about censorship pervade newspapers and magazines. They know that only a few months after publication of *The Satanic Verses* in late 1989, Salman Rushdie's book had been banned in many countries, and that because the Ayatollah Khomeini had determined that the book was blasphemous, Rushdie's life was to be forfeited. At about the same time, Senator Jesse Helms, a politician slightly less powerful than Khomeini, decided that Robert Mapplethorpe's homoerotic art was deeply offensive, particularly because government funds had paid for the Mapplethorpe exhibition. Thereafter, Helms was out to change guidelines for grants from the National Endowment for the Arts to prevent similar horrors.

Occasionally, although not as often as most of us would like, the attacks were so silly that newspaper reports made censorship sound foolish and gave ready an easy chuckle. In Mesa, Arizona, in late July 1990, a mother of two looked closely at the cover of Disney's videocassette of *The Little Mermaid* and found a castle tower that was clearly a phallic symbol. She called a local grocery chain, which pulled the video from its stores. Sanity returned when Disney executives admitted they were upset by the furor but refused to change the cover and the grocery stores went back to selling foodstuffs.

A bill that would have required people to speak kindly about fruits and vegetables in Colorado died after the governor refused to sign it. An apple grower who had noticed the bad press given to Washington apple growers over their use of chemicals to make the fruit look more attractive argued that the bill was needed to keep people from bad-mouthing produce. More people were amused than convinced by his arguments. Recently in Arizona, however, the governor signed an equally silly bill providing relief for families whose crops were criticized.

Far more common than tidbits of humor about censors are grim stories about censors and their fights to purify us all. School texts are rarely safe, as attacks across the United States on the Holt, Rinehart and Winston elementary series *Impressions* prove. Conservative parents in northern California, sometimes representing groups such as Citizens for Excellence in Education or the Traditional Values Coalition, maintained that the series (1) did not sufficiently emphasize good, old-

The daily press continues to report censorship problems with almost nauseating regularity.

fashioned American culture and values; (2) focused on occult and Satanic materials; and (3) removed traditional and classic stories in favor of the new and ephemeral. Other parents across the United States attended school board meetings and lambasted the series, maintaining the stories were violent, scary, Satanic, and generally inappropriate for children. Although the series was retained in almost all the several dozen attacks, opposing parents vowed to keep up the fight.

Teachers and librarians know that attacks on books and book banning are here to stay and are deadly serious, increasingly so in the last decade. Colin Campbell's words still ring true:

> A censorial spirit is at work in the United States, and for the past year or so it has focused more and more on books. Efforts to remove certain titles from school and public libraries, from paperback racks and bookstores, from the eyes of adults as well as children, have increased measurably.[1]

Obviously, not everyone who questions or objects to a book is a censor. Most parents are concerned about the welfare of their children but being forced to go to school to make a complaint may make them resentful or nervous or angry. If taking time from work were not enough reason to feel irritated, many parents have a built-in love-hate ambivalence toward schools. They may not have fond memories of

English teachers when they were young. They may worry about being talked down to by a much younger teacher or librarian. They may wonder if anyone will take them or their complaint seriously. When parents arrive at the school or the library, it is hardly surprising that they may feel hostile. That's easily misread by equally nervous teachers, who may see aggressive censors where there are only concerned parents.

Keeping this possibility of mistaken identity in mind, educators need to be considerate and reasonable and to listen more than they talk, at least for the first few minutes. Once objectors calm down and recognize that the teacher or librarian might possibly be human, then the educator will learn what is really troubling the parents. Everyone may learn, sometimes to the listener's surprise, that no one wants to ban anything, but parents do wonder *why* the teacher is using the book or *why* the librarian recommended it to their child. They may want their child to read something else but agree that they have no wish to control the reading of anyone else. The problem is easier to handle (not always easy, but certainly *easier*).

In such cases, teachers and librarians should remember that the announced objection may not always be the real objection. Censors might attack Huxley's *Brave New World* or Orwell's *1984* for their sexual references when the real objection is to the frightening political attitudes the authors displayed (or were thought to display). It is human nature to fear things we do not understand; hence the discomfort that many parents feel over the recent popularity of scary, supernatural books. An attack on the language in John Howard Griffin's *Black Like Me* may be only a subterfuge for a censor's hatred of African-Americans (and any minority group), whereas an attack on an oblique reference to masturbation in Judy Blume's *Deenie* may in reality be a protest against the liberal attitudes that parents sometimes believe pervade her books.

The underlying reasons for objections to particular books often are more significant than teachers or librarians may suspect. Sometimes the complaining parents do not even realize why a particular author or book makes them feel uncomfortable. This is why it's so important for parents to talk and for educators to listen. Parents who are worried about the moral climate facing their children are painfully aware that they have little power to change the material on television, and they cannot successfully fight the movies offered by local theaters or do away with local "adult" bookstores. Whom, then, can they fight? What can they change? An easy answer is to go to school and protect at least that little corner of their children's lives.

Thoughts of inflation and recession, fears of sexually transmitted diseases, threats of global warming and the depletion of the earth's resources, and faltering communication and affection among family members depress many of us most of the time, and sometimes these parental fears and worries are exploited for political gain. Parents are courted and brought into political action groups advocating censorship. The selling point of such groups is that there is little we can do to attack the gigantic problems spurred on by who knows what or whom. Either we give up or, in the case of censors, we strike back at the only vulnerable element in most communities, the schools. And why not attack schools, what with the rising militancy of teachers and the massive public criticism of schools' performances on SAT or ACT tests? And so the censors attack.

These individuals and groups—as opposed to sincere parents wanting what's best for their own children—are the objectors we define as censors. Their desire is not to talk and reason but to condemn, and as educators we feel a strong obligation to uncover their motives and to counter their claims.

The American Library Association has been on record against censorship since the 1920s, but its strongest statement first appeared in 1939 as the Library Bill of Rights. The document has periodically been tightened and strengthened, and the latest version can be found in the *Intellectual Freedom Manual,* 4th ed. The entire *Intellectual Freedom Manual* is filled with provocative ideas and helpful suggestions and should be required reading for librarians and English teachers alike.

The National Council of Teachers of English was a bit late entering the battle, but the first edition in 1962 of *The Students' Right to Read* set forth the NCTE's position and contained a widely used form for complaints, "Citizen's Request for Reconsideration of a Book." The 1972 edition expanded and updated the earlier edition. In 1982, the complaint form was amended to read "Citizen's Request for Reconsideration of a Work," and a complementary publication, *The Students' Right to Know* by Lee Burress and Edward B. Jenkinson, elaborated on the NCTE's position toward education and censorship.

A Brief History of Censorship

Some English teachers and librarians apparently believe the censorship of young adult reading began with the publication of J. D. Salinger's *The Catcher in the Rye.* But censorship goes far back in history, at least to Plato's 5th century B.C. masterpiece, *The Republic.* Plato argued that banishing poets and dramatists from his perfect state was essential for the moral good of the young. Writers often told lies about the gods, he maintained, but even when their stories were true, writers sometimes made the gods appear responsible for the evils and misfortunes of mortals. Plato reasoned that fiction was potentially emotionally disturbing to the young. Plato's call for moral censorship to protect the young is echoed by many censors today.

In *The Leviathan* in 1615, Thomas Hobbes justified the other basic case for censorship. Humanity was, in Hobbes's view, inherently selfish, venal, brutish, and contentious. Strife was inevitably humanity's fate unless the state established and enforced order. Hobbes acknowledged the right of subjects to refuse to obey a ruler's orders if he did not protect his people, but in all cases the sovereign had not merely the right but the duty to censor anything for the good of the state.

Between Plato and Hobbes and thereafter, history offers a multitude of examples of censorship for moral or political good: The Emperor Chi Huang Ti burned Confucius's *Analects* in 211 B.C.; Julius Caesar burned much of the Library of Alexandria in 48–47 B.C.; English officials publicly burned copies of William Tyndale's translation of the Bible in 1525; the Catholic Index of Forbidden Works was published in 1555; Prime Minister Walpole forced passage of a Licensing Act in

1737, which required that every English play be examined and approved before production.

America's premier censor, although hardly its last, appeared in the early 1870s. Anthony Comstock came from a religious family and before he was 18 had raided a saloon to drive out the devil and the drinkers. In June 1871, Comstock was so outraged by repeated violations of Sunday Closing Laws by saloons in his neighborhood that he reported them to the police. They ignored him, which taught him a good lesson about the futility of fighting city hall alone. Armed with the Lord's help and his own determination, Comstock secured the help of three prominent men and founded the Society for the Suppression of Vice in New York in 1872, and he was off and running. The following year he went to Washington, D.C., to urge passage of a federal statute against obscenity and abortion and contraceptive devices. That same year, he was commissioned a Special Agent of the Postmaster General, all without salary until 1906.

With the new law and Comstock's zeal and energy, he confiscated and destroyed "bad" literature and imprisoned evil authors and publishers almost beyond belief. By 1914, he had caused the arraignment of 3697 people with 2740 convicted or pleading guilty, total fines of $237,134.30, and prison sentences totaling 565 years, 11 months, and 20 days. In his last year of life, 1915, Comstock added another 176 arrests and 140 convictions. He also caused 15 suicides.[2]

Traps for the Young (1883) was Comstock's most famous work. By traps, Comstock meant the devil's work for young people—light literature, newspaper advertisements, saloons, literature obtained through the mail, quack medicine, contraceptives, gambling, playing pool, free love and anyone who advocated it, and artistic works (fine arts, classics of literature, photographic reproductions of art). Comstock was convinced that any young person who shot pool or smoked or chewed tobacco or drank alcohol or read dime novels or did anything else he disapproved of (and that catalogue was long indeed) was doomed to hell and to a life of crime and degradation.

Early librarians, as may be seen in "Fiction and Libraries" in Chapter Thirteen, were more likely pro-censorship than anti-censorship. As Arthur E. Bostwick wrote in 1910:

> In the exercise of his duties in book selection it is unavoidable that the librarian should act in some degree as a censor of literature. It has been pointed out that no library can buy every title that is published, and that we should discriminate by picking out what is best instead of by excluding what is bad.[3]

Mark Twain came under widespread attack for his ungenteel characters, but he was hardly the only writer to be critized for impropriety or immorality. Stephen Crane's *The Red Badge of Courage* was accused of lacking integrity and being inaccurate. At the sixth session of the American Library Association in 1896, a discussion of *The Red Badge of Courage* and whether it should be included in a list of ALA-recommended books brought forth comments that revealed more about the critics than about the book:

Mr. Larned: "What of Crane's *Red Badge of Courage?*"

A. L. Peck: "It abounds in profanity. I never could see why it should be given into the hands of a boy."

G. M. Jones: "This *Red Badge of Courage* is a very good illustration of the weakness of the criticism of our literary papers. The critics in our literary papers are praising this book as being a true picture of war. The fact is, I imagine, that the criticisms are written by young men who know nothing about war, just as Mr. Crane himself knows nothing about war. Gen. McClurg, of Chicago, and Col. Nourse, of Massachusetts, both say that the story is not true to the life of the soldier. An article in the *Independent,* or perhaps the *Outlook,* says that no such profanity as given in the book was common in the army among the soldiers. Mr. Crane has since published two other books on New York life which are simply vulgar books. I consider the *Red Badge of Courage* a vulgar book, and nothing but vulgar."[4]

It is more difficult to know how much censorship occurred in English classes of the nineteenth century because the major journal for English teachers, the *English Journal,* did not begin until 1912, but a few items may suggest that some English teachers endured or even encouraged censorship. Until 1864, Oberlin College would not allow Shakespeare to be studied in mixed classes. That Shakespeare was apparently of questionable value can be seen by an editorial in 1893 lauding students of Oakland High School who objected to using an unexpurgated edition of *Hamlet:*

All honor to the modest and sensible youths and maidens of the Oakland High School who revolted against studying an unexpurgated edition of *Hamlet!* The indecencies of Shakespeare in the complete edition are brutal. They are more than indelicacies, they are indecencies. They are no part of Shakespeare's thought, have no connection with the play, and can be eliminated with as little jar as could the oaths of a modern slugger. Indeed, Shakespeare's vulgarity was, to all intents and purposes, profanity, scattered promiscuously through the lines with no more meaning than so many oaths.[5]

An editorial writer in 1890 quoted from a contemporary account in the *Congregationalist* about books some young people had been reading:

In this series of papers we purposely avoid all mention of some thoroughly bad books chosen by our young friends. We remember hearing the principal of a young ladies' seminary, in trying to express her strong disapproval of a certain book, say impulsively to the pupils, "I think I should expel a girl if I found her reading such a work." Before the week closed no less than three copies were in surreptitious circulation. There is something in human nature which craves that which is prohibited. Just so surely as we gave the titles of books worthy of condemnation, some youth would thirst instantly for a knowledge of their contents.[6]

Would that present-day censors could recognize what this critic obviously recognized, that merely mentioning an objectionable title creates new readers.

One last incident a few years later: An English teacher reported on her use of *Treasure Island* with a junior high school class. Of the students who were enthusiastic, one student well on her way to becoming a literary snob wrote:

> *Treasure Island* should be read, firstly, because it is by a famous author, secondly, most people like it and, thirdly, because it is considered a classic.

Two other students objected. A boy wrote:

> I like a cleaner story. In this story there is too much bloodshed, drinking, and swearing.

A girl, however, pointed out the evil nature of the story and the nefarious and inevitable consequences of reading Stevenson's awful book:

> This story full of murder, fighting, and wiping blood off of knives is not suitable for boys and girls to read and if these kinds of books were not written there would not be so many boys go wrong. I don't think there should be any more books written like it, because it don't learn you anything and nowadays we should read books that do us some good.[7]

A modern censor might have said it more elegantly but hardly any better.

The State of Classroom and Library Censorship Today

Censorship was hardly a major concern of English teachers or school librarians (although it certainly was for public librarians) before the 1960s. Before World War II, it rarely surfaced in schools, although John Steinbeck's *The Grapes of Wrath* and *Of Mice and Men* caused furor in newspapers, especially Oklahoma and California, and when students began to read the books, the furor reached the schools. After World War II, Norman Mailer's *The Naked and the Dead* and J. D. Salinger's *The Catcher in the Rye* and other books "indicative of a permissive, lax, immoral society," as one censor noted, caught the eyes of adults and young adults alike. Granted, most objections were aimed at the writers and bookstores that stocked them, but teachers were now aware that they needed to be more careful about books they allowed students to read for extra credit or book reports. Two events changed the mild worry into genuine concern.

Paperback books seemed to offer little of intellectual or pedagogical value to teachers before World War II. Even after the war, many teachers blithely assumed paperbacks had not changed, and given the often lurid covers, teachers seemed to have a point, although it was more superficial than real. Administrators and parents continued to object even after the Bible, Plato's *Dialogues,* and *Four Tragedies of Shakespeare* proved to teachers and librarians that paperbacks had merit. Students discovered even earlier that paperbacks were handy to stick in a purse or back pocket, and paperback titles were appealing, not stodgy, as were most textbooks. So paperbacks came to schools, censors notwithstanding, and these cheap and ubiquitous books created problems galore for teachers.

Perhaps almost as important, young adult books before the late 1960s were generally safe, pure, and simplistic, devoid of the reality that younger people daily faced. Sports and going to the prom and getting the car for the big Friday night date loomed large as the major problems of young adult life in too many of these novels. Young people read them for fun, knowing that they were nothing more than escape reading with little relationship to reality or to anything of significance. Then in 1967, Ann Head's *Mr. and Mrs. Bo Jo Jones* and S. E. Hinton's *The Outsiders* appeared, and young adult literature changed and rarely returned to the good old days. Paul Zindel's *The Pigman* followed in 1968, and although all young adult books that followed were hardly great or honest, a surprising number were. English teachers and librarians who had accepted the possibility of censorship with adult authors popular with the young—Steinbeck, Fitzgerald, Heller, Hemingway, for example—now learned that the once safe young adult novel was no longer safe, and censorship attacks soon began. Head's and Hinton's and Zindel's books were denounced, but so were young adult novels as good as Robert Lipsyte's *The Contender* (1967), A. E. Johnson's *A Blues I Can Whistle* (1969), John Donovan's *I'll Get There. It Better Be Worth the Trip* (1969), and Jean Renvoize's *A Wild Thing* (1971)— and that was only the beginning.

Surveys of the state of censorship since 1963 reveal that censorship is either getting worse or fewer teachers and librarians are willing to lie quietly while the censor walks over them. Lee Burress's pioneer study "How Censorship Affects the School," in October 1963, was only the first of these surveys. Nyla H. Ahrens's doctoral study in 1965 was the first national survey. State surveys of Arizona censorship conditions appeared in the February 1969 and February 1975 *Arizona English Bulletin*. National studies appeared ever more often: L. B. Woods's "The Most Censored Materials in the U.S.," in the November 1, 1978, *Library Journal*; Burress's "A Brief Report of the 1977 NCTE Survey," in James Davis's *Dealing with Censorship*; and the much anticipated but disappointing *Limiting What Students Shall Read* (ALA, ASCD), in 1981. The 1982 survey of high school librarians by Burress found that 34 percent of the librarians reported a challenge to at least one book as compared to 30 percent in his 1977 survey. A survey of Canadian censorship by David Jenkinson published in the February 1986 *Canadian Library Journal* provided no optimism about censors. Two surveys by Donelson—one in the March 1985 *School Library Journal* of censorship for the previous 13 years and comparing conclusions from six previous surveys and another in the October—November 1990 *High School Journal* summarizing the censorship incidents in the *Newsletter on Intellectual Freedom* from 1952 through 1989—provide little comfort to teachers or librarians. Don Melichar's comparative study of surveys of Arizona classroom censorship in 1985 and 1994 is the most recent state or national survey that we know of.

Surveys make for dull reading and convey all too little about the individual teacher or librarian besieged by censors. The following reports of a few incidents from 1990 onward in newspapers or the *Newsletter on Intellectual Freedom* may suggest some of the emotional and pedagogical dilemmas faced by real people, who are too often alone and without allies, not even their fellow professionals.

1. *February 1990, Tempe, Arizona.* When the Tempe High School drama teacher decided to do *Little Shop of Horrors* for the school musical, a few parents objected. One mother said that the play's man-eating plant was an assault on the tradition of "wholesome family fare." She admitted she had not read the script, but she was sure there was something wrong about it. "I just think it's really in bad taste." Later, when she learned there was no connection between the musical and the picture she'd confused it with, *The Rocky Horror Picture Show,* she said, "Maybe I'm getting excited about something I shouldn't be."[8]

2. *April 1990, Idaho.* A teacher assigned *My Name Is Asher Lev* to her twelfth-grade English class. A day later, a student handed the book back to her teacher. The student explained, "My family and I don't believe in Israel and we hate Jews. My family wants me to read something else."[9]

3. *May 1990, Culver City and Empire, California.* Two school districts banned a new edition of "Little Red Riding Hood" in which Red carried a bottle of wine for Granny. An assistant superintendent said, "It gave the younger ones the wrong impression about alcohol."[10]

4. *August 1991, Charleston, West Virginia.* Middle-class parents objected to S. E. Hinton's *Rumble Fish* and *That Was Then, This Is Now* because the books were too frank. One parent said, "The words and subject matter are such that I don't think seventh-graders should be exposed to it. At that age group, they're going to be zeroing in on that instead of the message."[11]

5. *September 1991, San Ramon, California.* Two novels about homosexuality (Nancy Garden's *Annie on My Mind* and Frank Mosca's *All American Boys)* were donated to high school libraries by the Bay Area Network of Gay and Lesbian Educators. The vice-principals at two schools removed the books to "examine them," and that was the end of those books.[12]

6. *August 1991, Tempe, Arizona.* After a few parents objected to the showing of the R-rated film *Glory,* the school board voted not to allow the showing of R-rated films in classrooms. This was particularly intriguing because no formal complaint against *Glory* or any other film was ever filed. One of the three voting against use of R-rated films explained, "The time we have with students is precious. We should use that time to expose them to only the best and the brightest things. We don't have time to show R-rated films." One of two voting to allow some R-rated films rebutted, "I believe that we should expose kids to what's bright and beautiful, but I also believe we should produce kids that can survive in the world, and reality is not always that bright and beautiful."[13]

7. *1993, Rib Lake, Wisconsin.* The high school principal took a copy of Judy Blume's *Forever* from a student, browsed through it, and found "graphic descriptions of sex acts." The school superintendent removed the book from the library, and when the librarian objected, he said, "You're not in Alaska anymore. We have morals here."[14]

8. *1993, Octorara, Pennsylvania.* Two school board members proposed a policy that would prohibit the teaching of 18 activities and topics, including values clarification, death education, or any materials containing "profanity or sexual explicitness." Also forbidden would be discussion of "personal religious beliefs," "questionnaires on personal life, views and family," "critical appraisals of other individuals with whom the student has close family relationships,"

talk on "political affiliations and beliefs of the student and family," and discussion of "sexual behavior other than in the context of family values or reproduction." One community member commented after reviewing the policy, "This would exclude literature from Shakespeare to *The Red Badge of Courage* to *The Grapes of Wrath*." One teacher asked, "What's left to teach?"[15]

9. *1993, Simi Valley, California.* An objector to Theodore Taylor's *The Cay* said, "I have no qualms about book banning. Any book that offends any group should be taken out of the public libraries and schools."[16]

10. *November 1993, North Carolina.* A radio minister announced that beloved purple dinosaur Barney is leading "kids into a world of miracles and fantasy. It's a New Age philosophy which is the antithesis to the Scripture. Barney is teaching kids that we must accept everyone as they are—whether they're homosexuals or lesbians. He teaches alternative families."[17]

11. *May 1994, Tavares, Florida.* The Lake County School Board ordered teachers to teach young people that American culture is superior to any other. One man said the board acted in response to multiculturalism "being rammed down our throats." Another person said, "we need someone to look out for the Christian view" in our schools.[18]

12. *December 1994, Tempe, Arizona.* A student production of three one-act plays, particularly the play called "Sex Lives of Super Heroes" was stopped because the school board chair found some sexual scenes "objectionable." Although everyone seemed agreed that the way the chair handled the matter was illegal, most board members seemed willing to forgive him. Darlene Wedington-Clark, Tempe High's fine arts department chair, supported the board's actions and added, "If one person is offended, that's one too many. Everything out there has sexual innuendo and undertones. High school should be one place where students can come and not have to worry about that." Tempe High School teacher John Melis provided one intelligent comment: "It seems to me that our real problem is not a lack of morality but a fear of freedom."[19]

13. *January 1995, Elk Grove, California.* Objections by a few parents led Dana Cody of the Rutherford Institute to argue that the district was in violation of state education codes for using Lois Lowry's *The Giver*. Cody added, "It is not important if it is popular with the teachers if it conflicts with parents' beliefs. Parents have primary rule in school situations." A month earlier *The Giver* was temporarily banned in San Dimas, California.[20]

14. *1993–1995, Olathe, Kansas.* District officials removed Nancy Garden's *Annie on My Mind* from school libraries in 1993 even though librarians argued that the book was appropriate for high school students. A group of students and parents sued the district, charging that First Amendment rights had been violated. A five-day trial took place in September 1995 and a U.S. District judge ruled that the school officials had violated the First Amendment and ordered that the district return copies of the book to school library shelves by January 2, 1996.[21]

15. *November 1995, Gilbert, Arizona.* Administrators removed Maya Angelou's *I Know Why the Caged Bird Sings* from the sophomore English curriculum after parents complained that the book contained a description of rape. One mother said, "I feel it was definitely an R-rated book, and I don't think R-rated books

should be at the high school level." Her daughter added, "For people our age, we are too immature to handle that."[22]

16. *December 1995, Bellevue, Washington.* A senior who ridiculed his fellow students' preoccupation with sex and sports published "The Unofficial Newport High School Home Page" on the World Wide Web in February 1995. The principal of his school decided to punish the straight-A student by withdrawing support for his National Merit finalist candidacy. The principal also faxed letters to seven universities to which the student had applied, informing them that the school was withdrawing recommendations for admission to college. The ACLU threatened to sue, the school district apologized to the student, and a school official said, "The internet is unexplored territory for schools, and we now know that when a student uses his own equipment and on his own time, we should stay out of it."[23]

Some Assumptions About Censorship and Censors

Given the censorship attacks of the last twenty-plus years, we can safely make the following assumptions about censorship.

First, any work is potentially censorable by someone, someplace, sometime, for some reason. Nothing is permanently safe from censorship, not even books most teachers and librarians would regard as far removed from censorial eyes—not *Hamlet* or *Julius Caesar* or *Silas Marner* or *Treasure Island,* or anything else.

Second, the newer the work, the more likely it is to come under attack.

Third, censorship is capricious and arbitrary. Two teachers bearing much the same reputation and credentials and years of experience and using the same work will not necessarily be equally free from attack (or equally likely to be attacked). Some schools in conservative areas go free from censorship problems even though teachers may use controversial books. Other schools in relatively liberal areas may come under the censor's gun.

Fourth, censorship spreads a ripple of fear. The closer the censorship, the greater the likelihood of its effect on other teachers. If the newspaper coverage of the incident has been extensive, the greater the likelihood that schools many miles away will feel the effect. Administrators may gently (or loudly) let their teachers know it is time to be traditional or safe in whatever the teachers choose for the coming year.

Fifth, censorship does not come only from people outside the school. Administrators, other teachers or librarians, or the school board may initiate an incident. That often surprises some English teachers or librarians. It should not.

Sixth, censorship is, for too many educators, like cancer or a highway accident. It happens only to other people. Most incidents happen to people who know "it couldn't happen to me." It did and it will.

Seventh, schools without clear, established, school board–approved policies and procedures for handling censorship are accidents waiting to happen. Every school should develop a policy and a procedure that helps both educators and objectors when an incident arises. The aim of both policy and procedures should be to ensure that everyone has a fair hearing, not to stall or frustrate anyone.

SUE ELLEN BRIDGERS
On the Elimination of Choices

I admit to being slow about getting involved in censorship issues. When, early in my career, I heard tales of *Home Before Dark* being relegated to the "protected" shelf in some elementary school libraries, I shrugged it off. I was amused by the few critical letters I received, especially one that castigated me for the use of a single word which had kept the book out of a church library without letting me in on what the offensive word was. I could laugh off such nitpicking because I felt secure in my own belief system. I saw myself as a moral person writing about people struggling to find meaning in life. What could be suspect in that? Well, a lot.

Only a few months ago, *All Together Now* was withdrawn from an approved reading list, although all the seventh graders in that school district had read and enjoyed the book. I spoke with these children, examined the thoughtful, creative art projects they had done about the book, read some of the essays they had written in response to their reading. Their excitement and interest in my visits in their district was the kind of boost writers long for and yet, because of the protest of one parent who felt a minor character acted in a suggestive manner (flirty, she called it), next year's seventh graders won't be reading that book. A committee of administrators and teachers took the path of least resistance and as a result, several hundred children gave up an experience that is their right—the right to read, to think, to know.

What then do censors want? To eliminate our choices—my choices of what to write, teachers' choices of what to recommend or require, and the students' right to be exposed to new ideas and difficult questions and to practice making intelligent decisions based on what they've learned.

What do writers want? I want to write stories that compel me to grow, that force me to think beyond my own life in an exploration of another person's psyche, that stretch and strengthen my technical skills. I want to write without the threat of censorship at my shoulder. I want the confidence and the responsibility that freedom brings.

What do teachers want? Oh, I hope you want to open doors. I hope you want to know your students in personal ways that can be enhanced by reading and talking together. I hope you want to say good-bye every summer to kids whose reading and writing skills have improved.

And yet, I know that many of you are fearful and with reason. Stories of ruined careers, of administrators and school boards abandoning dedicated teachers to twist in the wind are not uncommon anymore. Books that are meaningful to young people and that reflect their personal struggles are bound to be questioned by people who want to eliminate for others the right to question.

The fact is that young adult literature of quality depends on you; it must be introduced and made accessible in the classroom. Many of us on this side of the books intend to keep on writing stories that explore both the emotional and the social issues that touch young people. We can do that as long as you are there on the other side reading, thinking, dreaming with your students. Both of us must meet the challenge by supporting each other, always aware that the kid with the book is what really matters.

Sue Ellen Bridgers's books include *Keeping Christina,* HarperCollins, 1993; *Permanent Connections,* HarperCollins, 1987; *Notes for Another Life,* Knopf, 1981; and *Home Before Dark,* Knopf, 1976.

Eighth, if one book is removed from a classroom or library, no book is safe any longer. If a censor succeeds in getting one book out, every other person in the community who objects to another book should, in courtesy, be granted the same privilege. When everyone has walked out of the library carrying all those objectionable books, nothing of any consequence will be left no matter how many books remain. Some books are certain to offend some people and be ardently defended by others. Indeed, every library has books offensive to someone, maybe everyone. After all, ideas do offend many people.

Ninth, educators and parents should, ideally, coexist to help each other for the good of the young, but the clash of parents with some educators appears to be sadly inevitable. Some people would prefer to see young adults *educated,* which means allowing them to think and wonder about ideas and to consider the consequences of those ideas. Others would prefer to see young people *indoctrinated* into certain community or family values or beliefs or traditions and to eschew anything controversial. With so little in common between these two philosophies of schooling, disagreement is not only natural but certain.

Censors seem unwilling to accept the fact that the more they attack a book, the greater the publicity and likelihood that more young adults will read the offensive book. In their drive to eliminate a book, censors create a wider circle of readers. In some cases with older or more obscure works, they revive something that has been virtually dead for years.

Censors do not believe that in trying desperately to keep young people pure and innocent they often expose those young people to the very thing the censors abhor. Several years ago, in the Phoenix area, a group violently objected to a scholarly dictionary that contained some "offensive" words. Worried that others might not believe all those degrading, evil, pernicious words could be so easily found in one work, censors compiled a sort of digest of "The Best Dirty Words in _____," duplicated the list, and disseminated it to anyone curious, including the very students censors claimed to be protecting. More than one censor has read parts of a book that would "warp any young person's mind" aloud at a school board meeting to prove the point while young students raptly listened.

Censors often have a simplistic belief that there is an easily established and absolute relationship between books and deeds. A bad book, however defined, produces bad actions. What one reads, one immediately imitates. To read profane language automatically leads young people to swear. Presumably, nonreading youngsters who swear must eagerly await more literate fellows to instruct them in the art of the profane. To read about seduction is to wish to seduce or to be seduced (although it is possible the wish may precede the book). To read about crime is to wish to commit that crime or at least something vaguely antisocial. Anthony Comstock loved to visit boys in jail because when he asked what led them into the world of crime, they told him exactly what he wanted to hear (as they knew full well), that dime novels and drinking and shooting pool were *the* sources of all their present misery.

Censors seem to have limited faith in the ability of young adults to read and think. Censors wonder if young people can handle controversial books such as Huxley's *Brave New World* or Salinger's *The Catcher in the Rye* because the young are so innocent and pure and untainted by contact with reality. That may have been what caused one censor who objected to Ann Head's *Mr. and Mrs. Bo Jo Jones* and Paul Zindel's *The Pigman* to announce to an audience, "Teenagers are too young to learn about pregnancy."

Censors alternately love and hate English teachers and librarians. Censors would appear to hate what educators use, but censors would also appear to approve of great literature, particularly the classics. Being essentially nonreaders, they know little about literature but that it must be uplifting and noble and fine. They may claim to have read the uplifting when they were young, "back when schools knew what they were doing," but they often cannot remember titles; when they do their comments suggest the book was read in an emasculated child's edition. Censors assume that classics have no objectionable words or actions or ideas. So much for *Crime and Punishment, Oedipus Rex, Hamlet, Madame Bovary, Anna Karenina,* and most other classics. For censors, the real virtue of great literature is that it is old, dusty, and hard to read, in other words, good for young people.

Censors care little what others believe. Censors sometimes seem to believe that they are ordained by God to root out evil, and they are divinely inspired to know the truth. Where teachers and librarians may flounder in searching for the truth, censors need not fumble, for they *know*. They are sincerely unable to understand that others may regard the censors' arrogance as sacrilegious, and they rarely worry because they claim to represent the side of morality. One censor counts for any number of other parents. When Judy Blume's *Deenie* was removed from an elementary library in the Cotati-Rohnert Park School District, California, in October 1982, a trustee said that a number of parents from a nearby college wanted the book retained, but "the down-to-earth parents who have lived in the district for quite awhile didn't want it,"[24] and that was clearly that. No one counted the votes, but no one needed to. Orwell was right when he wrote, "All animals are equal but some are more equal than others."

Censors would agree with Orwell's comment if not his ironic intention.

Finally, censors use language carelessly or sloppily. Sometimes they cannot possibly mean what they say. The administrator who said "We don't wish to have any controversial books in the bookstore or the library," either did not understand what the word *controversial* meant or was speaking gibberish (the native tongue of embarrassed administrators talking to reporters).

Three adjectives are likely to pop up in the censor's description of objectionable works—*filthy, obscene,* or *vulgar*—along with favored intensifiers such as *unbe-*

lievably, unquestionably, and *hopelessly,* although a few censors favor oxymoronic expressions like *pure garbage* or *pure evil.* Not one of the adjectives is likely to be defined operationally by censors who assume that *filth* is *unquestionably filth,* and everyone shares their definition. Talking with censors is, thus, often difficult, which may disturb others, although it is often a matter of sublime indifference to the censors. If talking is difficult, communicating with them is usually nigh unto impossible.

Attacks on Materials

Who Are the Censors?

There are three reasonably distinct kinds of censors and pressure groups: (1) those from the right, the conservatives; (2) those from the left, the liberals; and (3) an amorphous band of educators and publishers and editors and distributors who we might assume would be opposed to censorship. The first two groups operate from different guiding principles, or so one would assume. But it is sometimes easy for educators to be confused; whether the attack stems from the right or the left, the coercive methods, the censorial rhetoric, and the messianic fervor seem so similar. The third group is unorganized and functions on a personal, ad hoc, case-by-case approach, although people in the group are more likely than not to feel sympathetic to the conservative case for censorship.

An incredible number of tiny censorship or pressure groups on the right continue to *worry* educators (worry in the sense of alarm *and* harass). Many are better known for their acronyms, which often sound folksy or clever—for example, Save Our Schools (SOS); People of America Responding to Educational Needs of Today's Society (PARENTS); Citizens United for Responsible Education (CURE); Let's Improve Today's Education (LITE); American Christians in Education (ACE); and everyone's favorite, Let Our Values Emerge (LOVE). Chapter 9 in Ed Jenkinson's *Censors in the Classroom: The Mind Benders* summarizes quite well the major groups, big or small.

With few exceptions, these groups seem united in wishing to protect young people from insidious forces that threaten the schools, to remove any vestiges of sex education and secular humanism from classes or libraries, to put God back into public schools, and to restore traditional values to education. Few announce openly that they favor censorship of books or teaching materials, although individual members of the groups may so proclaim. Indeed, what is particularly heartening about the groups is that many of them maintain that they are anticensorship, although occasionally a public slip occurs. The president of the Utah chapter of Citizens for Decency was quoted as saying:

> I am opposed to censorship. We are not a censorship organization. But there are limits to the First Amendment. People have the right to see what they want on television, but that has nothing to do with the right to exhibit pornography on television. We're not stopping anyone from buying books and magazines or going to the movies they want. They just can't do it in Utah. Let them go to Nevada. Nobody there cares.[25]

Whether anyone from Nevada with a similar anticensorial attitude responded with a suggestion that people from Nevada seeking cheap thrills should go to Utah is unknown. Something similar to the preceding comment came from the Rev. Ricky Pfeil. Wheeler, Texas, apparently has its moral problems with objectionable movies like *Porky's* and *Flashdance* and *E.T.* (Pfeil's argument against the last-mentioned film was, "The film's an attempt to show something supernatural and it's not God. There's only one other power that's supernatural and that's Satan.") The good minister also is against censorship, as he said:

> You know, I am not for censorship. People have a right to see what they want or read what they want, but I'd just as soon they go to Los Angeles to get a copy of *Playboy* magazine. I'm responsible for here. Evil left unchecked will go rampant. God tells me what to do.[26]

Given the doublespeak of the Utah president and the Rev. Pfeil, readers will admire the honest and the original constitutional interpretation of the Rev. Vincent Strigas, co-leader of the Mesa (Arizona) Decency Coalition. Slashing merrily away at magazines that threatened the "moral fiber" of residents, the Rev. Strigas answered complaints about his approach:

> Some people are saying that we are in violation of First Amendment rights. I do not think that the First Amendment protects people [who sell] pornographic materials. The Constitution protects only the freedom to do what's right.[27]

Surely there is no ambiguity in that message.

Best known of all censors in the United States today are Mel and Norma Gabler, who operate a small but powerful company out of their Longview, Texas, home. Educational Research Analysts came about when the Gablers found a vast difference between their son's American history text and ones they remembered. Norma Gabler appeared before the State Board of Education in 1962 and went largely ignored. Upset, she came home and did her spadework on offensive textbooks. (Most texts seem to be offensive to the Gablers until they help writers and publishers to correct the material and remove secular humanism and anything that might prove offensive to Christians or any proponents of traditional values). Although the Gabler power seems to be diminishing, Educational Research Analysts continue to crank out thousands of pages of textbook analyses and reviews to aid any school or school board in selecting the best, the most proper, and the most accurate texts by the Gablers' standards. Readers who wish to know more about the Gablers or their organization should read William Martin's "The Guardians Who Slumbereth Not," a model of fair play reporting by a writer who does not agree with the Gablers on fundamental points but who clearly likes and admires their openness and caring.

Whatever else conservative groups may agree or disagree on, they seem united in opposing secular humanism and the New Age Movement and the teaching of evolution. Secular humanism is both too large and too fuzzy to handle adequately in a few paragraphs (or even a short chapter). Briefly, if inexactly, conservatives appear to define secular humanism as any teaching material that denies the existence of (or ridicules the worth of) absolute values of right and wrong. Secular humanism is said to be negative, anti-God, anti-American, anti-phonics, and anti-afterlife and pro-permissive, pro–sexual freedom, pro–situation ethics, pro-socialism, and pro–one worldism. Conservatives hopelessly intolerant about secular humanism often have problems explaining what the term means to outsiders, or even insiders, usually defining the presumably philosophical term operationally and offering little more than additional examples of the horror that secular humanism implies. Such was the case when secular humanism reared its ugly head at a meeting of the Utah Association of Women:

> One woman says with disgust that two recent school board members didn't know what secular humanism was; thus they weren't qualified to run for office. Lots of "tsks" run through the group until a young woman visitor apologizes for her ignorance and asks, Just what is secular humanism? There is an awkward silence. No one gives a definition, but finally they urge her to attend a UAW workshop on the subject. Later in the meeting, during a discussion of unemployment a vice-president says, "Our young people are only taught to do things that give them pleasure. That's secular humanism."[28]

Fortunately, for educators already concerned about the many pressure groups from the right, only one pressure group from the left need concern them, but that one group was once very worrisome. The Council on Interracial Books for Children was formed in 1965 to change the all-white world of children's books and to promote literature that more accurately portrayed minorities or reflected the goals of a multiracial, multiethnic society. They offer meetings and publications to expedite their goals, but for most teachers, the CIBC was best known for its often excellent *Bulletin.*

No humane person would disagree with the CIBC's goals. As it has maintained over the years, the CIBC does not censor teaching or library materials. It had, however, perhaps inadvertently, perhaps arrogantly, been guilty of coercing educators into not purchasing or stocking or using books offensive to the CIBC or its reviewers. Its printed articles have attacked Paula Fox's *The Slave Dancer,* Ouida Sebestyen's *Words by Heart,* and Harper Lee's *To Kill a Mockingbird.*

Noble as the CIBC was and well-intended as its goals, it appeared to be, inadvertently, censorious in action if not in theory. With the death of its founder and the suspension of the *Bulletin,* its influence seems muted.

The case for the racist-free classroom and library is carried to its absurd conclusion by Bettye I. Latimer in "Telegraphing Messages to Children about Minorities." After defining censorship as the "actual destruction of a book through banning, exiling, or burning it, so that no one has access to it," Latimer proclaims that she is "strongly opposed to censorship for adult readers, since adults are responsible for their own values," but that apparently does not hold true for young people:

> I am *not* suggesting censorship for books that are racist-oriented. I *am* suggesting that we remove these books to archives. This will permit scholars and researchers to have access to them. Since old racist books have no use in constructing healthy images for today's children, they need to be put in cold

storage. As for contemporary racist books, educational institutions ought to stop purchasing and thereby stop subsidizing publishers for being racist.

Finally, I would like to see librarians, teachers, and reading coordinators reeducate themselves to the social values which books pass on to children. I invite them to learn to use antiracist criteria in evaluating and assessing books.[29]

Amidst all the noble sentiments in these words, some people may sense a hint of liberal censorship or pressure at work. All censors, whatever their religious or sociological biases, *know* what is good and bad in books and are only too willing to *help* the rest of us fumbling mortals learn what to keep and what to exile (or put in the archives).

The third kind of censorship or pressure group comes from within the schools, teachers or librarians or school officials who either censor materials themselves or support others who do. Sometimes these educators do so fearing reprisals if they do not. Sometimes they do so because they fear being noticed, preferring anonymity at all costs. Sometimes they are fearful of dealing with reality in literature. Sometimes they regard themselves as highly moral and opposed to whatever they label immoral in literature. Sometimes they prize (or so claim) literary merit and the classics above all other literature and refuse to consider teaching or recommending anything recent or second-rate, however they define those terms. Fear permeates many of these people. A survey of late 1960s Arizona censorship conditions among teachers uncovered three marvelous specimens:

I would not recommend any book any parent might object to.

The Board of Education knows what parents in our area want their children to read. If teachers don't feel they can teach what the parents approve, they should move on.

The English teacher is hired by the school board, which represents the public. The public, therefore, has the right to ask any English teacher to avoid using any material repugnant to any parent or student.[30]

Lest readers assume that Arizona is unique in certifying these nonprofessionals, note these two Connecticut English Department Chairs quoted in Diane Shugert's "Censorship in Connecticut" in the Spring 1978 *Connecticut English Journal:*

At this level, I don't feel it's [censorship] a problem. We don't deal with controversial material, at least not in English class.

We have no problems at all in my department. The teachers order books directly and don't clear them with me or with a committee. But *I* receive the shipments. Copies of books that I think to be inappropriate simply disappear from the book room.[31]

So much for the good old days.

And at least one book distributor was only too willing to help librarians precensor books. The Follett Library Book Company of Crystal Lake, Illinois (not to be confused with Follett Publishing Company in Chicago), has for several years marked titles with a pink card *if* three or more customers had objected to the vocabulary or illustrations or subject matter of a book. The cards read:

> Some of our customers have informed us of their opinion that the content or vocabulary of this book is inappropriate for young readers. Before distributing this book, you may wish to examine it to assure yourself that the subject matter and vocabulary meet your standards.[32]

Publishers, too, have been guilty of rewriting texts or asking authors to delete certain words to make books or texts more palatable to highly moral librarians or communities. "Expurgation Practices of School Book Clubs" in the December 1983 *Voice of Youth Advocates* and Gayle Keresey's "School Book Club Expurgation Practices" in the Winter 1984 *Top of the News* uncovered censorship practices in Scholastic Book Club selections, as titles were changed and deletions of offensive words or ideas occurred between the hard-back edition and its publication in a paperback club edition.

What Do the Censors Censor?

The answer to the question of what censors censor is easy—almost anything. Books, films,[33] magazines, anything that might be enjoyed by someone is likely to feel some censor's scorn and moral wrath.

Some works, however, are more likely to be attacked.

A nearly ten-year survey of books listed as under attack in the *Newsletter on Intellectual Freedom* between May 1986 and September 1995 revealed that several books were repeatedly questioned. The most obvious was John Steinbeck's *Of Mice and Men*, but a few others were also frequently listed. Mark Twain's *Adventures of Huckleberry Finn,* J. D. Salinger's *The Catcher in the Rye*, Maya Angelou's *I Know Why the Caged Bird Sings*, Judy Blume's *Forever*, and Robert Cormier's *The Chocolate War* were all listed at least ten times. Nancy Garden's *Annie on My Mind*, Alice Walker's *The Color Purple*, Kurt Vonnegut's *Slaughterhouse-Five*, Robert Newton Peck's *A Day No Pigs Would Die*, John Gardner's *Grendel,* and *Go Ask Alice* followed soon thereafter.

Don Melichar's "Objections to Books in Arizona High School Classes" in the Fall 1994 *Arizona English Bulletin* revealed that the most widely attacked book was *Huck Finn*, but Steinbeck's *Of Mice and Men* and Harper Lee's *To Kill a Mockingbird* were also popular with the censors.

The most frequently challenged books in People For the American Way's *Attacks on the Freedom to Learn, 1994–1995* were these: Alvin Schwartz's *Scary Stories to Tell in the Dark, More Scary Stories to Tell in the Dark*, and *Scary Stories 3: More Tales to Chill your Bones*; Angelou's *I Know Why the Caged Bird Sings*; Lowry's *The Giver*; Eve Merriam's *Halloween ABC;* Katherine Paterson's *Bridge to Terabithia*; Cormier's *The Chocolate War*; Christopher and James Lincoln Collier's *My Brother Sam Is Dead*; and Steinbeck's *Of Mice and Men.*

While there's no guarantee that any one of these golden-goodies on the censor's hit list will come under attack soon, clearly some books are beloved of censors. There was a time when Salinger's *The Catcher in the Rye* led every list of censored books. *Go Ask Alice* occasionally threatened *Catcher*, but more and more *Of Mice and Men* and *Adventures of Huckleberry Finn* lead almost every list of censored works.

Racism raises its ugly head on censorship lists, with titles such as Claude Brown's *Manchild in the Promised Land* and Gordon Parks's *The Learning Tree* and Harper Lee's *To Kill A Mockingbird* appearing with nauseating regularity. There are the usual suspects on every list of censored books—Joseph Heller's *Catch–22*, Aldous Huxley's *Brave New World*, George Orwell's *Animal Farm* and *Nineteen Eighty-Four*, and William Golding's *Lord of the Flies*.

There are a few inevitable censorial favorites such as *The American Heritage Dictionary* or the much-hated story by Shirley Jackson, "The Lottery." Or modern plays such as Tennessee Williams's *The Glass Menagerie* or *Summer and Smoke* or Arthur Miller's *All My Sons* or *Death of a Salesman*.

Readers curious why a commonly censored title is not listed here should feel free to add whatever they wish. Anyone who wishes to expand the list could glance casually through any issue of the *Newsletter on Intellectual Freedom*.

Although most of the titles on these lists were published for adults, today's censors seem quite happy to attack books published for adolescents. Titles such as these now frequently are on lists of censored books, rarely near the top but still disturbingly present:

> Judy Blume's *Deenie, Forever*
> Bruce Brooks's *The Moves Make the Man*
> Alice Childress's *A Hero Ain't Nothin' But a Sandwich*
> Brock Coles's *The Goats*
> Robert Cormier's *After the First Death, The Chocolate War, Fade, I Am the Cheese*
> Chris Crutcher's *Athletic Shorts, Running Loose*
> Lois Duncan's *Killing Mr. Griffin*
> Paula Fox's *The Slave Dancer*
> Rosa Guy's *Ruby*
> Nat Hentoff's *The Day They Came to Arrest the Book*
> S. E. Hinton's *The Outsiders, Rumblefish, That Was Then, This Is Now*
> Ron Koertge's *The Arizona Kid*
> Ursula K. LeGuin's *A Wizard of Earthsea*
> Robert Lipsyte's *The Contender*
> Lois Lowry's *The Giver*
> Harry Mazer's *The Last Mission*
> Walter Dean Myers's *Fallen Angels*
> Katherine Paterson's *Bridge to Terabithia*
> Robert Newton Peck's *A Day No Pigs Would Die*
> Jerry Spinelli's *Space Station Seventh Grade*

Todd Stasser's *Angel Dust Blues*
Mildred Taylor's *Roll of Thunder, Hear My Cry*
Paul Zindel's *My Darling, My Hamburger, The Pigman*

Why Do the Censors Censor What They Do?

Why censors censor what they do is far more important and far more complex than what they censor. Unfortunately, for readers who want simple answers and an easy-to-remember list of reasons, the next paragraphs may be disappointing.

In "Censorship in the 1970s; Some Ways to Handle It When It Comes (and It Will)" in early 1974, Donelson listed eight different kinds of materials that get censored. Those that censors:

1. Deem offensive because of sex (usually calling it "filth" or "risqué" or "indecent").
2. See as an attack on the American dream or the country ("un-America" or "pro-commie").
3. Label peacenik or pacifistic (remember the Vietnam War had not yet become unpopular with the masses).
4. Consider irreligious or against religion or, specifically, un-Christian.
5. Believe promote racial harmony or stress civil rights or the civil rights movement ("biased on social issues" or "do young people have to see all that ugliness?").
6. Regard as offensive in language ("profane" or "unfit for human ears").
7. Identify as drug books, pro or con ("kids wouldn't hear about or use drugs if it weren't for these books").
8. Regard as presenting inappropriate adolescent behavior and therefore likely to cause other young people to act inappropriately.[34]

In an article entitled "Dirty Dictionaries, Obscene Nursery Rhymes and Burned Books," published in James E. Davis's 1979 *Dealing with Censorship,* Ed Jenkinson added fourteen more likely targets, including young adult novels, works of "questionable" writers, literature about or by homosexuals, role playing, texts using improper grammar, sexist stereotypes, and sex education. In a *Publishers Weekly* article the same year,[35] Jenkinson listed 40 targets, with new ones being sociology, anthropology, the humanities generally (if secular humanism is bad, so then must be humanism or anything that sounds like humanism, and that easily extends to humanities), ecology, world government, world history that mentions the United Nations, basal readers lacking phonics, basal readers with many pictures or drawings, situation ethics, violence, and books that do not promote the Protestant ethic or do not promote patriotism.

A year later, Jenkinson had expanded his list to 67, with additions including "Soviet propaganda," citizenship classes, African-American dialects, uncaptioned pictures in history texts, concrete poetry, magazines that have ads for alcohol or contraceptives, songs and cartoons in textbooks, and "depressing thoughts."[36] The last of the objections is truly depressing, apparently for censors and educators alike.

Some Court Decisions Worth Knowing

Legal battles and court decisions often seem abstract and dull and irrelevant to practical matters for too many educators, but several court decisions have been significant and have affected thousands of educators who hardly knew the battles had taken place, much less their disposition. A brief run-through of two kinds of decisions, those involving attempts to define obscenity and its supposed influence on readers and viewers and those directly involving schools and school libraries, may be helpful to readers.

Court Decisions About Obscenity and Attempting to Define Obscenity

Because censors frequently bandy the word *obscene* in attacking books, teachers and librarians should know something about the history of courts vainly attempting to define the term.

Although it was hardly the first decision involving obscenity, the first decision announcing a definition of and a test for obscenity came about in an English case in 1868. *The Queen v. Hicklin* (L.R. 3Q.B. 360) concerned an ironmonger who was also an ardent antipapist. He sold copies of *The Confessional Unmasked: Showing the Depravity of the Romish Priesthood, the Iniquity of the Confessional and the Questions Put to Females in Confession,* and although the Court agreed that his heart was pure, his publication was not. Judge Cockburn announced a test of obscenity that was to persist in British law for nearly a century and in American law until the 1930s:

> I think the test of obscenity is this, whether the tendency of the matter charged as obscenity is to deprave and corrupt those whose minds are open to such immoral influences, and into whose hands a publication of this sort may fall.

Clearly, but not exclusively, Cockburn was attempting to protect young people.

In 1913 in *United States v. Kennerly* (209 F. 119), Judge Learned Hand ruled against the defendant because his publication clearly fell under the limits of the Hicklin test, but he added:

> I hope it is not improper for me to say that the rule as laid down, however consonant it may be with mid-Victorian morals, does not seem to me to answer to the understanding and morality of the present time, as conveyed by the words, "obscene, lewd, or lascivious." I question whether in the end men will regard that as obscene which is honestly relevant to the adequate expression of innocent ideas, and whether they will not believe that truth and beauty are too pre-

cious to society at large to be mutilated in the interest of those most likely to pervert them to base uses.

Then in 1933 and 1934, two decisions (5 F. supp. 182 and 72 F. 2d 705) overturned much of the Hicklin test. James Joyce's *Ulysses* had been regarded as obscene by most legal authorities since its publication, largely for Molly Bloom's soliloquy. The novel was stopped by Customs officials and tried before Judge John M. Woolsey of the Federal District Court for Southern New York. Woolsey found the book "sincere and honest" and "not dirt for dirt's sake" and ruled that in matters determining what is obscene, the work *must* be judged as a whole, not on the basis of its parts. An appeal to the Federal Circuit Court of Appeals in 1934 led to Judge Learned Hand's upholding Woolsey's decision.

In 1957 in *Butler v. Michigan* (352 U.S. 380), Butler challenged a Michigan statute that tested obscenity in terms of its effect on young people, arguing that this restricted adult reading to that fit only for children. Mr. Justice Frankfurter agreed, and wrote:

The State insists that, by thus quarantining the general reading public against books not too rugged for grown men and women in order to shield juvenile innocence, it is exercising its power to promote the general welfare. Surely, this is to burn the house to roast the pig. . . . The incidence of this enactment [the Michigan statute] is to reduce the adult population of Michigan to reading only what is fit for children.

Frankfurter agreed with Butler and declared the Michigan statute unconstitutional.

Later in 1957, in *Roth v. United States* (354 U.S. 476), the U.S. Supreme Court announced that obscenity was not protected by the Constitution, for "implicit in the history of the First Amendment is the rejection of obscenity as utterly without redeeming social importance." (That phrase, "without redeeming social importance" was to cause problems for several years thereafter.) Reading for the majority, Justice Brennan added a new definition of obscenity:

Obscene material is material which deals with sex in a manner appealing to prurient interest.

And a new test:

Whether to the average person, applying contemporary community standards, the dominant theme of the material taken as a whole appeals to prurient interest.

Roth rejected the Hicklin test (already in patches) as "unconstitutionally restrictive of the freedoms of speech and press."

Jacobellis v. Ohio (84 S. Ct. 1676) in 1964 further refined the *Roth* test when Justice Brennan announced that the "contemporary community" standard referred to national standards, not local standards although Chief Justice Warren angrily dissented, arguing that community standards meant local and nothing more.

In 1966, in *Memoirs v. Attorney General of Massachusetts* (86 S. Ct. 975), Justice Brennan further elaborated on the *Roth* test:

> Under this definition, as elaborated in subsequent cases, three elements must coalesce: it must be established that (a) the dominant theme of the material taken as a whole appeals to prurient interest in sex; (b) the material is patently offensive because it affronts contemporary community standards relating to the description or representation of sexual matters; and (c) the material is utterly without redeeming social value.

The *Ginsberg v. New York* (390 U.S. 692) decision in 1968 did not develop or alter the definition of obscenity, but it did introduce the concepts of variable obscenity and caused some concern for librarians and English teachers. Ginsberg, who operated a stationery store and luncheonette, had sold "girlie" magazines to a 16-year-old boy in violation of a New York statute that declared illegal the sale of anything "which depicts nudity" and "was harmful" to anyone under 17 years of age. Ginsberg maintained that New York State was without power to draw the line at the age of 17. The Court dismissed his argument, sustained the New York statute, and wrote:

> The well-being of its children is of course a subject within the State's constitutional power to regulate.

The Court further noted, in lines that proved worrisome to anyone dealing in literature, classic, or modern or what-have-you:

> To be sure, there is no lack of "studies" which purport to demonstrate that obscenity is or is not "a basic factor in impairing the ethical and moral development of . . . youth and a clear and present danger to the people of the state." But the growing consensus of commentators is that "while these studies all agree that a causal link has not been demonstrated, they are equally agreed that a causal link has not been disproved either."

Those words were lovingly quoted by censors across the United States, although few of them bothered to read the citations in the decision that suggested the dangers of assuming too much either way about the matter.

Five U.S. Supreme Court decisions in 1973 brought forth a new test of obscenity. The most important, *Miller v. California* (413 U.S. 15) and *Paris Adult Theatre II v. Slaton* (413 U.S. 49), contained the refined test, one presumably designed to remove all ambiguities from past tests. That the test proved as ambiguous and as difficult to enforce and understand as previous tests should come as no surprise to readers. After attacking the 1957 *Roth* test, the majority decision read by Chief Justice Burger in *Miller* provided this three-pronged test of obscenity:

JUDY BLUME
On Censorship

When I began to write, more than twenty years ago, I didn't know if anyone would publish my books, but I wasn't afraid to write them. I was lucky. I found an editor and publisher who were willing to take a chance. They encouraged me. I was never told what I couldn't write. I felt only that I had to write the most honest books I could. Books that came from deep down inside—books about real people, real families, real feelings—books that left the reader hopeful (because I am basically an optimist), without tying up all the loose ends. It never occurred to me, at the time, that what I was writing was controversial. Much of it grew out of my own feelings and concerns when I was young.

There were few challenges to my books then, although I remember the night a woman phoned, asking if I had written *Are You There God? It's Me, Margaret.* When I replied that I had, she called me a Communist and slammed down the phone. I never did figure out if she equated Communism with menstruation or religion.

But in 1980, following the presidential election, everything changed. The censors crawled out of the woodwork, seemingly overnight, organized and determined. Not only would they decide what their children could read, but what all children could read. Challenges to books quadrupled within months. And we'll never know how many teachers, school librarians, and principals quietly removed books to avoid trouble.

I believe that censorship grows out of fear, and because fear is contagious, some parents are easily swayed. Book banning satisfies their need to feel in control of their children's lives. This fear is often disguised as moral outrage. They want to believe that if their children don't read about it, their children won't know about it. And if they don't know about it, it won't happen.

Today, it's not only language and sexuality (the usual reasons for banning my books) that will land a book on the censors' hit list. It's Satanism, New Age-ism, and a hundred other *isms,* some of which would make you laugh if the implications weren't so serious.

Books that make *kids* laugh often come under suspicion; so do books that encourage kids to think, or question authority; books that don't hit the reader over the head with moral lessons are considered dangerous. (My book, *Blubber,* was banned in Montgomery County, Maryland, for *lack of moral tone,* but in New Zealand it is used in teacher-training classes to help explain classroom dynamics.)

Censors don't want children exposed to ideas different from their own. If every individual with an agenda had his or her way, the shelves in the school library would be close to empty. I wish the censors could read the letters kids write.

(continued)

Dear Judy,
I don't know where I stand in the world.
I don't know who I am. That's why I read, to find myself.
Elizabeth, age 13

But it's not just the books under fire now that worry me. It is the books that will never be written. The books that will never be read. And all due to the fear of censorship. As always, young readers will be the real losers.

But I am encouraged by a new awareness. This year I've received a number of letters from young people who are studying censorship in their classes. And in many communities across the country, students from elementary through high school are becoming active (along with caring adults) in the fight to maintain their right to read and their right to choose books. *They* are speaking before school boards, and more often than not, when they do, the books in question are returned to the shelves.

Only when *readers* of all ages become active, only when *readers* are willing to stand up to the censors, will the censors get the message that they can't frighten us!

Copyright © 1992, Judy Blume

Judy Blume's books include *Here's To You, Rachel Robinson,* Orchard, 1993, *Tiger Eyes,* Bradbury, 1981; *Just As Long As We're Together,* Orchard/Watts, 1987; and *Then Again, Maybe I Won't,* Bradbury, 1971.

The basic guidelines for the trier of fact must be: (a) whether "the average person, applying contemporary community standards" would find that the work, taken as a whole, appeals to the prurient interest; (b) whether the work depicts or describes in a patently offensive way, sexual conduct specifically defined by the applicable state law; and (c) whether the work taken as a whole lacks serious literary, artistic, political or scientific value.

To guide state legislatures with "a few plain examples of what a state statute could define for regulation under the second part (b) of the standard announced in this opinion," the Court provided these:

(a) Patently offensive representations or descriptions of ultimate sexual acts, normal or perverted, actual or simulated.

(b) Patently offensive representations or descriptions of masturbation, excretory functions, and lewd exhibition of the genitals.

After this so-called Miller catalogue, Burger announced that "contemporary community standards" meant state standards, not national standards.

Paris Adult Theatre II underscored *Miller* and added more worrisome words about the dangers of obscenity and what it can lead to. Chief Justice Burger, again, for the majority:

But, it is argued, there is no scientific data which conclusively demonstrated that exposure to obscene material adversely affects men and women or their society. It is urged on behalf of the petitioner that, absent such a demonstration, any kind of state regulation is "impermissible." We reject this argument. It is not for us to resolve empirical uncertainties underlying state legislation, save in the exceptional case where that legislation plainly impinges upon rights protected by the Constitution itself. . . . Although there is no conclusive proof of any connection between antisocial behavior and obscene material, the legislature of Georgia could quite reasonably determine that such a connection does or might exist.

In other words, no proof exists that obscenity does (or does not) lead to antisocial actions (or nonactions), yet state legislatures can assume or guess that such a relationship may exist and pass legislation to that effect.

Justice Brennan dissented, noting that the dangers to "protected speech are very grave" and added that the decision would not halt further cases before the Court:

The problem is that one cannot say with certainty that material is obscene until at least five members of this Court, applying inevitably obscure standards, have pronounced it so.

To few observers' surprise, Brennan's prophecy proved correct. On January 13, 1972, police in Albany, Georgia, seized the film *Carnal Knowledge* (starring Jack Nicholson) and charged the manager with violating a state statute against distributing obscene material. He was convicted in the Superior Court, and the decision was affirmed by a divided vote in the Georgia State Supreme Court. In 1974, the U.S. Supreme Court announced its decision in *Jenkins v. the State of Georgia* (94 S. Ct. 2750), Justice Rehnquist reading the unanimous decision to reverse the Georgia Supreme Court opinion. Although *Carnal Knowledge* had been declared obscene by state standards and although it had a scene showing simulated masturbation, Rehnquist stated that "juries do not have unbridled discretion" in determining obscenity and that *Carnal Knowledge* had nothing that fell "within either of the two examples given in *Miller.*"

The history of litigation and court decisions about obscenity and its definition are hardly models of clarity or consistency. Anyone interested in more details of this frustrating but fascinating story should read that marvelous book by Felice Flanery Lewis, *Literature, Obscenity and Law.*

Court Decisions About Teaching and School Libraries

If the implications of court decisions about obscenity are a bit vague, decisions about teaching and school libraries are not notably better. Courts are notoriously leery of decisions involving schools and libraries, lest they be regarded as a national school board, but a few decisions, not unsurprisingly ambiguous, are worth noting about school libraries.

The U.S. Supreme Court had ruled in *Tinker v. the Des Moines (Iowa) School District* (393 U.S. 503) in 1969:

> First Amendment rights, applied in light of the special characteristics of the school environment, are available to teachers and students. It can hardly be argued that either students or teachers shed their constitutional rights to freedom of speech or expression at the schoolhouse gate.

But Courts, federal or state, seemed unwilling to extend those rights to the school library in *Presidents Council, District 25 v. Community School Board No. 25* (457 F. 2d 289) in 1972. A New York City school board voted 5–3 in 1971 to remove all copies of Piri Thomas's *Down These Mean Streets* from junior high libraries because of its offensive nature and language. The U.S. Court of Appeals, Second Circuit, held for the school board. The book, so the Court decided, had dubious literary or educational merit, and because the state had delegated the selection of school materials to local school boards and there was no evidence of basic constitutional impingement by the board, the Court saw no merit in the opposing view.

Presidents Council was cited for several years thereafter as the definitive decision, but because it was not a Supreme Court decision, it served as precedent only for judges so inclined.

A different decision prevailed in *Minarcini v. Strongsville (Ohio) City School District* (541 F. 2d 577) in 1977. The school board refused to allow a teacher to use Heller's *Catch–22* or Vonnegut's *God Bless You, Mr. Rosewater,* ordered Vonnegut's *Cat's Cradle* and Heller's novel removed from the library, and proclaimed that students and teachers were not to discuss these books in class. The U.S. District Court found for the school board, but on appeal to the U.S. Circuit Court of Appeals, the three-member panel reversed the lower court. Judge Edwards focused on the main issues of the case in eloquent words widely quoted and much admired by school librarians:

> A library is a storehouse of knowledge. When created for a public school it is an important privilege created by the state for the benefit of the students in the school. That privilege is not subject to being withdrawn by succeeding school boards whose members might desire to "winnow" the library for books the content of which occasioned their displeasure or disapproval. Of course, a copy of a book may wear out. Some books may become obsolete. Shelf space alone may at some point require some selection of books to be retained and books to be disposed of. No such rationale is involved in this case.

The opinion of the Court that library books gained a tenure of sorts and could not easily be culled by a school board was at odds with the parallel U.S. Circuit Court in *Presidents Council,* but again, the Ohio decision served as precedent only if judges in other Federal District Courts (or Federal Appeals Courts) wished to so use it.

A year later in *Right to Read Defense Committee of Chelsea (Massachusetts) v. School Committee of the City of Chelsea* (454 F. Supp. 703) in the U.S. District Court for Massachusetts, another decision supported the rights of students and libraries. The librarian of Chelsea High School ordered and made available a paperback anthology, *Male and Female under Eighteen,* containing a poem by a student, "The City to the Young Girl," which had, as the judge wrote, "street language." A parent felt the language was "offensive" and called the board chairman, who was also the editor of the local paper. The chair-editor concluded that the poem was "filthy" and contained "offensive" language and should be removed from the library. He scheduled an emergency meeting of the school committee to consider the subject of "objectionable, salacious and obscene material being made available in books in the High School Library" and wrote an article for his newspaper about the matter, concluding with these words:

> Quite frankly, I want a complete review of how it was possible for such garbage to even get on bookshelves where 14-year-old high school ninth graders could obtain them.

The superintendent urged caution and noted that the book could not be removed from the library without a formal review, but the chair was adamant. When the librarian argued that the poem was not obscene, the chair-editor wrote in his newspaper:

> [I am] shocked and extremely disappointed to have our high school librarian claim there is nothing lewd, lascivious, filthy, suggestive, licentious, pornographic or obscene about this particular poem in this book of many poems.

The school committee claimed "an unconstrained authority to remove books from the shelves of the school library." Although the judge agreed that "local authorities are, and must continue to be, the principal policymakers in the public schools," he was more swayed by the reasoning in *Minarcini* than in *Presidents Council.* He wrote:

> The Committee was under no obligation to purchase *Male and Female* for the High School Library, but it did. . . . The Committee claims an absolute right to remove *City* from the shelves of the school library. It has no such right, and compelling policy considerations argue against any public authority having such an unreviewable power of censorship. There is more at issue here than the poem *City.* If this work may be removed by a committee hostile to its language and theme, then the precedent is set for removal of any other work. The prospect of successive school committees "sanitizing" the school library of views divergent from its own is alarming, whether they do it book by book or one page at a time.
>
> What is at stake here is the right to read and be exposed to controversial thoughts and language—a valuable right subject to First Amendment protection.

What may yet prove the most significant decision about school libraries began in September 1975 when three members of the Island Trees (New York) School Board attended a conference sponsored by the conservative Parents of New York— United (PONY-U). After examining lists of books deemed "objectionable" by PONY-U, the three returned home, checked their district's school libraries, and found several suspect works—Bernard Malamud's *The Fixer,* Vonnegut's *Slaughter-house-Five,* Desmond Morris's *The Naked Ape,* Piri Thomas's *Down These Mean Streets,* Langston Hughes's edition of *Best Short Stories of Negro Writers,* Oliver La-Farge's *Laughing Boy,* Richard Wright's *Black Boy,* Alice Childress's *A Hero Ain't Nothin' But a Sandwich,* Eldridge Cleaver's *Soul on Ice,* and *Go Ask Alice.* In February 1976, the board gave "unofficial direction" that the books be removed from the library and delivered to the board for their reading.

Once the word was out, the board issued a press release attempting to justify its actions, calling the books "anti-American, anti-Christian, anti-Semitic, and just plain filthy" and argued:

> It is our duty, our moral obligation, to protect the children in our schools from this moral danger as surely as from physical or medical dangers.

When the board appointed a review committee—four members of the school staff and four parents—the board politely listened to the report suggesting that five books should be returned to the shelves and that two should be removed (*The Naked Ape* and *Down These Mean Streets*) and then ignored their own chosen committee. (The board did return one book to the shelves, *Laughing Boy,* and placed *Black Boy* on a restricted shelf available only with parental permission.) Stephen Pico, a student, and others brought suit against the board, claiming that their rights under the First Amendment had been denied by the board.

The U.S. District Court heard the case in 1979 and granted a summary judgment to the board. The court held that the state had vested school boards with broad discretion to formulate educational policy, and the selection or rejection of books was clearly within their power. The court found no merit in the First Amendment claims of Pico et al. A three-judge panel of the U.S. Court of Appeals for the Second Circuit (638 F. 2d 404) reversed the District Court's decision 2–1 and remanded the case for trial. The case then, although not directly, wended its way to the U.S. Supreme Court, the first such case ever to be heard at that level.

In a strange and badly fragmented decision—and for that reason it is unclear how certainly it will serve as precedent—Justice Brennan delivered the plurality (*not* majority) opinion in *Board of Education, Island Trees Union Free School District v. Pico* (102 S. Ct. 2799). He immediately emphasized the "limited nature" of the question before the court, for "precedents have long recognized certain constitutional limits upon the power of the State to control even the curriculum and classroom," and he further noted that *Island Trees* did not involve textbooks "or indeed any books that Island Trees students would be required to read." The case concerned only the removal, not the acquisition, of library books. He concluded the first section of his opinion by pointing out that the case concerned two questions:

First, does the First Amendment impose *any* limitations upon the discretion of petitioners to remove library books from the Island Trees High School and Junior High School? Second, if so, do the affidavits and other evidential materials before the District Court, construed most favorably to respondents, raise a genuine issue of fact whether petitioners might have exceeded those limitations?

Brennan proceeded to find for *Pico* (and ultimately for the library and the books):

> . . . we think that the First Amendment rights of students may be directly and sharply implicated by the removal of books from the shelves of a school library.
>
> Petitioners emphasized the inculcative function of secondary education, and argue that they must be allowed *unfettered* discretion "to transmit community values" through the Island Trees schools. But that sweeping claim overlooks the unique role of the school library. . . . Petitioners might well defend their claim of absolute discretion in matters of *curriculum* by reliance upon their duty to inculcate community values. But we think that petitioners' reliance upon that duty is misplaced where, as here, they attempt to extend their claim of absolute discretion beyond the compulsory environment of the classroom, into the school library and the regime of voluntary inquiry that there holds sway.
>
> Petitioners rightly possess significant discretion to determine the content of their school libraries. But that discretion may not be exercised in a narrowly partisan or political manner. . . . Our Constitution does not permit the official suppression of ideas. Thus whether petitioners' removal of books from their school libraries denied respondents their First Amendment rights depends upon the motivation behind petitioners' actions. If petitioners *intended* by their removal decision to deny respondents access to ideas with which petitioners disagreed, and if this intent was the decisive factor in petitioners' decision, then petitioners have exercised their discretion in violation of the Constitution.

Four pages follow before Justice Blackmun's generally concurring opinion and Justices Burger, Rehnquist, Powell, and O'Connor offered their stinging dissents, but it is clear that school librarians won something, although precisely what and how much will need to be resolved by future court decisions.

It is equally clear that secondary teachers lost something in *Island Trees*. In an understandable ploy, the American Library Association, the New York Library Association, and the Freedom to Read Foundation submitted an *Amicus Curiae* brief, which sought to distinguish between the functions of the school classroom and the school library, a distinction that worked to the advantage of the school librarian but certainly not to that of the classroom teacher. Apparently, Brennan bought the argument as readers can see, comparing Brennan's words with those from the following brief:

This case, however, is about a library, not a school's curriculum. This is an extremely important distinction for the evaluation of the First Amendment interests at stake here.

The school board below banned books from a library. Thus, this case does not present an issue concerning the board's control of curriculum, i.e., what is taught in the classroom. We freely concede that the school board has the right and duty to supervise the general content of the school's course of study.

Whether these words will cause serious disagreements between teachers and librarians remains to be seen. Certainly, that phrase, "we freely concede," has rankled a number of English teachers who recognized that *Island Trees* was a serious setback for intellectual freedom in the classroom, a point that was taken up in *Hazelwood* (108 S. Ct. 562, 1988) and later in *Virgil* (862 F. 2d 1517, 11th Cir., 1989).

Anyone who assumed that *Pico* quieted the waters of school censorship must have been surprised by five court decisions from 1986 through 1989. These decisions might have been expected to clear up the censorial waters; instead, they made the waters murkier.

On July 7, 1986, the U.S. Supreme Court announced its decision in *Bethel School District v. Fraser* (106 S. Ct. 3159, 1986) upholding school officials in Spanaway, Washington, who had suspended a student for using sexual metaphors in describing the political potency of a candidate for student government. Writing the majority opinion in the 7–2 decision, Chief Justice Burger said, "Surely it is a highly appropriate function of public school education to prohibit the use of vulgar and offensive terms in public discourse. . . . schools must teach by example the shared values of a civilized social order." To some people's surprise, Justice Brennan agreed with Justice Burger that the student's speech had been disruptive, although Brennan refused to label the speech indecent or obscene.

That decision worried many educators, but a lower court decision on October 24, 1986, frightened more teachers. *Mozert v. Hawkins County (Tennessee) Public Schools* (579 F. Supp. 1051, 1984) began in September 1983 when the school board of Hawkins County refused a request by parents to remove three books in the Holt, Rinehart and Winston reading series from the sixth-, seventh-, and eighth-grade program. The parents formed Citizens Organized for Better Schools and ultimately brought suit against the school board. U.S. District Judge Thomas Hull dismissed the lawsuit, but on appeal before the Sixth Circuit of the Court of Appeals, a panel of three judges remanded the case back to Judge Hull.

Not all the testimony in the trial during the summer of 1986 concerned humanism, particularly secular humanism, but so it seemed at times. Vicki Frost, one of the parents who initiated the suit, said that the Holt series taught "satanism, feminism, evolution, telepathy, internationalism, and other beliefs that come under the heading of secular humanism." Later she explained why parents objected to any mention of the Renaissance by saying that "a central idea of the Renaissance was a belief in the dignity and worth of human beings," presumably establishing that teaching the Renaissance was little more than teaching secular humanism.

Judge Hull ruled in favor of the parents on October 24, 1986, but the U.S. Sixth Circuit Court of Appeals overturned Hull's decision. Worse yet for the fundamentalist parents, the U.S. Supreme Court refused to hear an appeal of the Court of Appeals' ruling in February 1988. Beverly LaHaye, leader of the Concerned Women for America, who had filed the original suit in 1983 and whose group had helped finance the legal fees for the parents, said, "School boards now have the authority to trample the religious freedom of all children." Other people, notably educators, were grateful to the court for giving them the right to teach.

While *Mozert* worked its way through the courts, an even more troublesome and considerably louder suit was heard in Alabama. Judge Brevard W. Hand had earlier helped devise a suit defending the right of Alabama to permit a moment of silence for prayer in the public schools. The U.S. Supreme Court overturned Judge Hand's decision, so he devised another suit, *Smith v. School Commissioners of Mobile County, Alabama,* (655 F. Supp. 939, 1987), alleging that social studies, history, and home economics textbooks in the Mobile public schools unconstitutionally promoted the "religious belief system" of secular humanism, as Judge Hand wrote in his March 4, 1987, decision maintaining that 44 texts violated the rights of parents.

The decision was both silly and certain, but those who feared the bogeyman of secular humanism celebrated for a few weeks. Then, late in August 1987, the Eleventh U.S. Circuit Court of Appeals reversed Judge Hand's decision. The Court of Appeals did not address the question of whether secular humanism was a religion, but it did agree that the 44 texts did not promote secular humanism. Phyllis Schlafly said she was not surprised by the ruling, but it mattered little because the decision would be appealed to the U.S. Supreme Court. Oddly enough for a case that began so loudly, the plaintiffs were mute, the date for the appeal quietly passed, and all was silence.

The fourth case, *Hazelwood School District v. Kuhlmeier* (108 S. Ct. 562, 1988), will trouble many educators, although nominally the case was concerned with school journalism and the publication of a school newspaper. The case began in 1983 when the principal of a high school in Hazelwood, Missouri, objected to two stories in the school newspaper dealing with teenage pregnancy and divorce's effects on young people.

Associate Justice Byron White wrote the majority opinion in the 5–3 decision announcing that educators (i.e., administrators) are entitled to exercise great control over student expression. Although the case presumably dealt only with a school newspaper, White's words—inadvertently or not—went further. White wrote:

> The policy of school officials toward [the school newspaper] was reflected in Hazelwood School Board Policy 348.51 and the Hazelwood East Curriculum Guide. Board Policy 348.51 provided that "school-sponsored publications are developed within the adopted curriculum and its educational activities."

After commenting on needed school standards and the right of administrators to set standards, White added:

> This standard is consistent with our oft-expressed view that the education of the nation's youth is primarily the responsibility of parents, teachers, and state and local school officials, and not of federal judges.

Kirsten Goldberg warned only a month later that the consequences of *Hazelwood* would likely extend beyond school newspapers and be far more serious than most teachers had thought:

> Less than a month after the U.S. Supreme Court's decision expanding the power of school officials to regulate student speech, lower courts in three widely differing cases have cited the ruling in upholding the actions of school administrators.

The court decisions, which came less than a week apart, support a Florida school board's banning of a humanities textbook, a California principal's seizure of an "April Fool's" edition of a school newspaper, and a Nebraska school district's decision not to provide meeting space to a student Bible Club.

The Florida decision was particularly troubling and hinted that parallel decisions citing *Hazelwood* as precedent might be on the way. *Virgil v. School Board of Columbia County, Florida* (862 F. 2d 1517, 11th Cir., 1989) concerned a challenge to a school board's decision to stop using a humanities text in a high school class because it contained Chaucer's "The Miller's Tale" and Aristophanes's *Lysistrata,* two works to which parents had objected. After a formal complaint had been filed in April 1986, the school board appointed an advisory committee and then ignored that committee when it recommended keeping the text. Parents filed an action against the school board.

In the district court decision in January 1988, Judge Black agreed with the parents that the school board had overestimated the potential harm to students of Chaucer or Aristophanes, but she concluded that the board had the power as announced in *Hazelwood* to decide as it had.

The parents appealed to the Eleventh Circuit of Appeals, which, as in the district court, fell back on *Hazelwood* for precedent for curricular decisions, not merely those concerned with school newspapers. As Judge Anderson wrote in his decision of January 1989:

> In applying the *Hazelwood* standard to the instant case, two considerations are particularly significant. First, we conclude that the Board decisions at issue were curricular decisions. The materials removed were part of the textbook used in a regularly scheduled course of study in the school. . . . The second consideration that is significant in applying the *Hazelwood* standard to this case is that the motivation for the Board's removal of the readings has been stipulated to be related to the explicit sexuality and excessively vulgar language in the selections. It is clear from *Hazelwood* and other cases that this is a legitimate concern.

Judge Anderson found that the school board had acted appropriately, although in the last paragraph he and the court distanced themselves from the folly of the board's decision to ban two classics.

> We decide today only that the Board's removal of these works from the curriculum did not violate the Constitution. Of course, we do not endorse the

Board's decision. Like the district court, we seriously question how young persons just below the age of majority can be harmed by these masterpieces of Western literature. However, having concluded that there is no constitutional violation, our role is not to second-guess the wisdom of the Board's action.

Florida teachers must have been touched by those words.

Joan DelFattore's *What Johnny Shouldn't Read: Textbook Censorship in America* is a recent scholarly and readable work that admirably covers major court decisions involving teachers and librarians.

Extralegal Decisions

Most censorship episodes do not result in legal hearings and court decisions. Teachers or librarians come under attack and unofficial rumor-mongering charges are lodged because someone objects and labels the offending work "obscene" or "filthy" or "pornographic." The case is heard in the court of public opinion, sometimes before the school board, with few legal niceties prevailing. The censors (and too often the school board) almost never operate under any definitions of obscenity that a court would recognize, but their interpretations of the issues are operationally effective for their purposes. The book may not always be judged as a whole book (although individual parts may be juicily analyzed), and the entire procedure

See the bibliography at the end of this chapter for recent books related to censorship.

may be arbitrary and capricious. The decision, once announced, rapidly disposes of the offending book and frequently the teacher or librarian to boot, a variation of old-fashioned Western justice at work. Extralegal trials need not be cluttered with trivia such as accuracy or reasoning or fairness or justice. Many of the 18 censorship incidents described earlier in this chapter were handled extralegally.

Why would librarians or teachers allow their books and teaching materials to be so treated? Court cases cost a great deal of money, and unless a particular case is likely to create precedent, many lawyers discourage educators from going to the courts. Court cases, even more important, cause friction within the community and—surprising to many neophyte teachers and librarians—cause almost equal friction among a school's faculty. A teacher or librarian who assumes that all fellow teachers will automatically support a case for academic freedom or intellectual freedom is a fool. Many educators, to misuse the word, have little sympathy for troublemakers or their causes. Others are frightened at the prospect of possibly antagonizing their superiors. Others "know their place" in the universe. Others are morally offended by anything stronger than *darn* and may regard most of modern literature (and old literature) as inherently immoral and therefore objectionable to high school students' use. Others find additional or different reasons aplenty for staying out of the fray. And that, more likely than not, is the reason most censorship episodes do not turn into court cases.

What to Do Before and After the Censors Arrive

Certain steps should be taken by librarians and teachers, preferably acting in concert, to prepare for censorship.

Before the Censors Arrive

Teachers and librarians should have some knowledge about the history of censorship and why citizens would wish to censor (see the books and articles listed at the end of the chapter). They should keep up-to-date with censorship problems and court decisions and what books are coming under attack for what reason. That means they should read the *Newsletter on Intellectual Freedom, School Library Journal, English Journal, Journal of Youth Services in Libraries,* and *Voice of Youth Advocates,* along with other articles cited in the bibliography that concludes each issue of the *Newsletter.* A lot of work? Of course, but better than facing a censor totally ignorant of the world of censorship.

They should develop clear and succinct statements, devoid of any educational or library or literary jargon, on why they teach literature or stock books. These statements ought to be made easily available to the public, partly to demonstrate educators' literacy—always an impressive beginning for an argument—and to make parents feel that someone intelligent works in the school, partly because

See the bibliography at the end of this chapter for details about materials prepared by nonprofit organizations.

teachers and librarians have a duty to communicate to the public what is going on and why it goes on.

They need to develop and publicize procedures for book selection in the library or the classroom. Most parents have not the foggiest notion how educators go about selecting books, more or less assuming it comes about through sticking pins through a book catalogue. It might be wise to consider asking some parents to assist teachers and librarians in selection, partly to let parents learn how difficult the matter is, partly to use their ideas (which might prove surprisingly helpful).

They need to develop procedures for handling censorship, should it occur. The National Council of Teachers of English monographs *The Students' Right to Read* and *The Students' Right to Know* should prove helpful, as should the American Library Association's *Intellectual Freedom Manual,* both for general principles and for specific suggestions. Whether adopted from any of these sources or created afresh, the procedure should include a form to be completed by anyone who objects to any teaching material or library book and a clearly defined way in which the matter will be handled after completion of the form. (Will it go to a committee? How many are on the committee? Are people outside the school on the committee? How many teachers? How many administrators?) The procedural rules must be openly available for anyone to consult, the procedures must apply to everyone (no exceptions should be allowed, no matter whether the complainant is the local drunk or the school board president), every complainant must be treated courteously and promptly, and the procedures must be approved by the school board. If the board does not approve the procedures, they have no legal standing. If the school board is not periodically reminded of the procedures—say, every couple of years—it may forget its obligation. Given the fact that many school boards change membership slightly in three or four years and may change their entire composition within five or six years, teachers and librarians should take it upon themselves to remind the board. Otherwise, an entirely new board may wonder why it should support something it neither created nor particularly approves of.

Teachers who assign long works (other than texts) for common reading should write rationales, statements aimed at parents but open to anyone, explaining why the teacher chose *1984* or *Silas Marner* or *Manchild in the Promised Land* or *Hamlet* for class reading and discussion. Rationales should answer the following, although they should be written as informal essays, devoid of any educational jargon, not answers to essay tests: (1) Why would the teacher use this book with this class at this time? (2) What specific objectives—not couched in behavioral terms unless the teachers are anxious to alienate parents—literary or pedagogical, is the teacher aiming at? (3) How will this book meet those objectives? (4) What problems of style, tone, theme, or subject matter exist, and how will the teacher face them? Answering those questions should force teachers to take a fresh look at the book and think more carefully about the possibilities and problems inherent in the book. Rationales are *not* designed to protect the teacher by showing careful advance preparation before teaching, although clearly such rationales would be valuable should censorship strike. Rather, rationales should be written for public information easily available to anyone interested as part of the professional responsibility of teachers. Diane Shugert offers a number of sample rationales in the fall 1983 *Connecticut English Journal* and in "How to Write a Rationale in Defense of a Book" in James Davis's *Dealing with Censorship*.

Educators should woo the public to gain support for intellectual and academic freedom. Any community has its readers and former teachers interested in students' freedom to read. Finding them ahead of time is part of teachers' and librarians' jobs. Waiting until censorship strikes is too late. Pat Scales's ideas about working with parents in the November 1983 *Calendar* (distributed by the Children's Book Council) are most helpful. Scales was talking to a parent who helped in Scales's school library and who had picked up copies of Maureen Daly's *Seventeenth Summer* and Ann Head's *Mr. and Mrs. Bo Jo Jones* and wondered about students reading books with such provocative covers. Scales asked the mother to read the books before forming an opinion. From that experience came a program called "Communicate Through Literature" with monthly meetings to discuss with parents the reading that young adults do. Also, we should not forget about discussing the topic of censorship with our current students (Focus Box 12.1). They could easily be the parents who in a few years will be on the school board or on the library's board of trustees.

FOCUS BOX 12.1

Two Children's Novels and Seven Young Adult Novels About Kids and Censorship

The Day They Came to Arrest the Book by Nat Hentoff. Delacorte, 1982.   Almost a text of what happens when people of good will and different viewpoints debate whether *Huckleberry Finn* ought to be taught today, given the racial climate.

Freddy's Book by John Neufeld. Random House, 1973.   Young Freddy sees the word *fuck* written on the wall and wonders what it means and why it causes such intense and embarrassed reactions from adults he asks for help.

The Last Safe Place on Earth by Richard Peck. Delacorte, 1995.   Walden Woods seemed like a perfect place to live until a few narrow minded parents begin their work of trying to remove evil books from the school libraries to protect children.

A Matter of Principle by Susan Beth Pfeffer. Delacorte, 1982.   Seven students publish an underground high school newspaper, in part to get back at a teacher and an administrator. The principal threatens to suspend them.

Maudie and the Dirty Book by Betty Miles. Knopf, 1980.   Two sixth-grade girls read *The Birthday Dog* to first-graders, the children ask some questions about sex education, the girls are in trouble, and they learn something about community pressures and adults.

The Ninth Issue by Dallin Malmgren. Delacorte, 1989.   Students at Nathan Hale High try to breathe life into a dead school paper by taking up real and significant issues and learn that reality easily leads to controversy.

A Small Civil War by John Neufeld. Fawcett, 1982.   A small-town councilman attacks Steinbeck's *The Grapes of Wrath* and demands that it be removed from the tenth-grade English curriculum.

Strike! by Barbara Corcoran. Atheneum, 1983. Barry and his father take opposite sides, again, when the Committee for a Balanced Curriculum interferes with the curriculum and recommends that books be removed from the school library.

The Trouble with Mothers by Margery Facklam. Clarion, 1989.   It's bad enough that people know Luke because his mother teaches history. When she writes *The Passionate Pirate* under a pen name, things seem safe until the "Crusade for a Clean America" discovers his mother's book.

Educators should be prepared to take on the usual arguments of censors—for example, that educators are playing word games when we insist that we select and some parents try to censor. There is a distinction between *selection* and *censorship,* no matter how many people deliberately or inadvertently misuse or confuse the two. The classic distinction was drawn by Lester Asheim in 1952:

> Selection begins with a presumption in favor of liberty of thought; censorship with a presumption in favor of thought control. Selection's approach to the book is positive, seeking its values in the book as a book, and in the book as a whole. Censorship's approach is negative, seeking for vulnerable characteristics wherever they can be found anywhere in the book, or even outside it. Selection seeks to promote the right of the reader to read; censorship seeks to

protect not the right—but the reader himself from the fancied effects of his reading. The selector has faith in the intelligence of the reader; the censor has faith only in his own.

In other words, selection is democratic while censorship is authoritarian, and in our democracy we have traditionally tended to put our trust in the selector rather than in the censor.[37]

Finally, teachers and librarians should know the organizations that are most helpful if censorship does strike. Diane Shugert's "A Body of Well-instructed Men and Women: Organizations Active for Intellectual Freedom," in James Davis's *Dealing with Censorship,* has a long list of such groups. Following are six national groups every educator ought to know:

The American Civil Liberties Union, 132 W. 43rd St., New York, NY 10036

The Freedom to Read Foundation, 50 E. Huron St., Chicago, IL 60611

The National Coalition Against Censorship, 2 W. 64th St., New York, NY 10023

People for the American Way, 2000 M St., N.W., Washington, DC 20036

SLATE (Support for the Learning and Teaching of English), National Council of Teachers of English, 1111 Kenyon Road, Urbana, IL 61801

The Standing Committee on Censorship, c/o National Council of Teachers of English, 1111 Kenyon Road, Urbana, IL 61801

After the Censors Arrive

Teachers and librarians should begin by refusing to panic—easier said than done but essential. Censors always have one advantage. They can determine the time and the place for the attack. No matter how well prepared the teacher or the librarian, only the censor can say *when.*

Educators should not be too surprised or appalled to discover that not all their fellow teachers or librarians rush in with immediate support. If teachers and librarians assume they represent the entire cause by themselves, they are far better off and considerably less likely to be instantly disillusioned.

Educators ought to urge (or even require that) potential censors talk first to the teacher or librarian in question before completing the complaint form, not to stall the objectors but to assure everyone of fair play all around. Teachers or librarians may discover what others have before, that objectors sometimes simply want to be heard and their complaints treated with dignity and dispatch. Sometimes, teachers and librarians may even be able to talk calmly—once the need to battle has died down—with the objectors and to reason with them, which is not exactly the same as convincing them that the teachers or librarians are necessarily right. The objectors may even see why the offending work was assigned or recommended, sometimes even seeing the difficulty in choosing a book for a class or an individual. Many teachers and librarians, although by no means all, agree that if parents ask that their child not be required to read a certain book, educators must agree to find a substitute book. If a substitute book is to be found and if it is to meet a different fate than the first book, parents must help in selecting the new book. Most objectors deeply care about their children's education, and they understand why the substitute book should not be easier or shorter (thus rewarding the student) or harder and longer (thus unduly punishing the student). Finding another book approximately as long and as difficult as the original choice is no easy matter, but parents who demand substitutes must help, lest the teacher offend once more.

Librarians and teachers must treat objectors with every possible courtesy. Objectors should be expected to complete the school's forms detailing the objection, but the forms should be easily accessible and politely distributed. The complaint form should *never* be used to stall objectors. If it is so long that objectors get discouraged, the school may win one battle, but it will have produced one more disgruntled citizen, and at school bond time one irritated citizen and friends are quite enough to harm the cause of education.

Last, a committee (spelled out in detail before the censorship) meets to look at and discuss the complaint. After considering the problem but before arriving at a decision, the committee must meet with the teacher or librarian in question *and* the objectors to hear their cases. The committee then makes its decision and forwards it to the highest administrator in the school, who forwards it to the superintendent, who then forwards it to the school board. That body, already aware of the policy and procedures much earlier adopted to handle such matters, considers this objection and makes its decision, probably after at least one open meeting.

In no case and at no level should the actions of the educators or administrators or the school be viewed as pro forma. They should be considered as thoughtful actions to resolve a problem, not as an attempt to create newer and bigger ones. Objectors should feel that they have been listened to and courtesy has been extended them at all levels and all stages.

We believe that the school—classroom or library—must be a center of intellectual ferment in the community. This implies not that schools should be radical, but that they should be one place where freedom to think and inquire is protected, where ideas of all sorts can be considered, analyzed, investigated, and discussed, and their consequences thought through. We believe librarians and English teachers must protect these freedoms, not merely in the abstract but in the practical, day-by-day world of the school and library. To protect those freedoms, we must fight censorship, for without them no education worthy of the name is possible.

Notes

. . . .

[1]Colin Campbell, "Book Banning in America," *New York Times Book Review*, December 20, 1981, p. 1.

[2]Comstock's life and work have been the subject of many books and articles. Heywood Broun and Margaret Leech's *Anthony Comstock: Roundsman of the Lord* (Albert and Charles Boni, 1927) is amusing and nasty and still worth reading. A brief overview of Comstock's life can be found in Robert Bremner's introduction to the reprinting of *Traps for the Young* (Harvard University Press, 1967), pp. vii–xxxi. See also Paul S. Boyer's *Purity in Print: The Vice-Society Movement and Book Censorship in America* (Scribner, 1968) and Robert W. Haney's *Comstockery in America: Patterns of Censorship and Control* (Beacon Press, 1960).

[3]Arthur E. Bostwick, *The American Public Library* (Appleton, 1910), pp. 130–31.

[4]*Library Journal* 21 (December 1896): 144.

[5]"Unexpurgated Shakespeare," *Journal of Education* 37 (April 13, 1883): 232.

[6]"What Books Do They Read?" *Common School Education* 4 (April 1890): 146–47.

[7]Evaline Harrington, "Why Treasure Island?" *English Journal* 9 (May 1920): 267–68.

[8]*Tempe* (Arizona) *Daily News,* February 22, 1990, pp. A–1, A–7.

[9]*Idaho Language Arts News,* April 1990, p. 1.

[10]*Newsletter on Intellectual Freedom* 39 (July 1990): 128.

[11]*Newsleter on Intellectual Freedom* 41 (January 1992): 9.

[12]*Newsletter on Intellectual Freedom* 41 (January 1992): 5–6.

[13]*Tempe* (Arizona) *Daily News,* August 9, 1991, p. B–1.

[14]*Censorship News,* #47, Issue #1 of 1993, p.#1.

[15]*Forum: A Bulletin for People for the American Way* 4 (October 1993): 4

[16]*Attacks on the Freedom to Learn: 1992–1993 Report.* (People for the American Way, 1993), p. 48.

[17]*Arizona Republic,* November 25, 1993, p. E–3.

[18]*Phoenix Gazette,* May 25, 1994, p. A–1.

[19]*Tempe Daily News,* December 3 and 7, 1994, and "Tempe Community" in the December 12, 1994, *Arizona Republic.*

[20]*Newsletter on Intellectual Freedom* 44 (March 1995): 42.

[21]"Annie Goes Back to School," *School Library Journal* 42 (January, 1996): 13.

[22]*Arizona Republic,* November 18, 1995, pp. B–1, B–2.

[23]*New York Times,* December 24, 1995, p. 9.

[24]*San Francisco Examiner,* October 8, 1982, p. B-4.

[25]Louise Kingsbury and Lance Gurewell, "The Sin Fighters: Grappling with Gomorrah at the Grass Roots," *Utah Holiday* 12 (April 1983): 46.

[26]Lee Grant, "Shoot-Out in Texas," Calendar section, *Los Angeles Times,* December 25, 1983, p. 21.

[27]*Phoenix Gazette,* June 10, 1981, p. SE–6.

[28]Kingsbury and Gurwell, p. 52.

[29]Bettye I. Latimer, "Telegraphing Messages to Children About Minorities," *Reading Teacher* 30 (November 1976): 155.

[30]*Arizona English Bulletin* 11 (February 1969): 37.

[31]Diane Shugert, "Censorship in Connecticut," *Connecticut English Journal* 9 (Spring 1978): 59–61.

[32]*Publishers Weekly* 215 (April 30, 1979): 24.

[33]Kathleen Beck, "Censorship and Celluloid." *Voice of Youth Advocates* 18 (June 1995): 73–76.

[34]Ken Donelson, "Censorship in the 1970s: Some Ways to Handle It When It Comes (and It Will)," *English Journal* 63 (February 1974): 47–51.

[35]"Protest Groups Exert Strong Impact," *Publishers Weekly* 216 (October 29, 1979): 42–44.

[36]"Sixty-seven Targets of the Textbook Protesters," *Missouri English Bulletin* 38 (May 1980): 27–32.

[37]Lester Asheim, "Not Censorship but Selection," *Wilson Library Bulletin* 28 (September 1953): 67. See also Asheim's later article, "Selection and Censorship: A Reappraisal," *Wilson Library Bulletin* 58 (November 1983): 180–184. Julia Turnquist Bradley's "Censoring the School Library: Do Students Have the Right to Read?" *Connecticut Law Review* 10 (Spring 1978): 747–775, also draws a distinction between *selection* and *censorship.*

A Starter Bibliography on Censorship

BIBLIOGRAPHICAL SOURCES

McCoy, Ralph E. *Freedom of the Press: An Annotated Bibliography.* Southern Illinois University Press, 1968.

McCoy, Ralph E. *Freedom of the Press: A Bibliocyclopedia Ten-Year Supplement.* Southern Illinois University Press, 1979.

Newsletter on Intellectual Freedom. A bimonthly edited by Judith Krug with a sizable bibliography concluding each issue. Available from the American Library Association, 50 East Huron Street, Chicago, IL 60611.

TWO BASIC POLICIES

Burress, Lee, and Edward B. Jenkinson. *The Students' Right to Read,* 3rd ed. National Council of Teachers of English (NCTE), 1982. NCTE's official policy statement.

Intellectual Freedom Manual, 3rd ed. American Library Association (ALA), 1989. ALA's official policy statement along with a mass of material.

BOOKS

Ahrens, Nyla H. *Censorship and the Teaching of English: A Questionnaire Survey of a Selected Sample of Secondary Teachers of English.* Dissertation, Teachers College, Columbia University, 1965.

Ayers, Stephen Michael. *The Selection Process of the National Endowment for the Arts Theatre Program.* New York: Peter Lang, 1992.

Beahm, George, ed. *War of Words: The Censorship Debate.* New York: Andrews & McMeel, 1993.

Bolton, Richard. *Culture Wars.* New York: New Press, 1992. On the National Endowment for the Arts and all its problems, current and not so current.

Bosmajian, Haig A., ed. *Censorship: Libraries and the Law,* Neal-Schuman, 1983. Censorship cases.

Bosmajian, Haig A., ed. *The First Amendment in the Classroom,* 5 volumes. Neal-Schuman. No. 1, *The Freedom to Read,* 1987; No. 2, *Freedom of Religion,* 1987; No. 3, *Freedom of Expression,* 1988; No. 4, *Academic Freedom,* 1989; and No. 5, *The Freedom to Publish,* 1989. Censorship cases.

Boyer, Paul S. *Purity in Print: The Vice-Society and Book Censorship in America.* Scribner's, 1968.

Brown, Jean, ed. *Preserving Intellectual Freedom: Fighting Censorship in Our Schools.* Urbana, IL: National Council of Teachers of English, 1994. A rich collection of articles.

Bryson, Joseph E., and Elizabeth W. Detty. *The Legal Aspects of Censorship of Public School Library; and Instructional Materials.* Charlottesville, VA: Michie, 1982.

Burress, Lee, and Edward B. Jenkinson. *The Students' Right to Know.* National Council of Teachers of English, 1982.

Carmilly-Weinberger, Moshe. *Fear of Art: Censorship and Freedom of Expression in Art.* New York: Bowker, 1986.

Censorship Litigation and the Schools. American Library Association, 1983.

Davis, James E., ed. *Dealing with Censorship.* National Council of Teachers of English, 1979.

DelFattore, Joan. *What Johnny Shouldn't Read: Textbook Censorship in America.* Yale University Press, 1992. Court cases involving textbooks.

DeGrazia, Edward, ed. *Censorship Landmarks.* R. R. Bowker, 1969. Censorship cases.

DeGrazia, Edward, ed. *Girls Lean Backward Everywhere: The Law of Obscenity and the Assault on Genius.* New York: Random House, 1992.

DeGrazia, Edward, and Roger K. Newman. *Banned Films: Movies, Censors, and the First Amendment.* New York: Bowker, 1982.

Donnerstein, Edward, Daniel Linz, and Steven Penrod. *The Question of Pornography: Research Findings and Policy Implications.* New York: Free Press, 1987. Sometimes tough going but rewarding.

Eldridge, Larry D. *A Distant Heritage: The Growth of Free Speech in Early America.* New York University Press, 1993.

Fiske, Marjorie. *Book Selection and Censorship: A Study of School and Public Libraries in California.* University of California Press, 1968.

Foerstel, Herbert N. *Banned in the U.S.A.: A Reference Guide to Book Censorship in Schools and Public Libraries.* Westport, CT: Greenwood Press, 1994.

Geller, Evelyn. *Forbidden Books in American Public Libraries, 1876–1939: A Study in Cultural Change.* Greenwood Press, 1984.

Glasser, Ira. *Visions of Liberty: The Bill of Rights for All Americans.* Boston: Little, Brown, 1991.

Haight, Anne Lyons. *Banned Books,* 4th ed. R. R. Bowker, 1978.

Hall, Kermit L., ed. *The Oxford Companion to the Supreme Court.* New York: Oxford University Press, 1992. An encyclopedia of court cases and legal terms and Supreme Court Justices. Invaluable.

Hefley, James C. *Textbooks on Trial.* Victor Books, 1976. A defense of Mel and Norma Gabler's work.

Hentoff, Nat. *The First Freedom: The Tumultuous History of Free Speech in America.* Delacorte, 1980.

Hentoff, Nat. *Free Speech for Me—But Not for Thee: How the American Left and Right Relentlessly Censor Each Other.* New York: HarperCollins, 1992.

Homstad, Wayne. *Anatomy of a Book Controversy.* Phi Delta Kappa, 1996.

Jenkinson, Edward B. *Censors in the Classroom: The Mind Benders.* Southern Illinois University Press, 1979.

Jenkinson, Edward B. *The Schoolbook Protest Movement: 40 Questions and Answers.* Phi Delta Kappa Educational Foundation, 1986.

Karolides, Nicholas, Lee Buress, and John Kean, eds. *Censored Books: Critical Viewpoints.* Metuchen, NJ: Scarecrow Press, 1993. Essays and rationales on books under attack and ways of justifying using the books.

Kendrick, Walter. *The Sacred Museum: Pornography in Modern Culture.* New York: Viking, 1987.

Lewis, Felice Flanery. *Literature, Obscenity and Law.* Southern Illinois University Press, 1976. The best book on the topic.

Moffett, James. *Storm in the Mountains: A Case Study of Censorship, Conflict, and Consciousness.* Southern Illinois University Press, 1988.

Noble, William. *Bookbanning in America. Who Bans Books?—And Why?* Paul S. Eriksson, 1990.

Oboler, Eli, ed. *Censorship and Education.* H. W. Wilson, 1981.

Oboler, Eli, ed. *The Fear of the Word: Censorship and Sex.* Metuchen, NJ: Scarecrow Press, 1974.

O'Neil, Robert M. *Classrooms in the Crossfire: The Rights and Interests of Students, Parents, Teachers, Administrators, Librarians, and the Community.* Indiana University Press, 1981.

Reichman, Henry. *Censorship and Selection: Issues and Answers for Schools.* American Library Association, 1988.

Rehnquist, William H. *The Supreme Court: How It Was, How It Is.* New York: Morrow, 1987.

Rembar, Charles. *The End of Obscenity: The Trials of Lady Chatterley, Tropic of Cancer, and Fanny Hill.* New York: Random House, 1968. Proof that some lawyers can write.

Robbins, Jan C. *Student Press and the Hazelwood Decision.* Phi Delta Kappa Educational Foundation, 1988.

Robins, Natalie. *Alien Ink: The FBI's War on Freedom of Expression.* New York: Morrow, 1992.

Simmons, John, ed. *Censorship: A Threat to Reading, Learning, Thinking.* Newark, DE: International Reading Association, 1994. A fine collection of articles.

Thomas, Donald. *A Long Time Burning: The History of Literary Censorship in England.* New York: Praeger, 1969.

West, Mark, ed. *Trust Your Children: Voices Against Censorship in Children's Literature.* Neal-Schuman, 1988. Young adult authors speak out about censorship.

Zeigler, Joseph Wesley. *Arts in Crisis: The National Endowment for the Arts Versus America.* New York: A. Cappella Books, 1994.

ARTICLES

"Are Libraries Fair: Pre-Selection Censorship in a Time of Resurgent Conservatism," *Newsletter on Intellectual Freedom* 31 (September 1982): 151, 181–88. Comments by Cal Thomas, conservative syndicated columnist, and Nat Hentoff, *Village Voice* columnist.

Asheim, Lester. "Not Censorship, but Selection," *Wilson Library Bulletin* 28 (September 1953): 63–67. The most widely quoted statement on the distinction between selection and censorship.

Asheim, Lester. "Selection and Censorship: A Reappraisal," *Wilson Library Bulletin* 58 (November 1983): 180–84.

Avery, Kay Beth and Robert J. Simpson. "The Constitution and Student Publications: A Comprehensive Approach," *Journal of Law and Education* 16 (Winter 1987): 1–61.

Baker, Mary Gordon. "A Teacher's Need to Know Versus the Student's Right to Privacy," *Journal of Law and Education* 16 (Winter 1987): 71–91.

Bassett, John. "Huck and Tom in School: Conflicting Freedoms and Values," *Free Speech Yearbook* 27 (1989): 48–54.

Bernays, Anne. "I Don't Want to Read a Novel Passed by a Board of Good Taste," *Chronicle of Higher Education* 37 (March 6, 1991): B–1, B–3.

Booth, Wayne C. "Censorship and the Values of Fiction," *English Journal* 53 (March 1964): 155–164.

Bradley, Julia Turnquist. "Censoring the School Library: Do Students Have a Right to Read?" *Connecticut Law Review* 10 (Spring 1978): 747–775.

Briley, Dorothy. "Are the Editors Guilty of Precensorship?" *School Library Journal* 29 (October 1982): 114–115.

Broderick, Dorothy. "Censorship—Reevaluated," *School Library Journal* 18 (November 1971): 30–32.

Broderick, Dorothy. "Serendipity at Work," *Show-Me Libraries* 35 (February 1984): 13–14.

Bryant, Gene. "The New Right and Intellectual Freedom," *Tennessee Librarian* 33 (Summer 1981): 19–24.

Burger, Robert H. "The Kanawha County Textbook Controversies: A Study of Communication and Power," *Library Quarterly* 48 (April 1982): 584–589.

Burress, Lee A. "How Censorship Affects the School," Wisconsin Council of Teachers of English, *Special Bulletin No. 8* (October 1963): 1–23.

Campbell, Colin. "Book Banning in America," *New York Times Book Review* (December 20, 1981): 1, 16–18.

"Censorship: An American Dilemma," *Publishers Weekly* 230 (July 11, 1986): 30–46.

Clark, Todd, ed. "The Question of Academic Freedom," *Social Education* 39 (April 1975): 202–252.

Click, J. William, and Lillian Lodge Kopenhaver. "Few Changes Since *Hazelwood,*" *School Press Review* 65 (Winter 1990): 12–27.

Cornog, Martha. "Is Sex Safe in Your Library: How To Fight Censorship," *Library Journal* 118 (August 1993): 43–46.

Delp, Vaughn N. "The Far Right and Me: It's Not So Far Away and It's Not So Right," *Arizona English Bulletin* 37 (Fall 1994): 71–76.

Donelson, Kenneth L. "Shoddy and Pernicious Books and Youthful Piety: Literary and Moral Censorship, Then and Now," *Library Quarterly* 51 (January 1981): 4–19.

Donelson, Kenneth L. "Six Statements/Questions from the Censors," *Phi Delta Kappan* 69 (November 1987): 208–214.

Donelson, Kenneth L. "You Can't Have That Book in My Kid's School Library: Books Under Attack in the *Newsletter on Intellectual Freedom* 1952–1989," *High School Journal* 74 (October–November 1990): 1–7.

Donelson, Kenneth L. "Steps Towards the Freedom to Read," *ALAN Review* 20 (Winter 1993): 14–19.

Edwards, June. "Censorship in the Schools: What's Moral About the *Catcher in the Rye*? *English Journal* 72 (April 1983): 39–42.

Faaborg, Karen Kramer. "High School Play Censorship: Are Students' First Amendment Rights Violated When Officials Cancel Theatrical Productions?" *Journal of Law and Education* 14 (October 1985): 575–594.

FitzGerald, Frances. "A Disagreement in Baileyville," *New Yorker* 59 (January 16, 1984): 47–90.

Goldberg, Beverly. "On the Line for the First Amendment," *American Libraries* 26 (September 1995): 774–778. An interview with Judith Krug.

Glatthorn, Allan A. "Censorship and the Classroom Teacher," *English Journal* 66 (February 1977): 12–15.

Groves, Cy. "Book Censorship: Six Misunderstandings," *Alberta English '71* 11 (Fall 1971): 5–7. Reprinted in (Fall 1994) *Arizona English Bulletin*, pp. 19–20.

Hale, F. Dennis. "Free Expression: The First Five Years of the Rehnquist Court," *Journalism Quarterly* 69 (Spring 1992): 89–104.

Hentoff, Nat. "Any Writer Who Follows Anyone Else's Guidelines Ought to Be in Advertising," *School Library Journal* 24 (November 1977): 27–29.

Hentoff, Nat. "School Newspapers and the Supreme Court," *School Library Journal* 34 (March 1988): 114–16.

Hentoff, Nat. "When Nice People Burn Books," *Progressive* 47 (February 1983): 42–44.

Hildebrand, Janet. "Is Privacy Reserved for Adults? Children's Rights at the Public Library," *School Library Journal* 37 (January 1991): 21–25.

Hillocks, George, Jr. "Books and Bombs: Ideological Conflicts and the School—A Case Study of the Kanawha County Book Protest," *School Review* 86 (August 1978): 632–654.

Hirschoff, Mary-Michelle Upson. "Parents and the Public School Curriculum: Is There a Right to Have One's Child Excused from Objectionable Instruction?" *Southern California Law Review* 50 (1977): 871–959.

Holderer, Robert W. "The Religious Right: Who Are They and Why Are We the Enemy?" *English Journal* 84 (September 1995): 74–83.

Janeczko, Paul. "How Students Can Help Educate the Censors," *Arizona English Bulletin* 17 (February 1975): 78–80.

Jenkinson, David. "Censorship Iceberg: Results of a Survey of Challenges in Public and School Libraries," *Canadian Library Journal* 43 (February 1986): 7–21.

Jenkinson, Edward B. "Protecting Holden Caulfield and His Friends from the Censors," *English Journal* 74 (January 1985): 26–33.

Kamhi, Michelle Marder. "Censorship vs. Selection—Choosing the Books Our Children Shall Read," *Educational Leadership* 39 (December 1981): 211–215.

Keresey, Gayle. "School Book Club Expurgation Practices," *Top of the News* 40 (Winter 1984): 131–38.

Kingsbury, Louise, and Lance Gurwell. "The Sin Fighters: Grappling with Gomorrah at the Grass Roots," *Utah Holiday* 12 (April 1983): 42–61.

Kopenhaver, Lillian Lodge, David L. Martinson, and Peter Habermann. "First Amendment Rights in South Florida: View of Advisors and Administrators in Light of *Hazelwood*," *School Press Review* 65 (Fall 1989): 11–17.

MacLeod, Lanette. "The Censorship History of *The Catcher in the Rye*," *PNLA Quarterly* 39 (Summer 1975): 10–13.

MacRae, Cathi Dunn. "Watch Out for 'Don't Read This!'" *VOYA* 18 (June 1995): 80–87.

Martin, William. "The Guardians Who Slumbereth Not," *Texas Monthly* 10 (November 1982): 145–150.

Meeks, Lynn Langer. "Who Are the Censors, Why Do They Censor, and What Can We Do About It? *Idaho Language Arts Newsletter*, April 1990, pp. 1–4.

Melichar, Don. "Objections to Books in Arizona High School English Classes," *Arizona English Bulletin* 37 (Fall 1994): 3–13.

Moe, Mary Sheehy. "Selection and Retention of Instructional Materials—What the Courts Have Said," *SLATE*, August 1995, entire issue.

Moffett, James. "Hidden Impediments to Improving English Teaching," *Phi Delta Kappan* 67 (September 1985): 50–56.

Nelson, Jack L., and Anna S. Ochoa. "Academic Freedom, Censorship, and the Social Studies," *Social Education* 51 (October 1987): 424–427.

Niccolai, F.R. "Right to Read and School Library Censorship," *Journal of Law and Education* 10 (January 1981): 23–26.

O'Malley, William J. (S.J.). "How to Teach 'Dirty' Books in High School," *Media and Methods* 4 (November 1967): 6–11.

Orleans, Jeffrey H. "What Johnny Can't Read: 'First Amendment Rights' in the Classroom," *Journal of Law and Education* 10 (January 1981): 1–15.

Peck, Richard. "The Genteel Unshelving of a Book," *School Library Journal* 32 (May 1986): 37–39.

Peck, Richard. "The Great Library-Shelf Witch Hunt," *Booklist* 88 (January 1, 1992): 816–817.

Pico, Steven. "An Introduction to Censorship," *School Library Media Quarterly* 18 (Winter 1990): 84–87. Pico was the plaintiff in *Pico v. Island Trees*.

Pincus, Jonathan. "Censorship in the Public Schools: Who Should Decide What Students Should Learn?" *Free Speech Yearbook* 24 (1985): 67–84.

Pipkin, Gloria. "Challenging the Conventional Wisdom on Censorship," *ALAN Review* 20 (Winter 1993): 35–37.

Pipkin, Gloria. "Confessions of an Accused Pornographer," *Arizona English Bulletin* 37 (Fall 1994).

"Rationales for Commonly Challenged Taught Books," *Connecticut English Journal* 15 (Fall 1983): entire issue.

Reed, Michael. "What Johnny Can't Read: School Boards and the First Amendment," *University of Pittsburgh Law Review* 42 (Spring 1981): 653–657.

Robinson, Stephen. "Freedom, Censorship, Schools, and Libraries." *English Journal* 70 (January 1980): 58–59.

Rossi, John et al., eds. "The Growing Controversy Over Book Censorship," *Social Education* 46 (April 1982): 254–279.

Russo, Elaine M. "Prior Restraint and the High School Free Press': The Implications of *Hazelwood School District vs. Kuhlmeier,*" *Journal of Law and Education* 18 (Winter 1989): 1–21.

Schrader, Alvin M. "A Study of Community Censorship Pressures on Canadian Public Libraries," *Canadian Library Journal* 49 (February 1992): 29–38.

Shafer, Robert. "Censorship in Tucson's Flowing Wells School District Makes for a Nationally Publicized 'Non-Event,' " *Arizona English Bulletin* 37 (Fall 1994): 51–57.

Siegel, Paul. "*Tinkering* with *Stare Decisis* in the *Hazelwood* Case," *Free Speech Yearbook* 27 (1989): 97–103.

Simmons, John. "Censorship and the YA Book," *ALAN Review* 16 (Spring 1989): 14–19.

Simmons, John. "Proactive Censorship: The New Wave," *English Journal* 70 (December 1981): 18–20.

Simmons, John. "What Teachers under Fire Need from Their Principals," *ALAN Review* 20 (Winter 1993): 22–25.

Small, Robert C., Jr. "Censorship and English: Some Things We Don't Think About Very Often (but Should)," *Focus* 3 (Fall 1976): 18–24.

"Some Thoughts on Censorship: An Author Symposium," *Top of the News* 39 (Winter 1983): 137–153. Comments by Norma Klein, Judy Blume, Betty Miles, and others.

Stielow, Frederick J. "Censorship in the Early Professionalization of American Libraries, 1876 to 1929," *Journal of Library History* 18 (Winter 1983): 37–54.

Strike, Kenneth A. "A Field Guide of Censors: Toward a Concept of Censorship in Public Schools," *Teachers College Record* 87 (Winter 1985): 239–258.

Sutton, Roger. "What Mean We, White Man?" *Voice of Youth Advocates* 15 (August 1992): 155–158.

Tollefson, Alan M. "Censored and Censured: Racine Unified School District vs. Wisconsin Library Association," *School Library Journal* 33 (March 1987): 108–112.

Tyack, David B., and Thomas James. "Moral Majorities and the School Curriculum: Historical Perspectives on the Legalization of Virtue," *Teachers College Record* 86 (Summer 1985): 513–537.

Valgardson, W.D. "Being a Target," *Canadian Library Journal* 48 (February 1991): 17–18, 20.

Vonnegut, Kurt. "Why Are You Banning My Book?" *American School Board Journal* 168 (October 1981): 35.

Watson, Jerry J., and Bill C. Snider. "Educating the Potential Self-censor," *School Media Quarterly* 9 (Summer 1981): 272–276.

West, Celeste. "The Secret Garden of Censorship: Ourselves," *Library Journal* 108 (September 1983): 1651–1653.

Whaley, Elizabeth Gates. "What Happens When You Put the Manchild in the Promised Land? An Experiment with Censorship," *English Journal* 63 (May 1974): 61–65.

Whitson, James Anthony. "After *Hazelwood*: The Roles of School Officials in Conflicts over the Curriculum," *ALAN Review* 20 (Winter 1993): 3–6.

Wickenden, Dorothy. "Bowdlerizing the Bard," *New Republic* 192 (June 3, 1985): 18–19.

Chapter 13

A Brief History of Adolescent Literature

· ·

Although we would not argue with teachers and librarians that the best way to know adolescent literature is to read widely in contemporary books, a case can be made that professionals ought to know the history of their own fields for at least three reasons. First, they ought to know not merely where they are but also how they got there, and far too many teachers and librarians are unaware of their history. We were, for too many of us, miraculously born from nothing as a profession the day before yesterday. More than just being aware of a mixture of fascinating historical tidbits, knowing our common backgrounds gives us a sense of the past and a way of knowing why and how certain kinds of books have consistently proven popular and where books today came from.

Second, for anyone who cares about the mores and morals of our time reflected in adolescent books, there is a fascination in knowing how they came to be. There is no better way to see what adults wanted young people to accept as good and noble at any point in history than to examine adolescent books of the time. The analysis may breed some cynicism as we detect the discrepancies between the lessons taught by a Felsen or an Alger or a Stratemeyer Syndicate author and the truth about the world of the time, but the lessons are nonetheless important and not necessarily less sincere.

Third, and this may be difficult to believe for those who have not dipped into books out of the past, many of the older books are surprisingly fun to read. We're not suggesting that many deserve to be reprinted and circulated among today's young adults, only that librarians and teachers may discover that books as different as Mabel Robinson's *Bright Island* (1937) or John Tunis's *Go, Team, Go!* (1954) or John Bennett's *Master Skylark* (1897) are fun, or that other books such as Ralph Henry Barbour's *The Crimson Sweater* (1906) or Susan Coolidge's *What Katy Did* (1872) or Mary Stolz's *Pray Love, Remember* (1954) are not without their charm.

For the convenience of readers, this chapter is divided into roughly equal parts: 1800–1900, 1900–1940, and 1940–1966.

· ·

1800–1900: A Century of Purity with a Few Passions

Before 1800, literature read by children and young adults alike was largely religious. Such books as John Bunyan's *The Pilgrim's Progress* (1678) reminded young people that they were merely small adults who soon must face the wrath of God. In the 1800s, the attitude of adults toward the young gradually changed. The country expanded, we moved inevitably toward an urban society, medical knowledge rapidly developed, and young people no longer began working so early in their lives. The literature that emerged for young adults remained pious and sober, but it hinted at the possibility of humanity's experiencing a satisfying life here on earth. Books reflected adult values and fashions but of this world, not merely the next.

Alcott and Alger

Louisa May Alcott and Horatio Alger, Jr., were the first writers for young adults to gain national attention, but the similarity between the two ends almost as it begins. Alcott wrote of happy family life. Alger wrote about broken homes. Alcott's novels were sometimes harsh but always honest. Alger's novels were romantic fantasies. Alcott's novels are still read for good reason. Alger's novels are rarely read save by the historian or the specialist.

The second daughter of visionary Amos Bronson Alcott, Louisa May Alcott lived her youth near Concord and Boston with a practical mother and a father who was brilliant, generous, improvident, and impractical. The reigning young adult writer of the time was Oliver Optic (the pen name of William T. Adams), and Boston publishers Roberts Brothers were eager to find a story for young adults that would compete with Optic. Thomas Niles, Roberts's representative, suggested in September 1866 that Louisa May Alcott write a girls' book, and in May 1868 he gently reminded her that she had agreed to try.

She sent a manuscript to Niles, who thought parts of it dull, but other readers at the publisher's office disagreed, and the first part of *Little Women: Meg, Jo, Beth, and Amy. The Story of Their Lives. A Girl's Book* was published September 30, 1868. With three illustrations and a frontispiece for $1.50 a copy, *Little Women* was favorably reviewed, and sales were good, here and in England. By early November 1868, Alcott had begun work on the second part, which was published on April 14, 1869.

Little Women has vitality and joy and real life devoid of the sentimentality common at the time, a wistful portrait of the life and world Alcott must have wished she could have lived. The Civil War background is subtle, expressing the loneliness and never-ending war far better than many adult war novels, for all their suffering, pain, and horror. Aimed at young adults, *Little Women* has maintained steady popularity with them and children. Adults reread it (sometimes repeatedly) to gain a sense of where they were when they were children.

If *Little Women* is Alcott's best-known book, most of the recent research and criticism on Alcott has been devoted to the thrillers she wrote anonymously to make money for the family. Madeleine Stern has edited several collections of these thrillers (e.g., *Behind A Mask: The Unknown Thrillers of Louisa May Alcott; Plots and Counterplots: More Unknown Thrillers of Louisa May Alcott;* and *The Lost Stories of*

Louisa May Alcott). The most recent is edited by Kent Bicknell, *A Long Fatal Love Chase.*

Son of an unctuous Unitarian clergyman, Horatio Alger, Jr., graduated from Harvard at eighteen. Ordained a Unitarian minister in 1864, he served a Brewster, Massachusetts, church only to leave it two years later under a cloud of scandal and claims of sodomy, all hushed at the time. He moved to New York City and began writing full-time.

The same year, he sent *Ragged Dick; or, Street Life in New York* to Oliver Optic's magazine, *Student and Schoolmate,* a popular goody-goody magazine. Optic recognized salable pap when he spotted it, and he bought Alger's book for the January 1867 issue. Published in hardcover in 1867 or 1868, *Ragged Dick* was the first of many successes for Alger and his publishers, and it is still his most readable work, probably because it was the first from a mold that soon became predictably moldy.

The plot, as in most Alger books, consisted of semiconnected episodes illustrating a boy's first steps toward maturity, respectability, and affluence. Ragged Dick, a young bootblack, is grubby but not dirty, he smokes and gambles occasionally, but even the most casual reader recognizes his essential goodness. Through a series of increasingly difficult-to-believe chapters, Ragged Dick is transformed by the model of a young man and the trust of an older one into respectability. But where the sequence of events was hard to believe, Alger now makes events impossible to believe as he introduces the note that typified his later books. What pluck and hard work had brought to Dick is now cast aside as luck enters in—a little boy falls overboard a ferry, Dick saves the child, and a grateful father rewards Dick with new clothes and a better job. Some readers inaccurately label Alger's books "rags to riches" stories, but the hero rarely achieves riches, although at the close of the book he is a rung or two higher on the ladder of success than he has any reason to deserve. "Rags to respectability" is a more accurate statement about Alger's work.

Other Series Writers

The Boston publishing firm of Lee and Shepard established *the* format for young adult series, and to the distress of teachers, librarians, and parents, series books became the method of publishing for many young adult novels, although the format would be far more sophisticated a few years later when Edward Stratemeyer became the king of series books. If sales were any index, readers delighted in Lee and Shepard's 440 authors and 900 books published in 1887 alone.

Four series writers were especially popular. Under the pen name of Harry Castlemon, Charles Austin Fosdick wrote his first novel, *Frank the Young Naturalist* (1864), while in the navy. Castlemon's novels are close to unreadable today, but his books were popular well into the twentieth century. Oliver Optic, the pen name of William Taylor Adams, was a prolific writer of more than 100 books. *The Boat Club* (1885), his first book and the first of the six-book Boat Club series, ran through sixty editions.

Martha Finley (pen name of Martha Farquharson) wrote the amazingly popular Elsie Dinsmore series, twenty-eight volumes carrying Elsie from girlhood to grandmother. A favorite with young women who seemingly loved crying over every other page, Elsie is persistently and nauseatingly docile, pious, virtuous, sweet, humble, timid, ignorant, good, and lachrymose. Published in 1867 and running to an incredible number of editions after that, *Elsie Dinsmore* opened with the ever-virtuous and Christian Elsie awaiting the return of her cold father. His return proves again how unloving he is and how patient Elsie is. Elsie exhibits virtues no matter what happens to her, and much does, for she is no actor, but only a reactor.

Susan Coolidge (pen name of Sarah Chauncey Woolsey) wrote only a few books, but one series rivaled Alcott's books with many girls. *What Katy Did* (1872) featured tomboy Katy Carr, her widowed doctor father, her sisters and brothers, and an invalid aunt. Although too much of the book is concerned with retribution for Katy's obstinacy, Katy is prankish and fun and essentially good.

The Two Most Popular Types of Novels: Domestic and Dime Novels

In 1855, Nathaniel Hawthorne wrote his publisher bitterly lamenting the state of American literature:

> America is now wholly given over to a d--d mob of scribbling women, and I should have no chance of success while the public taste is occupied with their trash—and should be ashamed of myself if I did succeed. What is the mystery of these innumerable editions of *The Lamplighter,* and other books neither better nor worse?—worse they could not be, and better they need not be, when they sell by the 10,000?[1]

The trash was the domestic novel. Born out of belief that humanity was redeemable, the domestic novel preached morality; woman's submission to man; the value of cultural, social, and political conservatism; a religion of the heart and the Bible; and the glories of suffering.

Most domestic novels concerned a young girl, orphaned and placed in the home of a relative or some benefactor, who meets a darkly handsome young man with shadows from his past, a man not to be trusted but worth redeeming and converting. Domestic novels promised some adventure amidst many moral lessons. The heroines differed more in names than characteristics. Uniformly submissive to—yet distrustful of—their betters and men generally, they were self-sacrificing and self-denying beyond belief or common sense and interested in the primacy of the family and marriage as the goal of all decent women. Domestic novels were products of the religious sentiment of the time, the espousal of traditional virtues, and the anxieties and frustrations of women trying to find a role in a changing society.

Writing under the pen name of Elizabeth Wetherell, Susan Warner wrote more than twenty novels and the first domestic novel, *The Wide, Wide World* (1850). As much as forty years later, the novel was said to be one of the four most widely read books in the United States, along with the Bible, *The Pilgrim's Progress,* and *Uncle*

Tom's Cabin. An abridged edition was published in England in 1950 by the University of London Press, and the Feminist Press republished Warner's book in 1987.

The novel was rejected by several New York publishers. George Putnam was ready to return it but decided to ask his mother to read it. She did, she loved it, she urged her son to publish it, and the book was out in time for the Christmas trade. Sales slowly picked up, and the first edition sold out in four months. Translations into French, German, Swedish, and Italian followed, and by 1852, *The Wide, Wide World* was in its fourteenth printing.

The author's life paralleled that of her heroine, Ellen Montgomery. Warner's father was pathetically and persistently broke, and although the fictional world is not quite so ugly, Ellen's mother dies early, and her father is so consumed with family business that he asks Aunt Fortune Emerson to take over Ellen's life. Ellen, to her aunt's irritation, forms a firm friendship with the aunt's intended. Ellen's closest friend—the daughter of the local minister—is doomed to die soon and succeeds in doing just that. In the midst of life, tears flow. When Ellen and her friends are not crying, they are cooking. Warner's novel taught submission, the dangers of self-righteousness, and the virtues of a steadfast religion. Despite all the weeping, or maybe because of it, the book seemed to have been read by everyone of its time. E. Douglas Branch called it, "The greatest achievement of any of the lady novelists."[2]

Warner's popularity was exceeded only by Augusta Jane Evans Wilson for her *St. Elmo* (1867). Probably no other novel so literally touched the American landscape—13 towns were named, or renamed, St. Elmo, as were hotels, railroad coaches, steamboats, one kind of punch, and a brand of cigars. The popularity of Wilson's book may be gauged by a notice in a special edition of *St. Elmo* "limited to 100,000 copies." Only *Uncle Tom's Cabin* had greater sales, and Wilson was more than once called by her admirers, the American Brontë.

Ridiculously melodramatic as the plot of *St. Elmo* is, it was so beloved that men and women publicly testified that their lives had been permanently changed for the better by reading it. The plot concerns an orphaned girl befriended by a wealthy woman whose dissolute son is immediately enamored of the young woman, is rejected by her, leaves home for several years, returns to plead for her love, is again rejected, and eventually becomes a minister to win the young woman's hand. They marry, another wicked man reformed by the power of a good woman.

If domestic novels took women by storm, dime novels performed almost the same miracle for men. They began when two brothers, Erastus and Irwin Beadle, republished Ann S. Stephens's *Malaeksa: The Indian Wife of the White Hunter* in June 1860. The story of a hunter and his Indian wife in the Revolutionary War days in upper New York state may be as melodramatic as any domestic novel, but its emphasis is more on thrills and chills than tears, and it apparently satisfied and intrigued male readers. Indeed, 65,000 copies of the 6- by 4-inch book of 128 pages sold in almost record time. The most popular of the early dime novels, also set in the Revolutionary period, appeared in October 1860. *Seth Jones: or, The Captives of the Frontier* sold 60,000 copies the first day; at least 500,000 copies were sold in the United States alone, and it was translated into ten languages.

For several years, dime novels cost ten cents, ran about 100 pages in a 7- by 5-inch format, and were aimed at adults. Some early genius of publishing discovered that many readers were boys who could hardly afford the dime cost. Thereafter, the novels dropped to a nickel, although the genre continued to be called the *dime novel*. The most popular dime novels were set in the West—the West of dime novels increasingly meant Colorado and points west—with wondrous he-men like Deadwood Dick and Diamond Dick. Dime novels developed other forms, such as mysteries and even early forms of science fiction, but none were so popular or so typical as the westerns.

Writers of dime novels never pretended to be writing great literature, but they did write satisfying thrills and chills for the masses. The books were filled with stock characters. Early issues of the *Library Journal,* from 1876 onward for another thirty years, illustrate how many librarians hated dime novels for their immorality; but in truth dime novels were moral. The Beadles sincerely believed that their books should represent sound moral values, and what the librarians objected to in

These two half dime novels illustrate the promised action, the purple prose, and the erudite vocabulary of their day.

dime novels was nothing more than the unrealistic melodramatic plots and the stereotyped characters, more typical of the time than just the dime novel.

Bad Boy and Adventure Novels

Beginning with Thomas Bailey Aldrich's *The Story of a Bad Boy* in 1870, a new kind of literature developed around bad boys, imperfect but tough and realistic and anything but the good-little-boy figures in too many unrealistic books of the time. *The Story of a Bad Boy,* part-novel, part-autobiography, was an immediate success with readers and critics.

Mark Twain's *The Adventures of Tom Sawyer* (1876) and *Adventures of Huckleberry Finn* (1884) culminated and ended the genre. Aldrich and Twain told of real boys, sometimes moral or cruel or silly but always real. Other books once popular in the same strain, for example, George Wilbur Peck's *Peck's Bad Boy and His Pa* (1883), stressed silliness or prankishness to extremes.

A few adventure novels of the time deserve mention if for no other reason than that they remain readable even today. Noah Brooks's *The Boy Emigrants* (1876) is a romanticized but fascinating tale of boys traveling across the plains. Kirk Munroe is undeservedly ignored today, but his story of a young boy working in the mines, *Derrick Sterling* (1888), is great fun to read. John Bennett's *Master Skylark: A Story of Shakespeare's Time* (1898) is a witty, adventure-filled story, and John Meade Falkner's *Moonfleet* (1898) is almost as good a tale of piracy and derring-do as Robert Louis Stevenson's *Treasure Island* (1883).

Development of the American Public Library

The development of the public library was as rocky and slow as it was inevitable. In 1731, Benjamin Franklin suggested that members of the Junto, a middle-class social and literary club in Philadelphia, share their books with other members. That led to the founding of the Philadelphia Library Company, America's first subscription library. Other such libraries followed, most of them dedicated to moral purposes, as the constitution of the Salisbury, Connecticut, Social Library announced: "The promotion of Virtue, Education, and Learning, and . . . the discouragement of Vice and Immorality."[3]

In 1826, the governor of New York urged that school district libraries be established, in effect using school buildings for public libraries. Similar libraries were established in New England by the 1840s and in the Midwest shortly thereafter. Eventually, mayors and governors saw the wisdom of levying state taxes to support public libraries in their own buildings, not the schools, and by 1863, there were 1000 public libraries spread across the United States.

The first major report on the developing movement came in an 1876 document from the U.S. Bureau of Education. Part I, "Public Libraries in the United States of America, Their History, Condition, and Management," contained 1187 pages of reports and analyses on 3649 public libraries with holdings of 300 volumes or more.

That same year marks the beginning of the modern library movement. Melvil Dewey, then assistant librarian in the Amherst College Library, was largely responsible for the October 4, 1876, conference of librarians that formed the American Library Association the third day of the meeting. The first issue of the *American Library Journal* appeared the same year (it was to become the *Library Journal* the following year), the world's first professional journal for librarians. While there had been an abortive meeting in 1853, the 1876 meeting promised continuity the earlier meeting had lacked.[4]

In 1884, Columbia College furthered the public library movement by establishing the first school of Library Economy (later to be called Library Science) under Melvil Dewey's leadership. Excellent as these early public libraries were, they grew immeasurably under the impetus of Andrew Carnegie's philanthropy. A Scottish immigrant, Carnegie left millions of dollars for the creation of public libraries across the United States.

Fiction and Libraries

The growth of public libraries presented opportunities for pleasure and education of the masses, but arguments about the purposes of the public library arose almost as fast as the buildings. William Poole listed three common objections to the public library in the October 1876 *American Library Journal:* the normal dread of taxes; the more philosophical belief that government had no rights except to protect people and property—that is no right to tax anyone to build and stock a public library; and concern over the kinds of books libraries might buy and circulate.[5] In this last point, Poole touched on a controversy that raged for years, that is, whether a public library is established for scholars or the pleasure of the masses. Poole believed that a library existed for the entire community, or else there was no justification for a general tax. Poole's words did not quiet critics who argued that the library's sole *raison d'etre* was educational. Waving the banner of American purity in his hands, W. M. Stevenson maintained:

> If the public library is not first and foremost an educational institution, it has no right to exist. If it exists for mere pleasure, and for a low order of entertainment at that, it is simply a socialistic institution.[6]

Many librarians of the time agreed. Probably, a few agree even today.

The problem lay almost entirely with fiction. Indeed, the second session of the 1876 American Library Association meeting was devoted to "Novel Reading," mostly but not exclusively about young people's reading. A librarian announced that his rules permitted no fiction in his library. His factory-patrons might ask for novels, but he recommended other books and was able to keep patrons without supplying novels. To laughter, he said that he had never read novels so he "could not say what their effect really was."[7]

Teachers worried almost as much as librarians. A principal of a large endowed academy was approvingly quoted by a librarian for having said:

The voracious devouring of fiction commonly indulged in by patrons of the public library, especially the young, is extremely pernicious and mentally unwholesome.[8]

That attitude persisted for years and is occasionally heard even today among teachers and librarians.

1900–1940: From the Safety of Romance to the Beginning of Realism

During the first forty years of the twentieth century, the western frontier disappeared, and the United States changed from an agrarian society to an urban one. World War I brought the certainty that it would end all wars. The labor movement grew along with Ford's production lines of cars, cars, cars. President Hoover came along, then the Wall Street crash of 1929 and the Great Depression. By 1938, three million young people from age 16 through 25 were out of school and unemployed, and a quarter of a million boys were on the road. Nazi Germany rose in Eastern Europe, and in the United States, Roosevelt introduced the "New Deal." When the end of the Depression seemed almost in sight, the New York World's Fair of 1939 became an optimistic metaphor for the coming of a newer, better, happier, and more secure life. But World War II lay just over the horizon, apparent to some, ignored by most.

Reading Interests Versus Reading Needs

In the high schools, which enrolled only a tiny fraction of eligible students in the United States, teachers faced pressure from colleges to prepare the young for advanced study, which influenced many adults to be more intent on telling young people what to read than in finding out what they wanted to read. Recreational reading seemed vaguely time-wasting, if not downright wicked. Young people nevertheless found and read books, mainly fiction, for recreation. Popular choices were series books from Stratemeyer's Literary Syndicate, including Tom Swift, Nancy Drew, the Hardy Boys, Baseball Joe, and Ruth Fielding. Non-Stratemeyer series books were also popular, as were individual books written specifically for young adults, along with some classics and best-sellers selected by the Book-of-the-Month Club when it began in 1926 and the Literary Guild when it began a year later.

Arguments over what students choose to read have raged for years, and the end is unlikely to precede the millennium. In 1926, when Carleton Washburne and Mabel Vogel put together the lengthy *Winnetka Graded Book List,* they explained, "Books that were definitely trashy or unsuitable for children, even though widely read, have not been included in this list."[9] Apparently enough people were curious about the trashy or unsuitable to lead the authors to add two supplements.[10] *Elsie Dinsmore* was among the damned, and so were Edgar Rice Burroughs's *Tarzan of the*

Apes, Eleanor Porter's *Pollyanna,* Zane Grey's westerns, books from the Ruth Field-ing and Tom Swift series, Mark Twain's *Tom Sawyer Abroad,* and Arthur Conan Doyle's *The Hound of the Baskervilles. The Adventures of Sherlock Holmes,* however, was considered worthy of inclusion.

Representative of the other side of the argument is this statement by English professor William Lyon Phelps:

> I do not believe the majority of these very school teachers and other cultivated mature readers began in early youth by reading great books exclusively; I think they read *Jack Harkaway, an Old Sleuth,* and the works of Oliver Optic and Horatio Alger. From these enchanters they learned a thing of tremendous importance—the delight of reading. Once a taste for reading is formed, it can be improved. But it is improbable that boys and girls who have never cared to read a good story will later enjoy stories by good artists.[11]

Girls' Books and Boys' Books

Up to the mid–1930s, teachers and librarians frequently commented that girls' books were inferior to boys' books. Franklin T. Baker wrote that with the obvious exception of Alcott, girls' books of 1908 were "painfully weak" and lacking "inven-tion, action, humor."[12] Two years later, Clara Whitehill Hunt agreed that many girls' books were empty, insipid, and mediocre.[13] In 1935, Julia Carter broke into a review of boys' nonfiction with what appeared to be an exasperated *obiter dictum:*

> Will someone please tell me why we expect the *boys* to know these things and still plan for the girls to be mid-Victorian, and consider them hoydens beyond reclaiming, when instead of shrieking and running like true daughters of Eve, they are interested in snakes and can light a fire with two matches?[14]

Such writers as Caroline Dale Snedeker, Cornelia Meigs, Jeanette Eaton, Mabel Robinson, and Elizabeth Forman Lewis responded to these kinds of criticism by writing enough good girls' books that in 1937 Alice M. Jordan wrote as if the differ-ence in quality was a thing of the past:

> There was a time not long ago when the boys had the lion's share in the yearly production of books intended for young people. So writers were urged to give us more stories in which girls could see themselves in recognizable relation-ship to the world of their own time, forgetting perhaps that human nature does not change and the vital things are universal. Yet, nonetheless, the girls had a real cause to plead and right valiantly the writers have responded.[15]

Critics believed then, as they continued to insist for years, that girls would read boys' books, but boys would never read girls' books. At least part of the prob-lem lay with stereotypes of boys' and girls' roles as expressed by two writers. Clara Vostrovsky, author of the first significant reading interest study, went back to an-cient times for her stereotypes, suggesting that it was "probable" that the differ-ences in reading interests between boys and girls lay "in the history of the race."[16]

At least during the first half of the century, boys received the lion's share of attention from authors and publishers.

Psychologist G. Stanley Hall predicted reading interests of girls and boys on psychological differences:

> Boys love adventure, girls sentiment. . . . Girls love to read stories about girls which boys eschew, girls, however, caring much more to read about boys than boys to read about girls. Books dealing with domestic life and with young children in them, girls have almost entirely to themselves. Boys, on the other hand, excel in love of humor, rollicking fun, abandon, rough horse-play, and tales of wild escapades. Girls are less averse to reading what boys like than boys are to reading what girls like. A book popular with boys would attract some girls, while one read by most girls would repel a boy in the middle teens. The reading interests of high-school girls are far more humanistic, cultural and general, and that of boys is more practical, vocational, and even special.[17]

The simple truth, perhaps too obvious and discomforting to be palatable to some parents, English teachers, and librarians, was that boys' books were generally far superior to girls' books. That had nothing to do with the sexual or psychological nature of boys or girls but rather with the way authors treated their audience.

Many authors insisted on making their girls good and domestic and dull (if a heroine were allowed some freedom to roam outside the house, she soon regretted it or grew up, whichever came first), perhaps because they thought parents and librarians wanted books that way. Boys were allowed outside the house to find work and responsibilities, of course, but also to find adventure and excitement in their books.

Changing English Classroom

By 1900, the library played a significant role in helping young adults find reading materials. Although many librarians reflected the traditional belief that classics should be the major reading of youth, other librarians helped young adults find a variety of materials they liked, not trash, but certainly popular books.

This would rarely have been true of English teachers, saddled as they were with responsibility for preparing young adults for college entrance examinations. At first, these examinations simply required some proof of writing proficiency, but in 1860 and 1870, Harvard began using Milton's *Comus* and Shakespeare's *Julius Caesar* as alternative books for the examination. Four years later, Harvard required a short composition based on a question about one of the following: Shakespeare's *The Tempest, Julius Caesar*, and *The Merchant of Venice*, Goldsmith's *The Vicar of Wakefield*, or Scott's *Ivanhoe* and *The Lay of the Last Minstrel*.

In 1894, the prestigious Committee of Ten on Secondary School Studies presented its report, and English became an accepted discipline in the schools, although not yet as respectable as Latin. Chaired by controversial Harvard president Charles W. Eliot, the committee was appointed by the National Education Association in July 1892 and met later that year to determine the nature, limits, and methods appropriate to many subject matters in secondary school. Samuel Thurber of the Boston Girls' High School was unable to promote his belief that a high school curriculum should consist almost entirely of elective courses, but as chairman of the English Conference, his report liberalized and dignified the study of English. Two important recommendations were that English be studied five hours a week for four years and that uniform college entrance examinations be established throughout the United States.

The result was the publication of book lists, mainly classics, as the basis of entrance examinations. Plays and books such as Shakespeare's *Twelfth Night* and *As You Like It*, Milton's Books I and II from *Paradise Lost*, Scott's *The Abbot* and *Marmion* or Irving's *Bracebridge Hall* virtually became the English curriculum as teachers, inevitably concerned with their students' entry into college, increasingly adapted the English curriculum to fit the list.

National Council of Teachers of English Begins

Out of the growing protest about college entrance examinations, a group of English teachers attending a national Education Association Table formed a Committee on College Entrance Requirements in English to assess the problem through a national survey of English teachers. The committee uncovered hostility to colleges presumptuous enough to try to control the secondary English curriculum through the guise of entrance examinations. John M. Coulter, a professor at the University of Chicago, tried to sound that alarm to college professors, but without much success:

> The high school exists primarily for its own sake; and secondarily as a preparatory school for college. This means that when the high school interest and the college interest comes into conflict, the college interest must yield. It also means that the function of a preparatory school must be performed only in so far as it does not interfere with the more fundamental purpose of the high school itself.[18]

Some irate teachers recognized that the problem of college control would hardly be the last issue to face English teachers and formed the nucleus of the National Council of Teachers of English. The First Annual Meeting in Chicago on December 1 and 2, 1911, was largely devoted to resentment about actions of the National Conference on Uniform Entrance Requirements, particularly because that body had representatives from twelve colleges, two academies, and only two public high schools (principals, not English teachers). Wilbur W. Hatfield, then at Farragut High School in Chicago and soon to edit the *English Journal,* relayed instructions from the Illinois Association of Teachers of English that the new organization should compile a list of comparatively recent books suitable for home reading by students and that they should also recommend some books of the last ten years for study because the "present custom of using only old books in the classroom leaves the pupil with no acquaintance with the literature of the present day," from which students would choose their reading after graduation.[19]

James Fleming Hosic's 1917 report on the *Reorganization of English in Secondary Schools,* part of a larger report published under the aegis of the U.S. Bureau of Education, looked at books and teaching in ways that must have seemed muddle-headed or perverse to traditionalists. Looking at literature for the tenth, eleventh, and twelfth grades, Hosic chose works that pleased many, puzzled others, and alienated some. He explained that English teachers should lead students to read works in which they would, "find their own lives imaged in this larger life," and would gradually attain from the author's "clearer appreciation of human nature, a deeper and truer understanding. . . . It should be the aim of the English teacher to make [reading] an unfailing resource and joy in the lives of all."[20] Hosic's list included classics as well as modern works, such as Helen Hunt Jackson's *Ramona* and Owen Wister's *The Virginian* for the tenth grade, Rudyard Kipling's *The Light That Failed* and Mary Johnston's *To Have and To Hold* for the eleventh grade, and John Synge's *Riders to the Sea* and Margaret Deland's *The Awakening of Helena Richie* for the twelfth grade. Teachers terrified by the contemporary reality reflected in these books—and perhaps equally terrified by the possibility of throwing out age-old lesson plans and tests on classics—had little to fear. In many schools, nothing changed. *Silas Marner, Julius Caesar, Idylls of the King, A Tale of Two Cities,* and *Lady of the Lake* remained the most widely studied books. Most books were taught at interminable length in what was known as the "intensive" method with four to six weeks—sometimes even more—of detailed examination, while horrified or bored students vowed never to read anything once they escaped high school. A 1927 study by Nancy Coryell offered proof that the "intensive" method produced no better test results and considerably more apathy toward literature than the "extensive" method in which students read assigned works faster.[21] Again, however, in many schools nothing changed.

Fortunately, the work of two college professors influenced more English teachers. A 1936 study by Lou LaBrant on the value of free reading at the Ohio State University Laboratory School revealed that students with easy access to different kinds of books and some guidance read more, enjoyed what they read, and moved upward in literary sophistication and taste.[22] Earlier, University of Minnesota professor Dora V. Smith discovered that English teachers knew next to nothing about books written for adolescents. She began the long process of correcting that situation by establishing the first course in adolescent literature. She argued that it was unfair to both young people and their teachers "to send out from our colleges and universities men and women trained alone in Chaucer and Milton and Browning to compete with Zane Grey, Robert W. Chambers, and Ethel M. Dell."[23]

School Library

The development of the school library was almost as slow and convoluted as the development of the public library. In 1823, Brooklyn's Apprentice Library Association established a Youth Library where "Boys over twelve were allowed . . . as were girls whose access to the library were limited to one hour an afternoon, once a week." In 1853, Milwaukee School Commissioner Increase A. Lapham provided for a library open Saturday afternoons and recommended that schools spend $10 a year for books. Rules for the Milwaukee library were clear and more than a bit reminiscent of rules in some school and public libraries until the 1940s:

> (1) Only children over ten years old, their parents, teachers, and school commissioner could withdraw books; (2) books might be withdrawn between 2:00 P.M. and sunset on Saturdays and kept for one week; (3) withdrawals were limited to one book per person; and (4) fines were to be assessed for overdue or damaged books.[24]

Writers in the early years of the *Library Journal* encouraged the cultivation of friendly relations between "co-educators."[25] The National Education Association formed a Committee on Relations of Public Libraries to Public Schools, and its 1899 report announced that "The teachers of a town should know the public library, what it contains, and what use the pupils can make of it. The librarian must know the school, its work, its needs, and what he can do to meet them."[26]

A persistent question was whether schools should depend on the public library or establish their own libraries. In 1896, Melvil Dewey recommended to the National Education Association that it form a library department (as it had for other subject disciplines) because the library was as much a part of the educational system as the classroom.

The previous year, a branch of the Cleveland, Ohio, Public Library was established within Central High School, and in 1899, a branch of the Newark, New Jersey, Public Library was placed in a local high school. In 1900, Mary Kingston became the first library school graduate appointed to a high school library (Erasmus High School in Brooklyn). In 1912, Mary E. Hall, librarian at Girls' High School in Brooklyn, argued the need for many more professionally trained librarians in high school libraries:

> (1) The aims and ideals of the new high school mean we must stop pretending that high school is entirely college preparatory. "It realizes that for the great majority of pupils it must be a preparation for life." (2) Modern methods of teaching demand that a textbook is not enough. "The efficient teacher today uses books, magazines, daily papers, pictures, and lantern slides to supplement the textbook." (3) Reading guidance is easier for the school librarian than the public librarian. "The school librarian has the teacher always close at hand and can know the problems of these teachers in their work with pupils."[27]

In 1916, C. C. Certain, as head of National Education Association committee, began standardizing high school libraries across the United States. He discovered conditions so mixed, from deplorable (mostly) to good (rarely) that his committee set to work to establish minimum essentials for high schools of various sizes. Two reports from the U.S. Office of Education indicate the growth of high school libraries. A 1923 report found only 947 school libraries with more than 3000 volumes, and these were mostly in the northeastern part of the United States. Six years later, the 1929 report found 1982 school libraries with holdings of more than 3000 volumes, and the libraries were more equally spread over the country with New York having 211 such libraries and California having 191. The steady growth of high school libraries, however, slowed drastically during the Depression.

Edward Stratemeyer's Literary Syndicate

Whatever disagreements librarians and English teachers may have had about books suitable for young adults, they bonded together, although ineffectively, to oppose the books produced by Edward Stratemeyer and his numerous writers. Stratemeyer founded the most successful industry ever built around adolescent reading. In 1866, he took time off from working for his stepbrother and wrote on brown wrapping paper an 18,000-word serial, *Victor Horton's Idea,* and mailed it to a Philadelphia weekly boys' magazine. A check for $75 arrived shortly, and Stratemeyer's success story was under way. By 1893, Stratemeyer was editing *Good News,* Street and Smith's boys' weekly, building circulation to more than 200,000. This brought his name in front of the public, particularly young adults. Even more important, he came to know staff writers such as William T. Adams, Edward S. Ellis, and Horatio Alger, Jr. When Optic and Alger died leaving some uncompleted manuscripts, Stratemeyer was asked to finish the last three Optic novels, and he completed (or possibly wrote from scratch) at least eleven and perhaps as many as eighteen Alger novels.

His first hardback book published under his own name was *Richard Dare's Venture; or, Striking Out for Himself* (1894), first in a series he titled Bound to Succeed. By the close of 1897, Stratemeyer had six series and sixteen hardcover books in print. A major breakthrough came in 1898. After Stratemeyer sent a manuscript about two boys on a battleship to Lothrop and Shepard, one of the most successful publishers of young adult fiction, Admiral Dewey won his great victory in Manila Bay. A Lothrop editor asked Stratemeyer to place the boys at the scene of Dewey's victory. He rewrote and returned the book, and *Under Dewey at Manila; or, The War Fortunes of a Castaway* hit the streets in time to capitalize on all the publicity. Not one to miss an opportunity, Stratemeyer used the same characters in his next books, all published from 1898 to 1901 under the series title Old Glory. Using the same characters in contemporary battles in the Orient, Stratemeyer created another series called Soldiers of Fortune, published from 1900 through 1906.

By this time, Stratemeyer had turned to full-time writing and was being wooed by the major publishers, notably Grossett and Dunlap and Cupples and Leon. For a time he turned to stories of school life and sports, the Lakeport series (1904–1912), the Dave Porter series (1905–1919), and the most successful of his early series, the Rover Boys (30 books published between 1899 and 1926). These books were so popular that somewhere between 5 or 6 million copies were sold worldwide, including translations into German and Czechoslovakian.

Stratemeyer aspired to greater things, however. Between 1906 and 1910, he approached both his publishers, suggesting they reduce the price of his books to 50 cents. The publishers may have been shocked to find an author willing to sell his books for less money, but, as they soon realized, mass production of 50-centers increased their revenue and Stratemeyer's royalties almost geometrically. An even greater breakthrough came at roughly the same time, when he evolved the idea of his Literary Syndicate. Stratemeyer was aware that he could create plots and series faster than he could possibly write them. He advertised for writers who needed money and sent them sketches of settings and characters along with a chapter-by-chapter outline of the plot. Writers had a few weeks to fill in the outlines, and when the copy arrived, Stratemeyer tightened the prose and checked for discrepancies with earlier volumes of the series. Then the manuscript was off to the publisher and checks went out to the authors, from $50 to $100, depending on the writer and the importance of the series.

Attacks on Stratemeyer were soon in coming. Librarian Caroline M. Hewins criticized both Stratemeyer's book and the journals that praised his output:

> Stratemeyer is an author who misuses "would" and "should," has the phraseology of a country newspaper, as when he calls a supper "an elegant affair" and a girl "a fashionable miss," and follows Oliver Optic closely in his plots and conversations.[28]

Most librarians supported Hewins, but their attacks hardly affected Stratemeyer's sales. A far more stinging and effective attack came in 1913 from the Boy Scouts of America. Chief executive James E. West was disturbed by the deluge of inferior books and urged the organization's Library Commission to establish a carefully selected and recommended library to protect young men. Not long afterward, Chief Scout Librarian Franklin K. Mathiews urged Grosset and Dunlap to make better books available in 50-cent editions—to compete with Stratemeyer—and on

November 1, 1913, the first list appeared in a Boy Scout publication, "Safety First Week."

But that was not enough to satisfy Mathiews, who in 1914 wrote his most famous article under the sensational title "Blowing Out the Boy's Brains,"[29] a loud and vituperative attack, sometimes accurate but often unfair. Mathiews's attack was mildly successful for the moment, although how much harm it did to Stratemeyer's sales is open to question. Stratemeyer went on to sell more millions of books. When he died in 1930, his two daughters ran the syndicate, which still persists, presumably forever.

Series books were inevitably moral. Whatever parents, teachers, or librarians might have objected to about the unrealistic elements of the books or the poor literary quality, they would have agreed that the books were clearly on the side of good and right, if simplistically so. Series books—and many adult books as well—repeatedly underlined the same themes. Sports produced truly manly men. Foreigners were not to be trusted. School, education, and life should be taken seriously. The outdoor life was healthy, physically and psychologically. Good manners and courtesy were essential for moving ahead. Work in and of itself was a positive good and would advance one in life. Anyone could defeat adversity, any adversity, *if* that person had a good heart and soul. The good side (ours and God's) always won in war. Evil and good were clearly and easily distinguishable. And good always triumphed over evil (at least by the final chapter).

The Coming of the "Junior" or "Juvenile" Novel

Although for years countless books had been published and widely read by young adults, the term *junior* or *juvenile* was first applied to young adult literature during the early 1930s. Rose Wilder Lane's novel *Let the Hurricane Roar* had been marketed by Longmans, Green, and Company as an adult novel. A full-page blurb on the front cover of the February 11, 1933, *Publishers Weekly* bannered THE BOOK THAT MAKES YOU PROUD TO BE AN AMERICAN! and quoted an unnamed reader, presumably an adult, saying, "Honestly, it makes me ashamed of cussing about hard times and taxes." The tenor of the ad and ones to follow suggest an adult novel likely to be popular with young adults as well. It had been the same with the earlier serialization of the novel in the *Saturday Evening Post* and also with the many favorable reviews. Sometime later in 1933, Longmans, Green began to push the novel as the first of their series of "Junior Books," as they termed them.

That the company wanted to attract young adults to Lane's novel is not difficult to understand. Lane wrote of a threatening frontier world she had known in a compelling manner certain to win readers and admirers among young adults. *Let the Hurricane Roar* tells of newly married David and Molly and their life on the hard Dakota plains. David works as a railroad hand for a time, Molly waits for her baby to arrive, and both strive for independence and the security of owning their own 50-acre homestead. When they realize that dream and the baby is born, all looks well, but David overextends his credit, grasshoppers destroy the wheat crop, and no nearby employment can be found. David heads east to find work and later breaks his leg, leaving Molly isolated on the Dakota plains for a winter. Neighbors flee the area, and Molly battles loneliness, blizzards, and wolves before David returns. In summary, *Let the Hurricane Roar* sounds melodramatic, but it is not. In a short, quiet, and loving work, Lane made readers care about two likable young adults living a tough life in a hostile environment. The book's popularity is attested to by its 26 printings between 1933 and 1958 and a recent television production and reissue in paperback under the title *Young Pioneers*.

The development of publishing house divisions to handle books lying in limbo between children's and adults' books grew after *Let the Hurricane Roar*, although authors of the time were sometimes unaware of the "junior" or "juvenile" branches as was John T. Tunis when he tried to market *Iron Duke* in 1934 and 1935. After sending the manuscript to Harcourt, Tunis was invited into the president's office. Mr. Harcourt clearly did not want to talk about the book but instead took the startled author directly to the head of the Juvenile Department. He explained that Harcourt wanted to publish the book as a juvenile, much to Tunis' bewilderment and dismay, since he had no idea what a "juvenile" book was. Thirty years later, he still had no respect for the term, which he called the "odious product of a merchandising age."[30]

Books That Young Adults Liked

Among the most popular books before World War I were those featuring a small child, usually a girl, who significantly changed people around her. At their best, they showed an intriguing youngster humanizing sterile or cold people. At their worst (and they often were), they featured a rapturously happy and miraculously even-dispositioned child who infected an entire household—perhaps a community—with her messianic drive to improve the world through cheer and gladness.

The type began promisingly with Kate Douglas Wiggin's *Rebecca of Sunnybrook Farm* (1904). Nothing Wiggin wrote surpassed *Rebecca*, which sold more than 1.25 million copies between 1904 and 1975. Living in a small town during the 1870s, the optimistic heroine is handed over to two maiden aunts while her parents cope with a large family. She is educated despite her imperfections, high spirits, and rebelliousness and at the close of the books seems cheerfully on her way upward to a better life.

Anne of Green Gables (1908) by Lucy Maud Montgomery was a worthy successor. As in Wiggin's book, Anne travels to an alien society. Here a childless couple who wants to adopt a boy gets Anne by mistake. Anne changes the couple for the better, but they also change her, and Anne's delightfully developed character goes far to remedy any defects in the book.

Wiggin and Montgomery generally managed to skim the sea of sentimentalism, that fatal syrupy deep beloved by bad writers. Occasionally, Rebecca and Anne waded out dangerously far, but their common sense, their impulsiveness, and their ability to laugh at themselves brought them back to shore. After them came the disaster: authors and character so enamored of humanity, so convinced that all people were redeemable and so stickily and uncomplainingly sweet and dear that they drowned in goodness, while many readers gagged. Eleanor Porter wrote the genre's magnum opus and destroyed it with *Pollyanna* (1913). *Pollyanna* is usually remembered as a children's book, but it began as a popular adult novel, eighth among best-sellers in 1913 and second in 1914.

Westerns provided a different type of popularity. The closing of the West heightened interest in an exciting, almost magical, era. A few writers, aiming specifically at young adults, knew the West so well that they became touchstones for authenticity in other writers. In *Pawnee Hero Stories and Folk Tales* (1898) and *By Cheyenne Campfires* (1926), George Bird Grinnell established an honest and generally unsentimentalized portrait of Native American life. Both he and Charles A. Eastman often appeared on reading interest studies as boys' favorites. Joseph Altsheler wrote more conventional adventure tales, including *The Last of the Chiefs* (1909) and *The Horsemen of the Plains* (1910). Far more sentimental but much more popular was Will James's *Smoky, The Cowhorse* (1926), originally published as an adult novel but soon read by thousands of young adults and twice filmed to appreciative audiences. The best-written and most sensitive western for young people was Laura Adams Armer's *Waterless Mountain* (1931). Unfortunately, enthusiastic librarians and teachers had little success in getting teenagers to read this slow-moving and mystical story about a young Navajo boy training to become a Medicine Priest.

The first great writer to focus on the West and its mystique of violence and danger mixed with open spaces and freedom was Owen Wister, whose *The Virginian: A Horseman of the Plains* (1902) provided a model of colloquial speech and romantic and melodramatic adventure for novelists to follow. The best of Zane Grey's books—certainly the most remembered and probably the epitome of the overly romanticized western—was *Riders of the Purple Sage* (1912), which was filled with such classic elements as the mysterious hero, the innocent heroine, evil villains, and the open land. Although Grey has been criticized by librarians and teachers—who seem in general to have read little or nothing of his work—anyone who wishes to know the western dream must read Grey.

With more young adults attending school and with the steadily rising popularity of sports—especially college football and professional baseball—more school-sports stories appeared. William Gilbert Patten, under the pen name of Burt L. Standish, was the first to introduce a regular, almost mythic, sports character recognized throughout America—Frank Merriwell. The Frank Merriwell books began as short stories later fashioned into hardback books. Three other writers who stand out for their realistic sports books include Owen Johnson with his *The Varmint* (1910), *The Tennessee Shad* (1911), and *Stover at Yale* (1911), which attacks snobbery, social clubs, fraternities, and anti-intellectualism. Ralph Henry Barbour wrote an incredible number of fine books, beginning with *The Half-Back* (1899). He invented the formula of a boy attending school and learning who and what he might become through sports. William Heyliger followed in a similar pattern with *Bartley: Freshman Pitcher* (1911) and his Lansing and St. Mary's series.

School stories for girls never had a similar number of readers, but a few deserve reading even today, including Laura Elizabeth Richard's *Peggy* (1899) and

Marjorie Hill Allee's *Jane's Island* (1931) and *The Great Tradition* (1937). Best of them all is Mabel Louise Robinson's *Bright Island* (1937) about spunky Thankful Curtis who was raised on a small island off the coast of Maine and later attends school on the mainland.

1940–1966: From Certainty to Uncertainty

During the 1940s, the United States moved from the Depression into a wartime and then a postwar economy. World War II caused us to move from hatred of Communism to a temporary brotherhood, followed by Yalta, the Iron Curtain, blacklisting, and Senator McCarthy. We went from "Li'l Abner" to "Pogo" and from Bob Hope to Mort Sahl. Problems of the time included school integration, racial unrest, civil rights, and riots in the streets. We were united about World War II, unsure about the Korean War, and divided about Vietnam. We went from violence to more violence and the assassinations of John Kennedy and Malcolm X. The 25 years between 1940 and 1965 revealed a country separated by gaps of all kinds: generational, racial, technological, cultural, and economic.

Educators were as divided as anyone else. Reading interest studies had become fixtures in educational journals, but there was little agreement about the results. In 1946, George W. Norvell wrote, "Our data shows clearly that much literary material being used in our schools is too mature, too subtle, too erudite to permit its enjoyment by the majority of secondary-school pupils." Norvell offered the advice that teachers should give priority to the reading interests of young adults in assigning materials that students would enjoy and in letting students select a portion of their own materials based on their individual interests. He thought that three-fourths of the selections currently in use were uninteresting, especially to boys, and that "to increase reading skill, promote the reading habit, and produce a generation of book-lovers, there is no factor so powerful as interest."[31]

Other researchers supported Norvell's contention that young adults' choices of voluntary reading rarely overlapped books widely respected by more traditional English teachers. In 1947, Marie Rankin surveyed eight public libraries in Illinois, Ohio, and New York and discovered that Helen Boylston's *Sue Barton, Student Nurse* was the most consistently popular book.[32] Twelve years later, Stephen Dunning surveyed 14 school and public libraries and concluded that the ten most popular books were Maureen Daly's *Seventeenth Summer,* Henry Gregor Felsen's *Hot Rod,* Betty Cavanna's *Going On Sixteen,* Rosamund Du Jardin's *Double Date,* Walter Farley's *Black Stallion,* Sally Benson's *Junior Miss,* Mary Stolz's *The Sea Gulls Woke Me,* Rosamund Du Jardin's *Wait for Marcy,* James Summers's *Prom Trouble,* and John Tunis's *All American.*[33]

Near the height of the outpouring of published studies, Jacob W. Getzels assessed the value of reading interest surveys and found most of them wanting in "precision of *definition,* rigor of *theory,* and depth of *analysis.*"[34] He was, of course, right. Most reports were limited to a small sample from a few schools, and little was done except to ask students what they liked to read. The studies at least gave librarians and teachers insight into books young adults liked and brought hope that somewhere out there somebody was reading—a hope that for librarians and teachers needs constant rekindling.

In the mid–1950s, G. Robert Carlsen summarized the findings of published reading interest surveys as showing that young people select their reading first to reassure themselves about their normality and their status as human beings and then for role-playing:

> With the developing of their personality through adolescence, they come to a partially integrated picture of themselves as human beings. They want to test this picture of themselves in the many kinds of roles that it is possible for a human being to play and through testing to see what roles they may fit into and what roles are uncongenial.[35]

Carlsen's observations tied in with those of University of Chicago psychologist Robert J. Havighurst, who outlined the developmental tasks necessary for the healthy growth of individuals. (See Chapter One, p. 34, for the tasks that Havighurst thought crucial to adolescence.)

An outgrowth of the tying together of reading interests and psychology was an interest in bibliotherapy. In 1929, Dr. G. O. Ireland coined the term while writing about the use of books as part of his treatment for psychiatric patients.[36] By the late 1930s and early 1940s, articles about bibliotherapy became almost commonplace in education journals, and by the 1950s, the idea of using books to help readers come to terms with their psychological problems was firmly entrenched. Philosophically, it was justified by Aristotle's *Poetics* and the theory of emotional release through catharsis, a theory with little support except for unverifiable personal testimonials.

One clear and easy application of bibliotherapy was the free reading program (sometimes too clear and too easy for the inept psychologist/English teacher who, finding a new book in which the protagonist had acne, sought the acne-ridden kid in class saying, "You must read this—it's about you"). Lou LaBrant, popularizer of free reading, sounded both a recommendation and a warning when she wrote:

> Certainly I can make a much wiser selection of offerings if I understand the potential reader. . . . [but] This does not mean, as some have interpreted, that a young reader will enjoy only literature which answers his questions, tells him what is to be done. It is true, however, that young and old tend to choose literature, whether they seek solutions or escape, which offers characters or situations with which they can find a degree of identification.[37]

Rise of Paperbacks

Young adult readers might assume paperbound books have always been with us. Despite the success of dime novels and libraries of paperbacks in the late 1800s, paperbacks as we know them entered the mass market in 1938 when Pocket Books offered Pearl Buck's *The Good Earth* as a sample volume in mail-order tests. In the spring of 1939, a staff artist created the first sketch of Gertrude the Kangaroo with a book in her paws and another in her pouch. It became Pocket Books' trademark. A few months later, the company issued ten titles in 10,000-copy editions, most of them remaining best-sellers for years. Avon began publishing in 1941; Penguin entered the U.S. market in 1942; and Bantam, New American Library, Ballantine, Dell, and Popular Library began publishing in 1943. By 1951, sales had reached 230 million paperbacks annually. Phenomenal as the growth was, paperbacks were slow to appear in schools despite an incredible number of titles on appropriate subjects. Librarians complained that paperbacks did not belong in libraries because they were difficult to catalog and easy to steal. School officials maintained that the covers were lurid and the contents little more than pornography. As late as 1969, a New York City high school junior explained, "I'd rather be caught with Lady Chatterley in hardcover than *Hot Rod* in paperback. Hard covers get you one detention, but paperbacks get you two or three."[38]

Regardless of "official" attitudes, by the mid–1960s paperbacks had become a part of young adults' lives. They are easily available, comfortably sized, and inexpensive. Fortunately, not all school personnel were resistant. The creation of Scholastic Book Clubs and widespread distribution of Reader's Choice Catalogs helped paperbacks get accepted in schools and libraries. Eventually, Bantam and Dell's Yearling books became the major suppliers of books written specifically for young adults.

Changes and Growth in Young Adult Literature

From 1941 to 1965, the quality of young adult literature rose steadily, if at times hesitatingly and uncertainly. Series books, so popular from 1900 to the 1940s, died out—except for Stratemeyer Syndicate stalwarts Nancy Drew, the Hardy Boys, and the new Tom Swift, Jr., series. They were killed by increasing reader sophistication combined with the wartime scarcity of paper. Many of the books that replaced the series celebrated those wonderful high school years by focusing on dating, parties, class rings, senior year, the popular crowd, and teen romances devoid of realities such as sex. The books often sounded alike and read alike, but they were unquestionably popular.

Plots were usually simple, with only one or two characters being developed, while others were stock figures or stereotypes. Books dealt almost exclusively with white, middle-class values and morality. The endings were almost uniformly happy and bright, and readers could be certain that neither their morality nor their intelligence would be challenged.

Taboos may never have been written down, but they were clear to readers and writers. Certain things were not to be mentioned—obscenity, profanity, suicide, sexuality, sensuality, homosexuality, protests against anything significant, social or racial injustice, or the ambivalent feelings of cruelty and compassion inherent in young adults and all people. Pregnancy, early marriage, drugs, smoking, alcohol, school drop-outs, divorce, and alienation could be introduced only by implication and only as bad examples for thoughtful, decent young adults. Consequently, young adult books were often innocuous and pervaded by a saccharine didacticism.

Despite these unwritten rules, some writers transcended the taboos and limitations and made it possible for Stanley B. Kegler and Stephen Dunning to write in 1960, "Books of acceptable quality have largely replaced poorly written and mediocre books."[39] Among the authors bringing about this welcome change were four who appealed largely to girls (Florence Crannell Means, Maureen Daly, Mary Stolz, and James Summers) and four who appealed largely to boys (Paul Annixter, Henry Gregor Felsen, Jack Bennett, and John Tunis).

Means was unusual in developing minority protagonists. *Tangled Waters* (1936) about a Navajo girl on an Arizona reservation, *Shuttered Windows* (1938) about an African-American girl in Minneapolis who goes to live with her grandmother in South Carolina, and *The Moved Outers* (1945) about Japanese Americans forced into a relocation camp during World War II are rich portraits of young people with problems not easily solved.

During this period, Daly published only *Seventeenth Summer* (1942), which was incredibly popular and is still occasionally read, although by younger girls than its original audience. Daly was a college student when she wrote her story about shy and innocent Angie Morrow and her love for Jack Duluth during the summer between high school and college.

Stolz, the most prolific of the four, is still publishing. She writes magic, quiet, introspective books that appeal mostly to readers more curious about character than incident. Things happen in her books, but the focus is always on people—always lovingly developed. Her two best works are *Pray Love, Remember* (1945) and *A Love, or a Season* (1964). The former is a remarkable story of Dody Jenks, a popular and lovely and cold young woman who likes neither her family nor herself. The latter is a story of quiet and uneventful love suddenly turning torrid before either girl or boy is old enough to handle sex.

Summers's two best books are *Ring Around His Finger* (1957), a tale of young marriage told from the boy's point of view, and *The Limit of Love* (1959), a fine delineation of a sexual affair between two children. The girl begins to grow up, while the boy remains a boy dedicated to proving that the girl is ruining his life. Although both books were more about boys than girls, the readers were usually girls, curious about a boy's point of view. Critics worried about Summers's honesty, presumably fearing that young adult readers were too young to handle the emotional intricacies of sex.

Howard A. Sturzel, under the pen name of Paul Annixter, wrote widely but best known is *Swiftwater* (1950), a story mixing animals, ecology, symbolism, and some stereotyped characters into a rousing tale that remains a better than respectable book.

Felsen wrote run-of-the-mill prose, but not one of his fans cared because Felsen wrote about the joys and dangers of cars. *Hot Rod* (1950), *Street Rod* (1953), and *Crash Club* (1958) were widely read, often by boys who had never before read a book all the way through. Felsen was didactic, but his fans read for the material on cars and ignored his lessons. His best book was unquestionably *Two and the*

Town (1952) about a young couple forced to marry. Tired as the book seems now, it was a groundbreaker widely opposed by teachers and librarians.

Bennett, a South African journalist, wrote several remarkable books for young boys, including *Jamie* (1963), *Mister Fisherman* (1965), and *The Hawk Alone* (1965), a brilliant book that never received its due. It is about an old white hunter who has hunted everything, done everything, and outlived his time.

Tunis, an amateur athlete and sports reporter, was the best of these writers. *Iron Duke* (1938), his first young adult novel, is about a high school runner who wants to enter the big time at Harvard. What that book promised, *All American* (1942) delivered in its attack on prejudice aimed at both Jews and African-Americans and the win-at-all-costs attitude. *Yea! Wildcats* (1944) eloquently mixes basketball with incipient totalitarianism in a small Indiana town. *Go, Team, Go* (1954) is a fine story about the pressures brought to bear on high school coaches. Tunis preached too often, and sometimes the preaching was simply too much for readers to bear, but he knew sports and he cared deeply about boys and about games. At his best, he is still worth reading, and several of his books have recently been reissued.

Other Books Popular with Young Adults

Young adult reading during these 25 years fell loosely into the six areas of careers; sports and cars; adventure and suspense; love, romance, passion, and sex; society's problems; and personal problems and initiation.

Emma Bugbee, a reporter for the *New York Tribune,* began a deluge of career books with her *Peggy Covers the News* (1936). She wrote five Peggy Foster books that conveyed the ambivalent excitement and boredom of getting and writing the news. In presenting the picture of a young woman breaking into a male-dominated profession, the books served a purpose for their time. By far the most popular career books were about nursing, led by Helen Boylston's seven Sue Barton books followed by Helen Wells's 20 Cherry Ames books. Wells also wrote 13 books about flight stewardess Vicki Barr. Lucile Fargo's *Marion Martha* (1936) treated librarianship, and Christie Harris's *You Have to Draw the Line Somewhere* (1964) was about fashion designing.

Whatever freshness the vocational novel may once have had, by the late 1940s it was a formula and little more. Early in the book the insecure hero/heroine (more often the latter) suffers a mixture of major and minor setbacks but, undaunted, wins the final battle and a place in the profession. The novel passes rapidly and lightly over the job's daily grind, focusing instead on the high points, the excitement and events that make any job potentially, if rarely, dramatic.

We have already mentioned John Tunis and Henry Gregor Felsen in the sports and car category. Another notable is basketball writer John F. Carson with his *Floorburns* (1957), *The Coach Nobody Liked* (1960), and *Hotshot* (1961). C. H. Frick (pen name of Constance Frick Irwin) used clever plot twists to make her sports novels different. *Five Against the Odds* (1955) features a basketball player stricken with polio, and *The Comeback Guy* (1961) focuses on a too-popular, too-successful young man who gets his comeuppance and works his way back to self-respect through sports. Nonfiction was not yet as popular as it would become, but Jim Piersall's *Fear Strikes Out* (1955) and Roy Campanella's *It's Good to Be Alive* (1959) attracted young readers.

Until the late 1940s, interest in adventure or suspense was largely fulfilled by various kinds of war books, including vocational nonfiction such as Carl Mann's *He's in the Signal Corps Now* (1943) and vocational novels such as Elizabeth Lansing's *Nancy Naylor, Flight Nurse* (1944). More popular were true stories about battles and survivors, including Richard Tregaskis's *Guadalcanal Diary* (1943), Ernie Pyle's *Here Is Your War* (1943) and *Brave Men* (1944), Robert Trumbull's *The Raft* (1942), and Quentin Reynolds's *70,000 to One* (1946).

Perhaps as a reaction to the realities of war, the most popular series of books for both adults and young adults during the 1950s and 1960s centered about the fascinating James Bond, Agent 007. Ian Fleming caught the mood of the time with escapist excitement tinted with what appeared to be realities.

Also far removed from the grim realities of World War II were three historical novels that appealed to some young adults. Elizabeth Janet Gray's *Adam of the Road* (1942) revealed the color and music of the Middle Ages as young Adam Quartermain became a minstrel. Marchette Chute's *The Innocent Wayfaring* (1943) covers four days in June 1370 when Anne runs away from her convent school to join a band of strolling players, while in Chute's *The Wonderful Winter* (1954), young Sir Robert Wakefield, treated like a child at home, runs off to London to become an actor in Shakespeare's company.

Writers for young adults contributed several fine romances, including Margaret E. Bell's Alaskan story *Love Is Forever* (1954), Vivian Breck's superior study of young marriage in *Maggie* (1954), and Benedict and Nancy Freedman's *Mrs. Mike,* set in the northern Canadian wilderness. Elizabeth Goudge's *Green Dolphin Street* had everything working for it—a young handsome man in love with one of a pair of sisters. When he leaves and writes home his wishes, the wrong sister accepts. The true love, apparently overwhelmed by his unfaithfulness, becomes a nun. Passion, love, and adventure are all handled well by a first-rate writer. Kathleen Winsor was also one of a kind, although what one and what kind was widely debated. When her *Forever Amber* (1944) appeared, parents worried, censors paled, and young adults smiled as they ignored the fuss and read the book. Young people, especially in the last year or two of high school, have often been receptive to books about human dilemmas. Between 1940 and 1966, society changed rapidly and drastically with deeply disturbing consequences. There was a growing awareness that the democracy described in our Constitution was more preached than practiced. As the censorship applied to John Steinbeck's *The Grapes of Wrath* (1939) and *Of Mice and Men* (1937) lessened—although it never entirely disappeared—young readers read of the plight of migrant workers and learned that all was not well. Many were deeply disturbed by Alan Paton's stories of racial struggles in South Africa, *Cry the Beloved Country* (1948) and *Too Late the Phalarope* (1953). Still more were touched by the sentiment and passion of Harper Lee's *To Kill a Mockingbird* (1960) set in the American South.

Richard Wright and his books *Native Son* (1940) and *Black Boy* (1945) served as bitter prototypes for much African-American literature. The greatest African-American novel, and one of the greatest novels of any kind in the last fifty years, is Ralph Ellison's *Invisible Man* (1952). Existential in tone, *Invisible Man* is at different times bawdy (the incest scenes remind readers of Faulkner without being derivative), moving, and frightening, but always stunning and breathtaking.

Three African-American nonfiction writers are still read. Claude Brown painted a stark picture of African-American ghetto life in *Manchild in the Promised Land* (1965), whereas Malcolm X and Alex Haley, the latter better known for *Roots,* painted a no more attractive picture in *The Autobiography of Malcolm X* (1965). The most enduring work may prove to be Eldridge Cleaver's *Soul on Ice* (1968), an impassioned plea by an African-American man in prison who wrote to save himself.

Writings about African-Americans aimed at young adults were not long in coming. Lorenz Graham presented realistic African-American characters in *South Town* (1958), which today seems dated; *North Town* (1965); and *Whose Town?* (1969). Nat Hentoff's first novel for young adults, *Jazz Country* (1965), is a superb story of a white boy trying to break into the African-American world of jazz. It is an unusual topic, and perhaps neither African-Americans nor whites are comfortable with the themes or the characters, which is sad because Hentoff is a remarkable, compassionate, and honest writer. Nonfiction writing for young adults about African-Americans was mostly biographical. In the late 1940s and early 1950s, Shirley Graham wrote good biographies of Frederick Douglass, Benjamin Banneker, Phillis Wheatley, and Booker T. Washington. Elizabeth Yates won applause and the Newbery Award for *Amos Fortune, Free Man* (1950). Her account of a slave who gained freedom in 1801 and fought the rest of his life for freedom for other African-Americans has been attacked, however, by some groups as paternalistic, a word overused by African-American critics who assume that any white writer is inherently incapable of writing about African-Americans.

Intrigued and concerned as many young adults were about social issues and dilemmas, something far more immediate constantly pressed in on them—their own personal need to survive in an often unfriendly world. Anne Emery's books preached the status quo, especially acceptance of parental rules, but they also touched on personal concerns, with her best book being *Married on Wednesday* (1957). Mina Lewiton's *The Divided Heart* (1947) is an early study of the effects of divorce on a young woman, and Lewiton's *A Cup of Courage* (1948) is an honest and groundbreaking account of alcoholism and its destruction of a family. Later, Zoa Sherburne proved more enduring with her portrait of alcohol's effects in *Jennifer* (1959), although her best and most lasting book is *Too Bad About the Haines Girl* (1967), a superb novel about pregnancy, honest and straightforward without being preachy.

Something far more significant happened during this period, which was that the *bildungsroman,* a novel about the initiation, maturation, and education of a young adult, grew in appeal. Most bildungsroman were originally published for adults but soon read by young adults. Dan Wickenden's *Walk Like a Mortal* (1940) and Betty Smith's *A Tree Grows in Brooklyn* (1943) were among the first. None of these books won the young adult favor or the adult opposition as did J. D. Salinger's *The Catcher in the Rye* (1951). It is still the most widely censored book in American schools and still hated by people who assume that a disliked word (*that* word) corrupts an entire book. Holden Caulfield may indeed be vulgar and cynical and capable of seeing only the phonies around him, but he is also loyal and loving to those he sees as good or innocent. For many young adults, it is the most honest and human story they know about someone they recognize (even in themselves)—a young man caught between childhood and maturity and unsure which way to go. Whether *Catcher* is a masterpiece similar to James Joyce's *Portrait of the Artist as a Young Man* depends on subjective judgment, but there is no question that Salinger's book captured—and continues to capture—the hearts and minds of countless young adults as no other book has.

Many teachers and librarians would have predicted just as long a life for John Knowles's *A Separate Peace* (1961) and William Golding's *Lord of the Flies* (1955), but fame and longevity are sometime things, and despite many articles in *English Journal* about the literary and pedagogical worth of both books, they seem to be in a state of decline.

Rise of Criticism of Young Adult Literature

Today we take criticism of young adult literature as discussed in Chapter Ten for granted, but it developed slowly. In the 1940s, journals provided little information on, and less criticism of, young adult literature except for book lists, book reviews, and occasional references in articles on reading interests or improving young people's literary taste. The comments that did appear were often more appreciative than critical, but given the times and the attitude of many teachers and librarians, appreciation or even recognition may have been more important than criticism.

In 1951, Dwight L. Burton wrote the first criticism of young adult novels, injecting judgments along with appreciation as he commented on works by Dan Wickenden, Maureen Daly, Paul Annixter, Betty Cavanna, and Madeleine L'Engle. Concluding his article, Burton identified the qualities of the good young adult novel and prophesied its potential and future:

> The good novel for the adolescent reader has attributes no different from any good novel. It must be technically masterful, and it must present a significant synthesis of human experience. Because of the nature of adolescence itself, the good novel for the adolescent should be full in true invention and imagination. It must free itself of Pollyannaism or the Tarkington–Henry Aldrich–Corliss Archer tradition and maintain a clear vision of the adolescent as a person of complexity, individuality, and dignity. The novel for the adolescent presents a ready field for the mature artist.[40]

In 1955, Richard S. Alm provided greater critical coverage of the young adult novel.[41] He agreed with critics that many writers presented a "sugar-puff story of what adolescents should do and should believe rather than what adolescents may or will do and believe." He cited specific authors and titles he found good and painted their strengths and weaknesses in clear strokes. He concluded by offering teachers some questions that might be useful in analyzing the merits of young adult novels.

A year later, Emma L. Patterson began her fine study of the origin of young adult novels showing that "The junior novel has become an established institution."[42] Her command of history, her knowledge of trends in young adult novels, her awareness of shortcomings and virtues of the novels, and her understanding of the place of young adult novels in schools and libraries made her article essential reading for librarians and teachers.

Despite the leadership of Burton, Alm, and Patterson, helpful criticism of young adult literature was slow in arriving, but biting criticism was soon forthcoming. Only a few months after Patterson's article, Frank G. Jennings's "Literature for Adolescents—Pap or Protein?"[43] appeared. The title was ambiguous, but if any reader had doubts about where Jennings stood, the doubt was removed with the first sentence: "The stuff of adolescent literature, for the most part, is mealy-mouthed, gutless, and pointless." The remainder of the article added little to that point, and although Jennings overstated his case, Burton, Alm, Patterson, and other sensible supporters would have agreed that much young adult literature, similar to much adult literature, was second-rate or worse. Jennings's article was not the first broadside attack, and it certainly would not be the last.[44]

Much of the literature written for young adults from 1940 through 1966 goes largely and legitimately ignored today. Some writers are still read, however, and more important than mere longevity is the effect that these authors had on books appearing after 1966. Readers before then could not have anticipated S. E. Hinton's *The Outsiders* or Paul Zindel's *The Pigman,* which were to appear in only a year or two, much less Isabelle Holland's *The Man Without a Face,* Norma Klein's *Mom, The Wolfman and Me,* Rosa Guy's *Ruby,* or Robert Cormier's *The Chocolate War.* These iconoclastic, taboo-breaking novels and others of today would not have been possible had it not been for earlier novels that broke ground and prepared readers, teachers, librarians, and parents for contemporary novels.

Notes

[1]Caroline Ticknor, *Hawthorne and His Publisher* (Houghton Mifflin, 1913), p. 141.

[2]E. Douglas Branch, *The Sentimental Years, 1836–1860* (Appleton, 1934), p. 131.

[3]Jesse H. Shera, *Foundations of the Public Library: The Origins of the Public Library Movement in New England, 1629–1885* (The University of Chicago Press, 1949), p. 238.

[4]A brief summary of the 1853 and 1876 library conventions can be found in Sister Gabriella Margeath, "Library Conventions of 1853, 1876, and 1877," *Journal of Library History* 8(April 1973):52–69.

[5]William F. Poole, "Some Popular Objections to Public Libraries," *American Library Journal* 1(October 1876):48–49.

[6]W. M. Stevenson, "Weeding Out Fiction in the Carnegie Free Library of Allegheny, Pa.," *Library Journal* 22(March 1897):135.

[7]"Novel Reading," *American Library Journal* 1(October 1876):98.

8"Monthly Reports from Public Librarians upon the Reading of Minors: A Suggestion," *Library Journal* 24(August 1899):479.

9Carleton Washburne and Mabel Vogel, *Winnetka Graded Book List* (American Library Association, 1926), p. 5.

10Carleton Washburne and Mabel Vogel, "Supplement to the Winnetka Graded Book List," *Elementary English Review* 4(February 1927):47–52; and 4(March 1927):66–73.

11William Lyon Phelps, "The Virtues of the Second-Rate," *English Journal* 16(January 1927):13–14.

12Franklin T. Baker, *A Bibliography of Children's Reading* (Teachers College, Columbia University, 1908), pp. 6–7.

13Clara Whitehill Hunt, "Good and Bad Taste in Girls' Reading," *Ladies Home Journal* 27(April 1910):52.

14Julia Carter, "Let's Talk About Boys and Books," *Wilson Bulletin for Librarians* 9(April 1935):418.

15Alice M. Jordan, "A Gallery of Girls," *Horn Book Magazine* 13(September 1937):276.

16Clara Vostrovsky, "A Study of Children's Reading Tastes," *Pedagogical Seminary* 6 (December, 1899): 535.

17G. Stanley Hall, "Children's Reading: As a Factor in Their Education," *Library Journal* 33(April 1908):124–125.

18J. M. Coulter, "What the University Expects of the Secondary School," *School Review* 17(February 1909):73.

19Wilbur W. Hatfield, "Modern Literature for High School Use," *English Journal* 1(January 1912):52.

20*Reorganization of English in Secondary Schools*, Department of the Interior, Bureau of Education, Bulletin 1917, No. 2. (Government Printing Office, 1917), p. 63.

21Nancy Gillmore Coryell, *An Evaluation of Extensive and Intensive Teaching of Literature: A Year's Experiment in the Eleventh Grade*, Teachers College, Columbia University, Contributions to Education, No. 275 (Teachers College, Columbia University, 1927).

22Lou LaBrant, *An Evaluation of the Free Reading Program in Grades Ten, Eleven, and Twelve for the Class of 1935*. The Ohio State University School, Contributions to Education No. 2 (Ohio State University, 1936). See also Lou LaBrant, "The Content of a Free Reading Program," *Educational Research Bulletin* 16(February 17, 1937):29–34.

23Dora V. Smith, "American Youth and English," *English Journal* 26(February 1937):111.

24Graham P. Hawks, "A Nineteenth-Century School Library: Early Years in Milwaukee,"*Journal of Library History* 12(Fall 1977):361.

25S. Swett Green, "Libraries and School," *Library Journal* 16(December 1891):22. Other representative articles concerned with the relationship include Mellen Chamberlain, "Public Libraries and Public School," *Library Journal* 5(November–December 1880):299–302; W. E. Foster, "The School and the Library: Their Mutual Relations," *Library Journal* 4(September–October 1879):319–341; and Mrs. J. H. Resor, "The Boy and the Book, or The Public Library a Necessity," *Public Libraries* 2(June 1897):282–285.

26"The Report of the Committee on Relations of Public Libraries to Public Schools," *NEA Journal of Proceedings and Addresses of the 38th Annual Meeting* (The University of Chicago, Press, 1899), p. 455.

27Mary E. Hall, "The Possibilities of the High School Library," *ALA Bulletin* 6(July 1912):261–63.

28Caroline M. Hewins, "Book Reviews, Book Lists, and Articles on Children's Reading: Are They of Practical Value to the Children's Librarians?" *Library Journal* 26(August 1901):58. Attacks on series books, especially Stratemeyer's books, persisted thereafter in library literature. Mary E. S. Root prepared a list of series books not to be circulated by public librarians, "Not to Be Circulated," *Wilson Bulletin for Librarians* 3(January 1929):446, including books by Alger, Finley, Castlemon, Ellis, Optic, and others, the others being heavily Stratemeyer. Two months later, Ernest F. Ayers responded, "Not to Be Circulated?" *Wilson Bulletin for Librarians* 3(March 1929):528–529, objecting to the cavalier treatment accorded old favorites and sarcastically adding, "Why worry about censorship so long as we have librarians?" Attacks continue today. Some librarians and English teachers to the contrary, the Syndicate clearly is winning, and students seem to be pleased.

29Franklin K. Mathiews, "Blowing Out the Boy's Brains," *Outlook* 108(November 18, 1914):653.

30John Tunis, "What Is a Juvenile Book?" *Horn Book Magazine* 44(June 1968):307.

31George W. Norvell, "Some Results of a Twelve-Year Study of Children's Reading Interests," *English Journal* 35(December 1946):532, 536.

32Marie Rankin, *Children's Interests in Library Books of Fiction*, Teachers College, Columbia University, Contributions to Education, No. 906 (Teachers College, Columbia University, 1947).

33Stephen Dunning, "The Most Popular Junior Novels," *Junior Libraries* 5(December 15, 1959):7–9.

34Jacob W. Getzels, "The Nature of Reading Interests: Psychological Aspects" in *Developing Permanent Interests in Reading*, ed. Helen M. Robinson, Supplementary Education Monographs, No. 84, December

1956 (University of Chicago Press, 1956), p. 5.

[35]Robert Carlsen, "Behind Reading Interests," *English Journal* 43(January 1954):7–10.

[36]G. O. Ireland, "Bibliotherapy: The Use of Books as a Form of Treatment in a Neuropsychiatric Hospital," *Library Journal* 54(December 1, 1929):972–974.

[37]Lou LaBrant, "Diversifying the Matter," *English Journal* 40(March 1951):135.

[38]S. Alan Cohen, "Paperbacks in the Classroom," *Journal of Reading* 12(January 1969):295.

[39]Stanley B. Kegler and Stephen Dunning, "Junior Book Roundup—Literature for the Adolescent, 1960," *English Journal* 50(May 1961):369.

[40]Dwight L. Burton, "The Novel for the Adolescent," *English Journal* 40(September 1951):363–369.

[41]Richard S. Alm, "The Glitter and the Gold," *English Journal* 44(September 1955):315.

[42]Emma L. Patterson, "The Junior Novels and How They Grew," *English Journal* 45(October 1956):381.

[43]*English Journal* 45(December 1956):226–231.

[44]See, for example, Alice Krahn, "Case Against the Junior Novel," *Top of the News* 17(May 1961):19–22; Esther Millett, "We Don't Even Call Those Books!" *Top of the News* 20(October 1963):45–47; and Harvey R. Granite, "The Uses and Abuses of Junior Literature," *Clearing House* 42 (February 1968): 337– 340.

Titles Mentioned in the Text of Chapter Thirteen

Alcott, Louisa May. *Behind a Mask: The Unknown Thrillers of Louisa May Alcott*, ed., Madeleine Stern. Morrow, 1975.

Alcott, Louisa May. *Little Women: Meg, Jo, Beth, and Amy. The Story of Their Lives. A Girl's Book.* 1868.

Alcott, Louisa May. *Little Women: Meg, Jo, Beth, and Amy. Part Second.* 1869.

Alcott, Louisa May. *A Long Fatal Love Chase*, ed., Kent Bicknell. Random House, 1995.

Alcott, Louisa May. *The Lost Stories of Louisa May Alcott*, eds., Madeleine Stern and Daniel Shealy. Citadel, 1993.

Alcott, Louisa May. *Plots and Counterplots: More Unknown Thrillers of Louisa May Alcott*, ed., Madeleine Stern. Morrow, 1976.

Aldrich, Thomas Bailey. *The Story of a Bad Boy.* 1870.

Alger, Horatio. *Ragged Dick: or Street Life in New York.* 1867.

Allee, Marjorie Hill. *The Great Tradition.* 1937.

Allee, Marjorie Hill. *Jane's Island.* 1931.

Altsheler, Joseph. *The Horsemen of the Plains.* 1910.

Altsheler, Joseph. *The Last of the Chiefs.* 1909.

Annixter, Paul (real name Howard A. Sturzel). *Swiftwater.* A. A. Wyn, 1950.

Appleton, Victor (Stratemeyer Syndicate pseudonym). Tom Swift series, 1910–1935.

Armer, Laura. *Waterless Mountain,* 1931.

Barbour, Ralph Henry. *The Crimson Sweater.* 1906.

Barbour, Ralph Henry. *The Half-Back.* 1899.

Bell, Margaret Elizabeth. *Love Is Forever.* Morrow, 1954.

Bennett, Jack. *The Hawk Alone.* Little, Brown, 1965.

Bennett, Jack. *Jamie.* Little, Brown, 1963.

Bennett, Jack. *Mister Fisherman.* Little, Brown, 1963.

Bennett, John. *Master Skylark: A Story of Shakespeare's Time.* 1897.

Benson, Sally. *Junior Miss.* Doubleday, 1947.

Boylston, Helen Dore. *Sue Barton, Student Nurse.* Little, Brown, 1936.

Breck, Vivian. *Maggie.* Doubleday, 1954.

Brooks, Noah. *The Boy Emigrants.* 1876.

Brown, Claude. *Manchild in the Promised Land.* Macmillan, 1965.

Buck, Pearl. *The Good Earth.* John Day, 1931.

Bugbee, Emma. *Peggy Covers the News.* Dodd, Mead, 1936.

Burroughs, Edgar Rice. *Tarzan of the Apes.* 1914.

Campanella, Roy. *It's Good to Be Alive.* Little, Brown, 1959.

Carson, John F. *The Coach Nobody Liked.* Farrar, Straus & Giroux, 1960.

Carson, John F. *Floorburns.* Farrar, Straus & Giroux, 1957.

Carson, John F. *Hotshot.* Farrar, Straus & Giroux, 1961.

Castlemon, Harry (real name, Charles Austin Fosdick). *Frank the Young Naturalist.* 1864.

Cavanna, Betty. *Going on Sixteen.* Ryerson, 1946.

Chute, Marchette. *The Innocent Wayfaring.* Scribner, 1943.

Chute, Marchette. *The Wonderful Winter.* Dutton, 1954.

Cleaver, Eldridge. *Soul on Ice.* McGraw-Hill, 1968.

Coolidge, Susan (real name, Sarah Chauncey Woolsey). *What Katy Did.* 1872.

Cormier, Robert. *The Chocolate War.* Pantheon, 1974.

Daly, Maureen. *Seventeenth Summer.* Dodd, Mead, 1942.

Deland, Margaret. *The Awakening of Helena Richie*. 1906.

Doyle, Arthur Conan. *The Adventures of Sherlock Holmes*. 1891.

Doyle, Arthur Conan. *The Hound of the Baskervilles*. 1902.

DuJardin, Rosamund. *Double Date*. Longman, 1953.

DuJardin, Rosamund. *Wait for Marcy*. Longman, 1950.

Ellison, Ralph. *Invisible Man*. Random House, 1952.

Emery, Anne. *Married on Wednesday*. Ryerson, 1957.

Falkner, John Meade. *Moonfleet*. 1898.

Fargo, Lucile Foster. *Marian Martha*. Dodd, Mead, 1936.

Farley, Walter. *Black Stallion*. Random House, 1944.

Felsen, Henry Gregor. *Crash Club*. Random House, 1958.

Felsen, Henry Gregor. *Hot Rod*. Dutton, 1950.

Felsen, Henry Gregor. *Street Rod*. Random House, 1953.

Felsen, Henry Gregor. *Two and the Town*. Scribner, 1952.

Finley, Martha (real name, Martha Farquharson). *Elsie Dinsmore*. 1867. The series ran from 1867–1905.

Freedman, Benedict and Nancy. *Mrs. Mike*. Coward, McCann, & Geoghegan, 1947.

Frick, Constance H. *The Comeback Guy*. Harcourt Brace Jovanovich, 1961.

Frick, Constance H. *Five Against the Odds*. Harcourt Brace Jovanovich, 1955.

Golding, William. *Lord of the Flies*. Coward, McCann, 1955.

Goudge, Elizabeth. *Green Dolphin Street*. Coward, McCann, 1944.

Graham, Lorenz. *North Town*. Crowell, 1965.

Graham, Lorenz. *South Town*. Follett, 1958.

Graham, Lorenz. *Whose Town?* Crowell, 1969.

Gray, Elizabeth. *Adam of the Road*. Viking, 1942.

Grey, Zane. *Riders of the Purple Sage*. 1912.

Grinnell, George Bird. *By Cheyenne Campfires*. 1926.

Grinnell, George Bird. *Pawnee Hero Stories and Folk Tales*. 1899.

Guy, Rosa. *Ruby*. Viking, 1976.

Haley, Alex. *Roots*. Doubleday, 1976.

Harris, Christie. *You Have to Draw the Line Somewhere*. Atheneum, 1964.

Hentoff, Nat. *Jazz Country*. HarperCollins, 1965.

Heyliger, William. *Bartley: Freshman Pitcher*. 1911.

Hinton, S. E. *The Outsiders*. Viking, 1967.

Holland, Isabelle. *The Man Without a Face*. Lippincott, 1972.

Jackson, Helen Hunt. *Ramona*. 1884.

James, Will. *Smoky, the Cowhorse*. 1926.

Johnson, Owen. *Stover at Yale*. 1911.

Johnson, Owen. *The Tennessee Shad*. 1911.

Johnson, Owen. *The Varmint*. 1910.

Johnston, Mary. *To Have and to Hold*. 1900.

Joyce, James. *Portrait of the Artist as a Young Man*. 1914.

Klein, Norma. *Mom, the Wolfman and Me*. Random House, 1973.

Knowles, John. *A Separate Peace*. Macmillan, 1960.

Lane, Rose Wilder. *Let the Hurricane Roar*. 1933.

Lane, Rose Wilder. *The Young Pioneers* (reissue of *Let the Hurricane Roar*). 1976.

Lansing, Elizabeth. *Nancy Naylor, Flight Nurse*. Crowell, 1944.

Lee, Harper. *To Kill a Mockingbird*. Lippincott, 1960.

Lewiton, Mina. *A Cup of Courage*. McKay, 1948.

Lewiton, Mina. *The Divided Heart*. McKay, 1947.

Malcolm X and Alex Haley. *The Autobiography of Malcolm X*. Grove, 1965.

Mann, Carl. *He's in the Signal Corps Now*. McBride, 1943.

Means, Florence Crannell. *The Moved-Outers*. Houghton Mifflin, 1945.

Means, Florence Crannell. *Shuttered Windows*. Houghton Mifflin, 1938.

Means, Florence Crannell. *Tangled Waters: A Navajo Story*. Houghton Mifflin, 1936.

Montgomery, Lucy Maud. *Anne of Green Gables*. 1908.

Munroe, Kirk. *Derrick Sterling*. 1888.

Optic, Oliver (real name, William Taylor Adams). *The Boat Club*. 1855.

Paton, Alan. *Cry, the Beloved Country*. Scribner, 1948.

Paton, Alan. *Too Late the Phalarope*. Scribner, 1953.

Peck, George Wilbur. *Peck's Bad Boy and His Pa*. 1883.

Piersall, James Anthony, and Albert Hirschberg. *Fear Strikes Out* Little, Brown, 1955.

Porter, Eleanor. *Pollyanna*. 1913.

Pyle, Ernie. *Brave Men*. Holt, 1944.

Pyle, Ernie. *Here Is Your War*. Holt, 1943.

Reynolds, Quentin. *70,000 to One*. Random House, 1946.

Richards, Laura Elizabeth. *Peggy*. 1899.

Robinson, Mabel Louise. *Bright Island*. 1937.

Salinger, J. D. *The Catcher in the Rye*. Little, Brown, 1951.

Sherburne, Zoa. *Jennifer*. Morrow, 1959.

Sherburne, Zoa. *Too Bad about the Haines Girl*. Morrow, 1967.

Smith, Betty. *A Tree Grows in Brooklyn*. HarperCollins, 1943.

Standish, Burt L. (real name, William Gilbert Patten). Frank Merriwell series, 1901–1911.

Steinbeck, John. *The Grapes of Wrath*. Viking, 1939.

Steinbeck, John. *Of Mice and Men*. Viking, 1937.

Stevenson, Robert Louis. *Treasure Island.* 1883.

Stolz, Mary. *A Love, or a Season.* HarperCollins, 1953.

Stolz, Mary. *Pray Love, Remember.* HarperCollins, 1954.

Stolz, Mary. *The Seagulls Woke Me.* HarperCollins, 1951.

Stratemeyer, Edward. Dave Porter series. 1905–1919.

Stratemeyer, Edward. Lakeport series. 1904–1912.

Stratemeyer, Edward. Old Glory series. 1898–1901.

Stratemeyer, Edward. *Richard Dare's Venture; or, Striking Out for Himself.* 1894.

Stratemeyer, Edward. Rover Boys series. 1899–1926.

Stratemeyer, Edward. Soldiers of Fortune series, 1900–1906.

Stratemeyer, Edward. *Under Dewey at Manila; or, The War Fortunes of a Castaway.* 1898.

Stratemeyer, Edward. *Victor Horton's Idea.* 1886.

Summers, James. *The Limit of Love.* Ryerson, 1959.

Summers, James. *Prom Trouble.* Ryerson, 1954.

Summers, James. *Ring Around Her Finger.* Westminster, 1957.

Tregaskis, Richard. *Guadalcanal Diary.* Random House, 1943.

Trumbull, Robert. *The Raft.* Holt, 1942.

Tunis, John. *All-American.* Harcourt, 1938.

Tunis, John. *Go, Team, Go!* Morrow, 1954.

Tunis, John. *Iron Duke.* 1938.

Tunis, John. *Yea! Wildcats.* Harcourt, 1944.

Twain, Mark (real name, Samuel Clemens). *Adventures of Huckleberry Finn.* 1884.

Twain, Mark, *The Adventures of Tom Sawyer.* 1876.

Wetherell, Elizabeth (real name, Susan Warner). *The Wide, Wide World.* 1850.

Wickenden, Dan. *Walk Like a Mortal.* Morrow, 1940.

Wiggin, Kate Douglas. *Rebecca of Sunnybrook Farm.* 1904.

Wilson, Augusta Jane Evans. *St. Elmo.* 1867.

Winsor, Kathleen. *Forever Amber.* Macmillan, 1944.

Wister, Owen. *The Virginian: A Horseman of the Plains.* 1902.

Wright, Richard. *Black Boy.* HarperCollins, 1940.

Wright, Richard. *Native Son.* HarperCollins, 1940.

Yates, Elizabeth. *Amos Fortune, Free Man.* Aladdin, 1950.

Zindel, Paul. *The Pigman.* HarperCollins, 1968.

For information on the availability of paperback editions of these titles, please consult the most recent edition of *Paperbound Books in Print,* published annually by R. R. Bowker Company.

Appendix A

Book Selection Guides

. . . .

The following sources are designed to aid professionals in the selection and evaluation of books and other materials for young adults. We attempted to include sources with widely varying emphases, but, in addition to these sources—most of which appear at regular intervals—many specialized lists are prepared by committees and individuals in response to current and/or local needs. Readers are advised to check on the availability of such lists with librarians and teachers.

The ALAN Review. (Assembly on Literature for Adolescents, National Council of Teachers of English. Order from William Subick; NCTE; 1111 Kenyon Rd.; Urbana, IL 61801.)

> Since 1973, this publication has appeared three times a year. It is currently edited by Robert Small and Patricia P. Kelly and is unique in being devoted entirely to adolescent literature. Each issue contains "Clip and File" reviews of approximately 40 new hardbacks or paperbacks and several feature articles, news announcements, and occasional reviews of professional books.

Best Books for Junior High Readers by John T. Gillespie. (New York: R. R. Bowker, 1991, 567 pp.)

> Each of the 6,848 books listed in this collection for students ages 12 to 15 received two positive recommendations in standard reviewing sources. Fiction is arranged according to genre; nonfiction is arranged according to common subjects studied in junior high schools. Also recommended is Gillespie's *Best Books for Senior High Readers* (R. R. Bowker, 1991).

Best Videos for Children and Young Adults: A Core Collection for Libraries. (ABC-CLIO, 1990, 185 pp.)

> Annotations, evaluations, and suggestions for use are given for over 300 videos, excluding feature films and music videos.

Book Bait: Detailed Notes on Adult Books Popular with Young People, edited by Eleanor Walker. (4th ed., 1988. American Library Association; 50 E. Huron St.; Chicago, IL 60611.)

> A useful bibliography for bridging the gap between young adult and adult novels, this listing contains 100 books with extensive annotations that include plot summaries, discussions of appeal to teenagers, hints for book talks, and suggested titles for use as follow-ups. Arrangement is alphabetical by author; subject and title indexes are appended.

Booklist. (American Library Association; 50 E. Huron St.; Chicago, IL 60611.)

The size of the reviews of either books or media varies from 20-word annotations to 300-word essays. "Books for Young Adults" (ages 14 through 18) is a regular feature. Occasionally, books in both the children's and adult sections are also marked YA. A review constitutes a recommendation for library purchase, with stars being given to books having exceptionally high literary quality. *Booklist* publishes special-interest lists fairly regularly and also the best-book lists produced by various groups affiliated with the American Library Association.

Books for the Teen Age. (Annual ed. Office of Young Adult Services; New York Public Library. Order from Office of Branch Libraries; NYPL; 455 Fifth Avenue; New York, NY 10016.)

The 1,250 recommendations in this booklet come from the young adult librarians in the 80 branches of the New York Public Library. Annotations are minimal; grouping is by subject, with titles and authors indexed.

Books for You: A Booklist for Senior High Students, edited by Leila Christenbury and the Committee to Revise the Senior High Reading List. (11th ed., 1995. National Council of Teachers of English; 1111 Kenyon Rd.; Urbana, IL 61801.)

Part of NCTE's Bibliography Series, this booklist is published approximately every three years and includes only books published during the assigned years. The more than 1,000 annotations of both fiction and nonfiction are written to students and organized under some 50 categories.

Bulletin of the Center for Children's Books. (Editor, Betsy Hearne; Executive Editor, Roger Sutton. Published by the University of Illinois Press for the Graduate School of Library and Information Science; 54 E. Gregory Dr.; Champaign, IL 61820. Editorial offices at 1512 N. Fremont St., Suite 105; Chicago, IL 60622.)

This is the journal founded by Zena Sutherland and published by the University of Chicago Press until the recent closing of Chicago's Graduate Library School. In each issue, the *Bulletin* reviews approximately 60 new books for children and young adults. It has been known for the consistency of its reviews and for including discussions of developmental values and curricular uses.

Celebrate the Dream by the New York Public Library. (Order from Office of Branch Libraries; NYPL; 455 Fifth Ave.; New York, NY 10016.)

Books annotated in this guide explore the black experience in the United States and abroad.

Characters from Young Adult Literature by Mary Ellen Snodgrass. (Littlewood, CO: Libraries Unlimited, 1991.)

A collection of comments on YA material, ranging in time from Shakespeare's *Julius Caesar* (1598) to Norma Fox Mazer's *After the Rain* (1987), with stopovers in *The Chocolate War, A Day No Pigs Would Die, Gentlehands, The Outsiders, The Pigman, Summer of My German Soldier,* and *The Year without Michael.*

Children's Literature in Education: An International Quarterly. (Human Sciences Press; 233 Spring St., New York, NY 10013.)

This British/American cooperative effort is edited by Anita Moss from the United States and Geoff Fox from Great Britain. The editors show a preference for substantive analysis rather than pedagogical advice or quick once-overs. A good proportion of the articles are about YA authors and their works.

English Journal. (Editor, Leila Christenbury, National Council of Teachers of English; 1111 Kenyon Rd.; Urbana, IL 61801.)

Aimed at high school English teachers, nearly every issue contains at least a few reviews and/or articles about young adult literature.

High Interest—Easy Reading: A Booklist for Junior and Senior High School Students, edited by William G. McBride. (6th ed., 1990. National Council of Teachers of English; 1111 Kenyon Rd.; Urbana, IL 61801.)

Nearly 400 annotations are written so as to appeal directly to students. The books, mostly fiction, are grouped into 23 categories, including adventure, death, ethnicity, friendship, how-to, humor, love and romance, and social problems.

The Horn Book Guide to Children's and Young Adult Books and *Horn Book Magazine.* (The Horn Book, Inc.; 14 Beacon St.; Boston, MA 02108–3718. Magazine.)

Since 1924, the *Horn Book Magazine* has been devoted to the critical analysis of children's literature through both articles and reviews. Popular appeal takes a back seat to literary quality in the selection of titles for review. In a typical issue, seven or eight adolescent novels are reviewed under the heading of "Stories for Older Readers." A new service begun by the editors in 1990 is the *Horn Book Guide,* which gives brief annotations and a numerical ranking from 1 (outstanding) to 6 (unacceptable) for some 4,000 books published in the United States (including books published in Spanish), Canada, and Australia.

Journal of Adolescent and Adult Literacy. (International Reading Association; 800 Barksdale Rd.; Box 8139; Newark, DE 19711–8139.)

The audience for this journal is high school reading teachers. Although most of the articles are reports on research in the teaching of reading, some articles focus on reading interests and literature. Reviews of new young adult books are also included.

Journal of Youth Services in Libraries. (American Library Association; 50 E. Huron St.; Chicago, IL 60611.)

Articles cover both children's and YA literature as well as research and professional interests of librarians. Until 1987, the name was *Top of the News.*

Junior High School Library Catalog, edited by Richard H. Isaacson and Gary L. Bogart. (5th ed. H. W. Wilson Company; 950 University Ave.; Bronx, NY 10452.)

Designed as a suggested basic book collection for junior high school libraries, this volume is divided into two major parts. The first includes an annotated listing by Dewey Decimal Number for nonfiction, author's last name for fiction, and author's/editor's last name for story collections. The second part relists all books alphabetically by author, title, and subject. This outstanding reference tool for junior high school librarians is revised approximately every five years with frequent supplements.

Kirkus Reviews. (Kirkus Service, Inc.; 200 Park Ave. South; New York, NY 10003.)

Kirkus reviews are approximately 200 words long. The big advantage of this source is its timeliness and completeness, made possible by its being published on the first and the fifteenth days of each month.

Kliatt Young Adult Paperback Book Guide. (425 Watertown St.; Newton, MA 02158.)

Because teenagers prefer to read paperbacks, this source serves a real need by reviewing all paperbacks (originals, reprints, and reissues) recommended for readers ages 12 through 19.

A code identifies books as appropriate for advanced students, general young adult readers, junior high students, students with low reading abilities, and emotionally mature readers who can handle "explicit sex, excessive violence and/or obscenity." Reviews are arranged by subject. An index of titles and a directory of cooperating publishers are included.

New York Times Book Review. (New York Times Company; 229 W. 43rd St.; New York, NY 10036. 52 issues.)

The currency of the reviews makes this an especially valuable source. Also, because well-known authors are often invited to serve as critics, the reviews are fun to read.

Nonfiction for Young Adults: From Delight to Wisdom by Betty Carter and Richard F. Abrahamson. (Phoenix, AZ; Oryx Press, 1990.)

"You need this book," was the headline leading off the *School Library Journal* review of Carter and Abrahamson's book. We agree, as reflected by the number of times we refer to it.

Notable Children's Trade Books in the Field of Social Studies. (National Council for the Social Studies and the Children's Book Council. Single copies are available free of charge if an envelope stamped for three ounces is provided to the Children's Book Council; 568 Broadway; New York, NY 10012.)

This list is published each spring in *Social Education.* Many of the recommended books are appropriate for junior and early senior high students.

School Library Journal; (Cahners Publishing Co.; Bowker Magazine Group; 245 W. 17th St.; New York, NY 10011. Send to P.O. Box 1978, Marion, OH 43305–1978.)

The most comprehensive of the review media, *SLJ* reviews both recommended and not recommended books. Reviews are written by a panel of 400 librarians who are sent books, media, and/or computer materials appropriate to their interests and backgrounds. Starred reviews signify exceptionally good books.

Senior High School Library Catalog, edited by Ferne Hillegas and Juliette Yakkov. (13th ed. H. W. Wilson Company, 1987; 950 University Ave.; Bronx, NY 10452.)

Using the same format as the *Junior High School Library Catalog* (see earlier), this invaluable resource lists some books appropriate for both junior and senior high school collections as well as those aimed specifically at readers in grades 10 through 12. Like its companion volume, it is produced approximately every five years with frequent supplements.

Voice of Youth Advocates (VOYA). (Scarecrow Press; P.O. Box 4167; Metuchen, NJ 08840. Editorial correspondence to Dorothy M. Broderick; 1226 Cresthaven Dr.; Silver Spring, MD 20903.)

One of the aims of this publication, founded in 1978, is "to change the traditional linking of young adult services with children's librarianship and shift the focus to connection with adult services." Feature articles are especially good because they present viewpoints not commonly considered. About one-fourth of the journal is devoted to reviews in the categories of pamphlets, mysteries, science fiction, audiovisual, adult and teenage fiction and nonfiction, and professional books.

Young People's Books in Series: Fiction and Non-Fiction, 1975–1991, edited by Judith K. Rosenberg with C. Allen Nichols. (Littlewood, CO: Libraries Unlimited, 1992.)

Your Reading: A Booklist for Junior High and Middle School Students, edited by Barbara G. Samuels and G. Kylene Beers and the Committee to Revise the Junior High/Middle School Reading List. (1996. National Council of Teachers of English, 1111 Kenyon Rd.; Urbana, IL 61801.)

Part of the NCTE Bibliography Series, this one includes annotations of more than 1,000 recommended books published during 1988, 1989, and 1990.

Appendix B

Some Outstanding Books and Articles About Young Adult Literature

. . . .

The following represents our personal choices. We followed our ground rules of the first edition. That may explain why some works were included or excluded. Brief explanations are given where titles are not self-explanatory.

1. Books or articles were primarily about young adult literature, not on the psychology of the young, cultural milieu, literary history, or literary criticism.
2. Books or articles had to cover more than one author. No matter how good articles were on Cynthia Voigt or Leon Garfield or Robert Cormier, we ignored them in favor of articles with broader implications.
3. Books and articles had to excite us.
4. No books and articles were chosen to balance out the list. We chose what we did because we believe in them.
5. Readers will, again, find no books or articles by Nilsen or Donelson. Those desperate to see our work included will search in vain. Readers may continue to assume that we believe none of our work belongs in a list of "outstanding" works, that we long for professional oblivion, or that we are modest to a fault.

Books

Histories of Young Adult Literature

Avery, Gillian. *Childhood's Pattern: A Study of the Heroes and Heroines of Children's Fiction, 1770–1950.* London: Hodder and Stoughton, 1975.

Bingham, Jane, and Grayce Scholt. *Fifteen Centuries of Children's Literature: An Annotated Chronology of British and American Works in Historical Context.* Westport, CT: Greenwood Press, 1980.

Bratton, J. S. *The Impact of Victorian Children's Fiction.* Totowa, NJ: Barnes and Noble Books, 1981.

Cadogan, Mary, and Patricia Craig. *You're a Brick, Angela! A New Look at Girls' Fiction from 1839 to 1975.* London: Victor Gollancz, 1976. Still one of the most delightful and wittiest commentaries on girls' books.

Campbell, Patricia J. *Sex Education Books for Young Adults, 1892–1979.* New York: R. R. Bowker, 1979. Always accurate, often funny.

Children's Fiction, 1876–1984. 2 vols. New York: R. R. Bowker, 1984.

Crouch, Marcus. *The Nesbit Tradition: The Children's Novel in England 1945–1970.* London: Ernest Benn, 1972.

Crouch, Marcus. *Treasure Seekers and Borrowers: Children's Books in Britain 1900–1960.* London: Library Association, 1962.

Darling, Richard. *The Rise of Children's Book Reviewing in America: 1865–1881.* New York: R. R. Bowker, 1968. A fascinating study of early children's and YA books, book reviewing, and book reviewers.

Darton, F. J. Harvey. *Children's Books in England: Five Centuries of Social Use.* 2nd ed. Cambridge, England: Cambridge University Press, 1958. First published in 1932. Informative, if a bit stuffy.

Demars, Patricia, ed. *A Garland from the Golden Age: An Anthology of Children's Literature from 1850 to 1900.* Toronto: Oxford University Press, 1983.

Dyer, Carolyn Stewart and Nancy Tillman Romalov, eds. *Rediscovering Nancy Drew.* University of Iowa Press, 1995. Papers from the 1993 Nancy Drew conference.

Egoff, Sheila. *The Republic of Childhood: A Critical Guide to Canadian Children's Literature in English.* 2nd ed. Toronto: Oxford University Press, 1975.

Egoff, Sheila. *Worlds Within: Children's Fantasy from the Middle Ages.* Chicago: American Library Association, 1988.

Foster, Shirley and Judy Simons. *What Katy Read: Feminist Re-Readings of "Classic" Stories for Girls.* University of Iowa Press, 1995.

Girls' Series Books: A Checklist of Hardback Books Published 1900–1975. Children's Literature Research Collections, University of Minnesota Library, Minneapolis, 1978. Basic for any work with girls' series books.

Gorham, Deborah. *The Victorian Girl and the Feminine Ideal.* Bloomington: Indiana University Press, 1982.

Griswold, Jerry. *Audacious Kids: Coming of Age in America's Classic Children's Books.* New York: Oxford University Press, 1992. Audacious, as the title announces, sometimes irritating, and always worth reading.

Howarth, Patrick. *Play Up and Play the Game: The Heroes of Popular Fiction.* London: Eyre Methuen, 1973.

Hudson, Harry K. *A Bibliography of Hard Cover Boys' Books.* rev. ed. Tampa, FL: Data Print, 1977. Basic for any work with boys' series books (and fun to skim through).

Jackson, Mary V. *Engines of Instruction, Mischief, and Magic: Children's Literature in England from Its Beginnings to 1839.* Lincoln: University of Nebraska Press, 1989. Beautifully illustrated background material.

Kiefer, Monica. *American Children Through Their Books, 1700–1835.* Philadelphia: University of Pennsylvania Press, 1948.

Kloet, Christine A. *After Alice: A Hundred Years of Children's Reading in Britain.* London: Library Association, 1977. Published for an exhibition at the Victoria and Albert Museum of Childhood, 1977–1978.

MacLeod, Anne Scott. *A Moral Tale: Children's Fiction and American Culture, 1820–1860.* Hamden, CT: Archon Books, 1975.

Mason, Bobbie Ann. *The Girl Sleuth: A Feminist Guide.* Old Westbury, NY: Feminist Press, 1975. Perceptive, chatty, and witty words about girls' series books, especially Nancy Drew.

Meigs, Cornelia, et al. *A Critical History of Children's Literature.* rev. ed. Macmillan, 1969. Encyclopedic history of YA literature (and children's literature, of course) from the beginning.

Musgrave, P. W. *From Brown to Bunter: The Life and Death of the School Story.* London: Routledge and Kegan Paul, 1985.

Nye, Russel. *The Unembarrassed Muse: The Popular Arts in America.* New York: Dial, 1970.

Quigly, Isabel. *The Heirs of Tom Brown: The English School Story.* London: Chatto and Windus, 1982.

Reynolds, Kimberley. *Girls Only? Gender and Popular Children's Fiction in Britain, 1880–1910.* Philadelphia: Temple University Press, 1990.

Rowbotham, Judith. *Good Girls Make Good Wives: Guidance for Girls in Victorian England.* Oxford, England: Basil Blackwell, 1989.

Sloane, William. *Children's Books in England and America in the Seventeenth Century.* New York: Columbia University Press, 1955.

Townsend, John Rowe. *25 Years of British Children's Books.* London: National Book League, 1979. Not easily found but this 60-page pamphlet is worth the search.

Townsend, John Rowe. *Written for Children: An Outline of English-Language Children's Literature.* 3rd ed. New York: Lippincott, 1988. The most readable history.

Criticism of Young Adult Literature

Bauer, Marion Dane. *What's Your Story? A Young Person's Guide to Writing Fiction.* New York: Clarion, 1992.

Broderick, Dorothy M. *Images of the Black in Children's Fiction.* New York: R. R. Bowker, 1973. Racism in YA literature.

Cameron, Eleanor. *The Green and Burning Tree: On the Writing and Enjoyment of Children's Books.* Boston: Little, Brown, 1969.

Cameron, Eleanor. *The Seed and the Vision: On the Writing and Appreciation of Children's Books.* New York: Dutton, 1993.

Cart, Michael. *From Romance to Realism: 50 Years of Growth and Change in Young Adult Literature.* HarperCollins, 1996.

Carter, Betty, and Richard F. Abrahamson. *Nonfiction for Young Adults: From Delight to Wisdom.* Phoenix, AZ: Oryx Press, 1990.

Chambers, Aidan. *Introducing Books to Children.* 2nd ed. Boston: Horn Book, 1983.

Chambers, Aidan. *Reluctant Reader.* London: Pergamon Press, 1969. This reads better the older it gets. Sympathetic and practical ideas about getting hard-to-reach readers to read.

Children's Literature Review. Detroit: Gale Research Co., 1976–. A continuing series and an excellent source of material on YA books.

Christian-Smith, Linda K. *Becoming a Woman Through Romance.* London: Routledge and Kegan Paul, 1990.

Contemporary Literary Criticism. Detroit: Gale Research Co., 1973–. A continuing series.

Dixon, Bob. *Catching Them Young: Political Ideas in Children's Fiction.* London: Pluto Press, 1977.

Dixon, Bob. *Catching Them Young: Sex, Race and Class*

in Children's Fiction. London: Pluto Press, 1977.

Egoff, Sheila A. *Thursday's Child: Trends and Patterns in Contemporary Children's Literature*. Chicago: American Library Association, 1981. One of the great books in the field, basic reading.

Ettinger, John R., and Diana L. Spirt, eds. *Choosing Books for Young People*. Vol. 2: *A Guide to Criticism and Bibliography, 1976–1984*. Chicago: American Library Association, 1982.

Fisher, Margery. *The Bright Face of Danger*. London: Hodder and Hodder, 1986.

Fox, Geoff, et al., eds. *Writers, Critics, and Children*. New York: Agathon Press, 1976. Articles from *Children's Literature in Education*.

Harrison, Barbara, and Gregory Maguire, eds. *Innocence and Experience: Essays and Conversations on Children's Literature*. New York: Lothrop, 1987.

Hazard, Paul. *Books, Children and Men*. trans. Marguerite Mitchell, Boston: Horn Book, 1944. About all sorts of readers. A seminal book impossible to overrate.

Hearne, Betsy, and Marilyn Kaye, eds. *Celebrating Children's Books: Essays on Children's Literature in Honor of Zena Sutherland*. New York: Lothrop, 1981.

Hendrickson, Linnea. *Children's Literature: A Guide to the Criticism*. Boston: G. K. Hall, 1987.

Howard, Elizabeth F. *America as Story: Historical Fiction for the Secondary Schools*. American Library Association, 1988.

Hunt, Peter. *Criticism, Theory, and Children's Literature*. Oxford: Basil Blackwell, 1991.

Hunt, Peter. *An Introduction to Children's Literature*. New York: Oxford University Press, 1994. Far broader in scope than the title may suggest.

Hunter, Mollie. *The Pied Piper Syndrome and Other Essays*. New York: Charlotte Zolotow/HarperCollins, 1992.

Hunter, Mollie. *Talent Is Not Enough: Mollie Hunter on Writing for Children*. New York: Harper and Row, 1976.

Inglis, Fred. *The Promise of Happiness: Value and Meaning in Children's Fiction*. Cambridge, England: Cambridge University Press, 1981.

Kohn, Rita, compiler. *Once Upon . . . A Time for Young People and Their Books: An Annotated Resource Guide*. Metuchen, NJ: Scarecrow Press, 1986.

Lesnik-Oberstein, Karin. *Children's Literature: Criticism and the Fictional Child*. Oxford: Clarendon, 1994.

Lynn, Ruth Nadelman. *Fantasy Literature for Children and Young Adults*. New York: R. R. Bowker, 1989.

MacCann, Donnarae, and Gloria Woodward, eds. *The Black American in Books for Children: Readings on Racism*. Metuchen, NJ: Scarecrow Press, 1972.

Ray, Sheila G. *Children's Fiction: A Handbook for Librarians*. 2nd rev. ed. Leicester: Brockhampton Press, 1972.

Salmon, Edward. *Juvenile Literature as It Is*. London: Henry J. Drane, 1888. Forward-looking views on children's and YA books. A remarkable book.

Shields, Nancy E. *Index to Literary Criticism for Young Adults*. Metuchen, NJ: Scarecrow Press, 1988.

Sloan, Glenna. *The Child as Critic*. New York: Teachers College Press, 1975. Northrop Frye's theories applied to children's and YA literature.

Street, Douglas, ed. *Children's Novels and the Movies*. London: Ungar, 1984.

Sutherland, Zena. *The Arbuthnot Lectures: 1970–1979*. Chicago: American Library Association, 1980.

Tucker, Nicholas, ed. *Suitable for Children? Controversies in Children's Literature*. Berkeley: University of California Press, 1976.

Yolen, Jane. *Touch Magic: Fantasy, Faerie, and Folklore in the Literature of Childhood*. New York: Philomel, 1981.

Libraries and Young Adult Literature

Bodart, Joni. *Booktalking and School Visiting for Young Adult Audiences*. New York: H. W. Wilson, 1980. See also *Booktalk! Booktalks!* Wilson, 1993.

Bodart, Joni R. *Booktalk 2: Booktalking for All Ages and Audiences*. New York: H. W. Wilson, 1985. A continuing series.

Books for the Teen Age. New York Public Library, published annually.

Carr, Jo, ed. *Beyond Fact: Nonfiction for Children and Young People*. Chicago: American Library Association, 1982.

Edwards, Margaret A. *The Fair Garden and the Swarm of Beasts: The Library and the Young Adult*. rev. ed. New York: Hawthorn, 1974. Some of the problems but mostly the joys of working with YA's.

Eiss, Harry, ed. *Literature for Young People on War and Peace: An Annotated Bibliography*. New York: Greenwood Press, 1989.

Field, Carolyn W., ed. *Special Collections in Children's Literature*. Chicago: American Library Association, 1982.

Gillespie, John T. *More Juniorplots: A Guide for Teachers and Librarians*. New York: R. R. Bowker, 1977.

Gillespie, John T., and Diana L. Lembo. *Juniorplots: A Book Talk Manual for Teachers and Librarians*. New York: R. R. Bowker, 1967.

Gillespie, John T., and Corinne Naden. *Juniorplots 3: A Book Talk Guide for Use with Readers, Ages 12–16*. New York: R. R. Bowker, 1987.

Gillespie, John T. *Seniorplots: A Book Talk Guide for Use with Readers, Ages 15–18*. New York: R. R. Bowker, 1989.

Hinckley, Karen, and Barbara Hinckley. *America's Best Sellers: A Reader's Guide to Popular Fiction*. Bloomington: Indiana University Press, 1989.

Marshall, Margaret R. *Libraries and Literature for Teenagers.* London: Andre Deutsch, 1975.

Pelton, Mary Helen. *Reading Is Not a Spectator Sport.* Littlewood, CO: Libraries Unlimited, 1994. Aimed at anyone who works with kids and who wants kids to become readers. Specific, most helpful.

Rochman, Hazel. *Tales of Love and Terror: Booktalking the Classics, Old and New.* Chicago: American Library Association, 1987.

Roe, Ernest. *Teachers, Librarians, and Children: A Study of Libraries in Education.* Hamden, CT: Archon Books, 1965. Superb, maybe the best of the lot. First published in Australia.

Rosenberg, Betty. *Genreflecting: A Guide to Reading Interests in Genre Fiction.* 2nd ed. Littlewood, CO: Libraries Unlimited, 1987.

Spencer, Pam. *What Do Young Adults Read Next? A Reader's Guide to Fiction for Young Adults.* Detroit: Gale Research Co., 1994. Invaluable tool for finding almost any book that kids would like.

Taylor, Desmond. *The Juvenile Novels of World War II: An Annotated Bibliography.* Westport, CT: Greenwood Press, 1994.

English Classrooms and Young Adult Literature

Beach, Richard. *A Teacher's Introduction to Reader-Response Theories.* Urbana, IL: National Council of Teachers of English, 1993.

Beach, Richard, and James Marshall. *Teaching Literature in the Secondary School.* New York: Harcourt Brace Jovanovich, 1991.

Brown, Jean A. and Elaine C. Stephens. *Teaching Young Adult Literature: Sharing the Connection.* Belmont, CA: Wadsworth, 1995.

Burton, Dwight L. *Literature Study in the High Schools.* 3rd ed. New York: Holt, 1970. For many teachers and librarians, *the* book that introduced them to YA books.

Bushman, John H. and Kay Parks Bushman. *Using Young Adult Literature in the English Classroom.* New York: Merrill, 1993.

Carlsen, G. Robert. *Books and the Teen-Age Reader.* 2nd ed. New York: HarperCollins, 1980.

Chambers, Nancy, ed. *The Signal Approach to Children's Books.* Metuchen, NJ: Scarecrow Press, 1980. First published in England.

Corcoran, Bill, and Emrys Evans, eds. *Readers, Texts, Teachers.* Portsmouth, NH: Boynton/Cook, 1987. A great collection of criticism and pedagogy.

Crowley, Sharon. *A Teacher's Introduction to Deconstruction.* Urbana, IL: National Council of Teachers of English, 1989.

Evans, Tricia. *Teaching English.* London: Croom Helm, 1982.

Fader, Daniel. *The New Hooked on Books.* New York: Berkley, 1976. First published in 1966 and revised in 1968, Fader's book made English teachers take YA books seriously. The book lists are dated, but Fader's enthusiasm and caring aren't.

Farrell, Edmund J., and James R. Squire, eds. *Transactions with Literature: A Fifty-Year Perspective.* Urbana, IL: National Council of Teachers of English, 1990. Essays honoring Louise M. Rosenblatt.

Herz, Sarah K., and Donald R. Gallo. *From Hinton to Hamlet: Building Bridges between Young Adult Literature and the Classics.* Westport, CT: Greenwood, 1996.

Marshall, James D., Peter Smagorinsky, and Michael W. Smith. *The Language of Interpretation: Patterns of Discourse in Discussions of Literature.* NCTE Research Report No. 27. Urbana, IL: National Council of Teachers of English, 1995.

Moran, Charles, and Elizabeth F. Penfield, eds. *Conversations: Contemporary Critical Theory and the Teaching of Literature.* Urbana, IL: National Council of Teachers of English, 1990.

Ohanian, Susan. *Who's in Charge? A Teacher Speaks Her Mind.* Portsmouth, NH: Boynton/Cook, 1994. Brilliant, witty comments from a clearly great teacher.

Peck, David. *Novels of Initiation: A Guidebook for Teaching Literature to Adolescents.* New York: Teachers College, 1989.

Probst, Robert E. *Response and Analysis: Teaching Literature in Junior and Senior High School.* Portsmouth, NH: Boynton/Cook, Heinemann, 1988. A rarity: brilliant pedagogy with understandable and usable material on literary criticism.

Protherough, Robert, Judith Atkinson, and John Fawcett. *The Effective Teaching of English.* London: Longman, 1989. The best text today on teaching English.

Purves, Alan C., Theresa Rogers, and Anna O. Soter. *How Porcupines Make Love II: Teaching a Response-Centered Literature Curriculum.* New York: Longman, 1990.

Reed, Arthea J. S. *From Comics to Classics: A Parent's Guide to Books for Teens and Preteens.* Newark, DE: International Reading Association, 1985.

Reed, Arthea J. S. *Reaching Adolescents: The Young Adult Book and the School.* New York: Merrill, 1994.

Rosenblatt, Louise M. *Literature as Exploration.* 4th ed. New York: Modern Language Association, 1983.

Sample, Hazel. *Pitfalls for Readers of Fiction.* Chicago: National Council of Teachers of English, 1940. Too little known and appreciated, many insights into reading popular fiction.

Scholes, Robert. *Textual Power: Literary Theory and the Teaching of English.* New Haven, CT: Yale University Press, 1985.

Smagorinsky, Peter, and Melissa E. Whiting. *How English Teachers Get Taught: Methods of Teaching the Methods Class*. Urbana, IL: National Council of Teachers of English, 1995.

Thomson, Jack. *Understanding Teenager's Reading: Reading Processes and the Teaching of Literature*. Norwood, Australia: Australian Association for the Teaching of English, 1987.

Authors of Young Adult Literature

Berger, Laura Standley, ed. *Twentieth-Century Young Adult Writers*. Detroit: St. James Press, 1994.

Cech, John, ed. *American Writers for Children, 1900–1960. Dictionary of Literary Biography*. Vol. 22. Detroit: Gale Research Co., 1983.

Chevalier, Tracy. *Twentieth Century Children's Writers*. 3rd ed. New York: St. Martin's Press, 1989.

Commire, Anne, ed. *Something About the Author*. Detroit: Gale Research Co., 1971. A continuing series about authors and books. Indispensable.

Commire, Anne, ed. *Yesterday's Authors of Books for Children*. Detroit: Gale Research Co., 1977. Lives of authors who died before 1961.

de Montreville, Doris, and Elizabeth D. Crawford, eds. *Fourth Book of Junior Authors and Illustrators*. New York: H. W. Wilson, 1978.

de Montreville, Doris, and Donna Hill, eds. *Third Book of Junior Authors*. New York: H. W. Wilson, 1972.

Estes, Glenn E., ed. *American Writers for Children Before 1900. Dictionary of Literary Biography*. Vol. 42. Detroit: Gale Research Co., 1985.

Estes, Glenn E., ed. *American Writers for Children Since 1960: Fiction. Dictionary of Literary Biography*. Vol. 52. Detroit: Gale Research Co., 1986.

Estes, Glenn E., ed. *American Writers for Children Since 1960: Poets, Illustrators, and Nonfiction Authors. Dictionary of Literary Biography*. Vol. 61: Detroit: Gale Research Co., 1987.

Gallo, Donald R., ed. *Authors' Insights: Turning Teenagers into Readers and Writers*. Portsmouth, NH: Boynton/Cook; Heinemann, 1992.

Gallo, Donald R., ed. *Speaking for Ourselves: Autobiographical Sketches by Notable Authors of Books for Young Adults*. Urbana, IL: National Council of Teachers of English, 1990. From Joan Aiken to Paul Zindel, 92 sketches from important YA writers. A sequel, *Speaking for Ourselves, Too,* adds two-page statements from another 90 authors.

Hopkins, Lee Bennett, ed. *Pauses: Autobiographical Reflections of 101 Creators of Children's Books*. New York: HarperCollins, 1995.

Fuller, Muriel, ed. *More Junior Authors*. New York: H. W. Wilson, 1963.

Haviland, Virginia, ed. *The Openhearted Audience: Ten Authors Talk About Writing for Children*. Washington, DC: Library of Congress, 1980.

Helbig, Alethea K., and Agnes Regan Perkins. *Dictionary of American Children's Fiction,1859–1959*. Westport, CT: Greenwood Press, 1985.

Helbig, Alethea K., and Agnes Regan Perkins. *Dictionary of American Children's Fiction, 1960–1984*. Westport, CT: Greenwood Press,1986.

Helbig, Alethea K., and Agnes Regan Perkins. *Dictionary of British Children's Fiction*. Westport, CT: Greenwood Press, 1989.

Hipple, Theodore. *Writers for Young Adults* (three volumes). New York: Scribner's, 1997. A collection of critical essays written for young adults.

Holtze, Sally Holmes, ed. *Fifth Book of Junior Authors and Illustrators*. New York: H. W. Wilson, 1987.

Holtze, Sally Holmes, ed. *Sixth Book of Junior Authors and Illustrators*. New York: H. W. Wilson, 1989.

Huffman, Miriam, and Eva Samuels, eds. *Authors and Artists for Young Adults*. Detroit: Gale Research Co., 1989.

Jones, Cornelia, and Olivia R. Way. *British Children's Authors: Interviews at Home*. Chicago: American Library Association, 1976.

Kirkpatrick, D. L., ed. *Twentieth-Century Children's Writers*. 3rd ed. New York: Macmillan, 1990.

Kunitz, Stanley J. and Howard Hatycraft, eds. *The Junior Book of Authors*. 2nd ed. rev.: New York: H. W. Wilson, 1951.

Rees, David. *The Marble in the Water: Essays on Contemporary Writers of Fiction for Children and Young Adults*. Boston: Horn Book, 1980.

Rees, David. *Painted Desert. Green Shade: Essays on Contemporary Writers of Fiction for Children and Young Adults*. Boston: Horn Book, 1984.

Rees, David. *What Do Draculas Do? Essays on Contemporary Writers of Fiction for Children and Young Adults*. Metuchen, NJ: Scarecrow Press, 1990.

Roginski, Jim. *Behind the Covers: Interviews with Authors and Illustrators of Books for Children and Young Adults*. Littlewood, CO: Libraries Unlimited, 1985.

Roginski, Jim. *Behind the Covers: Interviews with Authors and Illustrators of Books for Children and Young Adults*. Vol. 2. Littlewood, CO: Libraries Unlimited, 1989.

Sarkissian, Adele, ed. *Writers for Young Adults: Biographies Master Index*. Detroit: Gale Research Co., 1984.

Townsend, John Rowe. *A Sense of Story: Essays on Contemporary Writers for Children*. Philadelphia: Lippincott, 1971.

Ward, Martha E., and Dorothy A. Marquardt, eds. *Authors of Books for Young People*. 3rd ed. Metuchen, NJ: Scarecrow Press, 1990.

Weiss, M. Jerry, ed. *From Writers to Students: The Plea-*

sures and Pains of Writing. Newark, DE: International Reading Association, 1979.

Wintle, Justin, and Emma Fisher, eds. *The Pied Pipers: Interviews with the Influential Creators of Children's Literature.* New York: Paddington Press, 1974.

Books of Readings About Young Adult Literature

Bater, Robert, ed. *Signposts to Criticism of Children's Literature.* Chicago: American Library Association, 1983.

Broderick, Dorothy M., ed. *The VOYA Reader.* Metuchen, NJ: Scarecrow Press, 1990. Articles from the *Voice of Youth Advocates.*

Egoff, Sheila, G. T. Stubbs, and L. F. Ashley, eds. *Only Connect: Readings in Children's Literature.* 2nd ed. New York: Oxford University Press, 1980.

Fox, Geoff, et al., eds. *Writers, Critics, and Children: Articles from Children's Literature in Education.* New York: Agathon Press, 1976.

Haviland, Virginia, ed. *Children and Literature: Views and Reviews.* Glenview, IL: Scott, Foresman, 1973.

Salway, Lance, ed. *A Peculiar Gift: Nineteenth Century Writings on Books for Children.* London: Kestrel, 1976.

Varlejs, Jana, ed. *Young Adult Literature in the Seventies: A Selection of Readings.* Metuchen, NJ: Scarecrow Press, 1978.

Articles in Periodicals

History and Young Adult Literature

Ashford, Richard K. "Tomboys and Saints: Girls' Stories of the Late Nineteenth Century." *School Library Journal* 26 (January 1980): 23–28.

Cantwell, Robert. "A Sneering Laugh with the Bases Loaded." *Sports Illustrated* 16 (April 23, 1962): 67–70, 73–76. Baseball novels for boys, particularly by Barbour and Heyliger.

Carlsen, G. Robert. "Forty Years with Books and Teen-Age Readers." *Arizona English Bulletin* 18 (April 1976): 1–5. From 1939 to 1976 in YA literature.

Crandall, John C. "Patriotism and Humanitarian Reform in Children's Literature, 1825–1860." *American Quarterly* 21 (Spring 1969): 3–22.

Edwards, Margaret A. "The Rise of Teen-Age Reading." *Saturday Review of Literature* 37 (November 13, 1954): 88–89, 95. The state of YA literature in the 1930s and 1940s and what led to it.

Evans, Walter. "The All-American Boys: A Study of Boys' Sports Fiction." *Journal of Popular Culture* 6 (Summer 1972): 104–121. Formulas underlying boys' school sports books, especially Barbour and the series books.

"For It Was Indeed He." *Fortune* 9 (April 1934): 86–89, 193–194, 204, 206, 208–209. An important, influential, and biased article on Stratemeyer's Literary Syndicate.

Geller, Evelyn. "The Librarian as Censor." *Library Journal* 101 (June 1, 1976): 1255–58. Social control as censorship in late-nineteenth-century library selection.

Geller, Evelyn. "Tom Sawyer, Tom Bailey, and the Bad-Boy Genre." *Wilson Library Bulletin* 52 (November 1976): 245–50.

Hutchinson, Margaret. "Fifty Years of Young Adult Reading, 1921–1971." *Top of the News* 29 (November 1973): 24–53. "A survey of the field (of) young adult reading for the past fifty years by examining articles indexed in *Library Literature* from its inception in 1921 ."

Kelly, R. Gordon. "American Children's Literature: An Historiographical Review." *American Literary Realism, 1870–1910* 6 (Spring 1973): 89–107.

Kolba, Ellen. "Stories for Sale." *English Journal* 69 (October 1980): 37–39.

Lapides, Linda F. "A Decade of Teen-Age Reading in Baltimore, 1960–1970." *Top of the News* 27 (Spring 1971): 278–291.

Morrison, Lillian. "Fifty Years of 'Books for the Teen Age.'" *School Library Journal* 26 (December 1979): 44–50.

Radnor, Rebecca. "You're Being Paged Loudly in the Kitchen: Teen-Age Literature of the Forties and Fifties." *Journal of Popular Culture* 11 (Spring 1978): 789–99. Ways in which YA writers for girls influenced young women.

Repplier, Agnes. "Little Pharisees in Fiction." *Scribner's Magazine* 20 (December 1896): 718–24. The didactic and joyless goody-goody school of YA fiction in the last half of the nineteenth century.

Trensky, Anne. "The Bad Boy in Nineteenth-Century American Fiction." *Georgia Review* 27 (Winter 1973): 503–17.

Vostrovsky, Clara. "A Study of Children's Reading Tastes." *Pedagogical Seminary* 6 (December 1899): 523–35. A pioneer account of the kinds of books young people read.

Criticism and Young Adult Literature

Abrahamson, Jane. "Still Playing It Safe: Restricted Realism in Teen Novels." *School Library Journal* 22 (May 1976): 38–39.

Aronson, Marc. "The Betrayal of Teenagers." *School Library Journal* 42 (May 1966): 23–25.

Aronison, Marc. "The YA Novel Is Dead,' and Other Fairly Stupid Tales," *School Library Journal* 41 (January 1995): 36–37.

Brewbaker, James M. "Are You There, Margaret? It's

Me, God—Religious Contexts in Recent Adolescent Fiction." *English Journal* 72 (September 1983): 82–86.

Campbell, Patty. "Perplexing Young Adult Books: A Retrospective." *Wilson Library Bulletin* 62 (April 1988): 20, 22, 24, 26. Campbell looks back on ten years of her YA column.

Carlsen, G. Robert. "For Everything There Is a Season." *Top of the News* 21 (January 1965): 103–110. Stages in reading growth.

Carlsen, G. Robert. "The Interest Rate Is Rising." *English Journal* 59 (May 1970): 655–59.

Cart, Michael. "Of Risk and Revelation: The Current State of Young Adult Literature." *Journal of Youth Services in Libraries* 8 (Winter 1995): 151–64.

Carver, Nancy Lynn. "Stereotypes of American Indians in Adolescent Literature." *English Journal* 77 (September 1988): 25–32.

Chambers, Aidan. "All of a Tremble to See His Danger." *Top of the News* 42 (Summer 1986): 405–22. The 1986 May Hill Arbuthnot Lecture.

Chambers, Aidan. "The Difference of Literature: Writing Now for the Future of Young Readers." *Children's Literature in Education* 24 (March 1993): 1–18.

Early, Margaret J. "Stages of Growth in Literary Appreciation." *English Journal* 49 (March 1960): 161–67. A seminal article.

Edwards, Margaret A. "A Time When It's Best to Read and Let Read." *Wilson Library Bulletin* 35 (September 1960): 43–47. Myths of buying books for young adults demolished.

Engdahl, Sylvia. "Do Teenage Novels Fill a Need?" *English Journal* 64 (February 1975): 48–52.

Evans, Dilys. "The YA Cover Story." *Publishers Weekly* 232 (July 24, 1987): 112–15. Differences between hardcover and paperback covers on YA books.

Gale, David. "The Business of Books." *School Library Journal* 42 (July 1996) 18–21. How publishing takes place, using a YA book as an example.

Garfield, Leon. "Historical Fiction for Our Global Times." *Horn Book Magazine* 64 (November/December 1988): 736–742.

Gauch, Patricia. "'Good Stuff' in Adolescent Fiction." *Top of the News* 40 (Winter 1984): 125–29.

Green, Samuel S. "Sensational Fiction in Public Libraries." *Library Journal* 4 (September–October 1879): 345–55. Extraordinarily forward-looking, intelligent comments about young adults and their books. The entire issue is worth reading, particularly papers by T. W. Higginson (pp. 357–59), William Atkinson (pp. 359–62), and Mellen Chamberlain (pp. 362–66).

Hamilton, Virginia. "Everything of Value: Moral Realism in the Literature of Children." *Journal of Youth Services in Libraries* 6 (Summer 1993): 363–77. The May Hill Arbuthnot Lecture.

Hanckel, Frances, and John Cunningham. "Can Young Gays Find Happiness in YA Books?" *Wilson Library Bulletin* 50 (March 1976): 528–34.

Hentoff, Nat. "Fiction for Teen-Agers." *Wilson Library Bulletin* 43 (November 1968): 261–64. The shortcomings of YA fiction.

Hentoff, Nat. "Tell It as It Is." *New York Times Book Review,* May 7, 1967, pp. 3, 51.

Hinton, Susan. "Teen-Agers Are for Real." *New York Times Book Review,* August 27, 1967, pp. 26–29. Brief and excellent.

Hipps, G. Melvin. "Adolescent Literature: Once More to the Defense." *Virginia English Bulletin* 23 (Spring 1973): 44–50. Nearly 30 years old and still one of the best rationales for adolescent literature.

"Is Adolescent Literature Worth Studying?" *Connecticut English Journal* 10 (Fall 1978). Robert P. Scaramella, "Con: At the Risk of Seeming Stuffy," pp. 57–58; Robert C. Small, Jr. "Pro: Means and Ends," pp. 59–63.

Janeczko, Paul B. "Seven Myths About Adolescent Literature." *Arizona English Bulletin* 18 (April 1976): 11–12.

Kaye, Marilyn. "In Defense of Formula Fiction: or, They Don't Write Schlock the Way They Used to." *Top of the News* 37 (Fall 1980): 87–90.

Kraus, W. Keith. "Cinderella In Trouble: Still Dreaming and Losing." *School Library Journal* 21 (January 1975): 18–22. Pregnancy in YA novels from Felsen's *Two and the Town* (1952) to Neufeld's *For All the Wrong Reasons* (1973).

Kraus, W. Keith. "From Steppin' Stebbins to Soul Brothers: Racial Strife in Adolescent Literature." *Arizona English Bulletin* 18 (April 1976): 154–60.

Martinec, Barbara. "Popular—But Not Just a Part of the Crowd: Implications of Formula Fiction for Teenagers." *English Journal* 60 (March 1971): 339–44. Formulaic elements of six YA novelists.

Matthews, Dorothy. "An Adolescent's Glimpse of the Faces of Eve: A Study of the Images of Women in Selected Popular Junior Novels." *Illinois English Bulletin* 60 (May 1973): 1–14.

Matthews, Dorothy. "Writing About Adolescent Literature: Current Approaches and Future Directions." *Arizona English Bulletin* 18 (April 1976): 216–19.

McDowell, Myles. "Fiction for Children and Adults: Some Essential Differences." *Children's Literature in Education* 4 (March 1973): 48–63.

Meek, Margaret. "Prologomena for a Study of Children's Literature, or Guess What's in My Head" in Michael Benton, ed., *Approaches to Research in Children's Literature.* Southhampton, England: University of Southhampton, 1980, pp. 29–39.

Meltzer, Milton. "Where Do All the Prizes Go? The Case for Nonfiction." *Horn Book Magazine* 52 (February 1976): 17–23.

Merla, Patrick. "'What is Real?' Asked the Rabbit One Day." *Saturday Review* 55 (November 4, 1972): 43–49. The rise of YA realism and adult fantasy, 20 years old and still valid.

Mertz, Maia Pank, and David A. England. "The Legitimacy of American Adolescent Fiction." *School Library Journal* 30 (October 1983): 119–23.

Nicholson, George M. "The Young Adult Novel History and Development." *CBC Features* 47 (Fall-Winter 1994). A significant article reprinted with permission in Chapter 1 of this text as a "People Behind the Books" feature.

Peck, Richard. "In the Country of Teenage Fiction." *American Libraries* 4 (April 1973): 204–207.

Peck, Richard. "Some Thoughts on Adolescent Literature." *News from ALAN* 3 (September–October 1975): 4–7.

Peck, Richard, and Patsy H. Perritt. "British Publishers Enter the Young Adult Age." *Journal of Youth Services in Libraries* 1 (Spring 1988): 292–304. Useful survey of British YA publishers.

Poe, Elizabeth Ann, Barbara G. Samuels; and Betty Carter. "Twenty-Five years of Research in Young Adult Literature: Past Perspectives and Future Directives." *Journal of Youth Services in Libraries* 28 (November 1981): 25–28.

Pollack, Pamela D. "The Business of Popularity: The Surge of Teenage Paperbacks." *School Library Journal* 28 (November 1981): 25–28.

Popkin, Zelda F. "The Finer Things in Life." *Harpers* 164 (April 1932): 602–11. Contrasts between what young adults like to read and what parents and other adults want kids to read.

Probst, Robert E. "Mom, Wolfgang, and Me: Adolescent Literature, Critical Theory, and the English Classroom." *English Journal* 75 (October 1986): 33–39.

Probst, Robert E. "Reader Response Theory and the Problem of Meaning." *Publishing Research Quarterly* 8 (Spring 1992): 64–73.

Root, Sheldon L. "The New Realism—Some Personal Reflections." *Language Arts* 54 (January 1977): 19–24.

Ross, Catherine Sheldrick. "Young Adult Realism: Conventions, Narrators, and Readers." *Library Quarterly* 55 (April 1985): 174–91.

Silver, Linda R. "Criticism, Reviewing, and the Library Review Media." *Top of the News* 35 (Winter 1979): 123–30. The entire issue on reviewing YA books is fine, particularly "What Makes a Good Review? Ten Experts Speak" (pp. 146–52) and Patty Campbell's "Only Puddings Like the Kiss of Death: Reviewing the YA Book" (pp. 161–62).

Spencer, Pam. "Winners in Their Own Right." *School Library Journal* 36 (July 1990): 23–27. Books that were overlooked on publication and which have since become standards.

Stanek, Lou Willett. "The Junior Novel: A Stylistic Study." *Elementary English* 51 (October 1974): 947–53.

Sutton, Roger. "The Critical Myth: Realistic YA Novels." *School Library Journal* 29 (November 1982): 33–35.

Townsend, John Rowe. "Didacticism in Modern Dress ." *Horn Book Magazine* 43 (April 1967): 159–64. Argues that nineteenth-century didacticism is remarkably like didacticism in modern YA novels.

Townsend, John Rowe. "Standards of Criticism for Children's Literature." *Top of the News* 27 (June 1971): 373–87.

Unsworth, Robert. "Holden Caulfield, Where Are You?" *School Library Journal* 23 (January 1977): 40–41. A plea for more books about males by males.

Wigutoff, Sharon. "Junior Fiction: A Feminist Critique." *The Lion and the Unicorn* 5 (1981): 4–18.

Wilson, David E. "The Open Library: YA Books for Gay Teens." *English Journal* 73 (November 1984): 60–63.

Using Young Adult Literature in Classrooms and Libraries

Abrahamson, Dick, and Eleanor Tyson. "What Every English Teacher Should Know About Free Reading." *ALAN Review* 14 (Fall 1986): 54–58, 69.

Abrahamson, Richard F. and Betty Carter, "What We Know About Nonfiction and Young Adult Readers and What We Need to Do about it." *Publishing Research Quarterly* 8 (Spring 1992): 34–40.

Broderick, Dorothy M. "Reviewing Young Adult Books: The *VOYA* Editor Speaks Out." *Publishing Research Quarterly* 8 (Spring 1992): 34–40.

Broderick, Dorothy M. "Serving Young Adults: Why We Do What We Do." *Voice of Youth Advocates* 12 (October 1989): 203–6.

Chelton, Mary K. "Booktalking: You Can Do It." *School Library Journal* 22 (April 1976): 39–43. Practical and fun to read and do.

Hopkins, Dianne McAfee. "Challenges to Materials in Secondary School Library Media Centers: Results of a National Survey." *Journal of Youth Services in Libraries* 4 (Winter 1991): 131–40.

Janeczko, Paul B. "Eight Things I've Learned about Kids and Poetry." *Publishing Research Quarterly* 8 (Spring 1992): 55–63.

"Seven Myths About Teaching Poetry, or, How I Stopped Chasing Foul Balls." *ALAN Review* 14 (Spring 1987): 13–16.

Lesesne, Teri S. "Developing Lifetime Readers: Suggestions from Fifty Years of Research." *English Journal* 80 (October 1991): 61–64.

McGee, Tim. "The Adolescent Novel in AP English: A Response to Patricia Spencer." *English Journal* 81 (April 1992): 57–58.

Mearns, Hughes. "Bo Peep, Old Woman, and Slow Mandy: Being Three Theories of Reading." *New Republic* 48 (November 10, 1926): 344–46.

Nelms, Ben F. "Reading for Pleasure in Junior High School." *English Journal* 55 (September 1966): 676–81.

Peck, Richard. "Ten Questions to Ask About a Novel." ALAN *Newsletter* 5 (Spring 1978): 1, 7.

Probst, Robert E. "Adolescent Literature and the English Curriculum." *English Journal* 76 (March 1987): 26–30.

Probst, Robert E. "Three Relationships in the Teaching of Literature." *English Journal* 75 (January 1986): 60–68.

Rakow, Susan R. "Young-Adult Literature for Honors Students." *English Journal* 80 (January 1991): 48–51.

Robertson, Sandra L. "Text Rendering: Beginning Literary Response." *English Journal* 79 (January 1990): 80–84.

Scharf, Peter. "Moral Development and Literature for Adolescents." *Top of the News* 33 (Winter 1977): 131–36. Lawrence Kohlberg's six stages of moral judgment applied to YA books.

Scoggin, Margaret C. "Do Young People Want Books?" *Wilson Bulletin for Librarians* 11 (September 1936): 17–20, 24.

Schontz, Marilyn Louise. "Selected Research Related to Children's and Young Adult Services in Public Libraries." *Top of the News* 38 (Winter 1982): 125–42. Includes an excellent list of sources.

Small, Robert C., Jr. "The Junior Novel and the Art of Literature." *English Journal* 66 (October 1977): 56–59.

Small, Robert C., Jr. "The Literary Value of the Young Adult Novel." *Journal of Youth Services in Libraries* 5 (Spring 1992) 277–85.

Small, Robert C. Jr. "Teaching the Junior Novel." *English Journal* 61 (February 1972): 222–29.

Thurber, Samuel. "An Address to Teachers of English." *Education* 18 (May 1898): 515–26. The best writer of his time, and one of the best English teachers of any time, on getting young people excited about literature.

Tuccillo, Diane P. "Leading Them to Books—for Life." *Publishing Research Quarterly* 8 (Spring 1992): 14–22.

Vogel, Mark, and Don Zancanella. "The Story World of Adolescents in *and* out of the Classroom." *English Journal* 80 (October 1991): 54–60.

ACKNOWLEDGMENTS

(p. 1) Jacket cover from *Shadow Boxer* by Chris Lynch, © 1995, reprinted by permission of HarperCollins. Jacket cover of *Deliver Us from Evie* by M. E. Kerr, © 1994, reprinted by permission of HarperCollins. Cover of Harper Trophy edition of *Grab Hands and Run* by Frances Temple, © 1993, Orchard/Watts, paperback cover reprinted by permission of HarperCollins. Jacket cover of *Plain City* by Virginia Hamilton, © 1993, reprinted by permission of Scholastic. Jacket cover of *The Monument* by Gary Paulsen, © 1991, reprinted by permission of Delacorte, a division of Bantam Doubleday Dell Publishing Group, Inc. Jacket cover of *Losing Joe's Place* by Gordon Korman, © 1990, reprinted by permission of Scholastic.

(p. 20) Jacket cover of *Cool Salsa: Bilingual Poems on Growing Up Latino in the United States* edited by Lori Carlson, © 1994, reprinted by permission of Holt. Jacket cover of *Eleanor Roosevelt: A Life of Discovery* by Russell Freedman, © 1993, reprinted by permission of Clarion.

(p. 26) Jacket cover of *Missing Angel Juan* by Francesca Lia Block, © 1993, reprinted by permission of HarperCollins. Jacket cover of *Make Lemonade* by Virginia Euwer Wolff, © 1993, reprinted by permission of Holt.

(p. 39) Taryn Nilsen

(p. 54) Jacket cover of *Summer on Wheels* by Gary Soto, © 1995, reprinted by permission of Scholastic. Jacket cover of *Talent Night* by Jean Davies Okimoto, © 1995, reprinted by permission of Scholastic.

(p. 75) Jacket cover of *When She Hollers* by Cynthia Voigt, © 1994, reprinted by permission of Scholastic. Cover of *Annotated Art* by Robert Cumming, © 1995, reprinted by permission of Dorling Kindersley. Jacket cover of *Scary Stories 3* by Alvin Schwartz, illustrations by Stephen Gammell, © 1991, reprinted by permission of HarperCollins. Cover of *After the First Death* by Robert Cormier, © 1979, Dell Laurel Leaf Paperback cover reprinted by permission of Bantam Doubleday Dell Publishing Group, Inc. Paperback cover of *Fell* by M. E. Kerr, © 1987, reprinted by permission of HarperCollins.

(p. 80) Beth Bergman, Sentinel/Enterprise

(p. 100) Jeff Thiebauth

(p. 130) Jacket cover of *The Best School Year Ever* by Barbara Robinson, © 1994, reprinted by permission of HarperCollins. Jacket cover of *Seventh-Grade Weirdo* by Lee Wardlaw, © 1992, reprinted by permission from Scholastic.

(p. 135) Photo courtesy of Mesa, Arizona, Public Library.

(p. 144) Jill Paton Walsh

(p. 161) Map from *The Stone and the Flute* by Hans Bemmann, translated by Anthea Bell for Penguin Book, 1987, © Hans Bemmann, 1987, originally published 1983, Edition Weitbrecht in K Thienemanns Verlag Stuttgart. Reproduced by permission of Penguin Books, Ltd.

(p. 178) Graham Mace

(p. 187) Jacket cover of *Catherine, Called Birdy* by Karen Cushman, © 1994, reproduced by permission from Clarion. Cover of *Maus II: A Survivor's Tale and Here My Troubles Began* by Art Spiegelman, © 1986, 1989, 1990, 1991 by Art Spiegelman. Reprinted by permission of Pantheon Books, a division of Random House, Inc.

(p. 212) Jacket cover of *Black Ice* by Lorene Cary, © 1991 by Lorene Cary, reprinted by permission of Alfred A. Knopf, Inc. Jacket cover of *Voices from the Civil War* by Milton Meltzer, © 1989, reprinted by permission of HarperCollins. Cover of *Malcolm X: By Any Means Necessary* by Walter Dean Myers, © 1993, reprinted by permission of Scholastic.

(p. 233) Cover of *How Things Work: Things We Make, Build, and Use: Scholastic First Encyclopedia*, © 1995, reprinted by permission of Scholastic. Cover of *How Sex Works* by Elizabeth Fenwick and Richard Walker, © 1994, reprinted by permission of Dorling Kindersley.

(p. 239) Cover of *Complete Baby and Child Care* by Dr. Miriam Stoppard, © 1995, reprinted by permission of Dorling Kindersley.

(p. 257) Cover of *The Chief* by Robert Lipsyte, © 1993, reprinted by permission of HarperCollins. Cover of *Arnold Schwarzenegger: Hercules in America* by Robert Lipsyte, © 1993, reprinted by permission of HarperCollins.

(p. 259) Anon Rupo

(p. 265) John Graves

(p. 274) Don Perkins

(p. 304) Adapted from "Booktalking: You Can Do It" by Mary K. Chelton. Reprinted with permission of Mary K. Chelton from *School Library Journal,* April 1976. R. R. Bowker Co./A Xerox Corporation.
(p. 314) Don Lewis
(p. 331) Cover of *Am I Blue?* edited by Marion Dane Bauer, © 1994, reprinted by permission of HarperCollins. Cover of *Center Stage: One-Act Plays for Teenage Readers and Actors* edited by Donald R. Gallo, © 1990, reprinted by permission of HarperCollins. Cover of *My Friend's Got This Problem, Mr. Candler* by Mel Glenn, © 1991, reprinted by permission of Houghton Mifflin.
(p. 345) N. V. Edris
(p. 391) Peter Simon

SUBJECT INDEX

CRITICS AND COMMENTATORS INDEX

AUTHOR AND TITLE INDEX